D1612222

THE NUCLEAR WEAPONS WORLD

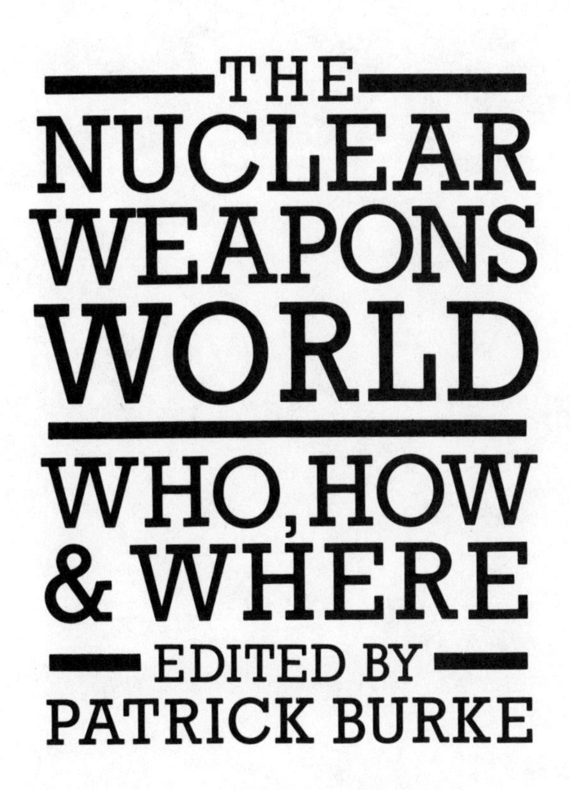

Greenwood Press
Westport, Connecticut

Published in the United States and Canada by
Greenwood Press, Inc., Westport, Connecticut

English language edition, except the United States and Canada,
published by Pinter Publishers Limited

First published 1988

Library of Congress Cataloguing in Publication Data:
Burke, Patrick.
The nuclear weapons world.
Includes index.
1. Nuclear weapons. 2. Military policy–Decision making, 3. Public officials–Directories. I. Title.
UZ64.B87 1989 355'.0217'0941 88-30078
ISBN 0-31326590-9 (lib. bdg, : alk. paper)

Library of Congress Catalog Card Number: 88-30078

ISBN 0-313-26590-9

Printed Great Britain

Contents

List of Figures

Foreword

There are two reasons why this book is being published. Firstly, to provide a more human and accessible insight into the highly technical world of weapons production and, secondly, to help improve accountability in nuclear weapons decisionmaking.

The work of the Oxford Research Group since 1982 has been devoted to gaining a clearer understanding of how decisions on nuclear weapons are made in the five major nuclear nations.

The initial study, *How Nuclear Weapons Decisions Are Made*, was published in 1986 and showed that politicians have very little control over the development and production of major weapons systems. The main reasons for this are, first, that politicians remain in office for comparatively short terms, while weapons systems are now so complex that they take fifteen or twenty years from drawing board to deployment and, second, that these systems are now so expensive that once a certain point in their development is passed, cancellation is seen as unacceptably wasteful. As a result, politicians have to rely on expert advice, and decisions are in fact shaped by groups of experts closely connected with the weapons: scientists and designers, intelligence analysts, military strategists, defence contractors and senior civil servants.

Nuclear Weapons: Who's In Charge?, published by the Oxford Research Group in 1987, took the investigation further and drew comparisions between the influence of the various decisionmaking groups in different countries. Through the study of published papers and speeches and lengthy interviews with decisionmakers, the initial conclusions were confirmed and a fuller picture built up of the types of pressure and influence which produce new weapons.

From these two studies, it emerged that a number of positions were of key importance in nuclear weapons decisionmaking. These key posts in the five countries have now been identified, and are presented in this book against a background explanation of the responsibilities held by the incumbents and by the departments or councils or committees in which they work.

A very large percentage of the people occupying these positions are not elected, and are thus not properly accountable for the decisions they take; nor are they known to the public. Yet the decisions being made or shaped by them will determine the future of the planet. The fragile mechanisms which have been set up to cope with this situation, to oversee and control defence production and expenditure, are not sufficiently strong to accomplish their task. In the Pentagon, for example, defence budget allocations are shifted from one project to another to allow an officially cancelled programme to stay alive. No president or prime minister has ever succeeded in terminating a technically feasible nuclear weapons system. One of the reasons why this has happened is because until now no one *outside* the decisionmaking system knew who was responsible for what, and to whom. This book is a step towards changing that situation.

Nuclear decisions and the weapons and strategy they concern are too mammoth, too complex and too intimidating a subject for most of us to grapple with. The more so because informed debate is rare, and because information is difficult to obtain. In Britain, Parliamentary questions receive evasive answers or no answers at all, and the rationale of official secrecy is used as a reason to reveal less and less about decisions on national defence: between 1981 and 1987, for example, the number of Open Government Documents published on defence fell from fifty-seven to two.

In the case of NATO, decisions on nuclear strategy into the next century are taken in secret by defence ministers meeting in the Nuclear Planning Group. These decisions are often not reported to, nor debated by, the parliaments of member nations until the decision has become a *fait accompli*. This deprivation of information leads inevitably to apathy and lack of interest in the voting public, followed by shock and resentment when they do learn the facts. One way of redressing this balance is to be open about who does have the information, and this book is a first attempt to do that.

As a first attempt, *The Nuclear Weapons World: Who, How and Where* will inevitably have gaps. We have worked entirely from unclassified information and, wherever possible with the co-operation of the departments and ministries concerned. Every attempt has been made to ensure accuracy, but because we are working with a very small staff and budget, there will inevitably be statements we have been unable to check. We will be very grateful to receive corrections or amplifications for future editions.

The work on this book was funded, as is all the work of the Oxford Research Group, by grants from charitable foundations – in this case from the Joseph Rowntree Charitable Trust, the Puckham Trust and the J.A.Clark Trust – to a total of £20,000. We are very grateful indeed for the support of these trusts.

Scilla Elworthy McLean
Oxford
August 1988

Contributors

John Beyer, currently working on a doctoral disitation at the University of Leeds on Chinese peasant writers; former Asia Researcher, Amnesty International.

Patrick Burke, Researcher, Oxford Research Group.

Julian Cooper, Lecturer on Soviet Technology and Industry at the Centre for Russian and East European Studies, University of Birmingham.

Gerard Holden, Research Officer, Science Policy Research Unit, University of Sussex; Associate Fellow, Transnational Institute, Amsterdam.

François Nectoux, Senior Lecturer in Economics and French, Faculty of Administrative Studies, South Bank Polytechnic, London.

Ken Resnik, Research Associate at the Center for Psychological Studies in the Nuclear Age (an affiliate of Harvard Medical School), Boston.

List of Abbreviations

ABM	Anti-Ballistic Missile
ACDA	Arms Control and Disarmament Agency
AMD-BA	Avions Marcel Dassault-Bréguet Aviation (Dassault)
CAS	Chinese Academy of Sciences
CB	Companion of the Order of the Bath
CBE	Commander of the Order of the British Empire
CBI	Confederation of British Industry
CBIM	Companion British Institute of Management
CBO	Congressional Budget Office
CDP	Chief of Defence Procurement
CDS	Chief of Defence Staff
CEA	Commissariat à l'Énergie Atomique
CEL	Centre d'Essais des Landes
CELAR	Centre Électronique de l'Armement
CEMA	Chef d'État-Major des Armées
CEMAA	Chef d'État-Major de l'Armée de l'Air
CEMM	Chef d'État-Major de la Marine
FAS	Forces Aériennes Stratégiques
FOST	Force Océanique Stratégique
CEng	Chartered Engineer
CERM	Centre d'Exploitation du Renseignement Militaire
CHEAr	Centre des Hautes Études de l'Armement
CERN	Controlle(rate), R & D Establishments, Research and Nuclear Programmes
CIA	Central Intelligence Agency
CMG	Companion of the Order of St Michael and St George
CNES	Centre Nationale d'Études Spatiales
CNRS	Conseil National de la Recherche Scientifique
COD	Central Organization for Defence
CRED	Conseil des Recherches et Études de Défense
CTB	Comprehensive Test Ban
C3I	Command, Control, Communications and Intelligence
D	Democrat
DARPA	Defense Advanced Research Project
DAT	Direction des Armements Terrestres
DCAé	Direction des Constructions Aéronautique
DCEN	Direction des Centres d'Experimentations Nucléaires

DEG	Direction aux Études Générales
DEI	Direction de l'Électronique et de l'Informatique
DEn	Direction des Engins
DFC	Distinguished Flying Cross
DGSE	Direction Générale de la Sécurité Extérieure
DM	Defence Policy Manpower and Materiel Group
DMO	Directive Minsterielle d'Orientation des Recherches
DoE	Department of Energy
DoD	Department of Defense
DPA	Délégué aux Programmes de l'Armement
DPAI	Direction des Programmes et Affaires Industrielles
DRET	Direction des Recherches et Études Techniques
DRI	Délégation aux Relations Internationales
DST	Direction de la Surveillance du Territoire
EMAT	État-Major de l'Armée de Terre
ENA	École Nationale d'Adminstration
EPC	Equipment Policy Committee
FATac	Force Aérienne Tactique
FRS	Fellow of the Royal Society
FTC	Federal Trade Commission
FY	Fiscal Year
GCB	Knight/Dame Grand Cross of the Order of the British Empire
GCMG	Knight/Dame Grand Cross of the Order of St Michael and St George
GIAT	Groupement Industriel des Armements Terrestres
GLCM	Ground-Launched Cruise Missile
HCDC	House of Commons Defence Committee
ICBM	Intercontinental Ballistic Missile
IEE	Institute of Electrical Engineers
IGA	Ingénieur Général de l'Armement
IMEMO	Institute of World Economy and International Relations
INF	Intermediate Nuclear Forces
INSTN	Institut National des Sciences et Techniques Nucléaires
IRTDI	Institut de Recherche Technologique et de Développement
IRF	Institut de Recherche Fondamentale
JC	Joint Command
JCS	Joint Chiefs of Staff
JD	Doctor of Jurisprudence
JS	Joint Secretariat
KCB	Knight Commander of the Order of Bath
KCMG	Knight Commander of the Order of St Michael and St George
MBA	Masters of Business Administration
MBFR	Mutual Balanced Force Reduction
MIRV	Multiple Independently Targetted Re-entry Vehicle
MIT	Massachusetts Institute of Technology
MoD	Ministry of Defence
MRCA	Multiple-Role Combat Aircraft
NPT	Non-Proliferation Treaty
OBE	Officer, Order of the British Empire
OT & E	Operational Test and Evaluation

OUR	Objectifs Unitaires de Recherches
PPBS	Planning, Programming and Budgeting System
PS	Permanent Secretary
PUS	Permanent Under-Secretary
QC	Queen's Council
R	Republican
ROTC	Reserve Officers Training Corps
SAB	Scientific Advisory Board
SAC	Strategic Air Command
SACEUR	Supreme Allied Commander Europe
SALT	Strategic Arms Limitation Talks
SCAI	Service Centrale des Affaires Industrielles
SEP	Société Européenne de Propulsion
SGDN	Secrétariat Général de la Défense Nationale
SGG	Secrétaire Général du Gouvernement
SHAPE	Supreme Headquarters Allied Command Europe
SIAr	Service de Surveillance Industrielle de l'Armement
SIOP	Strategic Integrated Operational Plan
SLBM	Submarine-Launched Ballistic Missile
SLCM	Sea-Launched Cruise Missile
SNLE (-NG)	Sous-marin Nucléaire Lanceurs d'Engins (Nouvelle Génération)
SNPE	Société Nationale des Poudres et Explosifs
START	Strategic Arms Limitation Talks
STen	Service Technique des Engins Ballistiques
STET	Service Technique des Engins Tactiques
STPE	Service Technique des Poudres et Explosifs
SWB	Summary of World Broadcasts

Preface

The format of *The Nuclear Weapons World: Who, How and Where* is simple. Each chapter is divided in two: in the first half the institutions in which decisions are made – commmittees, councils, ministries, and so on – are described; in some chapters this is followed by a case-study of decisionmaking; in the second half the names and biographies of the decisionmakers are listed. The two halves of each chapter are cross-referenced. Subject and name indices are also provided.

The chapter on the USA was researched and written by Ken Resnik; the chapter on the Soviet Union by Julian Cooper; the chapters on the UK and NATO by Patrick Burke, drawing on the Oxford Research Group's earlier work and research; the chapter on France by François Nectoux; the chapter on China by John Beyer; and the chapter on the Warsaw Treaty Organization by Gerard Holden.

In preparing this book we have received the assistance of many of the organizations described. We would like to acknowledge in particular the help of the Office of the Permanent Under-Secretary and of the Head of Secretariat (Policy Studies) in the UK Ministry of Defence, the press departments of the Foreign and Commonwealth Office and Her Majesty's Treasury, the Head of the Division of Defence Planning and Policy at NATO, the NATO Information Service, the National Defence Headquarters in Ottawa, the defence ministries in Copenhagen, The Hague, Oslo, Lisbon and Paris, the US Department of Defense and the CEA in France.

As editor, I would like to thank all my colleagues at the Oxford Research Group for their friendship and practical help without which this book would not have appeared on time. It was Scilla Elworthy McLean's idea to publish this material and she provided guidance and editorial advice throughout. John Hamwee, Rosie Houldsworth, Hugh Miall and Scilla edited the chapter on France. Julie Hudson typed the chapters on France, China and the Warsaw Treaty Organization. Tony Thomson, with help from Erica Parra and Anne Piper, researched material for the UK and the NATO chapters, often at short notice. I am also grateful, for helpful comments and discussions, to General Sir Hugh Beach and Malcolm McIntosh, and, for help with the compilation of the index, to John Poole. I would also like to thank, for various sorts of practical and moral support, Andrew Kilmister, Matthew Lockwood, Jon Lunn and Melissa Parker.

Patrick Burke
October 1988

~1~

The United States

INTRODUCTION

The United States, with its huge arsenal of nuclear weapons spread throughout the globe, is one of the two major players in the nuclear arms race. Yet little is known about how these weapons are chosen, who funds them, and why they are built. This is partially due to the complexity of the institutions and processes involved. The bureaucracies of both the federal government as a whole and the Department of Defense (DoD) in particular are huge and complex. Pentagon official Colonel Albert Spaulding described the Pentagon as 'An elephant. And you have to figure out how to eat this elephant. And you don't eat it all in one gobble. You know, you take it apart' (Public Broadcasting System, *Frontline*, 'Pentagon, Inc.', October 1985). The first real challenge the researcher faces is getting the request to the proper office, a procedure which can be frustrating and time consuming.

Probably too much is made of statistics describing how large and how rich the Department of Defense is, yet it is still worth noting that the DoD employs around 3 million people (roughly equivalent to the population of Chicago). Moreover, this figure does not include other members of the military–industrial complex, as it is now popularly known. In reality, the 'complex' includes those who work for the US intelligence services (over 100,000), the National Laboratories, the top military contractors, many employees of such agencies as the Department of Energy (DoE) and the National Aeronautic and Space Administration (NASA) who are involved in military projects, and researchers at universities throughout the USA. All told, the 'complex' is vast.

The military–industrial complex is well funded, and has been so especially during the Reagan years. Since 1979, the defence budget has increased 100 per cent, and now stands at around $300 billion. The term 'defence budget', however, is something of a misnomer, since it does not include the money spent for 'defence-related' activities that are carried out by agencies outside the Department of Defense. All told, defence and defence-related spending amounts to about 40 per cent of the federal budget and is equivalent to 9 per cent of the Gross National Product (GNP) (Gervasi, 1988).

Nuclear weapons decisionmaking in the United States is essentially a closed process little understood by the public and, indeed, by some in government. Complex jargon is employed to serve as *ex post facto* justification for new weapons systems for which there may be little justification. That the language and scope of the debate about nuclear weapons has become skewed is made clear by the universal acceptance of such terms as 'Department of Defense' and 'defence industry' as nonpejorative terms that describe the functions of these institutions, instead of politically-motivated phrases that imply a clear justification - 'national defence' - for more complicated issues. Levels of secrecy are deemed to be in the interests of the nation, which infact keep the people ignorant of actions taken in their name. Further, the subject of nuclear weapons strategy has become taboo for the ordinary citizen; nuclear strategy is viewed as the province of experts and wizards, and not suitable for debate by those who do not know all the details.

The reasons for this closure are multi-faceted, and it is increasingly difficult to distinguish causes from justifications. It is clear that the continued perception of hostility between the United States and the Soviet Union lies at the heart of politicians' justifications for the continued arms' build-up, but it is less clear that this hostility contributes any great impetus to new weapons systems. It is also clear that many institutions and millions of individuals have an interest in the continuation of the arms race. The military—industrial complex is not just a name, but a plethora of institutions which includes Congress, the Department of Defense, the defence industry, and various think-tanks and laboratories.

The factors which actually play a part in the nuclear weapons decisions that are made tend to be more narrow than the justifications offered to the public. They are generally the short-term interests of the institutions named above which revolve around funding and contests for power. Further, the magic of technological innovation has become a siren-call to the United States' defence establishment, providing its own impetus to the arms race.

The fact that the military—industrial complex and its bureacuracies are so large means that the decisionmaking process, both in policy and practice, is complex in the extreme. In trying to understand that process as it really occurs, it is important first to understand the formal decisionmaking process which apparently occurs in the US government. This is the model of decisionmaking which the government presents to the world, that which is encoded in policy directives and legislation, and put in concrete form in the many organizations which make up the government.

In the introduction, this process will be outlined. More complete descriptions of the functions of the various offices, where appropriate, can be found in the next section, as well as analysis of the actual power of some of these offices and institutions. For more complete descriptions of the formal decisionmaking process, see the Oxford Research Group's *How Nuclear Weapons Decisions Are Made*.

We are chiefly concerned here with two types of decisionmaking: that regarding nuclear (and by extension, military) strategy, and that regarding the development, procurement and deployment of nuclear weapons systems. In practice, these decisions, if not these processes, play a major role in shaping the world in which we live. Bearing this in mind, it seems obvious that a better understanding of these processes (formal and informal) and the outcomes they engender is important for those with a stake in these decisions. It is equally obvious that all of us have such a stake.

It is imperative to remember, however, that the following description of the formal decisionmaking process is not meant as a model of actual decisionmaking. It is worth noting that organizational charts are referred to by military personnel as 'wiring diagrams', which reflects the changing connections and short-circuiting of various offices in specific decisions. In describing the process, one is struck by the apparent rationality of it, but also its complexity. Yet a casual analysis is not enough, one must delve deeper to discover the inherent assumptions and biases which determine the process, and in turn warp it. Perhaps the clearest assumption underpinning the decisonmaking process is that of rational actors, all working with a common goal in mind: national defence. Further, the process rests on the assumption that this goal, national defence, is clearly defined and monolithic.

Yet these assumptions have different meanings for different people. In fact, 'national defence' means many things to many people. One of the things that the Pentagon has been strongly criticized for in recent years is a lack of articulation of long-term goals and strategy. Without this articulation, the assumption that the common goal of all players is the 'national defence' falls apart, for there is no reason to believe that there is a mutually shared vision of what constitutes the national defence. Further, with this lack of a common goal, our definition of rational actors changes. As Jim Falk has pointed out, 'When we talk about a rational actor it is possible to assume that he could make decisions solely in terms of his self-interest or alternatively in terms of the group interest' (Falk, 1985).

A Brief Description of the Decisionmaking Process

It is important to note that deadlines in the context of decisionmaking can be misleading. There is no one point when one of the groups discussed below can lean back and declare their work finished for the year. One of the central characteristics of the decisionmaking processes discussed below is that they are cyclical and ongoing.

Both military doctrine and procurement supposedly have as their cornerstone the military needs of the nation. Thus, what can be considered the first step in the decisionmaking process in both areas is the National Intelligence Estimate (NIE) which is put out by the intelligence community. It is common in the United States to identify the 'intelligence community' solely with the Central Intelligence Agency (CIA). While the CIA is certainly the largest and most visible member of this intensely secretive community, there are other agencies dedicated to intelligence functions (for a complete description of the intelligence community, see Richelson, 1985). Within the Department of Defense, these include the Defense Intelligence Agency (DIA) and the National Security Agency (NSA). In addition, each of the four military services has its own intelligence agency. The State Department Bureau of Intelligence and Research also performs significant intelligence functions.

National Intelligence Estimates are coordinated by the CIA, in particular by the Director of Central Intelligence (DCI), with the cooperation and input of the agencies mentioned above. The number of NIEs varies from year to year and administration to administration. During President Reagan's term of office there was a sharp increase in the number of NIEs produced each year. In 1982, for example, there were sixty-eight NIEs produced, as compared to eleven or twelve during the last years of the Carter Administration (Richelson, 1985, p.245). Only a few of these NIEs, usually what is known as the '11 series', will deal specifically with strategic military affairs.

From these NIEs is produced the 'threat assessment', which portrays the nuclear power levels of various nations, their nuclear research and development programmes, their budget allocations and deployment plans. There is controversy surrounding the threat assessment and the 'needs analyses' that results from it. Critics charge that the threat assessment is unrealistic and serves as an *ex post facto* justification for programmes the defence community would like to see funded; others reply that the threat assessments are indeed realistic, and that needs analyses are carefully weighed responses to those threats. There seems little doubt, however, that the public DoD publication, *Soviet Military Power*, is a public relations ploy designed to increase fears of the Soviet Union's military capability. Gervasi has argued that in this publication even the most basic facts are distorted (Gervasi, 1988). Suspicion has been directed at *Soviet Military Power* partly because the first edition, released in 1981, seemed designed to substantiate charges of Soviet military prowess and US weakness made by Reagan in the 1980 presidential campaign.

It is important to note here that 'nuclear weapons procurement' is actually two separate processes at every stage, a fact not usually reflected in public debate. The warhead (the actual explosive component) is developed and produced separately from the delivery system (the vehicle, such as a missile or launcher, which brings the warhead to a target). The technical characteristics of the warhead determine such things as yield (the 'power' of the weapon) and blast characteristics (how strong the blast is as compared to radiation effects, etc.). Delivery system characteristics, on the other hand, determine such factors as range (the distance the warhead can travel), accuracy and mobility. Warheads and delivery systems are designed independently of each other, not in the sense that the characteristics of the warhead are not taken into naccount when designing the delivery system (and vice versa), but in the sense that they follow different formal processes (for a readable explanation of the technical aspects of nuclear weapons, see Tsipis, 1983).

While the DoD determines the characteristics of both warheads and delivery systems, supposedly based on military needs, the actual design, testing, and production of nuclear warheads is undertaken by the Department of Energy (DoE) and funded - like other programmes - by the Congress. This allows the government to argue that decisions regarding nuclear warheads and their actual production remain under civilian control. This issue, along with the responsibilities of and relationship between the two agencies, will be discussed further below.

Warhead Acquisition

There are three formal phases in the warhead acquisition process: weapon concept, feasibility study and weapon development. Various components of both the DoE and DoD take part in each of the phases.

Phase 1, weapon concept, is basically a research phase. It may concern a new warhead or modification of an existing warhead.

Phase 2, the feasibility study, also establishes a formal contract between the two agencies (DoD and DoE) for production of a warhead. This is done when a 'request for research and engineering', which outlines the military characteristics of the proposed warhead, is submitted to the Office of the Secretary of Defense. DoD and DoE acceptance of such a request constitutes a contract. The next step is the undertaking of a Joint Feasibility Study, which is usually headed by the service developing the weapon. The study is undertaken with the cooperation of DoE. Both Phase 1 and Phase 2 are reviewed annually by the services and the Joint Chiefs of Staff.

Phase 3, weapon development, is dependent on the outcome of the feasibility study in phase 2. If the study concludes that the weapon is indeed feasible, the Secretary of Defense makes a 'Phase 3 development request' to the DoE through the Military Liaison Committee. A project officer is then appointed by the service which chaired phase 2. Other agencies within the Department of Defense may also designate someone to participate in the development project. During this phase, an agreement is also reached with the DoE concerning the division of responsibilities. Preliminary, interim and final reports on warhead development must be completed and reviewed by the Design Review and Acceptance Group (DRAAG), which is made up of representatives of each of the three services. If the DRAAG report is favourable, the Military Liaison Committee notifies DoE that production of the warhead may begin.

This procedure, as is noted above, results in the actual production of a new or modified warhead. This acquisition is based on the Warhead Annual Planning Cycle, which has four stages, described below.

Nuclear Weapon Development Guidance - this is submitted biennally by the Joint Chiefs of Staff to the Secretary of Defense. The guidance is based on the needs of the services for the next ten to fifteen years, and in addition lists the priorities for technological goals of the Unified and Specified Commands.

Annual Nuclear Weapons Development Guidance - this is prepared by the Department of Defense, and transmitted to the DoE through the Military Liaison Committee. The guidance defines development priorities and technological goals, and informs DoE what new warheads the DoD will want.

The Nuclear Weapons Stockpile Memorandum - this is prepared by the Defense Nuclear Agency (DNA) from the Development Guidance. The Stockpile Memorandum is an analysis and projection of stockpile needs. 'Stockpile' refers simply to the US stock of nuclear warheads, which is overseen by the DNA. The memorandum goes to the National Security Council (NSC) for Presidential approval.

Presidential Approval — this authorizes the stockpile for five years and grants long lead procurement authority for ten years beyond that.

It is rare that decisions on warheads are brought to public attention, partially due to the secrecy that surrounds this process. Recent allegations of safety problems at the Hanford Nuclear Reservation, a DoE facility, and the Rocky Flats plant, which manufactures plutonium 'triggers' for nuclear warheads and is managed by Rockwell International, have brought DoE nuclear facilities somewhat into the public spotlight.

Public attention is more frequently focused on a major weapons system. In the past several years allegations of impropriety in DoD procurement (ranging from the imfamous overpriced toilet seats to contractor indictments) has caused unusual public scrutiny of the system. In addition, more isolated controversies, such as the renewed debate over a suitable basing mode for the MX, or 'Peacekeeper', ICBM sometimes come to the public eye, most often because of congressional action.

As with the the process for warheads, there is both an acquisition process for delivery systems and an annual planning cycle, which is known as the Planning, Programming and Budgeting System (PPBS). We will first briefly examine the acquisition process.

The acquisition process is at this time in a state of flux due to DoD attempts to implement the 1986 Military Reform Act and the recommendations of the Packard Commission. While many changes have been carried out the final shape of the DoD acquisition process is still several months from being institutionalized at the time of writing (June 1988).

The acquisition process is primarily the province of the Defense Acquisition Board (DAB), a body constituted in October 1987 in response to the 1986 Military Reform Act. Its permanent members are: the Under Secretary of Defense for Acquisition; the Vice-Chairman of the Joint Chiefs of Staff; the Assistant Secretary of Defense, Comptroller; the Assistant Secretary of Defense (Production and Logistics); the Assistant Secretary of Defense (Program Operations); the Director of Defense Research and Engineering; the Director, Program Analysis and Evaluation; and the Acquisition Executives of the Army, Air Force and Navy. The Under Secretary of Defense chairs the DAB and the Vice-Chairman of the Joint Chiefs is its vice-chairman.

The DAB has ten permanent acquisition committees: the Science and Technology Committee; the Nuclear and Chemical Committee; the Strategic Systems Committee; the Conventional Systems Committee; the C3I Committee; the Test and Evaluation Committee; the Production and Logistics Committee; the Installations Support and Military Constructions Committee; the International Programs Committee; and the Policy and Initiatives Committee. The acquisition committees provide advice and support to the DAB and may be represented in DAB meetings where appropriate.

DAB approval is needed for all 'major defense acquisition programs'. These are defined as programmes which are not highly sensitive and classified (as defined by the Secretary of Defense) and either designated by the Secretary of Defense as major defence acquisition programmes because of urgency of need, development risk, joint funding, Congressional interest or other factors, or which will receive total expenditure for research, development, test and evaluation of more than $200 million or total expenditure on procurement of more than $1 billion. In this way DAB oversees the services responsible for development and production of their own weapons. At six stages, so-called 'milestones', DAB review and approval is required.

Milestone 0: this is concurrent with the Program Objectives Memoranda (POM) review described later in this introduction. At this point the DoD body responsible for new weapons systems must submit a Mission Need Statement (MNS) justifying the new system. Milestone 0 is known as Program Initiation—Need Decision and approves programme initiation and authorizes the budget for the system.

Milestone I: known as Concept Demonstration—Validation Decision. At this stage the appropriateness of the particular weapons programme is evaluated. DAB approval is required before the concept demonstration phase - in which the respective DoD body demonstrates the weapons system is feasible - can proceed. The relevant DoD body must also show at this point why alternative concepts are not being considered.

Milestone II: in this crucial stage the decision to proceed with full-scale development is taken. The DAB approves full-scale development of the weapons system and, occasionally, Low-Rate Initial Production (LRIP) of certain parts of the system. At this point the DAB also approves the 'program baseline agreement', which establishes functional specifications, cost and schedule goals, and thresholds. According to the DoD, deviations from a baseline agreement 'trigger a management review to either restore the program to baseline parameters, revise the baseline agreement, or cancel the program.'

Milestone III: At this point DAB approves the actual production of the weapons system. Testing and evaluation must be complete before this milestone is reached. If the programme is exceptionally large or the time between LRIP and full-rate production is very long, there may be a programme review before a Milestone III agreement.

Milestone IV: Logistics, readiness and support review. This usually takes place one—two years before initial deployment of a weapons system. This review identifies actions and resources needed to ensure the operational readiness of a weapons system when it is deployed.

Milestone V: 'Major upgrade or replacement of system decision'. This normally takes place five—ten years after the initial deployment of a weapons system. At this point the decision is taken whether the system's deficiencies in meeting its mission requirement warrant a major upgrade or whether it should be retired from service.

All DAB decisions are released by the Under Secretary of Defense for Acquisition as Acquisition Decision Memoranda (ADMs).

The Planning, Programming and Budgeting System (PPBS)

The PPBS is at the heart of Pentagon decision-making in terms of weapons procurement. The PPBS was introduced in 1961 and is the 'DoD's formal process for arriving at resource allocation decisions'(Committee on Armed Services, 1985). Since what weapons the DoD has built or is building to a certain extent dictates military strategy, PPBS also has some effect on military strategy. Though almost every office in the Pentagon participates in the PPBS to some extent, it is officially overseen by the Defense Resources Board (DRB). The DRB is made up of the Chairman of the JCS; the Under Secretary of Defense for Acquisition; the Acquisition Executives of the Army, Navy, and Air Force; the Department of Defense Comptroller; the Assistant Secretary of Defense (Production and Logistics); the Assistant Secretary of Defense (Program Operations); the Director of Defense Research and Engineering and the Director of Program Analysis and Evaluation. Other officials may also participate in DRB meetings, although they are not statutorily part of the board.

The PPBS starts with the release of the Defense Guidance by the Secretary of Defense. The Defense Guidance is the Secretary's 'official statement setting forth his perceptions of the military threat to the United States' vital interests and the strategy that the DoD should pursue to deal with that threat' (Rovner, 1982, p. 18).

The Defense Guidance is produced after the Joint Chiefs of Staff (JCS) submit the Joint Strategic Planning Document (JSPD) to the Secretary of Defense (SECDEF). The JSPD contains JCS views of threats to national security, and 'if-money-were-no-object' recommendations for US forces over the next seven years. At the same time, the views of the commanders of the Unified and Specified Commands on the same topic are solicited.

Once these recommendations have been analysed, draft copies of the Defense Guidance are circulated within the Department of Defense for comment by various offices. After these comments are collected, the official Defense Guidance is produced every January. The guidance informs each service of the goals that have been set for it and the amount of money it should plan to spend in the next five years to achieve those goals.

In response to the Defense Guidance, each of the three services submits what are known as Program Objective Memoranda (POMs). POMs set forth concrete proposals to fulfil the services' assigned goals. They also cover a five-year period, detailing how many weapons of what kind each service wants. This is where new weapons systems are submitted for consideration, and so there is intense competition and lobbying to be included in the POMs. The POMs are submitted in May, but 'POM development begins much earlier as the Services receive projections of future requirements from their major commands and other institutional "claimants" '(Rovner, 1982, p.490).

Prior to DRB review of the POMs, the JCS study them and submit to the DAB the Joint Program Assessment Memorandum (JPAM). The JPAM reviews the POMs and evaluates whether, taken as a whole, they will satisfy the requirements set forth in the Defense Guidance. At the same time, the commanders of the Specified and Unified Commands are once again invited to express their views on specific programme issues. This reflects an attempt in recent years to incorporate the commanders of the Specified and Unified Commands, who in fact frequently have operational control of weapons systems, into the decisionmaking process.

The decisions of the DRB are set forth in a series of Program Decision Memoranda (PDMs) signed by the Secretary or Deputy Secretary of Defense. In September, the actual budgeting process begins. Budgeting is overseen by the DoD Comptroller, who holds the rank of Assistant Secretary. Once this is finished, a document known as the SECDEF's Budget Request is produced and submitted to the Office of Management and Budget (OMB).

The Office of Management and Budget is an independent agency and is the President's primary vehicle for making budget decisions. The OMB is responsible for fashioning the President's Budget Request, which will be submitted to Congress in January. The OMB maintains an office and staff in the Pentagon. This gives the OMB constant representation in Pentagon budget decisions. While the OMB will sometimes change the DoD budget, it is not seen by the DoD as the 'axe-wielding' agency in the way that other departments often regard it.

The OMB works throughout the year, and its decisions are vital to all agencies. Budget policy is developed from March until May, at which time the OMB will set spending limits for the agencies. From July to September the OMB receives budget requests from the agencies, which are analysed from September to December. During this last period, the OMB will also hold hearings with the various agencies. Before the OMB writes the official request for Congress, the President will hear final appeals from an agency, if necessary.

At this point, the President's Budget Request will be sent to Congress for approval. Congressional action on the budget has come under intense scrutiny in recent years. This is largely due to growing concern - at times approaching hysteria - over the budget deficit. It has probably been heightened by repeated Presidential accusations that Congress - largely the Democratic Party - is responsible for the deficit. In truth, however, Congress and the Executive Branch share equally the responsibility for the budget and whatever problems it engenders.

Congressional action on the budget, and in particular the defence budget, is fairly complex. On paper, it follows a simple timetable (though this is rarely adhered to in practice): in January, the President's budget proposal is presented to Congress, accompanied by a plethora of press briefings and releases. The House and Senate budget committees start their hearings, considering testimony from major administration figures, who must defend the President's budget. By 15 April, the Budget Committees release the First Budget Resolution, which is then debated in the House and Senate. From 15 May until September the Authorization and Appropriations Committees make decisions regarding specific programmes. The House and Senate decisions must then be reconciled in joint conference, and the Second Budget Resolution is released in late September in time for the start of the new fiscal year, 1 October.

Most of the work done in Congress takes place in committees. This is obvious to anyone who has ever visited the galleries in either of the two Houses. Members of Congress wander in and out and chat with each other, usually while another member stands at the podium in order to get his or her speech into the *Congressional Record*. Several committees do work related to defence and the defence budget, and within these committees there are subcommittees which deal with more specific issues.

This simplified overview of the formal process of nuclear decisionmaking gives us some idea of both how weapons decisions are supposed to be reached and how they are reached. In order to understand how they are reached one must identify nodes of power, offices and institutions which usually have an influential voice in weapons decisions. This chapter does that as well as identifying individuals in powerful positions.

THE UNITED STATES GOVERNMENT

The US Government consists of three branches, the judicial, the executive and the legislative. Only the executive and the legislative branches play an important part in defence decisionmaking, although the judicial branch plays a part in isolated instances, such as when the Supreme Court ruled on the constitutionality of the Gramm-Rudman Act, which affected the defence budget.

Within the executive branch is the Executive Office of the President, which includes the

National Security Council and the Office of Management and Budget. The other agencies which play some part in defence decisionmaking within the executive branch are the Department of Defense, the Department of Energy, and the Department of State, which are executive departments. The heads of these agencies sit in the Cabinet, which is actually a creation of custom and tradition rather than law. Also within the executive branch are the independent establishments, which include the Central Intelligence Agency, the Arms Control and Disarmament Agency, and the National Aeronautics and Space Administration. In this study, the weapons laboratories are included with the executive branch. Although they are controlled by the Department of Energy, they are not formally considered part of the government.

The legislative branch consists of the Senate and the House of Representatives plus the agencies which support them, which include the General Accounting Office, the Congressional Budget Office, and the Office of Technology Assessment.

The Executive Branch

THE DEPARTMENT OF DEFENSE (DOD)
Address: The Pentagon, Washington, DC 20301

The Department of Defense was established, originally as the National Military Establishment, by the National Security Act of 1947 (see Figure 1.1). This act established the structure of the armed services and the DoD by combining the Navy Department and the War Department. The DoD was subsequently made an executive agency, essentially with the structure it has today, by the National Security Act Amendments of 1949. This act and its amendments shaped the structure of the United States military in many ways, and is at least in part responsible for the reliance which US military doctrine places on nuclear weapons (Eden, 1984). Today, the DoD stands at the centre of nuclear decisionmaking in the United States. In this section, some of the more important nodes of power within the DoD are identified.

Numerous proposals to reform the DoD have been put forward since its foundation. The most recent efforts were in 1985, when both the Armed Services Committee of the Senate and the Packard Commission, appointed by the President, conducted extensive studies into DoD organization. In part, the recommendations of these studies were enacted in the Nichols–Goldwater Department of Defense Reorganization Act of 1986 and the National Defense Authorization Act for FY 1987. These acts reflect continuing intense Congressional interest in procurement reform, which has been stirred by record-high military budgets, strong competition for federal budget monies, and public reaction to allegations of waste, fraud and inefficiency in procurement.

Criticism of the DoD has come from many quarters, and public concern was evident in the mid-1980s. It is questionable, however, whether structural reform of the DoD will have substantial effect on the arms race or on defence decisionmaking. Some of the forces which influence decisionmaking are to be found outside the Department of Defense - for instance, the so-called 'imperative' of technological development, contractor pressures, and the making and enactment of foreign policy. Other determinants of the arms race and defence decisionmaking, such as bureaucratic momentum, seem at least partially immune to structural changes.

In addition, there is the problem of what one defence critic has termed the DoD's 'culture of procurement'. In this 'culture of procurement,' he writes, 'the central function of the military has been perverted. Yes, the Pentagon is in business to devise war plans and understand the enemy and protect the nation; but before any of those things, it is in business to spend money'(Fallows, 1981, p.62).

The DoD has also been criticized for what is known as the 'revolving door'. The term 'revolving door' refers to the exchange of personnel between the DoD and the defence industry. Personnel turnover in the DoD is fairly high: General Accounting Office (GAO - see below) studies show that 30,126 employees left the DoD in FY 1983 and FY 1984. Of these, the GAO estimates that 5,100 of them were

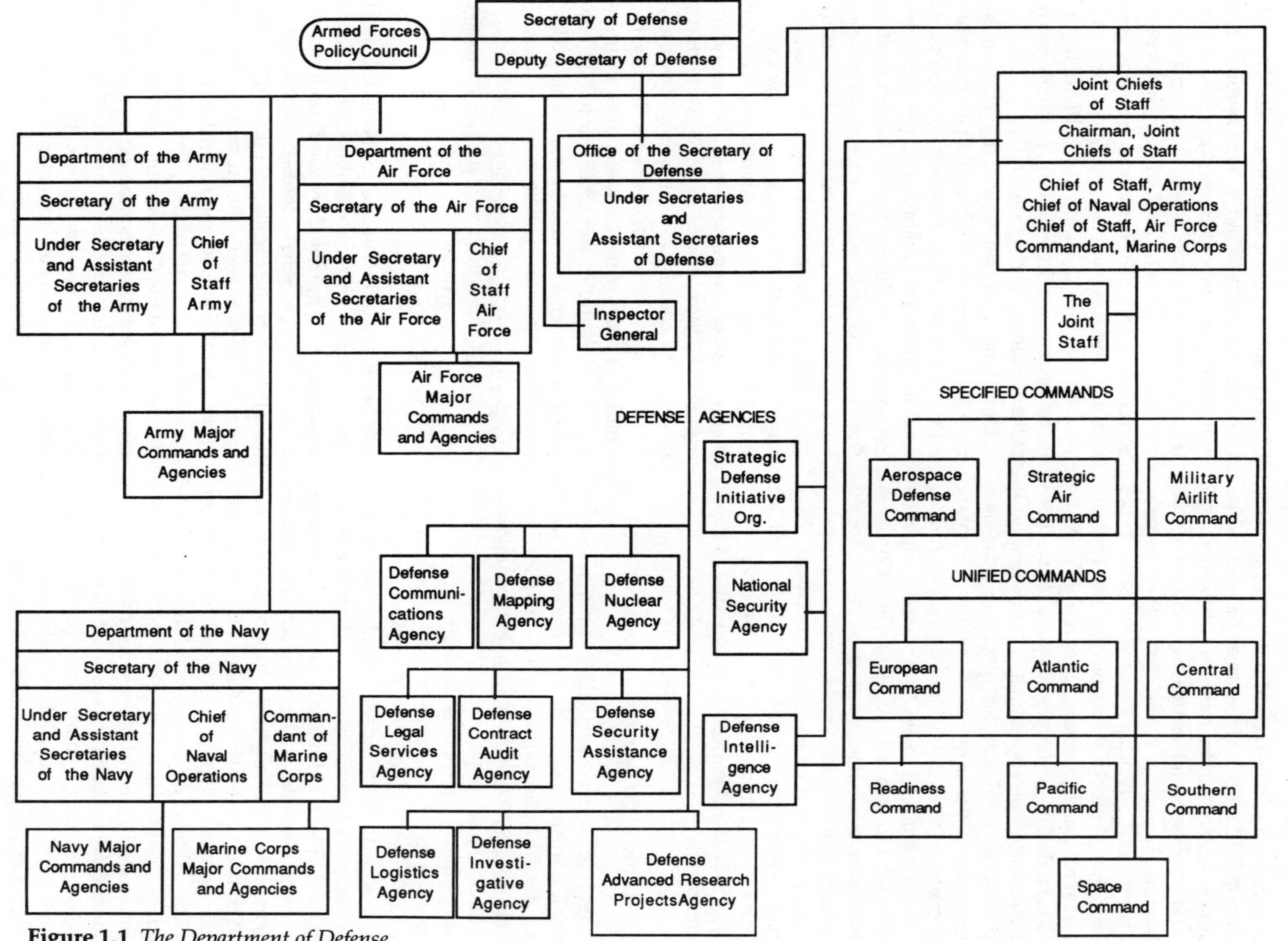

Figure 1.1 *The Department of Defense*

employed by a contractor for whom they were responsible when they were at the DoD. In a survey carried out by the GAO of former DoD employees who subsequently worked for contractors, 90 per cent considered this movement of personnel 'advantageous' for the DoD; 96 per cent thought it advantageous for the contractors (General Accounting Office, 1987). While GAO found no evidence of illegal activity, there was an obvious appearance of impropriety. It should be noted that the 'revolving door' also revolves in the opposite direction: corporate executives often leave defence contractors to take positions at the DoD where they might be of benefit to their former employers. Congress has recently implemented laws which forbid certain DoD employees from accepting remuneration from contractors for whom they had responsibility at DoD. This should at least partially ameliorate the 'revolving door' problem, although it is unlikely to solve the problem completely.

The Office of the Secretary of Defense (OSD)

'Office of the Secretary of Defense' is actually a misleading title, since the OSD actually encompasses the entire civilian leadership of the DoD, and not just the Secretary of Defense himself. The OSD was not particularly powerful when it was created in 1947 and more power was granted to it in the 1949 National Security Act amendments. The 1953 Reorganization Plan developed by President Eisenhower further concentrated power in the hands of the Secretary of Defense. However, basic problems concerning the role of the Secretary of Defense remained, especially with respect to his ability to control or modify the DoD and, to an extent, the services. The 1958 Amendments to the National Security Act were written to remove these problems, and their passage was hastened by open inter-service rivalry. These amendments clarified the authority of the Secretary of Defense to make it clear that he had 'direction, authority and control' over the DoD, including the power to make substantial organizational changes.

Today, the OSD has roughly 2,000 employees, and controls the Department of Defense substantially, if not absolutely. The OSD has also 'farmed out' a large portion of its work to the thirteen Defense Agencies, which report directly to the OSD. The OSD itself consists of the Secretary of Defense, the Deputy Secretary of Defense, the Under-Secretaries of Defense, the Assistant Secretaries of Defense, and the staffs of these offices. Although it is formally a civilian organization, naturally many military officers work at the OSD.

One of the chief criticisms of the Office of the Secretary of Defense has been that there is often little correspondence between the concepts used in policy formulation and the rationales for weapons acquisition. The Department of Defense, it is said, works with strategic concepts which in fact are broad enough to justify any weapons system, and strategic rationales for weapons systems are often merely *ex post facto* justifications for systems acquired for political and economic reasons. The restructuring which took place in 1986 was partly intended to address this problem. (The problem may also, however, be a product of the 'culture of procurement' - see above). Examining the structure of the OSD can tell us how weapons systems should be related to policy, but not whether they will be.

The Secretary of Defense (SECDEF)
Address: Room 3E880, The Pentagon, Washington, DC 20301
Tel: (202) 695-5261

The Secretary of Defense is probably the most visible and recognizable member of the defence bureaucracy. Appointed by the President and confirmed by the Senate, the Secretary serves at the pleasure of the President. Like the Department of Defense itself, the current position of Secretary of Defense was legislated in the National Security Act of 1947. The Secretary is a full member of the Cabinet, and the position is commonly seen as one of the most vital that an incoming administration has to fill. Most incoming Secretaries of Defense, however, are largely inexperienced in defence issues; on average, Secretaries remain only 2.4 years in office (McLean, 1986, p.55). Indeed, the criticism has been made that all the posts in the OSD are filled by inexperienced men and

women. Part of the blame for this state of affairs lies with the Senate, which has been reluctant to challenge the appointment of top DoD officials, even of those who are obviously unskilled in what is called 'defence management'. Critics argue that the lack of experience of the SECDEF and his senior officials not only makes them less efficient in their posts but also allows for their manipulation by the military and other, more experienced, officials in the DoD, and leads to a lack of accountability for the weapons systems initiated and policy decisions taken while they are in office. The dilemma here is that an experienced Secretary of Defense could only be chosen from the DoD, the defence industry or various think-tanks — that is, he would enter his post through the 'revolving door'.
(See biography of: Carlucci.)

The Deputy Secretary of Defense
Address: Room 3E994, The Pentagon, Washington, DC 20301
Tel: (202) 695-6532

The position of Deputy Secretary, the second highest civilian in the Department of Defense, is also probably the most flexible position. The power and responsibilities of the Deputy Secretary are highly dependent on the style and attitude of his immediate superior, the Secretary of Defense. The Deputy Secretary is formally responsible for the 'supervision and coordination' of the DoD, but how far his power extends depends on how involved the Secretary of Defense is in actually running the DoD.
(See biography of: Taft.)

The Under Secretary of Defense for Acquisition
Address: Room 3E1006, The Pentagon, Washington, DC 20301
Tel: (202) 695-2381

The Under Secretary of Defense for Acquisition is a new position, created by Congress in the Department of Defense Reorganization Act of 1986. The office of Under Secretary of Defense for Acquisition was created on the advice of the Packard Commission, of which Secretary of Defense Frank Carlucci was an influential member.

The formal responsibilities of the Under Secretary for Acquisition are to serve as the 'principal staff adviser to the Secretary of Defense for all matters relating to the acquisition system; research and development; production; logistics; command, control, communications and intelligence activities related to acquisition; military construction, and procurement'(*US Government Manual 1987—88, 1987, p.176*). In addition, the Under Secretary is responsible for the performance of the entire DoD acquisition system and chairs the Defense Acquisition Board (DAB). The Defense Science Board (see below) also reports to the Under Secretary. Informally, the Under Secretary is seen as the acquisition 'czar'.

Key Assistant: Principal Deputy Under Secretary - Vacant
(See biography of: Costello.)

Under Secretary of Defense for Policy
Address: Room 4E830, The Pentagon, Washington, DC 20301
Tel: (202) 697-7200

Secretary of Defense Carlucci intentionally let this post remain vacant after the resignation of its previous incumbent, Fred Ikle, who left the DoD soon after Secretary of Defense Caspar Weinberger resigned his post in December 1987. Ikle was seen as the last of the Reagan old guard, one of the conservative idealogues who had been with Reagan since the 1970s. Carlucci, it is believed, saw little point in filling the vacancy with so little of the Reagan administration's term left; he divided the responsibilities of the office among other officials.

The position, which was created in 1977, is one of two under secretaries and is the policy counterpoint to the Under Secretary for Acquisition. The Under Secretary for Policy is the principal staff assistant to the Secretary of Defense in all matters relating to policy. As such, the Under Secretary can have great influence on nuclear strategy (as, for instance, did Fred Ikle).

The direction of the DoD in the post-Reagan era will be in part dependent on who fills this post.

Key Assistants: Deputy Under Secretary (Policy) - Craig Alderman, Jr.; Deputy Under Secretary (Planning and Resources) - Dennis E. Kloske.

Assistant Secretary of Defense (Command, Control, Communications and Intelligence)
Address: Room 3E172, The Pentagon, Washington, DC 20301
Tel: (202)695-0348
Reports to: Under Secretary for Acquisition

The creation of this post - currently vacant - in 1984 reflected the Reagan Administration's continuing concern for command, control, communications and intelligence (C3I). This official serves as the principal adviser to the Secretary of Defense on matters involving C3I, which include telecommunications, intelligence, the early warning system, and command and control of forces. In addition, the Assistant Secretary is the primary DoD official charged with preparing and defending the DoD's C3I programme before the Congress. The Assistant Secretary is responsible for the direct supervision of the Defense Mapping Agency and the Defense Communications Agency, and has primary staff responsibility over the Defense Intelligence Agency and the National Security Agency/Central Security Service.

Under the Reagan Administration, C3I received a substantial portion of the defence budget in a somewhat controversial 'modernization' programme. Some claimed that US C3I, especially the early warning system, had become obsolete and dangerously vulnerable to sabotage or to destruction in the event of a nuclear attack attack on the USA. The same people also claimed that a 'survivable' C3I system is necessary for the USA to be able to launch an effective second strike after a Soviet attack. Critics, however, charged that the upgrading of the C3I system, and the attention it received under Reagan, was an indication of that Administration's plans to achieve the capability of waging and winning a protracted nuclear war.(For more information on C3I, see Bracken, 1983 and Ford, 1985; for information on the Reagan Administration's views on nuclear war, see Scheer, 1983.)

Key Assistants: Principal Deputy Assistant Secretary (C3I) - Thomas P. Quinn; Director, Strategic and Nuclear Forces C3 - Arthur H. Bertapelle; Director, Theater and Tactical C3 - Dick Howe; Deputy Assistant Secretary (Intelligence) - C. A. Hawkins; Deputy Assistant Secretary (Plans and Resources) - Nathaniel M. Cavalline.

Assistant Secretary of Defense (Production and Logistics)
Address: Room 3E808, The Pentagon, Washington, DC 20301
Tel: (202) 695-6639
Reports to: Under Secretary for Acquisition

This official is the Under Secretary for Acquisition's principal assistant in matters relating to procurement, including the development of procurement regulations and supervising procurement installations. As such, he has broad responsibility for *how* the DoD conducts business, but little effect on *what* it buys. The current incumbent, Katzen, is a replacement for Costello, who held this post before being appointed Under Secretary for Acquisition.

Key Assistants: Deputy Assistant Secretary (Procurement) - Eleanor P. Spector.
(See biography of: Katzen.)

Deputy Under Secretary of Defense (Research and Advanced Technology)
Address: Room 3E114, The Pentagon, Washington, DC 20301
Tel: (202) 695-5036
Reports to: Under Secretary for Acquisition, Director of Defense Research and Engineering

The Deputy Under Secretary for Research and Advanced Technology is charged with the overall management of science and technology programmes in the DoD. The Deputy Under Secretary also monitors in-house DoD laboratories and federal contract research centres. In addition, the Deputy Under Secretary is responsible for interaction and communication with the national scientific community.

Deputy Under Secretary of Defense (Strategic and Theater Nuclear Forces)
Address: Room 3E130, The Pentagon, Washington, DC 20301
Tel: (202) 697-9386

Reports to: Under Secretary for Acquisition, Director of Defense Research and Engineering

The Deputy Under Secretary for Strategic and Theater Nuclear Forces is responsible for overseeing research and engineering related to strategic and theatre nuclear forces.
(See biography of: Woodruff.)

Deputy Under Secretary of Defense (Test and Evaluation)
Address: Room 3E1060, The Pentagon, Washington, DC 20301
Tel: (202) 695-7171
Reports to: Under Secretary for Acquisition, Director of Defense Research and Engineering

(See biography of: Adolph.)

Director of Defense Research and Engineering
Address: The Pentagon, Washington, DC 20301
Tel: (202) 697-5095
Reports to: Under Secretary for Acquisition

This post was previously designated the Under Secretary of Defense for Research and Engineering and is one of the most powerful positions in the Pentagon. However, the same Act which created the Under Secretary for Acquisition redesignated it and subordinated its authority to that of the Under Secretary for Acquisition. The director now plays much more of a coordinating role than anything else, and has lost most of the authority the post previously had.
(See biography of: Duncan.)

Assistant Secretary of Defense (International Security Affairs)
Address: Room 4E830, The Pentagon, Washington, DC 20301
Tel: (202) 695-4351
Reports to: Under Secretary for Policy

This official is responsible for guidance in political-military activities related to international affairs, excluding NATO, the Soviet Union, and other European nations. Although this does not make the post especially important in nuclear decisionmaking, it merits inclusion because of the its current incumbent, Richard Armitage.
(See biography of: Armitage.)

Assistant Secretary of Defense (International Security Policy)
Address: Room 4E838, The Pentagon, Washington, DC 20301 Tel: (202) 695-0942
Reports to: Under Secretary for Policy

The Assistant Secretary for International Security Policy is responsible for policy on strategic international security matters involving NATO and European affairs, strategic and theatre nuclear force planning, and arms negotiations. In addition, he is responsible for formulating policy relating to the relationship between strategic and theatre force planning and budgets.
(See biography of: Lehman.)

Assistant Secretary of Defense (Comptroller)
Address: Room 3E822, The Pentagon, Washington, DC 20301
Tel: (202) 695-3237

The Comptroller provides assistance and advice to the Secretary of Defense on matters relating to programming and budgeting, and fiscal management. He is responsible for the supervision, direction and review of the planning and execution of the DoD's budget request. The Comptroller is also the chief 'numbercruncher' at the Pentagon, providing information to outside agencies.
(See biography of:Helm.)

Assistant Secretary of Defense (Legislative Affairs)
Address: Room 3E966, The Pentagon, Washington, DC, 20301
Tel: (202) 697-6210

The Assistant Secretary for Legislative Affairs maintains direct liaison between the DoD and other government agencies on all matters affecting the relationship between DoD and the Congress. The Assistant Secretary provides advice and assistance to officials of the DoD about Congressional aspects of DoD policies and plans, co-ordinates action the DoD takes in regard to Congressional consideration of DoD requests, and is responsible for providing information and witnesses requested by the Congress.

(See biography of: Carlisle.)

Director, Program Analyis and Evaluation
Address: Room 3E836, The Pentagon, Washington, DC 20301
Tel: (202) 695-0971
Reports to: Secretary of Defense

The Office of Program Analysis and Evaluation is responsible for formulating the force planning, fiscal guidance, programming guidance and policy guidance which DoD force planning and programme projections are based on. The office also evaluates military forces and weapons systems in relation to US objectives, projected threats, and budgetary constraints and priorities as established by the Secretary of Defense.

Key Aides: Principal Deputy - Michael Leonard; Deputy Director (Strategic Programs) - Michael Ioffredo.
(See biography of: Chu.)

Director, Operational Test and Evaluation
Address: Room 3E318, The Pentagon, Washington, DC 20301
Tel: (202) 697-3554
Reports to: Secretary of Defense

The Director of Operational Test and Evaluation (OT & E) is the principal adviser to the Secretary of Defense on DoD OT & E, that is, essentially, the testing of weapons systems. The director prescribes policies and procedures for the conduct of OT & E, and monitors OT & E programmes to assure compliance. The director also approves beforehand the adequacy of service test plans for major programmes, and reports on the effectiveness and suitability of a weapons system before it advances into full production. Operational test and evaluation of particular weapons systems by the DoD has been criticized as unrealistic and misleading. This office was created in 1985 to oversee testing and to deal with such criticism.

Key Assistants: Deputy Director (Resources and Administration) - Nicholas Toomer; Deputy Director (Test Plans and Assessments) - Don Greenlee.
(See biography of: Krings.)

Inspector General, Department of Defense
Address: The Pentagon, Washington, DC 20301
Tel: (202) 695-4249

The Office of the Inspector General is actually organizationally separate from the Office of the Secretary of Defense, and the Inspector General is responsible directly to the President. The Inspector General is responsible for initiating, conducting and supervising audits of and investigations into programmes and operations of the DoD. The Inspector General recommends policies to improve the efficiency of such programmes, and is responsible for informing the Secretary of Defense and the Congress of any deficiencies. The position was created by the Inspector General Act of 1978, which became effective in 1983.
(See biography of: Brown, J. G.)

The Joint Chiefs of Staff

The organization of the Joint Chiefs of Staff was created, with the DoD, by the National Security Act of 1947. Today it consists of the Chairman of the Joint Chiefs of Staff; the Chief of Staff, US Army; the Chief of Naval Operations; the Chief of Staff, US Air Force; and the Commandant of the Marine Corps. In addition, there is a Vice-Chairman of the Joint Chiefs who participates in all JCS meetings but may not vote. The Chairman of the Joint Chiefs is the principal military adviser to the President, the National Security Council, and the Secretary of Defense. The other chiefs are military advisers who can submit additional information on request, and may submit their opinion when it differs from that of the chairman. There is also a Joint Staff, run by the Director of the Joint Staff, which provides assistance to the chiefs. By law, this staff can be no larger than 1,627 after 1 October 1988.

The Joint Chiefs are responsible for assisting the President and Secretary of Defense in formulating strategy and in general planning for the armed forces, allocating resources to fulfil strategic plans, making recommendations for the assignment of responsibilities within the armed forces, comparing the capabilities of the armed forces with potential adversaries, and preparing and reviewing contingency plans which reflect policy guidance from the President and the Secretary of Defense. Although the Joint Chiefs have in theory equal power, the Commandant of the Marine Corps, whose service does not rely on nuclear weapons for prestige or budget allocations, usually does not participate in debates within the Joint Chiefs about nuclear weapons.

Since its foundation, the Joint Chiefs organization has been a focus of controversy and criticism. According to the Senate Armed Services Committee, at least twenty major studies of military organization over the last forty years have recommended organizational changes in the Joint Chiefs of Staff. Criticism has not only come from the outside. In 1982, the then Chairman of the Joint Chiefs of Staff, General David Jones, published an article entitled *Why the Joint Chiefs of Staff Must Change.* Shortly thereafter, the then Army Chief of Staff, General Edward Meyer, publicly voiced his dissatisfaction with the Joint Chiefs organization.

The Joint Chiefs of Staff have been criticized mainly for not being able to give timely and appropriate military advice to the President or Secretary of Defense. They have also been criticized for not being able to formulate strategy, for their inability to settle role and mission disputes within the armed forces, and for the requirement that each Chief wears 'two hats', namely that he is both a member of the Joint Chiefs and the chief of a particular service. This 'dual-hatting', it is charged, has been responsible for inter-service rivalry within the JCS, making it less effective.

The Congress took legislative action in 1985 and 1986 to remedy these problems, which resulted in the allocation of substantially more power to the Chairman of the Joint Chiefs, the creation of the post of Vice-Chairman, and several other changes. It remains to be seen, however, whether these changes have been successful in remedying the problems of the Joint Chiefs.

The Chairman of the Joint Chiefs of Staff
Address: Room 2E873, The Pentagon, Washington, DC 20301
Tel: (202) 697-9121

(See biography of: Crowe.)

Vice-Chairman, Joint Chiefs of Staff
Address: Room 2E860, The Pentagon, Washington, DC 20301
Tel: (202) 694-8948

The Vice-Chairman is responsible to the Chairman of the Joint Chiefs of Staff, and performs duties assigned by the Chairman with the approval of the Secretary of Defense. The Vice-Chairman acts as chairman in the event of a vacancy in the post of Chairman or if the Chairman is otherwise engaged. The Vice-Chairman attends all JCS meetings, but cannot vote unless he is acting as Chairman. While he holds the position, the Vice-Chairman outranks all members of the armed forces except for the Chairman.
(See biography of: Herres.)

Chief of Staff of the Army
Address: Room 3E668, The Pentagon, Washington, DC 20301
Tel: (202) 695-2077

In addition to being a member of the Joint Chiefs of Staff, the Army Chief of Staff is directly responsible to the Secretary of the Army for the efficiency of the Army and its readiness for military operations. He is the principal military adviser to the Secretary of the Army, and is responsible for the planning, development, execution, and analysis of Army programmes.
(See biography of: Vuono.)

Chief of Naval Operations
Address: Room 4E660, The Pentagon, Washington, DC 20301
Tel: (202) 695-6007

The Chief of Naval Operations is the senior military officer of the Department of the Navy, and exercises control over the Operating Forces of the Navy. He reports to the Secretary of the Navy, and is responsible for Navy manpower, material, weapons, and support facilities.
(See biography of: Trost.)

Chief of Staff of the Air Force
Address: Room 4E924, The Pentagon, Washington, DC 20301
Tel: (202) 697-9225

The Chief of Staff of the Air Force reports to the Secretary of the Air Force. The Chief of Staff is responsible for the efficiency and operational readiness of the Air Force.
(See biography of: Welch, L. D.)

Director, Joint Staff
Address: Room 2E936, The Pentagon, Washington, DC 20301
Tel: (202) 694-5221

The Joint Staff is charged with assisting the Joint Chiefs in carrying out their responsibilities. Officers serving on the Joint Staff are selected by the chairman of the Joint Chiefs in approximate equal numbers from the Army, Navy, Air Force and Marines. The Joint Staff is composed of both civilian employees and military officers. The Director, Joint Staff, is appointed by the chairman in consultation with the other chiefs and with the approval of the Secretary of Defense. The Joint Staff includes three departments of relevance to nuclear decisonmaking: the J-5 Strategic Plans and Policy directorate; the J-6 Command, Control and Communications directorate; and the J-8 Force Structure, Resource, and Assessment directorate.
(For Joint Staff biographies, see: Baldwin; RisCassi; Ryan; Tuttle.)

Defense Agencies

Though organizationally independent of the Department of Defense (DoD), the Defense Agencies operate under supervision of the DoD.

The Defense Advanced Research Projects Agency (DARPA)
Address: 1400 Wilson Boulevard, 8th Floor, Arlington, VA 22209
Tel: (202) 694-3007

DARPA is little known to the general public, but can be extremely important in influencing the decisions on what weapons the USA develops and builds. Although DARPA does not build weapons systems or decide which ones should be built, it engages in research which can prove important in the future. The agency carries out both basic and advanced applied research and development work that may be important to the Department of Defense; it also organizes prototype projects which embody technology that may be used by the DoD. DARPA also, on request, assists the services in their prototype projects. The agency's objective is 'to minimize the possibility of technological surprise by adversaries and offer potential for major increases in US defense capability' (Committee on Armed Services, 1985). DARPA reports to the Under Secretary of Defense for Acquisition. The director of DARPA is appointed by the Secretary of Defense. The position has been vacant since Robert Duncan became Director of Defense Research and Engineering.
(See biography of: Fields.)

The Defense Contract Audit Agency (DCAA)
Address: Building 4, Cameron Station, Alexandria, VA 22304
Tel: (202) 274-6785

Established in 1965, the DCAA is under the control of the Assistant Secretary of Defense (Comptroller). The agency provides accounting and financial advisory services to the DoD. These include evaluating the acceptability of costs claimed or proposed by contractors, and evaluating the efficiency and economy of contractor operations. This can make them influential in deciding which contractor may be chosen, providing other more powerful political factors are not at work.
(See biography of: Reed.)

The Defense Nuclear Agency (DNA)
Address: Washington, DC 20305
Tel: (202) 325-7095

Another little known agency, the DNA traces its history back to the Manhattan Project, which oversaw the development of the atomic bomb from 1942 to 1945. In 1946, the Atomic Energy Act abolished the Manhattan Project, and the military staff of the Project were transferred to the newly formed Armed Forces Special Weapons Project (AFSWP). The AFSWP was reorganized in 1959 and renamed the Defense

Atomic Support Agency (DASA). In 1971, DASA was redesignated the Defense Nuclear Agency.

The majority of DNA's responsibilities centres on research and testing into the effects of nuclear weapons. DNA is responsible for planning, supervising and co-ordinating Department of Defense (DoD) activity in this area. Further, DNA serves as the central DoD agency for the co-ordination of nuclear weapons development and testing with the Department of Energy (DoE). DNA is also responsible for managing the nuclear weapons stockpile, and, in theory, knows where every warhead is at all times. The agency provides advice and assistance to the Joint Chiefs and the services on all nuclear matters, including vulnerability, radiation and biomedical effects. DNA reports to the Under Secretary of Defense for Acquisition and the Chairman of the Joint Chiefs of Staff.
(See biography of: Atkins; Parker, J. T.)

National Security Agency/Central Security Service
Address: Fort George G. Meade, MD 20755
Tel: (301) 688-6311

The National Security Agency (NSA)/Central Security Service is one of the most secretive agencies in the US government. Even its letterhead is classified. The NSA was established by a Presidential Directive in 1952. The Central Security Service was established by a Presidential Memorandum in 1972. The Service prescribes security principles, doctrines and procedures for the US government, organizes and manages facilities for producing foreign intelligence information, organizes and manages research and engineering that may affect the goals of the National Security Agency, and operates the Department of Defense Computer Security Center. The post of director of the NSA/Central Security Service is currently vacant.

Strategic Defense Initiative Organization (SDIO)
Address: Washington, DC 20301,
Tel: (202) 695-7060

The Strategic Defense Initiative (SDI), more commonly known as Star Wars, has become a central focus of debate in US politics. It is a source of almost constant debate within the defence community, Congress, and the press. A 1988 unclassified report by the Office of Technology Assessment (OTA) which said, in part, that SDI would suffer a 'catastrophic failure' if it were ever deployed and used, was not released for seven months by the Pentagon, which then tried to discredit the report by saying it did not take into account very recent advances in technology. The Soviet Union is fiercely opposed to SDI, and it appears to be a major stumbling block in arms control negotiations. Ironically, this opposition to a certain extent has bolstered the Reagan Administration's arguments (which it in fact uses with nearly all weapons systems) that SDI is also a 'bargaining chip' which will force the Soviet Union to negotiate. On the face of it, this seems obviously false, since one of the ways to defeat an anti-ballistic missile system is to overwhelm it with warheads, which would necessitate the Soviets building more weapons.

The Congress has not been particularly enthusiastic about Star Wars, pointedly reducing budget money for SDI research and development. In the spring of 1988, SDI provisions in the Defense Authorization Act were debated in Congress; up to this point, however, Congress had been unwilling to completely cut SDI spending from the budget. Democrats, in general, oppose SDI while Republicans support it.

The Strategic Defense Initiative Organization was established in 1984, and will certainly try and prevent any attempts to abolish SDI funding. SDI has been a windfall in terms of money for many defence contractors and researchers, including universities, who will constitute a powerful constituency for the programme.

Officially, the function of the SDIO is to manage and conduct the research which will provide a basis for determining whether SDI is feasible. This has in fact been one of the Reagan Administration's trump cards, allowing it to argue that all the USA is doing is determining whether SDI is feasible or not, and that it would be foolish not to do the requisite exploratory research. In fact, the SDIO is clearly also an organization which promotes SDI and is staffed by people who believe that SDI is both feasible

and necessary. The SDIO reports directly to the Secretary of Defense.
(See biography of: Abrahamson, J. A.)

The Unified and Specified Commands

The Unified and Specified Commands represent the second of two distinct organizational levels in the Department of Defense: the operational level. The first is the policymaking level, which centres around the Pentagon. The Unified and Specified Commands are responsible for controlling operations whenever military forces are deployed. Unified and Specified Commands have broad and continuing missions.

Unified Commands have forces assigned to them from two or more services. The eight unified commands are: US European Command; US Atlantic Command; US Central Command; US Transportation Command; US Special Operations Command; US Pacific Command; US Southern Command; US Space Command.

Specified Commands consist of forces from one service. The three specified commands are: Strategic Air Command (SAC); Military Airlift Command (MAC); Forces Command.

The chain of command in the military runs from the President (constitutionally, Commander-in-Chief of the Armed Forces) and the Secretary of Defense to the Unified and Specified Commands. The chain of command is frequently misunderstood as including the Joint Chiefs of Staff. This is not the case. The Joint Chiefs are in the chain of command only in that they transmit orders from the President and the Secretary of Defense to the Unified and Specified Commands; they cannot actually *issue* these orders.

Service chiefs, however, do retain *de facto* influence over the operational commands. This is because the commanders of the operational commands rely significantly on the service chiefs for resource allocation as well as for subsequent career assignments.

Several other criticisms have been levelled at the operational commands, and specifically at the Unified Commands. One is that a unified commander has weak authority over the service component commands under his control. The root of this weak control is the interest the services have in retaining the integrity of their service operations, itself a reflection of the continuing rivalry between the services. Further, the service component commanders are dependent on the service chief, not the unified commander, for resources: unified commanders do not have much control over resource decisions; they find it hard to influence policymaking in the Department of Defense, and thus the decisions taken by policymakers about which resources have priority. In recent years the unified commanders have been given a role in the resource allocation decisionmaking process (see Introduction), but most commentators agree that the problem about their lack of influence in this area has not been completely solved.

This lack of influence is reflected in the fact that in terms of nuclear weapons decisionmaking, only one command, Strategic Air Command (SAC), merits extended discussion. It should be noted, however, that the US Atlantic Command can have some influence because it would be chiefly responsible if a war were to be fought in Europe.

The Strategic Air Command (SAC)
Address: The Pentagon, Washington, DC 20301
Tel: (202) 695-8048

SAC is the oldest and most powerful of the specified commands. SAC was established on 14 December 1946, although the term 'specified command' did not come into use until 1951. SAC is an Air Force command: it commands the Air Force's strategic missiles and bombers and exercises control over the targeting of the Navy's strategic submarine forces (a state of affairs the Navy resents). SAC is located at Offutt Air Force Base in Nebraska. Thus, for obvious reasons, SAC is very influential in the Air Force. The first commander of SAC, General Curtis Lemay (Curtis 'Boom-Boom' LeMay to his detractors), stands out as one of the more influential military leaders of the twentieth century. LeMay engaged in running battles with Presidents Eisenhower and Kennedy and their Secretaries of Defence over the size and

shape of US nuclear forces. The current Chief of Staff of the Air Force, Larry Welch, is a former commander of SAC. The influence of SAC in the Airforce is further enhanced by the fact that the commander of SAC also serves as director of the Joint Strategic Targeting Planning Staff, which selects targets and thus has some influence on the number of missiles the DoD recommends be built.
(See biography of: Chain.)

The Defense Science Board (DSB)
Address: Room 3D1020, The Pentagon, Washington, DC 20301
Tel: (202) 695-4157

The Defense Science Board is the senior independent advisory board to the Department of Defense. It can be highly influential. Founded in 1956 on the recommendation of the Hoover Commission, the Defense Science Board studies issues that are of high personal interest to the Secretary of Defense, the Under Secretary of Defense for Acquisition, or the Chairman of the Joint Chiefs of Staff. The Board has thirty-six members, four of whom, the chairmen of the Service advisory boards and of the Strategic Defense Initiative Organization, are ex-officio members. The remaining thirty-two are members-at-large who serve four-year terms. There is also a group of senior consultants to the DSB.

The Board operates by forming task forces to address tasks referred to it by the Under Secretary of Defense for Acquisition. The products of the task forces are a set of formal briefings for the full DSB and appropriate DoD officials, and a written report which contains findings and recommendations. The reports are submitted to the Under Secretary of Defense for Acquisition for approval. If approved, they are published as a Defense Science Board Report. In recent years, the DSB has issued reports such as *Military Applications of New Generation Computing Technologies*, *Chemical Warfare and Biological Defense*, *Small Intercontinental Ballistic Missile Modernization*, *Defense Nuclear Agency Management*, and *Soviet Imprecisely Located Targets for Strategic Systems*.

The DSB and other advisory panels have come under increasing criticism for a variety of reasons. Questions of conflict of interest have been raised by the General Accounting Office, the DoD Inspector General, and the House Government Operations Committee, as well as by independent critics. Yet a glance at the biographies of the DSB members shows that there are possible conflicts of interest for the many members of the panel who work for defense contractors. According to *Common Cause Magazine*, thirty-one members of the DSB, which deals with SDI, work for organizations which have SDI-related contracts (*Common Cause*, January—February 1987, pp. 33—5).

Pentagon advisory panels are also required by law to be 'balanced' in the points of view represented. This is plainly not the case with the DSB, where the views represented are essentially those of the DoD and defence contractors. Representative Jack Brooks (D, Texas), who chaired the House of Representatives study of advisory panels, has said that defence advisory panels 'in large part either acted as rubber stamps for the preconceived ideas of Department of Defense officials or, even worse, as forums where defense contractors could promote their own financial interest'(*Common Cause*, January-February 1987, pp. 33—5). These panels do have a function, but it often seems that function is to lend credence to whatever the DoD comes up with.
(See biographies of: Anders; Augustine; Bennett, I. L.; Bobrow; Braddock; Buchsbaum; Burnett; Cook; Currie; Decker; Deutch; DeLauer; Dougherty; Duffy; Everett; Fink; Fowler; Frieman; Fubini; Fuhrman; Heebner; Heilmeier; Hermann; Inman; Jones, A. K.; Kidd; Kresa; Lederberg; Lewis; Lucky; Miller, M. K.; Morrow; Parker, R. N.; Perry; Press; Rice; Rosenbaum; Rowen; Seitz; Shea; Shutler; Starry; Sullivan; Townes; Vessey; Williams, E. C.)

The Services

The Army, Navy, Air Force and Marines have been extensively criticized, since the late 1940s, for concentrating most of their energy on battling with each other for a larger share of the defence budget. Continuing inter-service rivalry, and continuing congressional and Presidential concern that this rivalry is detrimental both to the strength of the armed forces and to the efficacy of Department of Defense public relations, has fuelled much of the effort aimed at military reform.

This rivalry tends to spill over into the area of strategy decisions, since these decisions in part determine the priorities in the budget. In 1949, in what was known as the Admirals' Revolt, a group of high-ranking Navy officers publicly denounced the emerging US strategy, with its reliance on the atomic bomb, as immoral. It would seem that their horror was caused more by the recognition that atomic weapons did little to augment the Navy budget than by any real sense of moral revulsion, since at the time the atomic bomb was the sole property of the Air Force. This view is borne out by the fact that in 1951, when the Navy also started to develop an atomic arsenal, leaders of the Navy no longer had any objections to atomic weapons.

Most of the big battles over the budget have taken place between the Air Force and the Navy. As a former Air Force colonel once put it, 'The Air Force doesn't respond to what the Russians do. It reacts to what the Navy does'(Fallows, 1981, p.122). The Army, which recognizes that a drop in funding to the Air Force will probably benefit Army programmes, has usually supported the Navy. The Army possesses tactical nuclear weapons, but they do not represent a large portion of the Army budget. The Marine Corps, with no nuclear weapons to speak of and little influence in relation to the other services, has tended to stay on the sidelines or has supported the Navy, which provides the Marine Corps budget.

In recent years, the Air Force has still received the largest share of defence dollars, with the Navy running a very close second. In FY 1984, for example, 33.9 per cent of the defence budget went to the Air Force, with the Navy getting 31.7 per cent and the Army 23.9 per cent (defence-wide programmes and the budgets of the Defense Agencies account for the remainder). Since the first seven years of the Reagan Administration were a time of practically unrestrained growth in the defence budget, inter-service rivalry was muted by the perception that there was enough to go around for everyone. Currently, however, in a period when the defence budget is getting smaller, as former Army Chief of Staff General Edward C. Meyers has put it, 'the services start feeding on each other like a pack of piranhas'(*New York Times*, 6 November 1987).

Nuclear weapons are an important element in the inter-service battles over funding; according to the Washington DC Center for Defense Information, however, nuclear forces made up only 22.4 per cent of the defence budget in the period 1982—88, and inter-service fights centre around other parts of the budget as well.

The modern structure of the armed forces, including the independent Air Force, was created by the National Security Act of 1947. Although the services are referred to as Department of the Army, Department of the Air Force, and Department of the Navy, they are part of the Department of Defense and not executive departments.

Department of the Army
Address: see Department of Defense

The Army is the oldest service. It was established by the Continental Congress as the American Continental Army on 14 June 1775. The mission of the Army focuses on ground programmes, and therefore is not particularly influential in nuclear decisionmaking. The Army does, however, have most of the tactical nuclear weapons in the US arsenal. In most scenarios depicting a confrontation between the superpowers that leads to a nuclear war, it would be these weapons that would be used first.

Civilian control over the Army is exercised by the Secretary of the Army, who is responsible to the President and the Secretary of Defense. The Goldwater—Nichols Department of Defense Reorganization Act of 1986 resulted in a strengthening of the Office of the Secretary of the Army by shifting the functions of comptroller, acquisition, inspector general, and auditing from the Army Staff to the Office of the Secretary of the Army. This was intended to enhance civilian control over the Armed Forces. As with most of the Act, it is still too early to make any accurate judgements about its effectiveness.

Operational control over the Army rests with the Army Chief of Staff (see *Joint Chiefs of Staff*).

In fact, actual day-to-day control of the Army is usually delegated to the Vice-Chief of Staff.

The Secretary of the Army
Address: Room 3E718, The Pentagon, Washington, DC 20301
Tel: (202) 695-3211

The Secretary of the Army is responsible for conducting all affairs of the Department of the Army, including its organization, administration, and its operations. The Secretary of the Army is appointed by the President.
(See biography of: Marsh.)

Assistant Secretary of the Army (Research, Development, and Acquisition)
Address: Room 2E672, The Pentagon, Washington, DC 20301
Tel: (202) 695-6153

The Assistant Secretary (Research, Development, and Acquisition) is the key aide to the Secretary in terms of nuclear weapons decisionmaking. The assistant secretary is responsible for programming and budgetting for acquisition for the Army, management of Army research and development, and development test and evaluation.
(See biography of: Sculley.)

The Army Staff
The Army Staff is headed by the Army Chief of Staff, and is responsible for professional advice to the Secretary of the Army. The Army Staff is also responsible for recruiting, organizing, supplying, equipping, and training the Army. The Army Chief of Staff is considered the principal military adviser to the Secretary of the Army.

Army Vice-Chief of Staff
Address: Room 3E66, The Pentagon, Washington, DC 20301
Tel: (202) 695-4371
(See biography of: Brown, A. E.)

Department of the Navy

The Navy was created as the Continental Navy by the Continental Congress on 13 October 1775. The Department of the Navy and the Office of the Secretary of the Navy were created on 30 April 1798, when the Navy was taken out of the control of the Department of War. The Marine Corps is formally a separate service within the Department of the Navy. The Department of the Navy in its present form was created by the National Security Act Amendments of 1949.

In terms of influence over nuclear weapons decisionmaking, the Navy is secondary to the Air Force. Nevertheless, the Navy can have a powerful institutional voice in Department of Defense affairs. The last Secretary of the Navy, John Lehman, resigned amid controversy when he charged that recent budget cuts would prevent the Reagan Administration from fulfilling its goal of a 600-ship Navy. Plans for the 600-ship Navy have come under vociferous attacks from several quarters. Some critics argue that 600 is really an arbitrary number selected for political reasons, and not one based on an examination of actual military requirements. Others have said that the force projections produced by the Navy, which include the 600 ships, reflect a dangerous strategy which will waste valuable resources.

US naval strategy is predicated on the notion that in a war with the Soviet Union, the Navy should take offensive action which emphasizes strikes against both the Soviet Navy and its support structures. This in turn dictates that US Navy strikes will take place in enemy waters against its home territory. In strategic jargon, this is known as 'power projection'. The Navy both designs its ships and specifies the number and type of ships in order to meet the requirements of this strategy. One critic has pointed out that 'the Soviet Navy, by contrast, is designed to sink the American Navy'(Fallows, 1981, p.32). Critics also argue out that this strategy gives the Soviet Navy the opportunity to fulfil its mission by destroying the US Navy's (extremely expensive) aircraft carrier groups. Others have also said that this strategy will force the Soviets to use nuclear weapons, thus starting a war which will destroy not only the US Navy, but perhaps also the USA.

What the Navy likes about power projection is that it is expensive, thus requiring a large Navy budget, and that it allows the Navy to build the type of ship it wants.(It can also be argued that the preference for power projection is more a function of the Navy's competition with the Air Force than a product of its concern about the Soviet Union. The Air Force's centrepiece is power projection by long-range strategic bombers, the B-52, the B-1 and the B-2, or 'Stealth', bomber. If the Navy can argue successfully that it can project power more effectively than can the Air Force, its budget will be increased at the expense of that of the Air Force. The Air Force's intensive lobbying can also be interpreted as a response to this 'threat' from the Navy (see Case Study)). The type of ship most loved by the Navy is the aircraft carrier, which is huge, impressive, expensive, and requires an escort group of yet more ships. Such a group of ships is called a carrier battle group.

Civilian authority over the Navy rests with the Secretary of the Navy, who is appointed by the President. The Secretary of the Navy, who reports to the Secretary of Defense, is responsible for the policies and control of the Department of the Navy. The Under Secretary of the Navy and the Assistant Secretaries of the Navy are known as civilian executive assistants. Military control of the Navy and the Marines lies with the Chief of Naval Operations and the Commandant of the Marines, respectively. They are the principal military advisers to the Secretary on matters relating to their respective commands.

The Secretary of the Navy
Address: Room 4E686, The Pentagon, Washington, DC 20301
Tel: (202)695-3131
(See biography of: Ball)

The Assistant Secretary of the Navy (Shipbuilding and Logistics)
Address: Room 266, 2211 Jefferson Davis Highway, Arlington, VA 22202
Tel: (202)692-2202

The Assistant Secretary is responsible for all stages of the acquisition of ships funded by the budget appropriation 'Shipbuilding and Conversion, Navy'. He is also responsible for all Navy acquistion programmes after they reach the full-scale production decision. The Assistant Secretary is further responsible for policy and administration of the business and contractual aspects of Navy acquisition programmes.
(See biography of: Pyatt.)

The Assistant Secretary of the Navy (Research, Engineering and Systems)
Address: Room 4E768, The Pentagon, Washington, DC 20301
Tel: (202) 695-6315

The Assistant Secretary deals with matters related to Navy research, development, engineering, testing and evaluation. This includes management of programmes funded by the budget appropriation 'Research, Development, Test, and Evaluation, Navy'. In addition, the Assistant Secretary is responsible for Navy acquisition programmes through the full-scale production decision (DAB Milestone III) except for those which fall under the authority of the Assistant Secretary for Shipbuilding and Logistics.
(See biography of: Faught.)

The Office of the Chief of Naval Research
Address: see below

The Office of the Chief of Naval Research encompasses the Office of Naval Research and the Office of Naval Technology. The Chief of Naval Research is responsible to the Secretary of the Navy through the Assistant Secretary for Research, Engineering and Systems. The Chief of Naval Research serves as the principal adviser to the Assistant Secretary for Research, Engineering and Systems. The Office of Naval Research, established in August 1946, in addition to the responsibilites listed below, conducts research in conjunction with research conducted by other naval activities, and coordinates the Naval Basic Research Program. The Office of Naval Technology, established in October 1980, manages the Department of the Navy's Exploratory Development Program, including planning, programming, budgeting, and direction of the programme. In addition, this office manages the oversight activities in regard to the Industrial Independent Research and Development Program.

The Chief of Naval Research
Address: Room 907, 800 North Quincy Street, Arlington, VA 22203
Tel: (202) 696-4767

The Chief of Naval Research is responsible for

providing leadership and management to Department of the Navy research and exploratory development programmes; developing and formulating naval research and technology requirements based on current and projected Navy and Marine Corps long-range objectives; and co-ordinating naval research and promoting co-operative research between the Department of the Navy, other sectors of the Department of Defense, and other government research agencies.
(See biography of: Wilson, J. R.)

Director, Office of Naval Research
Address: Room 907, 800 North Quincy Street, Arlington, VA, 22203
Tel: (202) 696-4517
(See biography of: Saalfeld.)

Director, Office of Naval Technology
Address: Room 907, 800 North Quincy Street, Arlington, VA 22203
Tel: (202) 696-5115
(See biography of: Selwyn.)

Department of the Air Force

The Air Force is the youngest, but most powerful, of the services. It was established by the National Security Act of 1947, and designated a military department within the Department of Defense by the National Security Act Amendments of 1949. The Air Force, through the Strategic Air Command, controls the US arsenal of inter-continental ballistic missiles (ICBMs) and long-range strategic bombers. It can exert powerful influence within the Department of Defense (DoD) and the government as a whole. The Air Force has been criticized for its running battles with the Navy over the defence budget, and also for overstating the importance of its mission in order to gain a larger share of the budget. Questions have been raised, for instance, about the necessity of building new manned bombers like the B-1 and B-2 in the age of the ICBM. In fact, for this very reason, the Air Force stifled development of the ICBM in the early 1960s. Bombers are significantly slower than missiles, extremely expensive, require extensive facilities, and are less accurate. Some critics have said that the only purpose bombers would serve in the event of a nuclear war would be to 'bounce the rubble' of the Soviet Union and, lacking anywhere to land, fly off into oblivion. The Air Force and DoD have responded that bombers are more flexible and reliable than ICBMs. Bombers can be put into the air, out of danger, if warnings of a Soviet attack are issued. Bombers can also be recalled at any point in their flight if war is averted, which missiles cannot (see Case Study).

The Air Force is run by the Secretary of the Air Force, who is appointed by the President and reports to the Secretary of Defense. In addition to the Office of the Secretary of the Air Force, the department includes the Air Staff, which is led by the Air Force Chief of Staff, and the field organization, which includes the major commands, separate operating agencies, and direct reporting units.

The Secretary of the Air Force
Address: Room 4E871, The Pentagon, Washington, DC 20301
Tel: (202) 697-7376
(See biography of: Aldridge.)

Under Secretary of the Air Force
Address: Room 4E871, The Pentagon, Washington, DC 20301
Tel: (202) 697-1361

The Under Secretary of the Air Force is the principal assistant to the Secretary. He acts with the full authority of the Secretary in all matters involving the Department of the Air Force.
(See biography of: McGovern.)

Assistant Secretary for Acquisition
Address: Room 4E964, The Pentagon, Washington, DC 20301
Tel: (202) 697-6361

The Assistant Secretary for Acquisition is responsible for the formulation and execution of Air Force research and development programmes. Further, the assistant secretary is responsible for all decisions relating to the acquisition of weapons systems.

Key Assistants:
Deputy Assistant Secretary (Acquisition Management and Policy) - Daniel S. Rak; Deputy for Strategic Missile Systems and Strategic Defense

Initiative - Sydell P. Gold; Deputy Assistant Secretary (Command, Control, Communications, and Computer Systems) - Andrew E. Belinski; Deputy Assistant Secretary (Space Plans & Policy) - Charles W. Cook.
(See biography of: Welch, J. J.)

Air Staff

The Air Staff is a management organization under the Air Force Chief of Staff. It provides professional advice to the Office of the Secretary of the Air Force. Like most of the services, the Air Force day-to-day operations are usually the responsibility of the Vice-Chief of Staff.

Air Force Chief of Staff
Address: Room 4E924, The Pentagon, Washington, DC 20301
Tel: (202) 697-9225
(See biography of: Welch, L. D.)

Vice-Chief of Staff
Address: Room 4E936, The Pentagon, Washington, DC 20301
Tel: (202) 695-7911
(See biography of: Hatch.)

Chief Scientist of the Air Force
Address: Room 4E320, The Pentagon, Washington, DC 20301
Tel: (202) 697-7842
(See biography of: Sorenson.)

USAF Scientific Advisory Board
Address: Room 5D982, The Pentagon, Washington, DC 20301
Tel: (202) 697-4811
The USAF Scientific Advisory Board (SAB) exists to provide expertise to both the Secretary of the Air Force and the Air Force Chief of Staff. While the SAB recommendations are not binding, they provide the weight of scientific expertise to Air Force decisions on the development of weapons systems and the efficiency of current weapons systems. The SAB also studies emerging technologies which may be of interest to the Air Force.
(See biographies of: Abrahamson, George R.; Abramson; Airey; Allen; Altis; Bostrom; Bridges; Brown, W. M.; Buchanan; Cheathem; Clem; Cole; Covert; DeLauer; DePoy; Everett; Fillers; Fischer; Flanagan; Flax; Gabriel; Garmire; Geiger; Gerry; Getting; Gustavson; Happer; Heart; Heiser; Iorello; Kerrebrock; Key; Koff; Kopf; Kresa; Kurland; Lucky; Mills; Mitchell; Morrow; Murray; Naka; Pentecost; Perkins; Plummer; Rothaus; Rutan; Seebass; Selden; Shannon; Shevell; Smith, Harold P.; Snyder; Stear; Stubberud; Teller; Tenenbaum; Tennant; Tiffany; Toomay; Webb, Paul; Welch, Jasper A.; Welliver; Whitman; Williams, Max L.; Yang.) (The USAF provides only very short biographies of the members of its scientific advisory board.)

Air Force Major Commands
Strategic Air Command
(See Specified and Unified Commands)

Air Force Systems Command
Address: Andrews Air Force Base, MD 20334
The Air Force Systems Command is responsible for advancing aerospace technology, adapting the technology into operational systems, and acquiring advanced aerospace systems.
(See biography of: Skantze.)

Air Force Space Command
Address: Colorado Springs, CO 80914
The Air Force Space Command provides resource management and operation of assigned assets for space control, space force application, force enhancement, and strategic aerospace defence. The space command works closely with the United States Space Command, a unified command.
(See biography of: Padden.)

THE DEPARTMENT OF STATE
Address: 2201 C Street, NW, Washington, DC 20520
Tel: (202) 647-4000

The State Department is not particularly influential in nuclear weapons decisionmaking. It is only on the periphery of decisionmaking by virtue of the fact that it is the chief body in charge of foreign relations. Further, the Secretary of State is a member of the National Security Council. Offices within the State Department which are involved in decisionmaking are the Bureau of Intelligence and Research, the intelligence organization of the State Department, and the Bureau of Politico-Military Affairs, which develops guidance for

the State Department on matters relating to 'national security'.
(See biography of: Shultz.)

THE DEPARTMENT OF ENERGY
Address: 1000 Independence Avenue, SW, Washington, DC 20585
Tel: (202) 586-5000

The Department of Energy (DoE) is subordinate to other agencies in nuclear decisionmaking. The nuclear weapons programme takes a large share of the DoE budget (63 per cent in 1985), and the DoE largely controls warhead design, development, testing, and production. However, the department is not widely viewed in the USA as having any part in the defence build-up.

In theory, DoE control of the warhead design and production process ensures civilian control over nuclear weapons. Much has been made of this control since the end of World War II. Many observers, however, feel that the DoE functions at the whim of the services. There is indeed little evidence to suggest that the Department of Energy has acted in any way as a restraint on warhead design, nor that it attempts to.

The Department of Energy controls the weapons laboratories (see below) and also the facilities for production of nuclear warheads. The key communications point between the DoD and the DoE is the Military Liaison Committee. The key figure in the Department of Energy is the Assistant Secretary for Defense Programs.
(See biographies of: Herrington; Wade.)

The Weapons Laboratories

There are two national laboratories in the United States which are charged with design of nuclear warheads for the US nuclear arsenal: Lawrence Livermore National Laboratory and Los Alamos National Scientific Laboratory. Both are managed by the University of California. In addition, there is a third laboratory, Sandia National Laboratory, which is run by a subsidiary of the AT & T Corporation. Sandia concentrates on the survivability of warheads and other equipment and on the effects of nuclear explosions. Sandia is responsible for the design of non-nuclear components in nuclear warheads. It also administers the US nuclear testing programme. All three laboratories are known as GOCO (government-owned contract-operated) facilities. The employees of the laboratories are not employees of the US government, but of the contractors which run them. Control and funding of the laboratories is in the hands of the Department of Energy.

Los Alamos and Livermore have a combined budget of around $900 million. Of this, one-half to two-thirds is for nuclear weapons research. Los Alamos, the older of these two laboratories, was created in 1944 as part of the Manhattan Project, which built the first atomic bombs. Livermore was established in 1952, primarily at the request of scientist Edward Teller, to facilitate design of the hydrogen bomb, which work Teller felt was lagging at Los Alamos. Since that point, the two laboratories have had a competitive relationship, which often serves to facilitate advances in weapons technology at a rapid pace. The laboratories are not involved in the design or manufacture of delivery systems, nor the actual manufacture of warheads.

The role of the laboratories is not widely understood in the United States - nor indeed is their existence known of by many - although their management by the University of California has been a matter of controversy for many years both within that institution and generally in the state of California. The role and influence of the laboratories, however, has been a matter of debate within the defence community and Congress. It seems obvious that the laboratories exert some influence over the decisionmakers. As Hugh DeWitt, a physicist at Lawrence Livermore for nearly thirty years and a strong and outspoken proponent of the Comprehensive Test Ban (CTB), has said,

> The weapons-lab people enjoy very great influence with members of Congress and the higher levels of US government, and they always have. They are the experts. They have long experience of nuclear weapons design, and because so much of the work is classified they are almost the sole experts...Their pronouncements are of course

> couched in scientific and technical language which goes over the heads of the politicians, and there is little peer review of what they say.
>
> (*New Statesman*, 10 April 1987)

The laboratories have been vociferous opponents of the CTB, which would impede their work, and have been widely credited with dissuading President Carter from pursuing a five-year test ban with the Soviets in 1978 (see McLean, 1986, p.40; Zuckerman, 1983; *Bulletin of the Atomic Scientists*, April 1984, pp 40—2.) While it seems unquestionable that the laboratories do have influence over decisionmakers, and that the propriety of that interest is questionable, it also seems simplistic to say that the laboratories are the driving force behind the arms race.

THE PRESIDENT AND THE EXECUTIVE OFFICE OF THE PRESIDENT

Address: 1600 Pennsylvania Avenue, NW, Washington, DC 20500
Tel: (202)456-1414

The extent of power of the President of the United States in defence decisionmaking has been a matter of much debate. The President is Commander-in-Chief of the Armed Forces, the head of government, and the administrative head of the executive branch. Theoretically, the President should have absolute power over anything occurring in the executive branch, but this is rarely the case. The President must be responsive to numerous constituencies, including the public, Congress, the press, and a number of others in government. He cannot do without their co-operation at certain points in time. An incoming administration usually has an agenda that includes, but is larger than, defence issues. If the President alienates his constituency on defence issues, the whole of his or her agenda can be in trouble.

Further, the President is constrained in what he can do by his subordinates. They can use a variety of means to undermine his initiatives, and can also resign and cause embarrassment to his administration, as did Secretary of the Navy John Lehman under President Reagan. On the other hand, the President does have tremendous power. He sets the public tone for his administration, and he appoints subordinates to control departments.

The extent of the power of the presidency is connected with, of course, the character of the President. This has taken on special importance during the tenure of Ronald Reagan. Reagan is seventy-seven years old, and serious questions have been raised concerning his physical and mental health and his 'hands-off' style of management. These concerns have been compounded by embarrassing revelations, for example that he has used 'scripts' for White House meetings, that he has dozed off in cabinet meetings, and about his involvement in the Iran–Contra scandal.

The mere fact that the President's office is so high in the hierarchy limits his power. By the time a President is presented with a set of options, many important decisions have already been made. Further, it is far easier, in terms of weapons decisions, for a President to *initiate*, rather than to *cancel*, a programme. Unless the cancellation takes place early in the development cycle, an enormous amount of political power is required to override the constituency which backs a weapons system, a constituency which includes the relevant service, sections of the Office of the Secretary of Defense (OSD), members of Congress, and the weapons contractors. President Carter's cancellation of the B-1 (see Case Study) provides a vivid example of this. Reagan's initiation of the Strategic Defense Initiative (SDI), on the other hand, is a good example of the reverse.

SDI was initiated by President Reagan with the backing of a small group of advisers; most of the defence establishment and other policymakers were excluded from the discussions leading up to the 23 March 1983 speech in which Reagan first announced his ideas about SDI. The section of the speech which dealt with SDI was not written by his usual speechwriters but by a small group of staff in the National Security Council (who, in order to keep SDI secret, dubbed the section 'the annex').

Essentially, five people advised Reagan on SDI, only one of whom had any real knowledge of defence issues. This was Edward Teller, widely considered the 'father of the hydrogen bomb'. The others were brewer Joseph Coors, paper products magnate Karl Bendetsen, investor and rancher William A. Wilson, and food magnate Jacquelin Hume. It was they who convinced Reagan to launch the enormously expensive and controversial programme. The only senior adviser who appears to have had substantial knowledge of the proposed programme was the then Deputy National Security Adviser Robert McFarlane. Other senior officials were kept in the dark until practically the last minute. Secretary of State George Schultz was told about 'the annex' two days before the speech, as were the Joint Chiefs of Staff. Assistant Secretary of Defense Richard Perle received word about SDI two days before the speech was made. Under Secretary of Defense for Research and Engineering Richard DeLauer learned of SDI nine hours before the speech, as did Fred Ikle, Under Secretary of Defense for Policy. Secretary of Defense Caspar Weinberger learned of the speech four days, Science Adviser George Keyworth five days, before it was given.

While this is an example of what is known as 'top-down' leadership, it calls into question even more the sense of SDI. As one observer put it: 'You'd think that if the President proposed something absolutely off the wall, there'd be someone who would stand up and say "that's screwy." Well, there wasn't.'(*Philadelphia Enquirer*, 10 July 1985).
(See biography of: Reagan.)

The Office of Management and Budget (OMB)
Address: see below

The Office of Management and Budget is part of the Executive Office of the President of the United States. It was established in 1970. The OMB serves as the President's primary vehicle for budget decisionmaking. In the first Reagan Administration, it was under the control of David Stockman, a controversial Michigan Republican who was a primary shaper of the Reagan budget programmes and who, according to one congressional aide, 'permanantly changed the nature of the job'. Stockman had great influence on Reagan, and during his period in office the OMB rose in importance in decisionmaking. Under the current director, James C. Miller III, who is widely described as less influential and a subordinate player in the White House, the OMB has itself lessened in influence.

Formally, the OMB is responsible for assisting the President in preparation of the budget, supervising and controlling the administration of the budget, and planning, conducting, and promoting evaluation efforts which assist the President in the assessment of programme objectives, performance, and efficiency. The OMB is also a centre of lobbying efforts by departments within the government trying to protect their budgets, which the OMB reviews and changes after their submission by the departments. Congress also plays a part in OMB deliberations, as members of Congress or staff give OMB indications of Congressional support for various components in the budget.

Most agencies view the OMB as an adversary, but the OMB has a unique relationship with the DoD. It maintains a staff in the Pentagon to facilitate co-ordination of defence budgeting, and has an active hand throughout the decisionmaking progress. Some of this relationship is undoubtably due to the priority given to the defence budget in the Reagan Administration, but it is also a fact that the structural relationship between the OMB and the DoD influences the oversight of the defence budget.

Director of the Office of Management and Budget
Address: Executive Office Building, Washington, DC 20503
Tel: (202) 395-3080

Key Assistants: Deputy Director - Joseph R. Wright; Associate Director for Legislative Affairs (Senate) - Larry Burton; Associate Director for Legislative Affairs (House) - Gordon Wheeler; Associate Director for National Security and International Affairs - L. Wayne Arny; Deputy Associate Director, National Security Division - David Sitrin
(See biography of: Miller, J. C.)

The National Security Council (NSC)
Address: Old Executive Office Building, Washington, DC 20506

Tel: (202) 395-4974

The NSC was not a centre of attention in the United States until 1986, when it came under heavy fire for its role in the Iran–Contra scandal. Operating out of the White House basement, the NSC can be influential in the direction of nuclear weapons policy, but it does not have a particularly important role to play in the acquisition process. The NSC was created by the National Security Act of 1947, and was placed in the Executive Office of the President by Reorganization Plan No. 4 of 1949. The NSC has only four members, the President, the Vice-President, and the Secretaries of State and Defense. In addition, the Chairman of the Joint Chiefs of Staff serves as the NSC's military adviser, and the Director of Central Intelligence is its intelligence adviser. The National Security Council staff carry out most of the work of the Council. The most important figure is the National Security Advisor to the President, who effectively leads the NSC. The Secretary of Defense, Frank Carlucci, formerly held this position.

Formally, the responsibility of the National Security Council is to advise the President on the integration of foreign, domestic and military policies relating to national security. As such, the NSC is often the broker of inter-agency disputes.
(See biography of: Powell.)

INDEPENDENT AGENCIES

In the hierarchy of the government, the independent agencie are one level below the executive departments in the Executive Branch. We are concerned with three of the independent agencies.

Central Intelligence Agency (CIA)
Address: Washington, DC 20505

Chartered as part of the National Security Act of 1947, the CIA technically serves under the National Security Council (NSC). The CIA is the central co-ordination point for tasking, budget, resource allocation, priorities production and review for all intelligence work.

The Director of Central Intelligence (DCI) serves in the Cabinet, is appointed by the President and serves at his discretion. He is confirmed by the Senate. He is the principal adviser to the President and the NSC on foreign intelligence, and, formally, sets the intelligence community's objectives and policies.

According to Representative Bill Young, 'the intelligence community operated almost forever without having to report to anyone' (*International Herald Tribune*, 4 January 1985), though members of the House Permanent Select Committee on Intelligence say they believe it is no longer the 'rogue elephant' it was in the 1960s and 1970s.
(See biography of: Webster.)

The National Aeronautical and Space Administration (NASA)
Address: 600 Independence Avenue, SW, Washington, DC 20546
Tel: (202) 453-1000

The many military functions of NASA are not well-known in the USA. NASA is most often identified with the exploration of space, the moon landings, and recently, the space shuttle. The explosion of the space shuttle Challenger brought intense public scrutiny to bear on NASA, and led some wags to suggest that NASA stood for 'Not Another Space Accident'. In this public scrutiny, however, the military importance of the space shuttle programme and NASA was largely overlooked, or, for those who subscribe to grand conspiracy theories, suppressed.

Those who criticize SDI as the 'militarization of space' should widen their focus, for the militarization of space has in fact been under way since the early 1960s, and may indeed represent the future of the US military build-up. This is reflected in the recent formation of both the Air Force Space Command and the US Space Command. The Challenger disaster, along with the explosions of two Titan satellite-launching rockets, has thrown the space programme into some disarray, but these setbacks seem only temporary.

There is in fact resistance within the Air Force and the DoD to an emphasis on space. This is in part due to the bureaucratic law 'where you stand depends on where you sit', meaning that your position in controversies is determined by your position within the bureaucracy and what will help your budget. Further, as one Air Force officer complained, 'how many people have patted a satellite on the head? Everybody goes out and flies an F-15, a B-52. I call it the "stick and rudder psychosis". The senior leadership knows what it's like to fly an airplane...the leaders just aren't familiar with space systems' (Karas, 1983, p.22). This resistance is in fact one of the reasons for the military emphasis on NASA: defence-related work in space carried out by NASA comes out of NASA's budget and not the military budget. Carl Sagan has characterized this as 'a case of borrowing — or stealing — from the poor, namely NASA, to benefit the rich, namely the Department of Defense'. It is hard to say how much of the NASA budget supports DoD activities, but the General Accounting Office estimated that 20 per cent of the NASA budget supported the DoD.

NASA does not have much influence in defence decisionmaking, however. This is partly due to the fact that NASA needs DoD support for NASA budgets much more than the DoD needs NASA: essentially, the DoD can dictate to NASA what it wants (for more on the relationship between NASA and the DoD, see Karas, 1983, and Manno, 1984.)

NASA runs a variety of research laboratories, including the Ames Research Center, the Jet Propulsion Laboratory (operated by the California Institute of Technology), Langley Research Center, Lewis Research Center, and the National Space Technology Laboratory.

(See biography of: Fletcher.)

The Arms Control and Disarmament Agency (ACDA)

Address: 320, 21st St. NW, Washington, DC 20451

ACDA was established by President Kennedy in September 1961; its task is to promote arms control and disarmament. ACDA has never been very successful in carrying out its work, although it had some influence on the early SALT I negotiations. Under President Reagan, ACDA was largely reduced to repeating the Administration line on arms control.

The Legislative Branch

In theory, Congress is a powerful player in defence decisionmaking. The President, after all, submits a budget request to Congress: Congress has control over the relevant funds. Yet Congress rarely takes advantage of its power in this field; it seldom alters administration budget requests in substantial ways. Let us first look at how Congress works, and then at why it only infrequently exercises its budgetary powers.

Congress has two chambers, the House of Representatives (the House) and the Senate. The House has 435 members (Representatives), each of whom is elected from within a state for a two-year term. The number of Representatives from each state depends on the state's population; all states, however, must have at least one Representative. The Senate has 100 members (Senators), two from each state irrespective of the size of the state. Senators are elected for six-year terms.

For a number of reasons, Congressional politics can be enormously complex. First, the number of issues that Congress must deal with means that most members of Congress are generalists, or at most specialists in only one narrow issue. This means that most decisionmaking in Congress is done in the numerous committees and subcommittees.

Second, the rules of Congress mean that bills can be dealt with in many different ways: for instance, Congress members can manoeuvre votes on specific bills into being a referendum on a general issue; there are ways to expedite a vote on a bill; or, the Congress might vote on whether to even *consider* a measure — this way, a member who might be opposed to the measure but does not want to oppose it publicly can vote against considering it, thus preserving at least some political capital. In practice, the large number of rules and their complexity gives an advantage to senior members who have an intimate knowledge of rules and proceedings.

The timetable for Congressional decision-making on the budget, in theory at least, is as follows. In January of each year, the President submits his budget proposal to Congress. This is accompanied by a host of documents analysing the budget and expounding the virtues of the spending agencies (such as the DoD), widespread press coverage and a flurry of press briefings. By 15 April, the Budget Committees in each Chamber will draft the First Budget Resolution, which is then debated by the full membership of each Chamber. From 15 May to September, the authorizations and appropriations for each programme are decided, resulting in the Second Budget Resolution in late September. Differences between the House and Senate versions of the Resolution are decided in conference, and the Congress then passes the budget. New fiscal years start on 1 October, and if Congress has not passed a budget by then, it votes Continuing Resolutions.

There are two committees in each chamber which have primary responsibility for the defence budget. The House Armed Services Committee and the Senate Armed Services Committee decide on the authorization, which sets the overall legal limits on spending. The House Appropriations Committee and the Senate Appropriations Committee then decide on the actual spending within those limits. Further, within each of these committees there are sub-committees which deal with parts of the defence budget.

Why, then, does Congress not significantly alter Administration budget requests? The are four principal reasons for this. First, Congress exercises only what is known as 'micro-management'; that is, because the decisions that Congress makes on defence issues are extremely complex, Congressional committees become wrapped up in technological detail and debate at the expense of the overall picture. Specific decisions are debated in a vacuum; thus a decision on a particular weapons system is not made on the basis of an assessment about whether it fits into American strategy or defence objectives.

Second, because Congress has so many decisions to make, it does not examine closely the relatively small amounts of money that go into research and development of new weapons systems (and in a defence budget of $300 billion, 'relatively small' can refer to several million dollars). Yet it is precisely in the early stages that new systems accumulate the key supporters who can see them through full-scale development. Thus by the time Congress examines a system as a whole, there is a powerful political and financial constituency promoting it. Contractors, the Defense Department, and the armed services routinely lobby Congress for weapons systems.(Title 10 of the US Code makes it illegal for the armed forces to lobby Congress, a law which is often ignored. One method used to circumvent the law is for a member of Congress to invite a representative of one of the services to testify before a committee. As testifying is, technically, not lobbying, Title 10 has not been violated.)

Third, and related to the previous point, while a House member might be opposed in general to higher military spending, it is a safe bet that she or he will vote for a particular weapons system if this means that hundreds of thousands of jobs will be created in his or her district. Contractors therefore bid for, and the Department of Defense awards, contracts and sub-contracts 'strategically', i.e., in as many districts as possible so as to gain support from as many members as possible.

Fourth, there is also tremendous pressure on Congress from the public, often exacerbated by the Department of Defense and the Administration. Voting against a weapons system results in a flurry of accusations about being 'weak on defence' or 'soft on communism'. Frequently, Congress will deal with this by cutting funds from one weapons system while adding funds to another. For instance, most Democrats in Congress favour the Midgetman ICBM but oppose the MX ICBM (the DoD, on the other hand, favours the MX but opposes the Midgetman). Thus for FY 1989 the House cut funds from the MX and added funds to the Midgetman, thus deflecting charges of being 'soft on defence' and not cutting the military budget.

THE HOUSE OF REPRESENTATIVES

Personnel turnover in the House is higher than in the Senate, adding a further degree of complexity to its work. It is led by the Speaker of the House, a member of the majority party in the House, elected by members of that party. The current speaker is Jim Wright (D, Texas), who recently set off a power struggle within the Democratic Party by announcing he was leaving the post.

The chief strategist and floor spokesman is the House Majority Leader, currently Thomas S. Foley (D, Washington). The Majority Leader decides party strategy for getting issues important to the party leadership through the House. The House Democratic Caucus, currently led by Richard E. Gephardt (D, Missouri), supports him in this work. The caucus formulates party rules, selects the party leadership, and approves committee chairmen and party committee assignments which are recommended by the Democratic Steering and Policy Committee. The Democratic Steering and Policy Committee is the executive arm of the Majority Caucus. It is led by the Speaker of the House, the Majority Leader, and the Democratic Caucus Chairman. Its members are appointed by the Speaker. This committee has the all-important job of assigning party members to committees. While a party member can request to be on a particular committee, there is no guarantee this request will be met. Committee assignments often dictate what issues that member will deal with, his visibility, and his power in the Congress. The Steering and Policy Committee also recommends committee chairmen. Although this is no longer strictly based on seniority, the more senior members usually receive these assignments.

The House Republican leadership is headed by the House Minority Leader, currently Robert H. Michel (R, Illinois). Like his Democratic counterpart, the Minority Leader is the chief strategist and spokesperson for his party. The House Republican Conference is a caucus of all House Republicans. It formulates party rules and strategy, and approves committee assignments. The Conference also studies positions for the party to take on major legislation.

Republican committee assignments are dealt with by the House Republican Committee on Committees, chaired by the Minority Leader. Since the majority party appoints committee chairman, the Republican Committee on Committees does not at present have this responsibility.

(See biographies of: Aspin; AuCoin; Badham; Bateman; Bennett, C. E.; Bevill; Boggs; Boxer; Brennan; Bustamente; Byron; Chappell; Courter; Daniel; Darden; Davis, J.; Davis, R. W.; Dellums; Dickinson; Dicks; Dyson; Fazio; Foglietta; Hansen; Hefner; Hertel; Hochbruekner; Hopkins; Hunter; Hutto; Ireland; Kasich; Kyl; Leath; Livingston; Lloyd; McCloskey; McCurdy; McDade; Martin, D.; Martin, L. M.; Mavroules; Meyers; Miller, C. E.; Montgomery; Murtha; Nichols; Ortiz; Pickett; Price; Pursell; Ravenal; Ray; Robinson; Rowland; Sabo; Schroeder; Sisisky; Skelton; Smith, V.; Spence; Spratt; Stratton; Stump; Sweeney; Thomas; Watkins; Weldon; Wilson, C.; Young.)

THE SENATE

The Senate is officially presided over by the Vice-President, who is President of the Senate but does not have a vote unless the Senate is equally divided on a measure (an infrequent occurrence). In the absence of the Vice-President, which is frequent, the Senate is presided over by President Pro Tempore, currently John Stennis (D, Mississippi).

The majority party in the Senate, currently the Democrats, is led by the Senate Majority Leader, Robert Byrd (D, West Virginia). The Majority Leader is the chief strategist and floor spokesman for the majority party. Like his counterpart in the House, the post of Majority Leader gives Byrd an opportunity also to serve as a public spokesman for the Democrats, since he is frequently consulted by the press. The Majority Leader is assisted by the Senate Majority Whip, Alan Cranston (D, California). The Majority Whip helps to organize party strategy, and also serves as the vote-counter for upcoming legislation, which often affects strategy.

Party policy for Democratic senators is formulated by the Senate Democratic Policy Committee, which is also chaired by Robert Byrd and is dominated by conservative Democrats. Party positions on specific legislation are formulated by a subcommittee of the Democratic Policy Committee, the Legislative Review Committee. This committee is chaired by Dale Bumpurs (D, Arkansas).

Recommendations for committee assignments and chairmanships, which are as important in the Senate as in the House, are made by the Senate Democratic Steering Committee, which reports to the Majority Leader. Robert Byrd is also Chairman of that Committee, which is generally made up of the more senior members of the Senate Democrats.

The Republican counterpart to the Majority Leader is the Senate Minority Leader, Robert Dole (R, Kansas). The Minority Leader has been an important consultant to the White House since the Democrats took control of the Senate. He is assisted by the Senate Minority Whip, Alan K. Simpson (R, Wyoming). Republican Party policy is decided by the Senate Republican Policy Committee, which is chaired by William L. Armstrong (R, Colorado). The Committee also circulates summaries of major legislation and analyses of roll-call votes to Senate Republicans.

Republican Committee assignments are made by the Senate Republican Committee on Committees, chaired by Paul Trible (R, Virginia). Unlike the Democratic Steering Committee, the Committee on Committees meets only at the start of each new Congress to assign members to committees; after the assignments are made, the Committee on Committees becomes inactive. Since the Republicans are the minority party, the Committee on Committees does not assign chairmanships.

(See biographies of: Bennett Johnston; Bingaman; Burdick; Byrd; Chiles; Cochran; Cohen; D'Amato; DeConcini; Dixon; Domenici; Exon; Garn; Glenn; Gore; Gramm; Hatfield; Hollings; Humphrey; Inouye; Kasten; Kennedy; Leahy; Levin; McCain; McClure; Nunn; Proxmire; Quayle; Rudman; Sasser; Shelby; Specter; Stennis; Stevens; Symms; Thurmond; Warner; Weicker; Wilson, P.; Wirth.)

CONGRESSIONAL SUPPORT AGENCIES

Congress has set up a number of agencies to provide an independent flow of information to Congress. Because members of Congress tend to be generalists, due to the number of issues they have to deal with, the agencies can have an important influence on decisionmaking by Congress. The agencies are non-partisan; they are also often sharply critical of the Department of Defense. A brief description of each of them follows.

The Congressional Budget Office (CBO)

Address: House Office Building Annex 2, Second and D Streets, SW 4th Fl.
Washington, DC 20515
Tel: (202) 226-2600; Acting Director/Deputy Director: 226-2702; Assistant Director, National Security Division: 226-9200; Deputy Assistant Director for Weapons Analysis: 226-2900

The CBO was established by the Congressional Budget Act of 1974. It provides non-partisan analysis on a range of budgetary issues and outlines various fiscal, budgetary and programmatic options. The CBO does not present recommendations in its reports. Recent defence-related reports have included *An Analysis of Administration Strategic Arms Reduction and Modernization Proposals*, *Costs of the Trident Submarine and Missile Programs and Alternatives*, *Future Budget Requirements for the 600-Ship Navy*, and *Modernizing US Strategic Forces: The Administration's Program and Alternatives*. The CBO's reports are available to the public. Defence-related reports are produced by its National Security Division.

(See biographies of: Gramlich; Hale; Mayer.)

The General Accounting Office (GAO)

Address: 441 G Street, NW, Washington, DC, 20548
Tel (Reports Distribution): (202) 275-6241; Comptroller General: 275-5481; Assistant Comptroller/Director of National Security Division: 275-4418; Associate Director, C3I: 275-4841; Senior Associate Director, Dept. of the Air Force: 275-4268; Senior Associate Director, Dept. of the Army: 275-4141; Senior Associate Director, Dept. of the Navy: 275-6504;

Associate Director-in-Charge, Research, Development, Acquisition and General Procurement: 275-4587

Established in 1921, the GAO is the principal investigatory arm of Congress. The GAO generates a large number of reports on defence-related issues each year, all of which are available to the public. GAO reports are also sometimes valuable sources of the Department of Defense perspective, since the GAO usually distributes a draft of each report to the DoD for comment, and these comments are then included in the final report. Recent reports on defence-related issues from the GAO have included *DoD Acquisition Programs: Status of Selected Systems, Navy Acquisition: Cost and Performance of Various Antisubmarine Warfare Systems, Weapons Performance: Operational Test and Evaluation Can Contribute More to Decisionmaking*, and *Chemical Warfare: Progress and Problems in Defensive Capabilities*. The GAO reports which are distributed to the public are often unclassified versions of classified reports.

The Head of the GAO is the Comptroller of the United States, who is appointed by the President for a fifteen-year term (subject to confirmation by the Senate). GAO reports on defence-related issues are generally produced by its National Security and International Affairs Division (NSIAD).

(See biographies of: Bowsher; Conahan; Connor; Davis, R. A.; Finley; Landicho; Math.)

The Office of Technology Assessment (OTA)

Address: 600 Pennsylvania Avenue, SE, Washington, DC, 20510

Tel: (202) 228-6204; Director: 224-3695; Assistant Director, Energy, Materials, and International Security Division: (202) 224-6750

Established in 1972, the OTA does not generate the same volume of reports on defence-related issues as do the GAO or CBO. Its function is to provide early warning and analysis of emerging highly technical issues, in order to clarify the range of policy options and potential impacts of those options. It was the OTA which put out the groundbreaking *Effects of Nuclear War* study in 1977. Other defence-related studies by the OTA in recent years have included *Ballistic Missile Defense Technology, Seismic Verification of Nuclear Test Ban Treaties*, and *Anti-Satellite Weapons, Countermeasures, and Arms Control*. OTA reports are available to the general public.

The OTA is governed by a twelve-member board consisting of six Senators and six Representatives.

(See biographies of: Gibbons; Johns.)

THE DEFENCE CONTRACTORS

The corporations and universities which make up what is often referred to as the defence industry have no place in the formal decision-making process. They do, however, wield considerable power and influence, the extent and propriety of which have often been the subject of heated debate. This power is due in part to the size of the defence industry. As one author has put it, 'Almost every industry in the United States is a prime or sub-contractor with the Defense Department, or has some continuing or contingency relationship with the military' (Arkin, 1981, p.106). In spite of this, however, there are only a few corporations, mostly large aerospace firms, which are commonly identified as military contractors.

It would surprise many people to know of the part played by universities in the defence industry. The Defense Department (DoD) funds much of the university research done in the United States. Some of this is handled by agencies such as DARPA, which is at the centre of the Strategic Computer Initiative programme, under whose auspices almost all current US research into artificial intelligence (AI) is being carried out. In fact, two universities rank in the top 100 of DoD prime contractors for FY 1987: the Massachusetts Institute of Technology (fifty-first) and the Johns Hopkins University (fifty-third).

The defence industry wields power for a variety of reasons and through a variety of means. The first factor which deserves consideration — the 'revolving door' between the DoD and defence contractors — has been discussed above (see: Department of Defense).

It is difficult to say how much influence this exchange of personnel gives the defence industry, but it shows the commonality of interest between the DoD and the defence industry.

Further, the defence industry has an interest at stake at nearly every stage of a weapons systems development. Defence contractors do not merely sit and wait for the DoD to come up with weapons systems for them to build; rather, they have large research and development departments which investigate possibilities for new weapons. The majority of the DoD budget for research, development, testing and evaluation goes to industry, and most contractors also do research and development which is not subsidized by the government. Contractors will actively try to 'sell' a weapons system idea to the DoD or the armed forces, even though there may be no demonstrable military 'need' for such a weapon.

Defence contractors also constitute a powerful obstacle to the cancellation of weapons systems, especially in Congress. Industry has influence in Congress for a number of reasons. The first reason is that members of Congress often have military contractors located in the state or district they represent. A weapons system contract awarded to that contractor means jobs and revenue for constituents, for which the Congressional representative can take at least partial credit. Cancellation of a weapons contract means a loss of jobs, and being seen as responsible for throwing constituents out of work is a sure way to lose re-election. Defence contractors exploit this vulnerability by opening plants in the districts of powerful members of Congress in order to encourage or reward particular votes. Prime contractors also target Congressional districts and states when awarding sub-contracts on large contracts. As prime contractors decide which companies get the sub-contracts, which can be lucrative in their own right, subcontracts will often be awarded to 'politically strategic' companies throughout the nation.

Defence contractors also exert influence through financial means, in the form of both substantial campaign contributions and speaking fees. Most weapons contractors have political action committees (PACs) which donate money to both Congressional and Presidential campaigns. In 1983–84, for instance, General Dynamics contributed $256,031 to federal election campaigns. From 1983 to 1986, such PACs contributed $1.3 million to members of the House Armed Services Committee. While no one has proved that such contributions result in certain votes, it seems obvious that they would have some effect.

Further financial incentive is provided by the 'appearance fees' which defence contractors give to members of Congress. In 1985, House and Senate members reported receiving $387,613 in honoraria from weapons contractors. This money is often paid simply to tour a weapons plant and meet corporate officials.

It is important to recognize, however, that the defence industry is not monolithic. There is often fierce competition between companies for a particular contract, as a contract can mean millions of dollars in revenue for a company. Some critics have pointed out that contracts often seem to be awarded on the basis of need instead of merit. That is, they are often awarded to companies which have either recently failed in a commercial venture or phased out production of another weapons system. Since the defence industry is seen by most DoD officials as a national resource, there is an interest in keeping defence contractors afloat (see Gansler, 1980; Kotz, 1988).

Contractors will also compete in order to ensure one particular weapons system, rather than another, is built. The Northrop Corporation, contractor for the Stealth bomber, and Rockwell International, contractor for the B-1 bomber, waged a fierce battle when it seemed that the Reagan Administration and Congress were going to approve construction of either one or the other, but not both, of these two weapons systems. Contractors are also often identified with a particular service from which they receive the majority of their contracts, and will seek to protect the interests of that service and the weapons systems it wants built.

The following list includes some of the top prime contractors for FY 1986, according to the Department of Defense.

The Boeing Company
Address: 7755 Marginal Way South, Seattle, WA 98108
Tel: (206) 655-2121

Boeing, best-known for commercial aircraft, received over $3 billion in contracts for FY 1986. Boeing built the B-52 bombers and the Minuteman ICBM. It is also a sub-contractor for the Stealth and B-1B bombers.
(See biographies of: Miller, M. K.; Shrontz; Stamper.)

General Motors Corporation
Address: 3044 West Grand Boulevard, Detroit, MI 48202
Tel: (313) 556-5000

General Motors, although not well known as a military contractor, received over $5 billion worth of contracts in FY 1986. In fact, it is worth noting that all the major automobile manufacturers are involved also in military contracting, a point which sheds some light on the prevalance of the military in industry.
(See biographies of: Atwood; Smith, R. B.; Stempel.)

Honeywell Incorporated
Address: Honeywell Plaza, Minneapolis, MN 55408
Tel: (612) 870-5200

Honeywell, which received almost $2 billion in contracts for FY 1986, makes guidance systems and controls for the Minuteman, Trident and MX missiles. Honeywell also makes the ASROC anti-submarine missile, which is equipped with nuclear depth charges.
(See biographies of: Renier; Spencer; Wheaton.)

Lockheed Corporation
Address: 4500 Park Granada Boulevard, Calabasas, CA 91399
Tel: (818) 712-2000

Lockheed, which received almost $5 billion worth of contracts in FY 1986, has developed and manufactured the entire US sea-based missile fleet. Lockheed built the Polaris, Poseidon, and Trident I SLBMs, and is now building the Trident II. Lockheed also makes control systems for the Tomahawk.
(See biographies of: Araki; Fuhrman; Jones, D. C.; Kitchen.)

McDonnell Douglas Corporation
Address: P.O. Box 516, St. Louis, MO 63166
Tel: (314) 232-0232

McDonnell Douglas, which received over $6 billion in contracts in FY 1986, makes guidance systems for the Tomahawk GLCM and fire control systems for the Tomahawk GLCM and SLCM and the Harpoon anti-ship missile. McDonnell Douglas also makes a number of aircraft, including the AV-8B, the Harrier II, F-15 Eagle, F/A-18, and the F-4 Phantom.
(See biographies of: Little; McDonnell; Worsham)

Raytheon Company
Address: 141 Spring Street, Lexington, MA 02173
Tel: (617) 862-6600

Raytheon received just over $4 billion in contracts from the DoD in FY 1986. They make the Patriot surface-to-air missile, the Sidewinder and Sparrow air-to-air missile systems, and fire control systems for the Navy.
(See biographies of: Phillips; Picard; Shea; Shelley.)

Rockwell International
Address: 600 Grant Street, Pittsburgh, PA 15219
Tel: (412) 565-2000

Rockwell, which received over $5 billion in contracts in FY 1986, makes the B-1B bomber, the flight computer and guidance and control systems for the MX missile, and is the prime contractor for the space shuttle. Rockwell also manages facilities involved in the manufacture of nuclear warheads.
(See biographies of: Anderson; Beall; Iacobellis; Jeffs; McDivitt.)

United Technologies
Address: United Technologies Building, Hartford, CT 06101
Tel: (203) 728-7946

United Technologies received over $3 billion in contracts for FY 1986. Among other things, United Technologies builds jet engines for the F-15 and F-16 and helicopters.
(See biographies of: Daniell; Evans; Paul.)

CASE STUDY: DECISIONMAKING ON THE B-1 BOMBER

For several reasons, the case of the B-1 bomber is perhaps atypical of decisionmaking on nuclear weapons systems: the length of the controversy (nearly thirty years), the amount of public attention it received, and the fact that it was the focus of a major campaign by peace groups and one President. It is none the less a good example for our purposes because it clearly demonstrates the limits of power of the President and Congress, the importance of symbolism in defence politics, the importance of non-strategic reasons in deciding to produce weapons systems, the power the 'constituency' of a weapons system can have, and the independence of the services from the Department of Defense (DoD). Perhaps most important, decisionmaking on the B-1 clearly demonstrates the gap between public perception and the reality of decisionmaking.

Strategic air power, which the B-1 represents, has long been considered the 'heart' of the US Air Force. The Strategic Air Command (SAC) is the Air Force's showpiece, and its most powerful command. The Air Force and SAC have long been unhappy with SAC's former centrepiece, the B-52 bomber. The Air Force has contended that the B-52 is obsolete and, because of its age, potentially dangerous. Other studies have shown that the B-52H will be effective into the 1990s. But the B-52 has a more important failing than not being able to fulfil its mission: it does not increase the size of the Air Force budget and it has no symbolic value. The B-1 fulfils these 'missions'.

The Early Years: The Battle over the B-70 (1954–63)

The battle for the B-1 bomber began in 1954 under the code name WS-110. President Eisenhower was still in office, the defence budget was under $40 billion, and the B-52 was still in production at Boeing. WS-110 was a design project whose goal was to come up with a supersonic bomber that the Air Force could call its own. WS-110 was not a great success, however, and the Air Force cancelled the project in 1956.

In 1957, North American Aviation (the predecessor of Rockwell International) and Boeing made important breakthroughs in their work on a supersonic bomber. The date of these breakthroughs is significant: shortly after they were made, on 4 October 1957, the Soviets launched the Sputnik satellite. The psychological and symbolic effect on the USA was devastating, breaking US confidence in its superiority over the Soviet Union in science and technology. Under intense pressure from the public and the Democrats, Republican President Eisenhower approved an additional $2 billion for the 1958 defence budget. Two weeks after this approval was granted, the Air Force awarded a research and development contract to North American Aviation for a new bomber. Only a month later, the contract was expanded to include production of twelve test models and delivery of fifty new bombers to SAC by August 1964. The new bomber, known as the B-70 Valkyrie, was supposed to be able to fly at Mach 3 at an altitude of 70,000 feet for a distance of 7,000 nautical miles.

It is telling that Air Force officers referred to the B-70 as their 'manned missile': at this time, production of ICBMs was becoming likely, and Air Force officers regarded them as a threat to both the Air Force's budget and to its prestige.

Two years after Sputnik, Eisenhower decided to clamp down on defence spending. Although he had made his career in the military, Eisenhower saw runaway defence spending as a serious threat to the national budget. One of the weapons systems which faced the budget axe was the B-70 Valkyrie. In November 1959, Eisenhower met with a powerful coterie of defence advisers at the Augusta National Golf Club in Georgia to make a decision on the B-70. Present were the Secretary of Defense Neil McElroy; Dr George Kistiatowsky, Eisenhower's science adviser; General Nathan Twining, Chairman of the Joint Chiefs of Staff; and the service chiefs, including Air Force Chief of Staff General Thomas White.

McElroy and Twining presented their arguments for the B-70, but Eisenhower remained unconvinced. White then presented the Air Force's strategic case for the B-70: missiles had never been tested and therefore were not reliable; bombers, unlike missiles, could be recalled and thus gave the President more options; bombers would present complications for the enemy; and bombers could have an important psychological effect as symbols of military might. Eisenhower did not accept these arguments, telling White that 'we are talking about bows and arrows at the time of gunpowder when we speak of bombers in the missile age.' White then tried a different tack, stressing not the strategic role of the B-70, but its importance to the Air Force: 'There is a question of what is to be the future of the Air Force and of flying', he told Eisenhower,and 'this shift [to missiles] has a great impingement on morale. There is no follow-on aircraft to the fighter and no new opportunity for Air Force personnel'.

A few days later, Eisenhower all but killed the B-70, reducing the programme to one experimental plane without any weapons systems. The Air Force, however, had no intention of giving up on the B-70. With General White as their chief spokesperson, the Air Force took their case to Congress. Eisenhower was furious, and seriously considered firing White. He referred to the Air Force actions as 'damn near treason'. Yet the Air Force had powerful allies. One was North American Aviation, which saw it would lose a contract worth hundreds of millions of dollars if the B-70 did not go ahead. North American had bought itself some allies by judicious allocation of subcontracts for the B-70, including a $200 million contract for Boeing to build the plane's wings. However, these forces appeared unable to overturn Eisenhower's decision until the shadow of the 1960 presidential election fell on Eisenhower and his attempts to cut defence spending.

The 1960 election pitted Eisenhower's vice-president, Richard Nixon, against John F. Kennedy, one of the rising stars of the Democratic Party. Kennedy and the Democrats seized on the issue of defence spending, arguing that, under Eisenhower, it had been inadequate to the United States' needs. Eisenhower, as the election approached, decided to give Nixon a boost, and above all in California, where many jobs depended on the B-70. In July 1960, he announced an increase of $500 million in military spending, with $100 million going to revive the B-70. Then, in late October, just nine days before the election, the Air Force announced that an additional $155 million would go to a 'substantially augmented development program' for the B-70. Nixon won California, though he lost the election (by only just over 18,000 votes). The Air Force, however, had scored a clear victory. They had won a commitment to build at least four B70s: the programme was alive again. This victory was reflected in Eisenhower's final budget, which fully reinstated the B-70 development programme.

Though the B-70 had overcome the first attempt to cancel it, President Kennedy and his Secretary of Defense, Robert McNamara, soon proved to be not as sympathetic to the programme as the new Air Force Chief of Staff, Curtis LeMay, had hoped. LeMay was a former SAC commander who had almost single-handedly built SAC into the most powerful command in the Air Force. He was the commander of the group of Air Force generals, known as the 'bomber mafia', which saw strategic bombing as the heart and soul of the Air Force. Robert McNamara (a former president of Ford Motor Company) by contrast, regarded cost—benefit analysis as the key to making efficient decisions about defence and, to him, the B-70 did not look cost effective in the age of the ICBM. Going back on a campaign promise, Kennedy refused to expand the B-70 programme to production and seemed inclined to cancel it altogether.

In mid-1961, with their backs against the wall, the Air Force and North American Aviation thought they had found a way of overcoming opposition to the B-70: it would be redesigned and transformed - the first of several transformations it would undergo - into something called the RS-70. RS stood for 'reconnaissance strike', and the idea was that the plane would look for and then destroy important targets which had survived the 'first round' of a nuclear war. However, the technology for the RS-70 - a computerized radar which would simultaneously identify targets and direct missiles at them - had not yet been invented. Kennedy and McNamara refused to go along with this proposal.

The next champion for the B-70 emerged in 1962 in the shape of Carl Vinson, the powerful chairman of the House Armed Services Committee. For two years, Vinson and the Congress had authorized money to be spent on the B-70, but Kennedy and McNamara had simply refused to spend it. On 1 March 1962, Vinson's committee not only authorized $491 million for the B70, but 'ordered and directed' the executive branch to build it. This was a direct constitutional challenge to the power of the executive branch, and one Kennedy was not eager to accept. Aides told him he might lose on the House floor, and that such a battle could in any case ruin his legislative programme. On the eve of the battle, Kennedy and Vinson reached a compromise: Kennedy agreed to 'restudy' the bomber issue, and Vinson agreed to drop his challenge. For two more years Congress authorized money for the B-70, and for two more years that money went unspent.

It appeared that Kennedy and McNamara had won their fight with the Air Force. Yet that battle was not over.

The AMSA/FB-111 Debate (1963—69)

With the arrival of Lyndon Johnson in the White House, after Kennedy's assassination, a new round opened in the debate on a strategic bomber for the Air Force.

Johnson retained Robert McNamara as Secretary of Defense. Curtis LeMay was still Air Force Chief of Staff, but he and the Air Force had finally given up the B-70 for dead. Instead, they proposed another bomber be built, the advanced manned strategic airplane (AMSA). LeMay wanted only $55 million to initiate studies on the AMSA, but McNamara opposed even this request. Johnson was worried more about his upcoming election battle with Barry Goldwater in November 1964 than with the Air Force's new bomber, and continually put off making any decision about it.

After Johnson's (landslide) election victory in 1964, McNamara convinced him to refuse to fund the AMSA. McNamara successfully argued that developing multiple, independently targetable re-entry vehicle (MIRV) technology for missiles would be far more cost-effective than building bombers. However, McNamara, though unwilling to fund the AMSA, had also decided that he must reach some compromise with the Air Force on a new plane. He proposed that an enlarged version of the F111 fighter be built by General Dynamics and called the FB-111. McNamara told Johnson that 210 FB-111s would cost $1.5 billion, as opposed to $9—$11 billion for 200 AMSA bombers. Johnson, who was more concerned with his domestic 'Great Society' programme and the escalating war in Vietnam than with Air Force bombers, heartily supported McNamara's proposal. The Air Force, however, was still interested only in the AMSA bomber. This stalemate continued until 1969.

The B-1 Debate in the Nixon Years (1969—74)

In 1967 McNamara retired, and Johnson announced that he would not run for re-election. (Also in 1967, North American Aviation merged with Rockwell Standard Corporation forming a new company, North American Rockwell (re-named Rockwell International in 1973).) In January 1969, Richard Nixon took office as President. His choice for Secretary of Defense was Melvin Laird, a Wisconsin Republican and the ranking Republican on the House Defense Appropriations Subcommittee. The new Deputy Secretary of Defense was David Packard, one of the founders of the computer firm Hewlett-Packard. Laird and Packard divided between them the responsibility for DoD, with Laird handling Congress and the Vietnam War while Packard ran the DoD.

The Air Force, now led by Chief of Staff John Ryan (LeMay had retired in 1965) and Air Force Secretary Robert Seamans, were hopeful of finally getting a new strategic bomber. By this time, the debate over AMSA had gone on so long that some in the Air Force suggested that AMSA really stood for 'America's Most Studied Aircraft'. To signify a fresh start with the bomber, the Air Force renamed it the B-1 Excalibur, meant to be reminiscent of King Arthur's magic sword. The name Excalibur was dropped, however, when the Air Force realised that this was also the brandname of a popular make of condom.

Ryan, a former SAC commander, insisted to Packard that US strategy required a 'mixed force' (both bombers and missiles). He also pressed the need for a newer, more capable bomber than the B-52. Packard agreed, promising Ryan $200 million for the first year to get work off the ground.

PILOTS IN 'SHIRTSLEEVES'

The B-1, despite the new name, was not very different from the AMSA bomber. It was meant to cruise at high altitude at Mach 2.2, dropping to tree-top level for its attack run (this was, of course, different from the B-70, which was intended to attack at high altitude). The B-1 would also be equipped with so-called 'variable-sweep' wings that would sweep back for supersonic speed and low-level flying, and sweep forward for long-range cruising, take-offs and landings. A self-contained escape capsule would allow the entire crew to eject and land safely on land or water. The B-1 would have a range of six-thousand miles, carry twice as many weapons as the B-52, and be able to take off using less than 6,000 feet of runway.

The design for the B-1 dated from the requirements established in a six-month study in 1963 by Colonel David C. Jones and Lieutenant Colonel James Allen. Both were pilots and their requirements reflected a pilot's needs. One of these requirements (known to critics as 'desirements') was that the crew would be able to fly in 'shirt-sleeves' (most planes are flown by pilots in pressure suits, strapped into seats which can eject if the plane is in trouble). Hence the self-contained escape capsule, which would allow them to escape easily, without worrying about ejection seats and pressure suits.

Critics, including some within the Air Force and the DoD, considered many of the requirements to be 'gold-plating', unnecessary to the plane's mission. One such critic, Ivan Selin, the acting Assistant Secretary of Defense for Systems Analysis, tried to convince Deputy Defense Secretary Packard that the mission could be accomplished by a less complicated (and less expensive) subsonic bomber which would fire cruise missiles (long range, pilotless drones with warheads) at targets in the Soviet Union without having to fly into Soviet airspace. This concept is known as 'stand-off' bombing. Packard refused to accept Selin's arguments, believing that the Air Force knew best what sort of bomber they needed.

ROCKWELL GETS THE CONTRACT

The Air Force quickly selected three firms to compete for the B-1 contract: North American Rockwell, Boeing and General Dynamics. General Dynamics was already scheduled to build the Trident, a lucrative contract; Boeing was very successful with its commercial planes, and had just won a contract to build the B-747 transport plane; North American Rockwell, however, had just lost to McDonnell Douglas the competition to build the F15 fighter and its aircraft division was in serious trouble.

North American Rockwell board chairman, Willard Rockwell, wanted the company to drop out of the competition for the B-1, feeling there was little chance of success against Boeing. The recently-elected president of North American Rockwell, Robert Anderson, was able, however, to persuade him that the company should bid for the contract, and, in January 1970, Willard Rockwell sent the DoD the seventy-five volumes, totalling 9,772 pages, which made up the firm's bid for the contract.

North American Rockwell's efforts did not stop here. The company enlisted politicians and business leaders to plead its case. Senator George Murphy and Governor Ronald Reagan of California both interceded on Rockwell's behalf. Glennard Lipscomb of California, the ranking Republican on the House Defense Appropriations Subcommittee and close friend of Secretary of Defense Laird, telephoned or met Laird fifteen times to plead the Rockwell case. Without the contract, he told Laird, the company's aircraft division would close. Anderson of Rockwell went to the Pentagon to meet Packard, telling him that Rockwell needed the contract to survive.

Each of the companies could have built the B-1. Rockwell, however, had a head-start in the competition: not only did the company need the contract, but, as an important contributor to President Nixon's 1968 election campaign, it was favoured by the President and his advisers. Rockwell was awarded the contract in June 1970.

OPPOSITION TO THE B-1

Meanwhile, however, in the halls of Congress, trouble was brewing for Rockwell, the Air Force, and the B-1. Dissension over the Vietnam war, among other things, was causing Congress to take a more active role in foreign policy and defence matters. A group of legislators founded Members of Congress for Peace through Law (MCPL) and monitored weapons programmes on their own. In 1971, Representative John Sieberling (D, Ohio) and Senator George McGovern (D, South Dakota) wrote a report for MCPL which concluded that the B-1 was unnecessary.

These were merely the first ripples of Congressional dissent, however, and not enough to worry the Nixon Administration or the Air Force: the B-1 was not an expensive enough programme to merit serious concern in the Congress; the debate was still centred in the executive branch. Yet forces were now mobilizing in the *administration* that were opposed to the bomber. The effort was co-ordinated within the administration by Richard Stubbing, the budget examiner for Air Force programmes at the Office of Management and Budget. Stubbing was joined in his efforts by the DoD Office of Systems Analysis, the National Security Council staff, and the White House Office of Science and Technology: they all recommended that Nixon cancel B-1 development, or at the very least, eliminate the more expensive features of the plane. The Air Force's projected cost for the B-1, $8—$10 billion for 240, was very low, they said; North American Rockwell itself projected a cost of $20—$25 billion, while the Director of Research and Engineering at DoD projected the cost at $37—$40 billion.

Nixon did apparently consider cancelling the project and asked the Pentagon to reconsider the need for the bomber. Packard and Laird were furious. Packard threatened to resign if the B-1 were cancelled. Nixon, who wanted to avoid a confrontation with DoD, backed off and cancelled the review (he could afford to: the actual production decision lay far in the future).

OPPOSITION UNDERMINED

The presidential campaign of 1972, however, in which Nixon was planning to run for re-election, dramatically changed the fortunes of the B-1 within the administration. John Ehrlichman, Nixon's key adviser on domestic policy, felt that in order for Nixon to be re-elected, he had to win the southeastern and southwestern 'Sun-Belt' states and the way to do this was to retore some economic life to the region, especially since the Democrats were criticizing Nixon for the high national rate of unemployment. The fastest way to create jobs in the most important states in the region, Ehrlichmann realized, would be to award contracts in the aerospace industry. Nationwide, 1,253,000 defence workers had lost their jobs since the peak of the Vietnam War in 1969, including 207,000 in the aerospace industry. Part of this was due to Nixon's efforts to trim inflation, which had resulted in a two-year, $9 billion cut in the DoD budget. Creating jobs in aerospace, Ehrlichmann thought, might result in newspaper headlines like the one in the *Los Angeles Times* the day after Rockwell won the B-1 contract in 1970: '43,000 NEW JOBS'.

Out of these thoughts came a campaign named by some in the administration 'Keep California Green'. It called for 100,000 new defence jobs to be created in California by Labor Day 1972. The Office of Management and Budget identified defence contracts to which funds could be added without new Congressional authorization (mainly research and development contracts). North American Rockwell, and the B-1, were important beneficiaries of this plan: so the B-1 was safe, at least for the duration of the 1972 election.

The defence contractors reciprocated by making more than $3 million in secret contributions to Nixon's campaign. Willard Rockwell was approached for funds in 1971, when his company was fighting both for the B-1 and the contract to build the space shuttle, and North American Rockwell contributed $135,000 to Nixon's campaign. Although investigations during the Watergate affair revealed that many corporations did make illegal contributions, the gifts from Rockwell were legal.

During this time, when contractor dollars were pouring into the White House and government dollars pouring out to the contractors, the Nixon Administration negotiated the SALT agreement with the Soviets. Appearing before the Senate Foreign Relations Committee, Defense Secretary Laird bluntly announced the cost of arms control treaties: if the Congress did not approve 'strategic modernization', including the B-1 and Trident, he and the Joint Chiefs would not support the SALT agreement; Congress not only approved the B-1 and Trident, but $797 million in increased defence spending as well. (New jobs in the defence industry help not only to re-elect presidents, but also members of Congress.)

RESEARCH AND DEVELOPMENT PROBLEMS

Yet the saga of the B-1 was far from over. In Rockwell's Palmdale, California plant, a huge team was trying to turn the Air Force's sophisticated 'desirements' into reality. Snags developed almost immediately. The B-1 had the most demanding requirements ever, some of them requiring technology never used before on such a scale. Reports from Air Force officers assigned to monitor the plant (from Air Force Systems Command in Ohio) adopted a bleak tone after only a year. The project was already over budget and behind schedule, they warned - in stark contrast to the glowing progress reports given to Congress and the press by the B-1 Program Manager, Major General Douglas Nelson.

Senior Air Force officials were beginning to worry about the project. The officers from Systems Command were told by headquarters to stop reporting programme problems as these might fall into the wrong hands in Washington and result in the programme being scuttled. The Air Force then found a scapegoat for the critical reports: not Rockwell, nor the B-1, but the messenger of bad news: Lieutenant-Colonel Thomas H. Hobbs, manager of the B-1 Cost Schedule Control System and editor of the monthly status reports. Without warning or explanation, Hobbs was relieved of his duties at the plant and assigned to an empty office. His officer efficiency rating report, which previously had been 'outstanding', was downgraded by Systems Command Headquarters, and he was denied the promotion his command officer had reccomended. Eleven months later, Hobbs - a West Point graduate who had been decorated in both Korea and Vietnam - resigned from the Air Force.

At about the same time, senior officers in the Air Force were evaluating the Rockwell effort. According to the B-1 contract, Rockwell would receive a 'profit fee' based on the quality of the work done. The fee-award committee was headed by the Air Force Deputy Chief of Staff for Research, Development and Acquisition, General Otto Glosser. After a visit to Palmdale, Glosser recommended that Rockwell should get less than 40 per cent of the maximum allowable fee. Glosser's superiors were furious. 'What the hell are you trying to do, kill the program?', demanded on assistant secretary, and 'how do you think this going to look in Congress?' Rockwell received 95 per cent of the allowable fee, which made it seem as if the programme was proceeding almost perfectly. Critical reports from the DoD and Congress, however, did force Rockwell and the Air Force to bring in new programme managers in 1973.

The Ford Presidency (1974—76)

In 1974 the Nixon presidency disintegrated after the Watergate scandal, and Gerald Ford took office as President. His new Secretary of Defense was James Schlesinger, who had previously worked as a nuclear strategist at the RAND Corporation. A significant change took place in the Air Force, where the new Chief of Staff, General David C. Jones (the same man who had established the original requirements for the B-1 in 1963), was the first not to have gained the post through being commander of SAC.

Schlesinger supported the B-1, but also worried about its escalating cost. He warned Jones that if the costs went over $100 million per plane, he would abandon it. Though Jones had helped design the plane, he also now was worried about the B-1's costs and their effect on other Air Force programmes.

In December 1974, Jones convened a secret meeting of ten of the Air Force's twelve four-star generals. Its code name was Corona Quest, and the subject was the B-1. For forty-eight hours before the meeting, staff officers worked on budget and cost projections. The results were disastrous for the project: they showed that the B-1 would cost over $100 million per plane and require cuts in other Air Force programmes such as the A10, F-15 and F-16. The next day however, officers from Systems Command and from SAC told the participants in Corona Quest that the budget and cost projection figures were wrong: the costs of the plane had been overestimated and future Air Force budgets underestimated. By the time Corona Quest was over, the figures had become less threatening for the programme.

During the meeting, Jones had said that the B-1 could only continue if it had the complete support of all the commanders present. The support was forthcoming, but the budget figures produced in the meeting shocked the Air Force into at least modifying the project: the demand for an escape capsule was dropped, and the speed capability was reduced from Mach 2.2 to Mach 1.6. Further, the plane would now have to be flown at subsonic speeds in order to preserve the range of the bomber and conserve fuel.

THE BATTLE IN CONGRESS BEGINS

By now, however, the B-1 was running into serious opposition in Congress. The project manager at Rockwell, Bastian 'Buzz' Hello, realized that intense lobbying would be needed to convince Congress to continue funding for the B-1 in the 1975 Defense Authorization Act. The lobbying was co-ordinated by a small group from the Air Force and Rockwell who met in the Air Force Office of Legislative Liaison on the fourth floor of the Pentagon. The Rockwell team was led by Ralph J. (Doc) Johnson, the chief Rockwell lobbyist. Johnson was joined by John Rane, an aeronautical engineer from Rockwell, and they called their team the 'Doc and Johnny Show'. For crucial votes, 'Buzz' Hello would fly in from California. The Air Force lobby was directed by Lieutenant-General Marion Boswell, the assistant vice-chief of staff, assisted by Colonel Grant Miller, who directed day-to-day strategy. They were occasionally joined by John Grey, a representative from the Air Force Association, an organization of active and retired Air Force personnel and supporters (although technically the Air Force Association was not allowed to lobby, it could encourage its 150,000 members to put pressure on members of Congress in support of the B-1 through their local branches).

The lobbying coalition was born in response not only to the growing opposition in Congress to the B-1 and but also to the decentralization of Congressional power: Democratic reformers had succeeded in taking power away from committee chairmen, and contractors and the Pentagon now had to convince many more members to support their programmes than they would previously have had to.

The Air Force and Rockwell were joined in their lobbying efforts by the sub-contractors on the B-1. These included the Boeing Company, which had been selected to build offensive avionics for the plane. Like the other sub-contractors, Boeing was awarded the sub-contract more for political, rather than technical, reasons: after it had lost the competition for the prime contract, a lucrative sub-contract was intended to mollify both the company and the important Washington State 'senators from

Boeing', Scoop Jackson and Warren Magnuson. Rockwell had also chosen the LTV Corporation, based in Dallas, Texas, to build parts of the fuselage. Rockwell could have done this work itself, but the large Texas Congressional delegation included both John Tower, a Republican on the Senate Armed Services Committee, and Jim Wright, the House Democratic Majority Leader. It was hoped that a sub-contract for LTV would prove helpful in swaying the Texas delegation in favour of the B-1.

The Air Force also helped to bring two powerful unions, the United Automobile Workers (UAW) and the International Association of Machinists, into the B-1 coalition. Both unions had many members working in the aerospace industry, and on the B-1 in particular.

As the appropriations vote in June 1975 approached, the lobbying coalition was worried mainly about Senate Democrats. They targeted two Democratic senators to provide credible leadership in the Senate: John Glenn of Ohio and Sam Nunn of Georgia. Glenn was chosen because he enjoyed celebrity status as a former Marine pilot and astronaut, and Nunn was a member of the Armed Services Committee and had a reputation as an expert on defence issues. Neither senator had yet committed himself to the B-1. Glenn was lobbied hard by the UAW, a vital political supporter of his, and by General Electric, the largest employer in Ohio and the company which was manufacturing the engines for the B-1 in Evendale, Ohio. Despite these efforts, Glenn was not won over. Then one of his legislative aides told the Air Force and Rockwell that Glenn was not convinced of the need for a new nuclear strategic bomber, but thought the new bomber would be valuable in a conventional war. The Air Force leadership, dominated by SAC, was opposed to this use for the B-1, and did not even plan to install racks for conventional bombs in the plane. It decided, however, that Glenn's support was important enough to warrant making promises: General Kelly Burke, deputy to SAC Commander General Russell Dougherty, met with Glenn to express SAC's 'strong interest' in a conventional bombing role. Glenn insisted on a written assurance that the B-1 would be equipped for a conventional role. On the eve of the vote in the Senate, a letter from Defense Secretary Schlesinger promising that the B-1 would eventually be equipped for conventional bombs was hand-delivered to Glenn. Glenn read the letter aloud on the Senate floor and then voted in favour of the B-1.

Nunn was a more difficult figure to win over, since no major work on the B-1 was being done in Georgia. The lobbyists approached Dr Daniel Callahan, a friend of Nunn and president of the Middle Georgia chapter of the Air Force Association, a formidable advocacy group. Callahan spoke with Nunn and, for whatever reason, Nunn voted for the B-1.

The B-1 development programme was thus kept going, but other problems loomed. Since Congress had cut back on development funds for the bomber, B-1 project manager 'Buzz' Hello realized to his horror that the decision on actually producing the B-1 would come in 1976, the next presidential election year.

The 1976 presidential campaign started in 1975. Shortly before, in 1973, the coalition *against* the B-1 had begun to form itself. This coalition was mainly the creation of Peter Barrer, a staffer in the New England office of the US Quaker organization, the American Friends Service Committee (AFSC). Barrer and the AFSC were looking for a cause around which the peace movement could re-group; that the B-1 became the cause was due to an accident of geography: General Electric, subcontracted to build the engines for the B-1, had a large plant in nearby Lynn, Massachusetts.

The AFSC decided that, in addition to General Electric (GE), Rockwell and Boeing would be targeted. The AFSC joined with Clergy and Laity Concerned (CALC) in a campaign that became known as the Stop the B-1 Bomber/ National Peace Conversion Campaign. By June 1975, the campaign included the National Taxpayers Union (a conservative group), the Women's Strike for Peace, the Federation of American Scientists, the International Longshoremen's Union, Environmental Action and Common Cause. The campaign lobbied the 1976 Democratic presidential candidates intensively. It also lobbied heavily in Congress, trying to counter the efforts of the Air Force—Rockwell pro-B1 coalition.

In 1976, the Ford Administration asked Congress for $1.9 billion for the B-1 programme. This money was intended not only to allow development to be completed, but to start production of 244 bombers. If the money for production were passed, the programme would be unstoppable. In the House, Representative John Sieberling, co-author of the 1971 critical report about the B-1, with support from other Representatives, made a proposal which 'Buzz' Hello had feared: that the Congress delay making a decision on B-1 production. It would be inappropriate for Congress to take this decision in 1976, Sieberling and his allies argued, as testing would not be complete until late in the year. The decision should be put off until 1977 so that the next President could act with all the necessary information about the project at hand.

It was a brilliant move. Sieberling knew that Congress members would not do something as controversial as kill the B-1 programme in 1976, a presidential election year, but that voting to delay the B-1 decision was politically safe. On 8 April 1976, the House approved, by 210 votes to 177, Sieberling's amendment to the Defense Authorization to delay the production decision.

The focus of attention quickly shifted to the Senate. Here the battle against the B-1 was led by Senators William Proxmire, George McGovern and John Culver. It was co-ordinated by a staffer of Proxmire's, Ron Tammen. Proxmire and McGovern, both liberal and generally opposed to exorbitant defence spending, were natural choices for leading the fight against the B-1. Further, both came from states where there were practically no defence jobs. Culver, on the other hand, was a former Harvard fullback and Marine Officer, and usually supported military programmes from his seat on the Armed Services Committee. His leading role in the fight against the B-1 seemed to be a response to a personal slight by Rockwell: during his five terms in the House, Culver had been helpful to the Collins Radio Company, the largest employer in his district and in Iowa. When Rockwell bought Collins Radio in 1974, Culver had been shocked to hear the president of Collins criticizing him for comments raising questions about the B-1. After this incident, he took a special interest in the B-1 programme.

Like the Rockwell—Air Force coalition, the anti-B-1 forces focused their efforts on a few key senators: Scoop Jackson of Washington, Sam Nunn of Georgia, and Democrat Robert Byrd of West Virginia. Jackson was a contender for the presidential nomination, and knew that many liberal Democrats were adopting the battle against the B-1 as their own. Further, the Washington State-based Boeing Company had discovered a more lucrative opportunity than sub-contracts for the B-1: to convert their B-52s or 747s into a replacement for the B-1 and make a bomber that would fire cruise missiles from a 'stand-off' position. The Lockheed Corporation, based in Nunn's home state of Georgia, was interested in converting their C-5As for the same purpose. Both Nunn and Jackson voted to delay the production decision.

Byrd was in some ways an easier figure to convince than either Jackson or Nunn. As well as being the object of sustained lobbying by the anti-B-1 forces, Byrd was also scheduled to take over as Senate Majority Leader. He saw the B1 vote as a chance to assuage the worries liberal Democrats had about his record. Byrd cast his vote with the anti-B-1 forces. When the Senate voted on 20 May 1976, the amendment to delay the production decision, sponsored by Culver, passed by 44 votes to 37. (President Ford, having been attacked from the right by Republican contender Ronald Reagan, had made a point of giving his unqualified support to the B-1 bomber.)

Presidential candidate Jimmy Carter needed an issue that would boost support for his candidacy among liberals. His chief adviser, Stuart Eizenstadt, recognized that opposition to the B-1 could be this issue. On the day the production delay amendment was passed in the Senate, Eizenstadt told the *Wall Street Journal* that Carter, if elected, would oppose the B-1.

The B-1 was now becoming a symbolic issue: this was what 'Buzz' Hello had feared. The Air Force—Rockwell coalition was willing to cast the B-1 as as an economic or a strategic issue.

But if it became a litmus test of where someone stood on defence, votes would slip out of their control.

To a certain extent, the Congressional votes and Carter's opposition to the B-1 had produced an important victory for the anti-B-1 forces. But the the Stop the B-1 Bomber campaign was essentially a 'peace coalition', opposed in principle to new weapons systems and to the so-called 'war economy'. In Congress, however, debates over weapons systems are not usually cast in these terms. Members of Congress will usually not vote against a weapons system unless they can support a different weapons system as proof that they are not 'soft' on defence. Thus Congressional opponents of the B-1 turned to another weapons system: the cruise missile. They pointed out that cruise missiles could perform the same mission as the B-1, and were much cheaper.

The anti-B-1 forces now experienced some setbacks in Congress. They lost two votes, and had one last chance to try and make their amendment stick. This came in the Senate Appropriations Committee. The anti-B-1 forces expected a close vote, but thought that they would win 16 to 13. On 21 July, with twenty-eight members present, the vote seemed to go as expected - until Warren Magnuson of Washington voted. Magnuson, who had earlier voted in favour of the delay, now voted against it. The vote was tied 14—14, which would have meant the amendment would be lost. While Senator Proxmire stalled, his aide Ron Tammen raced to find Robert Byrd, the missing member. Byrd was found and cast his vote for delay. The amendment passed 15 to 14.

The circumstances of Magnuson's vote throw some light on how defence politics are played. Just before the vote, Magnuson - who was by most accounts somewhat frail and unsteady by this time - received a call from an Air Force general. The general implied that if the B-1 lost, the Boeing Company, Magnuson's most important supporter, would lose some valuable defence contracts: Magnuson switched his vote.

The B-1 Debate in the Carter Years (1976—80)

CARTER AND CONGRESS

In November 1976, Jimmy Carter beat Gerald Ford by a narrow margin. He took office in January 1977. Unlike his predecessors, Carter had extensive political and technical knowledge of defence issues. He examined defence proposals and the defence budget with an attention to detail that surprised many. The first serious defence issue that Carter had to deal with was the B-1 bomber. Both sides of the debate, at this point, could smell a victory. If Carter approved B-1 production and got it through the Congress, the production lines - ready and waiting at Rockwell's Palmdale plant - would start rolling. After fighting for the B-1 for two decades, the Air Force would finally get its new bomber. The anti-B-1 forces, on the other hand, had won important victories in Congress, and Carter had made campaign pledges against the B-1. They put much pressure on Carter to keep his pledges. The Air Force Chief of Staff, David Jones, was also making decisions: he told the Air Force that there would be no lobbying of Congress this year; in a break with tradition, the Air Force would let Carter make his decision and then accept it. The Rockwell lobbyists felt betrayed, but kept up their lobbying efforts independently of the Air Force. They felt the future of Rockwell was tied up with the future of the B-1.

The key committees in Congress, however, were not waiting. Efforts were already being made to advance the bomber. Carter ordered his Secretary of Defense, Harold Brown, to do yet another study on the B-1. Secretary of Defense Brown and Chief of Staff Jones both supported the B-1; both were also in difficult positions. To run the Pentagon effectively, Brown needed the co-operation of the leaders of the Air Force, who supported the bomber feverishly. In order to be effective within the administration, however, Brown could not alienate Carter. Jones was also in a tight spot: he was unwilling to support the B-1 if it would split the Air Force and cause damage to other programmes he favoured. They had to approach the new study cautiously, and not allow it to make a clear case for the B-1.

The study was named the Modernization of the Strategic Bomber Force Study; the group working on it was headed by Edward C. (Pete) Aldridge, the Assistant Secretary of Defense for Program Analysis. The group studied three options: a force of only B-1s, a mixed force of cruise missile-armed B-52s and 'penetrator' B-1s, and a force of only B-52s, some carrying cruise missiles and some used as 'penetrators'. The group's preliminary report was ready by April 1977: it advocated a 'mixed force' of B-1s and B-52s armed with cruise missiles.

The report was immediately leaked (despite being classified) to Rockwell officials by B-1 supporters in the Air Force. The officials were furious, as the study did not fully support the B-1. The Air Force had fought the cruise missile for years. The cruise missile programme had gone ahead only because Secretary of Defense Laird had ordered it to in 1972 and had placed a naval officer in charge of the programme to keep the Air Force from interfering. Now, as the Air Force had feared, the cruise missile threatened the B-1.

In 1976, Congress had dictated that the President had to make a decision on the B-1 by 30 June 1977. As that deadline approached, Carter came under siege from supporters and opponents of the B-1. He agreed to meet with Congressional delegations from both sides of the issue. It appeared that he was keeping his options open.

On 7 June, Carter met with the pro-B-1 contingent. This was led by George Mahon, the Texas Democrat and Chair of the House Appropriations Committee; John C. Stennis, a Democrat from Mississippi who chaired the Senate Armed Services Committee; Ernest Hollings, a Democrat from South Carolina; and Alan Cranston, a liberal Democrat who opposed many weapons systems, but not the B-1, which was built in his home state of California. The delegation argued that the B-1 would not be a destabilizing weapon, and reminded Carter that $3 billion was already invested in the bomber. Carter told them that if the B-1 was the best way of meeting the USA's strategic military needs, he would build it. But if B-52s with cruise missiles would be as effective and less expensive, they would be approved. Three days later, the anti-B-1 delegation met with Carter. The group included Senators Edward Kennedy of Massachusetts, George McGovern of South Dakota, Clifford Case of New Jersey, and Jacob Javits of New York. Senator John Culver of Ohio was spokesperson for the group. Culver argued that the B-1 would make only a marginal contribution to the country's defence effort, and that B-52s with cruise missiles would be more cost-effective. Further, Culver argued that the Soviets were not worried about the B-1 and it would thus be useless in arms control negotiations. The group also reminded Carter that he had come out against the B-1 during his campaign.

Secretary of Defense Brown told Carter that it was better to keep the B-1 option open, perhaps starting production slowly. He argued that not building the B-1 would make him more vulnerable to pressure to build the MX Missile.

There were, however, other, perhaps more important, pressures on Carter. The administration's programmes as a whole were in trouble in Congress. Many members of Congress considered Carter distant and thought he was treating them with contempt. Carter and his aides, on the other hand, felt that Congress was not giving the President's proposals proper attention, or changing them according to Congressional whims.

Vice-President Mondale, a veteran of the Senate, warned Carter that the more he gave in to the Congress, the more pressure Congress would put on him. Carter decided to make the B-1 a test case to prove his effectiveness as President. His cancellation of the B-1 would defy the wishes of many in Congress, and if he could push it through, it would prove that he was a strong President. On 30 June 1977, he announced that he was cancelling the B-1 programme, mainly because the 'B-1, a very expensive weapons system, basically conceived in the absence of the cruise missile factor, is not necessary.' (However, he did leave $460 million in the budget in development money for the B-1.) If he could convince Congress to go along with his decision, the B-1 looked like a dead letter.

Carter's cancellation of the B-1 programme was a vindication of the Stop the B-1 Bomber campaign, but the politics of defence dictated that Carter's decision made it much more likely that the cruise missile and the MX missile would be built.

In order to enact his decision, Carter first had battles to fight in Congress. The fight did not promise to be easy: two days before Carter's cancellation of the B-1 programme, the House had approved funds for building five more B-1s (numbers seven to eleven) in 1978; Carter had to convince Congress to rescind that funding. In addition, Congress had appropriated money the previous year to build bombers five and six, and Carter wanted these funds rescinded as well.

Air Force Chief of Staff David Jones was unwilling to campaign for the B-1 any longer. Rockwell and Congressional supporters of the B-1 were furious, because a 'guerrilla' lobbying campaign by the Air Force in Congress would have been very helpful to their cause. Jones, however, felt that the larger needs of the Air Force would suffer if he opposed Carter, and he had stated years earlier that he was unwilling to see this happen. Since the Air Force was officially no longer in the pro-B-1 campaign, the campaign by Rockwell and Congressional supporters moved out of the Pentagon and into the offices of Representative William V. Chappel, Jr., a Florida Democrat and ranking member of the House Defense Appropriations Subcommittee. Chappel, long-time anti-communist and defence advocates was disgusted with Jones' position. He took up the fight himself.

The job of lobbying against the B-1 was given to the Office of the Secretary of Defense (OSD) and Colonel Grant Miller (who had lobbied *for* the B-1 for three years) was transferred to the OSD to lead the lobbying. Bob Beckel, a White House aide, co-ordinated lobbying from the White House. The Carter Administration pulled out all stops in the campaign, hinting to members of Congress that if they did not support the White House, they might lose military bases in their home district. Beckel also arranged for the restoration of water projects and other public-works projects that Carter had scrapped, in return for support on the B-1.

The Rockwell pro-B-1 lobby also applied pressure, mostly on the issue of jobs. With Congressional elections due in just over a year's time, many members were vulnerable to both sides. The first votes in the House on rescinding funds for the five additional B-1s, though very close, were won by the administration (by 202 to 199 votes on 8 August and 204 to 194 on 20 October).

However, the Carter Administration had more trouble rescinding the funds which Congress had authorized in 1976 for planes five and six. On 6 December 1977, the House refused to rescind the funds by a vote of 191 to 166. If the production of those two planes went through, it meant that the Rockwell production lines would be open until 1980. Carter felt that his prestige and power were on the line, and continued to contest the issue against the advice of many of his aides. His perseverance was repaid: on 22 February 1978, the House cancelled production by a vote of 234 to 182.

KEEPING THE B-1 ALIVE

Rockwell recognized that it was in trouble. In 1978, Carter was at the peak of his popularity, and most observers felt he was sure to win re-election in 1980. Yet Rockwell refused to give up on a programme as potentially lucrative as the B-1. Rockwell stored (at government expense) the parts which had been purchased for the eleven planes. In addition, Rockwell stored 50,000 machine tools and 500,000 pounds of aluminium and titanium, the raw material for future planes.

The other key part of the B-1 effort, from Rockwell's point of view, was personnel. Programme manager 'Buzz' Hello and executive committee chairman Robert Anderson managed to keep 1,100 engineers on the payroll, while other personnel were 'loaned' to other companies on the understanding that if Rockwell needed them, they would return. Hello also hustled to find subcontracting jobs for Rockwell for which at least some of the workforce would be retained.

According to the government auditors, Rockwell also illegally charged B-1 expenses to other contracts. The company eventually reimbursed the government the sum of $1.5 million, although Rockwell never admitted to having broken the law.

The B-1, however, was still dead and Rockwell could not get the project started again without outside help. This help came from the Air Force, the Pentagon and Congress. In the Pentagon, Dr Hans Mark, Secretary of the Air Force, and Dr Seymour Zeiberg, Deputy Under Secretary of Defense for Research, Engineering, and Space, were determined to keep the B-1 alive. In the Air Force, help came from Lieutenant-General Thomas Stafford, Deputy Chief of Staff for Research and Development, and from his Director of Operations, Major-General Kelly Burke.

Working with Stafford and Burke, Mark and Zieberg slipped money for the B-1 programme into the Pentagon budget: items designated simply for research and development on 'advanced avionics', 'electronic-countermeasure studies', and the like, were spent on the bomber programme. (Carter, who read the defence budget line-by-line, would have cut any money intended for the programme. The budget was so vast that these designations were not questioned.) Together, the four men managed to spend $450 million on the programme, most of which went to Rockwell.

Only a few members of Congress knew about the hidden funding. They were led by Anthony Battista, staff director of the House Armed Services Subcommittee on Research and Development (where he still works). He was joined by the subcommittee's chairman, Richard Ichord of Missouri, and by the Ranking Republican Member, William Dickinson of Alabama. These three not only helped their allies in the DoD and the Air Force, they worked with Rockwell's 'Buzz' Hello on a plan to get the B-1 programme back on the road, this time 'disguised' as another plane. Carter had asked Congress to investigate an airplane which could carry and launch cruise missiles. Rockwell proposed the Strategic Weapons Launcher (SWL), which, with modifications — no swing wings, supersonic speed and cheaper — was the B-1.

Ichord and his subcommittee then refused to fund studies into an alternative to the SWL: a widebody transport plane converted into a cruise missile carrier. Kelly Burke (who replaced Stafford as deputy chief of staff for research and development in 1979), agreeing to demands from Congress members to hold a competition for a widebodied cruise missile carrier, pitted a modified B-1 against the designs for a plane called the C-X, a huge new 'super-transport'. To no one's surprise, the C-X lost. Officers in the Air Force also helped to stop another possible threat to the B-1 from Boeing: a proposal that powerful new engines be put in active B-52s, which would not only extend their service life but also make them more attractive as cruise missile carriers. When Boeing started to lobby Congress on this proposal, the Air Force warned them off and Boeing had good reason to heed the Air Force, since it was Air Force contracts which helped keep the company profitable. Not only did Boeing stop advancing the proposal for refurbishing B-52s, it also stopped advocating the refitting of their 747s as cruise missile carriers. This help from the Air Force and some Congress members kept the B-1 programme alive - and, for the time being, this was all Rockwell and their allies needed as they sat out the end of the Carter presidency.

CARTER'S POWER DECLINES

Sure enough, things began looking brighter for B-1 supporters in 1979. The Shah of Iran was overthrown and and sixty-six US personnel in Iran were seized as hostages at the US Embassy in Tehran. The episode was extremely embarrassing for the Carter Administration, and his opponents sensed that Carter's political power was waning.

Secretary of the Air Force Mark thought the time might be right for trying to bring back the B-1. In the Air Force 1980 budget request, a new bomber proposal was outlined. It was identified by the acronym CMCA, for cruise-missile-carrier aircraft. When the budget was reviewed by the OMB, however, B-1 opponents added the identification '(B-1)'. As the budget officers had expected, Carter quickly deleted the item from the budget.

When Carter denied the CMCA budget request, B-1 proponents decided to try a different tack. Speaking before the National Security Industrial Association, General Burke declared that the Air Force needed a new airplane. He explained that the plane the Air Force wanted was not just a 'penetrating bomber' (like the B-1), but something called a 'Long Range Combat Aircraft (LRCA)'. The LRCA would not only provide strategic bombing, Burke declared, but a variety of other missions as well. These missions included conventional tactical bombing, long-range sea surveillance and interdiction, minelaying, and anti-submarine warfare. These specifications were a departure from the usual Air Force requirements for its planes; nevertheless, the LRCA was still simply a manoeuvre to revive the B-1.

Events transpired to lend weight to the LRCA proposal. On 27 December 1979, the Soviet Union invaded Afghanistan. The invasion aroused consternation in the USA and helped to damage Carter's reputation badly: he retaliated to the invasion by declaring a grain embargo on the Soviet Union and pulling the USA out of the 1980 Moscow Olympics. More importantly, he withdrew the SALT II treaty from Senate consideration, its chances for ratification now finished; nevertheless, he was increasingly seen as being 'weak on defence'.

Air Force Secretary Mark felt that Carter would not be re-elected, and plans for bringing back the B-1 (still disguised as the LRCA) began to move ahead. Mark first convened a meeting of the top Air Force commanders at Maxwell Air Force Base (very much like the 1974 Corona Quest meeting). His goal was to unite the Air Force behind an attempt to bring back the B-1. By the time the meeting ended, the Air Force was unified in its support of the B-1, and ready to go public.

Mark asked the Air Force Scientific Advisory Board to study the bomber question at its annual summer meeting. Mark was looking for the blessing for the B-1 from the leaders in industry, academia and the military that the Scientific Advisory Board represented. The agenda was planned so that it would advance the idea for the modified B-1; the Advisory Board wrote a report endorsing it.

In the House, efforts were also under way to have the B-1 approved. B-1 proponents in Congress also recognized that Carter's strength had faded considerably. The House Armed Services Committee sent to the full House a proposal for the Strategic Weapons Launcher. On 14 May 1980, the House voted 297 to 119 to approve $600 million for Strategic Weapons Launcher (SWL) development and initial production.

The SWL fooled nobody, including President Carter. He told Democratic senators that if the Senate approved the SWL appropriation, he would veto the entire defence bill. Senate consideration began in late June. On 1 July, Senators Alan Cranston and John Glenn introduced an amendment that would advance the B-1 and allow Carter to save face; the amendment called for the President to present plans for a new bomber by 15 February 1981. The plans could be for either the LRCA (modified B-1), a 'stretched' FB-111, or an entirely new bomber (probably the so-called Stealth bomber).

Glenn and an aide, Robert Andrews, had worded the amendment so that the bomber specifications it contained could only be met by the B-1: the amendment not only listed multiple missions that the plane would have to accomplish, but dictated that at least one squadron would have to be ready for combat by February 1987. It would have been imposssible for the FB-111 to fulfil all the missions, and the Stealth bomber (which existed only on paper) could not be built by 1987. The Senate approved the amendment 53 to 37. In House—Senate conference, the Glenn–Cranston amendment was approved in its final form. The next President would have $350 million and a deadline of 15 March 1981 by which he would have to present a new plane. The scene was set for a revival of the B-1.

Meanwhile, the 1980 presidential campaign was heating up. A week after the Senate vote, the Republican platform committee called for 'a new manned strategic penetrating bomber'. Ronald Reagan, who won the Republican nomination in July 1980, was attacking Carter for being 'soft on defence' and accused him of leaving the USA vulnerable to Soviet attack.

Reagan called for building both the B-1 and new ICBMs. Although Carter tried to fight back, even adding funds to the defence budget, he was soundly beaten by Reagan in November 1980.

The Reagan Presidency: The B-1 is Approved (1981)

In January 1981, the cast in the fight over the B-1 changed again. Carter was no longer President. Representatives Richard Ichord and Bob Wilson retired from Congress and founded a lobbying firm. Among their first clients were Rockwell International and B-1 sub-contractors Boeing and Hughes Aircraft. Robert Andrews, the aide who had helped write the crucial 1980 Glenn—Cranston amendment, left government in 1982 to work for Rockwell as a pro-B-1 lobbyist in Congress.

THE STEALTH FACTOR

The new President, Ronald Reagan, appointed Caspar Weinberger as Secretary of Defense. Weinberger, known as 'Cap the Knife' because of his propensity for cutting budgets, was not well-versed in defence issues. He was, however, a tough and accomplished bureaucrat and used to getting his way. Weinberger's deputy secretary was Frank Carlucci.

When the Air Force leaders, led by Deputy Chief of Staff Kelly Burke, came to meet Weinberger and Carlucci, they expected all their plans to be approved without trouble. Reagan and Weinberger had, after all, already agreed to a $32 billion increase in the defence budget for 1981 and 1982, the Reagan transition team had endorsed every Air Force proposal, and Reagan's campaign rhetoric generally encouraged the Air Force to think they would have his team's support for their demands. However, Weinberger had already dismissed many members of the transition team, and his ideas on defence differed from those of the Air Force. At the meeting, Burke explained to Weinberger and Carlucci that the Air Force's top priority was producing one hundred of what was now called the B-1B (the B-1 with some modifications that eliminated most of its supersonic capability, increased its load of fuel, weapons and electronics, and had new features intended to make it less visible to Soviet radar). According to Burke, the B-1B would be supported by a modernized fleet of B-52s functioning as cruise missile carriers. In addition, they announced, production of 132 Stealth bombers (which would incorporate new technology that would make them invisible to the opponent's radar) would soon follow. Weinberger and Carlucci, to Burke's surprise, asked hostile questions about the necessity of building two bombers. When the Air Force representatives were unable to answer these questions to Weinberger's satisfaction, he left the meeting.

Weinberger had been strongly influenced by Harold Brown, Carter's Secretary of Defense, and by William Perry, Under Secretary of Defense for Research and Engineering under Brown. Both were advocates of the Stealth bomber, as was former Defense Secretary Melvin Laird, also consulted by Weinberger. Weinberger was interested in dropping the B-1 and building only the Stealth, thus saving billions of dollars.

The new Under Secretary of Defense for Research and Engineering, Richard DeLauer, spoke with the Air Force team after the abortive meeting. He warned them that they would have to make their programme more affordable by retiring B-52s as the B-1Bs were built. He also told the Air Force that they would have to find a reason for building *both* the B-1B and the Stealth bomber. So, to the surprise of the Air Force, the B-1 programme was again threatened, and this time because of an Air Force project.

Stealth research had originally been directed at fighter planes, with the work being done mainly by Lockheed. When Carter cancelled the B-1 in 1977, General Tom Stafford, the Air Force Deputy Chief of Staff for Research and Development, decided that the idea of a Stealth bomber might appeal to Carter. Using funds from what is known as 'black money', money for secret projects hidden in the defence budget, Stafford set Northrop Aviation and other firms to work on developing a Stealth bomber. Four years later, the Air Force found they had the possibility of building two bombers, but that each bomber had a different constituency and that each constituency did not want the other bomber built. The B-1B was supported by Republicans, the House of Representatives and Rockwell. The Stealth was supported by Democrats, the Senate and Northroop. The original proposal which the Air Force presented to Weinberger and Carlucci was designed to satisfy both constituencies. Rockwell claimed it could produce one hundred B-1Bs for $20 billion, the amount which the Air Force decided was the highest they could ask for: 132 Stealth bombers were requested because that meant the Air Force would build more Stealth bombers than B-1Bs, a measure designed to placate the Senate. Now, however, the Air Force would have to find a way to keep the Stealth from killing the B-1B even as the bombers' rival constituencies battled it out.

The battle between the B-1B and the Stealth would be fought on a variety of fronts. Secretary of Defense Weinberger, Deputy Secretary Carlucci and President Reagan would have to be convinced of the need for two bombers. Further, key members in Congress were undecided, and they would also come under pressure. The fight for the Stealth bomber was led by the chairman of the Board of Northrop, Thomas V. Jones, an old friend of Reagan. Jones was joined by T. A. Wilson, the chairman of Boeing, and Paul Thayer, the chairman of LTV Corporation. Both Boeing and LTV were subcontractors for the B-1B, but decided to push for the Stealth instead. If the Stealth bomber were built, it would be worth it for the two firms to sacrifice their B-1B contracts: not only would the Stealth contracts be more valuable financially, but, for Boeing at least, they represented a way for the company to pull ahead of the competition in technological expertise at government expense.

Jones, Wilson and Thayer told the House Defense Appropriations Committee that they could deliver the first squadron of fifteen Stealth bombers by 1987 (the deadline set by the Glenn-Cranston amendment) and that they could so at a fixed price. In May 1981, Jones said the same to Weinberger in a private meeting. Rockwell's 'Buzz' Hello thought these claims were ridiculous. He knew that the paper design for the plane had not even been approved yet: for Northrop to deliver the plane in four years, machine tools and parts would have to be ordered before blueprints existed.

When Weinberger held a meeting at Rockwell with Hello and his superiors, chairman of the board Robert Anderson and president Donald Beall, Anderson told him that Northrop's promises were unrealistic. Hello repeated the promise that Rockwell could build one hundred B-1Bs for $20 billion. Weinberger wanted to know if Anderson would guarantee that price and work on a fixed-price contract. Anderson refused, knowing that the cost overruns on such a contract could destroy the company.

By early June, it seemed that Weinberger was going to recommend that only the Stealth be built. The price for Rockwell stock plunged from $43 to $36.25 in ten days. Under Secretary of Defense Richard DeLauer asked Weinberger if he would consider the B-1B if Rockwell agreed to a fixed price. Weinberger, without making promises, said that he might. DeLauer quickly called Anderson, who was attending the Paris Air Show, and told him that unless he agreed to the fixed price, there would be no B-1B. Anderson reluctantly agreed to a fixed-price contract of $20.5 billion. Even though the contract had many loopholes and qualifications, it was a risk for Rockwell. Yet it allowed the B-1B to remain a candidate for production.

In the House, where support for the B-1B was strong, the approval of the plane was already progressing. By the time Anderson had agreed to a fixed-price contract in order to win DoD support for the plane, the House had already authorized $2.4 billion to begin production of the B-1B. In the Senate, the opposition to the B-1B was tougher, and senators facing re-election were being lobbied on the economic benefits the plane would produce.

Increasingly, lobbying efforts for the B-1B also focused on President Reagan. Supporters of the bomber had powerful arguments with Reagan, who had made campaign promises supporting the B-1. A group of Republican senators led by Howard Baker of Tennessee, the Majority Leader, met Reagan to tell him that not building the B-1B would be interpreted as an admission that Carter had been correct in cancelling the plane. The Stealth bomber and cruise missiles, the senators reminded Reagan, were *Democratic* alternatives that Carter had advocated.

Reagan's conservative supporters also stepped up their efforts. They pointed out that Reagan had failed to make a decision on any of the important aspects of the 'modernization' programme he had advocated. Not only the B-1B, but the MX missile and a new Trident missile were awaiting decisions by the President. Starting up production of the B-1B was the only visible action that the President could take, since the other programmes were either deadlocked or would take several years to produce results.

In late July, Reagan made his decision: he told Weinberger, who still had reservations about the B-1B, that the plane was going to be built. The decision was announced on 3 October 1981, at a press conference held to announce Reagan's strategic modernization programme. The administration would build one hundred B-1B bombers, along with 132 Stealth bombers at a later date. Reagan also called for one hundred MX missiles, to be based in 'hardened' underground silos, and for development of the Trident II SLBM. The strategic command, control and communications system would also be up-graded. The Air Force had received everything it had asked for.

But Reagan's programme still had to get through Congress, and the administration case for its modernization programme initially seemed weak. In November, testifying before the Senate Armed Services Committee, Weinberger said that the B-1B would not be able to penetrate Soviet defences after 1990, and that by 1988 or 1989 such penetration would entail a 'suicide mission'. CIA analyst Robert Huffstutler told the Senate that through 1990, the B-52s would be just as effective as the B-1B in penetrating Soviet defences. Further, the General Accounting Office and the Congressional Budget Office released reports which stated that the B-1B would cost far more than the Air Force had allowed for: one hundred B-1Bs would cost $35 to $40 billion, not the $20.5 billion promised by Rockwell and the Air Force.

The administration realized that it needed new justifications for the B-1B. The first such justification took the form of a joint letter issued on 11 November 1981 by Weinberger and Director of Central Intelligence William Casey. Refuting earlier testimony by both Weinberger and the CIA, the letter said that the B-1B would be able to penetrate Soviet defences well into the 1990s. The Air Force also changed its position. In early 1981, the Air Force had said that as the Stealth bombers were built, the B-1Bs would be converted to cruise missile carriers. Now, however, the Air Force said that both planes would be used together, creating what it called a 'a synergistic effect'. Congressional opposition to the two bomber programmes soon crumbled. There were more important battles to be fought, for instance over the MX missile. The House approved the programme on 18 November, and the Senate followed on 4 December. The Air Force and Rockwell were finally in business.

Conclusion

The story of the B-1 bomber illustrates much about defence politics and the ways in which nuclear weapons decisions are made. One could not, however, expect every weapons system to follow the same path to completion or abandonment. The characteristics of a weapons system, including its supporters, opponents and alternatives, often determines the route which the decisionmaking process will follow.

Since the B-1 would be a new strategic bomber, it was vital to the Air Force. For thirty years, as the fight for a new bomber developed, Air Force leaders identified such a plane with the future of the Air Force. It is hard to pinpoint the root cause of this identification. In the early period, it was due to the predominance of the 'bomber mafia' in the leadership of the Air Force. Later, however, the reasons were undoubtably more complicated. Some of them appear to have had more to do with the domestic, rather than strategic, consequences of the bomber's production. The B-1 would be a highly visible, very profitable victory for the Air Force. It would enlarge the Air Force budget, and help the Air Force in its long-running battle with the Navy for the 'top spot' in the nuclear arsenal. It would also be a good public relations tool for the Air Force, by providing both jobs for contractors and a 'sexy' new plane with which to attract pilots.

In order to get the B-1, the Air Force defied both the President and the Office of the Secretary of Defense, both by lobbying in Congress and in public and by secretly providing funds for the B-1 programme. They were assisted in this by the contractor for the B-1, Rockwell International.

For the contractors of weapons systems, millions of dollars in profit are involved. Since defence politics determine what defence contractors build, the contractors play politics with a vengeance. This takes the form not only of lobbying, but of political contributions and economic pressure.

Both the contractors and the military (and thus, by extension, the President) control valuable resources in terms of plants and bases. Members of Congress who support the military and the contractors are rewarded with both plants and bases, and opponents can come under heavy pressure to change their voting to keep these resources.

The story of the B-1 also shows both the extent and limitations of Presidential power. The plane was finally built by a President who supported it, but the support was in part forced. Further, those presidents who opposed the B-1 or its predecessors were only able to delay it, not kill it completely. The President of the United States can certainly prevent a weapons system from being built, but only for the term he or she is in office; weapons systems tend to have longer lives than elected officials.

Perhaps most importantly, the B-1 story illustrates the limits of public knowledge. Most of the decisions involving the B-1 were made without public knowledge. The forces which both support and oppose many other weapons systems work more quietly, and as with the B-1, the public only learns about the systems once they are virtually unstoppable, on the eve of production.

BIOGRAPHIES

Abrahamson, Dr. George R., Member USAF Advisory Board
(Vice-President, Physical Sciences Division, SRI International)
(See: USAF Scientific Advisory Board (Department of the Air Force).)

Abrahamson, James A., Lieutenant-General (USAF), Director, Strategic Defense Initiative Organization (SDIO)

General Abrahamson, a vocal advocate of SDI, was appointed director of the SDIO in April 1984. His education includes a BS from the Massachusetts Institute of Technology in 1955, and a MS in aeronautical engineering which he earned through the Air Force Institute of Technology programme at the University of Oklahoma in 1961. He also completed the Air Command and Staff College at Maxwell Air Force Base, Alabama, in 1966.

Abrahamson was commissioned as a second lieutenant in 1955, and completed flight training in May 1957. His initial assignment was as flight instructor in the Air Training Command. In 1961, he was assigned as spacecraft programme officer on the VELA Nuclear Detection Satellite Program at the Los Angeles Air Force Station in California. While assigned to Cannon Air Force Base in New Mexico, from October 1964 to August 1965, Abrahamson served two tours of duty in Vietnam and flew forty-nine combat missions.

Abrahamson graduated from the Aerospace Research Pilot School at Edwards Air Force Base in California in 1967, and was selected to be an astronaut with the Air Forces' Manned Orbiting Laboratory Program, where he served until the programme was cancelled in June 1969. He was then selected to serve on the staff of the National Aeronautics and Space Council in the Executive Office of the President. In March 1971, he was appointed director of the TV-guided, air-to-ground MAVERICK missile programme at Wright—Patterson Air Force Base in Ohio, where he served until June 1973, when he took command of the 495th Air Test Wing.

General Abrahamson was named Inspector General for Air Force Systems Command at Andrews Air Force Base, Maryland, in March 1974. In May 1976, he was appointed director for the F-16 air combat fighter programme at the Aeronautical Systems Division, Wright—Patterson Air Force Base. He became deputy chief of staff for systems of the Air Force Systems Command Headquarters in July 1980.

In November 1981, Abrahamson was appointed associate administrator for the space transportation system at the headquarters of the National Aeronautics and Space Administration (NASA) in Washington, DC. In this position, he was responsible for the space shuttle program. He stayed at this position until being appointed director of the SDIO in April 1984.
(See: Defense Agencies (Strategic Defense Initiative Organization).)

Abramson, Dr H. Norman, Member, USAF Scientific Advisory Board
(Vice-President, Engineering and Materials Science Division, Southwest Research Institute)
(See: USAF Scientific Advisory Board (Department of the Air Force).)

Adolph, Charles A., Deputy Under Secretary of Defense, (Test and Evaluation)
(See: Office of the Secretary of Defense (Department of Defense).)

Airey, Dr J. Richard, Member, USAF Scientific Advisory Board (Corporate Vice-President, Science Applications International Corporation
(See: USAF Scientific Advisory Board (Department of the Air Force).)

Aldridge, Edward C. 'Pete', Jr., The Secretary of the Air Force

Edward Aldridge was appointed Secretary of the Air Force by President Reagan in June 1986.

Aldridge, born in 1938, holds a BS in aeronautical engineering from Texas A & M University (1960). He also received an MS in aeronautical engineering from the Georgia Institute of Technology in 1962.

From 1962 until 1967, Aldridge held various staff and management positions with the Douglas Aircraft Company, Missile and Space Division (now McDonnel-Douglas Astronautics) in Santa Monica California and Washington, DC.

In 1967 Aldridge joined the Pentagon as an operations research analyst in the Office of the Assistant Secretary of Defense (Systems Analysis). In April 1969, he was appointed director, Strategic Defense Systems. In this position he was responsible for five-year planning of strategic defence systems, including the Safeguard Anti-Ballistic Missile (ABM) system and US air defences. Aldridge also served as an adviser to the Strategic Arms Limitation Talks (SALT) negotiations from 1969 to 1972. His efforts during this period earned him the Secretary of Defense Meritorious Civilian Service Award.

In 1972, Aldridge joined the LTV Aerospace Corporation, Vought Systems Division, a major defence contractor based in Dallas, Texas. He remained there until May 1973, when he was appointed a senior management associate, national security and international affairs, in the Office of Management and Budget.

In February 1974, Aldridge was named Deputy Assistant Secretary of Defense (Strategic Programs), in the Office of the Assistant Secretary of Defense (Program Analysis and Evaluation). In this position, he was responsible for advising the Secretary of Defense on the planning and evaluation of strategic weapons systems. During this period, he received the Department of Defense Distinguished Civilian Award. Aldridge was named Acting Assistant Secretary of Defense (Program Analysis and Evaluation) in February 1976.

Later in that same year, Aldridge was appointed the Director, Defense Planning and Evaluation.

(See: Department of the Air Force.)

Allen, Dr John L., Member, USAF Scientific Advisory Board

(John L. Allen Associates, Inc.)

(See: USAF Scientific Advisory Board (Department of the Air Force).)

Altis, Harold D., Member, USAF Scientific Advisory Board

(Private consultant)

(See: USAF Scientific Advisory Board (Department of the Air Force).)

Anders, William A., (Nuclear Engineer), Member at Large, Defense Science Board

Anders is currently senior executive vice-president for operations at Textron, Inc. He has an MS degree from the Air Force Institute of Technology. He was a crew member of Apollo 8; the Chairman of the Nuclear Regulatory Committee; and the U.S. Ambassador to Norway.

(See: Defense Science Board.)

Anderson, Robert, Chairman of the Executive Committee,Board of Directors, Rockwell International

Anderson, who retired from from the post of chairman of the board of directors and chief executive officer in February 1988, is considered to be one of the prime movers behind the B-1B bomber, built by Rockwell. Anderson received a BS in mechanical engineering from Colorado State University before joining the US Army in 1943. He served as a captain in the field artillery until 1946.

Anderson started his career with the Chrysler Corporation, earning a master's degree in automotive engineering from the Chrysler Institute of Engineering in 1948. After holding several engineering positions, Anderson was named chief engineer of the Plymouth Division in 1953, a post he kept for four years. In 1957, he became executive engineer for chassis, electrical and truck design for Chrysler's Central Engineering Division. In 1958, Anderson was named director of product planning and cost estimating, and went on to become vice-president of product planning in 1961 and group vice-president of corporate automotive manufacturing in 1964. He was appointed vice-president and general manager of the Chrysler-Plymouth Division in 1965.

Anderson moved to Rockwell in 1968 as corporate vice-president and president of the commercial products group. He was elected to the board of directors that same year. In 1969, he was named corporate executive vice-president and was elected president and chief operating officer in 1970. He became chief executive officer in 1974 and chairman in 1979.

Anderson is a trustee of the California Institute of Technology and of the American Enterprise Institute. He is also a member of the board of governors of the Ronald Reagan Presidential Foundation. In 1986, he was appointed to the President's Commission on Executive Exchange. He has also been a member of the Presidential Commission on Industrial Competitiveness.

(See: Defence Contractors.)

Araki, Minoru S., President, Space Systems Division, Lockheed Missiles and Space Company, Vice-President, Lockheed Corporation

Araki has held his present posts since March 1987. Previously, he served as vice-president and assistant general manager of the Space Systems Division (since 1985). He earned his BS in mechanical engineering in 1954 and his MS in mechanical engineering in 1955, both from Stanford University.

Araki joined Lockheed Missiles and Space Company as a senior scientist in 1958. He was appointed assistant cchief engineer, development, in 1975. He was named director of systems engineering a year later, and then became director of advanced systems in the Space Systems Division in 1978. He was appointed vice-president for advanced programmes and development in that division in 1981, and became vice-president and programme manager of the division's MILSTAR programmes in 1983.

Araki is a member of the American Institute of Aeronautics and Astronautics, the Institute of Electrical and Electronic Engineering, and the National Management Association.

(See: Defence Contractors.)

Armitage, Richard, Assistant Secretary of Defense (International Security Affairs)

Armitage is widely considered a highly influential figure in the Department of Defense, although mainly in the areas of covert operations and foreign aid, which fall outside his area of formal responsibility.

Armitage has served as Assistant Secretary since June 1983. He received his BS in engineering from the US Naval Academy in 1967 and was assigned to a US destroyer engaged in operations off the coast of Vietnam. Subsequently, Armitage served three in-country tours of Vietnam. He was also a senior counter-insurgency instructor at the Naval Amphibious School in Coronado, California.

In 1973, when US forces pulled out of Vietnam, Armitage resigned from the Navy to accept a position with the US defence attache's office in Saigon. Here he was an adviser to the South Vietnamese Navy and Marine Corps. After the fall of Saigon in 1975, Armitage worked in Washington as a consultant to the DoD. He also served in Tehran, Iran, on the staff of the US Defense Representative. From 1976 to 1978, Armitage returned to southeast Asia to pursue business interests. From March 1978 until May 1979, Armitage was administrative assistant to Senator Robert Dole of Kansas.

Later, Armitage worked in the foreign policy office of the Reagan presidential campaign and was appointed a member of the National Security Transition Team. He was also a senior adviser to the Interim Foreign Policy Advisory Board, which briefed Reagan on the major policy issues which would confront his administration. Prior to assuming his present position, Armitage was Deputy Assistant Secretary of Defense, International Security Affairs for East Asia and Pacific Affairs.

(See: Office of the Secretary of Defense (Department of Defense).)

Aspin, Les, Representative (D, Wisconsin), 1st District; Chairman, Armed Services Committee
Address: 2236 Rayburn House Office Building, Washington, DC, 20515
Tel: (202) 225-3031

Aspin was first elected to the House in 1971. He holds a BA from Yale University, an MA from

Oxford University, and a Ph.D. from the Massachusetts Institute of Technology. Before coming to the House, he was a professor of economics. As chairman of the Armed Services Committee, he is considered one of the most influential Democrats in the House on military affairs. He has a wider range of knowledge about defence issues than many members of the House. He is also chairman of the Defense Policy Panel, a subcommittee of the Armed Services Committee, and sits on the Research and Development Subcommittee. Aspin is known as a liberal and something of a proponent of arms control. He has a record of limited opposition to the MX missile and the B-1 bomber, and is considered a strong supporter of the Midgetman missile.

Aspin is also a member of the Arms Control and Foreign Policy Caucus, the Military Reform Caucus, and is co-chairman of the Defense Strategy Task Force of the Democratic Leadership Council.

Key Aides: Aspin has no aides specifically assigned to defense issues.

(See: The House of Representatives.)

Atkins, Mervin C., Deputy Director, Defense Nuclear Agency (DNA)

Atkins was appointed deputy director of the Defense Nuclear Agency in March 1983. He has a BS in physics from Texas A & M, an MS in physics from the University of Illinois, and a Ph.D. in nuclear science from the University of Michigan.

Atkins served in the US Air Force from 1952 until 1964, when he was discharged with the rank of major. From 1953 to 1957, he was a project officer and group leader in the materials laboratory at the Wright Air Development Center in Dayton, Ohio, where he specialized in nuclear radiation effects on aircraft materials. From 1960 until 1964, Atkins served at the Air Force Special Weapons Center and Air Force Weapons Laboratory at Kirkland Air Force Base in Albuquerque, New Mexico.

After leaving the Air Force in 1964, Atkins joined the AVCO Corporation as senior project scientist in the applications department, where he specialized in weapons effects and missile vulnerability and hardening. His other positions at AVCO were as assistant manager of the materials sciences department, manager of the engineering technology department, and director of environmental sciences and technology.

In February 1970, Atkins joined the Defense Nuclear Agency as assistant for experimental research, where he specialized in problems of survivability of missiles and silos and in underground nuclear testing. In March 1975, he became scientific assistant to the deputy director, in which post he was the principal assistant in planning and execution of the DNA research and development programme.

Atkins joined the Office of the Under Secretary of Defense for Research and Engineering in October 1978 as director of offensive and space systems. He was responsible for managment of strategic ballistic missile programmes, DoD participation in the space shuttle programme, and related programmes. He stayed in this position until his return to DNA. Atkins has also served as executive secretary of the President's Commission on Strategic Forces.

(See: Defense Agencies.)

Atwood, Donald J., Vice-Chairman of the Board, General Motors Corporation

Atwood is a member of the General Motors finance, executive and administration committees. He became vice-chairman in May 1987. Atwood is also president of GM Hughes Electronics (GMHE) and is also responsible for electronic data systems (EDS), the technical staffs, and the defence operations group. Atwood has a BS and an MS in Electrical Engineering, both from the Massachusetts Institute of Technology. While at MIT, he was on the technical staff of the instrumentation laboratory and was associated with the research which pioneered the development of inertial guidance systems. Atwood served in the US Army from 1943 to 1946.

Atwood joined GM in 1959 as an associate director of the Boston research and development laboratory of the AC Spark Plug division. In 1961 he became director of that laboratory.

He was transferred to AC's Milwaukee operation in 1962, and became director of that facility in 1969.

In 1970, Atwood was appointed director of the Indianapolis operations of the Detroit Diesel Allison division. He became director of the Transportation Systems division in 1974, and later in that year was named general manager of the Delco electronics division. He returned to the Detroit Diesel Allison division in 1978 as vice-president and general manager, and in 1981 became vice-president and group executive in charge of the worldwide truck and bus group. He was named president of GMHE in 1985.

Atwood is a member of the executive committee of the Massachusetts Institute of Technology, and a member of the board of directors of Charles Stark Draper Laboratory, Inc.
(See: Defence contractors.)

AuCoin, Les, Representative (D, Oregon), 1st District, Member, House Appropriations Committee, Subcommittee on Defense
Address: 2159 Rayburn House Office Building, Washington, DC, 20515
Tel: (202) 225-0855

AuCoin was elected to the House in 1974. He has a BA from Pacific University. From 1961 to 1964, he served in the US Army. He was a reporter with the *Portland Oregonian* from 1965 to 1966. From 1966 to 1973, he was public information director for Pacific University. He served in the Oregon State House of Representatives from 1970 until his election to the House. He sits only on the Appropriations Committee.
Key Aide: Bob Sherman, Legislative Assistant.
(See: The House of Representatives.)

Augustine, Norman A. (Aeronautical Engineer), Member at Large, Defense Science Board

Augustine is president of Martin Marietta Corporation, one of the USA's largest defence contractors. He is a past president of the American Institute of Aeronautics and Astronautics. He has been Under Secretary of the Army and Assistant Director of Defense Research and Engineering.
(See: Defense Science Board.)

Badham, Robert E., Representative (R, California), 40th District, Member, House Armed Services Committee
Address: 2427 Rayburn House Office Building, Washington DC, 20515
Tel: (202) 225-5611

Badham, who was a hardware company executive, was elected to the House in 1976. He is the Ranking Minority Member of the Procurement and Military Nuclear Systems Subcommittee. He also sits on the Seapower and Strategic and Critical Materials Subcommittee. Badham is a member of the executive committee of the House Republican Study Committee.
Key Aide: Earl Fain IV, Legislative Assistant.
(See: The House of Representatives.)

Baldwin, J. A., Vice-Admiral (USN), Director, J-5 Strategic Plans and Policy Directorate
(See: Joint Chiefs of Staff.)

Ball, William L. III, Secretary of the Navy

Ball was appointed Secretary of the Navy in February 1988, following the resignation of James Webb. Webb, a well-known Vietnam veteran and novelist, charged that Secretary of Defense Carlucci was abandoning the Administration's goal of having a 600-ship Navy.

Ball is a graduate of the Georgia Institute of Technology, and served as an officer in the Navy from 1969 to 1975. He originally came to Washington as an aide of former Senator Herman E. Talmadge, Democrat of Georgia.

In 1981, Ball served as chief clerk of the Senate Armed Services Committee. He was administrative assistant to Senator John Tower, Republican of Texas, from 1981 to 1985. In 1985, Ball became the Assistant Secretary of State for Legislative and Intergovernmental Affairs, the chief lobbying position at the State Department.

Ball became Assistant to the President for Legislative Affairs in February of 1986. In this position, which he held until his appointment

as Secretary of the Navy, he was the chief lobbyist for the White House on Capitol Hill. Unlike Webb, who was considered outspoken and frequently adversarial, Ball has a reputation for reaching behind-the-scenes compromises with Congress. He shares this reputation with Defense Secretary Carlucci. Ball is considered well-respected in Congress. He will be presiding over the Navy at a time when reductions in the defence budget have forced the Navy to cut back on programmes.
(See: Department of the Navy.)

Bateman, Herbert H., Representative (R, Virginia), 1st District, Member, House Armed Services Committee
Address: 1527 Longworth House Office Building, Washington, DC, 20515
Tel: (202) 225-4261

Bateman was an attorney before his election to the House in 1982. He holds a BA from the College of William and Mary and an LLB from Georgetown University. He is Ranking Minority Member of the Military Personnel and Compensation Subcommittee and sits on the Seapower and Strategic and Critical Materials subcommittee. Bateman is a member of the Defense Reform Task Force of the House Republican Research Committee and cochairman of the Congressional Space Caucus.

Key Aides: Rick Dykema, Legislative Assistant; Jim Hickey, Legislative Assistant.
(See: The House of Representatives.)

Batzell, Roger, Director, Lawrence Livermore National Laboratory

Batzell has been the director of Livermore since 1971. He earned his BS in chemical engineering from the University of Idaho in 1947, and his Ph.D. in nuclear chemistry from the University of California at Berkeley in 1951.

From 1943 until 1946, Batzell served in the Army Air Corps, the forerunner to the US Air Force. From 1947 to 1948, Batzell was employed with the General Electric Company, and from 1951 to 1953 he was a senior chemist with the California R & D Company.

In 1953, Batzell joined Livermore as assistant chemistry division leader. He moved on to be associate director of chemistry, testing, space reactors and biomedical research, before being named director in 1971.

Batzell's other experience includes the post of scientific adviser to the Office of Test Operations from 1960 to 1965. He was chairman of the NTS Planning Board from 1965 until 1971. From 1967 until 1968 he was on the board of visitors to the US Naval Radiological Defense Laboratory. From 1967 to 1971 he was on the Advisory Committee on Nuclear Materials and Safeguards, and he was Chairman of the Systems Vulnerability Task Force of the Defense Science Board in 1972. Batzell has also been a member of the US delegation for technical discussions with the Soviet Union, going to Vienna in 1969 and Moscow in 1970.
(See: Department of Energy.)

Beall, Donald R., Chairman and Chief Executive Officer, Rockwell International

Beall, who succeeded Anderson in February 1988, was president and chief operating officer for nine years prior to his election to his current position. He has earned a BS in metallurgical engineering from San Jose State University and an MBA from the University of Pittsburgh.

Beall began his career with Ford Motor Company, holding a number of managerial posts before coming to Rockwell as a member of the corporate staff in 1968. In 1969, he was named executive vice-president of the electronics group.

When Rockwell made its initial investment in Collins Radio Company in 1971, Beall was elected as Collins' executive vice-president. He joined the board of directors at Collins in 1972. Collins merged with Rockwell in 1973, and Beall was named executive vice-president of the Collins Radio Group. He became group president in 1974.

Beall was elected a Rockwell corporate vice-president in 1976, and also named president of electronic operations. In 1977, he became executive vice-president, holding this post until becoming president in 1979.

Beall is a past chairman of the board of governors of the Aerospace Industries Association and a board member of the Los Angeles World Affairs Council. He is a trustee of the University of Pittsburgh and a member of the board of overseers of the University of California—Irvine. Beall is also a member of the American Defense Preparedness Association and the Navy League of the United States.
(See: Defence Contractors.)

Bennett, Charles, E., Representative (D, Florida), 3rd District, Member, House Armed Services Committee
Address: 2107 Rayburn House Office Building, Washington, DC, 20515
Tel: (202) 225-2501

Bennett, who holds a BA and a JD from the University of Florida, was first elected to the House in 1949. He is chairman of the Seapower and Strategic and Critical Materials subcommittee. He also sits on the Procurement and Military Nuclear Systems subcommittee and the Acquisition Policy Panel. He is co-Chairman of the Military Reform Caucus. Bennett also is a member of the Merchant Marine and Fisheries Committee.

Key Aide J.H. Mooney, Legislative Assistant.
(See: The House of Representatives.)

Bennett, Ivan L., Jr. (Physician), Senior Consultant, Defense Science Board

Bennett is professor of medicine at the New York University Medical Center. He has been provost and dean of the New York University Medical Center, and also deputy director of the White House Office of Science and Technology.
(See: Defense Science Board.)

Bennett Johnston, J., Senator (D, Louisiana) Member, Senate Appropriations Committee, Defense Subcommittee, Chairman, Senate Appropriations Committee, Energy and Water Development Subcommittee
Address: Room SH-136, Hart Senate Office Building, Washington, DC, 20510
Tel: (202) 224-5824

Bennett was elected to the Senate in 1972 and faces re-election in 1990. Bennett is regarded as somewhat conservative. He has an LLB from the Louisiana State University Law School, and saw army service in the Judge Advocate General Corps from 1956 to 1959. He was a Louisiana State Representative from 1964 to 1968, and a State senator from 1968 until his Senate election.

Bennett is chairman of the Committee on Energy and Natural resources, and also serves on the Budget Committee and the Special Committee on Ageing.

Key Aide: Garry D. Reese, Legislative Assistant.
(See: The Senate.)

Bevill, Tom, Representative (D, Alabama), 4th District, Chairman, House Appropriations Committee, Subcommittee on Energy and Water Development

Address: 23202 Rayburn House Office Building, Washington, DC, 20515
Tel: (202) 225-4876

Bevill was elected to the House in 1966. He has a BS and an LLB from the University of Alabama. During World War II, from 1943 to 1946, he fought in Europe with the Army. He was a practising attorney from 1949 to 1966, and served in the Alabama State House of Representatives from 1958 until his election to the House. Bevill does not sit on any other committees.

Key Aide: Olivia Barton, Associate Staff.
(See: The House of Representatives.)

Bingaman, Jeff, Senator (D, New Mexico), Member of Senate Armed Services Committee
Address: Room SH-502, Hart Senate Office Building, Washington, DC, 20510
Tel: (202) 224-5521

Bingaman, who faces re-election in 1988, has a BA from Harvard University and a JD from Stanford University. He was elected to the Senate in 1982.

Bingaman is chairman of the Defense Industry and Technology Subcommittee, and is also on the Readiness, Sustainability and Support Subcommittee and the Strategic Forces and Nuclear Deterrence Subcommittee.

His other committee assignments are Energy and Natural Resources, Governmental Affairs, and the Joint Economic Committee.

Bingaman is on the Legislative Review Committee of the Senate Democratic Policy Committee, and is also a member of the Military Reform Caucus.

Key Aide: Ed McGaffigan, Legislative Assistant.
(See: The Senate.)

Bobrow, David S. (Political Scientist), Senior Consultant, Defense Science Board

A professor of government and politics at the University of Maryland, Bobrow received his Ph.D. from the Massachusetts Institute of Technology. He has served as special assistant, Behavioral and Social Sciences at the Office of the Director of Defense Research and Engineering and as acting director, Behavioral Sciences Office at DARPA. In addition, he has been senior social scientist, director's division, at Oak Ridge National Laboratory.
(See: Defense Science Board.)

Boggs, Lindy, Representative (D, Louisiana), 2nd District, Member, House Appropriations Committee, Subcommittee on Energy and Water Development

Address: 2353 Rayburn House Office Building, Washington, DC 20515
Tel: (202) 225-6636

Boggs was elected to the House in 1972. She graduated from Tulane University in 1935 and became a teacher. In 1976, she was chairman of the Democratic National Convention. She also serves on the Select Committee on Children, Youth, and Families.

Key Aide: Jan Schoonmanker, Legislative Director.
(See: The House of Representatives.)

Bostrom, Dr Carl O., Member, USAF Scientific Advisory Board (Director, Johns Hopkins Applied Physics Laboratory)
(See: USAF Scientific Advisory Board (Department of the Air Force).)

Bowsher, Charles, A., Comptroller General, General Accounting Office
(See: Congressional Support Agencies.)

Boxer, Barbara, Representative (D, California), 6th District, Member, House Armed Services Committee

Address: 307 Cannon House Office Building, Washington, DC 20515
Tel: (202) 225-5161

Boxer, a stockbroker and journalist before coming to the House in 1982, has a BA from Brooklyn College. She is often sharply critical of the DoD. Boxer sits on the subcommittees on Investigations, Research and Development, and on the Acquistion Policy Council. She is also a member of the Defense and International Affairs Task Force on the Budget Committee.

Key Aides: Donna Martin, Legislative Assistant; Maria Vegega, Legislative Fellow.
(See: The House of Representatives.)

Braddock, Joseph V. (Physicist), Member at Large, Defense Science Board

Braddock is senior vice-president of BDM International, a company he helped to found. He has a Ph.D. from Fordham University, and has taught physics as an assistant professor at Iona College.
(See: Defense Science Board.)

Brennan, Joseph E., Representative (D, Maine), Member, House Armed Services Committee

Address: 1428 Longworth House Office Building, Washington, DC, 20515
Tel: (202) 225-6116

Brennan, a past Governor of Maine, was elected to the House in 1986. He has received a BS from Boston College and a JD from the University of Maine. Brennan sits on the subcommittees on Research and Development, Seapower and Strategic and Critical Materials, and on the Acquisition Policy Panel. He is also a member of the Select Committee on Hunger.

Key Aides: E.H. 'Ned' Michalek, Legislative Director; Donald Mooers, Jr., Legislative Assistant.
(See: The House of Representatives.)

Bridges, Dr William, Member, USAF Scientific Advisory Board
(Carl F. Braun Professor of Engineering, California Institute of Technology)
(See: USAF Scientific Advisory Board (Department of the Air Force).)

Brown, General Arthur Edmond, Jr., Vice Chief of Staff, Army

Brown was named Vice Chief of Staff of the Army in June 1987. He has a BB in Engineering from the US Military Academy at West Point, and also earned an MPA from the University of Pittsburgh.

Brown was commissioned as a second lieutenant in the Army after his graduation in June 1953. After attending the US Army Infantry School for infantry officer training, he was assigned as a platoon leader with the 508th Airborne Infantry at Fort Benning, Georgia. He remained in this post until January 1954, when he returned to the Infantry School for ranger training. After a stint as platoon leader in Kentucky, Brown was sent to Europe as the reconnaissance officer for Company D of the 60th Infantry Regiment.

Brown returned to the United States in September 1956, and served in several posts before being assigned as an assistant professor of military science at Florence State College in Alabama in August 1958. After three years in this position, Brown attended the US Army Command and General Staff College from August 1961 to June 1962. Following his graduation, Brown spent a year in Vietnam as a Civil Guard/Self Defense Corps adviser with the Military Assistance Group.

On his return to the USA, Brown earned his MPA and then joined the US Army Combat Developments Command at Fort Beloir, Virginia. There he served in a variety of posts between 1964 and 1967 before returning to Europe as executive assistant to the United States representative to the NATO Military Committee, a post he held from July 1967 to July 1968. After his graduation from the US Army War College, Brown returned to Vietnam and served there from July 1969 to July 1970, including for a period as deputy senior adviser with the US Military Assistance Command. After his return to the USA, Brown spent three years as a faculty member at the US Army War College.

From August 1973 to February 1975, Brown was commander of the 1st Brigade of the 1st Infantry Division, based at Fort Riley, Kansas. He then was assigned to US Army Headquarters in Washington, first as Chief, Force Plans and Structure Division in the Force Programs and Structure Directorate of the Office of the Deputy Chief of Staff, and later as executive assistant to the Deputy Chief of Staff for Operations and Plans.

Brown spent two years, from 1978 to 1980, as assistant division commander of the 25th Infantry Division based at Schofield Barracks in Hawaii, and the following year as deputy superintendent of the US Military Academy. From September 1981 to June 1983, he was Commanding General of the US Army Readiness and Mobilization Region IV, based in Georgia. Prior to assuming his present duties, Brown spent four years as Director of Army Staff at US Army Headquarters.
(See: Department of the Army)

Brown, June Gibbs, Inspector General, Department of Defense

June Gibbs Brown was appointed Inspector General in 1987. Her education includes a BBA and an MBA from Cleveland State University, and a JD from the University of Denver School of Law. Brown is a career government employee, having held positions as chief of financial system design, Bureau of Land Management; system design project manager, Bureau of Reclamation; and director of the Audit and Quality Control Division at the Navy Finance Center. From 1979 to 1981, she was

Inspector General of the Department of the Interior and from 1981 to 1985 Inspector General of NASA. When appointed to her DoD post, Brown was serving as associate administrator for management at NASA.

Brown is a member of the board of advisers of the National Contract Management Association. She has served on the boards of directors of the Federal Law Enforcement Training Center and the Interagency Auditor Training Program at the Department of Agriculture Graduate School. In 1984, she was chairman of the Interagency Committee on Information Resources Management, and has been a member of both the President's Council on Integrity and Efficiency and the President's Council for Management Improvement.
(See: Office of the Secretary of Defense (Department of Defense).)

Brown, Dr William M., Member, USAF Scientific Advisory Board
(President, Environmental Research Institute of Michigan)
(See: USAF Scientific Advisory Board (Department of the Air Force).)

Buchanan, Dr Leonard F., Member, USAF Scientific Advisory Board
(Vice-President of Engineering and Program Development, General Dynamics Corporation)
(See: USAF Scientific Advisory Board (Department of the Air Force).)

Buchsbaum, Solomon J. (Physicist), Senior Consultant, Defense Science Board

Buchsbaum, who holds a Ph.D. from the Massachusetts Institute of Technology, is executive vice-president, customer systems, at Bell Laboratories. He is a past chairman of the White House Science Council. He has also been vice-president of Sandia Laboratories and chairman, Energy Advisory Board, at the Department of Energy.
(See: Defense Science Board.)

Burdick, Quentin N., Senator (D, North Dakota), Member, Senate Appropriations Committee, Energy and Water Development Subcommittee
Address: Room SH-511, Hart Senate Office Building, Washington, DC 20510
Tel: (202) 224-2551

Burdick was elected to the Senate in 1960. Prior to that, he served one term in the House of Representatives. He faces reelection in 1988. Burdick has a BA and an LLB from the University of Minnesota. From 1932 until his election to the House in 1958, Burdick was a practising attorney in North Dakota.

Aside from the Appropriations Committee, Burdick also sits on the Environment and Public Works Committee, the Select Committee on Indian Affairs, and the Special Committee on Aging.

Key Aide: Joan Timony, Legislative Assistant.
(See: The Senate.)

Burnett, James R. (Electrical Engineer), Member at Large, Defense Science Board

Burnett holds a Ph.D. from Purdue University and is currently vice-president and deputy general manager, electronics and defence, for TRW, Inc., another large defence contractor.
(See: Defense Science Board.)

Bustamante, Albert G. , Representative (D, Texas), 23rd District, Member, House Armed Services Committee

Address: 1116 Longworth House Office Building, Washington, DC 20515
Tel: (202) 225-4511

Bustamante, who was a judge before entering the House of Representatives, was elected to the House in 1984. He sits on the Procurement and Military Nuclear Systems subcommittee, and also the Military Personnel and Compensation subcommittee. His other committee assignment is Government Operations. Bustamante is chairman of the Congressional Hispanic Caucaus, and a member of the Military Reform Caucus and Congressional Space Caucus.

Key Aides: Sherry Babich, Office Manager; Jose Rosenfeld, Legislative Assistant.
(See: The House of Representatives.)

Byrd, Robert C., Senator (D, West Virginia) Senate Majority Leader, Member, Senate Appropriations Committee, Defense Subcommittee, Member, Senate Appropriations Committee, Energy and Water Development Subcommittee
Address: 311 Heart Building, Washington, DC 20510

Born in North Wilkesboro, North Carolina, in 1917, Byrd was educated at Beckley College, Concord College, Morris Harvey College, Marshall College and at the American University, from which he received his JD in 1963.

Byrd was a West Virginia State Delegate from 1946 to 1950, a West Virginia State Senator from 1950 to 1952 and a US Representative for West Virginia from 1952 to 1958. He entered the Senate for West Virginia in 1958. From 1971 to 1976 he was Majority Whip. In addition to the positions listed above, Byrd is an ex-officio member of the Select Committee on Intelligence. He is a delegate-at-large to the Democratic National Convention.
(See: The Senate.)

Byron, Beverley B., Representative (D, Maryland), 6th District, Member, House Armed Services Committee
Address: 2430 Rayburn House Office Building, Washington, DC 20515
Tel: (202) 225-2721

Byron, who holds a BA from Hood College, was elected to the House in 1978. She is a member of the Democratic Leadership Council and the Conservative Democratic Forum. Byron is the chairperson of the Subcommittee on Military Personnel and Compensation, and also sits on the Investigations Subcommittee. Byron also is a member of the Interior and insular Affairs Committee and of the Select Committee on Ageing.

Key Aide: Mark Kronenberg, Legislative Director.
(See: The House of Representatives.)

Carlisle, M. D. B., Assistant Secretary of Defense (Legislative Affairs)

Carlisle was appointed Assistant Secretary in April 1986. She graduated from Manhattanville College with a BA in 1975, and took the job of executive director of the Senate Steering Committee, where she worked until 1980. From 1981 until 1984, Carlisle was executive director of the Republican Conference in the Senate. Obviously, these experiences mean she has valuable contacts and knowledge of the Senate. From 1984 until her appointment as Assistant Secretary, Carlisle was executive director of the Council for National Policy, a non-profit foundation.
(See: Office of the Secretary of Defense (Department of Defense).)

Carlucci, Frank C., Secretary of Defense (SECDEF)

The current Secretary of Defense, Frank C. Carlucci, was appointed by President Reagan in autumn 1987 after the resignation of Caspar Weinberger. Carlucci has spent most of his life in government, and in many ways seemed an ideal choice for 'caretaker' of the DoD in the last days of the Reagan Administration. Carlucci, who grew up in Scranton, Pennsylvania, graduated from Princeton University and studied at Harvard Business School. He served two years in the Navy, and after working in some unremarkable jobs, joined the Foreign Service in 1956.

In a *New York Times* profile, Carlucci was described as one who 'has been known to embrace dangerous assignments'; it is widely believed that Carlucci was active in covert operations during his time in the foreign service, and in fact was expelled from his post as consul-general in Zanzibar for plotting to overthrow that nation's ruler (*New York Times*, 6 November 1987; *The Nation*, 20 December 1986; *Covert Action Information Bulletin*, Winter 1986). While serving in the Congo in the 1960s, Carlucci was beaten and stabbed by an angry mob after a car in which he was a passenger struck and killed a man.

Carlucci has long been associated with Weinberger, and served as Deputy Secretary of Defense from 1981 until 1983. Carlucci has also held top positions in the Office of Management and Budget, the Central Intelligence Agency, and the Department of Health, Education, and Welfare (now defunct). Under President Nixon, he served at the Office of Economic Opportunity, Nixon's domestic poverty programme. Carlucci worked briefly as president and chief executive officer of Sears World Trade Inc., a subsidiary of Sears Roebuck and Company, which has since been absorbed by another subsidiary. Although Carlucci did not distinguish himself at Sears, *Fortune* magazine noted that international traders had speculated that the company was a front for US intelligence activities (*Fortune*, 25 June 1984). In 1986, Carlucci became National Security Advisor, the top position at the National Security Council, after Vice-Admiral John Poindexter resigned amid the fallout from the Iran—Contra scandal.

Carlucci was widely praised, both in Congress and the press, after his appointments as National Security Advisor and Secretary of Defense. He is described as less ideological than Weinberger, as a pragmatist, and also as less combative than his predecessor, who had stormy relations with Congress and the press during his tenure as Secretary of Defense. 'Frank likes to compromise', one official has remarked. 'He likes to cut deals. Cap didn't like to compromise' (*New York Times*, 4 November 1987).

As Secretary of Defense, Carlucci has been much more involved in the day-to-day running of the Pentagon than was Weinberger. As Deputy Secretary, Carlucci was seen as the 'chief operating officer' of the DoD, while Weinberger was in charge of the presentation of the DoD's case in government. Carlucci has been involved in streamlining acquisition procedures at the DoD since he was deputy secretary, and in 1986 served on the Packard Commission, which recommended sweeping changes in the structure of the DoD.

Although Carlucci has been trying to integrate strategy and procurement since 1981, it remains to be seen how successful he has been. Without doubt, he has been influential at the Pentagon during a time when budget constraints have caused tough decisions to be made. On the other hand, with a relatively short time to serve as Secretary of Defense, it is worth wondering how long the changes he has made will last. Indeed, this depends more on who wins the 1988 election and Carlucci's successor than Carlucci himself.

(See: Office of the Secretary of Defense (Department of Defense).)

Chain, John T., Jr., General, Commander-in-Chief, Strategic Air Command (CINCSAC)

General Chain earned fame, or at least notoriety, not as commander of SAC, but as a Lieutenant-General and Director of the Bureau of Politico-Military Affairs at the State Department. Leslie Gelb, a *New York Times* reporter who had held the post of director before Chain, wrote an article revealing that the US had plans to drop nuclear depth charges off the Canadian and Caribbean coastlines in the event of a Soviet attack. Chain, incensed that Gelb would reveal classified information, ordered that Gelb's portrait be removed from where it hung with those of all the other directors of the Bureau of Politico-Military Affairs, and attacked Gelb publicly. Chain seemed to come off worse in the incident, however, and was widely lambasted in the press for his actions. Although it seemed to many that the incident would prevent Chain being given more important posts, he was soon promoted to full general and appointed chief of staff of NATO's Supreme Headquarters Allied Powers Europe (SHAPE), a powerful and prestigious command.

Chain graduated from Denison University in Ohio, where he was a member of ROTC. He originally intended to do a quick tour of duty and go into a law career, but ended up remaining in the Air Force. He was commissioned as a second lieutenant, and served combat duty in Vietnam. He has described his experiences in Vietnam as formative. After his return, he served as deputy commander for operations and, later, logistics.

Chain also served in numerous tactical air command roles at Langley Air Force Base in Virginia and George Air Force Base in California. He is a firm believer in the importance of nuclear weapons and of SAC, and is considered to be a smart political operator. He is also firmly convinced of the immediacy of the Soviet threat, and has said that 'The only thing keeping armies from marching across Europe has been the threat of nuclear weapons. Thanks to nuclear weapons, Europe is free' (*The World*, April 1987).
(See: Unified and Specified Commands.)

Chappell, Bill, Representative (D, Florida), 4th District, Chairman, House Appropriations Committee, Subcommittee on Defense, Member, House Appropriations Committee, Subcommittee on Energy and Water Development
Address: 2468 Rayburn House Office Building, Washington, DC 20515
Tel: (202) 225-4035

Chappell was elected to the House in 1968. He has a BA, an LLB, and a JD from the University of Florida. During World War II, he served in the Navy, and was later a captain in the Navy reserve. He was Marion County prosecuting attorney from 1950 to 1954. In 1954, he was elected to the Florida State House of Representatives, where he served until 1964. In 1966, he was again elected as a State Representative, and remained until his election to the House. He was unopposed in his last re-election bid in 1986. Chappell does not sit on any other committees.

Key Aides: Bill Goehring, Associate Staff; Berton R. 'Bud' Otto, Associate Staff.
(See: The House of Representatives.)

Cheathem, Thomas E., Member, USAF Scientific Advisory Board
(Harvard University)
(See: USAF Scientific Advisory Board (Department of the Air Force).)

Chiles, Lawton, Senator (D, Florida), Member, Senate Appropriations Committee, Defense Subcommittee
Address: Room SR-250, Russell Senate Office Building, Washington, DC 20510
Tel: (202) 224-5274

Chiles was elected to the Senate in 1970, after serving four years as a Florida state senator and eight years as a state representative. He is up for re-election this year. He has a BS and an LLB from the University of Florida. He saw combat in Korea with the Army. Chiles also serves on the Budget Committee, the Governmental Affairs Committee, and the Special Committee on Aging.

Key Aide: Ralph Shepard, Legislative Assistant.
(See: The Senate.)

Chu, David, Director, Program Analyis and Evaluation, Office of the Secretary of Defense

David Chu was appointed to his current post in May 1981. He received his BA in economics in 1965, and his Ph.D. in economics in 1972, both from Yale University. Chu served in the US Army from 1968 until 1970. He was an instructor at the US Army Logistics Management Center in Virginia from 1968 until 1969, and spent 1969 until 1970 working in the Office of the Comptroller, 1st Logistical Command, in South Vietnam.

From 1970 until 1978, Chu was an economist with the RAND Corporation, where he was appointed associate director of the economics department in August 1975.

Chu was the assistant director of the Congressional Budget Office for the National Security and International Affairs Division from 1978 until his appointment as director of Program Analysis and Evaluation.
(See: Office of the Secretary of Defense (Department of Defense).)

Clem, Robert G., Member, USAF Scientific Advisory Board
(Director of Systems, Sandia National Laboratories)
(See: USAF Scientific Advisory Board (Department of the Air Force).)

Cochran, Thad, Senator (R, Mississippi), Member, Senate Appropriations Committee,

Defense Subcommittee, Member, Senate Appropriations Committee, Energy and Water Development Subcommittee
Address: Room SR-326, Russell Senate Office Building, Washington, DC 20510
Tel: (202) 224-5054

Cochran, who faces re-election in 1990, was elected to the Senate in 1978. Prior to that, he had served in the House of Representatives from 1972. He has a BA and a JD from the University of Mississippi. Cochran served in the US Navy from 1959 to 1961. Before his election to the House, he was a private attorney. He also serves on the Agriculture, Nutrition and Forestry Committee and the Labor and Human Resources Committee.

Key Aide: Jack Haggard, Legislative Director.
(See: The Senate.)

Cohen, William S., Senator (R, Maine), Member, Senate Armed Services Committee
Address: Room SH-322, Hart Senate Office Building, Washington, DC 20510
Tel: (202) 224-2523

Cohen, who is known to be independent in his voting, was first elected to the Senate in 1978. His next re-election campaign will be in 1990. Cohen has a BA from Bowdoin College and an LLB from Boston University. Before coming to the Senate, he was an attorney, and served in the House of Representatives from 1972 to 1978. Cohen is the Ranking Minority Member of the Projection Forces and Regional Defense Subcommittee. He also sits on the Conventional Forces and Allied Defense Subcommittee and the Strategic Forces Subcommittee. Cohen is vice-chairman of the Select Committee on Intelligence, the position for which he is best-known, and serves on the Governmental Affairs Committee and the Special Committee on Aging. He is a member of the Senate Republican Policy Committee and the Military Reform Caucus.

Key Aides: James M. Bodner, Legislative Assistant; Robert P. Savitt, Congressional Assistant.
(See: The Senate.)

Cole, Julian D., Member, USAF Scientific Advisory Board
(Department of Mathematical Sciences, Renssalear Polytechnic Institute)
(See: USAF Scientific Advisory Board (Department of the Air Force.)

Conahan, Frank C., Assistant Comptroller/ Director of National Security Division, General Accounting Office
(See: Congressional Support Agencies.)

Connor, Henry W., Senior Associate Director, Dept. of the Army, General Accounting Office
See: Congressional Support Agencies.)

Cook, Vincent N. (Industrialist), Member at Large, Defense Science Board

Cook is an IBM vice-president and assistant group executive, Asia/Pacific Group. He holds an MA from American University. His past positions at IBM include president, Federal Systems Division (FSD); vice-president, Defense and Space Systems, FSD; vice-president and general manager, Command and Space Systems, FSD; and director, World Wide Military Command and Control System (WWMCCS) Architecture, FSD.
(See: Defense Science Board.)

Costello, Robert B., Under Secretary of Defense for Acquisition, Office of the Secretary of Defense

Robert Costello replaced Richard Godwyn, who resigned in September 1987 in disgust at the slow pace at which Department of Defense reforms were being implemented. Said one Pentagon bureaucrat of Godwyn, 'Congress told him to go forth and do good work, but everybody in this building told him to get lost.' Reflecting DoD official claims that Godwyn left because of personality conflicts and exaggerated expectations of his own power, William Taft IV, the Deputy Secretary of Defense, told Congress that 'There aren't any czars in Washington'. This atmosphere does not make it easier for Costello, who came into office with a *de facto* mandate to prove that the DoD can institute reforms.

Costello previously was Assistant Secretary (Production and Logistics) under Godwyn. His education includes bachelor's and master's degrees in civil engineering from Rennselaer Polytechnic Institute and a doctorate in civil engineering from Cornell University. He was formerly chief of missile engineering for the Allison Division of General Motors Corp., and later was executive director of materials management for General Motors. As Assistant Secretary, he worked for reform of the acquisition process and supported Godwyn.

Costello seems sympathetic to industry and is interested in instituting reforms mainly through doing away with or waiving rules which he believes raise the costs of weapons systems, thus giving more flexibility to industry. He has come in for some criticism from members of Congress, but newspaper reports also indicate that Congressional 'military experts' praise him.

Costello's chances of achieving any major revisions in Pentagon practices do not seem bright. It will be interesting to see if Congress and the public see his success, or lack of it, as a test case for military reform.

(See: Office of the Secretary of Defense (Department of Defense).)

Courter, Jim, Representative (R, New Jersey), 12th District, Member, House Armed Services Committee

Address: 2422 Rayburn House Office Building, Washington, DC 20515

Tel: (202) 225-5801

Courter, an attorney with a BA from Colgate University and a JD from Duke University, was elected to the House in 1978. He is considered one of the more influential conservatives on the Armed Services Committee. He is Ranking Minority member of the Acquisition Policy Panel, and also sits on the subcommittees on Procurement and Military Nuclear Systems and Research and Development. Courter is also a member of the Select Committee on Ageing. He is a member of the Military Reform Caucus and the executive committee of the House Republican Committee on Committees He is also a congressional observer at the Geneva arms talks.

Key Aides: Lisa Gaede, Legislative Assistant; Chris Harmon, Legislative Assistant.

(See: The House of Representatives.)

Covert, Professor Eugene E., Member, USAF Scientific Advisory Board (Director, Center for Aerodynamic Studies, Head, Department of Aeronautics and Astronautics, Massachusetts Institute of Technology)

(See: USAF Scientific Advisory Board (Department of the Air Force).)

Crowe, William T., Admiral (USN), Chairman of the Joint Chiefs of Staff

Admiral Crowe became Chairman of the Joint Chiefs of Staff (JCS) in October 1985. Since then, all four Chiefs have been replaced (each holds his post for a four-year term). Admiral Crowe is better known in public than past JCS chairmen: in 1987—88 he appeared on television fairly frequently, with the Secretary of Defense, to explain the circumstances surrounding the US attacks on Iranians in the Gulf. Admiral Crowe has had to contend with the new laws governing the Joint Chiefs, not always an easy job. In 1987, Admiral Crowe described the new laws as 'the dominating factor' in his work. During this period, Crowe was caught in a conflict between the then Secretary of Defense, Caspar Weinberger, and Secretary of State George Shultz. Weinberger insisted that the Chairman of the Joint Chiefs worked for him, and thus should not give advice to the National Security Council (NSC) except through him. Shultz argued that, as a member of the NSC, he had a right to hear Admiral Crowe's views, and invited Admiral Crowe to brief him directly. Crowe dealt with this by accepting Shultz's invitation, but informing Weinberger beforehand and briefing him right after the conversation. No such conflict has been reported between Carlucci and Schultz.

Admiral Crowe graduated from the US Naval Academy in 1946. He also has an MA in personnel administration from Stanford University and a Ph.D in politics from Princeton University.

His initial sea assignment was aboard the USS *Carmick*. In 1948, he went to the Naval Submarine School in New London, Connecticut. Following that, he served as flag lieutenant and aide to the Commander, Submarine Force, Atlantic Fleet. From 1952 to 1954 he served aboard the submarine USS *Clamagore*, and was assistant to the naval aide to the President from 1954 to 1956. He served as executive officer of the submarine USS *Wahoo* and commanding officer of the submarine USS *Trout* before being appointed commander of Submarine Division 31, in San Diego, California.

Significant shore assignments, before becoming an admiral, included aide to the Deputy Chief of Naval Operations (Plans and Policy); director of East Asia and Pacific Branch, Politico-Military Division, Office of the Chief of Naval Operations; senior US adviser to the Vietnamese Riverine Force; and director of the Office for Micronesian Status Negotiations, Department of the Interior.

In June 1974, Crowe was promoted to rear-admiral and appointed deputy director, Strategic Plans, Policy, Nuclear Security Affairs Divisions of the Office of the Chief of Naval Operations. From January 1975 until June 1976, he was director, East Asia and Pacific Region, in the office of the Assistant Secretary of Defense (International Security Affairs). From June 1976 until July 1977, he was commander of the Middle East Force, based in Bahrain in the Persian Gulf.

Crowe was promoted to vice-admiral in 1977, and was appointed deputy chief of Naval Operations, Plans, Policy, and Operations, as well as senior US military representative to the United Nations. In March 1980, he was promoted to admiral and became Commander, Allied Forces Southern Europe. In January 1983, he assumed the additional duties of Commander-in-Chief, US Naval Forces Europe. On 1 July 1983, Admiral Crowe became Commander-in-Chief, US Pacific Command, where he remained until his appointment as chairman of the Joint Chiefs Staff.

(See: Joint Chiefs of Staff.)

Currie, Malcolm R. (Electrical Engineer), Member at Large, Defense Science Board

Currie is president of the Delco Electronics Corporations, executive vice-president at the Hughes Aircraft Company, and group executive in the General Motors Corporation, Defense Division. He holds a Ph.D. from the University of California at Berkeley. In the past, Currie has been vice-president, research and development, at Beckman Instruments; group president, Hughes Aircraft Company; and director of Defense Research and Engineering.

(See: Defense Science Board.)

D'Amato, Alfonse M., Senator (R, New York), Member, Senate Appropriations Committee, Defense Subcommittee

Address: Room SH-520, Hart Senate Office Building, Washington, DC 20510

Tel: (202) 224-6542

D'Amato was elected to the Senate in 1980. A conservative, he faces re-election in 1992. D'Amato is in the midst of a controversy over his nominations for the Eastern District Federal Court, which some have charged are politically motivated. He received both his BA and his JD from Syracuse University. He has been Nassau County Public Administrator from 1965 to 1968, Nassau County Supervisor from 1971 to 1977, and was vice-chairman of the Nassau County Board of Supervisors from 1977 until his election to the Senate.

D'Amato sits on the Banking, Housing, and Urban Affairs Committee, the Small Business Committee, and the Joint Economic Committee.

Key Aide: Shawn Smallie, Legislative Assistant.

(See: The Senate.)

Daniel, Dan, Representative (D, Virginia), 5th District, Member, House Armed Services Committee

Address: 2308 Rayburn House Office Building, Washington, DC 20515

Tel: (202) 225-4711

Daniel was first elected to the House in 1969. He is a member of the Conservative Democratic Forum and co-chairman of the American Security Council. He is chairman of the Readiness Subcommittee. In addition to the Armed Services Committee, Daniel is a member of the Select Committee on Intelligence.
(See: The House of Representatives.)

Daniell, Robert F., Chairman, President,Chief Executive Officer and Chief Operating Officer, United Technologies

Daniell was elected president and chief operating officer of United Technologies in October 1984. He became chief executive officer in January 1986, and chairman in January 1987. He is a graduate of Boston University's College of Industrial Technology.

Daniell joined United Technologies in 1956 as a design engineer at Sikorsky Aircraft, a subsidiary. He later served as project manager for several programmes, including the US Air Force HH-3E 'Jolly Green Giant' helicopter and the Coast Guard HH-3F. In 1968, Daniell became programme manager for the S-61, S-62 and S-58 commercial helicopter programmes.

In 1971, Daniell was promoted to commercial marketing manager at Sikorsky. He was named vice-president—commercial marketing in 1974. In 1976, Daniell was appointed senior vice-president—marketing. During his time in that post, Sikorsky won development and production contracts for the Army UH-60A Blackhawk, the Navy CH-53E Super Stallion, and the Navy SH-60B Seahawk helicopters. Daniell was appointed executive vice-president in 1977. Soon after that, he was appointed president and chief executive officer of Sikorsky.

In December 1982, Daniell became a vice-president of United Technologies, and was appointed senior vice-president—defense systems (since renamed defense and space). He stayed in this post until his election as president.

Daniell is also a director of the Travelers Corporation and Shell Oil Company. He is a member of the board of trustees of Boston University.
(See: Defence Contractors.)

Darden, George (Buddy), Representative (D, Georgia), 7th, District, Member, House Armed Services Committee
Address: 1330 Longworth House Office Building, Washington, DC 20515
Tel: (202) 225-2931

Darden, who has a BA and a JD from the University of Georgia, was elected to the House in 1985. He sits on the subcommittees on Readiness and Research and Development. He is a member of the Conservative Democratic Forum and the American Security Council.

Key Aide: Richard Patrick, Legislative Assistant.
(See: The House of Representatives.)

Davis, Jack, Representative (R, Illinois), 4th District, Member, House Armed Services Committee
Address: 1234 Longworth House Office Building, Washington, DC, 20515
Tel: (202) 225-3635

Davis was elected to the House in 1986. Before that, he was a small business owner. He has a BS from Southern Illinois University. Davis sits on the subcommittees on Military Personnel and Compensation and Readiness.

Key Aide: Leslee DuBeau, Legislative Director.
(See: The House of Representatives.)

Davis, Richard A., Associate Director, C3I, General Accounting Office
(See: Congressional Support Agencies.)

Davis, Robert W., Representative (R, Michigan), 11th District, Member, House Armed Services Committee
Address: 2417 Rayburn House Office Building, Washington, DC 20515
Tel: (202) 225-4735

Davis, a funeral home director with a BS from Wayne State University, was elected to the House in 1978. He is a member of the subcommittees on Procurement and Military Nuclear Systems, Research and Development, and the

Acquisition Policy Panel. His other committee assignment is Merchant Marine and Fisheries.

Key Aides: Mark Ruge, Administrative Assistant; Cindy Lovett, Legislative Assistant.
(See: The House of Representatives.)

DeConcini, Dennis, Senator (D, Arizona), Member, Senate Appropriations Committee, Defense Subcommittee, Member, Senate Appropriations Committee, Energy and Water Development Subcommittee
Address: Room SH-328, Hart Senate Office Building, Washington, DC, 20510
Tel: (202) 224-4521

DeConcini, who is running for re-election in 1988, was elected to the Senate in 1976. He has a BA from the University of Arizona and an LLB from the University of Arizona law school. He served in the Army from 1959 to 1960, and the Army Reserve from 1960 to 1967. He was special counsel to the Governor of Arizona in 1965, and administrative assistant to the Governor from 1965 to 1967.

DeConcini sits on the Judiciary Committee, the Rules and Administration Committee, the Committee on Veterans' Affairs, the Select Committee on Indian Affairs, and the Select Committee on Intelligence.

Key Aide: Tim Roemer, Legislative Assistant.
(See: The Senate.)

Decker, Gilbert F., (Electrical Engineer), Ex-Officio Member, Defense Science Board, Chairman, Army Science Board

Decker is president of Penn Central Federal Systems Company. He has an MS from Stanford University and is a former vice-president, New Ventures, at TRW Inc.
(See: Defense Science Board.)

DeLauer, Richard (Engineer), Member at Large, Defense Science Board, Member, USAF Scientific Advisory Board

A recent Under Secretary of Defense for Research and Engineering in the Reagan Administration, DeLauer is currently president of the Orion Group, Ltd. DeLauer, who holds a Ph.D. from the California Institute of Technology, has also been executive vice-president of TRW, Inc. His other positions at TRW included vice-president and general manager, Systems Engineering and Integration; and director of the TITAN ICBM programme.
(See: Defense Science Board; USAF Scientific Advisory Board (Department of the Air Force).)

Dellums, Ronald V. , Representative (D, California), 8th District, Member, House Armed Services Committee
Address: 2136 Rayburn House Office Building Washington, DC 20515
Tel: (202) 225-2661

Dellums, who began his House service in 1971 (when Ronald Reagan was Governor of California), is one of the most liberal members of the House. He holds a BA from San Francisco State College and an MSW from the University of California at Berkeley. He is chairman of the Military Installations and Facilities Subcommittee and a member of the Investigations Subcommittee.

Key Aides: Robert Brauer, Special Counsel; Dan Lindheim, Legislative Counsel.
(See: The House of Representatives.)

DePoy, Dr Phil E., Member, USAF Scientific Advisory Board
(President, Center for Naval Analyses)
(See: USAF Scientific Advisory Board (Department of the Air Force).)

Deutch, John M. (Chemist), Senior Consultant, Defense Science Board

Deutch is provost of the Massachusetts Institute of Technology, where he is a past Dean of Science and Professor of Chemistry. He has served as Under Secretary at the Department of Energy and was a member of the President's Commission on Strategic Forces.
(See: Defense Science Board.)

Dickinson, William L., Representative (R, Alabama), 2nd District, Ranking Minority

Member, House Armed Services Committee
Address: 2406 Rayburn House Office Building, Washington, DC 20515
Tel: (202) 225-2901

Dickinson, an attorney and judge before being elected to the House in 1964, is the key Republican member of the Armed Services Committee. He has a BA and an LLB from the University of Alabama. Dickinson is the Ranking Minority Member of the Research and Development Subcommittee and the Defense Policy Panel. He also sits on the Military Installations Subcommittee and the Acquisition Policy Panel. He is a member of the executive committee of the House Republican Committee on Committees and co-chairman of the American Security Council.

Key Aide: Steve Conver, Defense Assistant.
(See: The House of Representatives.)

Dicks, Norman D., Representative (D, Washington), 6th District, Member, House Appropriations Committee, Subcommittee on Defense
Address: 2429 Rayburn House Office Building, Washington, DC, 20515
Tel: (202) 225-5916

Dicks was elected to the House in 1976. He has a BA and an LLB from the University of Washington. From 1973 until he was elected to the House, Dicks was an assistant to Senator Warren Magnuson of Washington. He only serves on the Appropriations Committee.

Key Aide: Terry Freese, Legislative Assistant.
(See: The House of Representatives.)

Dixon, Alan J., Senator (D, Illinois), Member, Senate Armed Services Committee
Address: Room SH-331, Hart Senate Office Building, Washington, DC, 20510
Tel: (202) 224-2854

Dixon, who has a BA from the University of Illinois and an LLB from Washington University, was an attorney before being elected to the Senate in 1980. He faces re-election in 1992.

Dixon is chairman of the Readiness, Sustainability and Support Subcommittee, and also serves on the subcommittees on Conventional Forces and Alliance Defense and Defense Industry and Technology. He also sits on the Banking, Housing, and Urban Affairs Committee and the Small Business Committee. He is considered somewhat conservative.

Key Aides: Charles C. Smith, Legislative Assistant; Mary Beth Dahm, Special Assistant.
(See: The Senate.)

Domenici, Pete V., Senator (R, New Mexico), Member, Senate Appropriations Committee, Energy and Water Development Subcommittee
Address: Room SD-434, Dirksen Senate Office Building, Washington, DC, 20510
Tel: (202) 224-6621

Domenici was elected to the Senate in 1972 and faces re-election in 1990. He has a BS from the University of New Mexico and an LLB from Denver University. He has been a teacher and an attorney. Domenici was a also a city commissioner in Albuquerque, New Mexico, from 1966 to 1968. He also sits on the Budget Committee, the Energy and Natural Resources Committee, and the Special Committee on Ageing.
(See: The Senate.)

Dougherty, Russell E., General, USAF (Retired), Member at Large, Defense Science Board

Dougherty is a former Commander-in-Chief of the Strategic Air Command and chief of staff, NATO Supreme Headquarters Allied Forces Europe. He is now an attorney with the firm Boothe, Pritchard & Dudley.
(See: Defense Science Board.)

Duffy, Robert A. (Aeronautical Engineer), Member at Large, Defense Science Board

A private consultant, Duffy holds a BS from the Georgia Institute of Technology. He is a former brigadier general in the Air Force and was vice-commander of the Space and Missile Systems Organization (SAMSO). Earlier, he served as deputy for re-entry systems at SAMSO, and

worked in the office of the Director of Defense Research and Engineering. He has also been president and chief executive of Charles Stark Draper Lab, Inc.
(See: Defense Science Board.)

Duncan, Robert C., Director of Defense Research and Engineering, Office of the Secretary of Defense

Robert Duncan graduated from the US Naval Academy in 1945 with a BS. He later earned a BS in aeronautical engineering from the US Navy Postgraduate School, and went on to receive a Master of Science and Doctor of Science degree, both in aeronautical engineering, from the Massachusetts Institute of Technology. He was a pilot of fighter and attack aircraft in the US Navy, and prior to this served two years aboard the USS *Bremerton* in the Pacific.

From 1960 to 1961, Duncan was the head of the Space Programs Branch in the office of the Chief of Naval Operations. From 1961 until 1963, he was special assistant to the Director of Defense Research and Engineering in the DoD. In 1964, Duncan joined NASA as the head of the Guidance Control Division at the Manned Spacecraft Center. From 1967 until 1968, Duncan was assistant director of the NASA Electronic Research Center.

Duncan joined the Polaroid Corporation in 1968 and was named assistant vice-president in 1969. In 1975, he was elected vice-president of engineering, a post he held until 1985. From 1968 until 1975, he was also programme manager for the SX-70 camera and film systems. In 1985, Duncan was appointed Director of DARPA, a post he held until his appointment as Director of Defense Research and Engineering in 1987.
(See: Office of the Secretary of Defense (Department of Defense).)

Dyson, Roy P., Representative (D, Maryland),1st District, Member, House Armed Services Committee
Address: 224 Cannon House Office Building, Washington, DC 20515
Tel: (202) 225-5311

Dyson, who earned his BA from the University of Maryland, was a lumber company executive before being elected to the House in 1980. He sits on the subcommittees on Military Personnel and Compensation, Procurement and Military Nuclear Systems, and Seapower and Strategic and Critical Materials. Dyson is also a member of the Merchant Marine and Fisheries Committee.

Key Aide: Todd A. Skipper
(See: The House of Representatives.)

Evans, William J., Vice-President, Deputy, Defense and Space Systems, United Technologies

Evans was elected as vice-president of United Technologies in September 1978, following his retirement from the post of fourstar general in the US Air Force. He was appointed deputy, defense and space systems in February 1985. He is responsible for monitoring current military plans and programmes.

Evans graduated from the US Military Academy in 1946 and the US Army War College in 1960. Evans flew more than 400 combat missions in Korea and Vietnam as a fighter pilot. He has also been assigned to tactical operations in the USA, Japan, and Europe. Evans also has Air Force experience in weapons systems research, development, and acquisition. He is a former commander of the US Systems Command, and when he retired from the Air Force he was Commander-in-Chief of the US Air Force in Europe and NATO Commander of Allied Air Forces, Central Europe.
(See: Defence Contractors.)

Everett, Robert R. (Electrical Engineer), Member at Large, Defense Science Board, Member, USAF Scientific Advisory Board

Everett is president emeritus at the MITRE Corporation. His past positions with MITRE include president, executive vice-president, and vice-president, technical operations. He has an MS from the Massachusetts Institute of Technology.

(See: Defense Science Board; USAF Scientific Advisory Board (Department of the Air Force).)

Exon, James J. , Senator (D, Nebraska), Member, Senate Armed Services Committee
Address: Room SH-330, Hart Senate Office Building, Washington, DC 20510
Tel: (202) 224-4224

Exon was governor of Nebraska from 1970 until 1978, when he was elected to the Senate. He has a BA from the University of Omaha, and was an office equipment retailer before he became governor. Exon faces re-election in 1990.

He is chairman of the Strategic Forces and Nuclear Deterrence Subcommittee. He also sits on the subcommittees on Manpower and Personnel and Projection Forces and Regional Defense. Exon is also a member of the Budget Committee, and the Commerce, Science, and Transportation Committee. A Deputy Majority Whip, Exon is also a member of the Senate Democratic Steering Committee.

Key Aide: Jeff Subko, Legislative Assistant.
(See: The Senate.)

Faught, Thomas F., Jr., Assistant Secretary of the Navy (Research, Engineering and Systems)

Faught, who served in the Marine Corps both as an enlisted man and an officer, received his BS in technology and business from Oregon State University, where he concentrated in industrial management, personnel and industrial analysis. He also holds an MBA from Harvard University, and did graduate work at the Massachusetts Institute of Technology on industrial applications of nuclear energy.

Faught joined the Ford Motor Company as an engineer, and later became a manufacturing manager. For ten years he worked for the international management consulting firm of Gould, Inc., Booz, Allen & Hamilton. He then became executive vice-president of the F & M Schaefer Corporation. In 1974, Faught joined Dravo Corporation, which is involved in project management, engineering, factory automation, construction, national resource development and materials handling systems manufacturing. He served as chief financial officer, chief administrative officer, and chief operating officer before being appointed president and chief executive officer in 1983.

Faught has served on the board of trustees of the Presbyterian University Hospital, WQED (Public Broadcasting and Television) and Carnegie Mellon University, all in Pittsburgh, Pennsylvania. In 1984, he was appointed by the President to the Advisory Committee of the Import-Export Bank of the United States, and became chairman of the committee in 1985.
(See: Department of the Navy.)

Fazio, Vic, Representative (D, California), 4th District, Member, House Appropriations Committee, Subcommittee on Energy and Water Development
Address: 2433 Rayburn House Office Building, Washington, DC 20515
Tel: (202) 225-5716

Fazio was elected to the House in 1978. He has a BA from Union College. Fazio has been an aide to Representative Ronald Cameron, and a consultant to the California State Assembly. He served in the assembly from 1975 until his election to the House. Fazio also sits on the Budget Committee, the Committee on Standards of Official Conduct, and the Select Committee on Hunger.
(See: The House of Representatives.)

Fields, Craig, Deputy Director for Research, Defense Advanced Research Projects Agency (DARPA)
(See: Defense Agencies.)

Fillers, Dr Robert W., Member, USAF Scientific Advisory Board
(Director, Material Sciences Laboratory, The Aerospace Corporation)
(See: USAF Scientific Advisory Board (Department of the Air Force).)

Fink, Daniel J., (Aeronautical Engineer), Senior Consultant, Defense Science Board

Fink is president of D. J. Fink Associates Inc. He has been deputy director of Defense Research

and Engineering (Strategic and Space Systems). He has also been senior vice-president for corporate planning and development, General Electric Company; and vice-president and group executive, Aerospace Group, General Electric.
(See: Defense Science Board.)

Finley, Harry L., Senior Associate Director, Dept. of the Air Force, General Accounting Office
(See: Congressional Support Agencies.)

Fischer, Dr Craig L., Member, USAF Scientific Advisory Board (Director of Clinical Laboratories, John F. Kennedy Memorial Hospital)
(See: USAF Scientific Advisory Board (Department of the Air Force).)

Flanagan, Dr James L., Member, USAF Scientific Advisory Board
(Head, Acoustics research Department, AT&T Bell Laboratories)
(See: USAF Scientific Advisory Board (Department of the Air Force).)

Flax, Dr Alexander H., Member, USAF Scientific Advisory Board
(President Emeritus, Institute for Defense Analyses)
(See: USAF Scientific Advisory Board (Department of the Air Force).)

Fletcher, James C., Administrator, NASA

Fletcher was appointed to be NASA administrator in May 1986. He previously held the same position from April 1971 to May 1977. Fletcher earned his BA in physics from Columbia University in 1940 and a Ph.D. in physics from the California Institute of Technology in 1948. After his graduation in 1940, Fletcher was a research physicist with the US Navy Bureau of Ordnance. In 1941, he became a special research assistant at Cruft Laboratory, Harvard University. In 1942, he became an instructor at Princeton University.

In 1948, Fletcher joined the Hughes Aircraft Company, where he stayed until 1954. He then joined the Ramo-Woolridge Corporation (now TRW) at the Guided Missile Research Division, which later became the Space Technology Laboratories. In 1958, Fletcher helped found the Space Electronics Corporation, where he was the first president. This later merged with a portion of Aerojet, becoming the Space General Corporation, where Fletcher was president and later chairman. Fletcher later served as systems vice-president of the Aerojet General Corporation.

In 1964, Fletcher became president of the University of Utah. He remained there until his first appointment as NASA administrator in 1971. After leaving NASA in 1977, Fletcher was the William K. Whiteford Professor of Energy Resources and Technology at the University of Pittsburgh, and also ran a consulting firm, James C. Fletcher & Associates.
(See: Independent Agencies.)

Foglietta, Thomas M., Representative (D, Pennsylvania), 1st District, Member, House Armed Services Committee
Address: 231 Cannon House Office Building, Washington, DC 20515
Tel: (202) 225-4731

Foglietta was elected to the House in 1980. He has earned a BA from St Joseph's University and a JD from Temple University, and was an attorney before his election. He sits on the Military Installations and Facilities Subcommittee and the Seapower and Strategic and Critical Materials Subcommittee. He is also a member of the Arms Control and Foreign Policy Caucus.

Key Aides: Phillip Rotondi, Administrative Assistant; Anne Keeney, Legislative Director.
(See: The House of Representatives.)

Fowler, Charles A., (Electrical Engineer), Chairman, Defense Science Board

Fowler, who holds a BS from the University of Illinois, runs C. A. Fowler, Associates. In the past, he has been a senior vice-president at the MITRE Corporation, a vice-president of the

Raytheon Company, and deputy director of Defense Research and Engineering (Tactical Warfare Programs).
(See: Defense Science Board.)

Frieman, Edward A. (Physicist), Member at Large, Defense Science Board

The director of the Scripps Institute of Oceanography, Frieman has a Ph.D. from the Polytechnic Institute of Brooklyn. He has been the executive vice-president of Science Applications, Inc., and the director of energy research at the Department of Energy. He also was a professor of astrophysical sciences at Princeton University.
(See: Defense Science Board.)

Fubini, Eugene G. (Physicist), Vice Chairman, Defense Science Board

Fubini hods a Ph.D. from the University of Rome and runs E. G. Fubini Consultants, Ltd. He has been a vice-president and group executive at the IBM Corporation; vice-president, Research and Systems Engineering, AIL Corporation; Deputy Director of Defense Research and Engineering; and Assistant Secretary of Defense.
(See: Defense Science Board.)

Fuhrman, Robert A. (Aeronautics Engineer), Member at Large, Defense Science Board, President and Chief Operating Officer, Lockheed Corporation

Fuhrman was elected president and chief operating officer in 1986. He has been a member of the board of directors since 1980 and chairman of the board of Lockheed Missiles and Space Company since 1979. He has a BS in aeronautical engineering from the University of Michigan, received in 1945, and earned an MS from the University of Maryland in 1952.

Fuhrman joined Lockheed Missiles and Space Company in 1958 as technical staff head of Polaris systems development. He became chief engineer in the Missile Systems Division in 1964, and vice-president and assistant general manager in the same division in 1966. He was elected a corporate vice-president and appointed general manager of the Missile Systems Division in 1969.

In 1970, Fuhrman became president of Lockheed—Georgia, and president of Lockheed—California in 1971. From 1973 to 1976, he was executive vice-president of Lockheed Missiles and Space Company. He became president of Lockheed Missiles and Space Company in 1976, becoming a senior vice-president of Lockheed Corporation at the same time.

In April 1983, Fuhrman was named group president of Lockheed Missiles, Space and Electronic Systems, and held this post until being elected to his current positions.

Fuhrman is a member of the National Academy of Engineering and a senior member of the American Astronautical Society. He is a fellow of the Society of Manufacturing Engineers. Fuhrman is also a member of the National and American Manufacturing Association, the National Defense Transportation Association, the Navy League, the Air Force Association, and the Association of the US Army.

A member of the Defense Science Board, Fuhrman is chairman of the Task Force on Defense Industrial Base. He is also a member of the Advisory Committee to the Subcommittee on Defense Industry and Technology of the Senate Committee on Armed Services.
(See: Defense Science Board; Defence Contractors.)

Gabriel, Dr Richard F., Member, USAF Scientific Advisory Board

(Chief Human Factors Engineer, Douglas Aircraft Company)
(See: USAF Scientific Advisory Board (Department of the Air Force).)

Garmire, Dr Elsa M., Member, USAF Scientific Advisory Board

(Director, Center for Laser Studies, University of Southern California)
(See: USAF Scientific Advisory Board (Department of the Air Force).)

Garn, Jake, Senator (R, Utah), Member, Senate Appropriations Committee, Defense Subcommittee, Member, Senate Appropriations Committee, Energy and Water Development Subcommittee
Address: Room SD-505, Dirksen Senate Office Building, Washington, DC 20510
Tel: (202) 224-5444

Garn was elected to the Senate in 1974, and faces re-election in 1992. Garn earned his BS from the University of Utah in 1955, and served in the Navy from 1956 to 1960. He was also a lieutenant-colonel in the Utah Air National Guard. Garn was mayor of Salt Lake City from 1972 until his election to the Senate. A conservative, Garn created controversy in 1985 by flying as a 'payload specialist' on the Space Shuttle Discovery in what was widely viewed as a public relations ploy.

Garn also sits on the Banking, Housing and Urban Affairs Committee and the Rules and Administration Committee.

Key Aides: Jeff Bingham, Administrative Assistant; Jackie Marie Clegg, Legislative Assistant.
(See: The Senate.)

Geiger, Rear-Admiral Robert K., USN (Retired), Member, USAF Scientific Advisory Board (Private consultant)
(See: USAF Scientific Advisory Board (Department of the Air Force).)

Gerry, Dr Edward T., Member, USAF Scientific Advisory Board
(J. Shafer Associates, Inc.)
(See: USAF Scientific Advisory Board (Department of the Air Force).)

Getting, Dr Ivan A., Member, USAF Scientific Advisory Board
(Private consultant)
(See: USAF Scientific Advisory Board (Department of the Air Force).)

Gibbons, John H., Director, Office of Technology Assessment
(See: Congressional Support Agencies.)

Glenn, John, Senator (D, Ohio), Member, Senate Armed Services Committee
Address: Room SH-503, Hart Senate Office Building, Washington, DC 20510
Tel: (202) 224-3353

Glenn, a former astronaut, made a bid for the Democratic Presidential nomination in 1979. He faces re-election to the Senate, to which he was first elected in 1974, in 1992. Glenn received a BS from Muskingham College. He is considered a conservative and a strong supporter of the military.

Glenn is chairman of the Manpower and Personnel Subcommittee. He also sits on the subcommittees on Conventional Forces and Alliance Defense and Strategic Forces and Nuclear Deterrence. Glenn is also chairman of the Governmental Affairs Committee and is on the Special Committee on Ageing. He is a member of the Senate Democratic Policy Committee.

Key Aides: Ron Grimes, Legislative Co-ordinator; Milton Beach, Legislative Assistant; Don Mitchell, Legislative Assistant.
(See: The Senate.)

Gore, Albert, Jr., Senator (D, Tennessee), Member of Senate Armed Services Committee
Address: Room SR-393, Russell Senate Office Building, Washington, DC 20510
Tel: (202) 224-4944

Gore, who was first elected to the Senate in 1984, ran a protracted campaign for the Democratic Presidential nomination in 1988. He faces re-election in 1990, and is considered a possible contender for the Presidential nomination in 1992. Gore, who served in the House of Representatives from 1976 until 1984, is generally conservative and sympathetic to the Department of Defense. He has a BA from Harvard University.

He serves on the subcommittees for Conventional Forces and Alliance Defense, Defense Industry and Technology, and Projection Forces and Regional Defense. He also sits on the Commerce, Science, and Transportation Committee, the Rules and Administration Committee, and the Joint Printing Committee.

Gore is a member of the Senate Arms Control Observer Group.

Key Aide: Leon Feurth, Legislative Assistant.
(See: The Senate.)

Gramlich, Edward M., Acting Director/Deputy Director, Congressional Budget Office
(See: Congressional Support Agencies.)

Gramm, Phil, Senator (R, Texas), Member of Senate Armed Services Committee
Address: Room SR-370, Russell Senate Office Building, Washington, DC 20510
Tel: (202) 224-2934

Gramm is best known for his part in the Gramm—Rudman Budget Reduction Act, a bill which invoked automatic cuts in the budget (including the military budget) to reduce the deficit. Gramm, a former professor of economics, was elected to the Senate in 1984 after serving six years in the House. He faces re-election in 1990.

A conservative, Gramm is the Ranking Minority Member on the Defense Industry and Technology Subcommittee. He also sits on the Conventional Forces and Alliance Defense Subcommittee and the Readiness, Sustainability and Support Subcommittee. His other committee assignment is on the Banking, Housing, and Urban Affairs Committee.

Gramm is on the Board of Visitors of the US Naval Academy and is co-chairman of the American Security Council.
(See: The Senate.)

Gustavson, Dr Martin R., Member, USAF Scientific Advisory Board
(Lawrence Livermore National Laboratory)
(See: USAF Scientific Advisory Board (Department of the Air Force).)

Hale, Robert F., Assistant Director, National Security Division, Congressional Budget Office
(See: Congressional Support Agencies.)

Hansen, James V. , Representative (R, Utah), 1st District, Member, House Armed Services Committee
Address: 1113 Longworth House Office Building, Washington, DC 20515
Tel: (202) 225-0453

Hansen was elected to the House in 1980. An insurance company executive before his election, he has a BA from the University of Utah. He sits on the subcommittees on Procurement and Military Nuclear Systems, Readiness, and the Acquisition Policy Panel. He is also a member of the executive committee of the House Republican Study Committee.

Key Aide: Kathlenn Gallegos, Chief Legislative Assistant.
(See: The House of Representatives.)

Happer, Dr William J., Member, USAF Scientific Advisory Board
(Professor, Department of Physics, Princeton University)
(See: USAF Scientific Advisory Board (Department of the Air Force).)

Hatch, Monroe W., Jr., General, Vice Chief of Staff, Department of the Air Force

Hatch was appointed Air Force Vice Chief of Staff in February 1987. He entered the US Naval Academy in 1951 and graduated in 1955. He also has an MS in aerospace engineering from the University of Oklahoma, earned in 1969, and completed the National War College in 1974.

After his graduation, Hatch was commissioned in the US Air Force and assigned to the 345th Technical Training Wing for guidance officer training. In 1956, he was transferred to the 587th Tactical Missile Group at Sembach Air Base, West Germany, as a squadron guided missile officer.

Hatch began pilot training in February 1958, and earned his pilot wings in January 1959. After B-47 combat crew training, he was assigned to the 321st Bombardment Wing at McCoy Air Force Base in Florida. In July 1961, he switched to B-52s and was a pilot with the 42nd Bombardment Wing at Loring Air Force Base in Maine.

In July 1964, Hatch was assigned as special projects officer and later programmes officer in the Advanced Technical Division at Strategic Air Command Headquarters. He served there until April 1965, when he became operations staff officer in the Astronautics Technology and Applications Office, under the Deputy Chief of Staff for Plans.

After his graduation from the University of Oklahoma in 1969, Hatch was assigned to the headquarters of the 7th Air Force at Tan Son Nhut Air Base in Vietnam. There he served as a T-39 courier pilot and as 7th Air Force standardization and evaluation flight examiner. On returning to the US in October 1970, Hatch was assigned to the Office of the Secretary of Defense as military assistant for strategic analysis in the office of the Deputy Director for Strategic and Space Systems, Under Secretary of Defense for Research and Engineering. From 1973 to July 1974, he attended the National War College, and then was assigned to the Aircraft Division, Directorate of Operational Requirements and Development, at Air Force Headquarters. In September 1978, Hatch became Deputy Director for Strategic Forces in the office of the Deputy Chief of Staff for Research, Development and Acquisition.

In June 1979, Hatch returned to SAC headquarters as Assistant Deputy Chief of Staff, eventually becoming SAC Chief of Staff in February 1983. He was appointed Inspector General of the Air Force in September 1984, and in August 1985 returned again to SAC, this time as Vice Commander-in-Chief. He was promoted to General on 30 January 1987.
(See: Department of the Air Force.)

Hatfield, Mark O., Senator (R, Oregon), Ranking Minority Member, Senate Appropriationa Committee, Energy and Water Development Subcommittee
Address: Room SH-711, Hart Senate Office Building, Washington, DC 20510
Tel: (202) 224-3753

Hatfield, who faces re-election in 1990, was elected to the Senate in 1966. He has a BA from Williamette University and an MA from Stanford University. From 1943 to 1946, he served in the Naval Reserves. From 1949 until 1956, Hatfield was a faculty member at Williamette University. In 1950, he was elected to the Oregon State House of Representatives, where he served until 1954. He was an Oregon State senator from 1954 to 1956. In 1956, he became Oregon secretary of state, a position he held for two years. From 1958 until his election to the Senate, Hatfield was Governor of Oregon. He is considered a conservative.

Hatfield is also Ranking Minority Member of the Appropriations Committee. He also serves on the Energy and Natural Resources Committee and the Rules and Administration Committee.
(See: The Senate.)

Heart, Frank E., Member, USAF Scientific Advisory Board

(Senior Vice President and Director, Computer Systems Division, BBN Laboratories Inc.)
(See: USAF Scientific Advisory Board (Department of the Air Force).)

Heebner, David R. (Electrical Engineer), Member at Large, Defense Science Board

Heebner is the executive vice-president of Science Applications International Corp. He has been a systems manager with the Hughes Aircraft Company. His government experience includes posts as assistant director of Sea Warfare Systems, office of the Director of Defense Research and Engineering; and Deputy Director of Defense Research and Engineering (Tactical Warfare Programs).
(See: Defense Science Board.)

Hefner, W. G. (Bill), Representative (D, North Carolina), 8th District, Member, House Appropriations Committee, Subcommittee on Defense

Address: 2161 Rayburn House Office Building, Washington, DC 20515
Tel: (202) 225-3715

Hefner was elected to the House in 1974. Prior to his election, he was a broadcasting executive. He only serves on the Appropriations Committee.

Key Aide: Ken Keefe, Associate Staff.
(See: The House of Representatives.)

Heilmeier, George H. (Electrical Engineer), Member at Large, Defense Science Board

Heilmeier holds a Ph.D. from Princeton University and is senior vice-president and chief technical officer, Corporate Research, Development and Engineering, at Texas Instruments Inc. He was a department head at RCA Laboratories; director of the office of Electronics and Physical Sciences in the office of the Director of Defense Research and Engineering; and director of the Defense Advanced Research Projects Agency (DARPA).
(See: Defense Science Board.)

Heiser, Dr William H., Member, USAF Scientific Advisory Board

(Vice President and Director, Propulsion Research Institute, Aerojet General)
(See: USAF Scientific Advisory Board (Department of the Air Force).)

Helm, Robert W., Assistant Secretary of Defense (Comptroller), Office of the Secretary of Defense

Helm was appointed to his current post in August 1984. Helm earned a BA from the University of Wisconsin—LaCrosse in 1973 and a master's from the Fletcher School of Law and Diplomacy. Helm served as the director of Defense Programs and Telecommunications Policy on the National Security Council from 1982 until his appointment as comptroller. Before that, Helm had worked for five years as senior defence analyst on the staff of the Senate Budget Committee. From 1975 until 1978, he was a professional staff member at the Los Alamos Laboratory, during which time he also served as a member of the US negotiating delegation at the arms control talks in Geneva.
(See: Office of the Secretary of Defense (Department of Defense).)

Hermann, Robert J. (Electrical Engineer), Member at Large, Defense Science Board

Hermann is vice-president, Systems Technology and Analysis, with the United Technologies Corporation. He has been assistant secretary of the Air Force and Deputy Under Secretary of Defense for Research and Engineering (C3I). He holds a Ph.D. from Iowa State University.
(See: Defense Science Board.)

Herres, Robert T., General (USAF), Vice Chairman, Joint Chiefs of Staff

Born in 1932, Herres took a BS at the US Naval Academy in 1954 and an MPA from George Washington University in 1965. In 1954 Herres assumed the post of second lieutenant with the USAF. He served with the 93rd Fighter-Interceptor Squadron, Kirtland Air Force Base, New Mexico from 1955 to 1958. He was a technical intelligence analyst, then a flying training superviser, in Europe from 1960 to 1964; a flight crew member with the Manned Orbiting Laboratory programme, in the Air Force Systems Command, Los Angeles, from 1967 to 1969, and a chief, flight crew division, with the same programme in 1969. From 1969 to 1970 he was deputy chief of staff, plans and requirements, at the Flight Test Center, Edwards Air Force Base, California. In 1973 he was commander of the 310th Strategic Wing at U-Tapao Royal Thai Air Force Base in Thailand.

From 1978 to 1979 Herres served as Assistant Chief of Staff, Communications and Computer Resources, USAF Headquarters, Washington and from 1979 to 1985 as Commander, Headquarters, Air Force Communications Command, Scott Air Force Base Illinois. He assumed his current position in 1985.
(See: Joint Chiefs of Staff.)

Herrington John S., Secretary of Energy

Herrington oversees the Department of Energy, including its involvement in defence-related activities. These include the management of the National Laboratories and the development, testing and production of nuclear warheads and reactors for nuclear-powered ships. The DoE also plays a significant role in the Strategic Defense Initiative.

Herrington became the fifth Secretary of Energy in February 1985. He has a BA in economics from Stanford University, earned in 1961, and has received LLB and JD degrees from the University of California Hastings College of Law. Before joining the administration, Herrington practised law in California, specializing in corporate, real estate, tax, and business law. He has been deputy district attorney of Ventura County, California, and a first lieutenant in the Marine Corps Reserves.

In October 1981, Herrington came to Washington as Assistant Secretary of the Navy, a position he held until February 1983. During that time, he was awarded the DoD Distinguished Service Medal. He then moved to the White House as Assistant to the President and Special Assistant to the Chief of Staff.

As Secretary of Energy, Herrington has been enthusiastic about high-risk basic research, and has steered funding in that direction. He is an advocate of the Superconducting Super Collider, a high energy particle accelerator project that is expensive and controversial. Herrington also signed a nuclear cooperation agreement negotiated by the Administration with the People's Republic of China that has been the subject of controversy in the United States.
(See: Department of Energy.)

Hertel, Dennis M. , Representative (D, Michigan), 14th District, Member, House Armed Services Committee
Address: 218 Cannon House Office Building, Washington, DC 20515
Tel: (202) 225-6276

Hertel was elected to the House in 1980. He received a BA from Eastern Michigan University and a JD from Wayne State University. He sits on the subcommittees on Military Installations and Facilities, Research and Development, and on the Acquisition Policy Panel. In addition, Hertel is a member of the Select Committee on Ageing and the Merchant Marine and Fisheries Committee. Hertel is the Michigan Congressional Delegation Whip and a member of the Military Reform Caucus.
(See: The House of Representatives.)

Hochbruekner, George J. , Representative (D, New York), 1st District, Member, House Armed Services Committee
Address: 1008 Longworth House Office Building, Washington, DC 20515
Tel: (202) 225-3826

Hochbruekner, formerly an electronics engineer, was elected to the House in 1986. He sits on the subcommittees on Readiness, Research and Development, and Seapower and Strategic and Critical Materials. He is also a member of the Committee on Science, Space, and Technology. Hochbruekner is a member of both the Arms Control and Foreign Policy Caucus and the Military Reform Caucus.

Key Aide: Victoria Holt, Senior Legislative Assistant.
(See: The House of Representatives.)

Hollings, Ernest F., Senator (D, South Carolina), Member, Senate Appropriations Committee, Defense Subcommittee, Member, Senate Appropriations Committee, Energy and Water Development Subcommittee
Address: Room SR-125, Russell Senate Office Building, Washington, DC 20510
Tel: (202) 224-6121

Hollings was elected to the Senate in 1966, and faces re-election in 1992. He has a BA from The Citadel and an LLB from the University of South Carolina. Hollings served in the Army during World War II. Hollings was Lieutenant-Governor of South Carolina from 1954 until 1958, when he was elected Governor, a post he held until coming to the Senate. He has also been a member of the South Carolina legislature, and served on the Hoover Commission on Intelligence Activities in 1954-55.

Hollinngs also serves on the Budget Committee, the Committee on Commerce, Science and Transportation, and is chairman of the Select Committee on Intelligence. He is known as a conservative Democrat who has an intimate knowledge of the Senate.

Key Aides: Ashley O. Thrift, Administrative Assistant; Linda Belton, Special Assistant.
(See: The Senate.)

Hopkins, Larry J., Representative (R, Kentucky), 6th District, Member, House Armed Services Committee
Address: 2437 Rayburn House Office Building, Washington, DC 20515
Tel: (202) 225-4706

Hopkins was elected to the House in 1978. He holds a BA from Murray State University and was a stockbroker before his election. Hopkins is the Ranking Minority Member of the Investigations Subcommittee, and also sits on the Subcommittee on Procurement and Military Nuclear Systems. His other committee assignment is Agriculture.

Key Aides: Rich Nagel, Legislative Assistant; Andy Vogeslang, Legislative Assistant; Mary Woodward, Legislative Assistant.
(See: The House of Representatives.)

Humphrey, Gordon J., Senator (R, New Hampshire), Member of Senate Armed Services Committee
Address: Room SH-531, Hart Senate Office Building, Washington, DC 20510
Tel: (202) 224-2841

Humphrey was an airline pilot before being elected to the Senate in 1978. He faces reelection in 1990. He has degrees from George Washington University and the University of Maryland. Humphrey, generally considered a strong military supporter, is Ranking Minority Member on the Readiness, Sustainability and Support Subcommittee. He also sits on the Projection Forces and Regional Defense Subcommittee and the Strategic Forces and Nuclear Deterrence Subcommittee. His other committee assignments are Judiciary and Labor and Human Resources.

Key Aide: Ron Kelly, Legislative Assistant.
(See: The Senate.)

Hunter, Duncan L. , Representative (R, California), 45th District, Member, House Armed Services Committee
Address: 133 Cannon House Office Building, Washington, DC 20515
Tel: (202) 225-5672

Hunter was elected to the House in 1981. He holds a JD from Western State University and was an attorney. He sits on the subcommittees on Research and Development and Seapower and Strategic and Critical Materials. Hunter is also a member of the Select Committee on Narcotics Abuse and Control.

Key Aide: Victoria Middleton, Legislative Director.
(See: The House of Representatives.)

Hutto, Earl, Representative (D, Florida), 1st District, Member, House Armed Services Committee
Address: 2435 Rayburn House Office Building, Washington, DC 20515
Tel: (202) 225-4136

Hutto was elected to the House in 1978. He holds a BS from Troy State University. He is chairman of the Special Operations Panel of the Readiness subcommittee, and a member of the Seapower and Strategic and Critical Materials Subcommittee. He also sits on the Merchant Marine and Fisheries Committee. Hutto is a member of the Conservative Democratic Forum.
(See: The House of Representatives.)

Iacobellis, Sam F., President, Aerospace Operations, Rockwell International

Acording to Rockwell International, Aerospace Operations accounts for about one third of Rockwell's sales. It includes North American Aircraft, Rocketdyne Division, Satellite and Space Electronics Division, and the Space Transportation Systems Division (which produced the space shuttle). Aerospace Operations also includes the National AeroSpace

Plane Program and management of the Rocky Flats plant (Colorado), which is part of the Department of Energy complex for producing nuclear warheads.

Iacobellis has a BS in mechanical engineering from California State University—Fresno and an MS in engineering from the University of California—Los Angeles. He joined Rockwell's predecessor, North American Aviation, in 1952 as an aircraft design engineer.

Iacobellis transferred to the Rocketdyne Division in 1957, eventually becoming vice-president of Advanced Programs in that division. In January of 1973, Iacobellis was named president of the Atomics International Group, which expanded to become the Energy Systems Group. He served in this position until 1981, when he joined North American Aerospace Operations (NAAO) as executive vice-president and B-1B Program Manager. He was named president of NAAO in 1984, while continuing with the management of the B-1B programme. He was appointed to his current position in January 1988, at the end of the B-1B production run.

(See: Defence Contractors.)

Inman, Bobby R., Admiral, USN (Retired), Senior Consultant, Defense Science Board

Inman is chairman and chief executive officer of Westmark Systems Inc. He also has been president and chief executive officer at the MCC Corporation. In addition, he has been deputy director of the Central Intelligence Agency, director of the National Security Agency, and vice-director (Plans, Operations, and Support) at the Defense Intelligence Agency.

(See: Defense Science Board.)

Inouye, Daniel K., Senator (D, Hawaii), Member, Senate Appropriations Committee, Defense Subcommittee

Address: Room SH-722, Hart Senate Office Building, Washington, DC 20510

Tel: (202) 224-3934

Inouye, who was elected to the Senate in 1962, is best-known for his role as chairman of the Select Committee on Secret Military Assistance to Iran and the Nicaraguan Resistance, the Iran—Contra Committee. Inouye served in the House from 1958 until his election to the Senate. He holds a BA from the University of Hawaii and a JD from George Washington University. He fought with the US Army in World War II, and was awarded the Distinguished Service Cross, Bronze Star and Purple Heart.

Inouye comes up for re-election in 1992, and it is considered unlikely that he will be unseated. He also serves on the Commerce, Science, and Transportation Committee and the select committee on Indian Affairs.

Key Aide: Frank Kelly, Legislative Assistant.

(See: The Senate.)

Iorello, Anthony J. Member, USAF Scientific Advisory Board (Group Vice President and Manager, Defense Systems Division, Hughes Aircraft Company)

(See: USAF Scientific Advisory Board (Department of the Air Force).)

Ireland, Andy, Representative (R, Florida), 10th District, Member, House Armed Services Committee

Address: 2416 Rayburn House Office Building, Washington, DC 20515

Tel: (202) 225-5015

Ireland, who holds a BS from Yale University, was a banker before his election to the House in 1976. He sits on the subcommittees on Investigations and Procurement and Military Nuclear Systems and the Acquisition Policy Panel. He is also a member of the Small Business Committee.

Key Aides: Elizabeth Mehl, Legislative Director; Joan Galvin, Legislative Assistant.

(See: The House of Representatives.)

Jeffs, George W., Corporate Vice President, Rockwell International, Executive Vice-President for Strategic Defense & Technology, President and Center Director, Strategic Defense Center

Jeffs holds a BS and an MS in aeronautical engineering, both from the University of Washington. He has been with Rockwell since 1947, and his company biography refers to him as 'one of the chief architects of America's accomplishments in space'. In his current position, Jeffs has overall responsibility for all company activities related to advanced defence systems, including all work on SDI.

Jeffs joined Rockwell in 1947 as a member of the Aerophysics Laboratory. He successively became section chief, advanced engineering; section chief, systems engineering; manager, corporate technical development and planning; vice-president and programme manager, paraglider programme; and corporate executive director, engineering.

In 1966, Jeffs joined the space division's Apollo team as assistant programme manager and chief programme engineer. In 1969 he was appointed vice-president and programme manager for Apollo command and service modules (CSM) programme. In 1973, he briefly became executive vice-president of the space division and programme manager of the Space Shuttle. He was appointed president of the space division in April 1974.

Jeffs became a Rockwell corporate officer in April 1976, responsible for directing the space transportation system, the space operations satellite systems, and propulsion divisions. In this post he played a major role in development of the Space Shuttle.

In September 1978, Jeffs became president of North American Aerospace Operations. He was appointed to his current position in 1988. Jeffs' awards include the NASA Distinguished Service Medal (twice), the Presidential Medal of Freedom, the NASA Public Service Award, NASA Certificate of Appreciation, Apollo Lunar Science Community Award and NASA Associate Administrator Commendation. Jeffs also has been a member of the Office of Technology Assessment Advisory Panel on Ballistic Missile Defense.

(See: Defence Contractors.)

Johns, Lionel S., Assistant Director, Energy, Materials, and International Security Division, Office of Technology Assessment

(See: Congressional Support Agencies.)

Jones, Anita K. (Computer Scientist), Member at Large, Defense Science Board

Jones, who holds a Ph.D. from Carnegie-Mellon University, is vice-president of development at Tartan Laboratories Inc. She has been a member of the Air Force Scientific Advisory Board and an associate professor of computer science at Carnegie-Mellon.

(See: Defense Science Board.)

Jones, Donald C., President, Missile Systems Division, Lockheed Missiles and Space Company, Vice-President, Lockheed Corporation

Jones was appointed president of the Missile Systems Division in August 1986. Prior to that he had been the division's vice-president and general manager since February 1986, when he was elected a vice-president of Lockheed Corporation.

Jones has a BS in chemical engineering from Fenn College (now Cleveland State University) and has taken advanced courses at UCLA, Sacramento State University, Northwestern University, and the US Armed Forces Institute. He spent three years in the Navy serving with a Regulus guided missile group as launching officer, personnel officer, and then assistant administrative officer.

After leaving the Navy, Jones came to Lockheed Missiles and Space Company in 1959 as a research specialist. He was promoted over the years, giving him managerial experience in engineering, propulsion and quality control positions.

Jones became deputy programme manager for the Trident I programme in 1978, and a year later director of US Operational Systems. Later in 1979, he was named vice-president of Operations. He became vice-president of engineering 1983.

Jones is a member of the American Institute of Aeronautics and Astronautics, the American Society for Quality Control, the Society of Logistics Engineers, the American Defense Preparedness Association and the Navy League.

(See: Defence Contractors.)

Kasich, John R., Representative (R, Ohio), Member, House Armed Services Committee
Address: 1133 Longworth House Office Building, Washington, DC 20515
Tel: (202) 225-5355

Kasich was elected to the House in 1982, having served previously in the Ohio Senate from 1979. He has a BA from Ohio State University. Kasich is the Ranking Minority Member of the Readiness Subcommittee, and also sits on the Investigations Subcommittee. He is a member of the Republican Committee on Committees.

Key Aide: Mike Lofgren, Legislative Assistant.
(See: The House of Representatives.)

Kasten, Robert W., Jr., Senator (R, Wisconsin), Member, Senate Appropriations Committee, Defense Subcommittee
Address: Room SH-110, Hart Senate Office Building, Washington, DC 20510
Tel: (202) 224-5323

Kasten was elected to the Senate in 1980, and faces re-election in 1992. He earned his BA from the University of Arizona, and his MBA from Columbia University. He has served both in the Wisconsin Air National Guard and the US Air Force. He was a Wisconsin State senator from 1972 until 1974, when he was elected to the US House of Representatives, where he served until his Senate election.

In addition to the Appropriations Committee, Kasten also sits on the Budget Committee, the Commerce, Science and Transportation Committee, and the Small Business Committee.

Key Aide: Jim Morhand, Legislative Assistant.
(See: The Senate.)

Katzen, Jack, Assistant Secretary of Defense (Production and Logistics), Office of the Secretary of Defense

Katzen graduated from the Carnegie Institute of Technology in 1942 with a BS. He held various positions at General Electric from 1956 until 1978, including that of general manager of Special Systems (1968—69), general manager of Advanced Programs (1969—71), manager of Strategic Planning and Review (1971—72), and manager of Far East Programs (1972—78). From 1978 until 1986, Katzen was corporate vice-president for the Avco Corporation, a defence contractor. In 1986, Katzen was appointed Deputy Assistant Secretary of Defense (systems), where he remained until his appointment as Assistant Secretary in January 1988.
(See: Office of the Secretary of Defense (Department of Defense).)

Kennedy, Edward M., Senator (D, Massachusetts), Member, Senate Armed Services Committee
Address: Room SR-315, Russell Senate Office Building, Washington, DC 20510
Tel: (202) 224-4543

Kennedy faces re-election in 1988, but should win easily. A liberal, Kennedy was elected to the Senate in 1962. He has made several unsuccessful tries for the Democratic presidential nomination, and many no longer consider him to have a significant chance for the presidency. An attorney before his election, Kennedy earned his BA from Harvard University and his LLB from the University of Virginia. On the Armed Services Committee, Kennedy is chairman of the Projection Forces and Regional Defense Subcommittee, and also serves on the subcommittees on Manpower and Personnel and Strategic Forces and Nuclear Deterrence. He is also a member of the Judiciary Committee and the Joint Economic Committee, and is the chairman of the Labor and Human Resources Committee.

Kennedy is a member of the Democratic Steering Committee and the Senate Arms Control Observer Group. He is also on the board of directors of the Office of Technology Assessment.

Key Aides: Bill Lynn, Legislative Assistant; Nancy Soderberg, Legislative Assistant.
(See: The Senate.)

Kerr, Donald M., Director, Los Alamos National Scientific Laboratory

Kerr, who assumed his post in 1979, is only the fourth director of Los Alamos. Previously, Kerr worked in the Department of Energy, including a stint as acting Assistant Secretary in the Office of Defense Programs. From 1966 until 1976, when he joined the Department of Energy, Kerr was employed at Los Alamos in a variety of positions. Originally, he was employed with the High Altitude Phenomenology Group, going on to become Assistant Division Leader for Field Tests and in 1975, Leader of the Energy Division. Kerr, who has a BS and an MS, earned his Ph.D. from Cornell University in 1966.

(See: Department of Energy.)

Kerrebrock, Professor Jack L., Member, USAF Scientific Advisory Board

(Associate Dean of Engineering, Massachusetts Institute of Technology)

(See: USAF Scientific Advisory Board (Department of the Air Force).)

Key, Edwin L., Member, USAF Scientific Advisory Board

(Senior Vice-President for Research and Engineering, The MITRE Corporation)

(See: USAF Scientific Advisory Board (Department of the Air Force).)

Kidd, Isaac C., Jr., Admiral, USN (Retired), Member at Large, Defense Science Board

Kidd graduated from the US Naval Academy and is now a private consultant. He has been chief of Naval Material and Commander-in-Chief of the Atlantic Fleet.

(See: Defense Science Board.)

Kitchen, Lawrence A., Chairman and Chief Executive Officer, Lockheed Corporation

Kitchen has been chairman and chief executive officer of Lockheed since 1 January 1986. Prior to that, he served ten years as the corporation's president and chief operating officer. He was elected to the board of directors in 1975.

Kitchen has a degree from Foothill College in California. During World War II, he served with the Marine Corps in aviation engineering maintenance. From 1946 to 1958, Kitchen was with the US Navy Bureau of Aeronautics in Washington, DC. During this time, he was designated an aeronautical engineer by the US Civil Service Commission.

In 1958, Kitchen began his career with Lockheed at Lockheed Missiles and Space Company. He advanced through a series of management positions before becoming manager of programme management controls at the Missile Systems Division in 1966. From 1968 to 1970, he was director of financial management controls for Lockheed Missiles and Space.

Kitchen moved to Lockheed—Georgia in 1970 as vice-president for finance and administration. He became president of Lockheed—Georgia in 1971.

Kitchen is a member of the American Institute of Aeronautics and Astronautics, the Navy League, the American Defense Preparedness Association, the National Management Association, the National Defense Transportation Association, the Association of the US Army, and the National Aeronautics Association. He is a member of the board of governors of the Aerospace Industries Association and a member of the Department of Defense Policy Advisory Committee on Trade. He is also a director of the Security Pacific Corporation.

(See: Defence Contractors.)

Koff, Bernard L., Member, USAF Scientific Advisory Board

(Senior Vice President, ITEK Optical Systems, Litton Corporation)

(See: USAF Scientific Advisory Board (Department of the Air Force).)

Kopf, Eugene, Member, USAF Scientific Advisory Board

(Senior Vice President, Rsearch and Business

Development, ITEK Optical Systems, Litton Corporation)
(See: USAF Scientific Advisory Board (Department of the Air Force).)

Kresa, Kent (Industrialist), Member at Large, Defense Science Board, Member, USAF Scientific Advisory Board

Kresa is president and chief operating officer of the Northrop Corporation, a large defence contractor. Formerly, he was group vice-president, Aircraft Group, Northrop, vice-president and general manager, Ventura Division, Northrop, and vice-president and manager, Northrop Research and Technology Center.
(See: Defense Science Board; USAF Scientific Advisory Board (Department of the Air Force).)

Krings, John E., Director, Operational Test and Evaluation, Office of the Secretary of Defense

Krings was appointed to this post when it was created in February 1985. He holds BS degrees in physics and chemistry from Louisiana State University, both of which he received in 1952. He was in the Reserve Officer's Training Program (ROTC) at Louisiana State and was commissioned in the US Air Force on graduation. He served in the Air Force until 1956 as a fighter pilot.

In 1956 he joined McDonnell-Douglas, the aerospace corporation and defence contractor, as a test pilot. From 1956 until 1960, he also served in the Air National Guard as pilot. In 1960, Krings attended the US Navy test pilot school, returning to McDonnell-Douglas to work in the F-4 Phantom development programme. He tested all models of the F-14 (fighter plane) and participated in the design and development of the F-15 Eagle. Krings received the Society of Experimental Test Pilots, 'Test Pilot of the Year Award' in 1975 for the spin tests on the F-15. In 1978, he flew the first flight of the F-18 Hornet.

In 1980, Krings became the director of flight operations for McDonnell-Douglas. He left this position in 1983 to become director of the United States Navy—United States Marine Corps Program at McDonnell-Douglas, a position he held until his appointment to the Department of Defense.
(See: Office of the Secretary of Defense (Department of Defense).)

Kurland, Dr Leonard T., Member, USAF Scientific Advisory Board
(Professor and Chairman, Department of Medical Statistics and Epidemiology, Mayo Clinic)
(See: USAF Scientific Advisory Board (Department of the Air Force).)

Kyl, Jon, Representative (R, Arizona), 4th District, Member, House Armed Services Committee
Address: 313 Cannon House Office Building, Washington, DC 20515
Tel: (202) 225-3361

Kyl, an attorney who holds a BA and an LLB from the University of Arizona, was elected in 1986. He sits on the Investigation and Military Personnel and Compensation subcommittees.

Key Aide: Jeff Schwartz, Legislative Assistant.
(See: The House of Representatives.)

Landicho, John, Senior Associate Director, Dept. of the Navy, General Accounting Office
(See: Congressional Support Agencies.)

Leahy, Patrick J., Senator (D, Vermont), Member, Senate Appropriations Committee, Defense Subcommittee
Address: Room SR-433, Russell Senate Office Building, Washington, DC 20510
Tel: (202) 224-4242

Leahy, who was elected to the Senate in 1974, is known mostly for his work on the Judiciary Committee. He faces re-election in 1992. He is considered liberal, and is generally outspoken. He has a BA from St Michael's College and a JD from Georgetown University Law Center. He was an attorney before coming to the Senate.

Leahy also sits on the Judiciary Committee and the Committee on Agriculture, Nutrition and Forestry.

Key Aide: Eric Newsome, Legislative Director.
(See: The Senate.)

Leath, Marvin, Representative (D, Texas), 11th District, Member, House Armed Services Committee
Address: 336 Cannon House Office Building, Washington, DC 20515
Tel: (202) 225-6105

Leath, who holds a BBA from the University of Texas, was elected to the House in 1978. He is a member of the Conservative Democratic Forum. He sits on the subcommittees on Military Installations and Facilities, Procurement and Military Nuclear Systems, and Readiness. He is also a member of the Budget Committee.

Key Aides: Doug Canatsey, Administrative Assistant; Jeff Bowden, Legislative Aide.
(See: The House of Representatives.)

Lederberg, Joshua (Geneticist), Member at Large, Defense Science Board

President of Rockefeller University, Lederberg holds a Ph.D. from Yale University. He is a Nobel Laureate in Medicine and chairman of the Department of Genetics at both Stanford University and the University of Wisconsin.
(See: Defense Science Board.)

Lehman, Ronald F., Assistant Secretary of Defense, (International Security Policy)

Before assuming his present position, Lehman was the Deputy Assistant Secretary of Defense for Strategic and Theater Nuclear Forces. Lehman received his BA from Claremont Men's College in 1968 and his Ph.D. from Claremont Graduate School in 1975. He saw combat in Vietnam, and was a major in the US Army, Military Intelligence Branch.

He has been involved in arms control negotiations in Geneva. He was a Public Affairs Fellow at the Hoover Institute on War, Revolution, and Peace, a conservative think-tank. Lehman has served in several Congressional posts. He has been a legislative assistant for Senator Dewey Bartlett of Oklahoma, a consultant to several other senators, and a member of the professional staff of the Senate Committee on Armed Services. In addition, he worked in the office of policy co-ordination of the office of the President-elect, Ronald Reagan.
(See: Office of the Secretary of Defense (Department of Defense).)

Levin, Carl, Senator (D, Michigan), Member, Senate Armed Services Committee
Address: Room SR-459, Russell Senate Office Building, Washington, DC 20510
Tel: (202) 224-6221

Levin, who was first elected to the Senate in 1978, survived a tough election challenge in 1984 from Jack Lousma, and faces re-election in 1990. He has a BA from Swarthmore College and a JD from Harvard University. Before coming to the Senate, he was a civil rights lawyer and member of the city council in Detroit. He is considered a liberal, and is often critical of the Department of Defense. He has strongly opposed the B-1 bomber and the MX missile. Levin is chairman of the Conventional Forces and Alliance Defense Subcommittee, and also a member of the subcommittees on Readiness, Sustainability and Support and Strategic Forces and Nuclear Deterrence. His other committee assignments are Governmental Affairs (where he is chairman of the Oversight of Government Management Subcommittee) and Small Business. A member of the board of visitors of the US Military Academy, Levin is also on the Steering Committee of the Arms Control and Foreign Policy Caucus.

Key Aides: Chuck Cutolo, Legislative Director; Greg Weaver, Legislative Assistant.
(See: The Senate.)

Lewis, Harold (Physicist), Senior Consultant, Defense Science Board

A professor of physics at the University of California at Santa Barbara, Lewis earned his Ph.D. at the University of California at

Berkeley. He has been a professor of physics at the University of Wisconsin. He was a member of the Advisory Committee on Reactor Safeguards at the Nuclear Regulatory Committee and a member of Technical Staff at Bell Laboratories.
(See: Defense Science Board.)

Little, Robert C., Vice-Chairman—Government Business, McDonnell Douglas Corporation

Little, who earned a BS in mechanical engineering from Texas A & M, has also been with McDonnell Douglas throughout his career. During World War II, Little served with the Army Air Corps, flying sixty-eight combat missions as a P-51 Mustang pilot.

After graduation in 1948, Little went to work for the McDonnell Aircraft Company as a flight test engineer. He also became an experimental test pilot and eventually chief test pilot. In 1960, Little became Program Manager for the F-4 Phantom, remaining in the post for four years.

In 1964, he was appointed director of sales for McDonnell Aircraft, and in 1968 became vice-president (marketing). Little came to the corporate office of McDonnell Douglas in 1972 as corporate vice-president (marketing). In 1973, he was elected to the board of directors. Little became corporate vice-president (engineering and marketing) in 1977. In 1980, he became corporate vice-president (operations and marketing). In 1984, Little became corporate vice-president—aerospace group executive, where he remained until assuming his current post in 1988.
(See: Defence Contractors.)

Livingston, Bob, Representative (R, Louisiana), 1st District, Member, House Appropriations Committee, Subcommittee on Defense
Address: 2412 Rayburn House Office Building, Washington, DC 20515
Tel: (202) 225-3015

Livingston was elected to the House in 1976. He has a BA and a JD from Tulane University, and also graduated from the Loyola Institute of Economics. Before studying at university, from 1961 to 1963, Livingston served in the Navy. He started practising law in 1968. He was assistant US attorney from 1970 to 1973, and chief special prosecutor in the Orleans parish District Attorney's office from 1974 to 1975. From 1975 until his House election, he was chief prosecutor in the Louisiana Attorney General's office.

Livingtson is also a member of the Select Committee on Intelligence.

Key Aide: Paul Cambon, Legislative Assistant.
(See: The House of Representatives.)

Lloyd, Marilyn, Representative (D, Tennessee), 3rd District, Member, House Armed Services Committee
Address: 2266 Rayburn House Office Building, Washington, DC 20515
Tel: (202) 225-3271

Lloyd, elected to the House in 1974, was a radio station executive before her election. She sits on the Subcommittee on Procurement and Military Nuclear Systems. Her other committee assignments are the Science, Space, and Technology Committee and the Select Committee on Ageing. Lloyd is a member of the Conservative Democratic Forum.

Key Aide: Steven Wright, Legislative Assistant.
(See: The House of Representatives.)

Lucky, Robert W. (Electrical Engineer), Ex-Officio Member, Defense Science Board, Chairman, USAF Scientific Advisory Board

Lucky has a Ph.D. from Purdue University. Currently, he is executive director, Research Communications Sciences Division, AT & T Bell Laboratories. He has also been director of the Electronic and Computer Systems Research Laboratory at Bell Labs.
(See: Defense Science Board; USAF Scientific Advisory Board (Department of the Air Force).)

McCain, John, Senator (R, Arizona), Member of Senate Armed Services Committee

Address: Room SR-111, Russell Senate Office Building, Washington, DC 20510
Tel: (202) 224-2235

McCain was elected to the Senate in 1986 and faces re-election in 1992. He served in the House of Representatives from 1982 to 1986. McCain received his BS from the US Naval Academy and was a combat pilot in Vietnam. He was shot down by the North Vietnamese in 1967 and spent the next six years as a prisoner of war before being released in 1973. There is a memorial in Vietnam marking the spot where he was captured. McCain sits on the Manpower and Personnel Subcommittee, the Projection Forces and Regional Defense Subcommittee, and the Readiness, Sustainability and Support Subcommittee. He is considered a strong military supporter. McCain's other committee assignments are on the Commerce, Science, and Transportation Subcommittee and the Select Committee on Indian Affairs. He is also a Deputy Minority Whip.

Key Aide: Pat Putignano, Legislative Assistant.
(See: The Senate.)

McCloskey, Frank, Representative (D, Indiana), 8th District, Member, House Armed Services Committee
Address: 127 Cannon House Office Building, Washington, DC 20515
Tel: (202) 225-4636

McCloskey, who has a BA and a JD from the University of Indiana, was elected to the House in 1982. He sits on the Investigations and Research and Development subcommittees. His other committee assignment is Post Office and Civil Service. McCloskey is a member of the Arms Control and Foreign Policy Caucus and the Military Reform Caucus.

Key Aide: Linda Tanzini, Legislative Assistant.
(See: The House of Representatives.)

McClure, James A. , Senator (R, Idaho), Member, Senate Appropriations Committee, Defense Subcommittee, Member, Senate Appropriations Committee, Energy and Water Development Subcommittee
Address: Room SH-309, Hart Senate Office Building, Washington, DC 20510
Tel: (202) 224-2752

McClure, who faces re-election in 1990, was elected to the Senate in 1972. He received his JD from the University of Idaho. He served in the US Navy from 1942 to 1946. He was prosecuting attorney of Payette County from 1950 to 1956, and served in the Idaho state Senate from 1960 to 1966, where he was Assistant Majority Leader in 1965—66. McClure was also chairman of the Idaho State Republican Committee in 1962. He was elected to the House of Representatives in 1966, and served there until his election to the Senate.

McClure was a member of the Iran—Contra Committee and also sits on the Energy and Natural Resources Committee and the Rules and Administration Committee.

Key Aide: Peter Flory, Legislative Assistant.
(See: The Senate.)

McCurdy, Dave, Representative (D, Oklahoma), 4th District, Member, House Armed Services Committee
Address: 409 Cannon House Office Building, Washington, DC 20515
Tel: (202) 225-6165

McCurdy was elected to the House in 1980. He was an attorney before his election, and has earned a BA and a JD from the University of Oklahoma. He is a member of the subcommittees on Military Installations and Facilities, Research and Development, and the Acquisition Policy Panel. He is also a member of the Select Committee on Intelligence and the Space, Science and Technology Committee. McCurdy is also a member of the House Democratic Steering and Policy Committee.

Key Aides: Howard Yourman, Chief Legislative Assistant; John Cuaderes, Legislative Assistant.
(See: The House of Representatives.)

McDade, Joseph M., Representative (R, Pennsylvania), 10th District, Member, House

Appropriations Committee, Subcommittee on Defense
Address: 2370 Rayburn House Office Building, Washington, DC 20515
Tel: (202) 225-3731

McDade was elected to the House in 1962. He has a BA from the University of Notre Dame and an LLB from the University of Pennsylvania. Before being elected to the House, McDade was an attorney. He is also Ranking Minority Member of the Committee on Small Business.

Key Aide: Deborah Weatherly, Administrative Assistant.
(See: The House of Representatives.)

McDivitt, James A., Senior Vice President, Government Operations, Rockwell International

McDivitt was appointed to his current position in January 1988. He has a BS in aeronautical engineering from the University of Michigan, earned in 1959. McDivitt joined the US Air Force in 1951 and was commissioned in 1952. He flew 145 combat missions during the Korean War, earning numerous decorations. He graduated from the US Air Force Experimental Test Pilot School in 1960.

In 1962, McDivitt was assigned to NASA as an astronaut. He was command pilot for Gemini IV in 1965, and commanded Apollo IX in 1969, establishing six world records for space flight. Later in 1969, he became Apollo Spacecraft Program Manager, with responsibility for Apollos 12—16. He retired from the Air Force in 1972 as a brigadier general.

After retiring from the Air Force, McDivitt became executive vice-president and a director of Consumer's Power Company of Jackson, Michigan. In 1975, he left to become executive vice-president of Pullman Inc. in Chicago.

McDivitt came to Rockwell in January 1981 as vice-president of strategic management. He has also been executive vice-president, electronic operations; executive vice-president, defense electronic operations; and senior vice-president of science and technology.
(See: Defence Contractors.)

McDonnell, John Finney, Chairman and Chief Executive Officer, McDonnell Douglas Corporation

McDonnell, who was elected chairman and chief executive of McDonnell Douglas in 1988, has been with the company throughout his career. He has a BS and an MS in aeronautical engineering from Princeton University.

After receiving his MS in 1962, McDonnell worked as a strength engineer with McDonnell Aircraft Company, a subsidiary of McDonnell Douglas. In 1963, he became a corporation analyst. He stayed in this position for two years, until 1965, before becoming a contract coordinator and administrator.

In 1968, McDonnell briefly moved to the Douglas Aircraft Company, another subsidiary, as assistant to the vice-president (finance). Later in 1968, he became vice-president of the McDonnell Douglas Finance Company.

McDonnell moved to the corporate office of McDonnell Douglas in 1971, becoming a staff vice-president (fiscal). In 1972, he was appointed corporate vice-president (finance and planning). In 1973, he was elected a director of the company by the board of directors, and was elected to the board's executive committee in 1975. Also in 1975, McDonnell became corporate vice-president (finance and development).

In 1977, McDonnell became corporate executive vice-president, and was elected president of McDonnell Douglas in 1980. In 1987, he also assumed the post of chief operating officer. He remained as president and chief operating officer before his election as chairman and chief executive officer in 1988. McDonnell serves on the board of trustees for Washington University and on the board of commissioners of the St Louis Science Center.
(See: Defence Contractors.)

McGovern, James F., Under Secretary of the Air Force

McGovern received his BS in engineering from the US Naval Academy in 1969 and his JD from the Georgetown University Law Center in 1978. He was appointed Under Secretary of the Air Force in November 1986.

After graduating from the Naval Academy, McGovern served as an active duty Navy fighter pilot until 1979, logging more than 2,000 flying hours. In 1979, after receiving his law degree, McGovern joined the law firm of Dickstein, Shapiro and Morin, where he specialized in corporate finance, particularly corporate mergers and asset acquisitions. In 1981, McGovern was appointed as general counsel to the Senate Committee on Armed Services, under the chairmanship of Senator John Tower (R, Texas). He became staff director and chief counsel to the committee in 1982, where he remained until his appointment as Under Secretary. McGovern is a member of the Marine Corps Reserve, and flies an F-4 Phantom operating out of Andrews Air Force Base. He is also qualified to fly the Air Force F-15 Eagle.

(See: Department of the Air Force.)

Marsh, John O. Jr., The Secretary of the Army

Marsh has set a record for time spent in office. Most secretaries have had relatively short terms, but Marsh has served since he was sworn in as the fourteenth Secretary of the Army on 30 January 1981.

Marsh, born in Virginia in 1926, entered the Army after graduating from high school in 1944. He attended infantry officer candidate school and was commissioned as a lieutenant in 1945, seeing active duty with the United States occupation forces in Germany. After leaving the Army, Marsh received his LLB from Washington and Lee University in Virginia in 1951. He was admitted to the Virginia Bar and practised law for twelve years in Strasburg, Virginia.

Marsh was elected to the US House of Representatives in 1963, serving four terms as a Democrat from Virginia's 7th District. He was a member of the House Appropriations Committee during that time. In 1971, after choosing not to run for a fifth term, Marsh opened a law office in Washington, DC.

Marsh became Assistant Secretary of Defense for Legislative Affairs in March 1973, and served in that post until January 1974, when he became Vice-President Ford's assistant for national security affairs. After Ford became President, Marsh was appointed counsellor, with cabinet rank, in August 1974. He remained in that position until President Carter took office in January 1977.

Marsh returned to private practice until his appointment as Secretary of Defense. From 1951 until 1976, Marsh served with the Virginia National Guard. He retired in 1976 with the rank of lieutenant-colonel. He has been awarded the Department of Defense Distinguished Public Service Medal, the American Legion Distinguished Public Service Medal, and the National Guard Distinguished Service Award.

(See: Department of the Army.)

Martin, David, Representative (R, New York), 26th District, Member, House Armed Services Committee

Address: 442 Cannon House Office Building, Washington, DC 20515
Tel: (202) 225-4611

Martin, who has a BA from the University of Notre Dame and a JD from Albany Law School, was an attorney before his election to the House in 1980. He is Ranking Minority Member of the Military Installations and Facilities Subcommittee, and also sits on the Readiness Subcommittee. Martin is a member of the Defense Reform Task Force of the Republican Research Committee and a member of the American Security Council.

(See: The House of Representatives.)

Martin, Lynn M., Representative (R, Illinois), 16th District, Member, House Armed Services Committee

Address: 1208 Longworth House Office Building, Washington, DC, 20515
Tel: (202) 225-5676

An English teacher with a BA from the University of Illinois, Martin was elected to the House in 1980. She sits on the Military Installations and Facilities and Research and Development subcommittees. Martin is also vice-chairperson of the House Republican Conference.

Key Aides: Fran McNaught, Administrative Assistant; John Anelli, Legislative Assistant.

(See: The House of Representatives.)

Math, Paul F., Associate Director-in-Charge, Research, Development, Acquistion and General Procurement, General Accounting Office
(See: Congressional Support Agencies.)

Mavroules, Nicholas, Representative (D, Massachusetts), 6th District, Member, House Armed Services Committee
Address: 2432 Rayburn House Office Building, Washington, DC 20515
Tel: (202) 225-8020

Mavroules was elected to the House in 1978. He is chairman of the Acquisition Policy Panel, and a member of the Investigations and Procurement and Military Nuclear Systems subcommittees. He is also a Congressional observer to the Geneva arms talks. His other committee assignment is the Small Business Committee. He is considered somewhat conservative.

Key Aides: Scott Parven, Legislative Assistant; Grace Pearson Waters, Legislative Assistant.
(See: The House of Representatives.)

Mayer, John, Deputy Assistant Director for Weapons Analysis, Congressional Budget Office
(See: Congressional Support Agencies.)

Meyers, John T., Representative (R, Indiana), 7th District, Ranking Minority Leader, Member, House Appropriations Committee, Subcommittee on Energy and Water Development
Address: 2372 Rayburn House Office Building, Washington, DC 20515
Tel: (202) 225-5805

Meyers was elected to the House in 1966. He has a BS from Indiana State University. Myers served in the Army from 1945 to 1946. From 1954 until his election to the House, Meyers worked as a trust officer for the Fountain Trust Company in Indiana. He also serves on the Post Office and Civil Service Committee and the Committee on Standards of Official Conduct.

Key Aide: David McCarthy, Legislative Assistant.
(See: The House of Representatives.)

Miller, Clarence E., Representative (R, Ohio), 10th District, Member, House Appropriations Committee, Subcommittee on Defense
Address: 2208 Rayburn House Office Building, Washington, DC 20515
Tel: (202) 225-5131

Miller was elected to the House in 1966. He was city councilman in Lancaster, Ohio, from 1957 to 1963, and mayor of Lancaster from 1963 until his election to the House. He sits on no other committees.

Key Aide: Connie Wilcox, Associate Staff.
(See: The House of Representatives.)

Miller, James C., III, Director, Office of Management and Budget

Miller, who took over the post in January of 1986, is viewed in the shadow cast by David Stockman and the book Stockman wrote entitled *The Triumph of Politics*. The *Washington Post*'s national weekly edition headlined an article on Miller with 'The Man Who Isn't David Stockman'. This is a fair assesment, since Miller has neither the knowledge nor the influence that Stockman brought to the job in 1981.

Miller, 45, holds a BA from the University of Georgia. He also received a Ph.D. in economics from the University of Virginia in 1969. He came to Washington shortly thereafter, working in the Department of Transportation. After that, he worked brief stints in the Brookings Institution and the American Enterprise Institute, both policy think-tanks. Miller then moved on to Texas A & M University, where he was an associate professor of economics. During this time, Miller wrote a book on airline deregulation, charging that government regulations led to higher rates, which brought him to the attention of figures in the Reagan Administration. On the recommendation of White House economic adviser Murray Weidenbaum, Miller was brought in to be director of the Office

of Government Procurement Policy at the Office of Management and Budget (OMB). Shortly thereafter, Miller became head of the Federal Trade Commission (FTC) to which he brought a firm belief in the power of the free market. A former chairman of the FTC has charged that while at the FTC Miller was responsible for 'the dismantlement of a great agency'.In 1986, Miller moved back to OMB as Director. He has not had good relations with the press, in contrast to Stockman, who used the press as a political weapon during his tenure.
(See: President and Executive Office of President.)

Miller, Mark K. (Mechanical Engineer), Member at Large, Defense Science Board

Miller is president of the Boeing Aerospace Company, a large defence contractor. He has been vice-president and general manager of Space and Information Systems at Boeing, and also executive vice-president of Program Management.
(See: Defense Science Board; Defence Contractors.)

Mills, Dr Harlan D., Member, USAF Scientific Advisory Board
(Director of Software Engineering and Technology, IBM Corporation)
(See: USAF Scientific Advisory Board (Department of the Air Force).)

Mitchell, Dr Jere H., Member, USAF Scientific Advisory Board
(Professor of Medicine and Psychology, Southwestern Medical School, University of Texas)
(See: USAF Scientific Advisory Board (Department of the Air Force).)

Montgomery, G. V. (Sonny), Representative (D, Mississippi), 3rd District, Member, House Armed Services Committee
Address: 2184 Rayburn House Office Building, Washington, DC 20515
Tel: (202) 225-5031

Montgomery was elected to the House in 1967. Before that, he was an insurance company executive. He holds a BS from Mississippi State University. He sits on the Millitary Installations and Facilities Subcommittee and the Military Personnel and Compensation Subcommittee. Montgomery is also a member of the Veterans' Affairs Committee. He is also a member of the Democratic Conservative Forum and co-chairman of the Coalition for Peace Through Strength.
(See: The House of Representatives.)

Moore, Robert A., Deputy Director for Technology, Defense Advanced Research Projects Agency (DARPA)
(See: Defense Agencies.)

Morrow, Walter E., Jr. (Electrical Engineer), Member at Large, Defense Science Board, Member, USAF Scientific Advisory Board, Director, MIT Lincoln Laboratory

Morrow holds an MS from MIT. He has been a professor of electrical engineering at MIT, and also associate director of Lincoln Laboratory.
(See: Defense Science Board; USAF Scientific Advisory Board (Department of the Air Force).)

Murray, Dr Dennis P., Member, USAF Scientific Advisory Board
(Head, Radar & Communications Systems Department, R&D Associates)
(See: USAF Scientific Advisory Board (Department of the Air Force).)

Murtha, John P., Representative (D, Pennsylvania), 12th, District, Member, House Appropriations Committee, Subcommittee on Defense
Address: 2423 Rayburn House Office Building, Washington, DC 20515
Tel: (202) 225-2065

Murtha was elected to the House in 1974. He has a BA from the University of Pittsburgh. He served in the US Marines during the Korean

War, and volunteered for a tour of duty in Vietnam (1966—67), where he was awarded the Bronze Star, two Purple Hearts and the Vietnamese Cross of Gallantry. Murtha was also a commander in the Marine Reserve Corps. From 1969 until his election to the House, he was a Pennsylvania State Representative.

Key Aide: Carmen Scialabba, Associate Staff.
(See: The House of Representatives.)

Naka, Dr Robert F., Member, USAF Scientific Advisory Board
(Vice President, Engineering and Planning, GTE Government Systems Corporation)
(See: USAF Scientific Advisory Board (Department of the Air Force.)

Nichols, Bill, Representative (D, Alabama), 3rd District, Member, House Armed Services Committee
Address: 2405 Rayburn House Office Building, Washington, DC 20515
Tel: (202) 225-3261

Nichols, who began his House service in 1967, is widely credited with helping to push through the Department of Defense Reorganization Act of 1986, which he also helped to write. He has a BS and an MA from Auburn University, and was a businessman before entering the House. A fairly conservative Democrat, he is chairman of the Investigations Subcommittee. Nichols is also a member of the Conservative Democratic Forum.
(See: The House of Representatives.)

Nunn, Sam, Senator (D, Georgia) Chairman, Senate Armed Services Committee
Address: Room SD-303, Dirksen Senate Office Building, Washington, DC 20510
Tel: (202) 224-3521

Nunn was first elected to the Senate in 1972. He does not face re-election until 1992. He is one of the most knowledgeable and influential senators on defence issues, and his name has come up frequently as a possible Secretary of Defense if the next administration is Democratic. There was also discussion of Nunn running as Vice-President with Michael Dukakis. Since Nunn is a southerner, and considered somewhat conservative, there has also been discussion of him running for the Presidency in 1992; there was also speculation that he would try for it in 1988.

Nunn has both a BA and an LLB from Emory University, and was a farmer and attorney before coming to the Senate. His appointment as Armed Services Committee chairman in 1985 was seen as a turning point for the committee, and it was thought that the committee would be willing thereafter to listen to more dissenting voices. While this has been true, most observers regard the committee as still solidly pro-Department of Defense.

Nunn is a strong supporter of military, but is also willing to question and criticize the Department of Defense. He is an opponent of the MX missile, a strong advocate of the Midgetman missile, and supported and opposed the B-1 at different points in its development.

As chairman of the Armed Services Committee, Nunn is an ex-officio member of all its subcommittees. Nunn also serves on the Governmental Affairs Committee, where he is chairman of the Permanent Subcommittee on Investigations. He is also on the Small Business Committee and the Select Committee on Intelligence. Further, Nunn is on the Senate Democratic Steering Committee, a member of the Military Reform Caucus, and co-chairman of the Senate Arms Control Observer Group. He is also director of the Democratic Leadership Council and cochairman of the Council's National Defense Strategy Task Force.

Key Aides: Jim Llewellen, Legislative Director; Bob Bayer, Legislative Assistant.
(See: The Senate.)

Ortiz, Solomon P., Representative (D, Texas), 27th District, Member, House Armed Services Committee
Address: 1525 Longworth House Office Building, Washington, DC 20515
Tel: (202) 225-7742

Ortiz was in law enforcement before being elected to the House in 1982. He sits on the subcommittees on Investigations, Military Installations and Facilities, and Seapower and Strategic and Critical Materials.

Key Aide: Robert Flint, Legislative Assistant.
(See: The House of Representatives.)

Padden, Maurice C., Major-General, Commander, Air Force Space Command

Padden became Commander of the USAF Space Command, headquartered at Peterson Air Force Base in Colorado, in October 1986. He has received a BA in English from Ohio State University in 1952 and an MA in counselling and guidance from Troy State University in 1974. He has also completed Squadron Officer School, Armed Forces Staff College, and the Air War College.

Padden joined the Air Force in 1953, and received his commission as a first lieutenant in 1954. From April 1954 to April 1958 he served as a navigation instructor at Ellington Air Force Base, Texas.

In May 1958, Padden entered B-47 navigator training, and was then assigned to the 340th Bombardment Wing at Whiteman Air Force Base, where he served as a combat crew member and wing staff officer until September 1963. He was then assigned to the 43rd Bombardment Wing as a B-58 Navigator.

Padden was assigned to SAC Headquarters in July 1965, where he served as test director for Automated Command and Control Systems and later as Deputy Chief of Staff for Operations. He graduated from Armed Forces Staff College in 1968 and briefly returned to SAC. In 1969, he was assigned as a B-52 strike planner at Tan Son Nhut Air Base in Vietnam.

Returning to the United States in July 1970, Padden was assigned as an aide-de-camp to the Air University Commander at Maxwell Air Force Base in California, and then served as executive officer from July 1971 to July 1973. After graduating from the Air War College in 1974, he served as deputy base commander at Norton Air Force Base and later Travis Air Force Base, both in California.

From February 1976 to June 1978, Padden served as Base Commander of Scott Air Force Base in Illinois before becoming Commander of the 443rd Military Airlift Wing at Altus Air Force Base, Oklahoma. He came to Washington in May 1980 as Deputy Director of Operations, National Military Command System, Organization of the Joint Chiefs of Staff, becoming Vice Director of Operations in 1983. In August 1985, Padden was assigned as Vice Commander in Chief of the North American Aerospace Defense Command and Vice Commander of the Air Force Space Command, before assuming his present post.
(See: Air Force Commands.)

Parker, John T., Director, Defense Nuclear Agency

Parker graduated from the US Naval Academy in 1955. He also holds an MA in administration from the George Washington University and has attended Guided Missile and Nuclear Engineering schools. He also attended the Industrial College of the Armed Forces. After his graduation from the Naval Academy, Parker served on the USS *D. H. Fox*, the USS *Dahlgren*, and the USS *Sellers*. He has also served as operations officer of Destroyer Division 262. Parker has commanded the USS *St. Clair County*, the USS *MacDonough*, and the USS *Piedmont*. From 1975 to 1977, Parker was chief of staff for the commander of the Sixth Fleet. His last sea tour was as commander of Service Group Two, the Mobile Logistic Support Force of the Atlantic Fleet. Parker has also served in the Bureau of Naval Weapons, the Naval Secretariat, and in the Office of the Chief of Naval Operations. He established the Cruiser-Destroyer Branch under the Deputy Chief of Naval Operations for Surface Warfare. After that, Parker served as director of the Surface Warfare manpower and Training Requirements Division and then as director of the Surface Warfare Division, where he was responsible for surface warfare requirements and plans.

Prior to his appointment as director of the Defense Nuclear Agency, Parker was assigned to the Office of the Chief of Naval Operations as the deputy director of Research, Development, Test and Evaluation.
(See: Defense Agencies.)

Parker, Robert N. (Electrical Engineer), Member at Large, Defense Science Board

Parker is president of the LTV Corporation's Missiles and Electronics Group, a defence contractor. He has been principal deputy director of Defense Research and Engineering. He has also been vice-president and general manager at Hoffman Electronics Corporation and Chief Engineer, Autonetics Division, at North American Rockwell.
(See: Defense Science Board.)

Paul, William F., Senior Vice-President—Defense and Space Systems, United Technologies

Paul was elected senior vice-president—defense and space systems in September 1985. He is responsible for the Sikorsky, Norden Systems, and Space Transportation divisions, as well as the Strategic Defense Systems Division, Space Station Program, Advanced Systems Division, and the Systems Technology and Analysis groups. Paul has a BS from the University of Bridgeport and an MS from Yale University.

Paul joined United Technologies through Sikorsky in 1955. He remained there until his appointment as senior vice-president, holding positions including vice-president of engineering, executive vice-president, and president. His company biography credits him with being 'responsible for the development of a new generation of [helicopters] including the United States Army Black Hawk'.
(See: Defence Contractors.)

Pentecost, Dr Eugene, Member, USAF Scientific Advisory Board

(Director of Industrial Liason, Vanderbilt University)
(See: USAF Scientific Advisory Board (Department of the Air Force).)

Perkins, Dr Courtland D., Member, USAF Scientific Advisory Board (Private consultant)
(See: USAF Scientific Advisory Board (Department of the Air Force.)

Perry, William J. (Mathmetician), Member at Large, Defense Science Board

Perry is a former Under Secretary of Defense for Research and Engineering who is now a managing partner with H & Q Technology Partners. He holds a Ph.D. from Pennsylvania State University. He has been president of ESL, Inc., a defence contractor, and director, Electronic Defense Labs, at GTE Sylvania.
(See: Defense Science Board.)

Phillips, Thomas L., Chairman and Chief Executive Officer, Raytheon Company

Phillips has been chief executive officer at Raytheon since 1968, and was appointed chairman of the board in 1975. He has a BS in electrical engineering and an MS in electrical engineering, both from Virginia Polytechnic Institute. He has also been awarded a variety of honorary degrees.

Phillips joined Raytheon in 1948 as an electronics design engineer and worked his way through the company, holding a series of engineering and then management positions. He was programme manager for the Hawk ground-to-air and Sparrow III air-to-air guided missile programmes, and in 1960 was elected vice-president of Raytheon and general manager of the Missiles and Space Division. He was appointed executive vice-president of Raytheon in 1961, and was elected president in 1964.

Phillips is also a director of the John Hancock Mutual Life Insurance Company, State Street Investment Company, and Knight-Ridder, Inc., the publishing conglomerate. He is also a trustee of Gordon College and a member of the executive committee of the United Ways of Eastern New England. Phillips is a member of the Business Council, the Business Roundtable, and the National Academy of Engineering. He is a Fellow of the American Institute of Aeronautics and Astronautics.

Phillips is director of the Laymen's National Bible Committee, Inc., and a member of the visiting committee of Memorial Church at Harvard University.
(See: Defence Contractors.)

Picard, Dennis J., Senior Vice-President, General Manager, Missile Systems Division, Raytheon Company

Picard holds engineering and management degrees from Northeastern University. He joined Raytheon in 1955 and has held various positions with the company in engineering and programme management. He has been director of the Data Acquisition Systems Directorate, where he was responsible for Raytheon's efforts at the Safeguard Missile Site Radar, the Coherent Radar System, and Cobra Dane.

In 1976, Picard was apppointed assistant general manager of operations for the Equipment Division. A year later he was appointed a vice-president of Raytheon. In 1981, Picard was appointed vice-president and deputy general manager of the Equipment Division. He was appointed to his present position in May 1985.

Picard is a member of the American Institute of Aeronautics and Astronautics, the Armed Forces Communication and Electronics Association, and the Association of the US Army. He is also the Director of the Children's Discovery Museum in Acton, Massachusetts; and a member of the Military Affairs Council for the North Suburban Chamber of Commerce, Burlington, Massachusetts

(See: Defence Contractors.)

Pickett, Owen P., Representative (D, Virginia), 2nd District Member, House Armed Services Committee

Address: 1429 Longworth House Office Building, Washington, DC 20515

Tel: (202) 225-4215

Pickett, an attorney who has earned a BS from Virginia Polytechnic Institute and and LLB from the University of Richmond, was elected to the House in 1986. His subcommittee assignments are Military Personnel and Compensation, Research and Development, and Seapower and Strategic and Critical Materials. Pickett is a member of the Congressional Space Caucus and on the board of visitors for the US Military Academy.

(See: The House of Representatives.)

Plummer, James W., Member, USAF Scientific Advisory Board

(Private consultant)

(See: USAF Scientific Advisory Board (Department of the Air Force).)

Powell, Colin L., Lieutenant-General, USA; National Security Advisor (National Security Council)

Powell was appointed National Security Advisor when Carlucci left the post to take over at the Pentagon. Ironically, he has said that the post of National Security Advisor should be held by a civilian, not a military officer. Powell is widely respected, both in the military and Congress, and has received glowing reports from the press. He is generally seen as a good Washington bureaucrat, who understands both the rules of the game and the players. His military biography has described him as having 'unlimited potential for executing key responsibilities at the highest levels of military—civilian interface'.

Born and raised in New York City, Powell joined ROTC when he was a student at the City University of New York. He was commissioned when he graduated in 1958. He was one of the early wave of Americans in Vietnam, serving as an adviser to the South Vietnamese Army in 1962—63. He returned to Vietnam in 1968, at the height of the war, and served until 1969 as an infantry battalion executive officer. He also served three years in Europe.

In 1971, Powell earned a master's degree in business administration from the George Washington University. He was then selected as a White House Fellow and was assigned as special assistant to the deputy director at the office of Management and Budget (OMB). It was in this post that he first came to the attention of Weinberger and Carlucci, who were later influential in getting him appointed to the National Security Council.

In 1973, after his time in Washington, Powell served as commander of an infantry battalion of the 2nd Infantry Division along the Demilitarized Zone in Korea. Upon his return to the United States, Powell was again sent to Washington, this time as an operations research analyst in the Office of the Assistant Secretary of Defense (Manpower, Requirements and Analysis). Following this, Powell commanded an air assault infantry brigade in the 101st Airborne Division at Fort Campbell in Kentucky.

In 1977, Powell was re-assigned to the Department of Defense. He first served as executive to the special assistant to the Secretary and Deputy Secretary of Defense, and later as senior military assistant to the Deputy Secretary of Defense. Powell was later appointed deputy commander at Fort Leavenworth, Kansas, after which he was called back to Washington in 1983 as military assistant to Secretary of Defense Weinberger. Following this assignment, Powell was commanding general of the Fifth Corps in West Germany for six months in 1986 before being appointed deputy national security adviser. Powell was initially reluctant to accept the post, but did so after a call from President Reagan. He served in this post until his appointment as National Security Advisor.

(See: President and Executive Office of President.)

Press, William H. (Astrophysicist), Member at Large, Defense Science Board

Press, who holds a Ph.D. from the California Institute of Technology, is now chairman of the Department of Astronomy at Harvard University. He was formerly a professor of astronautics and physics at Harvard.

(See: Defense Science Board.)

Price, Melvin, Representative (D, Illinois), 21st District Member, House Armed Services Committee

Address: 2110 Rayburn House Office Building, Washington, DC 20515

Tel: (202) 225-5661

Price has served in the House for since 1945. He is chairman of the Research and Development Subcommittee. He is considered to be somewhat influential on defence issues, owing partly to his intimate knowledge of Congress.

Key Aide: Kevie Tegler, Legislative Assistant.

(See: The House of Representatives.)

Proxmire, William, Senator (D, Wisconsin), Member, Senate Appropriations Committee, Defense Subcommittee

Address: Room SD-530, Dirksen Senate Office Building, Washington, DC, 20510

Tel: (202) 224-5653

A long-time critic of the Defense Department, Proxmire is probably best known for his 'Golden Fleece' awards, which he gives to the worst examples of what he considers to be government waste. Proxmire was first elected to the Senate in 1956, and faces re-election this year. He is very popular with the electorate, winning his last election by a margin of almost two to one.

Proxmire has a BA from Yale University, and an MBA and MPA from Harvard University. He served as a Wisconsin State assemblyman from 1951 to 1953, and ran unsuccessfully three times for the office of Governor of Wisconsin before being elected to the Senate. Proxmire is also chairman of the Committee on Banking, Housing, and Urban Affairs.

Key Aides: Ron Jannen, Administrative Assistant; Doug Walker, Legislative

(See: The Senate.)

Pursell, Carl D., Representative (R, Michigan), 2nd District, Member, House Appropriations Committee, Subcommittee on Energy and Water Development

Address: 1414 Longworth House Office Building, Washington, DC 20515

Tel: (202) 225-4401

Pursell was elected to the House in 1976. He has a BA and an MA from Eastern Michigan University. From 1957 to 1959, he served in the US Army. He has also been a captain in the Army Reserve. He has been a teacher, publisher, and real-estate agent, and from 1971 to 1976 served in the Michigan State Senate. He does not sit on any other committees.

Key Aide: David Mengebier, Legislative Assistant.

(See: The House of Representatives.)

Pyatt, Everett, The Assistant Secretary of the Navy (Shipbuilding and Logistics)

Pyatt took over as Assistant Secretary of the Navy (Shipbuilding and Logistics) on 3 August 1984. Pyatt graduated from Yale University in 1962 with a Bachelor of Engineering in electrical engineeering and a BS in industrial administration. He also has an MBA from the Wharton School of the University of Pennsylvania.

Pyatt has spent most of his career in government, beginning in 1969 when he entered the Management Intern Program. From 1969 to 1972, he participated in efforts supporting the US presence in Vietnam, in the US Middle East Task Group, evaluations of Soviet technology, and US weapons development planning processes as a member of special working groups. From 1973 to 1977, Pyatt served in a variety of roles with the Office of the Secretary of Defense.

In June 1977, Pyatt was appointed Principal Deputy Assitant secretary of the Navy for logistics, where he served until January 1980. He then moved to the Department of Energy, where he was Deputy Chief Financial Officer for project and business management. Prior to his appointment as Assistant Secretary, Pyatt was Principal Deputy Assistant Secretary of the Navy for Shipbuilding and Logistics.
(See: Department of the Navy.)

Quayle, Dan, Senator (R, Indiana), Member of Senate Armed Services Committee
Address: Room SH-524, Hart Senate Office Building, Washington, DC 20510
Tel: (202) 224-5623

Quayle, who was elected to the Senate in 1980, faces re-election in 1992. He has a BA from DePaul University and a JD from Indiana University. He served in the House of Representatives from 1976 until his election to the Senate, and before that was an attorney and newspaper publisher.

Quayle is the Ranking Minority Member of the Conventional Forces and Alliance Defense Subcommittee, and also sits on the Defense Industry and Technology Subcommittee and the Strategic Forces and Nuclear Deterrence Subcommittee. His other committee assignments are on the Budget Committee and the Labor and Human Resources Committee.

Key Aides: Henry Sokolski, Legislative Assistant; Karl Stegenga, Legislative Assistant.
(See: The Senate.)

Ravenal, Arthur, Jr., Representative (R, South Carolina), 1st District, Member, House Armed Services Committee
Address: 1730 Longworth House Office Building, Washington, DC 20515
Tel: (202) 225-3176

A businessman with a BA from the College of Charleston, Ravenal was elected to the House in 1986. He is on the subcommittees on Military Installations and Facilities and Military Personnel and Compensation.
(See: The House of Representatives.)

Ray, Richard, Representative (D, Georgia), 3rd District, Member, House Armed Services Committee
Address: 425 Cannon House Office Building, Washington, DC, 20515
Tel: (202) 225-5901

Ray, a former congressional aide, was elected to the House in 1982. He sits on the subcommittees on Military Personnel and Compensation, Procurement and Military Nuclear Systems, and Readiness, where he is the Chairman of the Evironmental Restoration Panel. His other committee assignment is Small Business.

Key Aides: Lee Culpepper, Legislative Director; Cindy Gillespie, Legislative
(See: The House of Representatives.)

Reagan, Ronald Wilson, The President of The United States

President Reagan was born on 6 February 1911 in Illinois. He graduated from Eureka College in Illinois in 1932 with a degree in economics and sociology.

After a brief career as a sports broadcaster and editor, Reagan moved to California to start a motion picture career. His film career includes fifty full-length films. During this time, he served in the Army Air Corps during World War II, making propaganda films. He served six terms as president of the Screen Actors Guild and two terms as president of the Motion Picture Industry Council.

In the 1950s, Reagan moved into television, working as production supervisor and host for 'General Electric Theatre'. In 1964—65, he was host of the series 'Death Valley Days'.

Reagan began his political career with his election as Governor of California in 1966. He was re-elected for a second term in 1970. It was after his second term that Reagan began laying the groundwork for his presidency, beginning a nationally syndicated radio commentary programme and a newspaper column. He also undertook an extensive speaking schedule. In 1974 and 1975, he served on the Presidential Commission investigating the CIA.

In November 1975, Reagan announced his bid for the 1976 Republican presidential nomination, which he lost to Gerald Ford. Reagan campaigned extensively for Ford in the 1976 election, which was won by Democrat Jimmy Carter. After the election, Reagan resumed his radio programme and newspaper column. He became a member of the Board of Directors of the Committee for the Present Danger,a neoconservative group, and founded a group called Citizens for the Republic.

Reagan announced his second bid for the Republication nomination in November 1979, this time defeating George Bush to gain the nomination. He was elected to the presidency on 4 November 1980, defeating Jimmy Carter, and was inaugurated in January 1981. He was re-elected in 1984, defeating Walter Mondale.

(See: President and Executive Office of President.)

Reed, William H., Director, Defense Contract Audit Agency (DCAA)

Reed was appointed as director of the DCAA in January 1986. He has a BA from Woodbury University and an MA in Management and Supervision from Central Michigan University. Reed has worked for DCAA since it was established in 1965. He held a number of of supervisory positions in its regional offices in Los Angeles and Boston. Before his appointment as director, Reed was regional director of the Boston region, a position he was appointed to in 1980.

Reed is chairman of the Association of Government Accountants' Financial Management Standards Board and serves on the board of advisers of the National Contract Management Association.

(See: Defense Agencies.)

Renier, James R., President and Chief Executive Officer, Honeywell Incorporated

Renier, who has a BS in chemistry from the College of St Thomas and a Ph.D. in physical chemistry from Iowa State University, was elected president and chief executive officer of Honeywell Incorporated in October 1987. He started his career after his graduation from college in 1951, working as a Research Associate at the Ames Laboratory of the Atomic Energy Commission at Iowa State University.

After earning his doctorate, Renier joined Honeywell in 1956 as a senior research scientist at the Corporate Research Center. In 1964, he became manager of space and armament systems, an operation of the Honeywell Aerospace Division. He was named general manager for Honeywell Systems and Research Center in 1965. A year later, Renier was named general manager of advanced communications systems for the Honeywell Communications and Data Products Division.

Renier was appointed vice-president of data systems operations for Honeywell Information Systems Inc. in 1970, and in 1974 was named Associate Group vice-president for the Honeywell Aerospace and Defense Group. In 1976, Renier was named vice-president and group executive, and appointed executive vice-president two years later.

In 1979, Renier was appointed president of Honeywell Control Systems, an operating unit of Honeywell Inc. He was named president and vice-chairman of Honeywell Information Systems in 1982. In 1985 Renier was appointed vice-chairman of Honeywell Inc, taking over as president and chief operating officer in May 1986 before becoming chief executive officer.

In addition to Honeywell, Renier is a member of the board of directors of the Northwestern National Life Insurance Company; the First Bank System, Inc.; and the Pillsbury Company. He is a trustee of the College of St Thomas and is a member of the foundation board of governors for Iowa State University.
(See: Defence Contractors.)

Rice, Donald B., (Economist & Engineer), Senior Consultant, Defense Science Board

Rice is president and chief executive officer at the Air Force's RAND Corporation, a think-tank which specializes in defence issues. Rice has been Assistant Director of the Office of Management and Budget, Deputy Assistant Secretary of Defense (Resource Analysis), and chairman of the National Commission on Supplies and Shortages.
(See: Defense Science Board.)

RisCassi, Robert W., Lieutenant-General (USA), Director, Joint Staff
(See: Joint Chiefs of Staff.)

Robinson, Tommy, Representative (D, Arkansas), 2nd District, Member, House Armed Services Committee
Address: 1541 Longworth House Office Building, Washington, DC, 20515
Tel: (202) 225-2506

Robinson was elected to the House in 1984. He was formerly in law enforcement. He is considered conservative, and sits on the subcommittees on Military Installations and Facilities and Readiness. He is also a member of the Education and Labor Committee, the Veteran's Affairs Committee, and the Select Committee on Ageing. Robinson is a member of the Conservative Democratic Forum.

Key Aide: David Huebler, Legislative Assistant.
(See: The House of Representatives.)

Rosenbaum, Harold (Astronautics), Member at Large, Defense Science Board

Rosenbaum is president of Rosenbaum Associates, Inc. He holds a Ph.D. from the Polytechnic Institute of Brooklyn, and is a former professional staff member, House Committee on Armed Services. He has also been a staff assistant to the general manager at the AVCO Systems Division.
(See: Defense Science Board.)

Rothaus, Dr Oscar S., Member, USAF Scientific Advisory Board (Department of Mathematics, Cornell University)
(See: USAF Scientific Advisory Board (Department of the Air Force).)

Rowen, Henry S. (Economist), Senior Consultant, Defense Science Board

Rowen, a past president of the RAND Corporation, is now a professor at Stanford University. He has also been Deputy Assistant Secretary of Defense (International Security Affairs).
(See: Defense Science Board.)

Rowland, John G., Representative (R, Connecticut), Member, House Armed Services Committee
Address: 512 Cannon House Office Building, Washington, DC 20515
Tel: (202) 225-3822

Rowland, a former insurance agent with a BA from Villanova University, was elected to the House in 1984. He sits on the Procurement and Military Nuclear Systems Subcommittee and the Readiness Subcommittee. He is also a member of the Veterans' Affairs Committee. Rowland is co-chairman of the Defense Spending Task Force of the Northeast-Midwest Congressional Coalition.

Key Aide: Dave Boomer, Legislative Assistant.
(See: The House of Representatives.)

Rudman, Warren B., Senator (R, New Hampshire), Member, Senate Appropriations Committee, Defense Subcommittee

Address: Room SH-530, Hart Senate Office Building, Washington, DC 20510
Tel: (202) 224-3324

Rudman, who faces re-election in 1992, was elected to the Senate in 1980. He is well-known as the Ranking Minority Member and vice-chairman of the Iran—Contra Committee, where he refused to support the Minority (Republican) Report, which was widely viewed as a whitewash. He has a BS from Syracuse University and an LLB from Boston College Law School. Rudman served in the US Army. He was New Hampshire Attorney-General from 1970 to 1976.

He also sits on the Budget Committee, the Governmental Affairs Commitee, the Small Business Committee, and the Select Committee on Ethics.

Key Aide: Jay Behuncik, Legislative Aide.
(See: The Senate.)

Rutan, Elbert L., Member, USAF Scientific Advisory Board
(President, Scaled Composites Inc.)
(See: USAF Scientific Advisory Board (Department of the Air Force).)

Ryan, Martin J., Jr., Major-General (USAF), Director J-8 Force Structure, Resource, and Assessment Directorate
(See: Joint Chiefs of Staff.)

Saalfeld, Fred E., Director, Office of Naval Research
(See: Department of the Navy.)

Sabo, Martin Olav, Representative (D, Minnesota), 5th District, Member, House Appropriations Committee, Subcommittee on Defense
Address: 2201 Rayburn House Office Building, Washington, DC 20515
Tel: (202) 225-4755

Sabo, who only sits on the Appropriations Committee, was elected to the House in 1978. He has a BA from Augsburg College. From 1960 until his election to the House, he was a Minnesota State Representative, which included a stint as Speaker from 1973 to 1978.
(See: The House of Representatives.)

Sasser, Jim, Senator (D, Tennessee), Member, Senate Appropriations Committee, Defense Subcommittee, Member, Senate Appropriations Committee, Energy and Water Development Subcommittee
Address: Room SR-298, Russell Senate Office Building, Washington, DC 20510
Tel: (202) 224-3344

Sasser, who faces re-election in 1988, was first elected to the Senate in 1976. Sasser has a BA from Vanderbilt University and a JD from the same school. He served in the Marine Corps from 1957 until 1963, after which he became an attorney. From 1973 until his election to the Senate, Sasser was chairman of the Tennessee Democratic State Committee.

Sasser sits on the Budget Committee, the Committee on Banking, Housing, and Urban Affairs, the Small Business Committee, and the Governmental Affairs Committee.
(See: The Senate.)

Schroeder, Patricia, Representative (D, Colorado), 1st District, Member, House Armed Services Committee
Address: 2410 Rayburn House Office Building, Washington, DC 20515
Tel: (202) 225-4431

First elected to the House in 1972, Schroeder ran an abortive exploratory campaign for the Democratic Presidential nomination in 1987. There is speculation that she might run again for the nomination in 1992. Schroeder holds a BA from the University of Minnesota and a JD from Harvard University. She sits on the Military Personnel and Compensation and the Research and Development subcommittees. Aside from Armed Services, Schroeder sits on the Judiciary and Post Office and Civil Service Committees, and also the Select Committee on Children, Youth, and Families. She is considered one of the more liberal House members, and is somewhat influential. She is a Deputy Majority Whip, Dean of the Colorado Congressional Delegation, and a member of the Steering Committee of the Arms Control and Foreign Policy Caucus.

Key Aide: Tom O'Donnel, Legislative Aide.
(See: The House of Representatives.)

Sculley, Jay Raymond, Assistant Secretary of the Army (Research, Development, and Acquisition)

Like his immediate superior, Army Secretary Marsh, Jay Raymond Sculley has also been in office for an exceptionally long period of time: he was confirmed by the Senate on 1 October 1981.

Scully graduated from Annandale High School in Virginia and entered the Virginia Military Institute (VMI) in 1958. He received a BS in civil engineering from VMI in 1962. Sculley has also earned an MSE in environmental engineering in 1970, and a Ph.D. in environmental engineering in 1974, both from Johns Hopkins University.

In 1962, after graduating from VMI, Sculley was an officer in the US Air Force until 1965. He then joined the DuPont Company, a large defence contractor, as a design engineer.

In 1970, Sculley joined the VMI faculty as an assistant professor of civil engineering, where he remained for four years. He was briefly general manager of Corrugated Services, Inc., a Texas paper re-cycling company, before returning to VMI in 1975. He was appointed a full professor in 1979. During his time at VMI, Sculley taught courses in computer science, operations research and traffic flow theory, as well as being involved in engineering research through VMI Research Laboratories, Inc. He was also coach of VMI's soccer team. He remained at VMI until his appointment as assistant secretary in 1981.
(See: Department of the Army.)

Seebass, Dr A. Richard, Member, USAF Scientific Advisory Board
(Dean, College of Engineering and Applied Sciences, University of Colorado)
(See: USAF Scientific Advisory Board (Department of the Air Force).)

Seitz, Frederick (Physicist), Ex-Officio Member, Defense Science Board, Chairman, SDI Advisory Group

Seitz holds a Ph.D. from Princeton University. He has been president of Rockefeller University, president of the National Academy of Sciences, and dean of the graduate school and vice-president of research at the University of Illinois.
(See: Defense Science Board.)

Selden, Dr Robert W., Member, USAF Scientific Advisory Board
(Los Alamos National Laboratory)
(See: USAF Scientific Advisory Board (Department of the Air Force).)

Selwyn, Philip A., Director, Office of Naval Technology
(See: Department of the Navy.)

Shannon, Robert R., Member, USAF Scientific Advisory Board
(Director, University of Arizona Optical Sciences Center)
(See: USAF Scientific Advisory Board (Department of the Air Force).)

Shea, Joseph F., (Engineer), Member at Large, Defense Science Board

Shea is senior vice-president—engineering, at the Raytheon Company, a defence contractor. He holds a Ph.D. from the University of Michigan. He has been vice-president and deputy director, engineering, with Polaroid; deputy director, manned space flight, NASA; and manager, advanced research and development, General Motors' AC Spark Plug Division.
(See: Defense Science Board.)

Shelby, Richard C., Senator (D, Alabama), Member of Senate Armed Services Committee

Address: Room SH-313, Hart Senate Office Building, Washington, DC 20510
Tel: (202) 224-5744

Shelby was elected to the Senate in 1986, and faces re-election in 1992. He has a BA and an LLB from the University of Alabama. Before coming to the Senate, he had served in the House of Representatives from 1978. Shelby is generally considered to be a conservative.

On the Armed Services Committee, he sits on the subcommittees on Conventional Forces and Alliance Defense; Manpower and Personnel; and Projection Forces and Regional Defense. He also serves on the Banking, Housing, and Urban Affairs Committee and the Special Committee on Ageing.

A member of the board of visitors for the US Military Academy, Shelby is also co-chairman of the American Security Council.

Key Aide: Terry Lynch, Legislative Assistant.
(See: The Senate.)

Shelley, R. Gene, President, Raytheon Company

Shelley became president of Raytheon in June 1986. He has a BS from the University of Arizona and an MS in electrical engineering from the Massachusetts Institute of Technology. He has also done graduate work at the University of Southern California, the University of California at Los Angeles, and Northwestern University. Prior to coming to Raytheon, Shelley was chief engineer of the Autonetics' Armament and Flight Control Division at North American Aviation (now Rockwell International), and was later president of Stoddard Aircraft Radio Company.

Shelley came to Raytheon in 1964 as manager of the Goleta, California operation, which later became the Electromagnetic Systems Division. He was appointed vice-president in October 1973. In April 1978, he was appointed group executive with responsibility for the Equipment Division, Electromagnetic Systems Division, Submarine Signal Division and two subsidiaries, Sedco Systems, Inc. and Raytheon Service Company. Shelley was elected senior vice-president in December 1979, the post he held before becoming president.
(See: Defence Contractors.)

Shevell, Professor Richard S., Member, USAF Scientific Advisory Board

(Department of Aeronautics and Astronautics, Stanford University)
(See: USAF Scientific Advisory Board (Department of the Air Force).)

Shrontz, Frank, Chairman and Chief Executive Officer, The Boeing Company

Shrontz was elected chief executive officer in April 1986, and chairman in January 1988. Shrontz has an LLB from the University of Idaho and an MBA from the Harvard Graduate School of Business Administration. He was also a Sloan Fellow at the Stanford Graduate School of Business Administration.

Shrontz joined Boeing in 1958, and worked there until he was appointed Assistant Secretary of the Air Force (Installations and Logistics) in October 1973. In February 1976 he was appointed Assistant Secretary of Defense. He returned to Boeing in January 1977 as corporate vice-president in charge of contract administration and planning.

In September 1978, Shrontz was apppointed vice-president and general manager of the 707/727/737 Division of the Boeing Commercial Airplane Company. In May 1982 he became vice-president—sales, in April 1984 president, of the Commercial Airplane Company.

Shrontz was elected president of Boeing in 1985, joining the board of directors at the same time. He is also a member of the board of directors of Citicorp.
(See: Defence Contractors.)

Shultz, George P., The Secretary of State

George Shultz was sworn in as the sixtieth Secretary of State on 16 July 1982. Shultz earned a BA in economics from Princeton University in 1942, and joined the Marine Corps upon graduation, serving until 1945. In 1949, Shultz was awarded a Ph.D. in industrial economics from the Massachusetts Institute of Technology

(MIT). He taught at MIT from 1948 until 1957, taking a leave of absence in 1955 to serve as a senior staff economist on the President's Council of Economic Advisors during the Eisenhower Administration.

In 1957, Shultz was appointed professor of industrial relations at the University of Chicago Graduate School of Economics. In 1962, he was named as dean of the Graduate School of Business. In 1968, Shultz took the position of fellow at the Center for the Advanced Study in the Behavioral Sciences at Stanford University.

Shultz began his government career under President Nixon, being appointed Secretary of Labor in 1969, where he served until June 1970. He then became Director of the Office of Management and Budget. In May 1972, he was appointed Secretary of the Treasury, where he remained until 1974. During this period he was also chairman of the Council on Economic Policy. In 1972, as chairman of the East—West Trade Policy Committee, Shultz went to Moscow to negotiate a series of trade protocols with the Soviet Union. He also represented the USA at the Tokyo meeting of the General Agreement on Tariffs and Trade.

In 1974, Shultz left Washington to join the Bechtel Corporation, one of the largest engineering firms in the world. When he was appointed Secretary of State, Shultz was president and a director of the Bechtel Group, Inc. He also taught part-time at Stanford University during this period. Before his appointment as Secretary of State, Shultz was chairman of President Reagan's Economic Policy Advisory Board. In May 1982, he met with leaders in Japan, Canada and Europe to help prepare for the Versailles Economic Summit. Shultz is the author of numerous books, including *Economic Policy Beyond the Headlines* (1978), *Workers and Wages in the Labor Market* (1970), *Management Organization and the Computer* (1960), and *The Dynamics of the Labor Market* (1951).

(See: Department of State.)

Shutler, Philip D., Lieutenant-General, USMC (Retired), Member at Large, Defense Science Board

Shutler is a private consultant. He has been director of operations, J-3, Joint Staff, and vice-director of the Joint Staff. He was also commander of the 4th Marine Amphibious Brigade.

(See: Defense Science Board.)

Sisisky, Norman, Representative (D, Virginia), 4th District, Member, House Armed Services Committee

Address: 426 Cannon House Office Building, Washington, DC 20515

Sisisky, who holds a BS from Virginia Commonwealth University, was a business executive before being elected to the House in 1982. He sits on the subcommittees on Investigations, Procurement and Military Nuclear Systems, Seapower and Strategic and Critical Materials, and on the Acquisition Policy Panel. He is also a member of the Small Business Committee and the Select Committee on Ageing. Sisisky is a member of the Congressional Space Caucus and the American Security Council (formerly the Coalition for Peace Through Strength).

(See: The House of Representatives.)

Skantze, Lawrence A., General; Commander, Air Force Systems Command

General Lawrence Skantze was born in 1928. He enlisted in the US Navy in 1946 and became a radio operator. In 1952, he received a BS in engineering from the US Naval Academy and was commissioned as a second lieutenant. He also has an MS in nuclear enginering from the Air Force Institute of Technology, earned in 1959. He has also completed Squadron Officer School and Armed Forces Staff College.

In 1953, Skantze earned his pilot wings at Reese Air Force Base in Texas and entered B-26 combat crew training. In February 1954 he was assigned to South Korea. He returned to the USA in 1955 as an aide to the commanding general of the 14th Air Force at Robins Air Force Base, Georgia. In 1959, after graduating from the Air Force Institute of Technology, Skantze became a project engineer with the joint Air Force–Atomic Energy Commission Nuclear Powered Airplane Project. From June 1963 to August 1965, he was assistant executive officer to the Under Secretary of the Air Force.

Skantze graduated from the Armed Forces Staff College in 1966, and worked until 1969 as director of system engineering and advanced planning in the Air Force Manned Orbiting Laboratory Program. In August 1969, he was assigned to Headquarters Air Force Systems Command as director of assignments. Later, he was appointed assistant for Senior Officer Management Systems Command HQ, where he remained until May 1971. He then became deputy for the AGM-69A Short Range Attack Missile (SRAM) at Wright-Patterson Air Force Base.

In June 1973, he was appointed systems programme director for the E-3A Airborne Warning and Control System (AWACS) at Hanscom Air Force Base in Massachusetts. In June 1979, he took command of the Aeronautical Systems Division at Wright-Patterson Air Force Base. Skantze then became Air Force Deputy Chief of Staff for Research, Development, and Acquisition in August 1982, where he remained until his present command.
(See: Air Force Commands.)

Skelton, Ike, Representative (D, Missouri), 4th District, Member, House Armed Services Committee
Address: 2453 Rayburn House Office Building, Washington, DC 20515
Tel: (202) 225-2876

Skelton has earned a BA and an LLB from the University of Missouri, and was elected to the House in 1976. On the Armed Servies Committee, he is a member of the subcommittees on Military Installations and Facilities, Military Personnnel and Compensation, and Procurement and Military Nuclear Systems. His other committee assignments are Small Business and the Select Committee on Ageing. Skelton is also chairman of the Congressional Rural Caucus.

Key Aide: Tommy Glakas, National Security Analyst.
(See: The House of Representatives.)

Smith, Dr Harold P., Jr., Member, USAF Scientific Advisory Board

(President, The Palmer Smith Corporation)
(See: USAF Scientific Advisory Board (Department of the Air Force).)

Smith, Roger B., Chairman and Chief Executive Officer, General Motors Corporation

Smith, who has a BA and an MBA from the University of Michigan, has been chairman and chief executive officer of General Motors since 1 January 1981. He started his career with General Motors (GM) in 1949 as a general accounting clerk in the Detroit Central Office. After a series of promotions, Smith became treasurer of the corporation in 1970. In 1971 he became vice-president in charge of the financial staff and a member of the administration committee.

In 1972 Smith became executive vice-president and group executive in charge of the non-automotive and defence group. He was elected executive vice-president in 1974, with responsibility for the financial, public relations, and industry—government relations staffs. He held this post until his election as chairman in 1981.

Smith also sits on the boards of directors of Johnson & Johnson and Citicorp. He is a trustee of the California Institute of Technology, and chairman of the Business Roundtable.
(See: Defence Contractors.)

Smith, Virginia, Representative (R, Nebraska), 3rd District, Member, House Appropriations Committee, Subcommittee on Energy and Water Development
Address: 2202 Rayburn House Office Building, Washington, DC 20515
Tel: (202) 225-6435

Smith was elected to the House in 1974. She has a BA from the University of Nebraska. From 1955 to 1974, she was a lecturer and national chairperson of American Farm Bureau Women. From 1950 to 1960, she was a member of the Nebraska State Normal Schools Board of Education. She was a delegate to the White House Congress on Children and Youth in 1960 and was chairperson of the Presidential Task Force on Rural Development in 1971—72. Smith does not sit on any other committees.

Key Aides: Brian McGrath, Legislative Assistant; Joe Western, Associate Staff.
(See: The House of Representatives.)

Snyder, Dr Harry L., Member, USAF Scientific Advisory Board

(Director, Human Factor Laboratory, Virginia Polytechnic Institute)
(See: USAF Scientific Advisory Board (Department of the Air Force).)

Sorenson, Harold W., Chief Scientist of the Air Force
(See: Department of the Air Force.)

Specter, Arlen, Senator (R, Pennsylvania), Member, Senate Appropriations Committee, Energy and Water Development Subcommittee
Address: Room SH-303, Hart Senate Office Building, Washington, DC 20510
Tel: (202) 224-4254

Specter, who was elected to the Senate in 1980 and faces re-election in 1992, is known as an independent. He often takes more liberal positions than his Republican colleagues. Specter has a BA from the University of Pennsylvania and an LLB from Yale University. He served in the US Air Force from 1951 to 1953. Specter was assistant district attorney of Philadelphia from 1959 to 1963, and district attorney from 1966 to 1974. He served as assistant counsel to the Warren Commission in 1964, and as special assistant attorney-general for the Pennsylvania Department of Justice from 1964 to 1965.

Specter also sits on the Judiciary Committee, the Veterans' Affairs Committee, and the Select Committee on Intelligence.
(See: The Senate.)

Spence, Floyd, Representative (R, South Carolina), Member, House Armed Services Committee
Address: 2406 Longworth House Office Building, Washington, DC 20515

An attorney with a BA and a JD from the University of South Carolina, Spence was elected to the House in 1970. He is the Ranking Minority Member of the Seapower and Strategic and Critical Materials Subcommittee and also sits on the Subcommittee on Military Installations and Facilities. Spence is also a member of the Standards of Official Conduct Committee and the Select Committee on Ageing. He is a member of the House Republican Policy Committee.
Key Aides: Craig Metz, Special Assistant; Marilyn King, Legislative Assistant.
(See: The House of Representatives).

Spencer, Edson W., Chairman of the Board, Honeywell Incorporated

Spencer became chairman of the board at Honeywell in May 1978, and stepped down from being chief executive officer in 1987. He is a graduate of Williams College and was a Rhodes Scholar at Oxford University (England) for two years. He has also served as an officer in the US Naval Reserve.

Spencer came to Honeywell in 1954, working in the Aeronautical Division. For five years, from 1959 to 1964, he was Honeywell's Far East regional manager in Tokyo. On his return to the USA, Spencer was named corporate vice-president of international operations.In 1969, he was appointed executive vice-president and elected to the board of directors. He was elected president and chief executive officer in 1974.

Spencer also serves on the board of directors of CBS, Inc. and Boise Cascade. He is a member of the board of trustees of the Carnegie Endowment for International Peace and serves as chairman of the board of trustees of the Ford Foundation.
(See: Defence Contractors.)

Spratt, John, Jr. , Representative (D, South Carolina), 5th District, Member, House Armed Services Committee
Address: 1118 Longworth House Office Building, Washington, DC 20515
Tel: (202) 225-4005

Spratt was elected to the House in 1982. He has a BA from Davidson College, an MA from Oxford University, and an LLB from Yale University. He sits on the subcommittees on Investigations and Procurement and Military Nuclear Systems, and on the Acquisition Policy Panel. Spratt is secretary-treasurer of the Arms Control and Foreign Policy Caucus.

Key Aide: Bob DeGrasse, Legislative Director.
(See: The House of Representatives.)

Stamper, Malcolm, Vice-Chairman, The Boeing Company

Stamper became vice-chairman of Boeing in February 1985. He served as a naval officer during World War II, and has a BS in electrical engineering from Georgia Tech. Stamper worked for General Motors for fourteen years before joining Boeing in 1962 as director of Aerospace Electronic Operations.

In June 1965 Stamper was elected vice-president of Boeing and named general manager of the Turbine Division. In 1966 he was appointed vice-president—general manager of the Boeing 747 Division, where he was responsible for running the 747 programme from start-up to its introduction.

Stamper became vice-president—general manager of the Commercial Airplane Group in April 1969. He was named senior vice-president-operations in May 1971. In September 1972, Stamper was elected president of Boeing and a member of the board of directors. He is also a member of the board of directors of the Nordstrom Company, the Travelers Insurance Companies and Chrysler Corporation.
(See: Defence Contractors.)

Starry, Donn A., General, USA (Retired), Member at Large, Defense Science Board

Starry is executive vice-president of Ford Aerospace and Communications Group, a defence contractor. He holds an MS from George Washington University. He was Commander-in-Chief of the US Readiness Command (one of the Unified Commands); commanding general, Fifth US Corps, US Army Europe and commanding general, US Army Armor Center.
(See: Defense Science Board.)

Stear, Dr Edwin B., Member, USAF Scientific Advisory Board

(Executive Director, The Washington Technology Center, University of Washington)
(See: USAF Scientific Advisory Board (Department of the Air Force).)

Stempel, Robert B., President and Chief Operating Officer, General Motors Corporation

Stempel has been president and chief operating officer of General Motors (GM) since September 1987. He has a BS in mechanical engineering from Worcester Polytechnic Institute and an MBA from Michigan State University.

Stempel joined GM in 1958, starting as a senior detailer in the chassis design department of the Oldsmobile division. He became a senior designer with Oldsmobile in 1962. In 1964 he became transmission design engineer. In 1969 he became a motor engineer, and was appointed assistant chief engineer in 1972. In 1973, Stempel was appointed special assistant to the president of General Motors. He later joined the engineering department of the Chevrolet division, and was named Chevrolet's director of engineering in 1975.

Stempel was elected a vice-president of General Motors in 1978, and was also appointed general manager of the Pontiac motor division. In 1980, he was appointed managing director of Adan Opel AG in West Germany, serving there two years before being appointed general manager of Chevrolet. In 1986, he became executive vice-president of GM, and also joined the board of directors. He remained in this post until assuming his present duties.

Stempel is also a trustee of the Worcester Polytechnic Institute.
(See: Defence Contractors.)

Stennis, John C., Senator (D, Mississippi), Member, Senate Armed Services Committee, Chairman, Senate Appropriations Committee, Defense Subcommittee, Member, Senate Appropriations Committee, Energy and Water Development Subcommittee

Address: Room SR-205, Russell Senate Office Building, Washington, DC 20510
Tel: (202) 224-6253

Stennis, who faces a re-election battle which he should win fairly easily this year, was first elected to the Senate in 1946. Before coming to the Senate, he was an attorney, and earned his BS from Missouri State University and his LLB from the University of Virginia. Stennis is considered a strong supporter of the Department of Defense. He is considered very influential, not only because he has an intimate knowledge of the Senate and because of his membership of the Armed Services Committee, but also because he is chairman of the Appropriations Committee and chairman of that committee's Defense Subcommittee. He is also a former Chairman of the Armed Services Committee.

Stennis is one of the characters in a story many consider all too typical of Congressional defence decisionmaking. In one Defense Appropriations Subcommittee meeting, Stennis was involved in a dispute with Senator Warren Magnuson of Washington over where three Navy Frigates would be built. Each Senator wanted two of the ships built in his state and one in the other's state. They finally settled the dispute by appropriating money for *four* frigates, with two to be built in each state.

On the Armed Services Committee, Stennis serves on the subcommittees on Readiness, Sustainability and Support, Strategic Forces and Nuclear Deterrence, and Projection Forces and Regional Defense. Stennis is also president *pro tempore* of the Senate and a member of the Senate Democratic Steering Committee.
(See: The Senate.)

Stevens, Ted, Senator (R, Alaska), Ranking Minority Leader, Member, Senate Appropriations Committee, Defense Subcommittee
Address: Room SH-522, Hart Senate Office Building, Washington, DC 20510
Tel: (202) 224-3004

Stevens was elected to the Senate in 1968 and faces re-election in 1990. He was Senate Majority Whip from 1980 to 1985. He has an LLB from Harvard Law School, and served in the Army Air Corps during World War II. Stevens was US attorney for the District of Alaska from 1953 to 1956, when he moved on to be legislative counsel to the Department of the Interior. From 1958 until 1960, he was assistant to the Secretary of the Interior. Stevens also served in the Alaska House of Representatives from 1964 until his election to the Senate.

He sits on the Commerce, Science and Transportation Committee and the Governmental Affairs Committee.

Key Aide: Wally Burnett, Legislative Director.

(See: The Senate.)

Stratton, Samuel S., Representative (D, New York), 23rd District, Member, House Armed Services Committee
Address: 2205 Rayburn House Office Building, Washington, DC 20515
Tel: (202) 225-5076

Stratton, who holds a BA from the University of Rochester, an MA from Haverford College and an MA from Harvard University, was elected to the House in 1959. He is chairman of the Procurement and Military Nuclear Systems Subcommittee, and also a member of the Investigations subcommittee. He is also chairman of the New York State Congressional Delegation.

Stratton is known as a strong supporter of the Defense Department, and is co-chairman of the American Security Council, which was formerly known as the Coalition for Peace Through Strength. He is also a member of the Conservative Democratic Forum.
(See: The House of Representatives.)

Stubberud, Dr Allen R., Member, USAF Scientific Advisory Board

(Professor of Electrical Engineering, University of California at Irvine)
(See: USAF Scientific Advisory Board (Department of the Air Force).)

Stump, Bob, Representative (R, Arizona), 3rd District, Member, House Armed Services Committee
Address: 211 Cannon House Office Building, Washington, DC 20515
Tel: (202) 225-4576

Stump, a farmer elected to the House in 1976, has a BS from Arizona State University. He sits on the Investigations and Research and Development subcommittees and on the Veterans' Affairs Committee. He is a member of the executive committee of the House Republican Committee on Committees.

Key Aide: Carl Commenator, Legislative Director.

(See: The House of Representatives.)

Sullivan, Leonard, Jr. (Aeronautical Engineer), Member at Large, Defense Science Board

A private consultant, Sullivan has been Assistant Secretary of Defense (Programme Analysis and Evaluation), Principal Deputy and Deputy Director of Defense Research and Engineering (Southeast Asia Matters), and manager of advanced systems with the Grumman Corporation, a defence contractor.
(See: Defense Science Board.)

Sweeney, Mac, Representative (R, Texas), 14th District, Member, House Armed Services Committee
Address: 1713 Longworth House Office Building, Washington, DC 20515
Tel: (202) 225-2831

Sweeney was director of administrative operations at the White House before his election to the House in 1984. He has a BA from the University of Texas. He sits on the subcommittees on Investigations and on Research and Development.
(See: The House of Representatives.)

Symms, Steven D., Senator (R, Idaho), Member of Senate Armed Services Committee
Address: Room SH-509, Hart Senate Office Building, Washington, DC 20510
Tel: (202) 224-6142

Symms, a former fruit grower, was elected to the Senate in 1980, and faces re-election in 1992. He also served in the House of Representatives from 1972 until his Senate election. Symms has a BS from the University of Idaho.

Symms sits on the subcommittees on Defense Industry and Technology, Manpower and Personnel, and Projection Forces and Regional Defense. His other committee assignments are on the Budget Committee, the Environment and Public Works Committee, and the Joint Economic Committee.

Key Aide: Andy Jazwick, Legislative Assistant.

(See: The Senate.)

Taft, William Howard, IV, Deputy Secretary of Defense, Office of the Secretary of Defense

Taft previously served as Deputy Secretary under Weinberger. He was expected by most observers to resign when Carlucci took over, but did not. It is worth noting that Carlucci took no action to dismiss him, and it now seems that he might remain in his post until the end of the Reagan Administration.

Taft, who received his BA in English from Yale and his JD from Harvard in 1969, was previously the general counsel to the Department of Defense (DoD). Taft also served under Ford and Nixon. From April 1976 to January 1977 he was general counsul to the Department of Health, Education, and Welfare (HEW). From 1973 until his appointment as HEW general counsel, Taft was Executive Assistant to the Secretary of HEW. Before this, starting in 1970, Taft was the principal assistant to Caspar Weinberger, who was then Director of the Office of Management and Budget. From 1977 until 1981, when he was appointed to be General Counsel of the DoD, Taft was in private practice.
(See: Office of the Secretary of Defense (Department of Defense).)

Teller, Dr Edward, Member, USAF Scientific Advisory Board

(Lawrence Livermore National Laboratory)
(See: USAF Scientific Advisory Board (Department of the Air Force.)

Tenenbaum, Dr Jay M., Member, USAF Scientific Advisory Board

(Schlumberger Palo Alto Research, Computer Aided Systems Laboratory)
(See: USAF Scientific Advisory Board (Department of the Air Force).)

Tennant, Samuel M., Member, USAF Scientific Advisory Board (Group Vice President, Programs, The Aerospace Corporation)

(See: USAF Scientific Advisory Board (Department of the Air Force).)

Thomas, Lindsay, Representative (D, Georgia), Member, House Appropriations Committee, Subcommittee on Energy and Water Development
Address: 431 Cannon House Office Building, Washington DC 20515

Born in Pierce County, Georgia, in 1943, Thomas was educated at the University of Georgia, where he received a BA. He was previously an investment banker with the firm of Johnson, Lane, Spence and Smith of Savannah, Georgia. He is currently a farmer. His military service includes a six-year period with the Georgia Air National Guard.

Thomas and his wife Melinda have three children.
(See: The House of Representatives.)

Thurmond, Strom, Senator (R, South Carolina), Member of Senate Armed Services Committee
Address: Room SR-218, Russell Senate Office Building, Washington, DC 20510
Tel: (202) 224-5972

Thurmond, a conservative and strong military supporter, was elected to the Senate in 1954. He faces a re-election campaign in 1990, although there is speculation that his current term will be his last. Thurmond has a BS from Clemson University, and was an attorney before coming to the Senate. He was also Governor of South Carolina from 1947 until 1951.

On the Armed Services Committee, Thurmond is the Ranking Minority Member of the Strategic Forces and Nuclear Deterrence Subcommittee. He also sits on the subcommittees on Conventional Forces and Alliance Defense and Readiness, Sustainability and Support. Thurmond is Ranking Minority Member of the Judiciary Committee, and also serves on the Labor and Human Resources Committee and the Veterans' Affairs Committee. He is also a member of the Senate Republican Policy Committee.

Key Aide: K. K. Cowan, Military Assistant.
(See: The Senate.)

Tiffany, Charles F., Member, USAF Scientific Advisory Board
(Vice President, Advanced Systems, The Boeing Military Airplane Company)
(See: USAF Scientific Advisory Board (Department of the Air Force).)

Toomay, Major-General John C., USAF (Retired), Member, USAF Scientific Advisory Board (Private consultant)
(See: USAF Scientific Advisory Board (Department of the Air Force).)

Townes, Charles H. (Physicist), Senior Consultant, Defense Science Board

Townes is professor of physics at the University of California Berkeley. A nobel laureate in physics, he earned his Ph.D. from the California Institute of Technology. He has been provost of the Massachusetts Institute of Technology and also vice-president of the Institute for Defense Analysis.
(See: Defense Science Board.)

Trost, Carlisle A. H., Admiral, Chief of Naval Operations

Admiral Trost, who was appointed in 1986 over the objection of then Secretary of the Navy John Lehman, raised a stir in April 1987 when he said that Lehman - who had just resigned - 'was not a balanced human being'. It was said at the time that the outburst, rare for a senior military officer, was either a reflection of the personal animosity between Trost and Lehman or an attempt by Trost to placate Senator Sam Nunn of Georgia, who might have been insulted by comments Lehman had made at his last press conference. Trost was not Lehman's but Weinberger's choice for the post of Chief of Naval Operations. Lehman favoured Admiral Frank B. Kelso II, who instead took over Trost's post as commander of the Atlantic Fleet.

A graduate of the US Naval Academy in 1953, Trost rose to the top post after being a submarine officer. This is somewhat unusual for the Navy, where submarines have long been regarded as inferior to surface ships in general, and aircraft carriers in particular.

After his graduation from the Naval Academy, Trost first saw service on a destroyer before attending submarine school. He was also trained in nuclear power. He then attended a military language school, studying German, before becoming a student at the University of Freiburg in West Germany.

Trost served on both attack and ballistic missile submarines, and was appointed to the command of the Polaris submarine *Sam Rayburn* in 1968. He was promoted to rear-admiral in 1973, and given command of a submarine group based in San Diego, California. Trost's other sea duty has included a tour as deputy commander of the Pacific Fleet, which has its headquarters in Hawaii, and also as commander of the Seventh Fleet in the Western Pacific. When he was appointed to his current post, Trost was serving as commander of the Atlantic Fleet, headquartered in Norfolk, Virginia, a post he took up in 1985.

Trost has also served several stints in Washington, which will help him in his current post. He has been a military assistant to the Secretary of Defense, and later an aide to the Secretary of the Navy. He has also served in the Navy Bureau of Personnel. From 1981 to 1985, Trost was director of Navy programme planning. In that post, he was considered instrumental in steering the Navy budgets, against some opposition, through Congress.
(See: Joint Chiefs of Staff.)

Tuttle, Jerry O., Vice-Admiral (USN), Director, J-6 Command, Control and Communications
(See: Joint Chiefs of Staff.)

Vessey, John W. Jr., General, USA (Retired), Member at Large, Defense Science Board

Vessey is a former Chairman of the Joint Chiefs of Staff and is now a private consultant. He holds an MS from George Washington University. He has also been Vice Chief of Staff, US Army Commander-in-Chief, Republic of Korea—US Combined Forces and Deputy Chief of Staff, Plans and Operations, US Army.
(See: Defense Science Board.)

Vuono, Carl E., General, Chief of Staff of the Army

Carl Vuono was appointed to his post in April 1987 by President Reagan. He was considered an unusual choice for the position as, at 53, he is the youngest of the Army's four-star generals, and he was only promoted to full general in 1986. Further, he is an artillery officer, while most of his predecessors in the post had been infantry or armoured corps officers.

Vuono graduated from the United States Military Academy at West Point in 1957. He commanded two artillery battalions in Vietnam. He has also led the 82nd Airborne Division's artillery, was assistant division commander of the First Infantry at Fort Riley, Kansas, and commanded the Eighth Infantry Division in West Germany. Vouno has served as executive officer to the Army Chief of Staff, and also as a Deputy Chief of Staff. In 1983, he took command of Fort Leavenworth and the US Army Command and General Staff College, the latter of which he is credited with bringing back to life. Before being appointed Chief of Staff, Vuono commanded the Army Training and Doctrine Command at Fort Monroe, Virginia.

Vuono has a solid reputation as a commander, and especially as one capable of training the Army well - which, according to some observers, was a factor in his appointment.
(See: Joint Chiefs of Staff.)

Wade, Troy E. II, Acting Assistant Secretary of Energy for Defense Programs

Wade was named Acting Assistant Secretary for Defense Programs in August 1987, after being appointed Principal Deputy Assistant Secretary for Defense Programs in June 1987. He is responsible for directing the research, testing and development programmes for nuclear warheads; he also manages the production of nuclear materials and is responsible for the security of weapons facilities.

Wade is a graduate of the College of Mechanical Engineering at the University of Colorado. He becamed involved in the US nuclear weapons programme in 1958, when he joined the staff of Lawrence Livermore National Laboratory. He joined the Atomic Energy Commission (the forerunner of the DoE) in 1968 at its Nevada Operations Office. There he served as Nuclear Safety Branch Chief, director of the Test Systems Division, assistant manager of operations, and finally deputy manager.

In July 1981, Wade came to Washington as the Principal Deputy Assistant Secretary of Energy for Defense Programs, a post he held until July 1983. He then became manager of the DoE Idaho Operations Office, where he was responsible for administering programmes involving research and development of defence materials production, reactor development and operations, and nuclear safety. He held this post until assuming his present duties.

Wade was also largely responsible for putting together the Nuclear Emergency Search Team (NEST), a response capability for nuclear emergencies. He was deputy commander of Operation Morning Light, the search for radioactive debris from the Soviet Cosmos satellite which crashed in Canada in 1978.
(See: Department of Energy.)

Warner, John W., Senator (R, Virginia), Ranking Minority Member, Senate, Member, Senate Armed Services Committee
Address: Room SR-421, Russell Senate Office Building, Washington, DC 20510
Tel: (202) 224-2023

Warner is probably best known for having married Elizabeth Taylor. More importantly, he is a powerful conservative Republican. Warner was first elected to the Senate in 1978, and faces a re-election campaign in 1990. He has a BS from Washington and Lee University and an LLB from the University of Virginia. Before being elected to the Senate, he was an attorney and farmer. Warner was also Secretary of the Navy from 1972 until 1974.

As the Ranking Minority Member, Warner is an ex-officio member of all subcommittees. He also serves on the Environment and Public Works Committee, the Rules and Administration Committee, and the Select Committee on Intelligence. A Deputy Minority Whip, Warner is also a member of the Senate Republican Policy Committee and the Senate Arms Control Observer Group.

Key Aides: Bill Wight, National Security Assistant.
(See: The Senate.)

Watkins, Wes, Representative (D, Oklahoma), 3rd District, Member, House Appropriations Committee, Subcommittee on Energy and Water Development
Address: 2348 Rayburn House Office Building, Washington, DC 20515
Tel: (202) 225-4565

Watkins was elected to the House in 1976. He has a BS and an MS from Oklahoma State University. He served in the Oklahoma National Guard from 1961 to 1967. From 1966 to 1968, he was executive director of the Kiamichi Development District of Oklahoma. He was a real-estate agent from 1968 until his election as Oklahoma State Senator in 1975. Watkins does not sit on any other committees.
(See: The House of Representatives.)

Webb, Dr Paul, Member, USAF Scientific Advisory Board (Private consultant)
(See: USAF Scientific Advisory Board (Department of the Air Force).)

Webster, William, H., Director of Central Intelligence

Born in 1924, Webster took a BA in 1947 from Amherst College and a JD from Washington University in 1949. He was admitted to the Missouri Bar in 1949. He served with the legal firm Armstrong, Teasdale, Kramer and Vaughan for much of the period 1949—70. From 1971—73 he was a judge in the US District Court, East Missouri. He was a member of the advisory committee on criminal rules from 1971 to 1978.

In 1978 Webster became director of the Federal Bureau of Investigation (FBI).
(See: Independent Agencies (Central Intelligence Agency).)

Weicker, Lowell P., Senator (R, Connecticut), Member, Senate Appropriations Committee, Defense Subcommittee
Address: Room SR-225, Russell Senate Office Building, Washington, DC 20510
Tel: (202) 224-4041

Weicker, who was elected to the Senate in 1970 and faces re-election this year, is known as a maverick who has often voted against the Reagan Administration. His last election was close (50.4 per cent to 46.1 per cent), and there is speculation that he will be forced out of office in 1988.

Weicker has a BA from Yale University and an LLB from the University of Virginia. He served in the Army from 1953 to 1955, and served in the Connecticut House of Representatives from 1963 until his election to the Senate.

Weicker also sits on the Energy and Natural Resources Committee, the Labor and Human Resources Committee, and the Small Business Committee.

Key Aide: Charles Murphy, Legislative Aide.
(See: The Senate.)

Welch, Major-General Jasper A., USAF (Retired), Member, USAF Scientific Advisory Board
(Jasper Welch Associates)
(See: USAF Scientific Advisory Board (Department of the Air Force).)

Welch, John J., Jr., Assistant Secretary for Acquisition, Air Force

Welch took over as Assistant Secretary of the Air Force for Acquisition in October 1987. He graduated from the Massachusetts Institute of Technology with a BS in engineering in 1951. After his graduation, Welch joined the Chance Vought Corporation of Dallas Texas (later Ling—Temco—Vought and now the LTV Corporation) as a junior engineer on aircraft and missile systems. He held a variety of engineering and programme management positions in flight test, missile operations, anti-submarine warfare, advanced programmes, and aircraft and missile product development, before becoming vice-president in 1965. As vice-president, he was director of all space defence systems programmes. He later became the vice-president and manager of all programmes and functional organizations at the Missiles and Space Division.

Welch temporarily left LTV in August 1969 to become chief scientist of the Air Force. He returned to LTV in September 1970 as vice-president of programmes for LTV Aerospace. He became a corporate vice-president in 1974, and was promoted to senior vice-president with responsibility for all corporate business development efforts in 1975. He stayed in that position until his appointment as Assistant Secretary.

Welch has held a variety of consultant positions with the Defense Science Board, the Air Force Scientific Advisory Board, the Army Science Board, the National Academy of Sciences Naval Studies, and Air Force Systems Command advisory groups. He has been a member of the board of visitors of the Defense Systems Management College and also a member of the Center for Strategic and International Studies Committees on Technology Transfer and Defense Futures. Welch is a member of the Air Force Association.
(See: Department of the Air Force.)

Welch, Larry D., General, Chief of Staff of the Air Force

The current Chief of Staff of the Air Force, General Larry D. Welch, was appointed in July 1986. Welch has a BA in business administration from the University of Maryland and an MS in international relations from the George Washington University. Welch has also completed the Armed Forces Staff College and the National War College.

Welch started his military career in 1951, when he joined the Kansas National Guard. He served with the 16th Armored Field Artillery until joining the Air Force in August 1953. In

November 1953, he started the aviation cadet programme and received his pilot wings and a commission as a second lieutenant. From 1955 until 1958, he served as a flight instructor. In 1958, he was assigned to Headquarters Air Training Command at Randolph Air Force Base in Texas.

From 1962 until 1966, Welch served in tactical fighter units in France and New Mexico. In March 1966, Welch transferred to Vietnam, where he flew combat missions in F-4Cs over North and South Vietnam and Laos. After returning from Vietnam in February 1967, Welch became a student at the Armed Forces Staff College. He finished at the college in July 1967 and was assigned to Air Force Headquarters in Washington, DC, in the office of the assistant chief of staff for studies and analysis. He remained there until 1971, when he went to the National War College.

Welch graduated from the War College in July 1972 and was assigned to the Tactical Air Command, where he served as deputy wing commander for operations, vice-commander, and wing commander. In August 1977, after promotion to brigadier general, Welch was assigned to Tactical Air Command Headquarters, where he served as inspector-general, deputy chief of staff for plans, and deputy chief of staff for operations. In June 1981, he was appointed commander of the 9th Air Force and also Air Force component commander of the Rapid Deployment Joint Task Force. Welch became deputy chief of staff for programmes and resources at Air Force Headquarters in November 1982, and became vice-chief of staff of the Air Force in July 1984. From August 1985 until his appointment as Chief of Staff, Welch was Commander-in-Chief of the Strategic Air Command and director of the Joint Target Planning Staff.

(See: Joint Chiefs of Staff; Department of the Air Force.)

Weldon, Curt, Representative (R, Pennsylvania), 7th District, Member, House Armed Services Committee

Address: 1233 Longworth House Office Building, Washington, DC 20515

Tel: (202) 225-2011

Weldon was elected to the House in 1986 after a career as a teacher. He holds a BA from West Chester University. He sits on the Subcommittees on Military Installations and Facilities, Military Personnel and Compensation, and Seapower and Strategic and Critical Materials. He is also a member of the Merchant Marine and Fisheries Committee.

Key Aide: Nancy Lifset, Legislative Director.

(See: The House of Representatives.)

Welliver, A. D., Member, USAF Scientific Advisory Board (Corporate Vice-President of Engineering and Technology, The Boeing Company)

(See: USAF Scientific Advisory Board (Department of the Air Force).)

Wheaton, Warde, F., President, Honeywell Defense and Marine Systems, Honeywell Incorporated

Wheaton graduated from the US Military Academy in 1950 and served in the Army Corps of Engineers. He came to Honeywell in 1957 as a contract administrator in the Ordnance Division. He was named director of marketing in that division in 1964.

In 1970, Wheaton was named general manager of the Apparatus Controls Division. He became director of the Medical Systems Center in 1974 and later became operations vice-president of the Government and Aeronautical Products Division. In 1977, Wheaton was appointed vice-president and general manager of the Defense Systems Division and a year later became vice-president and group executive of Honeywell's Aerospace and Defense business. In 1983 he became executive vice-president of Aerospace and Defense. He assumed his present position in January 1988.

(See: Defence Contractors.)

Whitman, Dr Robert V., Member, USAF Scientific Advisory Board

(Civil Engineering, Massachusetts Institute

of Technology)
(See: USAF Scientific Advisory Board (Department of the Air Force.)

Williams, Earle C. (Electrical Engineer), Ex-Officio Member, Defense Science Board, Chairman, Naval Research Advisory Committee

President and chief executive officer of BDM International Inc., Williams holds a BS from Auburn University. His other positions at BDM have been vice-president/general manager, director of operations, special projects director and senior engineer.
(See: Defense Science Board.)

Williams, Dr Max L., Jr., Member, USAF Scientific Advisory Board
(Air Force Institute of Technology)
(See: USAF Scientific Advisory Board (Department of the Air Force).)

Wilson, Charles, Representative (D, Texas), 2nd District Member, House Appropriations Committee, Subcommittee on Defense
Address: 2265 Rayburn House Office Building, Washington, DC 20515
Tel: (202) 225-2401

Wilson was elected to the House in 1972. He has a BS from the US Naval Academy, and served in the Navy from 1956 to 1960. In 1960, he was elected a Texas State Representative. From 1966 until his election to the House, he was a Texas State Senator. Wilson also serves on the Select Committee on Intelligence.

Key Aide: D'Anna Stanfield, Associate Staff.
(See: The House of Representatives.)

Wilson, John R., Jr., Rear-Admiral; The Chief of Naval Research

Wilson joined the Naval Reserve in 1950, where he served for a year before attending the US Naval Academy. He graduated from the Naval Academy in 1955 and earned his pilot wings in 1956. Wilson served with both fighter squadrons and a guided missile unit before going to Naval Test Pilot School in 1961.

After his graduation, Wilson was assigned as an aide and flag lieutenant to the commander of Carrier Division Four. He saw combat duty as a pilot in Vietnam before returning to the Naval Test Pilot School as operations officer in 1968. He later served with a variety of fighter squadrons, and was operations officer at the Naval Missile Center in Point Mugu, California. In 1976, Wilson was promoted to captain and became head of the Air Launched Guided Missile Branch at the Naval Air Systems Command Headquarters. He was designated rear-admiral (lower half) in 1982 and served as director for logistics and security assistance with the Commander-in-Chief, Pacific Fleet, from September 1982 to July 1984. From July 1984 to June 1986 he was commander of the Pacific Missile Test Center.

Wilson became deputy assistant for Navy ranges/field activities management at the Naval Air Systems Command in June 1986, and served there until January 1987. In December 1986, he was promoted to rear-admiral. From January 1987 to September 1987, when he assumed his present duties, Wilson was assistant commander for systems and engineering at the Naval Air Systems Command.
(See: Department of the Navy.)

Wilson, Pete, Senator (R, California), Member of Senate Armed Services Committee
Address: Room SH-720, Hart Senate Office Building, Washington, DC 20510
Tel: (202) 224-3841

Wilson, who is running a re-election campaign this year, was elected to the Senate in 1982. He has a BA from Yale University and a JD from the University of California at Berkeley. He was an attorney before coming to the Senate.

The Ranking Minority Member of the Manpower and Personnel Subcommittee, Wilson also sits on the Conventional Forces and Alliance Defense Subcommittee and the Strategic Forces and Nuclear Deterrence Subcommittee. Wilson also sits on the Agriculture, Nutrition, and Forestry Committee, the Commerce, Science, and Transportation Commttee, the Joint Economic Committee, and the Special Committee on Aging.

Wilson is also a Deputy Minority Whip and a member of the Senate Republican Committee on Committees.
(See: The Senate.)

Wirth, Timothy E., Senator (D, Colorado), Member of Senate Armed Services Committee
Address: Room SR-380, Russell Senate Office Building, Washington, DC 20510
Tel: (202) 224-5852

Wirth, who was elected to the Senate in 1986, served in the House of Representatives from 1974 to 1986. Before that, he was a corporate executive. Wirth has a BA and an M.Ed. from Harvard University and a Ph.D. from Stanford University.

Wirth sits on the subcommittees on Conventional Forces and Alliance Defense, Defense Industry and Technology, and Readiness, Sustainability and Support. He is also a member of the Banking, Housing, and Urban Affairs Committee, the Budget Committee, and the Energy and Natural Resources Committee. A Deputy Majority Whip, Wirth is also on the board of visitors of the US Air Force Academy.

Key Aide: Bob Griffith, Legislative Assistant.
(See: The Senate.)

Woodruff, Lawrence, Deputy Under Secretary of Defense, (Strategic and Theater Nuclear Forces), Office of the Secretary of Defense

Woodruff was appointed to his current post in October 1985. He has a BS and an MS in mechanical engineering, both from the University of California at Berkeley. In addition, he has a Ph.D. in mechanical engineering received from the University of California at Davis.

In 1964, Woodruff worked for the Boeing Company in the area of advanced thermal re-entry protection systems. In 1966, he moved to the Lockheed Missiles and Space Company, where he developed super-orbital re-entry heat shielding requirements.

From 1967 until 1980, Woodruff worked at Lawrence Livermore National Laboratory. His appointments there included deputy group leader/weapons effects and then deputy division leader/research engineering division. His special assignments included participation in two Defense Science Board task forces on ICBM basing and in the Air Force Scientific Advisory Board Summary Workshops on ICBM Basing and Verification.

In 1980, Woodruff joined TRW as assistant programme manager for concepts and plans at the Air Force's Ballistic Missile Office, a division of the Advanced Strategic Missile Systems Program. In 1981, Woodruff became manager of systems engineering operations supporting the Peacekeeper (MX) and Minuteman programmes. At the time of his appointment to his current post, Woodruff was the TRW programme manager for the Small ICBM (Midgetman) Program.
(See: Office of the Secretary of Defense (Department of Defense).)

Worsham, James E., Corporate Vice President—Aerospace Group Executive, McDonnell Douglas Corporation

Worsham, who came to McDonnell Douglas in 1982, has a BS in mechanical engineering from Vanderbilt University and an MS in mechanical engineering from the University of Arkansas. He was a captain in the US Army from 1943 to 1946.

After Worsham received his MS in 1950, he went to work for the General Electric Company as a design engineer. In 1965, he became GE1 project general manager. In 1970, Worsham became project general manager—advanced engines. He became vice president—military engines in 1973 and vice president-commercial engines in 1976. In 1981, Worsham was appointed vice president—market development.

Worsham came to McDonnell Douglas in 1982 as executive vice-president of the Douglas Aircraft Company and corporate vice-president of McDonnell Douglas Corporation. Later in 1982 he became president of Douglas Aircraft. He assumed his present duties in 1987.
(See: Defence Contractors.)

Yang, Dr Henry T. Y.,Member, USAF Scientific Advisory Board

(Dean, School of Engineering, Purdue University)
(See: USAF Scientific Advisory Board (Department of the Air Force.)

Young, Bill C. W., Representative (R, Florida), 8th District, Member, House Appropriations Committee, Subcommittee on Defense
Address: Rayburn House Office Building, Washington DC 20515

Young was elected to the House in 1970. From 1948 to 1957 he served in the Florida National Guard. He was a district assistant to Representative William Cramer from 1957 to 1960, when he was elected as a Florida State Senator. He served in the State Senate until his election to the House, including a stint as Minority Leader in 1966. Young only sits on the Appropriations Committee.

Key Aide: Douglas Gregory, Associate Staff.
(See: The House of Representatives.)

REFERENCES

Arkin, W. M., 1981, *Research Guide to Current Military and Strategic Affairs*, Institute for Policy Studies, Washington, DC/Transnational Institute, Amsterdam.

Bracken, Paul, 1983, *The Command and Control of Nuclear Forces*, Yale University Press, New Haven.

Committee on Armed Services, 1985, *Defense Organization: The Need for Change*, S. Prt., 99—86, 99th Congress, 1st Session, US Congress, Senate.

Eden, Lynn, 1984, 'Capitalist conflict and the state', in Bright, C. (ed.), *Statemaking and Social Movements: Essays in History and Theory*, University of Michigan Press, Ann Arbor, Michigan.

Falk, J., 1985, 'Beyond deterrence: logic behind the arms race', in *Metascience*, Vol. 3. pp 54—70.

Fallows, James, 1981, *National Defense*, Random House, New York.

Ford, Daniel, 1985, *The Button: The Pentagon's Strategic Command and Control System*, Touchstone, New York.

Gansler, J., 1980, *The Defense Industry*, The MIT Press, Cambridge, Mass.

Gervasi, T., 1988, *Soviet Military Power: The Pentagon's Propaganda Document Annotated and Corrected*, Vintage Books, New York.

General Accounting Office, 1987, *DoD Revolving Door: Post DoD Employment May Raise Concerns*, GAO/NSIAD—87—116, Government Printing Office, Washington, DC.

General Accounting Office, 1987, *Post DOD Employment: Evaluation of the Draft Regulation Implementing of 10 USC 2397b*, GAO/NSIAD—87—152BR, Government Printing Office, Washington, DC.

Karas, Thomas, 1983, *The New High Ground*, Touchstone, New York.

Kotz, Nick, 1988, *Wild Blue Yonder: Money, Politics and the B-1 Bomber*, Pantheon, New York.

Kurth, J. R., 'Why we buy the weapons we do', in Ferguson, T., and Rogers, J. (eds), 1984, *The Political Economy*, M. E. Sharpe, White Plains, N. Y.

Manno, Jack, 1984, *Arming the Heavens: The Hidden Military Agenda for Space*, Dodd, Mead and Co., New York.

McLean, Scilla (ed.), 1986, *How Nuclear Weapons Decisions Are Made*, Macmillan/Oxford Research Group, London.

Richelson, Jeffrey, 1985, *The U. S. Intelligence Community*, Ballinger Publishing Company, Cambridge, Mass.

Rovner, M., 1982, *Defense Dollars and Sense*, Common Cause, Washington DC.

Scheer, Robert, 1983, *With Enough Shovels: Reagan, Bush and Nuclear War*, Vintage, New York.

Tsipis, Kosta, 1983, *Arsenal: Understanding Weapons in the Nuclear Age*, Simon and Schuster, New York.

United States Government Manual 1987—88, 1987, Office of the Federal Register, Washington, DC.

Zuckerman, Lord Solly, 1983, *Nuclear Illusion and Reality*, Vintage, New York.

~2~

The Soviet Union

The principal bodies concerned with nuclear weapons decisionmaking in the Soviet Union are the Communist Party, the government, the armed forces, and the defence industry. The institutional framework for decisionmaking is known in the West in general terms, but many details of organizations and personnel remain obscure. Despite the very real improvement under Gorbachev in the provision of information, the policy of *glasnost'* has so far only to a limited degree extended to the military sphere. It is true that the INF treaty with its unprecedented provisions for on-site verification has led to the release of much hitherto classified information and that there has been Western access to such previously secret installations as the Semipalatinsk nuclear test site, the Shikhany chemical weapons base and the new Krasnoyarsk radar, but this welcome openness has had little impact on our understanding of decisionmaking processes and their actors. An additional complication of the post-Brezhnev years has been the very substantial renewal of personnel: a very high proportion of the leading officials discussed below have been appointed since Gorbachev came to power in March 1985. This extensive renewal creates difficulties for the Western analyst: firstly, biographical details are often sparse, or non-existent, for those of recent appointment, and, secondly, it is often difficult to identify the new office-holders. The latter applies with particular force to the leading scientists and designers of the defence industry. Nevertheless, it has proved possible to assemble biographical details for 109 leading individuals concerned in some way with nuclear-related decisionmaking, plus the names and posts of a further twelve for whom further details are not available.

The formal institutional framework of Soviet national security decisionmaking is shown in Figure 2.1. It must be emphasized that in practice there are probably also many important informal relationships, but while there is some evidence on these for an earlier period, virtually nothing is known for the present day. The principal bodies are the Communist Party, with its Central Committee Secretariat and Politburo, the Supreme Soviet, the Defence Council, the agencies of government under the Council of Ministers, including the ministries of the defence industry, the foreign ministry, and the Ministry of Defence, with its armed services.

Other agencies of note include the Academy of Sciences with its network of research establishments, including those concerned with foreign policy issues, and bodies concerned with peace and disarmament, including the Soviet Committee for the Defence of Peace. In order to place the officials in an institutional context, these agencies are briefly reviewed in the following section.

THE COMMUNIST PARTY OF THE SOVIET UNION

Address: Staraya Ploshchad' 4, Moscow 103132

The Soviet Union is a single party state. According to the latest edition of the Constitution (adopted in 1977), the Communist Party is the 'leading and guiding force in Soviet society and

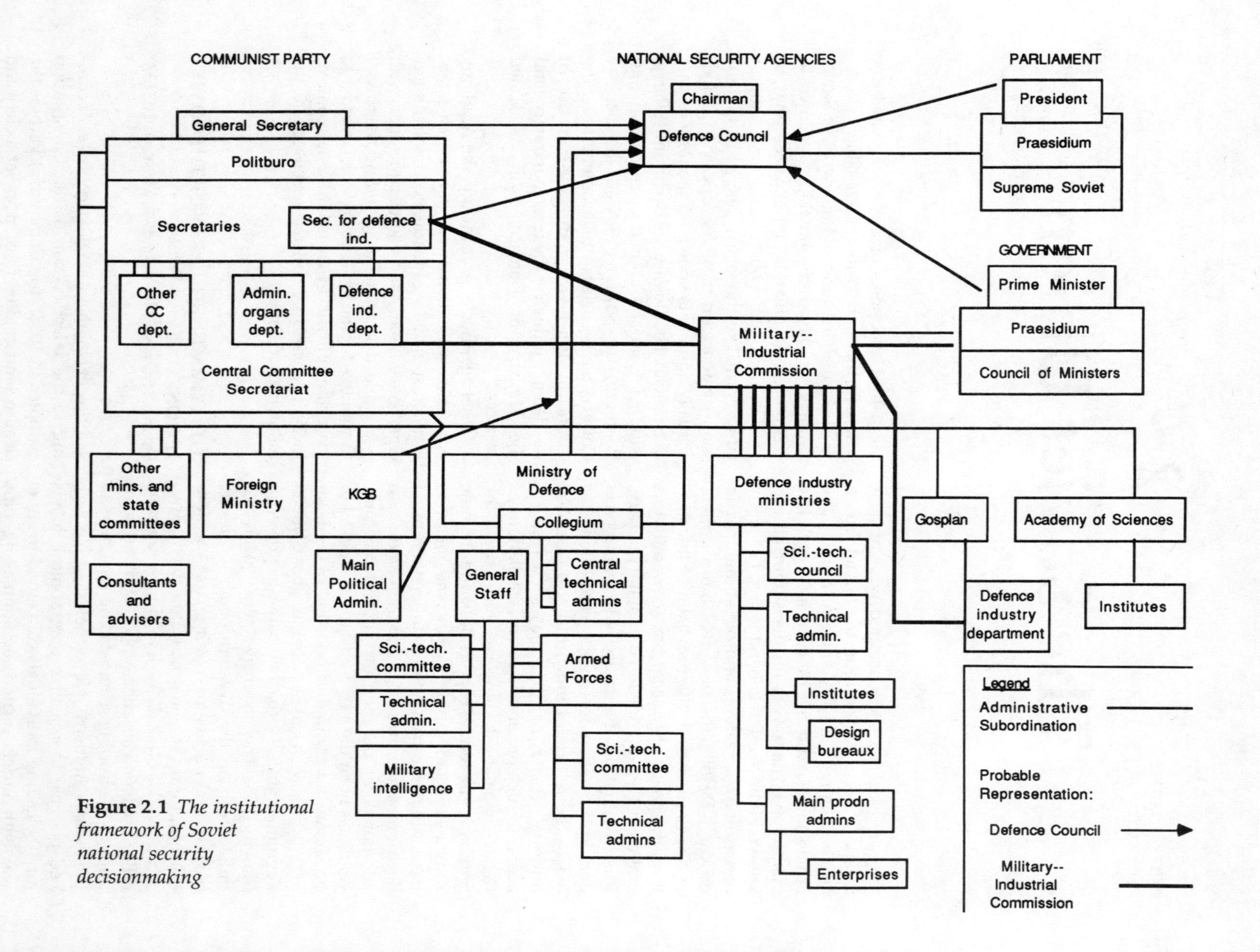

Figure 2.1 *The institutional framework of Soviet national security decisionmaking*

the nucleus of its political system...Armed with Marxism-Leninism [it] determines the general perspectives of the development of society and the course of the domestic and foreign policy of the USSR'(*Constitution (Fundamental Law) of the Union of Soviet Socialist Republics*, p.21). Membership of the Party currently stands at more than 19 million, drawn from all sections of society. At the base of the Party are the primary branches, some 450,000 in number, usually organized at places of work; at the apex are the Central Committee Secretariat and the Politburo. The organizational principle of the Party is democratic centralism, according to which all leading bodies are elected, the decisions of higher bodies are binding on those beneath, and once decisions are made they must be fulfilled by all concerned with the subordination of the minority to the majority. Throughout the Party a distinction is drawn between full and candidate membership, both for individual members and for membership of elected Party bodies. Full members enjoy all rights of membership; candidate members may be present at meetings and speak, but do not have the right to vote. Although appropriate information is not available in every case, it can be safely assumed that all 122 of the individuals reviewed are full Party members.

The Communist Party is constitutionally and organizationally separate from the system of government administration, but in practice the lines of demarcation are often blurred. The Party determines the main lines of domestic and foreign policy, mobilizes support for the fulfilment of these policies, and checks on the implementation of measures to put these policies into practice. It also exercises control over the appointment of leading personnel in the state administrative structure. The system of government is concerned with legislation and the execution of policy. Its top officials are simultaneously members of the leading organs of the Party and are thus involved in both policymaking and implementation. The Soviet Union has a highly politicized system of state administration: all government officials are expected actively to support and promote the policies of the Party and government departments have their own Party organizations to ensure that this occurs. This intimate relationship of Party and government means that some high-level state bodies effectively function as joint Party–government agencies, and the formal lines of demarcation are further blurred by the practice of adopting joint Party and government decrees on major issues of policy relating to the spheres of competence of state organizations (on the Soviet political system, see Lane, 1985).

The Congress

According to the Party's rules, the supreme body is the Congress, which takes place every five years. Some 5,000 delegates elected from Party organizations meet for almost a week to review the experience of the preceding period and adopt policy for the future. Foreign policy and security issues are considered in broad terms in the report of the General Secretary. The Congress usually approves the draft outlines of the forthcoming five-year plan for the economy and in so far as it incorporates projections of the growth of national income, industrial output, and investment and consumption, it must be based on some assessment of the level of defence expenditure considered appropriate in the light of the prevailing international situation. Congress elects the Central Committee. It also elects the Central Auditing Commission, which has responsibility for oversight of the Party's finances. Membership of this Commission is often a stepping-stone to membership of the Central Committee. While practices may change as the Gorbachev-led democratization proceeds, until now election to the Central Committee has been by secret ballot according to a single recommended list covering all the places on the Committee (the list being drawn up in advance by the Secretariat of the outgoing Central Committee). Almost without exception the leading figures identified here can normally expect to be elected as Congress delegates.

The Party rules also provide for the convening of Conferences between Congresses, although for many years this option was not taken up: the 18th Party Conference was held in 1941; the 19th in June 1988. The Conference can discuss major issues of policy and also renew part of the membership of the Central Committee.

The Central Committee

The Central Committee elected at the 27th Party Congress in March 1986 consisted of 304 full members and 172 candidate members. Of the total membership, almost 40 per cent are local, regional and national Party officials, and almost 20 per cent government ministers and chairmen of state committees, including those concerned with the defence sector. Military officers account for 7 per cent of the total and there are also a number of leading scientists and designers with military associations. According to the author's estimate, approximately 12 per cent of the total have direct military and defence industry associations. While women account for some 30 per cent of total Party membership, their representation on the Central Committee is a mere 4 per cent. Most leading Party and government officials can expect to be elected to the Central Committee simply by virtue of the importance of the posts they occupy. However, since 1986 the rapid renewal of personnel has meant that many of those elected have been removed from the posts that qualified them for membership, and their successors await election at the next Congress in 1991. Of the 122 officials and others reviewed here, seventy (57 per cent) are currently members of the Central Committee.

The Party Central Committee meets in plenary session at least twice a year to discuss major issues of policy. It also elects the members of the Politburo and the Central Committee Secretaries, including the General Secretary. Membership of the Central Committee is a matter of considerable prestige and must facilitate access to the real centres of power. For those in the spheres of science and industry it may bring benefits in terms of an enhanced ability to command resources and to resolve problems by direct resort to the highest authorities.

(See biographies of: Akhromeev; Arbatov; Baklanov; Basistov; Belousov, I. S.; Belyakov, O. S.; Biryukova; Chebrikov; Chernavin; Chernyaev; Demichev; Dobrynin; Dolgikh; Efimov; Finogenov; Frolov, I. T.; Frolov, K. V.; Gerasimov; Glushko; Gorbachev; Govorov; Gromyko; Gusev; Ivanovskii; Kolesnikov; Kolpakov; Kurkotkin; Lemaev; Ligachev; Lizichev; Luk'yanov; Lushev; Maksimov, Y. P.; Marchuk; Maslyukov; Medvedev; Nikonov; Ogarkov; Pervyshin; Primakov; Pugin; Razumovskii; Rodin; Ryzhkov; Savinkin; Shabanov; Shcherbina; Shcherbitskii; Shevardnadze; Shkabardnya; Silaev; Slyunkhov; Smyslov; Solomentsev; Solov'ev; Systsov; Talyzin; Tret'yak; Utkin; Vedernikov; Velichko; Velikhov; Voronin; Vorontsov; Vorotnikov; Yagodin; Yakovlev; Yazov; Zaikov; Zaitsev.)

The Politburo

Address: Communist Party of the Soviet Union (see above)

For the day-to-day running of the country the principal decisionmaking body is the Party Political Bureau, the Politburo, usually having from twenty to twenty-four members elected by a plenary meeting of the Central Committee. It normally meets every Thursday, the sessions being chaired by the General Secretary (Gorbachev), or, in his absence, the effective deputy General Secretary (Ligachev). At the time of writing the Politburo has thirteen full members and seven candidate members. The available evidence indicates that most decisions are reached by consensus, with votes rarely taken, which suggests that the full/candidate distinction probably has little practical significance.

The members of the Politburo are the leading officials of both the Party and government. Of the present twenty members, eight (Gorbachev, Ligachev, Zaikov, Yakovlev, Nikonov, Slyunkhov, Dolgikh and Razumovskii) are Party Secretaries. Zaikov is unusual in so far as he appears to combine an important Secretarial responsibility, oversight of the defence industry, with the post of First Secretary of the Moscow city Party Committee. The two other Party officials are the Ukrainian and Leningrad leaders (Shcherbitskii and Solov'ev), although there is evidence that those based outside Moscow do not attend all Politburo meetings. Finally on the Party side there is the Chairman of the Party Control Committee (Solomentsev); the Committee handles questions of discipline in the Party. On the government side, the members are the head of state (Gromyko) and his first deputy (Demichev), the Chairman of the Council of Ministers (Ryzhkov) and two of his first deputies (Maslyukov - Chairman of the State Planning Committee, and Talyzin - Chairman of the Bureau for Social Development), the Minister of Foreign Affairs (Shevardnadze), the Chairman of the KGB (Chebrikov), the Chairman of the Russian Soviet Federal Socialist Republic (RSFSR) Council of Ministers (Vorotnikov) and the Minister of Defence (Yazov), the latter being a candidate member. Other ministers and officials, including newspaper editors, also attend Politburo meetings when particular issues relating to their competence are under discussion.

The agenda of the Politburo meetings is prepared by the Secretariat and, given the overlapping membership of the two bodies, it is likely that many issues have been effectively resolved and decisions drafted in advance of the actual Politburo meetings. From the reports of meetings regularly published in the press it is clear that the agenda includes a very wide range of domestic and foreign policy issues. The Politburo analyses developments, establishes priorities, takes policy decisions and exercises oversight over the implementation of agreed policy. It is likely that major military-related issues are discussed, although there is uncertainty about the spheres of competence in military matters of the Politburo and the Defence Council. Major issues probably at least require Politburo ratification.

(See biographies of: Chebrikov; Demichev; Dolgikh; Gorbachev; Gromyko; Ligachev; Maslyukov; Nikonov; Razumovskii; Ryzhkov; Shcherbitskii; Shevardnadze; Slyunkhov; Solomentsev; Solov'ev; Talyzin; Vorotnikov; Yakovlev; Yazov; Zaikov.)

The General Secretary and His Assistants

Within the collective leadership of the Politburo the Party General Secretary is the dominant figure. Whereas other Secretaries have certain broadly defined spheres of competence, the General Secretary's brief extends to the entire range of issues facing the Soviet state. From the constitutional point of view, the General Secretary is simply the head of the ruling Party and not the head of state, the latter being the Chairman of the Presidium of the Supreme Soviet (Gromyko). Some past General Secretaries, e.g., Brezhnev, have occupied both posts, but Gorbachev has on many occasions effectively carried out the duties of head of state (e.g., the Washington summit meeting and the signing of the draft INF treaty) while remaining only Party leader.

In his work the General Secretary is aided by a group of assistants and a personal secretariat. The assistants appear to fulfil the role of a 'kitchen cabinet', advising the leader and writing speeches on his behalf. Gorbachev has assembled an impressive group of assistants, including prominent advocates of the 'new thinking' on domestic and foreign policy that characterizes his leadership (Frolov, Shakhnazarov and Chernyaev).

(See biographies of: Chernyaev; Frolov, I. T.; Gorbachev; Shakhnazarov.)

The Central Committee Secretariat

Address: Communist Party of the Soviet Union (see above)

The Secretariat is the principal administrative organ of the Party, its head office, and has within it a range of departments concerned with specific spheres of Soviet life, including the armed forces, and weapons development and production. According to the Party rules, the Secretariat is responsible to the Central Committee for directing 'current work, chiefly the selection of cadres and the organization of the verification of the fulfilment of decisions' (Lane, 1985, p.337, slightly modified translation). The Secretaries, currently twelve in number (excluding Gorbachev), are elected by the Central Committee and have responsibility for oversight of particular areas of work and the departments associated with them. The Secretaries have different levels of seniority. After the General Secretary, there is an effective deputy General Secretary with overall responsibility for the work of the Secretariat (currently

Ligachev), whose duties appear to include chairing the regular meetings of the Secretariat. These meetings, attended by the Secretaries and department heads, review matters of current concern and prepare materials for the Politburo. The evidence suggests that they are often attended by leading representatives of the media, foreign policy specialists, scientists and other leading officials. In the absence of the deputy leader, these meetings are chaired by a senior Secretary (currently Zaikov).

For military-related matters the Secretaries of greatest significance are those responsible for oversight of the defence industry (Zaikov appears to have overall responsibility, with the more recently appointed Baklanov exercising day-to-day oversight), of the so-called 'administrative organs' (the armed forces, security services and judiciary) (Luk'yanov), and of international affairs (Dobrynin). Other Secretaries of note include Yakovlev (ideology and propaganda), Slyunkhov (economic planning and management), Razumovskii (the Party's own organizational affairs, including appointments), Medvedev (relations with Eastern Europe and other ruling communist parties), Dolgikh (heavy industry) and Biryukova (social and welfare issues). Biryukova is notable for being the only woman in the top ranks of the Party leadership (and the sole woman in our set of 122 officials). It is unlikely that she has any direct involvement in defence-related decision-making, although she must have contact with the defence industry in so far as it is an important producer of consumer goods.

Within the Secretariat there is a Defence Industry Department (headed by Belyakov), which monitors the work of the military sector of economy (and the space programme). This department has various sections concerned with particular branches of the defence industry including, presumably, nuclear weapons, although the official responsible for the latter has not been identified. There is also a Department of the Administrative Organs (headed by Savinkin), which appears to exercise supervision over senior appointments in the armed forces, the KGB, police and judiciary. Another department concerned to some extent with military-related issues is that for science and educational establishments. This department (headed by Grigor'ev) oversees the work of the Academy of Sciences and the higher educational system, and it is notable that the obituaries of leading defence industry scientists and designers often include the signature of its head. Finally, there is the International Department (headed by Dobrynin), which in recent years appears to have become increasingly involved in arms control issues and to have appointed a number of military officers to its staff.

An important aspect of the Secretariat's work is its responsibility for the selection and placement of leading personnel. Many responsible posts within the institutions of the state are covered by the *nomenklatura* system, according to which those occupying them must be on a list approved by the central Party authorities. The *nomenklatura* system is likely to be of particular importance in militarily sensitive fields and probably covers all the officials reviewed below. The *nomenklatura* system is one of the crucial mechanisms by which the Party exercises its leading and guiding role in Soviet society. Another important mechanism is the adoption by the Central Committee of resolutions outlining measures to be implemented by lower Party organizations to tackle problems identified by the centre. These resolution are drafted by the Central Committee departments and the Secretariat and passed to the Politburo for approval. On significant questions concerning the work of state institutions, the Party will often secure the adoption of decrees in the name of both the Central Committee and the Council of Ministers (see below). Whereas the Party resolutions are binding only for other Party organizations, the joint decrees have the force of law.

The structure of the Party organs outlined above applies to the Soviet Union as a whole. Each of the Republics, except the largest, the Russian Soviet Federal Socialist Republic (RSFSR), has its own Party Central Committee, Politburo and Secretariat, and there are leading committees in the regions and cities. The Republics, and some regions and cities, have their own Party defence industry departments and it is likely that they maintain close links

with the central department in Moscow, keeping it informed of local problems.
(See biographies of: Baklanov; Belyakov, O. S.; Biryukova; Dobrynin; Dolgikh; Gorbachev; Grigor'ev; Medvedev; Larin; Ligachev; Luk'yanov; Nikonov; Razumovskii; Savinkin; Slyunkhov; Yakovlev; Zaikov.)

THE STATE

Questions of nuclear weapons and national security are handled by a number of institutions of the Soviet state. These include the Soviet parliament (Supreme Soviet), the government (Council of Ministers), the state security organization (KGB), and the various ministries and state committees, including those involved in weapons development and production.

The Supreme Soviet

Address: Kremlin, Moscow

According to the Constitution, the highest body of state authority competent to take decisions on all issues of national importance is the USSR Supreme Soviet. This parliamentary body with its elected deputies enacts laws, approves state plans for economic development, and decides the composition of the Council of Ministers. It has two chambers, the Soviet of the Union and the Soviet of Nationalities, with equal rights, each having 750 elected deputies, and a number of Standing Commissions, which can examine the work of government bodies and initiate and prepare new legislation. Thus both chambers have Commissions on Foreign Affairs, that of the former chaired by Ligachev, of the latter by Dobrynin. It was a joint session of these Commissions that began the discussion of the INF treaty in preparation for its ratification by the full Supreme Soviet. There is no Commission specifically for consideration of military matters.

Leading officials of the Party and government, and senior military officers, can normally expect to gain election to the Supreme Soviet. Of the set of 122 considered here, eighty-two (two-thirds) are deputies.

The Supreme Soviet normally meets for two sessions a year; continuity is provided by the Standing Commissions and, above all, the Soviet's Presidium, which between sessions is the supreme organ of state authority.
(See biographies of: Akhromeev; Arbatov; Anfimov; Baklanov; Basistov; Belousov, B. M.; Belousov, I. S.; Belyakov, O. S.; Belyakov, R. A.; Bespalov; Biryukova; Chebrikov; Chernavin; Chernyaev; Demichev; Dobrynin; Dolgikh; Durasov; Efimov; Finogenov; Frolov, I. T.; Gerasimov; Glushko; Gorbachev; Govorov; Grigor'ev; Gromyko; Gusev; Ivanovskii; Kolesnikov; Kolpakov; Kotel'nikov; Kovalev, S. N.; Kurkotkin; Lapygin; Ligachev; Lizichev; Lukonin; Luk'yanov; Lushev; Maksimov, Y. P.; Marchuk; Maslyukov; Medvedev; Nikonov; Ogarkov; Panichev; Pervyshin; Primakov; Pugin; Razumovskii; Rodin; Ryabev; Ryzhkov; Sagdeev; Savinkin; Semenikhin; Shabanov; Shcherbina; Shcherbitskii; Shestopalov; Shevardnadze; Shkabardnya; Silaev; Slyunkhov; Smyslov; Solomentsev; Solov'ev; Sorokin; Systsov; Talyzin; Tolstykh; Tret'yak; Tupolev; Utkin; Vedernikov; Velichko; Velikhov; Voronin; Vorontsov; Vorotnikov; Yagodin; Yakovlev; Yashin; Yazov; Zaikov; Zaitsev.)

The Presidium of the Supreme Soviet

Address: Supreme Soviet (see above)

The Presidium, which has approximately forty members, meets about once every two months. According to the Constitution, its Chairman (Gromyko) is the Soviet head of state, although in practice this position is often occupied by the Party General Secretary. The Presidium has extensive powers, including the right to appoint ministers, ratify international treaties, and declare war. The Constitution also states that the Presidium of the Supreme Soviet shall 'form the Council of Defence of the USSR and confirm its composition; appoint and dismiss the high command of the Armed Forces of the USSR' (*Constitution*, p. 89).
(See biographies of: Demichev; Gromyko; Shcherbitskii.)

The Defence Council

Address: not available

The existence of the Defence Council was not

revealed untill 1976, when it was disclosed that Brezhnev was its chairman. Later it became known that he had occupied this post since his election as General Secretary in 1964. There is some confusion as to its status. From a formal constitutional point of view it appears to be an organ of state administration (see Jones, 1984), and according to one Soviet work on administrative law it is headed by the Chairman of the Presidium of the Supreme Soviet (*Sovetskoe administrativnoe pravo*, 1981, p.375). But in practice it seems to be more like a joint Party—state organ; its chairman is the Party leader, Gorbachev. The membership of the Council has not been revealed, but is generally considered to include the Minister of Defence (Yazov), the Chairman of the Council of Ministers (Ryzhkov), and the head of the KGB (Chebrikov). Other members may include the Party number two (Ligachev), the Secretary for the defence industry (Zaikov) and the Chairman of Gosplan (Maslyukov). It is thought that the Chief of the General Staff (Akhromeev) serves as secretary to the Defence Council, preparing its agenda. Following the practice of the Politburo and Secretariat, it is likely that other officials attend meetings when required.

The Defence Council has wide powers with respect to all aspects of national security. From fragmentary evidence in Soviet sources it can be deduced that it co-ordinates the defence-related activities of state, Party and government agencies, reviews and decides all basic questions of the country's 'military development' and has an important role in arms control and disarmament decisionmaking. The Soviet term 'military development' refers to the entire system of economic, political and strictly military measures adopted by the state to enhance its military potential. It therefore concerns such questions as the structure and organization of the armed forces, military personnel and technical policy, and the procurement of weapons. It is likely that the Defence Council oversees the weapons acquisition process, at least for major systems, and provides overall direction and co-ordination of the work of the various agencies concerned, including the Military—Industrial Commission. What is not clear is the extent to which the Council refers decisions to the Politburo for ratification.

In the event of war, the Defence Council would probably be converted rapidly into the supreme organ of political and military leadership, similar to the State Committee for Defence which led the Soviet Union during the last war.

(See biographies of: Akhromeev; Chebrikov; Gorbachev; Ligachev; Maslyukov; Ryzhkov; Yazov; Zaikov.)

The Council of Ministers

Address: Kremlin, Moscow

The Council of Ministers is the Government of the Soviet Union, in the words of the Constitution, 'the highest executive and administrative body of state authority'. It is formed by the Supreme Soviet and consists of a chairman (Ryzhkov), who is in effect the Soviet Prime Minister, and several first deputy and deputy chairmen, this group constituting its Presidium, plus ministers and chairmen of state committees, and also the chairmen of the fifteen republican Councils of Ministers, making a total of some 130 members. The full Council meets quarterly; most of its authority is delegated to its Presidium, which meets weekly and has extensive powers, including the right to issue legally binding decrees and orders. All the national industrial ministries and the state committees concerned with planning, science and technology, and other economic matters, are subordinate to the Council of Ministers, as also are the Ministry of Defence, Ministry of Foreign Affairs, KGB and Academy of Sciences. The Council is charged with ensuring the direction of economic, social and cultural development, and with exercising general direction of the development of the armed forces. The Presidium does not include representatives of either the armed forces or the KGB, presumably because they have their own high-level body, the Defence Council, but does include the chairman of the Military-Industrial Commission.

(See biographies of: Belousov, I. S.; Gusev; Maslyukov; Ryzhkov; Shcherbina; Silaev; Talyzin; Tolstykh; Vedernikov; Voronin.)

The Military—Industrial Commission
Address: not available

The Commission of the Presidium of the USSR Council of Ministers for Military—Industrial Questions (often known in the West by its Russian initials, VPK (*voenno—promyshlennaya komissiya*)) is a body whose existence is rarely acknowledged in Soviet publications. Little is known about its organization and activities. Its chairman (Belousov) is a deputy chairman of the Council of Ministers and its members are known to include the ministers of the nine defence industry ministries (see below). Other members probably include the Party Secretary responsible for the defence industry (Zaikov or Baklanov), the head of the Defence Industry Department of the Central Committee (Belyakov O. S.), the State Planning Committee (Gosplan) first deputy head responsible for the defence sector (Smyslov), and some representatives of important branches of civilian industry, possibly on an associate member basis. The chairman is assisted by a first deputy and several deputies, but the identities of the present office-holders are not known.

It is likely that the VPK's functions include the following. Firstly, co-ordination of the activities of the ministries concerned with military production, including the defence-related work of nominally civilian ministries. Secondly, general oversight and checking on the fulfilment of Party and government decisions and the assignments of state plans. Thirdly, the preliminary consideration of draft plans for the development of the defence industry prepared in association with Gosplan and the ministries. Fourthly, co-ordination of weapons research and development. Fifthly, responsibility for weapons-related scientific and technical information, including material gathered abroad by the intelligence services and other agencies. Given this range of tasks it is likely that the VPK has a sizeable staff. As a commission of the Presidium of the Council of Ministers the VPK has a higher standing in the administrative hierarchy than the ministries and other bodies it co-ordinates. This, together with its high-level Party links, must endow the VPK with considerable authority and should ensure that it is able effectively to resolve inter-departmental disputes.

(See biographies of: Baklanov; Basistov; Belousov, I. S.; Belousov, B. M.; Belyakov; Doguzhiev; Finogenov; Koksanov; Kolesnikov; Pervyshin; Ryabev; Shimko; Smyslov; Systsov; Zaikov.)

The Ministries of the Defence Industry

The Soviet defence industry represents an important sector of the socialist planned economy (see Holloway, 1983). Most end-product weapons production and the manufacture of major assemblies and components is undertaken by enterprises subordinate to the nine industrial ministries generally considered as constituting the Soviet defence industry. The number of enterprises and the size of labour force employed in these ministries has not been revealed and is impossible to determine them with any accuracy from Soviet published sources. According to the US Department of Defence, more than 150 major final-assembly plants build weapons systems, with a further 150 supplying combat support equipment (including radar and communications systems) (*Soviet Military Power*, 1984, p.93). In addition, some militarily-related products and also materials, components and production equipment are supplied by enterprises of nominally civilian industrial ministries.

In many respect the defence industry is similar to its civilian counterpart. All enterprises and facilities are stateowned and administered by ministries subordinated to the Council of Ministers. The defence industry enterprise operates according to a plan setting out certain basic targets and is expected to economize on resources and make a profit, part of which is used to pay bonuses and provide welfare facilities for its work-force. However, there are some special features of the defence sector which mark it off from the rest of the economy and create conditions for its successful operation. It enjoys first priority in the supply of materials and equipment in terms of both quantity and quality. There are also special privileges for managers, technical personnel and workers in the form of somewhat higher rates of pay and larger bonuses, coupled with superior provision of housing and welfare services. Against these advantages must be set the very strict regime of secrecy, and limitations on the freedom to travel and publish. The conditions of secrecy are such that personnel working in the armaments industry are unlikely to receive open public recognition until after their retirement or death.

The following nine ministries are generally held to constitute the core of the Soviet defence industry:

Medium Machine-Building: Nuclear warheads and devices, uranium mining and processing; high-energy lasers. Minister: Ryabev; *Address*: Not available.

General Machine-Building: Strategic missiles, space launch vehicles and spacecraft. Minister: Doguzhiev; *Address*: Vtoraya Miusskaya ulitsa 4, Moscow.

Defence Industry: Ground forces equipment - tanks, other armoured combat vehicles, artillery, small arms and optical equipment. Minister: Finogenov; *Address*: Ulitsa Gor'koga 35, Moscow.

Machine-Building: Conventional ammunition, explosives and solid propellants. Minster: Belousov, B. M.; *Address*: Bogdana Klimel'nitskogo ulitsa 4, Moscow.

Aviation Industry: Military and civilian fixed-wing aircraft and helicopters; aerodynamic missiles. Minister: Systsov; *Address*: Ulanskii Pereulok 16, Moscow.

Shipbuilding: Naval and civilian ships and boats; naval accoustic systems and radars. Minister: Koksanov; *Address*: Sadovaya—Kudrinskaya ulitsa 11/13, Moscow.

Radio Industry: Radars and communications equipment; computers; guidance and control systems. Minister: Shimko; *Address*: Kitaiskii Proezd 7, Moscow 103074.

Communications Equipment Industry: Communications equipment; computers. Minister: Pervyshin; *Address*: Kitaiskii Proezd 7, Moscow 103074.

Electronics Industry: Electronic components; micro-computers and other electronic end products. Minister: Kolesnikov; *Address*: Kitaiskii Proezd 7, Moscow 103074.

Besides weapons and other military-related products all the above ministries also manufacture civilian products, sometimes on a substantial scale. Under Gorbachev this civilian role of the military sector is being enhanced. The products of the Ministry of General Machine-Building, for example, include tractors, trams, machine tools, robots, refrigerators, washing machines, prams, television sets, toys and medical equipment; of the Ministry of Medium Machine-Building, equipment for the dairy industry.

The industrial ministries have a common internal structure. The ministers have under them a first deputy and several deputies (though the names of these high-level personnel are often known, biographical details are sparse). Each ministry has a Collegium, a consultative body of the senior officials which reviews important policy issues and makes recommendations implemented through ministerial orders.

At this level there is also a Scientific and Technical Council, consisting of the leading scientists, designers and engineers of the industry. This Council attempts to secure a coherent technical policy for the ministry and examines research proposals and new technical projects. Under the minister are a number of functional administrations for planning, financial matters, labour, supply and other areas, including a main inspectorate for quality. For weapons development an important body is the Technical Administration, responsible for the oversight of the research and development effort of the ministry, and to which are subordinated the principal central research institutes. The head of this administration is a significant figure in the ministry and usually a member of its Collegium, but it is often difficult to identify the relevant officials. The ministries also have a number of Main Production Administrations, specialized by type of product, which control the industry's manufacturing facilities. These take the form of individual enterprises or, frequently, production associations, representing amalgamations of groups of enterprises under a single management. In the defence sector there are also many science-production associations: manufacturing facilities united with research and development organizations. The activities of the functional and production administrations are overseen by the deputy ministers, usually six to eight per ministry.

(See biographies of: Belousov, B. M.; Belyakov, R. A.; Bunkin; Doguzhiev; Finogenov; Koksanov; Kolesnikov; Lapygin; Pervyshin; Ryabev; Semenikhin; Shimko; Systsov; Tupolev.)

The Ministries for Nuclear Weapons and Missiles

Little is known about the nuclear weapons-producing Ministry of Medium Machine-Building (Minsredmash) and its leading personnel. The ministry was established in its present form in 1953; prior to this the nuclear weapons programme was managed by the First Main Administration of the Council of Ministers under the overall control of Beria, the head of state security. Minsredmash is responsible for all stages of the production of nuclear weapons from the extraction and processing of uranium ores to the manufacture of warheads and other devices. Uranium extraction is quite widely dispersed with major centres in the Ukraine and the Central Asian republics. The Chelyabinsk region in the Urals appears to be the principal centre for the fabrication of nuclear warheads and associated research and design. The leading scientist of this establishment, General E. I. Zababakhin, Academician, died in 1984, and his successor has not been identified. The ministry is known to have a major research facility at Sarova, near Arzamas in the Gor'kii region (apparently under the leadership of Academician Negin), and there has been speculation that its research includes investigation of high-energy lasers. Minsredmash also plays a major role in the civilian nuclear power programme: it has responsibility for the entire fuel cycle, with the exception of the commercial power stations themselves, the latter now managed by the Ministry of Nuclear Power, headed by Lukonin.

In 1956, with the development of civilian applications of atomic energy, part of the nuclear industry, in particular its research base, was transferred to a newly created State Committee for the Utilization of Atomic Energy. This move permitted a lowering of the barriers of secrecy and facilitated the extension of international contacts in the nuclear field. Today many leading nuclear research institutes are subordinated to this State Committee, including the Kurchatov Institute of Atomic Energy (Velikhov) and the Research Institute of Inorganic Materials (Nikiforov). The status of the State Committee is uncertain and there is a strong possibility that it is in effect a Main Administration of Minsredmash itself. There are two major nuclear test centres in the Soviet Union, both under military control. The oldest is located in the Semipalatinsk region in the deserts of eastern Kazakhstan. Its chief is known to be General A. D. Il'enko, but biographical details are not available. The second is on the island of Novaya Zemlya.

Created in 1965, the Ministry of General Machine-Building (Minobshchemash) is responsible for the development and production of solid- and liquid-fuel ballistic missiles, space launch vehicles and spacecraft. Its minister is now Doguzhiev and while the names of some of his deputies are known, there is an almost total lack of biographical details. The ministry has four Main Production Administrations - for missiles and space launchers, missile engines and motors, guidance systems, and ground equipment. According to the US Department of Defense, there are more than twenty plants building missile systems, supported by a network of enterprises supplying engines and other components (*Soviet Military Power*, 1984, p. 97). The former include major facilities at Dnepropetrovsk, building ICBMs, and at Votkinsk in the Urals, the latter building solid-fuel missiles, including the SS-25 and SS-20. There appear to be five major missile and rocket design bureaux. It is believed that the oldest, the former Korolev bureau at Kaliningrad near Moscow, is now principally concerned with space-related systems. The four missile bureaux are the former Yangel bureau in or near Dnepropetrovsk in the Ukraine, now headed by Utkin, the former Chelomei bureau near Moscow, the former Makeev bureau, specializing in sea-launched systems, and the former Nadiradze bureau, specializing in solid-fuel missiles. The present leaders of the latter three bureaux have not been identified. There are also major research and design centres for engines (including the leading centre headed for many years by Glushko) and guidance systems (Lapygin). The ministry also has a network of research centres, the most important being the NII-88 at Kaliningrad, the present director of which has not been identified.

The Soviet Union has three large launch centres: the best known, Baikonur (Tyuratam) in Kazakhstan, Plesetsk in the northern Archangel region, and Kapustin Yar near Volgograd. Overall control of these centres is in the hands of the military.

Other ministries of the defence industry build nuclear-related products. Several enterprises of the Ministry of Shipbuilding build nuclear submarines, with a major facility at Severodvinsk in the north. A leading designer of this industry is Kovalev. The Ministry of the Aviation Industry builds nuclear-capable fighters and bombers, leading designers including Tupolev and Belyakov, and also some categories of missiles. Shorter-range missile systems are also built at enterprises of the Ministry of the Defence Industry. Radar, early-warning, communications and control systems are built by the Ministries of the Radio and Communications Equipment Industries, leading scientists and designers including Semenikhin and Bunkin.

(See biographies of: Belyakov; Bunkin; Glushko; Doguzhiev; Kovalev (S. N.); Lapygin; Lukonin; Negin; Nikiforov; Protsenko; Semenikhin; Tupolev; Utkin; Velikhov.)

Other Industrial Ministries

In addition to the above nine core defence industry ministries, there are others which supply major inputs or military-related equipment. Under Gorbachev, groups of related ministries are now being co-ordinated by bureaux headed by deputy chairmen of the Council of Ministers, these new organizations apparently being modelled on the Military—Industrial Commission. Thus in the civilian engineering industry the eight ministries are being co-ordinated by the Bureau of Machine-Building, under the leadership of Silaev, formerly Minister of the Aviation Industry. The following ministries are included in this group:

Automobile Industry: Products include military trucks and missile transport-launch vehicles. Minister: Pugin; *Address*: Kuznetskii Most 21/5, Moscow 103265.

Heavy Machine-Building: Believed to produce some artillery systems and also equipment for the nuclear industry. Minister: Velichko; *Address*: Prospekt Kalinina 19, Moscow 121019.

Instrument Making: Control systems and computers. Minister: Shkabardnya; *Address*: Ulitsa Ogareva 5, Moscow 103009.

Electrical Engineering Industry: Supplies electrical equipment to the defence industry. Minister: Anfimov; *Address*: Prospekt Kalinina 19, Moscow 121908.

Machine Tool Industry: A major supplier of production equipment. Minister: Panichev; *Address*: Ulitsa Gor'kogo 20, Moscow 103789.

The chemical industry is also important as a supplier of inputs. Two ministries are responsible:

Chemical Industry: Minister: Bespalov; *Address*: Ulitsa Kirova 20, Moscow 101000.

Oil-refining and Petro-chemicals Industry: Products include rocket and aviation fuels. Minister: Lemaev; *Address*: Ulitsa Gilyarovskogo 31, Moscow 129832.

The chemical industry is co-ordinated by a Bureau under a Deputy Chairman of the Council of Ministers (Gusev). Ferrous and non-ferrous metals are supplied by the two metallurgical ministries:

Ferrous Metals Industry: Minister: Kolpakov *Address*: Ploshchad' Nogina 2/5, Moscow 103074.

Non-ferrous Metals Industry: Minister: Durasov *Address*: Prospekt Kalinina 27, Moscow 121019.

These ministries are co-ordinated by Vedernikov, Deputy Chairman of the Council of Ministers. Finally, there is a group of ministries for fuel and power, co-ordinated by a Bureau headed by Shcherbina. This group includes the civilian Ministry of Nuclear Power, whose minister is Lukonin (address not available).

(See biographies of: Anfimov; Bespalov; Durasov; Kolpakov; Lemaev; Panichev; Pugin; Shcherbina; Shkabardnya; Silaev; Vedernikov; Velichko;)

The State Planning Committee (Gosplan) and Other State Economic Agencies
Addresses: Gosplan: Prospekt Marksa 12, Moscow 103009; Gossnab: Orlikov Pereulok 5, Moscow 107801; Science and Technology Committee: Ulitsa Gor'kogo 11, Moscow 103009

The State Planning Committee (Gosplan) under the chairmanship of Maslyukov, formerly chairman of the Military—Industrial Commission, must play a large role in the weapons procurement process and national security decisionmaking. The development of the defence sector is planned like the rest of the economy and Gosplan has to ensure that the necessary resources are available to undertake military programmes and maintain the armed forces. Gosplan's military economic activities are overseen by one of the first deputy chairmen (Smyslov), and within the Committee are various sections concerned with particular branches of the defence industry, and also a summary department for overall co-ordination. The heads of these sections and departments have not been identified. Smyslov probably participates in the deliberations of the Military-Industrial Commission and can be assumed to have close relations with the Defence Industry Department of the Central Committee Secretariat.

Other state economic agencies must inevitably be involved to some extent in military economic affairs, in particular the State Committee for Material and Technical Supply (Gossnab), under the leadership of Voronin, a former Gosplan first deputy with responsibility for the defence sector. One of Gossnab's tasks will be ensuring that the defence industry and military receive material and equipment inputs of the requisite quality and quantity. The State Committee for Science and Technology under Tolstykh, formerly a leading figure of the electronics industry, appears to have a primarily civilian role, but must also have some involvement in military-related matters, if only in ensuring the general vitality of the country's R & D base. Other agencies likely to have some military role are the Ministry of Finance, the State Committees for Labour and Wages, Prices and Standards.

(See biographies of: Maslyukov; Smyslov; Tolstykh; Voronin.)

The Educational System
Address (State Committee for Higher Education): not available

Until 1988 there was a separate Ministry of Higher Education, but this has now absorbed into a State Committee for Public Education under the chairmanship of Yagodin, formerly the higher education minister. The higher educational system has an important role in the education and training of specialists for the defence sector and many of its establishments also undertake military-related research, often on a contract basis. Some of the leading technical higher educational institutes have long-standing links with the defence industry. Examples include the Moscow Bauman Higher Technical Institute and the Moscow Aviation Institute, both training many engineers and designers for the missile and space industries, the Leningrad Shipbuilding Institute, the Leningrad Mechanical Institute, which appears to have close links with the Ministry of the Defence Industry, and the Moscow Physical-Technical Institute, a major educational centre for the nuclear industry. It is a common practice for leading scientists and designers of the defence industry to undertake teaching at institutes and universities on a part-time basis.
(See biography of: Yagodin.)

The Academy of Sciences
Address: Leninskii Prospekt 14, Moscow 117901

Most of the country's basic research and an increasing amount of applied research in high technology fields is undertaken by research establishments of the USSR Academy of Sciences and the Republican Academies. Although Academy institutes do not appear to work on weapons as such, they undoubtedly do work of actual or potential military relevance. Indeed there is evidence that this involvement in military-related R & D has grown in recent years. Such research includes investigations in the fields of nuclear physics, lasers, computers, micro-electronics, new materials, and advanced manufacturing technologies. Considerable prestige is attached to election to the Academy; members include many leading scientists, designers and engineers directly associated with weapons R & D. The President of the Academy, Marchuk, is the leading spokesman of Soviet science. His first deputy is Kotel'nikov, while at least two of the vice-presidents (Velikhov and Frolov) have responsibilites which must involve them in military-related issues. Velikhov appears to serve as a science adviser to Gorbachev. The Academy also has a Sector of Applied Research, headed by Chuev, a shadowy body which appears to be directly concerned with military research questions. Much of the applied research and development for the defence industry is undertaken by institutes and design bureaux of the nine ministries discussed above. It is generally believed that approximately half the country's scientists and engineers are engaged in military-related R & D, and, according to the CIA, the defence industry ministries have approximately 450 R & D organizations, including some fifty major design bureaux. Some of the leading scientists and designers were noted above, but it must be stressed that our knowledge of even the most prominent figures is extremely limited and has deteriorated during the recent period as many leading personnel have been replaced.

(See biographies of: Basistov; Belyakov, R. A.; Bunkin; Chuev; Frolov, K. V.; Kotel'nikov; Kovalev, S. N.; Marchuk; Negin; Nikiforov; Sagdeev; Semenikhin; Tupolev; Velikhov.)

The Ministry of Foreign Affairs
Address: Smolenskaya-Sennaya Ploshchad' 32/34, Moscow 121200

Under Gorbachev the Ministry of Foreign Affairs has undergone substantial re-staffing following the replacement of Gromyko by Shevardnadze. Its new first deputy ministers are Kovalev and Vorontsov. The ministry is actively involved in arms control and disarmament negotiations and has a special department for these issues, headed by the experienced negotiator Karpov. Another leading negotiator is Obukhov who has played a prominent role at the Geneva talks in recent years. Some of the Soviet Union's disarmament efforts have been focused on the United Nations, and here a prominent role has been played by one of the deputy ministers, Petrovskii.

(See biographies of: Karpov; Kovalev, A. G.; Obukhov; Petrovskii; Shevardnadze; Vorontsov.)

Consultants and Advisers

A feature of the policy process in the Soviet Union in recent years has been the increasing role of specialist advisers. This has become particularly evident in the foreign policy field. Leading staff of such Academy institutes as the Institute of World Economy and International Relations (director, Primakov) and the Institute for the Study of the USA and Canada (director, Arbatov) prepare reports at the request of the Central Committee and may attend sessions of the Secretariat and Politburo. A notable feature of the Gorbachev period has been the growing involvement of the civilian staff of these foreign policy institutes in defence-related issues, previously the almost exclusive preserve of the uniformed military. Another organization that should be noted here is the Soviet Committee for the Defence of Peace, under the leadership of Borovik. This organization acts as a forum for discussion with foreign specialists and activists concerned with disarmament issues.

(See biographies of: Arbatov; Borovik; Primakov; Velikhov.)

The State Committee for Security (KGB)
Address: not available

The KGB under its chairman Chebrikov has wide involvement in issues of national security. It is a secret police and intelligence service and has responsibility for a section of the country's armed forces, the Border Guards. Its special troops control the movement and storage of nuclear weapons, guard strategic installations and control communications among the high-level Party officials and the upper ranks of the

military. It also has a counter-espionage presence within the armed forces and active involvement in the maintenance of security within the defence industry. Research institutes and enterprises engaged in military work have so-called First Departments, overseen by the KGB, which control access to classified documents, vet personnel, and ensure the security of contacts with outside organizations. Another activity of the KGB is the gathering of foreign scientific and technical intelligence, used to monitor Western developments and as a source of ideas applicable in the domestic weapons industry.
(See biography of: Chebrikov.)

THE MILITARY

The Ministry of Defence

Address: Ulitsa Kirova 37, Moscow 103160

The armed forces of the Soviet Union have a highly centralized command structure. The primary administrative organ is the Ministry of Defence, subordinate to the Council of Ministers, and headed by a minister (Yazov), three first deputies (Lushev, Akhromeev (Chief of the General Staff) and Kulikov (Commander-in-Chief of the Warsaw Pact Forces),[1] and eleven deputies, including the five service chiefs and those responsible for rear services (Kurkotkin), construction (Shestopalov), personnel (Sukhorukov), civil defence (Govorov), the chief inspectorate (Sorokin), and armaments (Shabanov). These senior officers are normally members of the Party Central Committee and the Supreme Soviet. The ministry has a high-level consultative body, the Collegium (or Main Military Council, as it used to be called), chaired by the minister, which considers questions relating to the development of the forces, their military and political training and personnel policy. Its recommendations are put into effect through orders of the ministry. A significant feature of the Soviet Ministry of Defence is that it does not have any high-level civilian participation, in contrast to both the British and US equivalents.
(See biographies of: Akhromeev; Chernavin; Efimov; Govorov; Ivanovskii; Kurkotkin; Lushev; Maksimov, Y. P; Shabanov; Shestopalov; Sorokin; Sukhorukov; Tret'yak; Yazov.)

The General Staff

Address: Ministry of Defence (see above)

The principal organ of management of the forces is the General Staff. The General Staff coordinates the activities of the various service branches, the rear services, civil defence and a number of chief directorates. According to the Soviet Military Encylopedia, the General Staff:

> thoroughly analyses and evaluates the evolving military–political situation, determines the trends of development of the means of waging war and the methods of their use, organizes training of the armed forces and carries out necessary measures for securing their high combat readiness to repulse any possible aggression. The further development of military theory occupies an important place in the activity of the General Staff. It directs military scientific work, elaborates the most important regulations and topical problems of Soviet military science, and introduces the achievements of the latter into the practice of operational and combat training of troops and staff.
> *(Sovetskaya Voennaya Entsiklopediya*, 1976, p.513)

The Chief of the General Staff, Akhromeev, is assisted by first deputies (including Lobov) and deputies, one of whom (Grivosheev) heads the Military Intelligence Directorate (GRU).

The GRU gathers information on potential adversaries and assists the General Staff in preparing threat assessments which help to determine force requirements and procurement needs. The General Staff also has a Military Science Directorate concerned with issues of military theory and and directorates for operations, foreign military assistance, communications and external relations. It also has a directorate concerned with treaties and negotiations, headed by Chervov, who is a frequent spokesman on disarmament issues.

There is no doubt that the General Staff is an extremely important body in national security decisionmaking. Under Gorbachev its role appears to have been further enhanced: Akhromeev has played a very prominent role in disarmament matters and in the articulation of the emerging new Soviet military doctrine with its strong emphasis on defence. He also appears to be close to Gorbachev. In contrast, Yazov, the Minister of Defence, is relatively inexperienced and has played less of a public role.

Following the precedent of 1941—45, in the event of war the General Staff, together with the Party General Secretary in his capacity as Supreme Commander of the Armed Forces, would constitute the headquarters of the Supreme High Command for military leadership of the war effort.

(See biographies of: Akhromeev; Chervov; Grivosheev; Lobov.)

Central Technical Administrations

Addresses: Ministry of Defence (see above)

One of the Deputy Ministers of Defence (Shabanov) has responsibility for armaments and as such leads the weapons acquisition process from the military side. He heads an Armaments Directorate (or Administration) with what appears to be a substantial staff, including two first deputies (only one, Kolosov, currently identified) and several deputies. This directorate is the principal centre for questions of military technical policy. Shabanov also leads the work of a number of other directorates concerned with the procurement of specific types of weapons. These include the Main Rocket and Artillery Directorate and the Main Armour Directorate (tanks and armoured vehicles). It is possible that there is a special directorate concerned with nuclear weapons, but details are not available. These technical directorates, in association with the equivalent directorates of the service arms, can be expected to play an active role in the procurement process, with duties including the identification of new weapons requirements, project selection and approval, and the acceptance testing of newly developed systems. Another central directorate leads the work of military educational establishments, some of which undertake weapons-related research.

(See biography of: Shabanov.)

The Armed Forces

Addresses: Ministry of Defence (see above)

The five principal service branches are subordinate to the General Staff; their commanders-in-chief are deputy ministers of defence. The Services are the Strategic Rocket Forces (Maksimov), the Ground Forces (Ivanovskii), the Navy (Chernavin), the Air Force (Efimov), and the Air Defence Forces (Tret'yak). The Soviet Union has conscript armed forces, with all able-bodied males liable to military service.

The Soviet nuclear capability is shared between the different services, with the principal strategic and tactical capabilities in the hands of the Strategic Rocket Forces (ground-based systems), the Navy (the submarine-based missiles, plus naval aviation) and Air Force (strategic bombers and nuclear-capable tactical air forces). In addition, the Ground Forces possess shorter-range missiles and battlefield nuclear systems, and the Air Defence Forces control the early-warning system and the Moscow anti-ballistic missile system, the interceptor missiles of which carry nuclear warheads. From the point of view of nuclear capability the Strategic Rocket Forces are the most important. It is possible to identify its first deputy and deputy commanders, but biographical details are sparse.

In each of the services there is a deputy commander-in-chief responsible for armaments and questions of procurement. They probably head special directorates which work in association with the central technical directorates of the Ministry of Defence. Their responsibilities include the issuing of requirements for new weapons, the general oversight of the R & D process, the acceptance testing of prototypes of new systems, and probably the leadership of some weapons-related investigations undertaken by their own research institutes. The services also appear to have their own Scientific and Technical Committees, which probably elaborate issues of technical policy and review proposals for new weapons development. It is also the various technical directorates of the services that provide the military representatives (*voenpredy*) who monitor the work of industrial research and production facilities to see that specifications and quality standards are observed. Again, the identities of the deputy commanders for armaments are known, but few biographical details are available.

A feature of the Soviet command structure since the early 1980s has been the formation of Theatres of Military Operations. These four principal theatre commands represent very senior posts within the military, second only to the deputy ministers. The Western theatre is headed by the controversial figure of Marshal Ogarkov; the South Western by Gerasimov, and the Southern by Zaitsev. The Far Eastern Theatre commander has not been identified.

Most senior and middle-ranking officers of the forces are members of the Party. The Party's presence in the forces is organized through the Main Political Administration, the chief of which, Lizichev, appears to have the effective status of a first deputy minister of defence. The Administration has close links with the Central Committee and is concerned with questions of political education and the general political and moral training of the troops to prepare them for combat. Each of the services has its own Political Directorate, its chief being the equivalent of a first deputy commander-in-chief.

The Soviet military has its own network of educational establishments, including many higher military command and technical schools and academies. Some of these are also centres of research, including the Dzerzhinskii Academy of the Strategic Rocket Forces (chief, Kotlovtsev) and the Zhukovskii Military Aviation Engineering Academy of the Air Force.

(See biographies of: Bazhenov; Chernavin; Efimov; Gerasimov; Ivanovskii; Kochemasov; Kotlovtsev; Leonov; Lizichev; Maksimov, A. A.; Maksimov, Y.P.; Malinovskii; Mikhalkin; Nedelin; Novoselov; Ogarkov; Rodin; Ryazhskikh; Shilovskii; Shishkov; Tret'yak; Volkov; Yashin; Zaitsev.)

CONCLUDING REMARKS

The above is intended to situate the officials whose biographies follow. It will be apparent that there are many gaps in our knowledge and that many leading figures and the jobs remain shrouded in secrecy. The sample of 122 individuals does nevertheless provide insights into the backgrounds of the occupants of posts concerned with national security in the USSR. Some general characteristics are worthy of note. There is an overwhelming male predominance, with only a single woman in the sample. There is also a predominance of Russians: for those for whom information on nationality is available, only nine (less than 10 per cent) are of other nationalities, and six of these are Ukrainians. If a similar review had been undertaken at the end of the Brezhnev period it would have been found that the overwhelming majority would have been in their sixties or seventies. Under Gorbachev there has been a striking rejuvenation; a high proportion of the officials concerned are in their fifties or early sixties, or younger, and have occupied their posts for only a brief period. It is also a well-educated group. More than one-third (forty-two) have higher degrees (candidate or doctor of science) and twenty are candidate or full members of the USSR Academy of Sciences. As noted above, all are Party members, and the majority also members of the Central Committee and Supreme Soviet. It is to be hoped that further pursuit of the policy of *glasnost'* will make possible the identification of more members of this important elite group of Soviet society, permitting a better understanding of decision-making processes that so vitally affect not only Soviet citizens, but the whole of humanity.

BIOGRAPHIES[2]

Akhromeev, Sergei Fedorovich, Marshal of the Soviet Union, First Deputy Minister of Defence, Chief of General Staff

As Chief of General Staff of the Soviet Armed Forces, Sergei Akhromeev has become known in the West as a participant in arms control talks and a right-hand man of Gorbachev at the Reykyavik and Washington summit meetings. He was appointed in September 1984 after serving as first deputy chief (under Nikolai Ogarkov) from May 1979. Akhromeev was born in 1923 and joined the Army in 1940. During the war he saw active service at the front in Leningrad where he served throughout the prolonged siege. In 1952 he graduated from the Military Academy of Armour-Tank Troops and then occupied a series of command posts, broken by a period of study at the Military Academy of the General Staff (1967). Between 1972 and 1974, Akhromeev was Chief of Staff of the Far Eastern Military District; he then transferred to the General Staff as chief of a main directorate. It was from this post that he rose to become first deputy chief of General Staff in 1979. A Party member since 1943, he was elected a candidate member of the Central Committee in 1981 and two years later was elevated to full membership. In 1979 he was given the rank of Army General and in 1983 Marshal of the Soviet Union. He is a Lenin Prize winner (1980) and a Hero of the Soviet Union (1982). In 1984 he was elected a deputy of the Supreme Soviet. From his meetings with Western statesmen and military leaders it is apparent that Marshal Akhromeev is a very competent and intelligent chief of General Staff, who appears to share Gorbachev's concern for new thinking in international relations and military doctrine.
(See: Central Committee; Supreme Soviet; Defence Council; Ministry of Defence; General Staff.)

Anfimov, Oleg Georgievich, Minister of the Electrical Engineering Industry

Anfimov was appointed minister in July 1986, having previously served as a Secretary of the Latvian Party Central Committee. Alongside its basic civilian work the Electrical Engineering Industry supplies equipment and components to the defence industry and armed forces. Anfimov was born in 1937 and from 1952 to 1956 studied at a Novocherkassk technical college. At some later point he graduated from the Riga Polytechnic Institute. He began work as a fitter at the Riga electrical engineering works, and after service in the Navy returned to it, rising from foreman to deputy director for economic affairs. In 1971 he became director of the Riga experimental works for mechanization equipment, and from 1980 director of the Riga electrical engineering works. In 1983 he was elected Secretary of the Riga city Party Committee; in 1985 Secretary of the republican Central Committee. He has been a Party member since 1959, but is not a member of the Central Committee. He is now a delegate of the Supreme Soviet.
(See: Supreme Soviet; Other Industrial Ministries.)

Arbatov, Georgii Arkad'evich, Director of the Institute of the USA and Canada, USSR Academy of Sciences

Perhaps the best-known of all the Soviet Union's foreign policy specialists, Georgii Arbatov has headed the Academy's USA Institute since its foundation in 1967. He was prominent in the Brezhnev period, but there is some evidence that his influence has waned somewhat under Gorbachev, with Primakov playing an increasingly prominent role. He was born in 1923 and graduated from the Moscow Institute of International Relations in 1949, having served in the Army between 1941 and 1944. His academic qualifications include doctor of history (1966), professor (1970), corresponding member of the Academy of Sciences (1970), and full member (1974). Between 1949 and 1960 Arbatov undertook editorial work with a number of periodicals, including the Party's theoretical journal, *Kommunist*. In 1960 he went to Prague as an observer on the journal *Problems of Peace and Socialism*, returning to Moscow in 1962 as head of a sector at the Institute of World Economy and International Relations. Between 1964 and 1967 Arbatov

worked in the Central Committee Secretariat. A Party member from 1943, Arbatov was elected to the Central Auditing Commission in 1971 and in 1976 became a candidate member of the Central Committee, rising to full membership five years later. Since 1974 he has served as a Supreme Soviet delegate.
(See: Central Committee; Supreme Soviet; Consultants and Advisers.)

Baklanov, Oleg Dmitrievich, Secretary, Central Committee (CC) of the Communist Party of the Soviet Union (CPSU) with responsibility for oversight of the defence industry

Oleg Dmitrievich was elected Secretary of the Central Committee in February 1988, a beneficiary of the removal of Boris Elt'sin as head of the Moscow city Party organization. Elt'sin's replacement, Zaikov, was previously Secretary responsible for oversight of the defence sector. A Ukrainian, Baklanov was born in 1932 and obtained a degree from the All-Union Correspondence Course Power Institute, eventually in 1969 obtaining the qualification of candidate of the technical sciences. For twenty-five years he worked at the Khar'kov instrument-making works of the missile industry, rising from the shop floor to director, and then in 1975 became general director of a production association based on the works. A deputy minister of the Ministry of General Machine-Building from 1976, five years later he became first deputy minister and in 1983 minister. He joined the Party in 1953 and was elected a full member of the Central Committee in 1986. In 1984 he was elected a deputy of the Supreme Soviet. A Hero of Socialist Labour, Baklanov is also a Lenin Prize winner.
(See: Central Committee/Secretariat; Supreme Soviet; Military–Industrial Commission.)

Basistov, Anatolii Georgievich, position not known

The nature of Basistov's post is not clear, but there is no doubt that he is a prominent military technology specialist and it is possible that he now occupies a leading position in the Military—Industrial Commission. In both 1984 and 1987 he spoke at the celebration of the Day of the Air Defence Forces; in 1987 he was a prominent signatory of the obituary of Pleashakov, the former Minister of the Radio Industry. His field of scientific interest is given as 'complex informational systems'. These fragments of evidence suggest that he is a radar or early warning systems specialist. Basistov was born in 1920 and graduated from the Leningrad Military Aviation Academy in 1944. Between 1944 and 1950 he served in the armed forces, and then worked as an engineer, becoming a laboratory head and later a deputy chief designer. He is a doctor of the technical sciences and a corresponding member of the Academy of Sciences (1984). A Party member since 1945, in 1986 he was elected to the Central Committee as a candidate member - providing additional evidence of his importance in Soviet military technology. In 1968 he was made a Hero of Socialist Labour.
(See: Central Committee; Military—Industrial Commission; Academy of Sciences.)

Bazhenov, Pavel Ivanovich, Colonel-General; Deputy Commander-in-Chief of the Ground Forces, Chief of Main Directorate for Armaments

Identified in the post early in 1984.
(See: Armed Forces.)

Belousov, Boris Mikhailovich, Minister of Machine-Building

Before his appointment as minister responsible for the conventional munitions industry in June 1987, Belousov's career was in the Ministry of the Defence Industry. He was born in 1934 and studied at the Taganrog Radio-Technical Institute. In 1958 he began work at the vast Izhevsk machine-building works, a major production facility of the defence industry. Here he rose from senior engineer to Secretary of the Party committee, before switching to head a department of the local regional Party committee. In 1976 Belousov was appointed director of the Izhevsk Mechanical Works and in 1980 became a deputy minister of the Defence Industry, later rising to first deputy. He joined the

Party in 1963. In 1988 he was elected to the Supreme Soviet.
(See: Supreme Soviet; Military—Industrial Commission; Ministries of the Defence Industry.)

Belousov, Igor Sergeevich, Deputy Chairman, USSR Council of Ministers, Chairman of the Military—Industrial Commission of the Presidium of the USSR Council of Ministers

Igor Belousov was appointed chairman of the Military-Industrial Commission in February 1988, replacing Maslyukov when the latter was made chairman of Gosplan. Born in 1928, Belousov graduated as an engineer from the Leningrad Shipbuilding Institute in 1952 and then worked his way up from foreman to chief engineer of the Baltic shipyard in Leningrad, one of the principal enterprises of the shipbuilding industry. In 1967 he moved to another leading shipyard, the Leningrad Admiralty works, where he worked as chief engineer until his appointment as deputy minister of the shipbuilding industry in 1969. As a leading figure of Leningrad industry Belousov will have come into contact with Grigorii Romanov, then a rising figure in the local Party organization and a fellow graduate of the Shipbuilding Institute, and probably also L. N. Zaikov, at the time a factory director. In 1976 Belousov became first deputy minister and in January 1984 minister of the shipbuilding industry. A Party member from 1955, he was elected a full member of the Central Committee in 1986. In 1984 he was elected to the Supreme Soviet. Belousov is a Hero of Socialist Labour and has been awarded both Lenin and State Prizes (1969).
(See: Central Committee; Supreme Soviet; Council of Ministers; Military—Industrial Commission.)

Belyakov, Oleg Sergeevich, Head of the Defence Industry Department, Central Committee (CC) of the Communist Party of the Soviet Union (CPSU)

Belyakov became head of the Defence Industry Department in 1985, having served from 1983 as assistant to one of the Secretaries of the Central Committee. This was probably Romanov, at the time Secretary with responsibility for oversight of the defence industry, and given Belyakov's Leningrad background it is possible that he is a Romanov protégé. Born in 1933, he had a military education, graduating from the Leningrad Dzerzhinsky Higher Military-Naval Engineering School in 1958. Until 1964 he occupied engineering posts and then switched to Party work. In 1972 he moved from Leningrad to Moscow to take up a post in the Central Committee Secretariat, becoming deputy head of the Defence Industry Department in 1981. A Party member from 1961, Belyakov was elected to full membership of the Central Committee in 1986. Since 1986 he has been a deputy of the Supreme Soviet.
(See: Central Committee/Secretariat; Supreme Soviet; Military–Industrial Commission.)

Deputy Heads of the Defence Industry Department

Very little is known about Belyakov's deputies and the identity of the Department's First Deputy is not known. Deputy Heads include Viktor Vasil'evich Kozlov, responsible for oversight of the aviation industry and in the 1960s director of the Novosibirsk aircraft factory; N. M. Luzhin, who oversees the shipbuilding industry, in the early 1970s chief engineer of the Leningrad Admiralty shipyard; and N. A. Shakhov, who appears to have responsibility for oversight of the ground forces equipment industry. There must also be a Secretariat official responsible for oversight of the nuclear weapons industry.

Belyakov, Rostislav Apollosovich, General Designer of the Ministry of the Aviation Industry, Head of the Mikoyan Experimental-Design Bureau.

Rostislav Belyakov is head of the Mikoyan design bureau, famous for its MIG fighter aircraft. He was born in 1919 and studied at the Moscow Aviation Institute, from which he graduated in 1941. From then on he worked in the Mikoyan bureau, rising from a junior engineer-design post to head of a design team,

and later first deputy general designer. In 1971 he was made general designer. A doctor of the technical sciences, in 1974 Belyakov was elected a corresponding member of the USSR Academy of Sciences; in 1981 a full member. A Party member since 1944, he has served as a Supreme Soviet delegate since 1974. His many awards include a Lenin Prize (1972) and a State Prize (1952). His contribution to the aircraft industry and the country's defence have been marked by two awards of Hero of Socialist Labour (1971 and 1982).
(See: Supreme Soviet; Ministries of the Defence Industry; Ministries for Nuclear Weapons and Missiles; Academy of Sciences.)

Bespalov, Yurii Aleksandrovich, Minister of the Chemical Industry

Bespalov was appointed minister in August 1986 after a period of work in the Party Central Committee Secretariat. He was born in 1939 and studied at the Kazan Chemical-Technological Institute and, later, the Academy of Social Sciences of the Central Committee. At some point he gained the qualification of doctor of the technical sciences. He started work in 1961 at enterprises of the Ministry of the Chemical Industry, rising from engineer to department head, and in 1971 was appointed chief engineer of the Plastpolimer science-production association near Leningrad, one of the leading centres of the Soviet plastics industry. In 1979 he switched to the Party Central Committee, occupying various posts in its Chemical Industry Department, and in 1984 he was promoted to deputy head of the department. Bespalov joined the Party in 1967, but is not a member of the Central Committee. He is a delegate of the Supreme Soviet.
(See: Supreme Soviet; Other Industrial Ministries.)

Biryukova, Aleksandra Paulovna, Secretary, Central Committee (CC) of the Communist Party of the Soviet Union (CPSU)

The most senior woman in the Soviet leadership, Aleksandra Biryukova was elected a Central Committee Secretary in March 1986. Born in 1929, her early career was associated with the textile industry. After study at the Moscow Textile Institute, from which she graduated in 1952, she worked as foreman, and then head, of a production shop of a Moscow textile factory. Between 1959 and 1963 she was a leading technical specialist of the textiles administration of the Moscow city Economic Council. From 1963 Biryukova worked as chief engineer at one of the country's leading textile works, the Moscow Trekhgornaya Manufaktura combine. In 1968 she left the textile industry to become a secretary of the All-Union Central Council of Trade Unions, serving in this post until 1985, when she was promoted to deputy chairman of the Council. Biryukova joined the Party in 1956, was elected to the Central Committee as a candidate member in 1971 and as a full member in 1976. She has been a deputy of the Supreme Soviet since 1986. Biryukova's responsibilities as Central Committee Secretary relate mainly to the oversight of light industry and consumer matters. It is unlikely that she has any involvement in military-related decisionmaking.
(See: Central Committee/Secretariat; Supreme Soviet.)

Borovik, Genrikh Aviezerovich, Chairman of the Soviet Committee for the Defence of Peace

Genrikh Borovik replaced Georgii Zhukov as Chairman of the Soviet Peace Committee in March 1987. Born in 1929, Borovik is a journalist who has written on a range of international themes, including terrorism and the situation in Chile. From 1983 he served as a member of the board of the Soviet copyright agency, VAAP.
(See: Consultants and Advisers.)

Bunkin, Boris Vasil'evich, Director of a Research Institute of the Ministry of the Radio Industry

Academician Bunkin has been described as the leader of a large research organization and a specialist on the theory of radar and radio control systems. He was born in 1922 and graduated from the Moscow Aviation Institute

in 1947. He remained at the Institute until 1950, but his subsequent career has not been disclosed, although it is known that he heads a faculty of the Moscow Physical-Technical Institute. He is a doctor of the technical sciences (1950) and was elected to the Academy of Sciences in 1968 as a corresponding member, in 1974 as a full member. Bunkin joined the Party in 1953. His importance can be judged from the fact that he has twice been made a Hero of Socialist Labour (1958 and 1982). Other awards include a Lenin Prize (1980) and a State Prize (1970). Boris Bunkin has a brother Fedor Vasil'evich Bunkin (born 1929), a corresponding member of the Academy, a deputy director of the Academy's Institute of General Physics and a leading authority on lasers.
(See: Ministries of the Defence Industry; Ministries for Nuclear Weapons and Missiles; Academy of Sciences.)

Chebrikov, Viktor Mikhailovich, Army General; Chairman, State Committee for Security (KGB), Member of Politburo

Viktor Chebrikov replaced Yurii Andropov as chairman of the KGB (State Security Committee) when the latter became General Secretary in December 1982. Chebrikov, born in 1923, pursued a Party career in Dnepropetrovsk in the Ukraine (a city well-known for its Brezhnev associations) before transferring to KGB work in 1967. He served in the Army between 1941 and 1946 and saw active war service. After graduation from the Dnepropetrovsk Metallurgical Institute in 1950, he undertook Party work in one of the districts of the town. Between 1955 and 1958 he led Party work at a metallurgical factory in Dnepropetrovsk, and then became Second Secretary of the city Party Committee. After two years as head of a department of the regional Party organization, he was appointed First Secretary of the city Committee in 1961. After two years in the post he became a Secretary of the regional Party Committee in 1964, and in 1965, Second Secretary. In 1967 Chebrikov moved to Moscow to take up the post of Chief of the Personnel Directorate of the KGB; by the autumn of the following year he was a deputy chairman of the Committee. Later, at a time not revealed, he was promoted to first deputy chairman. In 1983, after his promotion to chairman of the KGB, he was given the rank of Army General.

Chebrikov joined the Party in 1944, was elected to the Central Committee as a candidate member in 1971 and as a full member ten years later. In December 1983 he was made a candidate member of the Politburo; in April 1985, under Gorbachev, a full member. He has been a deputy of the Supreme Soviet since 1974. A Hero of Socialist Labour, Chebrikov is also a State Prize winner (1980).
(See: Central Committee; Politburo; Supreme Soviet; Defence Council; State Committee for Security (KGB).)

Chernavin, Vladimir Nikolaevich, Admiral of the Fleet; Deputy Minister of Defence, Commander-in-Chief of Navy

Appointed in December 1985, Chernavin replaced the powerful Admiral Gorshkov, who had served as Navy commander-in-chief for thirty years. Born in 1928, Vladimir Chernavin joined the Navy in 1947. He studied at the Leningrad Frunze Higher Naval School and later at the Military-Naval Academy (1965) and the Military Academy of the General Staff (1969). After occupying a series of command posts he was appointed chief of staff of the Northern Fleet in 1974, rising to commander in 1977. At the end of 1981 Chernavin was appointed chief of the main naval staff, a post he occupied for five years before his appointment as Gorshkov's successor. In 1983 he was promoted to Admiral of the Fleet. Chernavin joined the Party in 1949 and was elected a candidate member of the Central Committee in 1981; a full member in 1986. Since 1969 he has been a deputy of the Supreme Soviet. In 1969 he was made a Hero of the Soviet Union.
(See: Central Committee; Supreme Soviet; Ministry of Defence; Armed Forces.)

Chernyaev, Anatolii Sergeevich, Assistant to the General Secretary

Chernyaev was identified as one of Gorbachev's assistants early in 1986. He is a foreign

policy specialist with particular expertise on Britain. Born in 1921, he graduated from Moscow University in 1947 as a historian and obtained a candidate degree in 1950. Before this he had served in the Army throughout the war. After teaching at the University for three years he joined the International Department of the Central Committee. Here he worked until 1986, except for a short interval in 1958—61 when he joined the editorial staff of the Prague-based journal *Problems of Peace and Socialism*. From 1970 Chernyaev was a deputy head of the department, specializing in the United Kingdom and the Commonwealth. He joined the Party in 1942 and was elected to the Central Auditing Commission in 1976, to the Central Committee as a candidate member in 1981, and as a full member in 1986.
(See, Central Committee; General Secretary and his Assistants.)

Chervov, Nikolai Fedorovich, Colonel-General; Chief of the Negotiations Directorate of the General Staff

Chervov has become known in recent years as a frequent speaker at press conferences on questions of disarmament. He appears to have occupied the post since 1982. At the 1985 Geneva summit he was the sole representative of the military, suggesting that he is now a figure of some importance in Soviet arms control policy.
(See: General Staff.)

Chuev, Yurii Vasil'evich, Colonel-General, Head of the Sector of Applied Problems, USSR Academy of Sciences

Little is known about Chuev except that he is the author of various works on military-related technologies, in particular studies of the application of operations research to military affairs. He is a professor, doctor of the technical sciences, and an unsuccesful candidate for corresponding membership of the Academy of Sciences. The Sector of Applied Problems appears to co-ordinate the Academy's military R & D effort and as such may have some role in the nuclear weapons programme. Chuev has occupied the post since the mid-1970s.
(See: Academy of Sciences.)

Demichev, Petr Nilovich, First Deputy Chairman, Presidium USSR Supreme Soviet, Candidate Member of Politburo

Petr Demichev is one of the longest-serving members of the Soviet leadership, having been a candidate member of the Politburo since 1964. Before his appointment in 1986 to his present post as first deputy chairman (under Gromyko) he was Minister of Culture for almost twelve years, and before that a Secretary of the Party Central Committee from 1961. Born in 1918, Demichev joined the Army in 1937 and studied at a military academy. In 1944 he graduated from the Moscow Chemical-Technological Institute and worked there until 1945 when he switched to Party work in one of the districts of Moscow. Between 1950 and 1956 he was an official, first of the Moscow city Party Committee and then of the Central Committee. In 1953 he completed a course of study at the Higher Party School. After two years as a Secretary of the Moscow regional Party Committee, he served for a period as the administrator of affairs of the Council of Ministers, before returning to Party work in 1959 as First Secretary of the Moscow regional Committee. In 1960 he gained promotion as First Secretary of the Moscow city Committee, but in 1961 was elected a Secretary of the Central Committee, a post in which he served until 1974 when he became the Minister of Culture. A Party member from 1939, Demichev was elected to the Central Committee in 1961 and has remained a member ever since. He has also been a Supreme Soviet deputy since 1960 and was a member of its Presidium between 1962 and 1966 and again from 1986.
(See: Central Committee; Politburo; Presidium of Supreme Soviet.)

Dobrynin, Anatolii Fedorovich, Secretary, Central Committee (CC) of the Communist Party of the Soviet Union (CPSU), Head of CC International Department

The election of Anatolii Dobrynin as Secretary of the Central Committee and his appointment as head of the International Department in March 1986 was an important step in the evolution of a new foreign policy under Gorbachev. Dobrynin, a highly experienced diplomat with an excellent knowledge of the West, replaced the 80-year-old Boris Ponomarev, who had occupied the post since 1955. Born in 1919, Dobrynin graduated from the Moscow Aviation Institute in 1942 and then studied at the Higher Diplomatic School of the Foreign Ministry, from which he graduated as a historian in 1946. Between 1947 and 1952 he worked as an official of the Ministry of Foreign Affairs, and then for the next three years undertook diplomatic work at the Soviet Embassy in Washington. On his return to Moscow he worked as an assistant to the foreign minister (Gromyko), then from 1957 to 1960 served as a deputy general secretary of the United Nations in New York. In 1962 he became Soviet ambassador to the United States, a post he held until 1986. Dobrynin has been a Party member since 1945 and was first elected to the Central Committee as a candidate member in 1966. In 1971 he became a full member. He has been a deputy of the Supreme Soviet since 1986. His awards include Hero of Socialist Labour (1982). With Dobrynin as head of the International Department and the less-experienced Shevardnadze as foreign minister, it is likely that the Party's role in foreign policy decisionmaking has been enhanced under Gorbachev.
(See: Central Committee/Secretariat; Supreme Soviet.)

Doguzhiev, Vitalii Khusseinovich, Minister of General Machine-Building

The replacement of Baklanov when he was elected a Secretary of the Central Committee, Doguzhiev was appointed minister in March 1988, having previously served as first deputy under Baklanov. Doguzhiev is a member of one of the Soviet Union's smaller national minorities, the Adygeitsy from the Caucasus. He was born in 1935 and studied at Dnepropetrovsk University, from which he graduated in 1958. He then worked as head of a team in a design office, head of a shop, and eventually director of a machine-building factory. In 1983 he was appointed deputy minister of the missile-producing Ministry of General Machine-Building and four years later became first deputy minister. Doguzhiev has been a Party member since 1965; he is not a member of the Central Committee. His awards include the title of Hero of Socialist Labour.
(See: Military—Industrial Commission; Ministries of the Defence Industry; Ministries for Nuclear Weapons and Missiles.)

Dolgikh, Vladimir Ivanovich, Secretary, Central Committee (CC) of the Communist Party of the Soviet Union (CPSU), Candidate Member of Politburo

A long-serving Secretary of the Central Committee, Dolgikh has occupied his post since December 1972, but has been a candidate member of the Politburo since only 1982. Dolgikh, born in 1924, trained as a metallurgical specialist and rose to prominence as a leading figure of the Siberian non-ferrous metals industry. After service in the war he graduated from the Irkutsk Mining and Metallurgical Institute in 1949 and then worked until 1958 at a non-ferrous metals plant in Krasnoyarsk, rising to the post of chief engineer. He then moved to the vast Noril'sk mining and metallurgical combine, at first as chief engineer, and later, from 1962, as director. In 1968 he gained the qualification of candidate of the technical sciences. From 1969 until his appointment as a Central Committee Secretary in 1972 he served as First Secretary of the Krasnoyarsk regional Party committee. In the period 1976 to 1984 Dolgikh headed the Heavy Industry Department of the Central Committee and today his responsibilities still appear to focus on oversight of civilian heavy industry. A Party member since 1942, he was elected to the Central Committee in 1971. Since 1966 he has served as a Supreme Soviet deputy. Dolgikh has twice been made a Hero of Socialist Labour: in 1965 and 1984.
(See: Central Committee/Secretariat; Politburo; Supreme Soviet.)

Durasov, Vladimir Aleksandrovich, Minister of the Non-Ferrous Metals Industry

Durasov has headed the Ministry of Non-Ferrous Metals Industry since October 1986; it is of considerable importance to the defence industry as the supplier of aluminium and other light metals and alloys used by the missile and aviation industries, and also titanium, now being widely employed in submarine building. Durasov was born in 1935 and studied at the Urals Polytechnic Institute, graduating in 1958 (a year before Ryzhkov left the same institute). After a brief period as a research worker at the Institute of Metallurgy of the Urals branch of the Academy of Sciences, he started work at the Yuzhuralnikel combine. He was there for almost tweny years, rising from foreman to director. In 1978 he moved to Moscow to study at the Academy of the National Economy, from which he graduated in 1980. Until the summer of 1983 Durasov was a deputy minister of the Non-Ferrous Metals Industry, but then switched to the Central Committee's Department of Heavy Industry as a deputy head, and it from here that he was appointed minister three years later. A Party member from 1964, Durasov is not a member of the Central Committee. After his promotion he was elected to the Supreme Soviet.

(See: Supreme Soviet; Other Industrial Ministries.)

Efimov, Aleksandr Nikolaevich, Marshal of Aviation, Deputy Minister of Defence, Commander-in-Chief of Air Forces

Efimov was appointed Air Force commander-in-chief in December 1984, having previously served for fifteen years as first deputy commander. He was born in 1923 and joined the armed forces at the beginning of the war in 1941. During the war he served in the Air Force at the front and for his combat exploits was twice made a Hero of the Soviet Union. After the war he studied at the Military-Aviation Academy, from which he graduated in 1951. Later, after serving in various command posts, he studied at the Military Academy of the General Staff, at some point gaining the qualification of candidate of the military sciences. In command posts until 1969 he was then appointed first deputy commander of the Air Forces and given the rank of Marshall of Aviation in 1975. Efimov joined the Party in 1943 and was elected a full member of the Central Committee in 1986. He served as a deputy of the USSR Supreme Soviet in 1946—50 and again from 1974.

(See: Central Committee; Supreme Soviet; Ministry of Defence; Armed Forces.)

Finogenov, Pavel Vasil'evich, Minister of the Defence Industry

Appointed minister in January 1979, Pavel Finogenov is the oldest of the defence industry ministers. Born in 1919, he has spent his entire working life in the ground forces equipment industry. He began work in 1941 as a foreman and went on to occupy management posts at a factory. In 1953 he graduated from the Leningrad Mechanical Institute, a leading centre for training weapons industry engineers, where he studied on a part-time basis. He became chief engineer and then director of a factory before gaining promotion in 1960 to the post of deputy chairman of the Vladimir regional Economic Council. Between 1963 and 1965 he served as chief of an administration of the State Committee for Defence Technology, the forerunner of the Ministry of the Defence Industry. When the ministry was created in 1965 Finogenov was appointed deputy minister, rising to first deputy minister in 1973. He joined the Party in 1943 and was elected to the Central Committee in 1981. Since 1979 he has served as a deputy of the Supreme Soviet. Finogenov was made a Hero of Socialist Labour in 1976 and has been awarded both Lenin and State Prizes.

(See: Central Committee; Supreme Soviet; Ministries of the Defence Industry.)

Frolov, Ivan Timofeevich, Assistant to the General Secretary

After a period as editor of the Party's principal theoretical journal *Kommunist*, during which it was strikingly revitalized, Ivan Frolov was identified as one of Gorbachev's assistants in

May 1987. Frolov is one of the country's leading philosophers — in 1987 he was also elected president of the USSR Philosophical Society — and a leading exponent of the 'new thinking' in both domestic and international affairs. Born in 1932, he graduated from Moscow University in 1953. In 1966 he gained a doctorate in philosophy, was made a professor in 1970 and a corresponding member of the Academy of Sciences in 1976. Between 1956 and 1962 he was engaged in editorial work on the journal *Voprosy Filosofii* (Questions of Philosophy), and then moved to Prague to work on the journal *Problems of Peace and Socialism*. Between 1965 and 1968 he was assistant to one of the Central Committee Secretaries, and then was appointed editor of *Voprosy Filosofii*. He was removed from this post in 1977 and made secretary of the journal *Problems of Peace and Socialism*. In 1979 Frolov was made a deputy director of the Systems Research Institute under its director Zhermen Gvishiani, a prominent exponent of the new concern for 'global problems', a concern shared by Frolov. Between 1980 and 1986 Frolov chaired the Academy of Science's council on the philosophical and social problems of science and technology. A particular concern of Frolov has been the philosophy of science, especially as related to biology. A Party member since 1960, he was elected to the Central Committee in 1986 and in the same year also became a delegate of the Supreme Soviet.
(See: Central Committee; General Secretary and his Assistants; Supreme Soviet.)

Frolov, Konstantin Vasil'evich, Vice-President of the USSR Academy of Sciences, Academic Secretary of the Division of Machine-Building, Mechanics and Control Processes of the Academy of Sciences

Academician K. V. Frolov became head of the Machine-Building Division and vice-president of the Academy in 1985. Born in 1932, he began his working life as a fitter before studying at the Bryansk Institute of Transport Machine-Building from which he graduated in 1956. He returned to industry for two years as an engineer at a Leningrad factory before switching to a research career at the Institute of Machine Sciences in Moscow. Here he rose from postgraduate student (obtaining his doctorate in 1970) to a laboratory head and in 1975 director, a post he has occupied ever since. This institute of the Academy of Sciences is the leading Soviet centre for basic research in the field of engineering. Frolov's own specialization is research into vibration technologies. In 1976 he was elected a corresponding member of the Academy and eight years later a full member. A Party member from 1965, Frolov was elected to the Central Committee as a candidate member in 1986. There have been rumours that in 1986 Frolov was a rival candidate to Marchuk for the presidency of the Academy.
(See: Central Committee; Academy of Sciences.)

Gerasimov, Ivan Aleksandrovich, Army General; Commander-in-Chief of the South-Western Theatre of Military Operations

Gerasimov appears to have commanded the South-Western Theatre since its organization in 1984 (its headquarters are at Bel'tsy in Moldavia). He was born in 1921 and joined the Army in 1938. After active service during the war he occupied command posts and then studied at the Military Academy of the Armoured Forces (1955). In 1966 he graduated from the Military Academy of the General Staff. Between 1973 and 1975 Gerasimov commanded the Northern Group of Troops and then became commander of the Kiev Military District. It was from this post that he was appointed commander of the South-Western Theatre. A Party member from 1942, he was elected to the Central Committee as a candidate member in 1976, and as a full member in 1986. He is also a member of the Ukrainian Party Central Committee and a member of the Supreme Soviet since 1970.
(See: Central Committee; Supreme Soviet; Armed Forces.)

Glushko, Valentin Petrovich, General Designer of Liquid-propellant Rocket Engines

Academician Glushko has been the leading figure in Soviet liquid-fuel rocket engine design for almost sixty years. A Ukrainian born in Odessa in 1908, he graduated from Leningrad University in 1929. From then he on worked on the design of rocket engines at the Gas Dynamics Laboratory in Leningrad, creating the first Soviet liquid-fuel engine in 1930—31. From the early 1930s Glushko has been the head of the principal experimental design bureau for liquid-propellant rocket engines, located in the post-war years near Moscow. He worked closely with Korolev in establishing the Soviet missile and space programme and led the development of all the main engines installed in Soviet space launch vehicles and probably also in most liquid-propellant missiles. In 1953 Glushko was elected a corresponding member of the Academy of Sciences; five years later a full member. He joined the Party relatively late, in 1956, and since 1976 has been a full member of the Central Committee. Since 1966 he has served as a Supreme Soviet deputy. Glushko's many awards include Hero of Socialist Labour (1956 and 1961), Lenin Prize (1957) and State Prize (1967 and 1984). In terms of age and experience Glushko is the most senior figure of the Soviet space and missile programmes.

(See: Central Committee; Supreme Soviet; Ministries for Nuclear Weapons and Missiles.)

Gorbachev, Mikhail Sergeevich, General Secretary, Central Committee (CC) of the Communist Party of the Soviet Union (CPSU), Chairman of the Defence Council, Supreme Commander of Soviet Armed Forces, Member of Politburo

Mikhail Gorbachev was elected General Secretary of the CPSU in March 1985 following the brief post-Brezhnev interregnums of Andropov and Chernenko. In contrast to his predecessors he was young, vigorous and well-educated. It soon became apparent that Gorbachev's leadership not only differed in style, but also in substance: he was committed to a far-reaching modernization of Soviet society involving genuine economic reform, democratization and a new approach to international relations. Born in 1931 of peasant family background in the village of Privol'noe in Stavropol' province, Gorbachev began his working life in 1946 as an assistant combine-harvester operator. In 1950 he left Stavropol' province to study at the law faculty of Moscow University, from which he graduated in 1955. Already a Komsomol activist, in 1952 he joined the Communist Party and was soon on the Party Committee of the University. In 1955 he returned to Stavropol' and until 1962 was engaged in Komsomol work, rising to the position of First Secretary of the province's Komsomol organization. For the next few years Gorbachev's principal concern was agriculture. Working in the agricultural department of the Party Committee of Stavropol' province, he became its head in 1963. Simultaneously, he undertook a correspondence course in agronomy at the local Agriculural Institute, graduating in 1967. In 1966 he was elected First Secretary of the Stavropol' city Committee, two years later Second Secretary of the provincial Committee, and in 1970 its First Secretary, a post he retained until 1978. In November of that year he made the decisive move to Moscow as Central Committee Secretary with responsibility for agriculture. After the death of Brezhnev, Gorbachev took on broader Secretarial duties: under Chernenko he was effectively deputy leader, and while Chernenko was ill, acting General Secretary. Elected to the Central Committee as a full member in 1971, he became a candidate member of the Politburo in 1979 and a full member from October 1980. He has served as a Supreme Soviet delegate since 1970. In his rise to power Gorbachev had no direct experience of military affairs. In this respect he differs from Brezhnev, who for a period was responsible for Party supervision of the defence industry. As General Secretary he now chairs the Defence Council and has the title of Supreme Commander of the Armed Forces.

One aspect of the Gorbachev leadership that has gained attention in the West is the prominent role played by his wife, Raisa Maximovna (nee Titarenko, b. 1932), who formerly taught philosophy at Moscow University. They have a daughter, Irina, in her mid-thirties, who works as a doctor.

(See: Central Committee/Secretariat; Politburo, General Secretary and his Assistants; Supreme Soviet; Defence Council.)

Govorov, Vladimir Leonidovich, Army General; Deputy Minister of Defence, Chief of Civil Defence

Govorov was identified as Chief of Civil Defence in July 1987, having previously served for three years as chief of the Ministry of Defence's Main Inspectorate. He was born in 1924, the son of a famous Marshal, and joined the Army in 1942, seeing active service during the war. After the war he studied at the Frunze Military Academy (1949) and later the Academy of the General Staff (1963). After a series of staff and command posts in 1969 he became first deputy commander of the Group of Soviet Forces in Germany. Two years later he became commander of the Baltic Military District, and in 1972 commander of the Moscow Military District. Between 1980 and 1984 Govorov was commander of the Far Eastern Theatre of Military Operations, and it was from this post that he was appointed deputy minister and chief inspector in the summer of 1984. A Party member from 1946, he was elected to the Central Committee as a candidate member in 1976, and as a full member in 1981. Since 1970 he has served as a Supreme Soviet delegate. In 1984 he was made a Hero of the Soviet Union.
(See: Central Committee; Supreme Soviet; Ministry of Defence.)

Grigor'ev, Valentin Aleksandrovich, Head of the Department of Science and Higher Education of the Central Committee (CC) of the Communist Party of the Soviet Union (CPSU)

Grigor'ev was appointed to his present post in 1987 after previously serving as a deputy head of the department. He was born in 1929. A doctor of the technical sciences, he was elected corresponding member of the Academy of Sciences in 1981 (Department of Physical-Technical Problems of Power Engineering). Grigor'ev is not a member of the Central Committee, but was elected to the Supreme Soviet in June 1987.
(See: Central Committee Secretariat; Supreme Soviet.)

Grivosheev, Grigorii Fedorovich, Colonel-General; Deputy Chief of the General Staff, Chief of the Main Intelligence Directorate

Early in 1988 Grivosheev was tentatively identified in the West as the new chief of the GRU, the Soviet military intelligence agency. At the time of writing this appointment had not been confirmed by a Soviet source. He replaced Ivashutin, who occupied the post for almost twenty-five years and is known to have retired. Little is known about Grivosheev, except that in the spring of 1987 he was appointed chief of staff of the Soviet Ground Forces, having previously served as chief of staff of the Group of Soviet Forces in Germany. He was identified in the latter post in September 1984, and prior to that was chief of staff of the Turkestan Military District; as such he may well have been involved in the Afghan war.
(See: General Staff.)

Gromyko, Andrei Andreevich, Chairman of the Presidium of the USSR Supreme Soviet, Member of Politburo

The veteran former Foreign Minister was elected to his present post in July 1985 and serves as the formal head of state. Gromyko, born in 1909, is by far the oldest Politburo member and it is unlikely to be long before his retirement is announced. By education an economist, he studied at the Economics Institute (1932) and the Research Institute of Agricultural Economics (1936), gaining a doctorate in 1956. Between 1936 and 1939 he worked at the Institute of Economics of the Academy of Sciences, but then transferred to diplomatic work. From 1943 to 1946 Gromyko served as Soviet ambassador in the United States; from 1946 to 1948 as the Soviet Union's permanent representative on the United Nation's Security Council, with the rank of deputy foreign minister. In 1949 he was appointed first deputy foreign minister, a position he occupied until 1957, broken in 1952—53 by a period as Soviet ambassador in Britain. In 1957 Gromyko was appointed foreign minister and remained in the post for the next twenty-eight years. A Party member from 1931, he was elected a candidate member of the Central Committee in 1952 and a full member in 1956. Since 1973 he has been a member of the Politburo. He has served as a Supreme Soviet deputy since 1960. Gromyko's

many awards include Hero of Socialist Labour (twice, in 1969 and 1979), the Lenin Prize and a State Prize (1984). Gromyko appears to have played an important role in securing the election of Gorbachev as General Secretary, and as the longest serving member of the present leadership it is likely that he still exercises influence.
(See: Central Committee; Politburo; Supreme Soviet; Presidium of the Supreme Soviet.)

Gusev, Vladimir Kuz'mich, Deputy Chairman, USSR Council of Ministers, Chairman of the Bureau for the Chemical-Timber Industry Complex

Appointed a deputy chairman of the Council of Ministers in June 1986, Gusev is responsible for overall co-ordination of the ministries of the chemical, petrochemical, timber, paper and pulp industries. He was born in 1932 and graduated from Saratov University in 1957. Later he also studied at the Saratov Economic Institute (1969). In 1972 he gained the degree of candidate of the technical sciences. From 1957 he worked in enterprises of the Saratov region, rising to the post of chief engineer; in 1970 he was appointed director of the chemical fibres combine in the town of Engel's near Saratov. He then switched to Party work, becoming First Secretary of the Engel's city Committee and, in 1976, quickly rose from Second Secretary to First Secretary of the Saratov regional Committee. In 1985 he was appointed first deputy chairman of the Russian Soviet Federal Socialist Republic (RSFSR) Council of Ministers (under Vorotnikov) and it was from this post that he rose to deputy chairman of the USSR Council of Ministers in the following year. A Party member from 1963, he was elected to the Central Committee in 1981. He served as a Supreme Soviet delegate for a time in the 1960s and again from 1979.
(See: Central Committee; Supreme Soviet; Council of Ministers.)

Ivanovskii, Evgenii Fillipovich, Army General, Deputy Minister of Defence, Commander-in-Chief of Ground Forces

Appointed in February 1985, Evgenii Ivanovskii is the oldest of the five service commanders. A Belorussian, he was born in 1918 and joined the Army in 1936. In 1939—40 he fought in the Soviet—Finnish war and then studied at the Military Academy of the Armour-Tank Forces. During the war Ivanovskii was in combat service with tanks. In 1958 he graduated from the Military Academy of the General Staff and then served in a series of command posts, rising to commander of the Moscow Military District in 1968. In 1972 Ivanovskii was appointed commander-in-chief (C-in-C) of the Group of Soviet Troops in Germany and occupied this important post until the end of 1980, when he became commander of the Belorussian Military District. Five years later he was promoted C-in-C of the Ground Forces. A Party member from 1941, Ivanovskii was elected a full member of the Central Committee in 1981. Since 1970 he has been a deputy of the Supreme Soviet. Given his age it is likely that Ivanovskii will be replaced before long.
(See: Central Committee; Supreme Soviet; Ministry of Defence; Armed Forces.)

Karpov, Viktor Petrovich, Head of the Administration for Questions of Arms Limitation and Disarmament, Ministry of Foreign Affairs

Viktor Karpov has become known in the West for his leadership of Soviet delegations at major disarmament talks, including SALT II and START in Geneva. In the summer of 1986 he was identified as head of the new administration of the Foreign Ministry concerned with arms control and disarmament. Born in 1928, Karpov graduated from the Moscow Institute of International Relations in 1951. After a period of research work (he eventually became a candidate of science in law) he joined the staff of the Ministry of Foreign Affairs in 1955. Between 1962 and 1966 Karpov worked at the Soviet Embassy in Washington. He participated in the SALT I talks and during the 1970s held the post of Ambassador on Special Assignment concerned with disarmament issues.
(See: Ministry of Foreign Affairs.)

Kochemasov, Stanislav G., Lieutenant-General, First Deputy Commander-in-Chief, Strategic Rocket Forces

Appointed in 1987.
(See: Armed Forces.)

Koksanov, Igor Vladimirovich, Minister of the Shipbuilding Industry

Koksanov has enjoyed rapid promotion following the appointment of his predecessor, I. S. Belousov, as chairman of the Military—Industrial Commission in February 1988. Koksanov was born in 1928 and like Belousov studied at the Leningrad Shipbuilding Institute, graduating one year earlier than Belousov in 1951. For ten years he served in the Navy, then in 1961 transferred to industry, first as a deputy chief designer of ships at a design bureau and later as the deputy chief of an administration of the Ministry of the Shipbuilding Industry. In 1973 Koksanov was promoted to the Party Central Committee Secretariat where he worked as the head of a sector (probably in the Defence Industry Department). He served in this post until his appointment as first deputy minister of the shipbuilding industry in 1985. He is thus one of three defence industry ministers (the other two being Ryabev and Shimko) appointed under Gorbachev with extensive experience of work in the Party Central Committee Secretariat. Koksanov joined the Party in 1954 and is a State Prize winner.
(See: Military—Industrial Commission; Ministries of the Defence Industry.)

Kolesnikov, Vladislav Grigor'evich, Minister of the Electronics Industry

Appointed minister in November 1985, Vladislav Kolesnikov succeeded the late A. I. Shokin, one of the founders of the Soviet electronics industry. From 1971 to 1985 he served as Shokin's first deputy. Born in 1925, Kolesnikov began his working life in 1941 as a fitter at the Tula gun factory and from 1948 worked at the Voronezh radio components factory where he rose to deputy chief designer. From 1954 he occupied a series of posts at a factory producing semi-conductor devices, rising to director in 1967. In 1960 he graduated from the Voronezh Polytechnic Institute where he had studied on a part-time basis. In 1969 Kolesnikov was appointed general director of the Voronezh Elektronika production association, one of the leading associations of the Soviet electronics industry. It was from this post that he moved directly to the first deputy minister position in 1971. A candidate of the technical sciences (obtained in 1966), Kolesnikov was elected to the USSR Academy of Sciences as a corresponding member in 1984 — the only minister of the defence industry to gain election to the Academy. He joined the Party in 1961 and was elected a full member of the Central Committee in 1986. In October 1986 he was elected a deputy of the Supreme Soviet. The recipient of many government awards, including Hero of Socialist Labour (1975), Kolesnikov is both a Lenin Prize (1966) and State Prize (1984) winner. He must be considered one of the most experienced of all the leaders of the Soviet defence industry.
(See: Central Committee; Supreme Soviet; Military—Industrial Commission; Ministries of the Defence Industry.)

Kolpakov, Serafim Vasil'evich, Minister of Ferrous Metallurgy

Kolpakov, a ferrous metallurgy specialist, was appointed minister in July 1985. Born in 1933, he began work in 1951 at the Ashinsk metallurgical works in the Chelyabinsk region. Between 1954 and 1957 he served in the Army and then worked at the Lipetsk tractor factory. From there he moved to Moscow to study at the Institute of Steels and Alloys, from which he graduated in 1963. Later, in 1985, he obtained a doctorate in the technical sciences. Between 1963 and 1978 Kolpakov worked at the Novolipetsk metallurgical combine, one of the foremost steel works of the country, rising from foreman to director (1970). In 1978 he was promoted to deputy minister; in 1981, first deputy minister. A Party member from 1956, he was elected to the Central Committee in 1986. In 1984 he was elected to the Supreme Soviet.

Kolpakov's awards include two State Prizes (1969 and 1978).
(See: Central Committee; Supreme Soviet; Other Industrial Ministries.)

Kotel'nikov, Vladimir Aleksandrovich, First Vice-President of the USSR Academy of Sciences

A prominent specialist in the field of communications and radio technology, Kotel'nikov has served as Academy first vice-president since 1979. Since 1954 he has headed the Academy's Institute of Radio Engineering and Electronics. Kotel'nikov was born in 1908 and studied at the Moscow Power Institute from which he graduated in 1931. He then worked at a number of institutes and contributed to the war effort by his work on new communications systems. He was elected a full member of the Academy of Sciences in 1953, and a vice-president of the Academy in 1970. Kotel'nikov is well known for his research into radioastronomy and has played an active role in the Soviet space programme. Since 1981 he has headed the Interkosmos organization responsible for leading international space research projects. A Party member from 1948, he has served as a deputy of the Supreme Soviet since 1979. Kotel'nikov is the recipient of many government awards: Hero of Socialist Labour (1969 and 1978), Lenin Prize (1964) and Stalin Prize (1943 and 1946).
(See: Supreme Soviet; Academy of Sciences.)

Kotlovtsev, Nikolai N., Lieutenant-General, Director of the Dzerzhinskii Military Academy of the Strategic Rocket Forces

Appointed in late 1987 following the death of the previous director, F. P. Tonkikh, Kotlovtsev heads the leading educational establishment serving the Strategic Rocket Forces. Formerly the principal artillery Academy, the Dzerzhinskii Academy in Moscow trains command and technical personnel.
(See: Armed Forces.)

Kovalev, Anatolii Gavrilovich, First Deputy Minister of Foreign Affairs

A career diplomat and specialist on Western Europe, Kovalev has been one of Shevardnadze's first deputies since May 1986. He was born in 1923 and graduated from the Moscow Institute of International Relations in 1948. After graduation he joined the staff of the Foreign Ministry and from 1949 worked in Soviet organizations in the GDR. In 1955 he returned to the ministry in Moscow and occupied a series of posts before becoming head of the First European Department in 1965. In 1971 Kovalev became a deputy minister and headed the Soviet delegation to the Conference on European Security and Cooperation between 1973 and 1975. A Party member from 1945, he was elected to the Central Auditing Commission in 1986.
(See: Ministry of Foreign Affairs.)

Kovalev, Sergei Nikitovich, General Designer, Shipbuilding, Leningrad

Academician Kovalev is possibly the Soviet Union's principal ship design specialist and may well be responsible for leading work on the creation of nuclear submarines. He was born in 1919 and has been involved in ship design and research since 1943, based in the country's main ship-building centre, Leningrad. A doctor of the technical sciences (1973), Kovalev was elected to the Academy of Sciences in 1981. He joined the Party in 1962 and was elected to the Supreme Soviet in 1985. His contribution is indicated by the fact that he has twice been made a Hero of Socialist Labour, most recently in 1984.
(See: Supreme Soviet; Ministries for Nuclear Weapons and Missiles; Academy of Sciences.)

Kurkotkin, Semen Konstantinovich, Marshal of the Soviet Union, Deputy Minister of Defence for Rear Services

Kurkotkin has occupied his present post since 1972. He was born in 1917 and joined the Army in 1937. He saw active service during the war, rising to commander of a brigade. After the war he occupied various command posts and studied at the Military Academy of the Armoured and Mechanized Troops (1951), and later at the

Military Academy of the General Staff (1958). Between 1968 and 1971 he was commander of the Caucasian Military District and then served as commander-in-chief of the Group of Soviet Forces in Germany. A Party member from 1940, Kurkotkin was elected to the Central Committee as a candidate member in 1971, and as a full member in 1976. Since 1970 he has been a delegate of the Supreme Soviet. In 1981 he was made a Hero of the Soviet Union.
(See: Central Committee: Supreme Soviet; Ministry of Defence.)

Lapygin, Vladimir Lavrentevich, General Designer, General Director of a science-production association, Moscow

There is no doubt that Vladimir Lapygin is a major figure of the Soviet missile/space equipment industry, although his precise role has not been revealed. In the author's view it is likely that he heads the leading rocket control systems organization, headed for many years by Nikolai Pilyugin, one of the close collaborators of the Soviet rocketry pioneer, Sergei Korolev. Pilyugin died in August 1982 and in the same year Lapygin was appointed General Designer. Born in 1925, Lapygin began work in 1941 as a welder at an aircraft factory. In 1952 he graduated from the Moscow Aviation Institute and then worked in a research organization, rising to deputy chief. In 1963 he was appointed deputy chief designer of a research institute; later, first deputy chief designer. He is a doctor of the technical sciences and is known to be the author of works on the control of space vehicles. In both 1984 and 1987 he stood for election to the USSR Academy of Sciences, but failed to be elected as a corresponding member. In October 1982 he was elected a deputy of the Supreme Soviet. Lapygin's involvement with missiles is confirmed by the fact that in November 1986 he was a main speaker at the celebration of the Day of the Rocket Forces.
(See: Supreme Soviet; Ministries of the Defence Industry.)

Larin, Ivan Alekseevich, Major-General, First Deputy Head, Administrative Organs Department of the Central Committee (CC) of the Communist Party of the Soviet Union (CPSU)

Larin was appointed in 1986, having previously served as chief of the political administration of the Leningrad Military District. This Leningrad connection suggests that Zaikov may have had influence over the appointment.
(See: Central Committee Secretariat.)

Lemaev, Nikolai Vasilevich, Minister of the Oil Refining and Petrochemicals Industry

Lemaev became minister in October 1985 after briefly serving as first deputy. The ministry he heads produces fuel for aircraft and other military equipment, and also rubber, tyres and other petro-chemical products. He was born in 1929 and graduated from the Ufa Oil Institute in 1956. In 1983 he gained his doctorate in the technical sciences. His working life began in 1950 at the Novoufimsk refinery, where he rose from a senior operator to deputy chief engineer. Between 1960 and 1963 Lemaev was deputy head of the chemical industry administration of the Tatar Economic Council, and then became director of the Nizhnekamsk petrochemicals combine. In 1977 this became the Nizhnekamskneftekhim association with Lemaev as its general director. It was from this post that he became first deputy minister of the chemical industry in March 1985, and minister seven months later. He joined the Party in 1955 and was elected to the Central Committee in 1986. In 1980 he was made a Hero of Socialist Labour.
(See: Central Committee; Other Industrial Ministries.)

Leonov, Leonid Mikhailovich, Colonel-General Engineer, Deputy Commander-in-Chief of the Air Defence Forces, Chief of the Main Armaments Directorate (?)

Identified in the post autumn 1981.
(See: Armed Forces.)

Ligachev, Igor Kuzmich, Secretary, Central Committee (CC), Communist Party of the Soviet Union (CPSU), Member of Politburo

Igor Ligachev was elected a Secretary of the Central Committee in December 1983, at the time when Andropov was General Secretary, and a full member of the Politburo in April 1985, shortly after Gorbachev's election as General Secretary. Born in 1920 in Siberia, he began his working life in the aviation industry. After graduating from the Moscow Aviation Institute in 1943, he worked for a year as an engineer at the Novosibirsk Aircraft Factory, but then switched to Komsomol work, rising to the post of Novosibirsk regional First Secretary before turning to Party work in 1949. Between 1949 and 1961 Ligachev occupied a series of Party and Soviet posts in Novosibirsk, becoming a Secretary of the regional Party organization in 1959. In 1951 he graduated from the Central Committee's Higher Party School, where he had studied on a correspondence course basis. In 1961 he transferred to Moscow to serve as deputy head of the Propaganda and Agitation Department of the Central Committee. In 1965 Ligachev returned to Siberia as First Secretary of the Tomsk regional Party committee, a position he occupied until April 1983 when he returned to Moscow to head the Central Committee's Department of Party Organizational Work. Ligachev joined the Party in 1944 and was elected a candidate member of the Central Committee in 1966, and a full member in 1976. Since 1966 he has been a Supreme Soviet deputy. As Gorbachev's first deputy in the Party Secretariat, Ligachev is known to chair the weekly Secretariat meetings and is undoubtably a powerful figure in the Soviet leadership. There has been speculation in the West that he is more conservative than Gorbachev, but while there may be differences of emphasis there is no evidence to suggest any fundamental disagreement on the necessity for far-reaching reforms. Given his position it is likely that Ligachev is a member of the Defence Council.

(See: Central Committee/Secretariat; Politburo; Supreme Soviet; Defence Council.)

Lizichev, Aleksei Dmitrievich, Army-General, Chief of the Main Political Administration of the Soviet Armed Forces

In the summer of 1985 Lizichev replaced the elderly General A. A. Epishev as chief of the Main Political Administration. A career political officer, he was born in 1928 and joined the Army in 1946. In 1949 he left a military college and undertook political work in the forces. He then studied at the Lenin Military-Political Academy, graduating in 1957. Between 1965 and 1975 he served as deputy, then first deputy, chief of the political administration of the Moscow Military District and also first deputy chief of the political administration of the Group of Soviet Forces in Germany. From 1975 to 1980 Lizichev headed the political administration of the Transbaikal Military District and then for two years served as a deputy chief of the Main Political Administration. In the summer of 1982 he was appointed chief of the political administration of the Group of Soviet Forces in Germany, a position he held for three years. A Party member from 1949, Lizichev was elected to the Central Committee as a full member in 1986, and has served as a Supreme Soviet delegate since 1984.

(See: Central Committee; Supreme Soviet; Armed Forces.)

Lobov, Vladimir Nikolaevich, Colonel-General, First Deputy Chief of the General Staff

Lobov was identified as a first deputy chief of the General Staff in May 1987, after having previously served as Commander of the Central Asian Military District from the autumn of 1984. He was born in 1935.

(See: General Staff.)

Lukonin, Nikolai Fedorovich, Minister of Nuclear Power

The Ministry of Nuclear Power was created in July 1986 in the wake of the Chernobyl disaster. It is responsible for running the civilian nuclear power stations, but it is not known whether it has any role at all in military-related nuclear matters. The first minister, Lukonin, is an experienced specialist of the nuclear industry. Born in 1928, he studied at the Odessa Electrical Engineering Institute of Communications. He then worked in managerial and technical posts, becoming director of the Leningrad Nuclear Power Station in 1976. This station was the first

based on the RBMK-1000 reactor of the type involved in the Chernobyl accident. In 1983 he transferred to Lithuania to direct the Ignalina Power Station, the first to employ the RBMK-1500 reactor, a larger capacity version of the RBMK-1000. Lukonin is a Hero of Socialist Labour and a Lenin Prize winner. A Party member, he was elected to the Supreme Soviet in 1987.
(See: Supreme Soviet; Ministries for Nuclear Weapons and Missiles; Other Industrial Ministries.)

Luk'yanov, Anatolii Ivanovich, Secretary, Central Committee (CC) of the Communist Party of the Soviet Union (CPSU)

Anatolii Luk'yanov was elected Secretary of the Central Committee in January 1987, having previously occupied the post of head of the General Department of the Central Committee Secretariat. He was born in 1930 and began work at a very young age in 1943 at an engineering factory. After the war he studied law at Moscow University, graduating in 1953. There is speculation that Luk'yanov may have become acquainted with Gorbachev at this time: the latter graduated from the same law faculty in 1955. Until 1961 he served as consultant to a juridical commission of the USSR Council of Ministers. There is then a gap in his official biography until 1969, when he became deputy head of a department of the Presidium of the Supreme Soviet. In 1976—77 Luk'yanov worked in the Central Committee Secretariat before taking up the post of chief of the Secretariat of the Presidium of the USSR Supreme Soviet. In 1983, under Andropov, he was appointed first deputy head of the General Department of the Central Committee, rising to head of the department, under Gorbachev, in the autumn of 1985. A Party member from 1955, Luk'yanov was elected to the Central Auditing Commission in 1981 and to the Central Committee as a full member in 1986. Since 1987 he has been a Supreme Soviet deputy. Luk'yanov's responsibilities appear to include supervision of the Administrative Organs Department and this may give him some influence in personnel policy for the Armed Forces. He also exercises general Party oversight of the legal system, militia and, possibly, the KGB.
(See: Central Committee/Secretariat, Supreme Soviet.)

Lushev, Petr Georgievich, Army General; First Deputy Minister of Defence

Lushev was appointed first deputy minister of Defence in July 1986 after serving for a year as Commander-in-Chief (C-in-C) of the Group of Soviet Forces in Germany. Born in 1923, he enlisted in the Army in 1941 and saw active service during the war. Between 1973 and 1975 he was first deputy commander of the Group of Soviet Forces in Germany and as such served under Ivanovskii, the present C-in-C of the Ground Forces. He was then appointed commander of a series of Military Districts: Volga (1975—77), Central Asian (1977—80), and finally Moscow (1980—85), before becoming C-in-C of the Group of Soviet Troops in Germany. Lushev joined the Party in 1951 and was elected to the Central Committee as a full member in 1981, the year in which he gained his present military rank. Since 1979 he has served as a deputy of the Supreme Soviet. In 1983, on the occasion of his sixtieth birthday, he was made a Hero of the Soviet Union.
(See: Central Committee; Supreme Soviet; Ministry of Defence.)

Maksimov, A. A., Colonel-General; Chief of Main Administration for Guided Weapons Systems, Strategic Rocket Forces (?)
(See: Armed Forces.)

Maksimov, Yurii Pavlovich, Army General, Deputy Minister of Defence, Commander-in-Chief of Strategic Rocket Forces

A surprise appointment given his background, Yurii Maksimov became Commander-in-Chief of the Strategic Rocket Forces in July 1985, shortly after the Gorbachev succession. He was born in 1924 and joined the Army in 1942, seeing active service at the front during the war. After the war he studied at the Frunze Military

Academy (1950) and from then on, apart from a period at the Military Academy of the General Staff (1965), occupied command posts in the Army, with no experience of the Rocket Forces. In 1978 Maksimov became first deputy commander of the Turkestan Military District and in the following year its commander. This military district (with headquarters in Tashkent) has been important for its role in the Afghanistan conflict and Maksimov can be assumed to have had active involvement in the Soviet action. In 1984 he was appointed Commander-in-Chief of the Southern Theatre of Military Operations and it was from this post that he was promoted to head the Strategic Rocket Forces. Maksimov joined the Party in 1943 and was elected to the Central Committee at first as a candidate member in 1981 and then as a full member in 1986. He has served as a deputy of the Supreme Soviet since 1979. His present rank of Army General was obtained in 1982 and in the same year Maksimov was made a Hero of the Soviet Union.

(See: Central Committee; Supreme Soviet; Ministry of Defence; Armed Forces.)

Malinovskii, G. N ., Colonel-General, Deputy Commander-in-Chief Strategic Rocket Forces, Chief of Main Directorate of Combat Training *(See: Armed Forces.)*

Marchuk, Gurii Ivanovich, President of USSR Academy of Sciences

Gurii Marchuk was elected president of the USSR Academy of Sciences in 1986, replacing the 83-year-old A. P. Aleksandrov. This important new post followed six years as chairman of the State Committee for Science and Technology. A Ukrainian, Marchuk was born in 1925. After serving in the Army between 1943 and 1945 he studied mathematics at Leningrad University, graduating in 1949. He obtained his doctorate in the physical and mathematical sciences in 1956 and six years later was elected a corresponding member of the Academy of Sciences. From 1952 Marchuk occupied a research post at the Academy's Geophysical Institute, but soon moved to the Physico-Energy Institute at Obninsk. Here he was engaged in mathematical analysis for nuclear reactor design, including work on the first civilian power reactor which went into operation in 1954. In 1962 he moved to the new scientific centre of the Academy at Novosibirsk as deputy director of its Institute of Mathematics, but in the following year he was appointed director of the Computing Centre of the Siberian Division of the Academy. In 1969 Marchuk became deputy chairman of the Siberian Division of the Academy; six years later chairman and simultaneously one of the Academy's vice-presidents. Thus before his appointment to head the State Committee for Science and Technology in January 1980 Marchuk had gained considerable experience as a science administrator. In 1976 he was elected a full member of the Academy. Academician Marchuk joined the Party in 1947 and was elected a candidate member of the Central Committee in 1976, rising to full member in 1981. He has served as a deputy of the Supreme Soviet since 1979. His awards include Hero of Socialist Labour (1975), the Lenin Prize (1961) and a State Prize (1979). As Academy President Marchuk has the task of revitalizing the country's fundamental research effort and improving the Academy's links with industry.

(See: Central Committee; Supreme Soviet; Academy of Sciences.)

Maslyukov, Yurii Dmitrovich, First Deputy Chairman, USSR Council of Ministers, Chairman of Gosplan, Candidate Member of Politburo

Maslyukov's appointment as chairman of Gosplan in February 1988 was the most striking example to date of a process which has become a feature of the post-Brezhnev period: the transfer of leading defence sector administrators to major positions in the civilian economy and in state economic bodies of general responsibility. Born in 1937 at Leninabad, Tadzhikistan, Maslyukov is one of the youngest members of the Soviet leadership. After study at the Leningrad Mechanical Institute, from which he graduated in 1962, he occupied a series of technical posts at a research institute concerned with production technology, rising

to the position of deputy director. In 1970 he became chief engineer of the motor vehicle plant of the Izhevsk machine-building association of the Ministry of the Defence Industry, before promotion in 1974 to the post of chief of the ministry's technical administration. Five years later he became a deputy minister, but in 1982 left the ministry to become first deputy chairman of Gosplan with responsibility for planning the defence industry. From this post in November 1985 he was appointed chairman of the Military—Industrial Commission. Maslyukov joined the Party in 1966 and in 1986 was elected a full member of the Central Committee. Following his transfer to Gosplan, in February 1988 he was elected a candidate member of the Politburo. He is also a member of the Supreme Soviet, elected in 1984. Now Maslyukov has the difficult task of leading the implementation of the economic reform.
(See: Central Committee; Politburo; Supreme Soviet; Defence Council; Council of Ministers; State Planning Committee (Gosplan).)

Medvedev, Vadim Andreevich, Secretary, Central Committee (CC) of the Communist Party of the Soviet Union (CPSU), Head of CC Department for Liaison with Communist and Workers' Parties of Socialist Countries

Elected Secretary of the Central Committee in March 1986, Vadim Medvedev has major responsibility for relations with the Eastern European socialist countries. Born in 1929, Medvedev has had a career combining academic and Party work. He studied economics at Leningrad University, graduating in 1951, and then worked at the University until 1956. From 1956 to 1961 he was employed as an economist at the Leningrad Institute of Rail Transport Engineers, and then transferred to the Leningrad Technological Institute, where he headed a department until his election as a Secretary of the Leningrad city Party Committee in 1968. By this time he was a doctor of economics and a professor. From 1970 to the spring of 1978 Medvedev was a deputy head of a department of the Central Committee Secretariat in Moscow, but then returned to academic life as rector of the Central Committee's Academy of Social Sciences. He remained in this post until August 1983, when he was appointed head of the Central Committee's Department for Science and Educational Establishments, replacing the conservative S. P. Trapeznikov, who had occupied the post for most of the Brezhnev period. It was from this post that he was made a Secretary in 1986. Medvedev is the author of many works on political economy and is known as a reform-minded economist. In 1984 he was elected a corresponding member of the USSR Academy of Sciences. A Party member from 1952, Medvedev was elected to the Central Auditing Commission in 1976, and to the Central Committee as a full member in 1986.He is also a deputy of the Supreme Soviet, elected in 1984.
(See: Central Commmittee/Secretariat; Supreme Soviet.)

Mikhalkin, Vladimir Mikhailovich, Colonel-General, Commander of the Missile Troops and Artillery of the Ground Forces

Mikhalkin has occupied his present post since July 1983, having previously served as first deputy commander. He joined the Army in July 1941 and trained at an artillery school and later the Military Artillery Academy. He rose to his present post after occupying a series of command posts in the artillery troops.
(See: Armed Forces.)

Nedelin, V. S. , Colonel-General, Deputy Commander-in-Chief Strategic Rocket Forces, Chief of Main Directorate of Educational Establishments

Born in 1928.
(See: Armed Forces.)

Negin, Evgenii Arkad'evich, Director of a research institute, Gor'kii region

Academician Evgenii Negin appears to be a leading specialist of the Soviet nuclear industry. It is known that the Ministry of Medium Machine-Building has a major research facility

in the Gor'kii region and it seems likely that Negin is its director. It may be significant that Negin was one of the signatories of the obituary of Academician E. I. Zababakhin, who died in 1984. Zababakhin was in charge of research at an institute in the Chelyabinsk region, and appears to have been a leading specialist on nuclear warheads for missiles. The few available details of Negin's research profile (a specialist in mechanics and gas dynamics) suggest similar interests to those of Zababakhin. He was born in 1921 and graduated from the Zhukovskii Military-Air Force Engineering Academy in 1944. From 1948 he was engaged in research, design and organizational work. A doctor of the technical sciences (1958), he was elected to the Academy of Sciences as a corresponding member in 1974, and as a full member in 1979. A Party member, he joined in 1943. Negin has many official awards, including Hero of Socialist Labour (twice, in 1954 and 1962), Lenin Prize (1959) and State (Stalin) Prize (1951 and 1953). The dating of some of these awards again suggests involvement in the nuclear weapons programme.
(See: Ministries for Nuclear Weapons and Missiles; Academy of Sciences.)

Nikiforov, Aleksandr Sergeevich, Director of the All-Union Research Institute of Inorganic Materials of the State Committee for the Utilization of Atomic Energy

Nikiforov has headed this important nuclear research institute since 1984 following the death of its founder Academician A. A. Bochvar, one of the pioneers of Soviet plutonium research and production. Born in 1926, Nikiforov graduated from the Moscow Institute of Steel and Alloys in 1948 and then worked at an enterprise, rising to chief engineer. In 1975 he gained his doctorate and in 1977 he became deputy director of the institute. In 1981 he was elected a corresponding member of the Academy of Sciences and in 1987 was elevated to full membership of the Academy. Nikiforov is a specialist in the chemistry and technology of processing nuclear materials, and chairs the inter-agency council for the problem of processing and storing radioactive wastes. Nikiforov joined the Party in 1952. In 1971 he was made a Hero of Socialist Labour and he has also been awarded a Lenin Prize (1962) and two State Prizes (1953 and 1975). He is a deputy of the Moscow city soviet.
(See: Ministries for Nuclear Weapons and Missiles; Academy of Sciences.)

Nikonov, Viktor Petrovich, Secretary, Central Committee (CC) of the Communist Party of the Soviet Union (CPSU), Member of Politburo

In April 1985 Viktor Nikonov was elected Central Committee Secretary with responsibility for agriculture and in June 1987 he was elected a full member of the Politburo. Born in 1929, Nikonov graduated as an agronomist from the Azov-Chernomorsk Agricultural Institute in 1950 and then worked as chief agronomist of a machine-tractor station, deputy director of a school of agronomy, and a director of a machine-tractor station in the Krasnoyarsk region. In 1958 he transferred to Party work as deputy, then head of the agricultural department of the Krasnoyarsk regional Party Committee. After a period as an instructor of the Central Committee, between 1961 and 1967 he worked as Second Secretary of the Tatar regional Party committee, and next as First Secretary of the Marii regional committee. In 1979 Nikonov was appointed deputy minister of agriculture and chairman of the national agro-chemicals organization, Soyuzsel'khozkhimiya. He worked in this post until 1983, when he was made minister of agriculture of the RSFSR. A Party member from 1954, Nikonov was elected to the Central Committee as a candidate member in 1971 and as a full member in 1976. He has been a Supreme Soviet deputy since 1966.
(See: Central Commitee/Secretariat; Politburo; Supreme Soviet.)

Novoselov, F. I., Vice-Admiral, Deputy Commander-in-Chief of the Navy, Chief of the Main Directorate of Shipbuilding and Armaments
(See: Armed Forces.)

Obukhov, Aleksei Aleksandrovich, Ambassador on Special Assignment, Ministry of Foreign Affairs

Aleksei Obukhov is one of the Soviet Union's leading disarmament negotiators, a participant in the SALT and START talks and more recently leader of the Soviet delegation at the Geneva INF and strategic arms talks. Born in 1937, he graduated from the Moscow Institute of International Relations in 1961. After a period of research, he joined the staff of the Ministry of Foreign Affairs in 1965, serving for a period at the Soviet embassy in Thailand. Between 1968 and 1973 he worked in the South Asia Department of the Foreign Ministry and then transferred to the USA Department, eventually becoming head of its disarmament section. In 1981 Obukhov was identified as a deputy head of the USA Department. Obukhov is a candidate of the historical sciences and a Party member.

(See: Ministry of Foreign Affairs.)

Ogarkov, Nikolai Vasil'evich, Marshal of the Soviet Union, Commander-in-Chief of the Western Theatre of Military Operations

Marshal Orgarkov's abrupt dismissal from his post of Chief of the General Staff in September 1984 generated considerable discussion in the West. Prior to his removal he had voiced concern about the need to respond to the rapid development of conventional weapons and questioned the military utility of large-scale nuclear forces. There is evidence that thet Chernenko leadership was disturbed by Ogarkov's forthright expression of views on questions usually the prerogative of the Party. However, Ogarkov retained a very important command post as Chief of the Western Theatre, an appropriate posting given his known advocacy of the formation of theatre command stuctures. Born in 1917, he joined the Army in 1938 and graduated from the Military-Engineering Academy in 1941. After war service he occupied a series of staff and command posts and then studied at the Academy of the General Staff (1959). After two years with the Group of Soviet Troops in Germany, he served in the Belorussian Military District, rising to first deputy commander. Between 1965 and 1968 Ogarkov commanded the Volga Military District, and then became first deputy chief of the General Staff and chief of its Main Operations Directorate. Between 1974 and the beginning of 1977 he was a deputy minister of defence, before becoming chief of the general staff. A Party member from 1945, Ogarkov was elected to the Central Committee as a candidate member in 1966, and has been a full member since 1971. Since 1966 he has also been a delegate of the USSR Supreme Soviet. His awards include Hero of the Soviet Union (1977) and a Lenin Prize (1981).

(See: Central Committee; Supreme Soviet; Armed Forces.)

Panichev, Nikolai Aleksandrovich, Minister of the Machine Tool and Tooling Industry

The machine tool industry is a major supplier of production equipment to both the civilian economy and the defence sector. Panichev was appointed to his present post in July 1986 having previously served as first deputy minister. He is a Belorussian. Born in 1934, he graduated from the Leningrad Kalinin Polytechnic Institute and later also from the Academy of the National Economy (the principal management school for senior administrators). After service in the Army from 1953 to 1955 he studied at a technical school before starting work as a machine tool operator at the Il'ich machine tool factory in Leningrad in 1957. At this works he became a designer and, later, head of a production shop. In 1967 he transferred to the Leningrad Sverdlov machine tool building association as Deputy Secretary and then Secretary of its Party committee. In 1975 Panichev returned to the Il'ich works (a leading producer of precision grinding equipment) as director and head of its design bureau. Five years later he was appointed head of the machine tool ministry's all-union industrial association for precision machine tools. A year later, in 1981, he became a deputy minister. Panichev has been a Party member since 1955. He is not a member of the Central Committee, but in 1987 was elected a delegate of the Supreme Soviet.

(See: Supreme Soviet; Other Industrial Ministries.)

Pervyshin, Erlen Kirchovich, Minister of the Communications Equipment Industry

Appointed minister at the age of forty-one in April 1974, when the communications equipment industry became separated from the radio industry, Pervyshin is the longest serving minister of the defence sector. Born in 1932, he graduated from the Moscow Communications Electrical Engineering Institute in 1955 and then occupied a series of posts concerned with the installation of radio communications systems, rising to chief of an installations organization of national scope in 1965. In 1969 he became general director of a scientific-production association before being appointed a deputy minister of the radio industry in the following year. Pervyshin joined the Party in 1959 and gained election to the Central Committee as a candidate member in 1976. In 1986 he became a full member. Since 1974 he has served as a deputy of the Supreme Soviet. In 1971 Pervyshin became a candidate of the technical sciences and in 1978 was awarded a State Prize. Pervyshin is one of the better-known defence sector ministers, partly because of his long service, but also because his ministry is responsible for the production of many consumer electronic goods, including television sets much criticized in recent years for their poor reliability.
(See: Central Committee; Supreme Soviet; Military—Industrial Commission; Ministries of the Defence Industry.)

Petrovskii, Vladimir Fedorovich, Deputy Minister of Foreign Affairs

Vladimir Petrovskii was appointed a deputy minister in 1986 and is now one of the leading Soviet officials involved in disarmament issues. Born in 1933, he graduated from the Moscow Institute of International Relations in 1957, later becoming at candidate of science in law and a doctor of the historical sciences. After graduation he served until 1961 as a member of the Soviet mission to the United Nations in New York. He then returned to Moscow and after a brief interval in the International Organizations Department of the Foreign Ministry, worked until 1964 in the Ministry's Secretariat. Between 1964 and 1970 he served as a member of the Department of Political and Security Council Affairs in the United Nations Secretariat, and then returned to the ministry, where he was engaged in policy issues concerning the United States. In 1979 he was identified as head of the International Organizations Department of the Foreign Ministry. He is a Party member. Petrovskii is the author of books on American foreign policy and disarmament issues. In 1987 he caused a stir in the West by revealing at a UN session, for the first time, some details of the scope of the Soviet defence budget, with an indication that more details of its true scale may be revealed in the future.
(See: Ministry of Foreign Affairs.)

Primakov, Evgenii Maksimovich, Director of the Institute of World Economy and International Relations (IMEMO), USSR Academy of Sciences

Evgenii Primakov is now one of the Soviet Union's leading foreign policy specialists and a prominent advocate of the 'new thinking' of the Gorbachev period. Born in 1929, his career has combined both academic and media work. A graduate of the Moscow Institute for Eastern Studies (1953), he went on to become at doctor of economics (1969), professor (1972), a corresponding member of the USSR Academy of Sciences (1974), and a full member in 1979. Between 1956 and 1962 he occupied editorial posts in the State Committee for Radio and Television and then moved to *Pravda* as an observer, deputy editor, and foreign correspondent. In 1970 Primakov was appointed deputy director of IMEMO. He occupied this post until 1977, when he was made director of the Academy's Institute for Eastern Studies (Primakov is the author of many works on Middle Eastern and Asian affairs). In 1985 he was appointed to his present post as director of IMEMO. A Party member since 1959, he was elected to the Central Committee as a candidate member in 1986. In March 1987 he was elected to the Supreme Soviet. His awards include a State Prize (1980). It is believed that Primakov is close to Gorbachev and has served as an adviser to the Soviet leader.
(See: Central Committee; Consultants and Advisers.)

Protsenko, Aleksandr Nikolaevich, Chairman of the State Committee for the Utilization of Atomic Energy

At some time in late 1987 or early 1988 Alexandr Protsenko replaced the elderly Andronik Petros'yants as chairman of the State Committee for the Utilization of Atomic Energy. Petrosyants had headed the committee from 1962. Unfortunately, few biographical details of Protsenko are available. It is known that he is a doctor of the technical sciences and an unsuccessful candidate in 1987 for election to the Academy of Sciences as a corresponding member in the Division of Physical and Technical Problems of Energy, suggesting that he may be a reactor specialist. In April—May 1988 he headed a Soviet delegation to the USA to investigate explosion detection methods at the Nevada nuclear test site as part of a joint US-Soviet effort to improve verification techniques.
(See: Ministries for Nuclear Weapons and Missiles.)

Pugin, Nikolai Andreevich, Minister of the Automobile Industry

The products of the motor industry, for which Pugin has been responsible since 1986, include armoured vehicles and also transporters for missiles. Born in 1940, he is one of the youngest Soviet ministers. Almost his entire working life has been associated with the Gor'kii automobile works (GAZ), one of the leading truck-building plants of the country, the products of which include armoured personnel carriers and military trucks. Between 1954 and 1958 he studied at an industrial technical school and then started work as a machine tool operator at the GAZ factory. After occupying a series of posts he became deputy head of a production shop. In 1967 Pugin graduated from the Gor'kii Polytechnic Institute. In 1975 he became chief engineer of the gear-box factory of the GAZ association and then in 1981 was promoted to technical director of the truck factory. Two years later he was general director of the whole GAZ production association. His ministerial appointment in 1986 was from this management post: an unusually rapid promotion, bypassing the normal deputy minister position. Pugin joined the Party in 1965 and was elected to the Central Committee in 1986. He has served as a Supreme Soviet deputy since 1984. His awards include a State Prize (1985).
(See: Central Committee; Supreme Soviet; other Industrial Ministries.)

Razumovskii, Georgii Petrovich, Secretary, Central Committee (CC) of the Communist Party of the Soviet Union (CPSU), Candidate Member of Politburo

One of the younger members of the leadership, Razumovskii was elected a Secretary of the Central Committee in March 1986 and a candidate member of the Politburo in February 1988. Since the summer of 1985 he has been head of the important Organizational Party Work Department of the Central Committee, responsible for Party organizational and personnel matters. Born in 1936, Razumovskii graduated from the Kuban Agricultural Institute in 1958 and then worked for a short time as an agronomist on a collective farm. Throughout his career he has had close association with the Krasnodar region. After serving in various district Party posts in the region, in 1967 he became head of a department of the regional Party committee. Between 1971 and 1973 he worked in Moscow in the Central Committee Secretariat, but then returned to Krasnodar as chairman of the executive committee of the regional Soviet. In 1981 he again moved to Moscow for a period of work in the USSR Council of Ministers, but returned in 1983 to become First Secretary of the Krasnodar regional Party committee, replacing Vorotnikov in the post. It was from this position that Razumovskii was appointed head of the Organizational Party Work Department in 1985. A Party member from 1961, he was elected a full member of the Central Committee in 1986. Since 1970 he has served as a deputy of the Supreme Soviet. Razumovskii's rapid rise under Gorbachev suggests that he is a committed supporter of reform.
(See: Central Committee/Secretariat; Politburo; Supreme Soviet.)

Rodin, Viktor Semenovich, Colonel-General, Chief of the Political Administration of the Strategic Rocket Forces

Rodin was appointed to his present post in 1985. Born in 1928 he was in engaged in Komsomol and Soviet work in the Penza region from 1946, before joining the Army in 1949. Since 1951 he has held a series of political posts in the Army, punctuated by periods of study: at the Lenin Military Political Academy (graduated in 1964) and then the Academy of the General Staff (1969). Between 1975 and 1984 he served as chief of the political administrations of three military districts, including Turkestan (1977—82) and Kiev (1982—84). From 1984 until his present appointment he was chief of the political administration of the Southwestern Theatre of Military Operations. He joined the Party in 1950 and was elected a candidate member of the Central Committee in 1986.
(See: Central Committee; Armed Forces.)

Ryabev, Lev Dmitrievich, Minister of Medium Machine-Building

In November 1986 the veteran Efim Slavskii, who had headed the nuclear weapons industry for almost thirty years, was replaced by his first deputy, Lev Ryabev. Ryabev was born at Vologda, north of Moscow, in 1933 and studied at the Moscow Engineering-Physics Institute, the leading higher educational centre for the nuclear industry. After graduation in 1957 he worked as an engineer at a research institute of the Ministry of Medium Machine-Building, rising to deputy director and, finally, director. The institute concerned appears to have been a major research facility of the Ministry located near Arzamas, south of the city of Gorkii. For a three year period (1969—72) Ryabev left the institute to head a department (not identified) of the Gorkii regional Committee of the Party, and this Party experience was probably important in the decision to appoint him head of a sector (not identified) of the Central Committee Secretariat in Moscow in 1978. After six years in this post, in 1984, Ryabev was appointed a deputy minister of the nuclear weapons industry, rising to first deputy minister in July 1986. Just four months later he became minister. This rapid promotion was an outcome of the Chernobyl accident: A. G. Meshkov, the first deputy from 1982 and the evident chosen successor of Slavskii (he was elected a candidate member of the Central Committee in the spring of 1986) was the most senior official to be dismissed following the accident. Ryabev joined the Party in 1958. He is a State Prize winner and since March 1987, deputy of the Supreme Soviet.
(See: Supreme Soviet; Military—Industrial Commission; Ministries of the Defence Industry.)

Ryazhskikh, A. A. , Lieutenant-General, Deputy Commander-inChief Strategic Rocket Forces, Chief of Armaments Administration
(See: Armed Forces.)

Ryzhkov, Nikolai Ivanovich, Chairman of the USSR Council of Ministers, Member of Politburo

Nikolai Ryzhkov was appointed Chairman of the Council of Ministers (Prime Minister) in September 1985. He has an industrial background, with experience of economic planning. All his early career was linked with Sverdlovsk in the Urals. Born in 1929, he graduated from the Urals Polytechnical Institute in 1959 and from then until 1975 worked at the Urals Heavy Machine-Building Factory (Uralmashzavod), a vast multi-product enterprise, the output of which is reported to include artillery systems. Here Ryzhkov rose from foreman, to chief engineer (1965), and then director (1970). In the latter post he gained a reputation as an effective and forward-looking administrator. In 1975 he was appointed first deputy minister of Heavy and Transport Machine-Building, a post he held until February 1979, when he became a first deputy chairman of the State Planning Committee (Gosplan). In November 1983 Ryzhkov was elected a Secretary of the Party Central Committee and in this post also headed the Economic Department of the Secretariat. It was from this position that he was appointed Chairman of the Council of Ministers. A Party member since 1956, he was elected to the Central Committee as recently as 1981. In April 1985, shortly after Gorbachev's accession, without a candidate period, he was elected a full member of the Politburo. Since 1974 he has been a Supreme Soviet deputy. His awards include two State Prizes (1969 and 1979). As head of government, Ryzhkov now has responsibility for overall leadership of the implementation of the economic reform and many other aspects of the *perestroika*. A less colourful figure than Gorbachev, Ryzhkov gives the impression of being a very competent administrator. His post will ensure that he sits on the Defence Council.

(See: Central Committee; Politburo; Supreme Soviet; Defence Council; Council of Ministers.)

Sagdeev, Roald Zinnurovich, Director of the Institute of Space Research, USSR Academy of Sciences

Academician Sagdeev has headed the leading Soviet space research institute since its establishment in 1973. He has become known in the West through his role in joint research projects and also as an author of critical works on the US Strategic Defence Initiative. He was born in 1932 and graduated from Moscow University as a physicist in 1955. From 1956 he worked at the Kurchatov Institute of Atomic Energy, specializing in plasma physics and thermonuclear fusion. Between 1970 and 1973 he worked at the Institute of High Temperature Physics of the Academy of Sciences. In 1968 Sagdeev was elected a full member of the Academy; in 1987 he was made a member of the US National Academy of Sciences. He joined the Party relatively late, in 1977. Perhaps in recognition of his increasingly prominent role in questions of disarmament, in early 1987 Sagdeev was elected to the Supreme Soviet. In 1984 he was awarded a Lenin Prize.

(See: Supreme Soviet; Academy of Sciences.)

Savinkin, Nikolai Ivanovich, Head of the Administrative Organs Department of the Central Committee (CC) of the Communist Party of the Soviet Union (CPSU)

Nikolai Savinkin is one of the few leading officials to have survived from the Brezhnev period. He was appointed to his present post in 1968, having worked in the Central Committee Secretariat from 1950. Born in 1913, he studied at a technical school for agricultural mechanization (1932) and then undertook Komsomol work. In 1935 he switched to political work in the Army and during the war served as a political worker at the front. After the war Savinkin studied at the Lenin Military-Political Academy, from which he graduated in 1950, and then immediately started his career as a Central Committee official. He joined the Party in 1937 and in 1966 was elected to the Central Auditing Commission. From 1971 to 1981 he was a candidate member of the Central Committee and since 1981 a full member. Savinkin has served as a deputy of the Supreme Soviet since 1970.

(See: Central Committee/Secretariat; Supreme Soviet.)

Semenikhin, Vladimir Sergeevich, General Designer and Director of a Research Institute of the Ministry of the Radio Industry

Semenikhin is known to head a large Moscow research institute of the radio industry, but the exact scope of its work has not been revealed. According to one account, Semenikhin is concerned with computerized control systems. The fact that he was elected to the Supreme Soviet in 1984 indicates that he occupies a position of some importance in the country's R & D system. He was born in 1918 and graduated from the Moscow Energy Institute in 1941. From then until 1946 he worked at a factory in Sverdlovsk, rising to head of a shop. From 1946 he worked at a research institute in Moscow as an engineer, becoming its director and scientific leader in 1963. Between 1971 and 1974 Semenikhin was a deputy minister of the radio industry. A doctor of the technical sciences (1964), he became a professor in 1966, a corresponding member of the Academy of Sciences in 1968, and a full member in 1972. A Party member since 1945, he has served on the Moscow city Committee. His awards include Hero of Socialist Labour (1981) and a State Prize.

(See: Supreme Soviet; Ministries of the Defence Industry; Ministries for Nuclear Weapons and Missiles; Academy of Sciences.)

Shabanov, Vitalii Mikhailovich, Army General, Deputy Minister of Defence for Armaments

Vitalii Shabanov's career is not typical of that of a senior Soviet officer in so far as he has worked in both the industrial and military sectors: he was appointed to his present post in 1978 after serving for four years as deputy minister of the radio industry. Born in 1923, he joined the Army in 1941, served with a fighter regiment at the front and graduated from the Leningrad Military-Aviation Academy in 1945. For the next four years he worked as an engineer at an Air Force research establishment, apparently engaged in acceptance testing of aircraft radar systems. From 1949 to 1972 Shabanov worked in the radio industry in a series of engineering and design posts, eventually reaching the level of deputy general designer. In 1964 he gained the qualification of candidate of the technical sciences. Between 1972 and 1974 he was general director of a scientific-production association before being appointed deputy minister of the radio industry in 1974. Shabanov gained his present military rank in 1981 and in the same year was made a Hero of Socialist Labour. A Party member since 1947, he was elected a candidate member of the Central Committee in 1981 and elevated to full membership in June 1983. Since 1984 he has been a deputy of the Supreme Soviet. Awards include a State Prize in 1953 and a Lenin Prize in 1963. Shabanov is now one of the longest serving of the top leaders of the Soviet armed forces. Shabanov is known to have two first deputies, one of them Colonel-General S. F. Kolosov, about whom nothing is known.
(See: Central Committee; Supreme Soviet; Ministry of Defence; Central Technical Administrations.)

Shakhnazarov, Georgii Khozroevich, Assistant to the General Secretary

Shakhnazarov was identified as one of Gorbachev's assistants in the spring of 1988, having previously served since 1986 as first deputy head of the Central Committee Department for Liaison with Communist and Workers' Parties of Socialist Countries. He is a well-known author of books on political science, international issues, futurology and global problems, the latter an interest he shares with I. T. Frolov, with whom he has collaborated. Born in 1924, Shakhnazarov shares with Gorbachev a legal education, having a doctorate in law. Between 1972 and 1986 he served as a deputy head of the Central Committee's Liaison Department. Since 1974 he has also been president of the Soviet Political Science Association. A Party member, Shakhnazarov is not a member of either the Central Committee or the Supreme Soviet.
(See: General Secretary and his Assistants.)

Shcherbina, Boris Evdokimovich, Deputy Chairman, USSR Council of Ministers, Chairman of the Bureau for the Fuel and Energy Complex

Boris Shcherbina came to the attention of Western observers for his prominent role as head of the goverment commission investigating the Chernobyl accident. He was appointed a deputy chairman of the Council of Ministers in 1984, and was identified as Bureau chairman at the end of 1986. His responsibilities include oversight of the Ministry of Atomic Energy, created in the wake of the Chernobyl disaster. A Ukrainian, born in 1919, Shcherbina graduated from the Kharkov Institute of Rail Transport Engineers in 1942 and from the Ukrainian Party School in 1948. After a period of Komsomol work, he occupied junior Party posts in the Khar'kov region, becoming a Secretary of the city Committee in 1950. In 1951 he moved to Siberia, becoming a Secretary, then Second Secretary of the Irkutsk regional Committee. In 1961 Shcherbina became First Secretary of the Tyumen regional Committee, an important post at a time of the rapid expansion of the local oil and gas industries. He remained here until 1973 when he was appointed Minister of Construction of Oil and Gas Industry Enterprises. This was a short-lived appointment: in the following year he became deputy chairman of the Council of Ministers. A Party member from 1939, Shcherbina was elected to the Central Committee as a candidate member in 1961 and as a full member in 1976. Since 1962 he has

served as a Supreme Soviet delegate. In 1983 he was made a Hero of Socialist Labour.
(See: Central Committee; Supreme Soviet; Council of Ministers.)

Shcherbitskii, Volodomyr Vasil'evich, First Secretary, Central Committee (CC) of the Communist Party of the Soviet Union (CPSU), Ukraine, Member of Politburo

Shcherbitskii has been the Ukrainian Party leader since May 1972 and a full Politburo member since 1971. Despite his age, closeness to Brezhnev, and criticism of the work of the Ukrainian Party organization, he has remained in the post under Gorbachev. A Ukrainian, born in 1918, Shcherbitskii was involved in Komsomol work from 1934 and graduated from the Dnepropetrovsk Chemical-Technological Institute in 1940. He served in the Army during the war and from 1945 occupied technical and Party posts at factories in the Dnepropetrovsk area. In 1952 he was elected First Secretary of the Dneprodzerzhinsk city Committee, and then from 1955 to 1957 and again from 1963 to 1965, First Secretary of the Dnepropetrovsk regional Committee. The period 1957 to 1961 was spent as a Secretary of the Ukrainian Party Central Committee; 1961—63 and 1965—72 as Chairman of the Ukrainian Council of Ministers. Shcherbitskii joined the Party in 1941, was elected to the Central Auditing Commission in 1956, and the Central Committee in 1961. Between 1961 and 1963 and again from 1965 he was a candidate member of the Politburo, making him the longest-serving of all the current members. A deputy of the Supreme Soviet since 1960, he has been a member of its Presidium since 1972. His awards include the title Hero of Socialist Labour, awarded twice, in 1974 and 1977, and a Lenin Prize.
(See: Central Committee; Politburo; Supreme Soviet; Presidium of Supreme Soviet.)

Shestopalov, Nikolai Fedorovich, Marshal of Engineering Troops; Deputy Minister of Defence for Construction and the Billeting of Troops

Responsible for military construction since 1978, Shestopalov's career has been concerned exclusively with engineering and construction activities. He was born in 1919 and joined the Army in 1937. In 1941 he graduated from the Military-Engineering Academy and then served in engineering and construction services during the war and after. In 1961 he became head of a construction administration; in 1963 deputy commander of a military district with responsibility for construction. He then became chief of a military construction administration and eventually first deputy head of construction of the Ministry of Defence. Shestopalov joined the Party in 1951, but is not a member of the Central Committee. In 1984 he was elected to the Supreme Soviet.
(See: Supreme Soviet; Ministry of Defence.)

Shevardnadze, Eduard Amrosievich, Minister of Foreign Affairs, Member of Politburo

In a surprise appointment, the Georgian Eduard Sheverdnadze in July 1985 replaced the veteran Andrei Gromyko as foreign minister. During the preceding three years he had been First Secretary of the Communist Party of the Georgian republic, in which post he had gained the reputation of an innovator and also a forthright opponent of corruption. Since his appointment the initially inexperienced Shevardnadze has gained in stature in the post and come to symbolize the evolving new Soviet foreign policy. His relaxed and flexible style is in marked contrast to that of his dour and unbending predecessor. Born in 1928, Shevardnadze began his career in 1946 as a Komsomol official. In 1951 he completed a course at the Georgian Party school and by 1957 had become First Secretary of the republic's Komsomol organization, a post he retained until 1961. Simultaneously, he studied at the Kutaisi Pedagogical Institute, from which he graduated in 1959. From 1961 he headed district Party committees, but in 1964 was appointed first deputy minister of Internal Affairs for the republic, becoming minister in the following year. After this period heading the police force, he was elected First Secretary of the Tbilisi city committee in 1972, and later the same year First Secretary of the Georgian Party Committee. A Party member from 1948, in 1976 Shevardnadze

was elected to the Central Committee and in November 1978 was made a candidate member of the Politburo. Following his appointment as Foreign Minister, in July 1985 he was elevated to full Politburo membership. He has been a Supreme Soviet deputy from 1974. In 1981 Shevardnadze was made a Hero of Socialist Labour.
(See: Central Committee; Politburo; Supreme Soviet; Ministry of Foreign Affairs.)

Shilovskii, Vladimir P. , Lieutenant-General; Deputy Commander-in-Chief, Strategic Rocket Forces

Appointed 1987 (?), after previously serving as Commander of the Western Army of the Strategic Rocket Forces.
(See: Armed Forces.)

Shimko, Vladimir Ivanovich, Minister of the Radio Industry

One of the new, young Gorbachev appointees, Shimko, born in 1938, was appointed minister of the radio industry in November 1987 following the death of P. S. Pleshakov, who had held the post from 1974. After graduation from the Moscow Power Institute in 1960, he spent eight years in the radio industry, first as a design engineer at an enterprise and later as senior member of a research institute. In 1968 Shimko switched to work in the Central Committee Secretariat, apparently in its defence industry department, where he became a deputy chief in 1983. It was from this Party post that he was promoted to minister at the end of 1987. A Party member from 1964, Shimko is not a member of the Central Committee.
(See: Military—Industrial Commission; Ministries of the Defence Industry.)

Shishkov, N. G., Colonel-General of Aviation, Deputy Commander-in-Chief of the Air Force, Chief of the Main Armaments Directorate
(See: Armed Forces.)

Shkabardnya, Mikhail Sergeevich, Minister of Instrument Making, Control Systems and Means of Automation

Shkabardnya's ministry, the Ministry of Instrument Making, usually known as Minpribor, is responsible for the production of control instruments, control computers and other equipment for automation, some of which find application in the military sector. He has occupied the post since 1980, having previously served as a deputy minister. Born in 1930, Shkabardnya studied at the Novocherkassk Polytechnic Institute and on graduating in 1954 worked at the Krasnodar factory of electrical measuring instruments. Here he rose to chief engineer before gaining promotion in 1968 to chief engineer and deputy head of one of the ministry's main administrations. From 1974 he served as head of Minpribor's scientific and technical administration, later rising to deputy minister. Shkabardnya has academic qualifications: candidate of the technical sciences (1971), doctor (1980) and professor (1986). A Party member from 1960, include a State Prize (1976).
(See: Central Committee; Supreme Soviet; Other Industrial Ministries.)

Silaev, Ivan Stepanovich, Deputy Chairman, USSR Council of Ministers, Chairman of the Bureau for Machine-Building

Ivan Silaev was appointed chairman of the Bureau of Machine-Building when it was created at the end of 1985. He is a transferee from the defence sector, having previously served as minister of the aviation industry. Born in 1930, he graduated from the Kazan Aviation Institute in 1954. For the next twenty years he worked at the Gor'kii aviation works (a leading producer of military aircraft), rising from foreman to chief engineer, and finally becoming director in 1971. Between 1974 and 1977 he was a deputy minister of the aviation industry, and then for three years first deputy minister. In 1980 Silaev was made minister of the machine tool industry, but this proved to be a short-lived appointment. Following the death of the aviation industry minister in early 1981, Silaev took over the post. A Party member from 1959, he was elected to the Central Committee in 1981. He has served as a Supreme Soviet deputy since 1980. In 1975 he was made a Hero of Socialist Labour; in 1972 he was awarded a Lenin Prize. As chairman of

the Bureau for Machine-Building of the Council of Ministers, Silaev is responsible for the overall co-ordination liaision with the defence industry and the Military-Industrial Commission.
(See: Central Committee; Supreme Soviet; Council of Ministers; Other Industrial Ministries.)

Slyunkhov, Nikolai Nikitovich, Secretary, Central Committee (CC) of the Communist Party of the Soviet Union (CPSU), Member of Politburo

Nikolai Slyunkhov was elected a Secretary of the Central Committee in January 1987 and heads the Secretariat's economic committee, which has the important task of monitoring the introduction of the economic reform. At the time of his election he was made a candidate member of the Politburo; in June 1987 he was elevated to full membership. Slyunkhov, a Belorussian born in 1929, is one of the three non-Russians in the Politburo. Most of his early working life was associated with the Minsk tractor factory where he worked from 1950. By 1960 he had risen from foreman to chairman of the works trade union committee. He then served as director of the Minsk spare parts factory and in 1962 graduated from the Belorussian Institute of Agricultural Mechanization. From 1965 he was director of the tractor factory, but then switched to Party work as First Secretary of the Minsk city committee. In 1974 he moved to Moscow as a deputy chairman of Gosplan, returning to Minsk in 1983 as First Secretary of the Belorussian Party Central Committee. He joined the Party in 1954 and was elected to the Central Committee in 1986. Slyunkhov was a delegate of the Supreme Soviet for a period during the early 1970s and again since 1979; between 1983 and 1987 he was a member of its Presidium. He is a Hero of Socialist Labour (1974) and a State Prize winner. There is little doubt that Slyunkhov is a rising figure of the Soviet leadership, but he faces a difficult task in overseeing the economic reform.
(See: Central Committee/Secretariat; Politburo; Supreme Soviet.)

Smyslov, Valentin Ivanovich, First Chairman of Gosplan (for the Defence Sector)

Smyslov was appointed to his present post in 1985 after a career in the shipbuilding industry. Like Belousov, chairman of the Military–Industrial Commission, he was born in 1928, but graduated from the Leningrad Shipbuilding Institute one year earlier in 1951 (at the same time as Igor Koksanov, the shipbuilding minister). From then until 1969 he occupied a series of engineering and administrative posts in the Penza and Tartar regions. For eight years he headed the Sudozagranpostavka association, a foreign trade organization of the shipbuilding industry. In 1977 Smyslov was appointed chief of an administration of the Ministry of the Shipbuilding Industry and four years later became a deputy minister, rising to first deputy before his transfer to Gosplan in 1985. He joined the Party in 1956 and was elected to the Central Committee as a full member in 1986. In 1979 he won a State Prize.
(See: Central Committee; Supreme Soviet; Military—Industrial Commission; State Planning Committee (Gosplan) and other state economic agencies.)

Solomentsev, Mikhail Sergeevich, Chairman, Party Control Committee, Member of Politburo

After Gromyko, Mikhail Solomentsev is the second oldest Politburo member and has occupied his present post since June 1983, having previously served since 1971 as chairman of the RSFSR Council of Ministers. In the post-Brezhnev period the Control Committee, the Party's disciplinary body, has played an important role in tackling corruption and other abuses by Party members. Solomentsev was born in 1913 and from 1930 worked on a collective farm. In 1940 he graduated from the Leningrad Polytechnic Institute and then worked at factories in Lipetsk and Chelyabinsk, rising to the post of director. Between 1954 and 1957 he undertook Party work in the Chelyabinsk region as a Secretary and then Second Secretary of the regional committee. In 1957 he became chairman of the Chelyabinsk Economic Council, but in 1959 moved to Kazakhstan as First Secretary of the Karaganda regional Party Committee. In 1964 after two years as Second Secretary of the Kazakhstan

Party Central Committee, Solomentsev became First Secretary of the Rostov regional Party organization. From 1966 to 1971 he was a Secretary of the Central Committee and head of one of its departments. It was from this post that he became chairman of the RSFSR Council of Ministers in 1971. A Party member from 1940, he was elected to the Central Committee in 1961 and to the Politburo as a candidate member in 1971. With his present appointment he was elevated to full membership in 1983. A deputy of the Supreme Soviet since 1960, Solomentsev has twice been made a Hero of Socialist Labour, in 1973 and 1983. There is no doubt that Solomentsev is one of the most experienced members of the present leadership but given his advanced age it is likely that he will retire in the near future.
(See: Central Committee; Politburo; Supreme Soviet.)

Solov'ev Yurii Filipovich, First Secretary, Leningrad Regional Party Committee, Candidate Member of Politburo

In July 1985 Solov'ev replaced Zaikov as the Leningrad regional Party First Secretary, having earlier served for several years as the city Party leader. He was born in 1925 and after military service during the war, 1943—44, studied at the Leningrad Institute of Rail Transport Engineers, from which he graduated in 1951. Between 1952 and 1973 Solov'ev worked in the construction organization of the Leningrad Metro, rising to chief engineer and then, from 1967, head of the organization. After a brief period as a deputy chairman of the Leningrad city soviet executive committee, in 1974 he became a Secretary, then Second Secretary of the Leningrad city Party Committee. In 1978 he became First Secretary. At this time he must have had regular contact with both Romanov, the regional Party First Secretary, and Zaikov. Before his election to his present post, Solov'ev served briefly in 1984 as USSR Minister for Industrial Construction. He joined the Party in 1955 and was elected to the Central Committee in 1976. In March 1986 he was elected a candidate member of the Politburo. A Supreme Soviet deputy since 1979, in 1986 he became a member of its Presidium.
(See: Central Committee; Politburo; Supreme Soviet.)

Sorokin, Mikhail Ivanovich, Army General, Deputy Minister of Defence, Chief of the Main Inspectorate

Sorokin was appointed chief of the Defence Ministry's Inspectorate in the summer of 1987, replacing Govorov, who became chief of civil defence. Prior to his promotion, Sorokin had been first deputy commander of the Western Theatre of Military Operations, under Nikolai Ogarkov. He was born in 1922 and joined the Army in 1941, seeing active service during the war. In 1949 he graduated from the Frunze Military Academy; in 1964 from the Academy of the General Staff. After a series of command posts, in 1974 he became first deputy commander of the Far Eastern Military District, and from 1976 commander of the Leningrad Military District. From the end of 1981 until 1984 he appears to have been commander of the Soviet troops in Afghanistan. A Party member from 1943, he was a candidate member of the Central Committee between 1981 and 1986, but was not re-elected at the 27th Party Congress. Sorokin has served as a Supreme Soviet delegate since 1980.
(See: Supreme Soviet; Ministry of Defence.)

Sukhorukov, Dmitrii Semenovich, Army General, Deputy Minister of Defence for Personnel

Sukhorukov replaced Yazov in the post in the summer of 1987, having previously served since 1979 as commander of the Parachute Troops. Born in 1922, he enlisted in the Army in 1939 and participated in the war. Most of his postwar career has been associated with the parachute troops, in both staff and command posts. In 1958 Sukhorukov graduated from the Frunze Military Academy, and then served as a commander, first of a regiment and then of a unit. In 1969 he became a deputy commander of the Parachute Troops, but in 1971 again commanded a unit. Between 1974 and 1976 he served as first deputy commander of the Transcaucasian Military District, and then until his

appointment as commander of the Parachute Troops in 1979, he served as commander of the Central Group of Troops in Czechoslovakia. A Party member since 1944, Sukhorukov is not a member of the Central Committee.
(See: Ministry of Defence.)

Systsov, Apollon Sergeevich, Minister of the Aviation Industry

Systsov was appointed minister in November 1985 after serving as first deputy minister from January 1981. Born in 1929, he began work in 1948 at an aircraft factory, where he worked until 1975, rising from the shop floor to chief engineer. He graduated from the Tashkent Polytechnical Institute in 1962, which suggests that the factory concerned was the Tashkent aviation works. In 1975 he became general director of a major new production facility of the industry then under construction at Ulyanovsk. The Ulyanovsk Aviation-Industrial Complex, as it is known, is now producing the world's largest heavy transport plane, the An-124. From this post he rose directly to the first deputy minister position. A Party member from 1961, Systsov was elected a full membe of the Central Committee in 1986. He is also a member of the USSR Supreme Soviet, elected 1986, and a winner of a State Prize (1973).
(See: Central Committee; Supreme Soviet; Military—Industrial Commission; Ministries of the Defence Industry.)

Talyzin, Nikolai Vladimirovich, First Deputy Chairman, USSR Council of Ministers, Chairman of the Bureau for Social Development, Candidate Member of Politburo

In October 1985 Nikolai Talyzin, a former minister of communications, replaced the elderly Baibakov as chairman of the State Planning Committee (Gosplan), and shortly thereafter he was elected a candidate member of the Politburo. Baibakov had held the post for most of the Brezhnev period and was widely regarded as a conservative. But in February 1988, in what must be seen as a demotion, Talyzin was himself replaced (by Maslyukov) and moved sideways to head the Council of Ministers' Bureau for Social Development, retaining his Politburo membership. He was born in 1929 and began work in industry in 1944. After graduation from the Moscow ElectroTechnical Institute of Communications in 1955 he worked at the State Radio Institute, rising to the post of deputy director. In 1965 Talyzin was appointed deputy minister, later first deputy minister, of communications, and in 1975 he became the minister. As he rose he gained academic qualifications: a doctorate in the technical sciences in 1970; a professorship in 1976. In 1980 Talyzin was promoted to become a deputy chairman of the Council of Ministers and in this capacity served as the USSR's permanent representative in the socialist countries' economic community, the CMEA. It was from this post that Talyzin was promoted to first deputy chairman of the Council of Ministers and chairman of Gosplan in 1985. A Party member from 1960, he was elected to the Central Committee as a candidate member in 1976 and as a full member in 1981. Since 1979 he has been a member of the Supreme Soviet. Awards include two State Prizes, gained in 1968 and 1975.
(See: Central Committee; Politburo; Supreme Soviet; Council of Ministers.)

Tolstykh, Boris Leont'evich, Deputy Chairman of the USSR Council of Ministers, Chairman of the State Committee for Science and Technology

Tolstykh took up his present appointment in February 1987, when the previous chairman of the Committee, Marchuk, was elected president of the USSR Academy of Sciences. He has had a rapid advancement. Born in 1936, he studied at Voronezh University, later gaining a doctorate in the technical sciences. From 1959 he worked as an engineer at a Voronezh electronics factory, rising to chief engineer. In 1977 he became general director of the Voronezh Elektronika association - the post occupied a few years earlier by Kolesnikov, the present minister of the electronics industry. In December 1985 Tolstykh was appointed a deputy minister. He joined the Party in 1970 and

was elected a deputy to the USSR Supreme Soviet in 1979. A Hero of Socialist Labour, Tolstykh is also a State Prize Winner. Given his background, it is likely that one of his tasks as chairman of the State Committee for Science and Technology is improved cooperation between the R & D of the military and civilian sectors, especially in the new information technologies.
(See: Supreme Soviet; Council of Ministers; State Planning Committee and other state economic agencies.)

Tret'yak, Ivan Moiseevich, Army General, Deputy Minister of Defence, Commander-in-Chief of Air Defence Forces

Tret'yak was appointed to his present post in June 1987 in the wake of the Rust affair, which led to the dismissal of Koldunov, the commander of the Air Defence Forces from 1978. It was an unusual appointment in so far as Tret'yak had previously had an army career with no previous experience of air defence. A Ukrainian, born in 1923, he joined the Army in 1939 and fought in the war, being made a Hero of the Soviet Union in 1945. In 1949 he graduated from the Frunze Military Academy; in 1959 the Academy of the General Staff. In the 1950s and early 1960s he occupied a series of command and staff posts, rising to commander of troops of the Belorussian Military District in 1967, and from 1976 commander of troops of the Far Eastern Military District. His first deputy from 1976 to 1979 was Yazov, the present defence minister. From 1984 to 1986 he served as commander-in-chief of the Far Eastern Theatre of Military Operations before being promoted in July 1986 to deputy minister of defence and chief inspector of the armed forces. Tret'yak joined the Party in 1943 and was elected a candidate member of the Central Committee in 1971; since 1976 he has been a full member. He has served as a deputy of the USSR Supreme Soviet since 1970. In 1982 he was made a Hero of Socialist Labour.
(See: Central Committee; Supreme Soviet; Ministry of Defence; Armed Forces.)

Tupolev, Andrei Andreevich, General Designer of the Ministry of the Aviation Industry, Head of the Tupolev Experimental-Design Bureau

The son of the eminent aircraft designer A. N. Tupolev, Andrei Tupolev has been general designer since 1973, following his father's death at the end of the preceding year. He was born in 1925 and started work in the Tupolev bureau as a designer in 1942. In 1949 he graduated from the Moscow Aviation Institute and then returned to the bureau as a leading designer. In 1963 Tupolev became a chief designer and is known to have played a prominent role in the development of the Tu-144 supersonic transport plane. A doctor of the technical sciences, he was elected to the Academy of Sciences as a corresponding member in 1979 and as a full member in 1984. In 1959 he joined include a Lenin Prize (1980) and a State Prize (1967).
(See: Supreme Soviet; Ministries of the Defence Industry; Ministries for Nuclear Weapons and Missiles; Academy of Sciences.)

Utkin, Vladimir Fedorovich, General Designer of a Missile/Rocket Design Bureau

Vladimir Utkin heads one of the principal design bureaux of the Soviet missile industry. This design organization, based in Dnepropetrovsk in the Ukraine, was founded and headed for many years by M. K. Yangel. It has been responsible for such missiles as the SS-4 and SS-5 (to be eliminated under the terms of the INF treaty) and the SS-17 and SS-18 ICBMs. Utkin appears to have taken over its leadership following Yangel's death in 1971. Born in 1923, he joined the army in 1941 and saw active service during the war. He then studied at the Leningrad Military-Mechanical Institute, graduating in 1952. From then on, in the words of his cryptic official biography, 'he occupied engineering and technical posts in the engineering industry'. In 1967 he gained a doctorate in the technical sciences, in 1972 was elected a corresponding member of the Ukrainian Academy of Sciences, and in 1976 a full member of the latter. In 1984 he was elected to

the USSR Academy of Sciences. A Party member from 1945, Utkin was elected to the Central Committee of the Ukrainian Communist Party in 1971, and to the USSR Central Committee in 1976. At present he is the sole missile designer on this leading Party committee. Since 1972 he has been a deputy of the USSR Supreme Soviet. His awards include Hero of Socialist Labour (twice, in 1969 and 1976), a Lenin Prize (1964) and a State Prize (1980). Given his post and membership of leading Party and government bodies, it is likely that Utkin is consulted on at least some matters relating to weapons policy.
(See: Central Committee; Supreme Soviet; Ministries for Nuclear Weapons and Missiles.)

Vedernikov, Gennadii Georgievich, Deputy Chairman, USSR Council of Ministers

Appointed to his present post in June 1986, Vedernikov is responsible for oversight of the metallurgical industry in which he has spent much of his career. Born in 1937, he studied at the Siberian Metallurgical Institute (1960) and then worked at the Chelyabinsk iron and steel works, rising from foreman to shop head. In 1970 he became Second Secretary of one of the district Party Committees of Chelyabinsk, but returned to the steel works in 1973, eventually becoming deputy director. Between 1978 and 1980 he served as Second, then First, Secretary of the Chelyabinsk city Party Committee, and then became a Secretary of the regional Committee. At this time he was studying on an external basis at the Central Committee's Academy of Social Sciences, from where he graduated in 1982. In 1983—84 he worked in the Central Committee Secretariat, but then returned to Chelyabinsk as First Secretary of the regional Party Committee. Here he remained until his promotion in 1986. He joined the Party in 1965 and was elected to the Central Committee in 1986. In 1984 he became a delegate of the Supreme Soviet.
(See: Central Committee; Supreme Soviet; Council of Ministers; other industrial ministries.)

Velichko, Vladimir Makarovich, Minister of Heavy Machine-Building

At the end of 1983 Velichko was appointed minister of power machine-building, but in 1987 this ministry was merged with the heavy machine-building ministry to form the new, enlarged ministry which Velichko now heads. The very wide product range includes items of military equipment, including some artillery systems and diesel engines for armoured vehicles. Velichko himself is an interesting example of a transfer from the military sector. Born in 1937, he graduated from the Leningrad Mechanical Institute in 1962. From then until 1975 he worked at the large Bol'shevik factory in Leningrad, an enterprise of the missile-producing Ministry of General Machine-Building. Here he rose from assistant foreman to deputy director (in 1967) and director (1971). In 1975 he was appointed first deputy minister of the power engineering industry, responsible for electric power equipment. A Party member from 1962, Velichko was elected to the Central Committee in 1986, and to the Supreme Soviet in 1984. In 1977 he was awarded a State Prize.
(See: Central Committee; Supreme Soviet; Other Industrial Ministries.)

Velikhov, Evgenii Pavlovich, Vice-President of the USSR Academy of Sciences, Academic Secretary of the Division of Informatics, Computing and Automation of the Academy of Sciences

Academician Evgenii Velikhov has become one of the best-known Soviet scientists. Head of the new Informatics Division of the Academy from its creation in 1985, for many years deputy director of the Kurchatov Institute of Atomic Energy, and science adviser to Gorbachev, Velikhov has represented the USSR at many international forums, including those concerned with nuclear disarmament. Born in 1935, he graduated from Moscow University in 1958. He obtained his doctorate in 1964 and four years later was elected a corresponding member of the Academy of Sciences. After graduation he worked at the Kurchatov Institute, becoming deputy director in 1971 and head of its branch institute at Troitsk, known for its laser research. Velikhov has worked in the

fields of plasma physics, thermonuclear fusion and high-powered lasers. In 1974 he was elected a full member of the USSR Academy of Sciences and three years later one of its vice-presidents. He joined the Party in 1971 and was elected a candidate member of the Central Committee in 1986. He is also a deputy of the Supreme Soviet, elected in 1984. On his fiftieth birthday he was made a Hero of Socialist Labour and is also the recipient of Lenin and State Prizes. Velikhov is a participant in the Pugwash movement and is chairman of the committee of the organization Soviet Scholars for Peace, against the Nuclear Threat.
(See: Central Committee; Supreme Soviet; Academy of Sciences; Ministries for Nuclear Weapons and Missiles; Consultants and Advisers.)

Volkov, Aleksandr P. , Lieutenant-General; Deputy Commander-in-Chief Strategic Rocket Forces

Volkov was appointed in 1987, having previously served as commander of the Eastern Army of the Strategic Rocket Forces.
(See: Armed Forces.)

Voronin, Lev Alekseevich, Deputy Chairman of the USSR Council of Ministers, Chairman of the State Committee for Material and Technical Supply

Appointed head of the state supply system in November 1985, Lev Voronin has a background similar to that of Gosplan chairman Maslyukov. Born in 1928, he graduated from the Urals Polytechnic Institute in Sverdlovsk in 1949 and then for ten years occupied junior and middle management posts at a local machine-building factory. Between 1959 and 1963 he was chief engineer at two factories in the Urals and then served as chief of an administration of the economic council of the Central Urals economic region. In 1965, when the regional economic councils created under Khrushchev were abolished, Voronin was appointed director of the Krasnogorsk mechanical works south of Moscow, a leading producer of optical equipment under the Ministry of the Defence Industry. In 1968 he became head of the ministry's planning administration and four years later a deputy minister. After a brief period as first deputy minister in October 1980 he switched to Gosplan, where he initially served as first deputy chairman for the defence sector before taking on wider responsibilities. A Party member from 1953, he was elected a full member of the Central Committee in 1981. He has served as a deputy of the Supreme Soviet since 1979.
(See: Central Committee; Supreme Soviet; Council of Ministers; State Planning Committee (Gosplan) and other state economic agencies.)

Vorontsov, Yulii Mikhailovich, First Deputy Minister of Foreign Affairs

Appointed in the spring of 1986, Yulii Vorontsov is one of the new team of foreign ministry officials formed under Gorbachev. He has experience of work in the United States, India and Western Europe. Born in 1929, he graduated from the Moscow Institute of International Relations in 1952. He then worked for a period in the Ministry of Foreign Affairs before becoming a representative of the USSR at the United Nations. Between 1966 and 1977 Vorontsov served in the Soviet embassy in Washington under Ambassador Dobrynin; he then took up the post of ambassador to India. He held this post until 1983 when he was appointed ambassador to France. A Party member since 1956, he was elected to the Central Committee in 1981. In 1987 he replaced Karpov as head of the Soviet delegation at the Geneva talks on strategic and space weapons.
(See: Central Committee; Supreme Soviet; Ministry of Foreign Affairs.)

Vorotnikov, Vitalii Ivanovich, Chairman, Russian Soviet Federal Socialist Republic (RSFSR) Council of Ministers, Member of Politburo

Vorotnikov was appointed to his present post in June 1983 and almost simultaneously was elected a candidate member of the Politburo. By the end of 1983 he had been promoted to full Politburo membership and there is little doubt that Vorotnikov is one of the leaders whose career was effectively blocked under Brezhnev.

He was born in 1926 and began his working life in 1942 in the aviation industry, occupying a series of posts at a Kuibyshev aircraft factory and graduating from the local Aviation Institute in 1954. From 1960 to 1967 he undertook Party work as a Secretary and then Second Secretary of the Kuibyshev regional Party Committee. For four years he served as chairman of the Kuibyshev regional Soviet before moving in 1971 to Voronezh as First Secretary of the regional Party organization. From 1975 Vorotnikov was first deputy chairman of the RSFSR Council of Ministers, but in 1979 was made Soviet ambassador to Cuba. In 1982 he returned as First Secretary of the Krasnodar regional Party Committee, replacing Medunov, a corrupt associate of Brezhnev. This was a brief appointment as in 1983 he became chairman of the RSFSR Council of Ministers. Vorotnikov joined the Party in 1947 and was elected to the Central Committee in 1971. Since 1970 he has been a deputy of the Supreme Soviet. In 1986 he was made a Hero of Socialist Labour.

(See: Central Committee; Politburo; Supreme Soviet.)

Yagodin, Gennadii Alekseevich, Chairman of the State Committee for Public Education

In March 1988 the Soviet educational system was reorganized. Three separate ministries were abolished and replaced by a single State Committee. Yagodin, minister of higher education since 1985, was appointed its first chairman. Born in 1927, Yagodin graduated from the Moscow Chemical-Technological Institute in 1950. After a brief period of Komsomol work he spent the next ten years at the Institute engaged in teaching and research. Beween 1962 and 1966 he served as deputy general director of the International Atomic Energy Agency in Vienna. He then returned to the Institute, becoming a dean of a faculty and eventually, in 1973, rector. In 1971 Yagodin defended his doctorate in chemistry, and in 1976 was elected a corresponding member of the USSR Academy of Sciences. It was from his rectorate that he was promoted to minister of higher education in 1985. A Party member from 1948 he was elected to the Central Committee in 1986. In the same year he also became a deputy of the Supreme Soviet. In 1985 he was awarded a State Prize. As chairman of the new State Committee Yagodin is charged with leading the modernization of the Soviet educational system, including efforts to improve the quality of training of scientists and engineers, and measures to enhance the research role of the higher educational system.

(See: Central Committee; Supreme Soviet; Educational system.)

Yakovlev, Aleksandr Nikolaevich, Secretary, Central Committee (CC) of the Communist Party of the Soviet Union (CPSU), Member of Politburo

Aleksandr Yakovlev has enjoyed rapid promotion under Gorbachev and must now be considered one of the principal figures of the Soviet leadership. Having been the director of an Academy institute in 1985, he was elected a Secretary of the Central Committee in March 1986, became a candidate member of the Politburo in January 1987, and a full member in June. In academic terms he is the most highly qualified member of the top leadership: a doctor of history (1967), professor (1969) and corresponding member of the Academy of Sciences (1984). Yakovlev was born in 1923 and saw active service during the war between 1941 and 1943. Invalided out of the forces, he studied at the Yaroslavl Pedagogical Institute, graduating in 1946, and then undertook Party work in the Yaroslavl region. From 1953 he worked in the Central Committee Secretariat, eventually becoming head of the Propaganda Department. During this time Yakovlev studied at the Central Committee's Academy of Social Sciences, graduating in 1960. His domestic career was checked in 1973, when he was appointed Soviet ambassador to Canada, a post he retained until after the death of Brezhnev. In 1983 he was appointed director of the Academy's Institute of World Economy and International Relations; in 1985 head of the Central Committee's Department of Propaganda. Now, as a senior Secretary of the Central Committee, Yakovlev oversees the work of this department and has responsibility for the process of ideological

renewal. A Party member since 1944, he was elected a member of the Central Auditing Commission in 1971, and of the Central Committee in 1986. He has been a Supreme Soviet deputy since 1984.
(See: Central Committee/Secretariat; Politburo; Supreme Soviet.)

Yashin, Yurii Alekseevich, Colonel-General, First Deputy Commander-in-Chief, Strategic Rocket Forces

Born in 1930, Yashin joined the Army in 1948. At some point he studied at the principal educational establishment for training Strategic Rocket Forces specialists, the Dzerzhinskii Military Academy in Moscow. An engineer, Yashin has a doctorate in the technical sciences and is known to have participated in the testing of some of the early Soviet missile systems. He was appointed to his present post in 1981. Yashin has been a Party member since 1957 and a deputy of the USSR Supreme Soviet since 1984.
(See: Supreme Soviet; Armed Forces.)

Yazov, Dmitrii Timofeevich, Army General, Minister of Defence

The unexpected appointment of Yazov as minister of defence in May 1987 followed the dismissal of his predecessor Sokolov in the wake of the Rust landing in Red Square. It was a remarkably rapid promotion: only in January 1987 had he been transferred to Moscow from the far east as Deputy Minister of Defence for Personnel. Dmitrii Yazov was born in 1923 near Omsk in Siberia. He enlisted in the Red Army in 1941 and fought on the Volkhov and Leningrad fronts during the war. After the war he served as a company and corps commander and then graduated from the Frunze Military Academy in 1956. After a period as a regimental commander in the Leningrad Military District he graduated from the Military Academy of the General Staff in 1967. After occupying command posts in Siberia and the Caucasus, Yazov worked in the Main Personnel Directorate of the Ministry of Defence between 1974 and 1976. He then served as first deputy commander of the Far Eastern Military District and in 1979 as commander of the Soviet forces in Czechoslovakia. Between 1980 and 1984 he commanded the Central Asian Military District and in this position is likely to have played an active role in the Soviet action in Afghanistan. In 1984 he was appointed commander of the Far Eastern Military District. There is speculation that Yazov came to Gorbachev's attention during the latter's visit to the Far East in July 1986. A Party member from 1944, Yazov was elected a candidate member of the Central Committee in 1981 and was elevated to full membership in June 1987, when he also became a candidate member of the Politburo. Since 1984 he has been a Supreme Soviet deputy.
(See: Central Committee; Politburo; Supreme Soviet; Defence Council; Ministry of Defence.)

Zaikov, Lev Nikolaevich, Secretary, Central Committee (CC) of the Communist Party of the Soviet Union (CPSU), First Secretary, Moscow City Committee CPSU, Member of Politburo

Lev Zaikov is the Politburo member with the greatest experience of the defence industry. He was appointed a Secretary of the Central Committee in July 1985 and, in November 1987, First Secretary of the Moscow city Party Committee, replacing Boris El'tsin. He currently holds both posts. As Central Committee Secretary, Zaikov's responsibilities include oversight of the defence sector, and the fact that he has remained a Secretary while heading the Moscow Party may mean that he retains an interest in this field, possibly supervising Oleg Baklanov, the present Secretary for the defence industry. Zaikov was born in 1923 and began his working life in 1940 as a fitter at a military factory. In 1944 he moved to another Leningrad enterprise where he rose from foreman to director (1961). In 1963 he graduated from the Leningrad Engineering-Economics Institute. Zaikov served as factory director until 1971, when his enterprise, apparently concerned with militarily-related electronics, was incorporated in a production association. He became general director of this larger unit, which in 1974 became the science-production association

Leninets. From 1976 Zaikov was chairman of the Leningrad city Soviet and then from 1983 replaced Grigorii Romanov as First Secretary of the Leningrad regional Party Committee. It was from this position that he became a Central Committee Secretary under Gorbachev in July 1985. A Party member from 1957, he was elected to the Central Committee in 1981. In March 1986 he was elected a full member of the Politburo. From 1979 he has served as a Supreme Soviet deputy; from 1984 to 1986 as a member of its Presidium. In 1971 he was made a Hero of Socialist Labour. Given his background and experience, it is likely that Zaikov is involved in defence-related decisionmaking. One of the features of economic policy under Gorbachev has been the attempt to harness defence sector skills to the modernization of the civilian economy: Zaikov appears to have been directly involved in this reorientation of the defence industry. Zaikov himself has revealed that in Ligachev's absence he chairs the weekly Central Commitee Secretariat meetings, making him the third-ranking Party leader after Gorbachev and Ligachev.
(See: Central Committee/Secretariat; Politburo; Supreme Soviet; Defence Council; Military—Industrial Commission.)

Zaitsev, Mikhail Mitrofanovich, Army General; Commander-in-Chief of the Southern Theatre of Military Operations

Since the summer of 1985 Zaitsev has occupied the Southern Theatre command post (with headquarters in Baku) after more than four years as Commander-in-Chief of the Group of Soviet Troops in Germany. He was born in 1923, joined the Army in 1941 and saw active service during the war. In 1954 he graduated from the Military Academy of the Armoured Troops and later, in 1965, from the Military Academy of the General Staff. After a series of command and staff posts he was appointed first deputy commander of the Belorussian Military District in 1972, and Commander in 1976. In December 1980 he moved to the German command post. Having joined the Party in 1941, Zaitsev was elected to the Central Committee in 1981. He has been a Supreme Soviet delegate since 1980. In 1983 he was made a Hero of the Soviet Union.
(See: Central Committee; Supreme Soviet; Armed Forces.)

NOTES

1. For biography of Kulikov, see Chapter 7.
2. The biographies have been compiled from a range of sources, predominantly Soviet, in particular encylopedias and other reference works. These are listed below. The Soviet reference works provide only a limited range of basic information and this accounts for the rather formal and repetitive nature of most of the biographies. A long-standing feature of Soviet political culture is the absence of discussion of details of the personal lives of leading officials. It should also be noted that it is difficult to find detailed biographical information on Soviet officials who are not members of either the Party Central Committee or the USSR Supreme Soviet.

REFERENCES

Constitution (Fundamental Law) of the Union of Soviet Socialist Republics, 1977, Novosti Press Agency, Moscow.

Holloway, D., 1983, *The Soviet Union and the Arms Race*, Yale University Press, New Haven and London.

Jones, E., 1984, *The Defence Council in Soviet Leadership Decision-making*, Occasional Paper No. 188, Kennan Institute for Advanced Russian Studies, Washington D. C.

Lane, D., 1985, *State and Politics in the USSR*, Blackwell, Oxford.

Soviet Military Power, 1984 (3rd edn), US Government Printing Office, Washington D. C.

Sovetskaya Voennaya Entsiklopediya, Vol. 2, 1976, Voenizdat, Moscow.

Sovetskoe administrativnoe pravo, 1981, Yuridicheskaya Literatura, Moscow.

Sources for Biographies

Deputaty Verkhovnogo Soveta SSSR (Deputies of the USSR Supreme Soviet), 1984, Moscow.

Ezhegodnik Bol'shoi Sovetskoi Entsiklopedii, 1987 (Yearbook of the Great Soviet Encylopedia), 1987, Moscow.

Sovetskii Entsiklopedicheskii Slovar' (Soviet Encylopedia of Words), (4th edn), 1984, Moscow.

Voennyi Entsiklopedicheskii Slovar' (Military Encylopedia oft Words), 1986, Moscow.

These sources have been supplemented by information from the Soviet press (in particular *Pravda*, *Izvestiya* and *Krasnaya Zvezda*).

~3~

The United Kingdom

The institutions in the United Kingdom in which decisions to produce nuclear weapons are made are the Cabinet and the Cabinet Office, the Ministry of Defence (which is also the headquarters of the armed forces), the intelligence services, the Treasury, the Foreign and Commonwealth Office, and the various firms which manufacture defence equipment and nuclear material. In addition, the USA plays an important role, as does NATO. Parliament, through which the government is constitutionally accountable to the electorate, has no significant role in nuclear weapons decision-making, though this is not unique to this area of policy.

In this chapter these institutions are described, their roles in the nuclear weapons production decisionmaking process assessed, and profiles of key individuals in the decision-making process are provided.

GOVERNMENT

The Cabinet

Address: see Cabinet Office

The Cabinet is the highest elected policymaking body in the country. The full Cabinet is made up of approximately twenty-two men and women: the Prime Minister; senior departmental ministers; and some non-departmental ministers. While its membership is public, it meets in private and its proceedings are confidential. It normally meets about once a week. Most of its work is done in committees (see below); only the ministers and civil servants responsible for the work allocated to a committee sit on it. The Cabinet is serviced by its own branch of the civil service, the Cabinet Office (see below). Most legislative as well as administrative initiative comes from Cabinet. In order to initiate policy, however, the Cabinet depends on the advice and research of the civil service in both the Cabinet Office and the ministerial departments; and it must always work within the constraints of inherited policy. Thus, for instance, while approval at Cabinet level was essential for the Trident programme to proceed, the approval was to a certain extent pre-empted by the research work which had already been done at the then Atomic Weapons Research Establishment at Aldermaston, by the fact that British dependence on US technology left little room for consideration of alternative weapons systems (See NATO and the USA) and, above all, by the unquestioned assumption that Britain required a 'nuclear deterrent'. The Cabinet may be the supreme decisionmaking body in the country; its decisions, at least about nuclear weapons, however, tend to be made between a very limited number of choices.

THE PRIME MINISTER

Address: 10 Downing Street, London SW1
Tel: 01-270-3000

Constitutional theorists and Cabinet observers have spilt much ink over the influence on policymaking, in the Cabinet and in the government as a whole, which the Prime Minister – and particularly the current one, Margaret Thatcher – enjoys.

The Prime Minister has considerable power to shape and run the Cabinet according to his views. He effectively makes all the appointments to ministerial office (Crown ministers are appointed by the Monarch on the recommendation of the Prime Minister). He also appoints senior civil servants – a feature of Mrs Thatcher's period in office has been her appointment of senior civil servants known to be sympathetic to her views – and can strongly influence how the tasks of government should be distributed among different departments. The Prime Minister can ask ministers to resign, can recommend to the Monarch that they be dismissed and can 're-shuffle' the Cabinet.

The Prime Minister also presides over full Cabinet meetings and is thus normally able to control the discussions in Cabinet and the decisionmaking process in it; this is done by the Prime Minister's right to decide the order and content of Cabinet business, and by using consensus, rather than vote-taking, to make decisions. And though the Cabinet Secretariat (in the Cabinet Office) services the whole Cabinet, it has a special relationship with and allegiance to the Prime Minister; this is particularly true of the Secretary to the Cabinet. In addition, only the Prime Minister has the constitutional right to recommend that Parliament be dissolved and new elections called and is not required to discuss this with the Cabinet. Consequently, some commentators argue that political power in the UK lies not with 'Cabinet government' but with 'prime Ministerial government'. The restraints on the Prime Minister should not be under-estimated: Cabinet colleagues have to be carried on policy issues, as do backbench MPs; factions in the party have to be kept sweet; dissolving Parliament is risky, particularly if the government has a slender majority; and the Prime Minister, like all ministers, relies heavily on the civil service for advice. Nevertheless, the Prime Minister does have greater say in the decisionmaking process than other ministers. This is particularly so in the present Cabinet; indeed, Margaret Thatcher can be said to have redefined the role of Prime Minister.

Since Mrs Thatcher was first elected in 1979, the conduct of Cabinet government has reflected her stated desire to lead a 'conviction government' in which she would not 'waste time having any internal arguments' (Hennessy, 1986, p. 94). The bare statistics of Cabinet business show that discussion has a less important role in Cabinet than under her predecessors: Cabinet rarely meets more than once a week (compared with twice-weekly under Attlee and Churchill); the number of Cabinet papers produced annually has been on average one-sixth of the total produced in the late 1940s and early 1950s; and the number of Cabinet committees created in the six years from 1979 to 1985 – 160 – was about the same as that produced in three years (April 1976–79) under Prime Minister Callaghan. A considerable degree of Cabinet and Cabinet committee work is, instead, now done by ministerial correspondence; in addition, a number of *ad hoc* groups have been formed which do not find their way into the Cabinet Secretary's committee book and thus probably operate under even closer prime ministerial direction than do some registered Cabinet committees: for example, an important one dealing with monetary policy and delicate decisions affecting the money market, described by one observer as a 'flexible, amoeba-like group whose composition changes according to circumstances. "It's more of a habit of working than an approach"'.

In addition to re-moulding the Cabinet machine, Mrs Thatcher has, since 1979, carefully but steadily removed from senior positions ministers whose reflect the old consensual Tory tradition of governing.

Commentators point out that however clear Margaret Thatcher is (or appears to be) about her own views and in neither needing nor wanting to resolve matters by collective discussion, she like other Prime Ministers, must have the support of at least the senior members of her Cabinet. Where she pursues goals without such support she risks public rows, and even damaging splits, as in the dispute over the future of the Westland company in 1985–86, during which two senior ministers resigned their posts. It may be too bold to say that she is practising not even 'prime ministerial', but 'presidential government, in which she operates like a sovereign in court' (Hennessy, 1986,

p. 99). Nevertheless, in Cabinet as in government as a whole, her worldview has a profound influence on policy.
(*See biography of: Thatcher.*)

THE CABINET COMMITTEES

The Cabinet committees have been called the 'working parts' of British central government. As we have noted, about 160 had been created by the Thatcher government between 1979 and the winter of 1985–86.

There are two basic types of Cabinet committee: *Standing* committees, which are permanent for the duration of the Prime Minister's of office and *Ad Hoc* committees, which are convened to deal with a single issue or on occasion, like the 'Star Chamber', which meets every autumn to resolve the ministries' competing budgetary claims (see Office of Management and Budget, Ministry of Defence). Committees can be either *ministerial*, in which case civil servants attend only as minute-takers; *official*, which only civil servants attend, and which either shadow ministerial committees, or do the spadework for them; or *mixed*, made up of both civil servants and ministers. The Ad Hoc committees are numbered and prefixed with MISC for miscellaneous, for example MISC 7, the committee which took the decision in 1979–80 to replace the Polaris weapons system with Trident. In addition, under Mrs Thatcher a number of unregistered *ad hoc* groups have been formed to handle specific issues (see above).

Margaret Thatcher has acknowledged the existence of four committees: the four main Standing committees on Home and Social Affairs, Legislation, economic strategy and Oversea and Defence Policy, respectively. The membership of the last committee includes the Prime Minister, the Chancellor of the Exchequer (Nigel Lawson), the Secretary of State for Defence (George Younger) and the Foreign Secretary (Sir Geoffrey Howe). The Chief of the Defence Staff (after December 1988: Air Marshall Sir David Craig) may also attend its meetings.

The practice of decisionmaking in committee, rather than full Cabinet, obviously means that not all ministers have a say in every decision made. In fact, according to Sir Geoffrey Howe, 'there are very few discussions of Government decisons by full Cabinet' (Hennessy, 1986, p.105). However, the fiction of full Cabinet participation in government decisionmaking is upheld by the tradition of 'collective responsibility', which requires Cabinet members neither to criticize nor to disassociate themselves from government policy decisions, whether taken in full Cabinet or in committee, and whether they have been party to them or not. Ministers may even be ignorant of the existence of the committee in which the decision was made. Thus, the Conservative government's decision to approve the Trident programme was simply presented to the Cabinet, with a short briefing and no time for debate, after it had been worked out in Ad Hoc committee MISC 7.
(*See biographies of: Craig; Howe; Lawson; Thatcher; Younger.*)

The Cabinet Office
Address: 70 Whitehall, London SW1A 2AS
Tel: 01-270-3000

The Cabinet Office consists of the Cabinet Secretariat, the Management and Personnel Office, the Establishment Officers' Group and the Central Statistical Office. The Cabinet Office has been described as the 'engine room' of British central government. It is the Secretariat to which this epithet particularly applies.

The Secretariat's basic function is to service the Cabinet policymaking process, namely the committee system, with advice on which fora are suitable for particular topics, and on whether new committees should be established, and with more mundane tasks such as minute taking. The Cabinet Secretary and his private office and senior staff members play a major part in the first, advisory process. These functions give the Cabinet Office an influence over the way in which policy is discussed.

Mrs Thatcher's contempt for collectivist working practices, evident in her approach to Cabinet discussion (see above), is apparent in her attitude to the Secretariat. Under her, it has been in less demand from politicians and outsiders than under her recent predecessors. Senior Whitehall officials are as likely to approach her Downing Street private office as the Secretariat to find out what is going on. Margaret Thatcher 'is not the sort of person who uses the official machinery to do things for her'(Hennessy, 1986, p. 22).

The Secretariat is made up of about one hundred civil servants, all of whom, except for the Cabinet Secretary, are on secondment from the ministries. The Secretariat is in fact a federation of six secretariats, each with its own head. Two of these play a role in defence decisionmaking: the Oversea and Defence Secretariat, which is led by a senior Foreign Office diplomat and combines foreign and defence policymaking with the output of the intelligence agencies; and the Security and Intelligence Secretariat (the 'most sensitive of all the secretariats' (Hennessy, 1986, p. 25), which is headed by Sir Colin Figures, the Coordinator of Intelligence and Security (see Defence Intelligence). The Economic, European, Home Affairs and Science and Technology Secretariats make up the group.
(*See biographies of Butler; Figures.*)

SECRETARY OF THE CABINET
Address: see Cabinet Office

The Secretary of the Cabinet, Sir Robin Butler, is the chief civil servant in the Cabinet Office. His is 'the most powerful job in Whitehall, first because he has the ear of the PM and works cheek by jowl with her and second because he is responsible for the whole of the Civil Service and recommends people for key appointments' (*The Times*, 9 July 1987). His office at 70 Whitehall is linked to 10 Downing St.

Although the PM seeks advice from the whole range of government departments, her Cabinet Secretary is her closest adviser. He calibrates the flow of business through Cabinet and its committees. On security matters he is the one who liaises with the intelligence services and advises the Prime Minister on the most sensitive and secret aspects of government. He chairs the Permanent Secretaries' Committee on Intelligence Services (PSIS – see Defence Intelligence).
(*See biography of: Butler.*)

Civil Service

Government departments are the main instruments for giving effect to government policy when Parliament has passed the necessary legislation.

The departments can be grouped loosely in three types: *executive units*, which provide a service to the public directly, like the Department of Health and Social Security (DHSS), or indirectly, like the Department of Education and Science (DES); *common service units*, like Her Majesty's Stationary Office (HMSO), which provide a support service for other departments; and central units, which perform some central co-ordinating or research role, like the Ministry of Defence, the Foreign and Commonwealth Office, the Treasury or the Cabinet Office. In addition, ministers and some senior civil servants have a *private office*. This consists of a small team which provides a wide range of administrative support for its busy superior. The minister's private office is headed by a private secretary who is often a successful younger civil servant using this post as a stepping-stone to promotion. In addition, the minister's office will have in it the parliamentary private secretary; she or he will be an unpaid backbench MP who does much of the routine work which the minister is simply too busy to do. Each Secretary of State is assisted by one or two second-rank ministers of state and a parliamentary under-secretary. Together, these three form a ministerial team which is the total governmental presence in the ministry.

Government departments are staffed by civil servants, of which there are currently approximately 600,000. Although civil servants work under the authority and direction of the ministers of the department to which they are appointed, constitutionally they are servants of the Crown. Formally, civil servants are politically neutral. In the words of a government publication: 'Stability of administration is ensured by the political neutrality of the civil service: a change of minister, whether due to changes within the administration or to a government being formed by a different political party, does not involve a change of staff.'

The extent to which the civil service does or not play an active political role in the administration of the country is, however, a subject of continuing debate. The object of this debate is the top 0.01 per cent (about 650 people) of the civil service, the so-called Whitehall 'mandarins' who are at the centre of the policymaking process and who bear the titles of Permanent Secretary, Deputy Secretary and Under-Secretary (Grades I, II and III respectively in the civil service hierarchy). Permanent Secretaries (Permanent Under Secretaries in the Ministry of Defence and the Foreign and Commonwealth Office) are the officials in charge of a government department.

Two factors hinder discussion of the policymaking role of civil servants. First, there is the Official Secrets Act, which forbids civil servants from disclosing any aspect of their work. This means that the work they carry out with and for ministers remains private and that they are not allowed to reply to public criticism made of them by ministers. Secondly, by the tradition of ministerial responsibility. This dictates that a minister takes responsibilty for all that is done in and by his or her government department; it thus encourages civil servants to conceal in public their roles in the formulation of policy and thus remain unaccountable for their part in policy formation (for instance when being questioned by Parliamentary Select Committees — see Parliament). Nevertheless, it is possible to assess the potential influence which civil servants can have on the policymaking process. This influence can take four forms:

1: *Permanence and expertise*. Departmental ministers do not often serve in office for more than three years. Often they will be appointed without having any expert knowledge of the department's business. By contrast, civil servants, almost without exception, serve in their particular department for life and are thus able to develop not only expertise in their field but also a network of contacts and in-depth working knowledge of the administrative machinery. This combination of permanence and expertise has led to many departments becoming attached to certain policies which they appear to have suported over many years and under different governments. These 'departmental polices' are not, of course, publicly acknowledged but they do exist.

2: *Information and advice*. One of the senior civil servants' most important tasks is the collection of and presentation to the minister of relevant information, on the basis of which the minister will make the relevant political decision. This stage of processing or filtering the information provides an opportunity for influence. Furthermore, civil servants have the opportunity to determine the framework within which any information is presented and interpreted. Lord Armstrong, former head of the civil service, has said: 'Obviously I had a great deal of influence. The biggest and most pervasive influence is in setting the framework within which the questions of policy are raised. We, while I was in the Treasury, had a framework of the economy which was basically neo-Keynesian. We set the questions which we asked ministers to decide arising out of that framework and it would have been enormously difficult for my minister to change the framework; so to that extent we had great power.'

3: *Delegation*. Ministers have to delegate a lot of their heavy work load to civil servants. It is a constitutional fiction that politicians take the political decisons and civil servants implement them in an objective and impartial manner. A rigid distinction cannot be made between policy and administration: so, for example, a civil servant who is on a Cabinet sub-committee is involved in policymaking and administration. On occasion, decisionmaking power will be delegated to civil servants.

4: *Bureaucratic resistance*. James Prior, speaking of his time as Secretary of State for Employment, has said that civil servants 'could slow [the policy] down by raising constant objections, saying that every single policy issue, however small, had to be cleared in a minute sort of way, and having endless discussions on it...[Second, they] could stir up other departments to raise all sorts of objections when it went to Cabinet Committee or Cabinet. [Third,] they could…and this undoubtedly does happen…have some discreet briefing of various organizations in the country to raise questions of 'Was this right?' and so on…[Lastly], of course, it somehow does get into the newspapers. I'm not saying that there would be deliberate leaks, but there would certainly be nods and winks given that the policy the minister was pursuing was perhaps rather dangerous and not according to the advice he was receiving. I think there would be a number of ways in which that could be done, and if the civil service does get at odds with a minister, then it is not very easy for either to operate very effectively.'

The Ministry of Defence
Address: The Ministry of Defence, Main Building, Whitehall, London SW1A 2HB
Tel: 01-218-9000

The Ministry of Defence (MoD) is 'concerned with the 'control, administration, equipment and support of the Armed Forces. The research, development, production and purchase of weapons systems for the Armed Forces is the concern of the Procurement Executive of the Ministry of Defence' (*Civil Service Year Book*, 1988, p.113). With 195,000 civilian staff – one-third of the British civil service — the MoD is the largest government department. In addition, it has the 325,000-strong armed forces on its payroll. It is British industry's single largest customer: defence equipment expenditure sustains about 225,000 jobs directly and about 185,000 indirectly.

The Ministry of Defence (MoD) in its present shape was created in 1963. The dominant feature of the post-war history of the Central Organization of Defence, as the mainly Whitehall-based bureacracy which runs Britain's armed forces is termed in the specialist literature, has been its increasing centralization. If in 1946 the Central Organization of Defence (COD) and the armed forces constituted a loose-knit federal structure, in the late 1980s there is considerable central control over defence policymaking and defence budgeting. Consequently, civilian advisers play a much greater role in defence decisionmaking than they did forty years ago. The single services, which used to enjoy considerable independence in policymaking and budgeting, are now primarily responsible only for their own management. And even in this respect, their autonomy has been reduced as, in this process of centralization, single service-oriented formulation of defence policy and management has been gradually replaced by policymaking and management in terms of *functions* which can be carried out across the armed forces (also known as 'defence-wide' planning).

The first post-war reform, in which the MoD was actually called in to existence, took place in 1946 in the aftermath of wartime co-operation between the services. By the mid-1950s, various issues had exposed the COD's organizational weaknesses and raised questions as to where, and at what level, responsibility lay for the planning and execution of defence policy. These issues included the development, production and control over nuclear weapons; rapid increases in the costs and technical complexity of new weapons; Britains's involvement in the Western alliance and the retreat from Empire; and pressures to effect overall economies in defence while improving military efficiency and reducing waste and duplication. A further reform took place in 1963 with the subsumption of the service ministries — Admiralty, Air Ministry and the War Office – under the MoD; nevertheless, the services retained a certain degree of autonomy from central control.

In the 1960s, under Labour governments committed to exercising greater control over defence spending, the trend towards functionalization continued; in the same decade, a steady increase in the cost and complexity of weaponry led, in 1972, to the creation of a centralized procurement structure, the Procurement Executive.

Under the first and second Thatcher governments (1979–87), government concern with cutting the level of public spending and with improving efficiency and productivity of government departments led to a further defence review, begun under Secretary of State John Nott in 1981–82 and completed under his successor Michael Heseltine in 1984–85 (entitled,

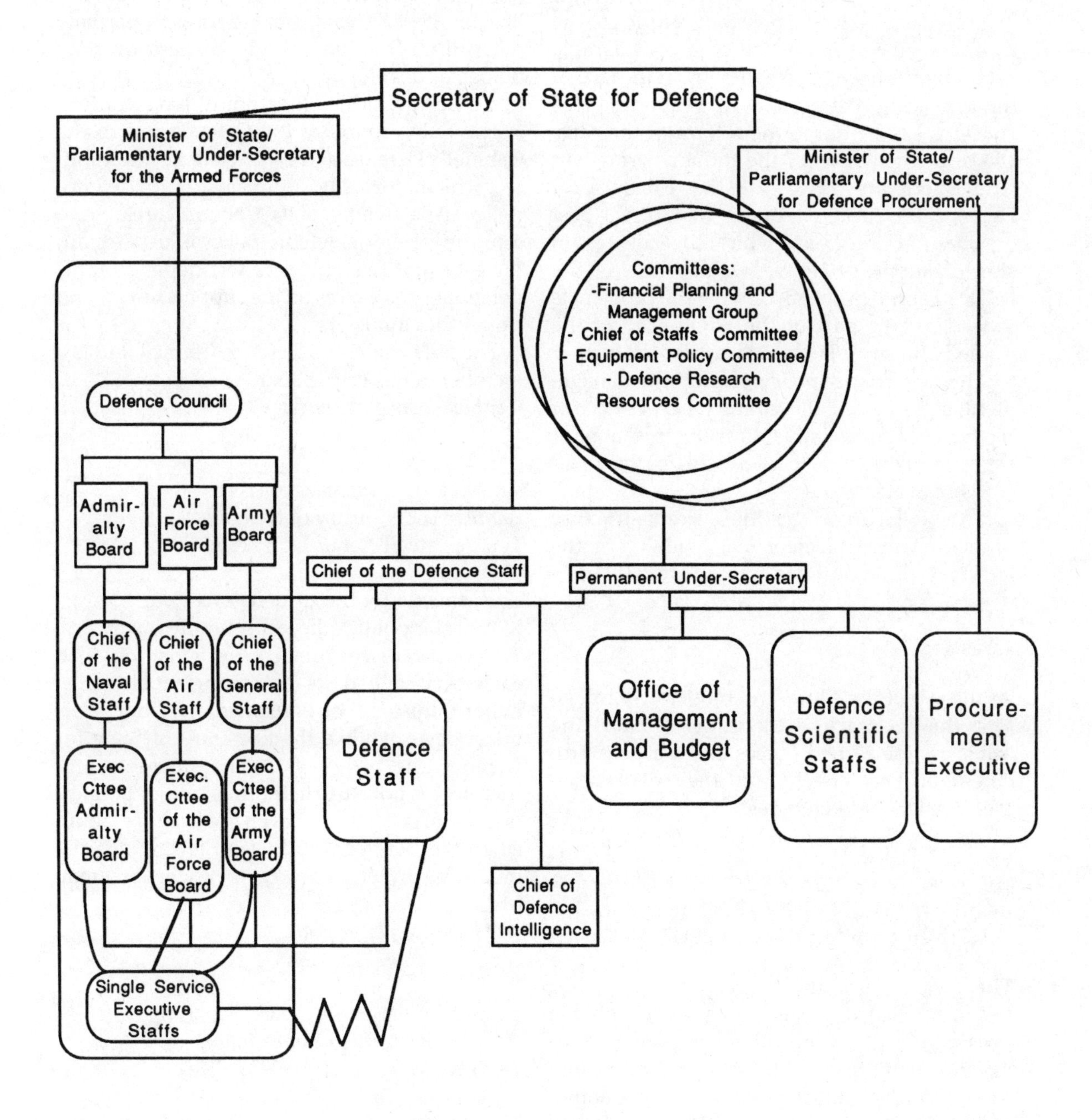

Figure 3.1 *The Central Organization of Defence*

by Heseltine, the MINIS (Management Information for Ministers System) reform).

As we have seen, the post-war reforms of the COD have been motivated to a considerable extent by the need to save money in the face of the increasing cost of modern weaponry. This concern was central to the reform of the early 1980s. In the words of the former Permanent Under-Secretary (PUS) at the Ministry of Defence, Sir Clive Whitmore, 'Making the best of financial resources which are always in shorter supply than we would wish is the MOD's central problem. Solving the problem is indeed a large part of the *raison détre* of the unified Ministry'. The need was also felt further to integrate defence policymaking and management, in the light of the 'country's experience of modern warfare' (The Central Organisation for Defence, 1984, p.1) particularly in the Falklands/Malvinas war.

In the following pages, the current structure of the Ministry of Defence, as modified by the latest reform, is outlined (see Figure 3.1).

MINISTERS

At the top of the MoD structure sit five ministers: the Secretary of State for Defence, the Ministers for Armed Forces and Defence Procurement, respectively, and their two Parliamentary Under-Secretaries.

THE SECRETARY OF STATE FOR DEFENCE
Address: see The Ministry of Defence
Tel (Private Secretary): 01-218-2111

The functions of the Secretary of State for Defence (SSD), George Younger MP, include providing political control of and giving political direction to the MoD, representing the position of the Ministry in Cabinet or Cabinet committees (on the Defence and Oversea Policy Committee (DOPC) he does this with the Chief of Defence Staff) and answering to Parliament for the actions of his department. His ability to lead the MoD politically will depend on the strength of his personality: as we have seen, senior civil servants have the power to influence substantially the sorts of political decisions that are taken. In addition, in procurement matters (whether nuclear or conventional), he, like his civil servants, has decisions partially determined for him by the process of technological development over which neither he nor other politicians (by choice) have control.

The SSD reports to the Cabinet and to the Cabinet's Defence and Oversea Policy Committee which, formally, is in charge of defence policy. As a member of the Cabinet, he can have a key influence on defence policy issues. Again, the extent of this influence will depend on his personality as well as on the support he can find from other ministers.

The SSD chairs the Defence Council and is a member of its Service Boards (see below).
(*See biography of: Younger.*)

MINISTER FOR THE ARMED FORCES
Address: see Ministry of Defence
Tel (Private Secretary): 01-218-6385

The Minister for the Armed Forces, Ian Stewart MP, is the political head of the three services. This post replaces previous systems, in which each service had its own representative, at either ministerial or Parliamentary Under-Secretary level. Unlike the Secretary of State for Defence, he is not a Cabinet member and therefore is not party to the most senior political nuclear decisions. He sits on the Defence Council and its Service Boards. Ian Stewart's Parliamentary Under-Secretary is Roger Freeman MP.
(*See biography of: Stewart.*)

MINISTER FOR DEFENCE PROCUREMENT
Address: see Ministry of Defence
Tel (Private Secretary): 01-218-2452

The Minister for Defence Procurement, currently Lord Trefgarne, is the political head of the Procurement Executive. His approval is required throughout the procurement process for equipment projects which exceed £25 million in R&D costs and £50 million in production costs. Like the Minister for the Armed Forces, he is not a Cabinet member. He sits on the

Defence Council and its Service Boards. Lord Trefgarne's Parliamentary Under-Secretary is David Heathcote-Amory MP.
(*See biography of: Trefgarne.*)

DEFENCE COUNCIL

The Defence Council is, formally, a senior committee in the MoD with the peacetime role of advising and assisting in defence policy decisions. To this end it brings together civilian and military personnel: the Secretary of State for Defence (SSD), his four junior ministers, the Permanent Under-Secretary of State, the three Service Chiefs of Staff, the Chief of the Defence Staff, the Vice Chief of the Defence Staff, the Chief of Defence Procurement, the Chief Scientific Adviser and the Second Permanent Under-Secretary of State. However, despite its prominent position in the MoD hierarchy, in practice the DC exists only on paper. Some question its effectiveness even when it does meet regularly.

PERMANENT UNDER-SECRETARY
Address: see Ministry of Defence
Tel (Personal Assistant): 01-218-2392

The Permanent Under-Secretary's organization in the MoD is the section which runs day-to-day matters in the department. The Permanent Under-Secretary (PUS), Sir Michael Quinlan, is the most powerful civil servant in the MoD. The PUS is one of the two principal advisers to the Secretary of State for Defence (the other is the Chief of the Defence Staff – see below). Formally, he is the permanent head of the department and the Principal Accounting Officer and his responsibilities include:

– the organization and efficiency of the Ministry, including the management of all civilian staff and the co-ordination of its business;

– the long-term financial planning and budgetary control of the defence programme, the associated allocation of resources, and the proper scrutiny of all proposals which will require expenditure; and

– providing advice on the political and parliamentary aspects of the Ministry's work and relations with other government departments (The Central Organisation for Defence, 1984, p.3).

The following report to the PUS: the Chief Scientific Adviser (CSA), the Chief of Defence Procurement (CDP), the Chief Defence Equipment Collaboration and the Second Permanent Under-Secretary (PUS). The PUS is a member of the Defence Council.
(*See biography of: Quinlan.*)

CHIEF OF THE DEFENCE STAFF
Address: see Ministry of Defence
Tel (Aide-de-Camp): 01-218-6190

One of the most radical, and controversial, changes in the MINIS reform of 1985–85 concerned the reponsibility of the Chief of Defence Staff (CDS), the military head of the MoD (from December 1988: Air Marshal Sir David Craig). Whereas previously individual service chiefs of staff had greater say in policymaking and had their own political representatives in Parliament, MINIS left them little policymaking authority and deprived them of their political spokespersons. The service chiefs – Admiral Sir William Staveley GCB (Navy); General Sir John Chapple (Army); Air Chief Marshall Sir Peter Harding (RAF), from December 1988 – sit on the Chiefs of Staff Committee, which the CDS chairs. He is responsible for passing on their collective view to the Secretary of State for Defence. His, however, is the most important voice on the committee and he also has the right to tender independent military advice on strategy, forward policy, resource allocation, commitments and operations. The individual Service Boards and their executive subcommittees are now responsible only for the management of their respective services and are subordinated to the CDS and the Defence Staff (see below). Further, the CDS is now appointed by the Secretary of State for Defence and the Prime Minister; the post will no longer rotate according to the principle of 'Buggins's turn' among the three service chiefs. This change gives the central political authorities greater control over the direction of defence policymaking. The CDS also plans and directs the work of

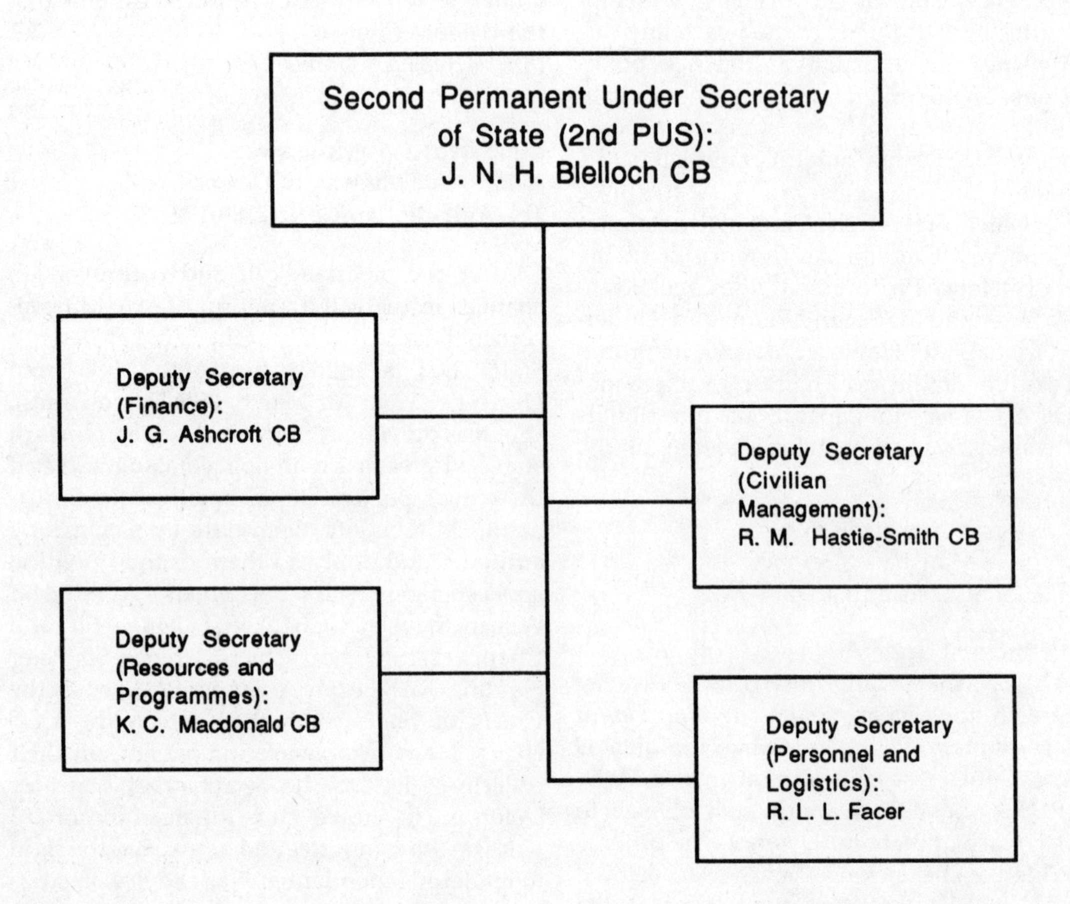

Figure 3.2 *The Office of Management and Budget (MoD)*

the Defence Staff (see below).
(See biographies of: Chapple; Craig; Harding; Staveley.)

THE OFFICE OF MANAGEMENT AND BUDGET
Address:see Ministry of Defence

The establishment of the Office of Management and Budget (OMB), the central finance office of the MoD (see Figure 3.2), was one of the more radical innovations of the MINIS reorganization of the MoD. Under the previous system, service chiefs drew up their own budgets; the function of the OMB is to exercise greater central scrutiny of resource allocation and expenditure. The OMB is part of the Permanent Under-Secretary's Organization and is responsible directly to the PUS. Its work is directed by the Second Permanent Under-Secretary of State, Sir John Blelloch KCB. He sits on the Defence Council and on the Service Executive Committees and reports to the PUS. The OMB is organized into four areas:

– *Resources and Programmes*, which co-ordinates MoD long-term costing. This department vets proposals for the PUS. It is headed by K. C. Macdonald CB.

– *Finance*, which is responsible for the financial management, cost control, parliamentary accountability of the MoD defence programme. It is led by J. G. Ashcroft CB.

– *Personnel and Logistics*, led by R. L. L. Facer, which scrutinizes expenditure proposals on personnel and logistics areas (e.g., claims, defence lands).

– *Civilian Management*, which deals with training and conditions for civilian staff and industrial relations with the MoD. It is headed by R. M. Hastie-Smith CB.

The work of the OMB is formally overseen by the Financial and Planning Management Group (FPMG), one of the four senior committees in the MoD on which sit the eight most senior officials in the MoD: the Permanent Under-Secretary (who chairs it), the Chief of Defence Staff, the Chief of Naval Staff, the Chief of General Staff (Army), the Chief of Air Staff, the Chief of Defence Procurement, the Vice Chief of Defence Staff and the Second Permanent Under-Secretary, the head of the OMB. The head of the Programme and Budget Division in the Resources and Programmes sector of the OMB is secretary to the FPMG. The FPMG was created in 1977. Formally, it has the final say in the allocation of defence pounds among the various departments. Its recommendations are passed on to the Secretary of State for Defence. Some observers, however, are sceptical of the real influence which the FPMG has over budgetary decisionmaking.

Budgeting for Defence

Putting together an MoD budget – for nuclear weapons as well as for all non-nuclear equipment – is a long, complicated process, throughout which political criteria help determine how funds should be allocated.

As in all government departments, defence budgeting takes place within the framework of the Public Expenditure Survey (PES), a system which attempts to relate public spending to the size of the Gross Domestic Product and tries to plan it over the medium future.

The overall budgetary process is cyclical. Each year, the Treasury notifies the departments of its forecasts for the economy (of which it prepares a medium-term one, covering five years ahead, and a short-term one, for the next year only) and of its overall guidelines on the total of public expenditure. Ministries then cost their existing and continuing programmes, as well as any new commitments for which they have approval.

Within the MoD, the budgeting process begins when the OMB prepares a planning document (which does not become public) called the 'Long Term Costings' (LTC), which projects the total planned expenditure of the Ministry for the next ten years. This paper represents a compromise between the financial demands of the three services (the Second PUS sits on the Service Executive Committees where he is presented with these demands) and forms the basis of the Ministry's bid for resources. Once the LTC have been agreed within the

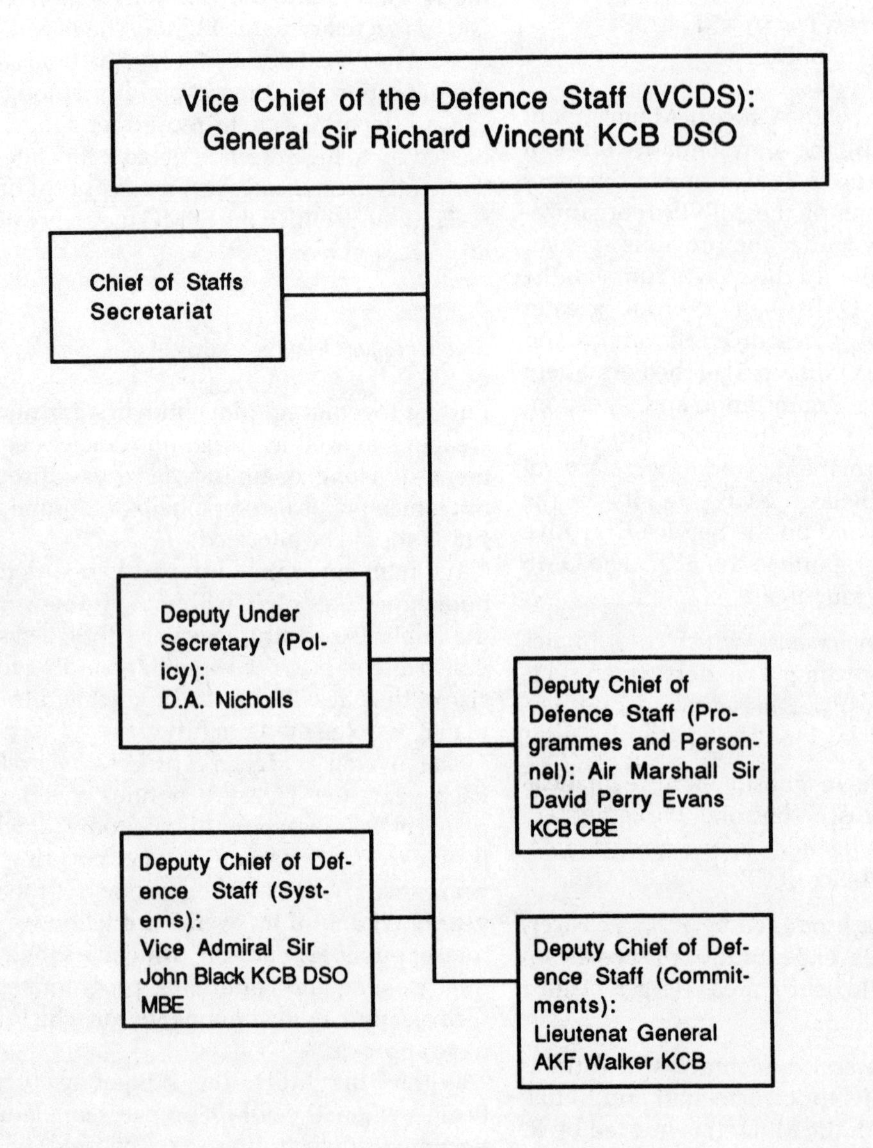

Figure 3.3 *Defence Staff (MoD)*

MoD, they are considered both by the Treasury and by an interdepartmental committee of finance officers called the Public Expenditure Committee (PESC), which draws its membership from the Treasury, the Bank of England, the Inland Revenue and the Customs and Excise and is chaired by the Permanent Secretary to the Treasury. The PESC reviews the spending plans of all the government ministries and looks for ways of reconciling them with the (always smaller) funds available. The PESC's report, the Public Expenditure Survey, provides the information for the review of planned expenditure by the 'Star Chamber' Cabinet Committee (see: Cabinet). The 'Star Chamber' further resolves conflicts between ministries' spending plans and the Treasury's limit for total public expenditure. The resolution is reached by political bargaining between ministers. Nuclear weapon expenditure is not systematically reviewed during this process.

The government then publishes its expenditure plans in the Annual Defence Estimates, which Parliament approves. Though the House of Commons debates the Estimates for a few days, it is unable to submit expenditure plans on nuclear-related projects to any rigorous examination as the Estimates contain no detailed information about them (see Parliament).

After Parliament has voted the funds, further formal approval is required from the Treasury before the MoD can spend those earmarked for nuclear weapons. In the Treasury, defence spending is dealt with by the Defence Policy Manpower and Materiel Group, known as DM (See Treasury). Ultimately, spending decisions about major weapon items will be taken by Cabinet sub-committee, such as the MISC 7 committee which approved the Trident programme (though, as we have noted, it would have been difficult for the Cabinet not to have approved the Trident).

(*See biographies of: Ashcroft; Blelloch; Facer; Hastie-Smith; Macdonald.*)

DEFENCE STAFF

Address: see Ministry of Defence

As we have noted, the 1984–85 MINIS reform of the MoD gave greater say in defence policymaking to the central Defence Staff compared with the individual service staffs. The Defence Staff (see Figure 3.3) is the MOD's internal think-tank or policy unit: in the words of the 1984 Defence White Paper, it has the 'duty of finding the best solution to the problems of the day, whether of an operational nature, [or to do with] strategic planning, defence policy or equipment priorities'. Service chiefs are subordinate to the Defence Staff. However, uniformed men seconded from services into central staffs will be influenced in the work they do and advice they give by the knowledge that their careers are in the respective service, not in Whitehall.

The Defence Staff's immediate chief of staff is the Vice Chief of Defence Staff; it is responsible to both the Chief of the Defence Staff and to the Permanent Under-Secretary. It is headed by the Vice Chief of the Defence Staff (VCDS), General Sir Richard Vincent KCB DSO, who has one of the most powerful posts in the MoD. The VCDS, who is of the same seniority as the service chiefs, is a member of the Chief of Staffs Committee and of the Defence Council. The Defence Staff is divided into four sections:

– *a systems* grouping, headed by Deputy Chief of Defence Staff (DCDS) Vice Admiral Sir Jeremy Black, which is responsible for the formulation of operational concepts, the determination of operational requirements for equipment, and for setting the aims of the military research programme;

– *a commitments* grouping, headed by DCDS Lieutenant General Sir Anthony Walker KCB, which formulates policy defence commitments, including joint and single-service plans for operational deployments and transition to war, and issues directives for operations and major exercises;

– *a programmes and personnel* grouping, headed by DCDS Air Marshal Sir David Parry Evans KCB CBE, which determines military priorities in the allocation of resources and provides central co-ordination of service personnel matters; and

– *a policy and programmes* grouping, headed by a

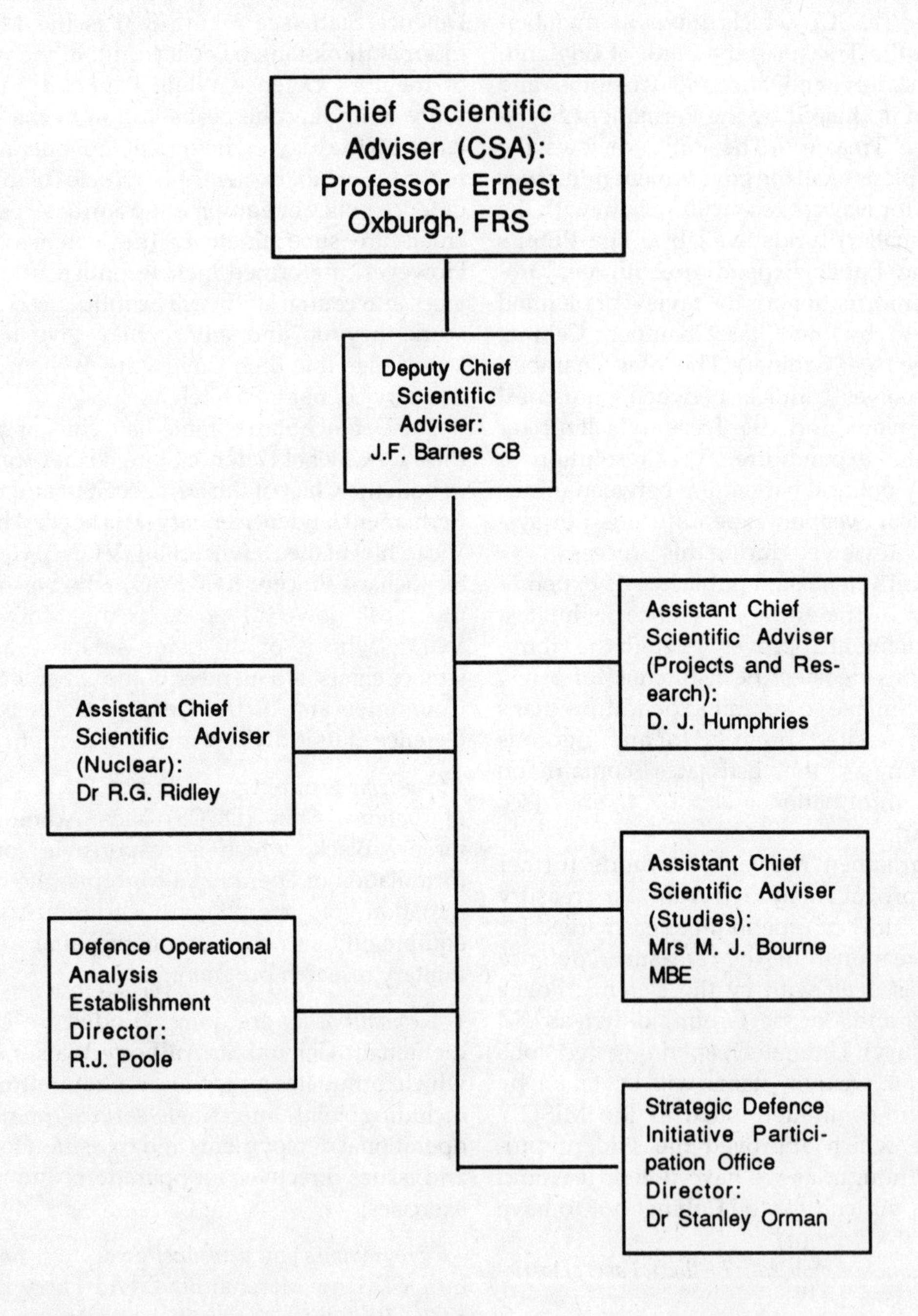

Figure 3.4 *Defence Scientific Staffs (MoD)*

Deputy Under-Secretary of Secretary (Policy and Programmes), D. A. Nicholls, which does long-term thinking about the strategic, policy and operational aspects of both conventional and nuclear deterrence. The Deputy Under-Secretary is the British representative on the NATO High Level Group, an important position, as the HLG formulates NATO's nuclear decisions, e. g., the 1979 'dual-track' decision to deploy cruise and Pershing II missiles and seek disarmament negotiations with the Soviet Union (see Chapter 6). A previous holder of the post was Michael Quinlan, now Permanent Under-Secretary at the MoD (see above). He was appointed in mid-1977 and carried out much of the preparation for the Trident decision. This is therefore a key post in nuclear weapons decisionmaking.

(*See biographies of: Black; Nicholls; Parry Evans; Vincent; Walker.*)

DEFENCE SCIENTIFIC STAFFS
Address: see Ministry of Defence

The Defence Scientific Staffs is led by the Chief Scientific Adviser (CSA), Professor Ernest Oxburgh (see Figure 3.4). Below him is the Deputy Chief Scientific Adviser (DCSA), J. F. Barnes. The CSA reports directly to the Permanent Under-Secretary. Before the 1984–85 MINIS reorganization of the MoD, each Service had a Chief Scientist advising on its particular weapons plans; this centralization of scientific advice thus represented a further loss of influence for the service chiefs. The function of the Scientific Staffs is to provide advice to the military on potentially useful research and technological programmes, in contrast to CERN (see below) which is responsible for actual research and production. The CSA chairs the Equipment Policy Committee (see Procurement Process), one of the four senior committees in the MoD. The Scientific Staff is divided into five sections:

– *Projects and Research*, led by ACSA D. E. Humphries, which provides advice on new projects and changes in R & D programmes, i.e., on the technical likelihood of the success or failure of a weapon;

– *Capabilities*, headed by ACSA Mrs M. J. Bourne OBE, which co-ordinates operational analysis, which is advice on whether a technologically feasible weapon is operationally required;

– *The Defence Operational Analysis Establishment (DOAE)* in West Byfleet, led by R. J. Poole. The DOAE does 'modelling', in which weapons 'mixes' are examined: this includes wargaming and and analysing the cost-effectiveness of various solutions to military problems;

– *Nuclear*, led by Dr R. G. Ridley, which advises on the implications of new technological developments for nuclear defence policy; and

– *the Strategic Defence Initiative (SDI) Participation Office (SDIPO)*, which helps British firms gain contracts in the US SDI programme. This is run by the its Director-General, Dr Stanley Orman. The SDI Participation Office was set up to help British firms gain contracts in the US SDI programme.

(*See biographies of: Barnes; Humphries; Orman; Oxburgh; Poole; Ridley.*)

PROCUREMENT EXECUTIVE
Address: see Ministry of Defence

The MoD's Procurement Executive (PE) is concerned with the 'research, development, production and purchase of weapons systems and equipment for the Armed Forces' (Civil Service Yearbook, 1988, 113) (see Figure 3.5). Its size (40,242 personnel, i.e., 20 per cent of the Ministry's civilian staff) belies its significance: it administers more than £8 billion per annum, that is, approximately 45 per cent of the UK's annual defence budget. The MoD is British industry's single largest customer.

The head of the Procurement Executive is the Chief of Defence Procurement, Peter Levene. To him report the Controller, Research and Development Establishments, Research and Nuclear Programmes (CERN), D. M. Spiers CB; the Systems Controllers of each of the three Service Controllerates (see below)); the Head of Defence Sales, in charge of overseas sales; and

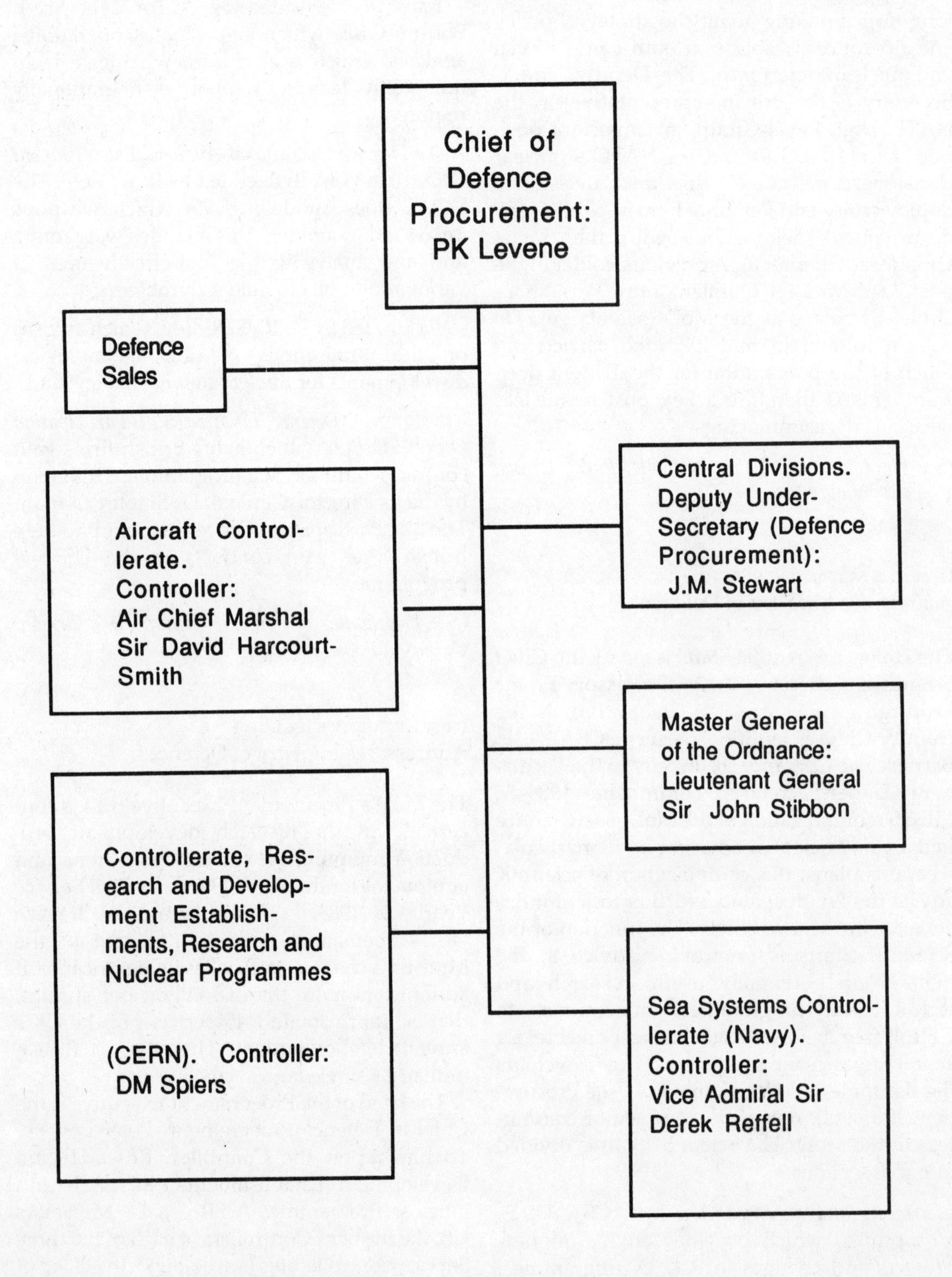

Figure 3.5 *Procurement Executive (MoD)*

the Deputy Under-Secretary of State (Defence Procurement).

The Procurement Process

The term 'procurement process' describes the military production cycle from the original proposal for a weapon or other piece of military equipment through its approval, research, development to production itself. Many different departments and institutions have a say in the procurement process: the Defence Staff, the Office of Management and Budget, Research and Development Establishments (see below), the individual services, and the relevant defence manufacturers. The largest projects are considered by the Equipment Policy Committee (EPC). On the EPC sit the Chief Scientific Adviser (its chairperson), the Deputy Chief Scientific Adviser, the Vice Chief of Defence Staff, the Deputy Under-Secretary (Defence Procurement), the Deputy Under-Secretary Resources and Programmes (from the Office of Management and Budget),two Deputy Chiefs of Defence Staff, responsible for Programmes and Personnel and Systems respectively, the three Systems Controllers, CERN and the Head of Defence Sales. In addition, the Treasury, the Foreign Office, the Department of Trade and Industry and the 10 Downing Street Policy Unit have a right to send representatives to the committee.

Formally, the process begins with *concept formulation*, in which operational staffs in the Defence Staff and the services, with assistance from industry and research establishments in the MoD (see below), outline broadly the need for and purpose of a new weapon or other piece of equipment. If a concept is approved by the Chief of Defence Staff, operational staffs develop it into a *Staff Target*, with advice taken from industry where necessary. This is presented to the Procurement Executive, which initiates a *feasibility study*. Such a study is usually carried out by a defence contractor, or by several in competition. If the project proves feasible, the Staff Target is expressed as a more detailed *Staff Requirement*. The next stage is *Project Definition*, in which costs, performance and potential technical problems are examined again in depth, final characteristics are agreed, and plans for full development and an outline plan for production are drawn up. The length of this stage depends on the size and technical complexity of the project. Like the feasibility study stage, project definition will normally be conducted competively by firms. The penultimate stage is *full development*, which includes performance and safety trials. The final stage is *production*. The formal description of the procurement process, places emphasis on the origins of the process in the perceived need by the military for a piece of equipment. However, technological innovation, in an R & D Establishment or in a defence firm, will, in fact, often be the principal stimulus for a new weapon. Lord Zuckerman, former Chief Scientific Adviser in the MoD and to the government, has written, 'Except in the short term, so called "operational requirements" are always formulated around technological promises'. New combat concepts are themselves often shaped by technological developments. (See also Defence Contractors.)

All equipment proposals with estimated R & D costs of over £25 million and production costs over £50 million (like the Tornado programme: 385 aircraft at a cost of £19 million each) are submitted to the EPC, which advises the Minister on which weapons items to include in the procurement programme.

Before Michael Heseltine became Secretary of State for Defence in 1983, defence manufacturers enjoyed a — for them — very beneficial relationship with the MoD, resulting from the 'cost-plus' contract system. According to this system, the MoD paid the firm extra costs incurred both in R & D and production and in deadline overrun. In other words, there was no incentive for a firm to finish a project as cheaply as possible and on time. The VC10 tanker is an example: in 1974 the MoD decided it needed the tankers to refuel fighter planes in the air. Originally, British Aerospace (BAe) estimated the conversion would cost £40 million spread over the 1978, 1979 and 1980 budgets. Only in 1978, however, did BAe complete its feasibility study to convert nine VC10 airliners into a flight refuelling tankers. By 1981, the estimate had increased to £100 million for delivery in 1983.

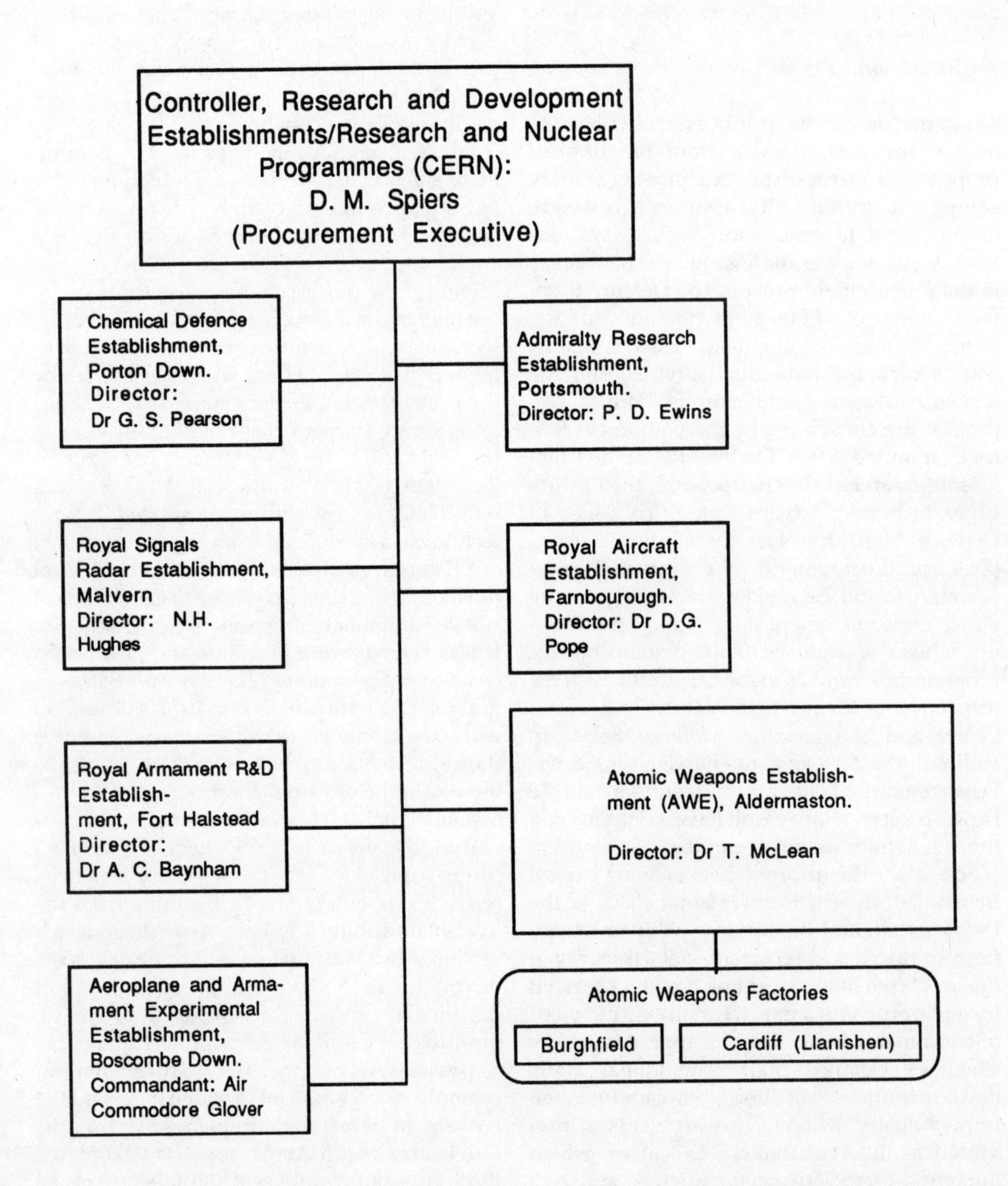

Figure 3.6 *Controllerate, Research and Development Establishments, Research and Nuclear Programmes (CERN) (MoD)*

Heseltine brought in a new Chief of Defence Procurement, Peter Levene (see below), in order to stop such obvious wastage in the defence budget.

Cost overruns by defence contractors were – and are – part of a larger problem, which we have already noted, namely of the steadily increasing cost of defence equipment. The MoD has been trying to solve this problem in two ways: first, by adopting a more commercial attitude to procurement, which includes awarding contracts competitively where possible, by moving away from the cost-plus contract system, and by generally placing responsibility and risk for the contract with the contractor; second, by collaborating more with allies in defence production. Britain was involved in thirty-seven collaborative projects in 1988, including the Tornado fighter-bomber. (*See biographies of: Harcourt-Smith; Levene; Reffell; Spiers; Stibbon.*)

Controllerate of Research and Development Establishments/ Research and Nuclear

There are seven research and development centres in the Research and Development Controllerate, headed by the Controller, D. M. Spiers (see Figure 3.6): the Admiralty Research Establishment at Portsmouth; the Atomic Weapons Establishment at Aldermaston; the Royal Aircraft Establishment at Farnborough; the Royal Signals and Radar Establishment at Malvern; the Aeroplane and Armament Experimental Establishment at Boscombe Down; the Royal Armament Research and Development Establishment at Fort Halstead; and the Chemical Defence Establishment at Porton Down. Of these seven, only one, the Atomic Weapons Establishment (AWE), has its *raison d'étre* work on nuclear weaponry. The Admiralty, Aircraft and Signals establishments do work which is of importance for Britain's nuclear weapons programmes and brief descriptions of their tasks are found below. It is arguable, however, that, because most of their work is in the conventional sector (with the exception of the AWE), none of the R & D establishments have a strong vested interest in the maintenance of a British nuclear 'deterrent'.

The Admiralty Research Establishment (ARE)
Address: Portsdown, Cosham, Hants, PO6 4AA

ARE was formed on 1 September 1984 by combining the Admiralty Surface Weapons Establishment, the Admiralty Underwater Weapons Establishment and the Admiralty Marine Technology Establishment. Its current director is P. D. Ewins.

ARE's responsibility is to conduct R & D into all aspects of military marine technology. This includes work on reducing noise in ships and submarines and on the design of ship and submarine hull forms; research into radar, electronic warfare, communications, weapon control, command and control, and navigation sytems; and research into acoustic propagation through the ocean.
(*See biography of: Ewins.*)

Atomic Weapons Establishment
Address: Aldermaston, Reading, Berkshire RG7 4PR

The research, development and production of a nuclear warhead begins at the Atomic Weapons Establishment (AWE) at Aldermaston in Berkshire. Its director is Dr Thomas McLean.

Aldermaston is the site of all major nuclear warhead research and development work in Britain. According to evidence given to the House of Commons Defence Committee (HCDC), it's functions are:

– to develop nuclear warheads for future UK strategic and theatre weapons;

– to manufacture fissile components for UK nuclear warheads; and

– to provide support in certain areas for the UK defence non-nuclear programme.

The only two other sites involved in nuclear warhead production are the Royal Ordnance Factory (ROF) at Llanishen, Cardiff, where radioactive materials are machined, and the ROF at Burghfield, near Aldermaston, where nuclear weapons are finally assembled.

Out of Aldermaston have come the original Polaris and the Chevaline 'front-ends' for the Polaris missile and the WE-177 nuclear free-fall bomb/depth-charge. Aldermaston scientists are currently working on the Trident submarine missile warhead and have begun research on a nuclear warhead for a new 'stand-off' weapon for aircraft to replace free-fall bombs. The stand-off missile will be produced in collaboration with other NATO allies.

Aldermaston regularly pre-empts the political and even the central bureaucratic decisions about nuclear weapons production. The rhythm of technological development requires the AWE scientists to push for and even to begin work on new warheads in order to keep their jobs at the research centre irrespective of outside political developments. The early research on Trident, begun when the Chevaline research programme was over, was one factor which determinined the political decision to proceed with the system. This decision in turn created a need for a new large production complex at Aldermaston (the A90: see below). The need to use the capacity of the complex will in turn give Aldermaston directors extra leverage when they argue in future for new nuclear warhead work.

Aldermaston is under the control of the MoD. The Director reports directly to the Chief of Defence Procurement (CDP) on matters of production programmes and to the Controller of Research and Development (R&D) Establishments, Research and Nuclear (CERN) for all R&D programmes. Aldermaston' s staff currently numbers 5,000 and it has an annual budget of about £120 million.

Aldermaston is divided into five major departments, each sub-divided into separate divisions and each supported by its own engineering, technical, supply and health and safety services:

– the *Warhead Development Department*, which is the cornerstone of Aldermaston. The demands of its team dictate the sort of work carried out in the other departments. It is divided into four sections: the Mechanical Engineering Services Division which maintains close technical and programme links with the AWE workshops and with the ROF factories and is also responsible for nuclear testing, carried out in the USA; the *Weapons Electronics Division*, responsible for R & D of both nuclear and conventional weapons electronics, for monitoring the effects of nuclear radiation on electronic components; the *Assembly Division*, which includes in its work the study of conventional explosive triggers and mathematical theoretical analysis of explosions; the *Special Projects Division*, which provides systems and project management on suitable research and development programmes and carries feasibility studies on future weapons systems.

– the *Mathematical Physics Department*, which studies and calculates, with the aid of computers, structural changes in materials and warhead mechanisms during explosions. As the temperature and pressures of nuclear explosions far exceed what can be created in a laboratory most information about their nature can only be derived from theory. AWE is the only British establishment with expertise in this field.

– the *Applied Physics Department*, which develops the specialized optical-mechanical electronics equipment needed to monitor nuclear explosions and evaluates lasers as weapons.

– the *Materials Department*. This has four divisions: *Chemistry*, *Chemical Technology*, *Explosives* and *Metallurgy*. The Explosives division researches high explosives for the MoD generally, while the Metallurgy division deals with plutonium, uranium and beryllium.

– the *Engineering Services Department*, which designs and constructs new plants and buildings, carries out maintenance work,and so on.

AWE also has a *test department* at Foulness which is licensed to fire the heaviest charges permissible in Britain.

Currently the A90 complex is being built at an estimated cost of £230 million to replace AWE's A-1 building. Modelled on the Los Alamos Scientific Laboratory in the USA, the A90 will have four large bays with laboratories able to handle weapon-grade plutonium. Two of the bays will be used to manufacture Trident warheads. In the third, research into a new generation of nuclear warheads is being carried out, while in the last plutonium is recovered from obsolete bombs.

Royal Ordnance Factories at Burghfield and Llanishen, Cardiff

ROF Cardiff sits in the middle of a housing estate in Caerphilly Road, Llanishen. Its function is to shape and assemble depleted uranium (U235) and beryllium into the precisely-shaped components needed for nuclear weapons 'triggers' and 'reflectors' used to maximize the efficiency of the explosive device. This also entails the recycling of old nuclear weapons and of radioactive materials. ROF Burghfield, a few miles from Aldermaston, is where British nuclear warheads and bombs are finally assembled. Day-to-day management of both factories rests with the Director, Atomic Weapons Factories.
(*See biography of: McLean.*)

Royal Aircraft Establishment (RAE)
Address: Farnborough, Hants, GU14 6TD

Described by the MoD as the largest R & D establishment in Europe, RAE, whose current director is Dr G. G. Pope, carries out and coordinates research into all aspects of aerospace activities, with the exception of radar. These include: aerodynamics, communications, computation, electrical engineering, materials, mechanical engineering, optics and space. Most of the scientific staff are engaged in gas turbine technology research.

RAE is in overall charge of research done in industry and the universities under contract to the MoD's Procurement Executive. It has close links with industry (e.g., with British Aerospace) and with the universities of Reading, Surrey and Sussex. RAE participates in the development programmes of multinational projects, such as the Tornado fighter-bomber, as well as in collaborative research, and acts as the technical agency in the exchange of information agreed to by governments.

The main section at RAE responsible for nuclear-related developments is the Special Weapons Departments. This department had overall control of the work done at RAE on Chevaline, the new front-end for the Polaris SLBM developed in the 1970s, in conjunction with the then prime contractor, Hunting Engineering.
(*See biography of: Pope*)

Royal Signals and Radar Establishment (RSRE)
Address: South Site, St Andrew's Road, Malvern, Worcs, WR14 3PS

RSRE, whose current director is N. H. Hughes, is the MoD's principal electronic warfare research and development establishment. The work at RSRE has far-reaching implications: electronics, especially advanced computer technology, is currently transforming military strategy and operations. The Navy's Type-23 frigate, for example, has up to 200 microcomputers on board to control its weapon and sensor systems, amounting to half the total cost of the ship's production.

RSRE has two main departments:

– the *Applied Physics Department*, which is divided into the Physics Group, the Optics and Guided Weapons Group and the Electronic Devices Group. These three groups cover a range of research programmes, including the up-dating of radar; electronic counter-measures; laser research; development of new materials for electronic application; infra-red research for night vision application; and guided weapon research.

– the *Systems Department*, which is divided into the Airborne Radar Group, the Computing and Ground Radar Group and the Communications Group. The work of these three groups includes radar; guided weapon research; evaluation of weapons systems; defence communications systems, including satellites; and computing and software.

(*See biography of: Hughes.*)

Systems Controllerates

The three service controllerates in the Procurement Executive — the Sea Systems Controllerate, the Land Systems Controllerate and the Aircraft Controllerate — deal with the purchase of all equipment for the services. Each is headed by a Controller: Vice Admiral Sir Derek Reffell KCB (Sea Systems); Lieutenant General Sir John Stibbon KCB OBE (Army); Air Chief Marshal Sir David Harcourt-Smith KCB DFC (Aircraft). Services can use any controllerate:

so, if the Navy needs aircraft it turns to the Aircraft Controllerate. The Strategic Systems Executive, which handles the procurement of submarine-based nuclear weapons systems, is in the Sea Systems Controllerate.
(*See biographies of: Harcourt-Smith; Reffell; Stibbon.*)

The Treasury
Address: Parliament Street, London SW1P 3AG
Tel: 01-270-3000

The Treasury has a total staff of 3,800, of whom about 1,400 work in the central Treasury. The Prime Minister is the First Lord of the Treasury. Its effective head, however, is the Chancellor of the Exchequer (Nigel Lawson MP), helped by the Chief Secretary (John Major MP), and a varying number of junior ministers. The senior officials at the Treasury are the Permanent Secretary (Sir Peter Middleton), the two Second Permanent Secretaries and the Chief Economic Adviser.

The Treasury negotiates with the MoD, as it does with other departments, a total annual budget for defence. Within this total, the MoD may allocate funds as it sees fit, though projects with development costs of over £12.5 million and production costs of over £25 million must be submitted to the Treasury for approval. The Defence Policy and Materiel Group (DM) is responsible for this work. It is under the supervision of two Assistant Secretaries and one Under-Secretary (S. A. Robson), who report directly to the Second Permanent Under-Secretary (J. Anson). With a staff of only twenty-four, however, the DM is ill-equipped to counter the arguments of the well-staffed departments in the MoD.
(*See biographies of: Anson; Lawson; Major; Middleton; Robson.*)

Foreign and Commonwealth Office
Address: Downing Street, London SW1A 2AL
Tel: 01-270-3000

In 1981 the then Foreign Secretary, Lord Carrington, stated that 'Arms Control is part of our national security policy. Our arms control endeavours and our defence effort are two different but complementary ways of achieving the same end: peace with freedom to pursue our legitimate national interests around the world'. This claim for complementarity does not, however, mean that Britain's arms control and defence policies are formulated with reference to each other. Rather, while arms control policy is cleared with the Ministry of Defence, the MoD does not clear its defence policy with the Foreign Office (FCO) for its arms control implications.

The FCO does not have a direct influence on decisionmaking about nuclear weapons production, nor on the formulation of nuclear weapons strategy. Foreign Secretary Sir Geoffrey Howe and Permanent Under-Secretary Sir Patrick Wright have greater say in these matters by virtue of their membership of the Cabinet and the Permanent Secretaries Committee on Intelligence and Security (PSIS, see Defence Intelligence), respectively. In addition, the Foreign Office contributes to the maintenance of the close relationship between the United Kingdom and the USA. Foreign Office officials are responsible for negotiating details of UK-US co-operation on nuclear weapons projects; for example, a Foreign Office team (under Robert Wade-Geary) was in charge of negotiating the Trident Sales Agreement of 10–14 July 1980.
(*See biographies of: Howe; Wright.*)

Defence intelligence

Defence intelligence is information about the military activities of actual or potential opponents. It includes information about research, development, production and deployment of weaponry; about budget allocations; troop manoeuvres; and about developments in tactics and strategy. No nation's military effort is based solely on the information received about the opponent; nevertheless military intelligence is crucal in sustaining in the effort.

'Intelligence' is properly known as 'evaluated information' — i.e., raw data which has been analysed. Only after it has been analysed does it acquire value. The process of intelligence acquisition and application has two stages: first, the data is gathered ('collected') by a variety of means, including satellite, radio frequency monitoring and espionage; then it is 'evaluated' and fed into the policymaking process. Information currently gathered includes defence, political and economic intelligence. In Britain, collection and analysis of most information are carried out by separate institutions.

The bulk of — though not necessarily the most useful — intelligence is gathered today from 'open' sources, namely foreign press and broadcast reports, scientific and technical publications, and day-to-day observation by overseas diplomats and defence attachés. Most 'secret' intelligence — that supposedly gathered without the enemy's knowledge — is acquired electronically by signals intelligence (SIGINT). Perhaps only 10 per cent of intelligence is now gathered by the traditional methods of human espionage.

The basic source for military intelligence in the West, especially for data on the WTO, is the US intelligence community, which has unparallelled access to a wide range of information collection systems, such as satellites, electronic spying and so on (see below). It would be wrong to assume that at some stage in the process there exists data in a pure, 'hard', form; all information must be analysed to be understood, and will therefore be interpreted according to the analyst's assumptions and world views. As one commentator has written: 'Even the most honest and rigorous analyst cannot totally exclude the effects of normative assumptions and ideological preferences from any stage of the process' (Smith, 1980, p.68).

THE INTERNATIONAL INTELLIGENCE NETWORK

Several British intelligence and security institutions are part of a vast global intelligence-gathering and exchange network, which comprises the USA, the UK, Canada, the remaining NATO countries, Japan, South Korea, the People's Republic of China, Taiwan, the ASEAN countries, Papua New Guinea, Israel and South Africa (for comprehensive information about the global intelligence network see Richelson & Ball,1985; for UK–USA links, see Campbell, 1984).

The closest links in this network are between the first five countries, the so-called UKUSA nations, after the treaty of the same name signed in 1947. There are hundreds of agreements which cover the exchange of intelligence information among the UKUSA countries. The Treaty itself (which has not been published: it is described by one commentator as 'quite likely the most secret agreement ever entered into by the English-speaking world') covers one of the most significant areas, namely signals intelligence or SIGINT. Signals intelligence encompasses a wide range of technical (non-human) intelligence. Its two main types are: *communications intelligence* (COMINT), which is technical and intelligence information (diplomatic, commercial, political, and military) gathered from the interception of foreign communications (telephone, radio-telephone, radio or satellite); and *electronic intelligence* (ELINT) which is information gathered from electromagnetic radiations, such as the emanations of radars. ELINT allows, for example, air fields, ships at sea and anti-ballistic missile (ABM) systems to be located. SIGINT information is collected by satellites, from aircraft and from land-based systems. Between them, the five UKUSA nations have divided up the world into areas of primary SIGINT collection responsibility; the five SIGINT agencies are: the US National Security Agency (NSA); Britain's Government Communications Headquarters (GCHQ, see below); the Canadian Communications Security Establishment (CSE); Australia's Defence Signals Directorate (DSD) and, in New Zealand, the Government Communications Security Bureau (GCSB). An historian of the NSA has described how the American SIGINT agency had the ability to pick up and transcribe the radio-telephone conversations of top Soviet officials driving to the Kremlin in their limousines (*Sunday Times*, 31 October 1982).

Ocean surveillance is another major area of secret intelligence-gathering and exchange among the UKUSA nations. This surveillance is carried out by underwater sonar systems, land-based systems, satellites, aircraft and submarines. A third area is the USA-UK division of the world for the purposes of monitoring foreign radio broadcasts. Other spheres of co-operation include 'human intelligence' collection (i.e., spying), covert action and counter-intelligence.

Co-operation and exchange on SIGINT among the five UKUSA nations is supposed to be essentially unqualified. However, a formal hierarchy exists within the network: the USA and the UK are currently designated as First Parties, the other nations as Second Parties. The SIGINT agencies of the other NATO countries, Japan and South Korea are 'Third Parties' and the provisions of the Agreement are apparently 'much less generous' with respect to them. Presumably the countries which are not Parties are on even less generous terms with the Treaty signatory nations. In fact, the USA dominates the SIGINT network, and for a number of reasons: it has a far greater signals intelligence collection capability than the other member countries and as a result collects more and better intelligence; it subsidizes to a great extent UK and Australian SIGINT activities; and, as the most powerful military nation in the Western world, it will probably have a significant influence in determining intelligence collection priorities. The US security and intelligence agencies account for perhaps 90 per cent of the total budgets and personnel of all the UKUSA countries, while the British agencies account for about 8 per cent and the Australian, Canadian and New Zealand agencies *together* account for about 2 per cent. A former officer of the US National Security Agency, has said: '[all] information comes to the US, but the US does not totally reciprocate in passing all the information to the other powers'. Such a dominance in intelligence collection and distribution would be likely also to obtain in ocean surveillance.

There are a wide range of channels through which the intelligence gathered by the UKUSA nations is circulated around the network. The principal such channel is the liaison officer stationed at embassies and high commissions of co-operating countries and the Special Liaison Office at the headquarters of co-operating agencies. The liaison officers are responsible for, *inter alia*, the physical exchange of intelligence information and material.

In addition to the network of liaison officers there are several joint communications stations and channels, from which the users communicate with their headquarters and many of the most important intelligence collection stations are also jointly staffed and operated — for instance, in Britain, the joint US–UK satellite Control Facility at Oakhanger and the SIGINT satellite ground station at Menwith Hill, North Yorkshire.

Examples of the close co-operation between UKUSA agencies include the presence of a Special US Liaison Office (SUSLO) and SUSLO communications centre beside the US Naval headquarters in Grosvenor Square and a large SUSLO detachment of US National Security Agency and US Navy staff at the UK Government Communications Headquarters (GCHQ) in Cheltenham, UK (see below); GCHQ officials work at the National Security Agency headquarters at Fort Meade, Maryland.

The UKUSA intelligence and security community, described as 'one of the largest bureacracies in the world', keeps over 250,000 people in full-time employment worldwide, and has a total budget of US$16–18 billion.

BRITISH INTELLIGENCE AND SECURITY AGENCIES

Five agencies form the bulk of the British security and intelligence community: the Government Communications Headquarters (GCHQ); the Defence Intelligence Staff (DIS) in the Ministry of Defence; the Secret Intelligence Service (MI6); the Security Service (MI5); and the Special Branch of the Metropolitan Police (Scotland Yard, London) (see Figure 3.7). The first four are part of the global intelligence network and the first three (GCHQ; DIS; MI-6) are the primary institutional conduits through which military intelligence is fed into the British defence policymaking processes. These are described below. The formal head of the British intelligence services is the Prime Minister, assisted by various Cabinet and Ministerial Committees. MI6 and GCHQ are formally under the administration of the Foreign Office, MI5 under that of the Home Office, and the Defence Intelligence Staff under that of the

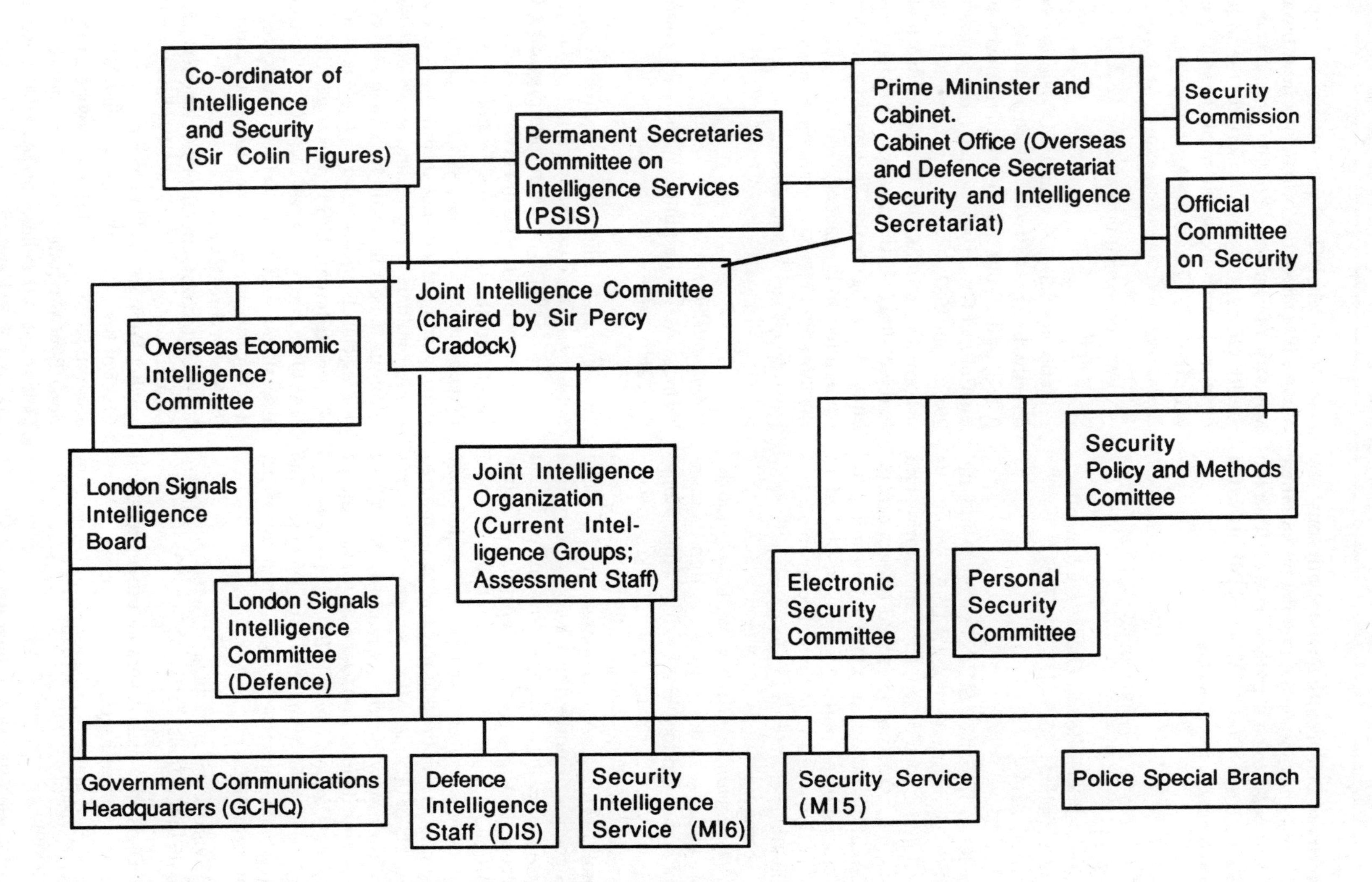

Figure 3.7 *Management Structure of British Intelligence and Security.*

Ministry of Defence. All operate with considerable autonomy, however, and the bulk of their work appears to be kept hidden even from the most ministers. Only GCHQ and DIS are listed in Civil Service Yearbooks.

Government Communications Headquarters (GCHQ)
Address: Priors Road, Oakley, Cheltenham, Gloucesteshire GL5 5 AJ
Tel: 0242-221491

GCHQ is the UK's SIGINT agency and the British signatory to the UKUSA Treaty. Its mission has been described as monitoring and decoding 'all radio, telex and telegram communications in and out of Britain, including the messages of all foreign embassies based in Britain, finance and industrial companies, and individuals of interest to the state agencies' — i.e. communications intelligence (COMINT) (*New Statesman*, 29 October 1982). It also carries out similar activities abroad through its intercept stations in locations such as Hong Kong, Cyprus, West Germany, Malta, Turkey, Ascension Island, Diego Garcia in the Indian Ocean (jointly with NSA). The area of the globe assigned to it under the UKUSA Treaty (see above) is Eastern Europe, the Soviet Union west of the Ural Mountains, Africa and China.

GCHQ and its associated units are believed to receive some £300 million a year for their operations, four times as much as the combined budgets of MI5 and MI6. Its current director is Sir Peter Marychurch. Its world-wide staff of 10,000 are divided into four directorates, one of which, *Directorate of SIGINT Operations and Requirements*, is central to GCHQ's work. This directorate contains GCHQ's main divisions. These include:

–J Division, one of the biggest, which intercepts Soviet Bloc signals;

–K Division which covers all other areas and commercial messages;

– H Division, which actually does the code-breaking;

– Z Division, through which detailed UKUSA and other SIGINT requirements are determined. It receives target requests from the UK Ministry of Defence, Foreign and Commonwealth Office, the military services, as well as from trade and economic ministries. It liaises with the US, Canadian, Australian and New Zealand SIGINT agencies; and

– X Division which operates the GCHQ Computer system.

It appears that J, K, H and Z Divisions report directly to the Current Information Groups (CIGs) of the Joint Intelligence Organization in the Cabinet Office (see below) (*New Statesman*, 29 October 1982).

Formally, the GCHQ is responsible to the Foreign Office. In practice, it is an independent body reporting to the Permanent Secretaries Committee on Intelligence Services (PSIS) and the Joint Intelligence Committee (see below). (*See biography of: Marychurch.*)

Defence Intelligence Service
Address: Main Building, Whitehall, London SW1 2HB

The Defence Intelligence Service (DIS) is in the Ministry of Defence. Its staff numbers between 800 and 1,200. Its tasks include providing the Ministry of Defence planners with regularly updated 'threat assessments', mainly of Warsaw Pact countries. For this, a wide range of remote sensing and surveillance technologies is used, though military attachés and other personnel continue to be important. In addition to collaborating closely with several US agencies and the US armed forces, DIS co-operates with other NATO countries and with NATO's own threat assessment staff in Brussels. DIS has a reputation for providing 'worst case' assessments of the Soviet threat.

The Director-General of Intelligence (DGI), Lieutenant General Sir Derek Boorman, reports to the Permanent Under-Secretary and the Chief of the Defence Staff (see Figure 3.8). He also reports to the Joint Intelligence Organization. Beneath him is the Assistant Chief of Defence Staff (Intelligence) (ACDS (I)), Air Vice Marshall R. J. Kemball.

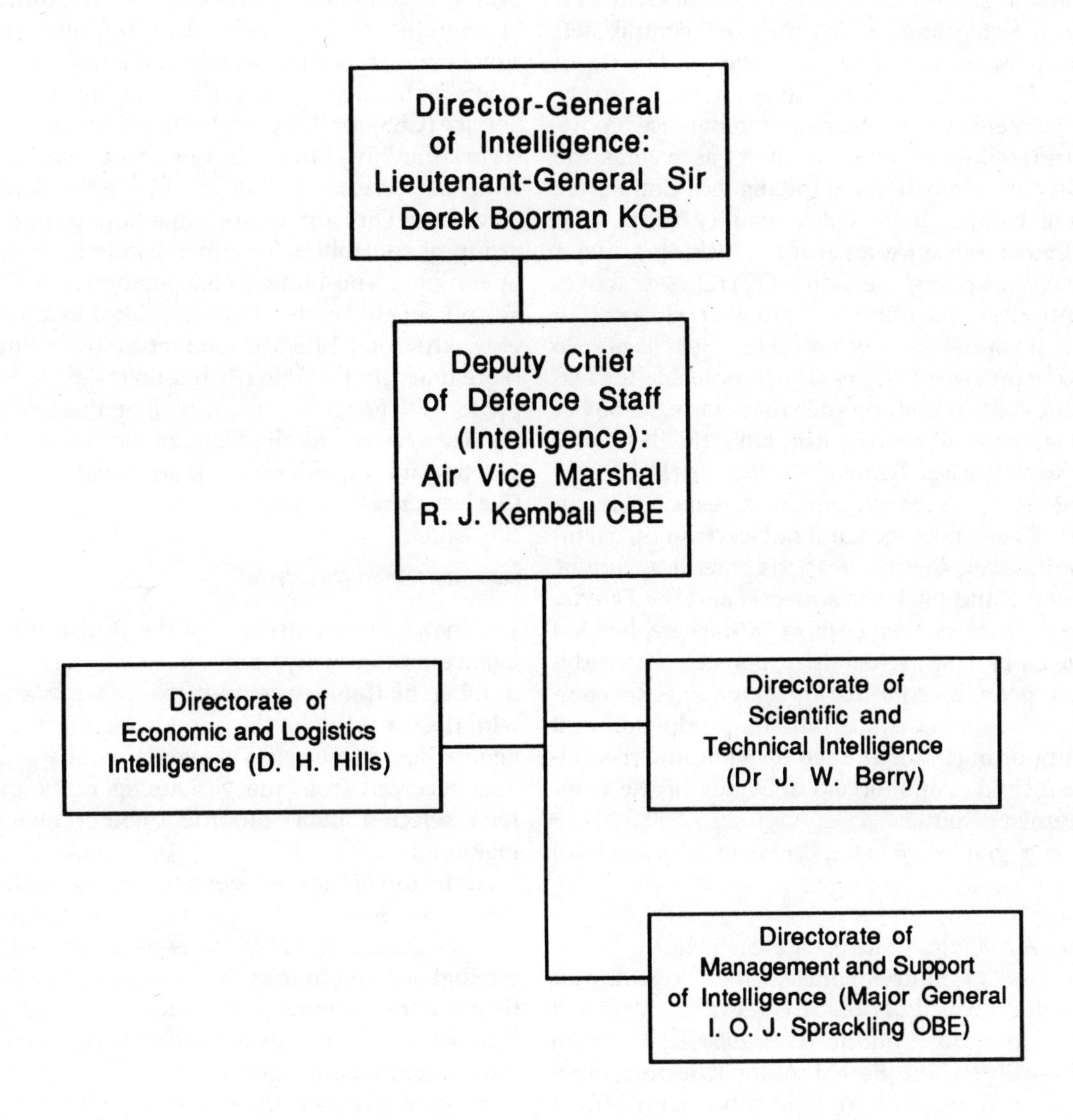

Figure 3.8 *Defence Intelligence Staff (DIS) (MoD)*

The DIS is subdivided into three directorates: the *Directorate of Management and Support of Intelligence (DMSI)*, headed by Major General I. O. J. Sprackling, which provides central staff support for the DGI and the ACDS (I) in handling intelligence business (except current intelligence). It co-ordinates intelligence reporting required by DIS customers as well as the DIS input into the Joint Intelligence Committee (see below). It provides military support to other intelligence agencies – including major 'eavesdropping' posts for GCHQ (see above) and the MI6 training school at Gosport in Hampshire (see below)(*New Statesman*, 26 November 1982). It is also responsible for DIS long-term studies on such matters as US-Soviet relations and strategic arms talks; the *Directorate of Scientific and Technical Intelligence (DSTI)*, led by Dr J. W. Berry, which is responsible for producing intelligence about electronics, chemical and biological weapons, missiles, atomic energy and the basic sciences; and the *Directorate of Economic and Logistics Intelligence*, headed by D. H. Hills, which is responsible for studying general economic developments in communist countries; armaments production and supporting industries world-wide; and the military and economic aid activities of the communist countries.
(*See biographies of: Berry; Boorman; Hills; Kemball.*)

The Secret Intelligence Service /SIS (MI6).
Address: Century House, 100 Westminster Bridge Road, London SE1; (also: 60, Vauxhall Bridge Road, London SE1; 296–302 Borough High Street, SE1; Fort Monkton, Gosport (sabotage and demolition); joint office with MI5 at 140 Gower St, London W1).

SIS is one of the three agencies (the others are MI5 and the Special Branch) in which intelligence is collected not primarily by machines but by humans. Despite its title ('MI' stands for military intelligence) the collection of defence intelligence is only one of its tasks: it also recruits foreigners living in the United Kingdom for espionage work when they return to their native countries; and, abroad, its wide range of activities include counter-intelligence operations (i.e., penetrating the opponent's organization) and covert action (e.g., assisting in the attempted subversion or overthrow 'unfriendly' governments). It is the only UK agency which both collects and analyses data.

SIS is headed by the Chief of the Secret Service (CSS), or 'C', Christopher Curwen. The second-ranking official in SIS is the Director, who supervises its day-to-day operations. Under the Director are four directorates and a group of controllers for supervision of foreign operations. The budget and personnel of SIS are not made public. One unofficial estimate gives the total MI6/MI5 budget at somewhat more than £100 million (Richelson & Ball, 1985, pp.15–16). Formally, the Chief of the Secret Service reports to the Foreign Secretary. In practice, it is an independent organization.
(*See biography of: Curwen.*)

MANAGEMENT STRUCTURE

The management strucure of the British intelligence and security community consists of a number of Cabinet committees and posts — with the exception of the London Signals Intelligence Board (see below) — which evaluate the data received from the various agencies and feed selected data into the Cabinet policy-making process.

At the top of the management structure is the *Permanent Secretaries' Committee on Intelligence Services (PSIS)*. The PSIS supervises the British intelligence community as a whole, and particularly the budgets of the intelligence organizations, and approves interdepartmentally recommended intelligence priorities.

It receives reports from the Joint Intelligence Committee (JIC), the Overseas Economic Intelligence Committee (OEIC), the London Signals Intelligence Board (LSIB, see below) – and possibly also the Official Committee on Security. From the PSIS go intelligence assessments to goverment ministers. The PSIS is chaired by the Secretary of the Cabinet, Sir Robin Butler, and its other members are the Permanent Secretaries of the Foreign and Commonwealth Office (Sir Patrick Wright), Defence (Sir Michael Quinlan), Treasury (Sir Peter Middleton), Trade and Industry, Home Office and the Chief of the Defence Staff (Air Chief Marshall Sir David Craig). The Coordinator of Intelligence and Security (see below) is an ex-officio member of the PSIS.

The Joint Intelligence Committee is part of the Cabinet Office. The JIC and its subordinate elements in the *Joint Intelligence Organization (JIO)* are responsible for the production of British 'national' intelligence on foreign and defence affairs, combining information from each service, allied intelligence and open sources. Their analyses are presented every week in the 'Red Book' to the Cabinet, individual ministers and the Chiefs of Staff. The JIO is made up of an *Assessment Staff* and *Current Intelligence Groups (CIGs)*. The Assessment Staff's work has been described as 'preparing both short- and long-term assessments in support of government policy', in preparation of which 'it utilizes the output of various agencies both within and outside the intelligence community'; the geographically-based CIGs maintain day-to-day world-wide coverage of current intelligence The JIC is chaired by a Foreign and Commonwealth Office Under-Secretary, Sir Percy Cradock GCMG, who is seconded to the Cabinet Office and listed in the 1988 *Civil Service Year Book* as 'Foreign Affairs Adviser' in the Prime Minister's Office. Membership of the JIC consists of two Foreign Office representatives, the Chief of MI6, the Director-General of Intelligence, the Director-General of the Security Service, the Assistant Chief of the Defence Staff (Intelligence), the Director of GCHQ and the Chairman and Deputy Chairman of the Assessments Staff. One observer has described the JIC as 'operating almost like a fifth intelligence agency' (i.e., in addition to GCHQ, DIS, MI5 and MI6). It has representatives abroad in Washington, Ottawa and Canberra, in addition to the other services' 'ambassadors'. Liaison representatives from the other UKUSA nations, USA, Canada, Australia and New Zealand, attend JIC meetings.

The Overseas Economic Intelligence Board concentrates on economic and non-military scientific and technical intelligence. Its membership consists of representatives of GCHQ, DIS, MI6, MI5, the Department of Trade and the Treasury. *The London Signal Intelligence Board* (LSIB) monitors the work of GCHQ. It is headed by the Chief of the Secret Service and attended by the Directors of the Intelligence of each of the services as well as by the Director of the Government Codes and Cipher School (GCCS). Apparently, a sub-committee of the LSIB, the London Signals Intelligence Committee (Defence), deals with military signals intelligence matters.
(See biographies of: Butler; Cradock; Craig; Middleton; Quinlan; Wright.)

The Coordinator of Intelligence and Security

The Coordinator of Intelligence and Security, who is appointed on the basis of long experience in intelligence, is an adviser who provides top-level guidance on intelligence priorities and resources. This is a Cabinet Office post (concealed in *Who's Who* under the title 'Deputy Secretary, Cabinet Office'). Previous Coordinators have been former heads of MI5 and MI6 and a former head of GCHQ. The current Coordinator, Sir Colin Figures, is a former MI6 Chief. The Coordinator's basic tasks have been described as preparing 'an annual review of intelligence for the PSIS [which] looks at intelligence in the previous twelve months and suggests the broad lines of future requirements and priorities and proposes any necessary action'; scrutinizing 'the annual financial estimates and five-year forecasts of the individual intelligence agencies [and presenting] them to the PSIS with his recommendations'; conducting 'enquiries on various intelligence subjects which he, the Secretary of the Cabinet or the PSIS may deem necessary'; and generally advising and encouraging the intelligence community, particularly the machinery within the Cabinet Office (see above). The Joint Intelligence Secretariat (see below) provide staff suport for the Coordinator. The Coordinator, the Chair of the Joint Intelligence Committee and the Chairperson of the OEIC (see below) have been described as making up an intelligence 'triumvirate'.
(See biographies of: Figures.)

DEFENCE CONTRACTORS

Like some other advanced industrial states,

Britain has a 'military-industrial complex'. This is not, however — as this term is sometimes used to suggest — a shadowy conspiracy between arms corporations, which determine weapons procurement, strategy and military spending, and key individuals in the bureaucracy. Rather, the British defence industry, the military and the bureaucracy share a requirement for continuing and regular weapons production; this requirement is based on two shared fundamental political-strategic assumptions: first, that, for reasons of national security, Britain should be self-sufficient in arms production and, second, that advanced technology is also a security requirement; and the results of this are that there is a structural pairing of the armed forces and arms industries and that major weapons suppliers become influential in determining what weaponry is produced and in setting the overall level of military expenditure (Smith, D. & Smith, R., 1983, pp. 74–5). As we have noted, approximately 43 per cent of the defence budget in 1988–89 will be spent on defence equipment (see Procurement Executive). In 1986–87, 110 UK-based contractors were paid £5 million or more by the MoD. For some of them, exports are an essential source of revenue. A summary of the companies with the largest MoD contracts (i.e., who received over £100 million in 1986–87) follows. It should be noted that many items listed below will be used in dual-capable systems, such as communication systems.

British Aerospace (BAe) plc
Address: 11 Strand, London, WC2N 5JT
Tel: 01-930-0120

British Aerospace is the largest contractor to the MoD. The military projects in which they are prime contractors include the Sea Harrier FSR Mark 1 for the Royal Navy, currently being replaced by an updated Sea Harrier Mark 2; joint development and production, with the US firm McDonnell Douglas, of the Harrier VSTOL (Vertical Stationary Take-Off and Landing); the Tornado MRCA (Multi-Role Capable Aircraft) fighter-bomber, built with partners in Italy and West Germany; the European Fighter Aircraft, which will be built over the next ten years in collaboration with Messerschmitt-Bölkow-Blohm (MBB) of West Germany, Aeritalia in Italy and CASA of Spain; and the Skynet military communications satellite. BAe's turnover in 1987 was £4,075 million, of which £3,322 million was in military aircraft and support services, weapons and electronic systems and in space and communications. Exports (which includes some work done on collaborative projects) made up almost 70 per cent of the total.
(*See biographies of: Lygo; Smith.*)

Ferranti plc
Address: Bridge House, Park Road, Gatley, Cheadle, Cheshire, SK8 4HZ

Ferranti are specialists in military electronics. Electronic systems are an essential part of the modern battlefield on land and at sea; they provide command and control, communications, detection, intelligence-gathering, data-processing, navigation and other facilities without which fighters, tanks and ships would be inert bits of metal. Ferranti's current military contracts include work on weapon effectiveness studies; work on sonars; Action Information and Fire Control Systems for the Trident nuclear submarines; Foxhunter radar, nose radar, map displays and video cameras for the Tornado MRCA; and the 2050 sonar for Royal Navy frigates. Ferranti's turnover in 1986-7 was £628.7 million.
(*See biographies of: Alun-Jones; de Ferranti.*)

General Electric Company (GEC) plc
Address: 1 Stanhope Gate, London, W1A 1EH
Tel: 01-493-8484

GEC is the leading British electronics group. Military contracts in the electronic systems and component fields for which GEC and GEC subsidiaries are the prime contractors include the FLIR night vision system for the Tornado and Harrier II fighters; Seafox high-frequency communications equipment for submarines; the Sky Shadow ECM for the Tornado; Zeus

electronic warfare equipment for the Harrier II GR5; the Foxhunter airborne radar system; the FACE accurate targeting command and control system; and the Type 1022 naval radar. GEC subsidiary Easams Ltd has been awarded three contracts in the US Strategic Defence Initiative programme. GEC's turnover in 1987 was £5,939 million of which £2,016 million was in electronic systems and components.
(See biographies of: Hilsum; Prior; Weinstock.)

Hunting Associated Industries plc
Address: Reddings Wood, Ampthill, Bedford, Bedfordshire, MK45 2HD
Tel: 0525-406202

Hunting is a major engineering firm. Its contracts include work on the Trident warhead.
(See biography of: Hunting.)

The Plessey Co. plc
Address: Vicarage Lane, Ilford, Essex, IG1 4AQ
Tel: 01-478-3040

Plessey is a major manufacturer of electronic equipment. Its prime contracts include extra low frequency communications systems; the Ptarmigan digital communications system; the Type 2016 Fleet Escort sonar; Type 2054 sonar for the Trident nuclear submarine; the Clansman battlefield communications system; and the Wavell data processing system. Plessey's turnover in 1987 was £1,429.7 million.
(See biographies of: Clark; Tovey.)

Racal Electronics plc
Address: Western Road, Bracknell, Berkshire, RG12 1RG
Tel: 0344-481222

Racal's contracts include production of the type 72 doppler radar for the Tornado MRCA; 6-90 series communications control systems and fire control systems and airborne dopler radar for the Sea Harrier FRS Mark 1; command and control unit for the Type 22 frigate; and navigation equipment for the Sea King helicopter.
(See biography of: Harrison.)

Rolls Royce Ltd
Address: 65 Buckingham Gate, London, SW1E 6AT
Tel: 01-222-9020

Rolls Royce is a major manufacturer of aero engines. Its military contracts include work on engines for the planned European Fighter Aircraft; on the Pegasus engine for the jets Harrier I and Harrier II; on the engine for the Tornado MRCA; and on engines for the Type 22 frigates. Its subsidiary, Rolls Royce Associates, set up in 1959 to build nuclear Pressurized Water Reactors (PWRs) for submarines, is working in a consortium which includes Babcock, Foster Wheeler and Vickers Shipbuilding and Engineering Ltd (see below) on the PWR Mark 2 for the Trident nuclear submarine. Rolls Royce's turnover in 1987 was £2,059 million, of which £592 million was on military aero engine work.
(See biographies of: Robins; Tombs.)

Thorn-EMI plc
Address: Thorn-EMI House, Upper St Martin's Lane, London WC2H 9ED
Tel: 01-836-2444

Thorn-EMI is a major producer of military electronics. Its contracts include the Searchwater airborne radar for Nimrod aircraft and Sea King helicopters; the type 2054 sonar for the Trident SSBN; radar simulators for the RAF; and data distribution systems for the Type 23 frigate. Thorn-EMI's turnover in 1987 was £3,185 million.
(See biography of: Wilkins.)

Vickers Shipbuilding and Engineering Ltd
Address: Barrow-In-Furness LA14 1AF
Tel: 0229-23366

Vickers S & E's contracts include construction work on the submarines, missile tubes and, in the Rolls Royce consortium (see above), on the PWRII of the Trident nuclear submarines and on the Type 22 frigate.

Westland plc
Address: Westland Works, Yeovil, Somerset

BA20 2YB
Tel: 0935-75222

Westland plc is Britian's major helicopter manufacturer. Its military contracts include work on the Gazelle helicopter (with Aérospatiale of France), the EH-101 anti-submarine helicopter; the Harrier I and Harrier II fighters; the Sea Harrier FRS Mark II; and the Tornado MRCA. Westland's turnover in 1987 was £387.6 million. (*See biography of: Cuckney.*)

UK–US RELATIONS

By comparison with relations between other pairs of sovereign states, the relationship between the United States and the United Kingdom has been intimate and informal enough to warrant the epithet 'special'.

While sentimental attachments, cultural affinities, historical traditions, similar institutions and a common language have all helped to cement this 'special relationship', it is the awareness of the mutuality of interests between the two nations and in particular of the contribution each can make to the other's security which is its main *raison détre*. A wide spectrum of political and economic issues help to constitute this 'partnership'; at its core, however, is the defence relationship between the two countries (See Baylis, 1984; Campbell, 1984).

From the British point of view, the most important aspect of the defence relationship has been and is the collaboration in the production of nuclear weapons systems. This wide-ranging collaboration dates from the signing of the July 1958 'Agreement for Cooperation on Uses of Atomic Energy for Mutual Defence Purposes' and its May 1959 amendment. The Agreement specified three major areas of co-operation: a general exchange of information, equipment and materials; exchange of specific information on the development of delivery systems for atomic weapons and the weapons themselves; and the transfer to Britain of a submarine reactor and limited quantities of nuclear fuel. The Agreement has resulted in the supply by the USA to the UK of missiles for Britain's submarine-based nuclear forces, help with the construction of the submarines, and with the re-entry vehicles and warheads in the missiles, help with the construction of other nuclear weapons, and assistance with related intelligence and with navigation and communication. The Skybolt ballistic missile, which was to be bought complete from the USA after the cancellation of the Blue Streak missile programme in 1960 was the first missile system the USA agreed to supply to the UK. The second was the Polaris missile system, currently operational, bought from the USA in 1963 after the cancellation of Skybolt; Britain has 102 Polaris A3 missiles which were bought 'off-the-shelf' from the USA under the Polaris Sales Agreement. Polaris was followed by the Trident missile system, which is being supplied to Britain on a similar basis to that on which Polaris missiles were supplied under the Polaris Sales Agreement. Trident is intended to replace Polaris in the mid-1990s. The four nuclear submarines, the re-entry systems and nuclear warheads for the missiles of both the Polaris and the Trident systems are largely designed and built in Britain. However, the USA has provided significant help in these areas as well: in addition to the assistance on nuclear propulsion reactors given under the 1958 Agreement, it has given the UK certain essential materials for the construction of submarines (e.g., zirconium, hafnium, highly enriched uranium: the last in exchange for British plutonium from civil and military reactors) and even, apparently, the high-stress steel for the submarine hulls. In addition,the submarines depend on the use of US trial facilities at Cape Canaveral, Florida, and the Eastern US Test Range, California. It is widely assumed that the re-entry vehicles are tested in American test flight facilities, as Britain has none.

In the case of warheads, not only has all British nuclear warhead testing since 1958 been done at the USA's underground test site in Nevada, but Britain has also received vital materials for use in warhead production, such as highly enriched uranium, polonium and, in the past tritium (the fuel for a thermonuclear — hydrogen — bomb). Duncan Campbell has claimed that, since 1957, all the nuclear warheads assigned to British forces have been either designed and manufactured in the US (battlefield and intermediate-range weapons), manufactured in the UK (probably) after a US design, (including various free-fall bombs and the first Polaris missile warhead), or designed and manufactured in Britain but dependent on US design information (the Polaris missile's second — Chevaline — warhead and the Trident missile warhead) (Campbell,1984, pp. 101–6). He also comments that though the 1958 Agreement did prohibit the exchange of actual 'atomic weapons', it nevertheless did allow the USA to supply Britain with a 'virtual do-it-yourself kit for bombs' (Campbell, 1984, p.101). The Mutual Defence Agreement has been updated regularly since 1958, the last time in 1984 for ten years.

Britain has no satellite surveillance capability of its own. In as much as intelligence information about Soviet targets and strategic defences is derived from satellite surveillance, it seems likely that Britain relies for this on the USA. Whether Britain could obtain similiar information from other sources (e.g., SIS, DIS), or whether such information is vital, is difficult to estimate (see Defence Intelligence). Britain may also rely on the USA in the areas of submarine navigation and communication. The UK has bought SINS navigation equipment from the USA and some reports suggest that the submarines also use US navigation satellites and submarine beacons to check their position, provided by the SINS system. Whether the UK has or can produce similar navigation equipment and is able to confirm submarine positions from other sources is not known. Britain also relies heavily on the USA for help with targeting its nuclear weapons. (For UK-US co-operation on intelligence, see Defence Intelligence.)

BRITAIN AND NATO

British defence policy is organized almost entirely within the framework of the Atlantic Alliance. Over 90 per cent of Britain's annual military budget is devoted to British commitments in NATO.

The three British services operate nuclear forces: the Royal Air Force, free-fall bombs ; the Navy, free-fall bombs, depth-charges and the Polaris submarine weapons system, the largest component of Britain's nuclear arsenal; the Army, tactical (battlefield) nuclear weapons. Under the terms of the 1962 Nassau agreement, these are all assigned to NATO use, 'except where Her Majesty's Government may decide that supreme national interests are at stake'. Despite the commitment to NATO, however, the decisions to procure and deploy the Polaris and Trident weapons systems were not the subject of NATO discussion.

Like most other NATO members Britain participates in all NATO fora (see Chapter 6).

PARLIAMENT

Formally, Parliament is the supreme legislative authority in Britain. As we have noted, however, the bulk of legislation is initiated in Cabinet: Parliament is little more than a rubber stamp for government policies. It has overseeing, investigative and legislative functions, but these are strictly circumscribed by the constitutional and political context of British politics: the party which wins the the majority of seats in the House of Commons at a general election normally forms the government; once in the Commons, members of the government party are under great pressure to support the government. This division along political party lines means that the Commons cannot function properly as a legislature able and willing to control the executive.

Members of Parliament have no role in the decisionmaking process about nuclear weapons production. Nevertheless, it is worth looking briefly at the limited work in this area which MPs can perform, namely that of monitoring various aspects of government defence policy, as it represents one of very few channels through which the electorate can find out about this policy. There are three fora in which MPs can carry out their monitoring role: in the chamber of the House of Commons; in the Defence Select Committee; and in the Public Accounts Committee.

In the chamber of the House, Opposition parties can open up nuclear weapons issues for discussion by calling a special debate. Divisions over defence issues within the main Opposition party, the Labour party, has meant it has been reluctant to do this: since the resulting vote would be won by the government, the debate would simply be an opportunity for the government to expose the inconsistencies in the Labour Party's defence policy. MPs also have the opportunity, once a year, to debate government policy when the Defence Estimates are published. The value of the Estimates is limited by the fact that they do not contain detailed breakdowns of the cost of each stage (research, development, testing and production) of each weapons system, as do, say, those received by the legislators of the US Congress. Thus detailed parliamentary scrutiny, let alone control, of government defence spending is not possible.

The Defence Committee is one of fourteen Select Committees established in 1979 to monitor the work of fourteen government ministries. It is made up of eleven backbench MPs, chosen in proportion to the distribution of seats in the House, and a small full-time staff, supplemented by specialist advisers. Like the other Select Committees, the Defence Committee has no legislative function; it is only able to advise the ministry on a course of action. Though it may send for 'persons, papers and records', it has no statutory right to summon ministers. Ministers may also withhold information from the committee in the 'national interest' and may rule that civil servants should not appear before it, as happened when former MI5 chief Sir Anthony Duff was forbidden to appear before the Defence Committee by Margaret Thatcher. What the Defence Committee can do is to elicit, and make available to both Parliament and the general public, *some* information which would otherwise have remained concealed. Thus, it has published lengthy and reasonably detailed reports on, for example, the Trident programme, other procurement projects, the Defence Estimates, and so on (though it should be noted that a substantial proportion of the committee's hearings take place in camera and are not published). By comparison with what is made publicly available in the USA through Congress, the British public gets a raw deal from its supreme representative body. Finally, though the Defence Committee's remit is to 'examine the administration, policy and expenditure' of the MoD, and may recommend changes in these areas, it has no power to enforce them.

By comparison with the Select Committees, the Public Accounts Committee has considerable powers. Established in 1862, it is staffed by fifteen backbenchers and has its own 600-strong staff of auditors — headed by the Comptroller and Auditor General — which examines the accounts of each government department to ensure they tally with the funds allocated by Parliament. The PAC has a tradition of scrutinizing government spending carefully for efficiency and economy; many of its reports have embarrassed government, and senior civil servants prepare meticulouly for its hearings. The PAC's power, however, is limited to examining expenditure after it has been allocated; its remit is not to influence the extent and distribution of expenditure before its allocation.

BIOGRAPHIES

Alun-Jones, Sir (John) Derek, Managing Director and Chief Executive, Ferranti plc

Alun-Jones was born in 1933 and educated at Lancing College and St Edmund Hall, Oxford, where he took an honours degree in jurisprudence.

His commercial career began with Philips Electrical in 1957. In 1960 he joined Expandite, becoming its managing director in 1966 at the young age of 33. He moved to Burmah Industrial Products as managing director in 1971, and then to Ferranti in 1975. He has a number of other directorships, including of Royal Insurance, the Society of British Aerospace Contractors, Reed International and GKN. He was knighted in 1987.

Alun-Jones married in 1960 and has two sons and three daughters. He likes shooting and fishing.
(*See: Defence Contractors.*)

Anson, John, CB, Second Permanent Secretary (Public Expenditure), Her Majesty's Treasury
Tel: 01-270-5643

Anson oversees the work of the Treasury's Defence Policy, Manpower and Materiel Group. Born in 1930, and educated at Winchester and Cambridge, Anson worked first in the Treasury from 1954–to 1968. From 1968–1971 he was financial counsellor at the British Embassy in Paris and from 1971–1974 Assistant Secretary and then Under-Secretaryin the Cabinet Office. He returned to the Treasury in 1974, where he served as Under-Secretaryuntil 1977. Between 1980 and 1983 he was Economic Minister at the British Embassy in Washington DC and the UK Executive Director with the International Monetary Fund and the World Bank.
(*See: Her Majesty's Treasury.*)

Ashcroft, James Geoffrey, Deputy Under-Secretary of State, Finance, Office of Mangement and Budget, Ministry of Defence
Tel: (Personal Assistant) 01-218-6188

Born in 1928, Ashcroft was educated at Cowley School, St Helens, and Cambridge. He worked in the Ministry of Supply from 195 to 1959 and in the Ministry of Aviation from 1959 1961. From 1961 to 1964 he was in the Ministry of Defence and again from 1965 to 1968 and 1970 to 1973. He took two years off, from 1968 to 1970, to work at the International Institute for Strategic Studies in London. From 1973 to 1974 he was an Under-Secretary with the Pay Board; from 1974 to 1976 an Assistant Under-Secretary of State in the Management Services in the MoD's Procurement Executive; and from 1976 to 1984 Assistant Under-Secretary of State, General Finance, in the MoD. He assumed his current post in January 1985. He has published papers on international collaboration in military logistics.
(*See: Office of Management and Budget (MoD).*)

Barnes, James Frederick CB, Deputy Chief Scientific Adviser, Ministry of Defence
Tel: (Private Secretary – A.J. Radcliffe) 01-218 2468

Jim Barnes was born on the 8 March 1932 in Calverley, Yorkshire. He was educated at Almondbury Grammar School, Huddersfield, Taunton's School, Southampton, and at Queen's College, Oxford, from which he graduated with a first class honours degree in engineering sciences in 1953. In 1953 he joined the Bristol Aeroplane Company where he worked on ramjet performance analysis. In 1955 he joined the civil service and worked first as a scientific officer in the performance and projects department at the National Gas Turbine Establishment at Pyestock. He was gradually promoted until he became senior principal scientific officer on individual merit for his research work on the mechanical behaviour of turbine blades.

In 1970 he was appointed assistant director, Engine R & D, at the Ministry of Aviation Supply; in 1972, on promotion to the rank of deputy chief scientific officer, he was seconded to HM Diplomatic Service in Washington as Counsellor (Science and Technology), at an important time in UK–US relations on strategic nuclear weapons. On his return from Washington, he was promoted to Under-Secretary at the MoD and appointed Director General Establishment Resources Programme C; this post put him in charge of all the air-associated research in the Procurement Executive, including that related to weaponry. After that he moved to the post of Deputy Director (Weapons) at RAE Farnborough. In 1979, a year later, he was promoted to Deputy Secretary and became Deputy Chief Scientific Adviser (Projects) in the Department of Defence Science, in which post he advised the Chief Scientific Adviser on defence projects. He was Deputy Controller, Establishments and Research, from 1984 to 1986, in which position his responsibilities extended over all MoD research, including at AWRE Aldermaston.

In November 1986 Barnes was appointed to his present post of Deputy CSA and head of the newly formed MoD Scientific Group.

He is a member of the Council on Christian Approaches to Defence and Disarmament, a lay member of two synods, and a church warden at All Saints, Farringdon. In 1965 he was awarded a James Clayton Fund Prize by the Institute of Mechanical Engineers. He is a Fellow of the Royal Aeronautical Society and of the Institution of Mechanical Engineers. He has contributed to several books and learned journals on mechanical engineering, in particular gas turbine technology, heat transfer and stress analysis.

Barnes was awarded the CB in the Birthday Honours 1982. He lists his recreations in Who's Who as 'making things'. He has been married since 1957 to Dorothy Jean Drew, and they have one son and two daughters.

(*See: Defence Scientific Staffs (MoD).*)

Beetham, Marshall of the Royal Air Force Sir Michael, GCB, CBE, Chairman, General Electric Company (GEC) plc Avionics Ltd

Born in 1923 into a military family, Sir Michael was educated at St Marylebone Grammar School and joined the RAF as a trainee pilot in 1941. He served in the 50, 57 and 35 squadrons, Bomber Command, during the war, and subsequently moved through various commands at home and abroad, as well as Air Ministry posts, until in 1968 he became Director of Operations (RAF) at the MoD for two years. From 1970 to 1972 Sir Michael was commandant of RAF Staff College, and from 1972 to 1975 Assistant Chief of Staff (Plans and Policy) at Supreme Headquarters Allied Powers Europe (SHAPE). He was then appointed Commander-in-Chief, Strike Command, for one year, and in 1976–77 was Commander-in-Chief RAF Germany and Commander of the 2nd Tactical Allied Force. He became Chief of Air Staff in 1977, a post which he retained for five years. In the same period he was also Air aide-de-camp to the Queen.

In October 1982 Sir Michael retired as Chief of Air Staff, and in 1984 joined the board of GEC-Marconi Avionics. He became its chairman in 1986. He is also on the board of Brixton Estate plc, and has been chairman of the trustees of the RAF Museum since 1983.

He is married with a son and a daughter, and his hobbies are golf and tennis.

(*See: Defence Contractors.*)

Berry, Dr James William, Director of Scientific and Technical Intelligence, Ministry of Defence
Tel: 01-218 0528

Born in 1931, Dr Berry studied at Manchester University (BSc) and Leeds University (PhD) before joining in 1956 the Royal Signals and Radar Establishment (RSRE) at Malvern. In 1960 he went to the Admiralty Surface Weapons Establishment, Portsdown, where he became head of the computer division in 1972. From 1976 to 1979 he was director of Long Range Surveillance and Command and Control Projects, and, 1979–82, director general of Strategic Electronic Systems at the MoD.

Dr Berry is married with three daughters and lists his hobbies as music, walking and bird-watching.

(*See: Defence Intelligence Service (Defence Intelligence).*)

Black, Vice-Admiral, Sir (John) Jeremy, KCB, DSO, MBE, Deputy Chief of Defence Staff (Systems), Ministry of Defence
Tel: (Personal Assistant) 01-218-2531

Born in 1932, Sir Jeremy entered the Royal Naval College at Dartmouth in 1946. He served in the Korean war and the Malayan Emergency in the early 1950s. He qualified in gunnery in 1958 and in 1960 took command of his first ship, *HMS Fiskerton*, followed by commands on *HMS Decoy* in 1969 and *HMS Fife* in 1977. After a spell in 1979 at the Royal College of Defence Studies he went on to become Director of Naval Operational Requirements, Naval Staff, from 1980 to 1981. During the Falklands/Malvinas war he took command of *HMS Invincible*; he became Flag Officer, First Flotilla, from 1983 to 1984. He returned to the MoD as Assistant Chief Naval Staff (Policy) in 1984 and assumed his present post in 1986.

Sir Jeremy is married with two sons and one daughter and lists his hobbies as sailing and history.
(*See: Defence Staff (MoD).*)

Blelloch, John Niall Henderson, Second Permanent Under-Secretary, (Head of Office of Management and Budget), Ministry of Defence
Tel: (Personal Assistant) 01-218-6014

Blelloch was born in 1930, educated at Fettes College and Caius College, Cambridge, and in 1958 married Pamela Blair. He entered the War Office as assistant principal in 1954, was private secretary to successive parliamentary undersecretaries between 1956 and 1958 and became principal in 1958. He was in the MoD from 1964 to 1980 becoming Assistant Secretary in 1968, Assistant Under-Secretary (Air) in the Procurement Executive in 1976 and Assistant Under-Secretary in the Defence Staff in 1979. From 1980 to 1982 he was Deputy Secretary in the Northern Ireland Office. In 1982 he returned to the MoD where he was, until 1984, Deputy Under-Secretary of State (Policy and Programmes). He took up his current post in 1984. He lists his interests as 'golf, squash, skiing, learning the piano'. He is a member of the Roehampton club and of the Mid-Surrey Golf clubs.
(*See: Office of Management and Budget (MoD).*)

Boorman, Lieutenant General Sir Derek, KCB, Chief of Defence Intelligence, Ministry of Defence
Tel: (Secretary) 01-218-6427

Born in 1930, Sir Derek went to Sandhurst and was commissioned into the Staffordshire Regiment in 1950. After a spell at Staff College in 1968 and more Army service he went in 1977 to the Royal College of Defence Studies. From 1978 to 1979 he was director of public relations for the Army.

Between 1980 and 1982 Sir Derek was director of military operations and from 1982 to 1985 Commander of British Forces Hong Kong and major general of the Brigade of Gurkhas.

He is married with two daughters and one son and lists his hobbies as shooting, gardening and music.
(*See: British Intelligence Services (Defence Intelligence).*)

Butler, Sir Robin, Secretary to the Cabinet

Robin Butler was born in 1938. He was a pupil at Harrow and a student at University College, Oxford. He came top in the Civil Service exam in 1961 and joined the Treasury in the same year. 'His subsequent career has been a mixture of the nitty-gritty of the Treasury and in the centre of government in Whitehall' (*Financial Times*, 9 July 1987). In 1964–65 he was private secretary to the Financial Secretary to the Treasury; 1965–69, secretary to the budget committee and seconded to the Bank of England ; in 1971–72 he was seconded to the Cabinet Office's 'Think Tank', the Central Policy Review Staff. He was private secretary to Prime Ministers Edward Heath (1972–74) and Harold Wilson (1974–75). In 1975 he took up the post of Assistant Secretary in charge of the general expenditure intelligence division at the Treasury and from 1977–80 he was Under-Secretary of the department's general expenditure policy group. From 1982 to 1985 he was Margaret Thatcher's principal private secretary. In 1985 he was appointed Second Permanent Secretary (Public Expenditure) in the Treasury.

The Times has said of Butler that 'throughout his career as a Civil Servant he has always been regarded as one of the Chosen Few who could one be day be selected for the highest post of all, Secretary of the Cabinet.' (*The Times*, 9 July 1987.) Butler has, unusually, earned the approval of politicians from left and right: 'respected and liked' by Prime Ministers Heath, Wilson and Margaret Thatcher and 'described as outstanding in the books of Labour advisers such as Joe Haines, as well as in the private comments of current ministers. Friends of Mr Butler do not regard him as an ideologue or Thatcherite, but rather as a classic example of the Civil Service sense of duty. His appointment 'contradicts the misleading view that Margaret Thatcher only appoints sympathizers to top Whitehall posts' (*Financial Times*, 9 July 1987).

In 1962 Butler maried Gillian Lois Galley. They have three children.
(*See: Cabinet Office; Secretary to the Cabinet.*)

Chapple, General Sir John (Lyon), KCB CBE, Chief of the General Staff, Ministry of Defence
Tel: (Aide-de-Camp) 01-218-7873; (Military Assistant) 01-218-7114

General Sir John Chapple took up the post of Chief of the General Staff in September 1988. Sir John was born in 1931. He began his military career as a National Serviceman in 1949, leaving after two years to read Modern Languages and History at Cambridge. In 1954 he joined the 2nd King Edward VII's Own Gurkha Rifles (The Sirmoor Rifles) and served with them in Malaya, Borneo and Hong Kong. From 1970 to 1972 he commanded the battalion in Singapore and Hong Kong. From 1972 to 1973 he had a Staff College appointment, after which he returned to Cambridge as a Services' Fellow. From 1974 to 1976 he worked at the MoD and in 1976 took command of 48 Gurkha Infantry Brigade. From 1978 to 1979 he was principal staff officer to the Chief of Defence Staff; from 1980 to 1982 Commander, British Forces Hong Kong, and Major-General, Brigade of Gurkhas; and from 1982 to 1984 director of military operations with membership of the Defence Reorganization planning team (MINIS). In 1984 he became Deputy Chief of the Defence Staff (Programmes and Personnel) with responsibility for, among other things, pay and conditions for all three services. In 1987 he was appointed Commander in Chief of United Kingdom Land Forces. His rise has been unusual in that he has spent very little time with the British Army on the Rhine (BAOR) in West Germany.

SIr John is a Life Fellow of the Zoological Society, the Linean Society and the Royal Geographical Society. He is on the Council of the National Army Museum and is chairman of the Society for Army Historical Research. He is also active in various organizations connected with wildlife and conservation, including the World Wildlife Fund.

He and his wife Annabel have one son and three daughters.
(*See: Chief of the Defence Staff (MoD).*)

Clark, Sir John (Allen), Chairman and Chief Executive, the Plessey Company plc

Born in 1926, Clark was educated at Harrow and Cambridge, and saw military service in the World War II. He received his early industrial training with Metropolitan Vickers and Ford Motor Co.; he has been with Plessey since 1949. He was director and general manager of Plessey Ireland in 1950, and, at the age of 27, appointed to the main board of the Plessey Company in 1953. Four years later he was made general manager of the Plessey Components Group, and in 1962 managing director of the main company. The steady rise continued, with his appointment as deputy chairman in 1967, and chairman in 1970. Clark is also a director of the Banque Nationale de Paris, a member of the Engineering Industries Council and a former member of the National Defence Industries Council. He was knighted in 1971, and awarded the Portuguese Order of Henry the Navigator in 1973.

Clark has one son and one daughter by his first marriage, and a daughter and two sons by

his second marriage. In his spare time he enjoys horse riding and shooting.
(*See: Defence Contractors*)

Cradock, Sir Percy GCMG, Adviser to the Prime Minister on Foreign Affairs; Chair, Joint Intelligence Committee

Born in 1923, Sir Percy received his degree from Cambridge University. He joined the Foreign and Commonwealth Office (FCO) in 1954. From 1954 to 1957 he served in Britain; from 1957 to 1962, he was First Secretary in Kuala Lumpur, Hong Kong and Peking successively. After three years back in the Foreign Office, he returned to Peking in 1966, serving counsellor and head of chancery (1966–68) and chargé d'affaires (1968–69). He was head of planning staff at the FCO from 1969 to 1971 and Under-Secretary in the Cabinet Office from 1971 to 1975. He was ambassador to the German Democratic Republic from 1976 to 1978; the leader of the UK delegation to the Comprehensive Test Ban discussions at Geneva from 1977 to 1978; and ambassador to the People's Republic of China from 1978 to 1983. In 1984, as a Deputy Under-Secretary to the Foreign Office, he supervised negotiations on Hong Kong. He took up his current post, which he holds on secondment from the FCO, in 1984.
(*See: Management Structure (Defence Intelligence).*)

Craig, Sir David (Brownrigg), Air Chief Marshal, GCB, OBE; Chief of Defence Staff (CDS), Ministry of Defence
Tel: (Personal Staff Officer) 01-218-6314

Air Chief Marshal Sir David Craig took up his post as Chief of the Defence Staff (CDS) in December 1988. He will replace Admiral Sir John Fieldhouse. Sir David was born in 1929 and educated at Radley College and at Lincoln College, Oxford. He was commissioned into the Royal Air Force in 1951 and completed tours as a qualified flying instructor on Meteors and as a Hunter pilot in Fighter Command before being posted to the Air Minstry as a specialist in the guided weapons field.

After attending Staff College at Andover in 1962, Craig returned to flying duties in Vulcans as commanding officer of No. 35 Squadron from 1963 to 1965. From 1965 to 1968 he served as military assistant to the Chief of Defence Staff in the Ministry of Defence.

He was promoted to group captain in 1968 and was station commander at the RAF College, Cranwell, until 1970, when he was posted to Headquarters Far East Command. He was Director of Plans and Operations at the Headquarters until its closure in October 1971. From there he went to Cyprus and, with the rank of air commodore, commanded RAF Akrotiri from January 1972 to December 1973. In 1974 he completed the Royal College of Defence Studies course and then took up the post of Assistant Chief of Air Staff (Operations) in March 1975. He became Air Officer Commanding No.1 Group in July 1978, and Vice Chief of the Air Staff in May 1980. In September 1982 Craig became Air Officer Commander-in-Chief Strike Command and thus also Commander-in-Chief United Kingdom Air Force.

The choice of Sir David as CDS attracted critcism from some in the Ministry of Defence, who favoured Sir Nigel Bagnall, then Chief of the General Staff. One source was quoted as saying that Craig 'had been chosen because ministers would have "an easy ride" with him' (*The Independent*, 9 February 1988). SIr David's defenders have argued that, with three years at the top of the RAF, he is an astute and effective officer. He is credited with bringing the RAF through one of its most potentially difficult periods of recent years: the decision to write off £1billion spent on the Nimrod Airborne Early Warning System.

Sir David is married and has two children. He lists his recreations as fishing, shooting and golf.
(*See: Chief of the Defence Staff (MoD.*)

Cuckney, Sir John, Chairman, Westland Group plc

Born in 1925, the son of Air Vice-Marshal E. J. Cuckney, Sir John Cuckney was educated at Shrewsbury and St Andrews University. After

military service in World War II, he was attached to the then War Office, as civil assistant to the General Staff, until 1957. His appointments in the public sector include: chief executive of the Property Services Agency at the Department of Environment (1972–74); and chairman of International Military Services (an MoD company) (1974–78). In addition to his position with Westland, Cuckney is currently also chairman of the Investors in Industry Group and a director of the Midland Bank.
(*See: Defence Contractors.*)

Curwen, Sir Christopher Keith, KCMG, Chief of the Secret Service (MI6)

Sir Christopher Curwen was appointed Chief of the Secret Service (MI6) at the end of 1985. Born in April 1929, he served in Malaya with the 4th Queens Own Hussars from 1948 to 1949 – where he apparently 'fought with distinction against Communist guerrillas' – and joined the Foreign Office in 1952. His foreign postings included Bangkok (1954 and 1961) – where he learnt Thai – and Kuala Lumpur (1963). It is not clear when Curwen joined MI6. In 1968 he became one of MI6's representatives in Washington. One colleague from that period, Peter Spendlove, said: 'MI6 is a very good and discreet service and Chris Curwen was a very quiet, unassuming but efficient officer. He was a very gentle chap. I can't think of anyone more low-key than him.' (*Sunday Times*, 15 December 1985.) Curwen's appointment as head of MI6 was interpreted at the time as evidence of Mrs Thatcher's determination to control MI6 after it had provided faulty information in the months leading up to the Argentinian invasion of the Falklands/Malvinas islands in 1982.

Christopher Curwen has been married twice and divorced one. He has one son and two daughters from his first marriage and one son and one daughter from his second marriage. He lists his hobbies ' books, gardening, motoring'. He lives in a modest, semi-detached house and travels to work in a chauffeur-driven, bullet-proof car.

de Ferranti, Basil, Chairman, Ferranti plc

Born in 1930, Basil de Ferranti was educated at Eton and Cambridge. He served with the 4th/7th Royal Dragoon Guards in 1949–50, and as a departmental manager in his father's firm in 1954–57. He was Conservative MP for Morecambe and Lonsdale Division of Lancaster from 1958 to 1964, and Parliamentary Secretary in the Ministry of Aviation in 1962. From 1957 to 1962 he was director of overseas operations for Ferranti Ltd. He then moved to International Computers Ltd., of which he became managing director in 1964, and later director. He was a member, and for a time chairman, of the Economic and Social Committee, European Communities, from 1973 to 1979, and chairman of the European Movement (British Council) from 1980 to 1982. He has been a Member of the European Parliament (first for Hampshire West, and since 1984 for Hampshire Central) since 1979.

Basil de Ferranti has been married three times, with three children from his first marriage and one from his second. He lists his hobbies as skiing and sailing.
(*See: Defence Contractors.*)

Ewins, P. D., CEng, MRAeS, Director, Admiralty Research Establishment, Ministry of Defence

Ewins graduated in aeronautical engineering from Imperial College in London in 1964 and received a Master of Science degree from Cranfield College Institute of Technology in 1966. He joined the Royal Aircraft Establishment (RAE) at Farnborough, in the MoD's Procurement Executive, in 1966, where for ten years he carried out research into the application of new materials to aerospace structures. In 1980 he was posted to the the Procurement Executive of the MoD under the Chief Scientist (RAF), where he was responsible for operational and effectiveness studies in support of RAF operational planning and procurement programmes. In 1982 he returned to the RAE, where as senior principal scientific officer in the post of superintendent of the Helicopters Division, he had responsibility for structures and aerodynamic research and development and helicopter advice and project support to the Services and to the Aircraft Controller.

From 1984 to 1987 Ewins worked in the Cabinet Office as head of the Personnel Management Division. On his return to the MoD he was appointed Director (Nuclear) Projects, in which post he was responsible to the Deputy Controller (Nuclear) under the Controller R & D Establishments, Research and Nuclear Programmes (CERN), for the procurement of all nuclear weapon payloads, including Trident and Polaris (Chevaline), and for advice to CERN and Central Staffs on future nuclear projects.
(See: Controllerate of Research and Development Establishments, Research and Nuclear/Procurement Executive (MoD).)

Facer, Roger L. L., Deputy Under-Secretary (Personnel and Logistics), Office of Management and Budget, Ministry of Defence

Born in 1933, and educated at Rugby and Oxford, Facer joined the then War Office as Assistant Principal in 1957. From 1958 to 1961 he was Private Secretary to the Permanent Under-Secretary. From 1966 to 1968 he served in the Cabinet Office. From 1970 to 1972 he was head of Defence Secretariat 13 in the MoD. From 1972 to 1973 he was a research associate at the Institute of International Strategic Studies in London and from 1973 to 1975 counsellor on defence to the British delegation to the Mutual and Balanced Force Reduction (MBFR) talks in Vienna. From 1976–9 he was Private Secretary to the Secretary of State for Defence. He assumed his current position in 1987.
(See: Office of Management and Budget (MoD).)

Figures, Sir Colin (Frederick), KCMG, OBE, The Co-ordinator of Intelligence and Security

Sir Colin Figures was appointed Co-ordinator of Intelligence and Security by Prime Minister Thatcher in 1986. Born in July 1925, he served in the Worcestershire Regiment from 1943 to 1948 and joined the Foreign Office in 1951. From 1953 to 1956 he was attached to Control Command in West Germany. His other foreign postings included: Amman, Jordan (1956–58); Warsaw (1959–62); and Vienna (1966–69). Apart from that he apparently served in Britain. For much, if not all, of his career, he will probably have been working for MI-6, of which he became the Chief in 1982.

He lists his recreations as 'watching sport, gardening, beachcombing'. He is married and has three children.
(See: Management Structure (Defence Intelligence).)

Harcourt-Smith, Air Chief Marshal Sir David, KCB, DFC, Controller Aircraft, Procurement Executive, Ministry of Defence

Born in 1931, the son of an Air Vice Marshal, Harcourt-Smith was educated at Felsted School, which he left to study at RAF College. He was commissioned in 1952. He attended staff college from 1962 to 1963, and was appointed commanding officer of No. 54 Squadron in 1963. From 1965 to 1967 he was the personal staff officer to the Air Officer Commanding-in-Chief of the Technical Training Command. He then joined the Defence Planning Staff for one year, before taking command of No. 6 Squadron in 1969 to 1970. From 1970 to 1972 he worked with the Central Tactics and Trials Organization. He then commanded RAF Brüggen from 1972 to 1974. From 1974 to 1976 he was Director of Operational Requirements, after which he spent a year at the Royal College of Defence Studies. From 1978 to 1980 he was commandant of the RAF College at Cranwell, then Assistant Chief of Air Staff (Operational Requirements) until 1984. In 1984–85 he was Air Officer Commanding-in-Chief, RAF Support Command. He was appointed to his present post in 1986.

Harcourt-Smith is married with two sons and one daughter. He lists his hobbies as tennis, walking and golf.
(See: Systems Controllerates/Procurement Executive (MoD).)

Harding, Sir Peter (Colin), Air Chief Marshal, KCB, CBIM, FRAeS; Chief of the Air Staff, Ministry of Defence
Tel: (Personal Staff Officer) 01-218-6314

Air Marshal Sir Peter Harding became Chief of the Air Staff in December 1988. He was born in London in 1929. He joined the Royal Air Force (RAF) in 1952. In October 1952, on completion of his initial pilot training, he was appointed to a commission. After further training he joined No. 12 (Canberra) Squadron as a pilot and later trained as a flying instructor. In 1957 Harding was posted to Cranwell as a qualified flying instructor and in 1960 went to Australia on an exchange posting where he flew with No. 1 (Canberra) Squadron of the Royal Australian Air Force (RAAF). He returned to England in 1963 to attend the RAF Staff College at Bracknell.

After a tour as a personnel officer in the Air Secretary's department in the Ministry of Defence (MoD), Harding was posted in 1966 to No. 18 (Wessex) Squadron, Gutersloh, as Officer Commanding. He was promoted to wing commander in 1968 and returned to England with No. 18 Squadron where he was based first at Acklington and later at Odiham. In 1969 he was posted to the MoD for duty with the Defence Policy Staff. After attending the Joint Services Staff College, Latimer, he was promoted to group captain in 1970 and returned to the MoD as Director of Air Staff Briefing. In 1974 he was appointed station commander, Bruggen.

On promotion to air commodore in 1976, Harding took up the appointment of Director of Defence Policy (A) in the MoD. In 1978 he was appointed Assistant Chief of Staff (Plans and Policy Division) to the Supreme Allied Commander Europe (SACEUR) at NATO's Supreme Headquarters Allied Powers Europe (SHAPE), with the rank of Air Vice Marshal; on his return to Britain in 1981 he became air officer commanding No.11 Group. On promotion to Air Marshal he was appointed Vice Chief of the Air Staff, a post he held from August-December 1984. He took up the appointment of Vice Chief of the Defence Staff in January 1985. In August 1985 he took up the posts air officer commanding-in-chief, RAF Strike Command and Commander-in-Chief, United Kingdom Air Forces.

Harding's interests include bird-watching, walking, bridge and pianoforte. He and his wife Sheila have three sons and one daugher.
(*See: Chief of Defence Staff (MoD).*)

Harrison, Sir Ernest Thomas, Chairman and Chief Executive, Racal Electronics plc

Born in 1926, Harrison was educated at Trinity Grammar School in Wood Green, and later qualified as a chartered accountant. He joined Racal in its early days as secretary and chief accountant in 1951, and was made a director seven years later. By 1961 he was deputy managing director. He has been chairman and chief executive since 1966. In 1981 he was elected Businessman of the Year, and in the same year he received his knighthood.

From 1964 to 1976 Harrison was active in the National Savings movement, for which services he was awarded the OBE. He has received four honorary doctorates. He is married with two daughters and three sons. He owns racehorses and in his spare time enjoys gardening and soccer.
(*See: Defence Contractors.*)

Harrowby, 7th Earl of, Dudley Danvers Granville Coutts Ryder,
Chairman, Dowty Group plc

Born in 1922, Harrowby was educated at Eton, and saw military service in the World War II. He has been director of a number of companies and banks, and chairman of the Olympia Group, the Powell Duffryn Group, National Westminster Unit Trust Managers, and Orion Bank. In addition to his chairmanship of the Dowty Group, he is currently chairman of the International Westminster Bank, National Westminster Investment Bank, Bentley Engineering Company and the National Biological Standards Board. He is deputy chairman of Coutts and Co and the National Westminster Bank. Harrowby has served on a number of public bodies, including the Fulham and Kensington Hospital Group, the Central Council for the Care of Cripples, the Committee of Management of the Institute of Psychiatry, and the University of Keele. Currently, he is a member of the Trilateral Commission, a governor of the Atlantic Institute for International Affairs and a trustee of the Psychiatry Research Trust.

Harrowby is married with a daughter and a son, and has homes in London, Stafford and Gloucestershire.

(*See: Defence Contractors.*)

Hastie-Smith, Richard Maybury, CB, Deputy Under-Secretary of State (Civilian Management), Office of Management and Budget, Ministry of Defence
Tel: (Personal Assistant) 01-218-3003

Born in 1931, Hastie-Smith was educated at Cranleigh and Cambridge. He joined the then War Office in 1955 and became private secretary to the Permanent Under-Secretary in 1957. He was Assistant Private Secretary to the Secretary of State from 1958 to 1960 and again from 1965 to 1968. In 1975 he was appointed Under-Secretary. From 1979 to 1981 he worked in the Cabinet Office. He was appointed to his current post in 1981.
(*See: Office of Management and Budget (MoD).*)

Hills, David Henry, Director of Economic and Logistic Intelligence, Defence Intelligence Service, Ministry of Defence
Tel: 01-218-5723

Born in 1933, Hills was educated at Varndean School, Brighton, and Nottingham University. He served in the Army Intelligence Corps from 1954 to 1956, after which he entered the MoD. He was director of marketing in the MoD's Defence Sales Organization from 1979 to 1982. He lists his recreation as gardening.
(*See: British Intelligence agencies (Defence Intelligence.*)

Hilsum, Professor Cyril, Director of Research, General Electric Company plc (GEC)

Cyril Hilsum was born in 1925 and educated at Raines School, London, and University College, London, where he received his doctorate. In 1945 he joined the Royal Naval Scientific Service, going on to the Admiralty Research Laboratory in 1947. For fourteen years from 1950 he worked at the Services Electronics Research Laboratory on infra-red research and on semi-conductors. From 1964 to 1983 Hilsum worked at the Royal Signals and Radar Establishment on compound semi-conductors and then on flat panel electronic displays. In 1983 he joined General Electric as their chief scientist, becoming director of research two years later. He is a force on the Scientific and Economic Research Council.

Hilsum is proud of his inventions and shows visitors a recent one: an electronic safe which records when it was opened. To his great scorn, no manufacturer has yet seen the obvious value and importance of this device. He speaks with obvious pleasure of work he has done which has contributed to scientific knowledge and technological advances and – most enthusiastically – of the rewards of working with a close group of bright scientists. He draws a very sharp distinction between defence science and nuclear defence science, and does not see himself as at all involved in the nuclear area – although GEC through its associates and subsidiaries designs and makes vital components for nuclear delivery systems, including electronics for Polaris submarines and avionics for Tornado. Indeed he is somewhat scathing of the scientific credentials and abilities of nuclear scientists, and of their immunity from the criticism and challenge of their peers. He is equally scathing about the reluctance of some university scientists to do work funded by the MoD.

In addition to his work at GEC, Cyril Hilsum is also visiting professor in applied physics and electronics at the University of Durham. He is married with two daughters, and enjoys ballroom dancing and tennis.
(*See: Defence Contractors.*)

Howe, The Rt Hon Sir Geoffrey, QC, MP, Secretary of State for Foreign and Commonwealth Affairs
Tel: 01-270-2057

Born in 1926, in Port Talbot, Glamorgan, Geoffrey Howe is the son of a coroner and a JP. His grandfather was a tinplate worker and pioneeer trade unionist. He won an exhibition to Winchester and went on to Cambridge, where he studied classics. After a period as lieutenant in the Royal Signals, he moved to the Bar, becoming a barrister in accident and company law. He was chairman of the Cambridge University Conservative Association and a founder-member and later chairman of the Bow Group. In 1964 he was elected MP for Bebington, and became Opposition front-bench spokesman on social services. In 1970 he was appointed Solicitor-General by Edward Heath, and in 1972 became Minister for Trade and Consumer Affairs. In 1974 he became Opposition spokesman on treasury and economic affairs. He stood for the leadership of the Conservative Party in 1975, which election Margaret Thatcher won. Mrs Thatcher appointed him Shadow Chancellor and, following her victory in 1979, Chancellor of the Exchequer. In this post he was known for his 'dry' deflationary policies, presiding over a period of record unemployment and strict public expenditure control. He became Foreign Secretary in 1983, in Mrs Thatcher's second government, when she dismissed his predecessor, the 'wet' Francis Pym.

A soporific speaker, Geoffrey Howe was called a 'dead sheep' by his Labour opponent Denis Healey, a sobriquet that stuck. Nevertheless, he is dogged and industrious, and has surprised observers by admitting that he retains ambitions to succeed Mrs Thatcher. As Foreign Secretary he was credited with the succesful agreement with the Chinese government on the future of Hong Kong. He was also responsible for announcing a ban on unions at GCHQ, which raised a political storm. It has been his fate to be seen as Mrs Thatcher's puppet, overrruled mercilessly by a Prime Minister with an avowed dislike of the Foreign office who has increasingly taken foreign policy as her own prerogative. In March 1985 he made an important speech (at the Royal United Services Institute) criticizing SDI, when he cautioned that 'research may acquire an unstoppable momentum of its own', and that 'the process of moving towards a greater emphasis on active defence' might generate 'dangerous uncertainty'. He had to tone down these views following an expression of support by Mrs Thatcher for SDI research. He was overruled on sanctions for South Africa, the role of the Western European Union, Anglo-Irish relations and membership of the European Monetary Union. He has been critical of the Soviet Union, particularly of its so-called 'peace offensive', warning the public against being taken in by 'a speciously attractive timetable for abolishing nuclear weapons by the end of the century.' (*The Times*, 18 March 1986) Mr Howe is a proponent of Anglo-French nuclear co-operation, and has spoken of a 'crying need' for greater European co-operation on arms production and procurement.

(*See: Cabinet Committees; Foreign and Commonwealth Office.*)

Hughes, Nigel Howard, Director, Royal Signals and Radar Establishment (RSRE), Ministry of Defence

Born in 1937, Hughes was educated at St Paul's School and Oxford. He was a pilot officer with the RAF from 1956 to 1958. From 1961 to 1973 he worked at the Royal Aircraft Establishment (RAE) branch at Bedford; and from 1973 to 1980 at RAE Farnborough, first as head of the Radio and Navigation division, then as head of the Flight Systems Department. He worked in the MoD Central Staffs between 1980 and 1982. He was Assistant Chief Scientific Adviser (Projects) from 1982 to 1984 and Deputy Chief Scientific Adviser from 1985 to 1986. He assumed his current position in 1986. He is a Rolls Royce enthusiast and an amateur radio buff.

(*See: Controllerate of Research and Development Establishments, Research and Nuclear Programmes/ Procurement Executive (MoD).*)

Humphries, David Ernest, Assistant Chief Scientific Adviser (Projects and Research), Ministry of Defence

Born in 1937, Humphries was educated at Brighton College and went to Corpus Christi College, Oxford, with a scholarship. He joined the Royal Aircraft Establishment (RAE) Farnborough in 1961, working first in the Materials Department and then the Avionics

Department, before becoming head of the Inertial Navigation Division in 1974. In 1975 he became head of Bombing and Navigation Division and, in 1978, head of the Systems Assessment Department. From 1981 to 1983 Humphries was Director General, Future Projects, in the Procurement Executive of the MoD. In 1983 he was appointed Chief Scientist for the RAF and Director General of Resources. From 1984 to 1986 he was Director General Resource Technology in the Procurement Executive. He was appointed to his present post in 1986.

Humphries is married with one son and one daughter. He lists his recreations as music, playing the organ and building organs.
(See: Defence Scientific Staffs (MoD).)

Hunting, (Lindsay) Clive, Chairman, Hunting Group of Companies.

Born in 1925, Hunting was educated at Loretto School in Edinburgh and Trinity Hall, Cambridge. He served with the Royal Navy from 1944 to 1947, going on to Cambridge afterwards and graduating in 1950. He joined the Hunting Group in the same year, aged 25. He became vice-chairman in 1962, and chairman in 1975.

He is married with one son and one daughter. He enjoys yachting and fishing in his spare time.
(See: Defence Contractors.)

Kemball, Air Vice Marshal Richard John, Asssistant Chief of Defence Staff (Intelligence), Defence Intelligence Service, Ministry of Defence
Tel: 01-218-7481

Born in 1939, Kemball was educated at Uppingham school. He was commissioned into the RAF in 1957. He was officer commanding, No. 54 Squadron, in 1977 and officer commanding, RAF Laarbruch, in 1979. From 1983 to 1985 he was the commandant of the Central Flying School as well as, from 1984 to 1985, aide-decamp to the Queen. From 1985 to 1986 he was commander of the British forces in the Falkland/Malvinas islands. He lists his recreations as shooting, tennis, cricket and gardening.
(See: British Intelligence Agencies (Defence Intelligence).)

Lawson, Rt Hon Nigel, MP, Chancellor of the Exchequer
Tel: 01-270-4330

Nigel Lawson was born in 1932, the son of a London tea merchant and grandson of a Jewish Latvian immigrant. His mother's father was a senior partner in a firm of City stockbrokers. He was brought up in a comfortable and wealthy home in Hampstead.

War broke out when he was seven, and he was evacuated and moved several times. At the end of the war he went to Westminster School, from which he won a scholarship to Oxford. He read PPE and graduated with first-class honours. His tutor, Roy Harrod, described him as one of the most brilliant students he has ever had, though he was more interested in philosophy than economics at the time. After graduation he did national service.

In 1956 he started a career as a financial journalist, joining the *Financial Times* and becoming City Editor of the *Sunday Telegraph* in 1961 and Editor of the *Spectator* in 1966. He became a political adviser to the Conservative Party in 1973 and was elected MP for Blaby in 1974. He was an Opposition Whip from 1974 to 1979. He became Financial Secretary to the Treasury in Mrs Thatcher's first government in 1979, and became a spokesman for tight controls on public spending. In 1983 he became Chancellor of the Exchequer. His policies of tight monetary control and control of public spending have been credited with reducing inflation and the restoration of economic growth, and blamed for contraction of manufacturing and a sharp rise in unemployment after 1979.

He is married with three children His tastes include jazz and Mozart.
(See: Cabinet Committees; HM Treasury.)

Levene, Peter Keith, Chief of Defence Procurement, Ministry of Defence

Educated at City of London School and with a BA in economics and political science from Manchester University, 46-year-old Peter Levene has had a reputation as a skilful and hard-working entrepeneur since he was 21. It was at that age, in 1963, that he joined United Scientific Holdings (USH), a small army surplus company selling binoculars and watches. Within five years USH had gone public as a spares wholesaler and Levene was its managing director. Of those early days, a former colleague has said: 'Levene got orders nobody else could. He knew how to sell' (*Observer*, 31 March 1985). USH expanded considerably after that. By the end of the 1970s, it was heading the league-table of private company growth. Levene was now making deals all over the world, and above all in Singapore, Egypt and the USA. In 1981 USH joined the big defence manufacturers' club, when Levene paid £27 million for Alvis, British Leyland's armoured car subsidiary. In 1984 USH was worth £153 million on the stockmarket.

Levene first came to the attention of the then Secretary of State for Defence (SSD), Michael Heseltine, in 1983, when he was lobbying for Alvis through the Defence Manufacturers' Association (of which he was then vice-chairman). In 1984 Heseltine appointed him as (unpaid) 'special personal adviser' and asked him to report on the privatization of the Royal Dockyards. He then wrote a report for the SSD on military spares (which Heseltine refused to release to the House of Commons Select Committee on Defence). He concluded his six-month assignment at the MoD with the chairmanship of a review of the Procurement Executive. In December 1985, Heseltine appointed him Chief of Defence Procurement, a move that aroused much controversy because of the £95,000 annual fee Levene was to receive.

Levene has said that the 'primary task' of the Procurement Executive is 'simple: to acquire for the armed forces the equipment they need to maintain their effectiveness and credibility against the developing threat, to acquire that equipment when it is needed, and to do so at a price that can be afforded within the resources available. To meet that objective we must concentrate on getting the best possible value for money throughout the whole range of procurement' (Levene,1987, p.3). In order to get 'value for money', he argued, greater emphasis must be put on 'more and sharper competition' and the PE must be made more 'commercially minded'. One major step he has taken since his appointment is to reduce the number of contracts awarded by the MoD on a 'cost-plus' basis, replacing them with 'firm-price' and 'fixed-price' contracts. With cost-plus contracting the contractor can spend more than the sum agreed and be repaid. In evidence to the House of Commons Select Committee on Defence, Levene said that his aim was to save about 10 per cent of the then annual procurement budget over five years. In the same hearing Levene stated that in his post he would not influence whether or not a particular weapon or item of equipment would be purchased: 'my real responsibility is that when the decision has been made to procure a certain type of equipment [or] if a decision has been made to go ahead with a certain programme, it is up to me to make sure that it is procured in the most attractive and efficient and cost-effective way possible for that particular service'.

Another area in which Levene has pushed ahead is international collaboration: 'There is no doubt that we must pursue collaboration. The armed forces want equipment which is interoperable and standardized. With the pace of technological change, we cannot continue to afford expensive national development programmes leading to small, uneconomic production runs. Collaboration can cut out wasteful duplication.' (Levene, 1987.)
(See: Procurement Executive (MoD).)

Lygo, Admiral Sir Raymond (Derek), KCB, Chief Executive, British Aerospace plc

Born in 1924, Lygo was educated at the Valentine's School, Ilford, at Ilford County High School and at Clark's College, Bromley. He worked for *The Times* between the ages of 16 and 18 and joined the Royal Navy as a naval airman in 1942. Sir Raymond rose up in the ranks of the Navy, and in 1969 was given the command of *HMS Ark Royal*. He was Vice-Chief of Naval Staff from 1975 to 1978. In 1978 the year he joined British Aerospace as managing director of the Hatfield/Lostock Division, becoming the Group Department chairman in 1980. From 1980 to 1982 he was chairman and chief executive of the Dynamics Group. He assumed his present position in 1983. He will also chair the new space and communications business, one of BAe's three divisions which are to be turned into separately managed and autonomous businesses.

Sir Raymond is director of the CBI Educational Foundation and Appeal President of the National Deaf-Blind and Rubella Association. He is married with two sons and one daughter. In his spare time he enjoys building, gardening and joinery.
(See: Defence Contractors.)

Mabberley, J. C., Deputy Controller (Nuclear), Controllerate of Research and Development Establishments, Research and Nuclear Programmes, Ministry of Defence

Mabberley graduated with first-class honours in applied physics from City University, London, in 1968. Since then, he has worked as a civil servant on various aircraft and weapon system programmes, most recently at the MoD HQ in Whitehall.
(See: Controllerate of Research and Development Establishments, Research and Nuclear Programmes/ Procurement Executive (MoD).)

Macdonald, Kenneth Carmichael, CB, Deputy Under-Secretary of State (Resources and Programmes), Office of Management and Budget, Ministry of Defence
Tel: (Personal Assistant) 01-218-6014

Born in 1930, Macdonald was educated at Hutchesons' Grammar and Glasgow University, from which he received an MA in Classics. He served in the RAF from 1952 to 1954. In 1954 he became Assistant Principal in the Air Ministry. From 1956 to 1957 he was assistant private secretary to the Secretary of State in the Air Ministry; from 1958 to 1961, private secretary to the Permanent Secretary. In 1962 he went to the Treasury, where he remained until he moved to the MoD in 1965. From 1973 to 1975 he was Counsellor (Defence) to the UK delegation to NATO. In 1975 he became Assistant-Under Secretary in the MoD and in 1980 Deputy Under-Secretary. He assumed his current post in 1985. He lists golf as his recreation.
(See: Office of Management and Budget (MoD).)

McLean, Dr Thomas Pearson, Director, Atomic Weapons Establishment, Ministry of Defence

Born in Paisley in August 1930, McLean was educated at the John Neilson Institution, Paisley, and at Glasgow University, from which he received a BSc and a PhD. In 1955 he joined the Royal Radar Establishment (which in 1976 became the Royal Signals and Radar Establishment), where he was made head of the Physics Group in 1973, and deputy director in 1977. In 1980 he became an Under-Secretary at the MoD, with the position of Director General Air Weapons and Electronic Systems. From 1984 to 1986 McLean was Director of the MOD's Royal Armaments R & D Establishment, after which he was appointed Deputy Controller, Aircraft (1986–87) He was appointed to his present post in 1987, succeeding Peter Jones.

McLean was Honorary Professor of Physics at Birmingham University between 1977 and 1980. He is married with two daughters. He lists his hobbies as music and Scottish country dancing.
(See: Controllerate of Research and Development Establishments, Research and Nuclear Programmes/ Procurement Executive (MoD).)

Major, Rt Hon John, MP, Chief Secretary to the Treasury
Tel : 01-270-4339

John Major was born in 1943, when his father, a former high-wire trapeze artist, was aged 66. He grew up in two rooms in Brixton in South London. He left Rutlish Grammar School when he was 16 and worked in an insurance company, as a labourer and was unemployed before joining the Standard Chartered Bank. He joined the Young Conservatives in Brixton and was elected to Lambeth Borough Council in 1968. There he introduced the policy of selling council houses to owner-occupiers. He entered Parliament in 1979 and was the first of that year's intake to reach Cabinet level rank, when he became Chief Secretary to the Treasury in 1987. In that post he clashed with the MoD over the 1987 public expenditure review, which cut planned defence expenditure by 6 per cent. Nuclear projects are not at risk, although several conventional programmes have been stretched out.

In 1982 he attacked the 'silly, sincere and misguided women' demonstrating against cruise missiles, who he said were delaying multilateral disarmament. He urged the eviction of anti-cruise campers from Molesworth base in 1984.

He is married with two children.
(*See: Cabinet Committees; HM Treasury*.)

Marychurch, Sir Peter (Harvey), KCMG, Director, Government Communications Headquarters (GCHQ)

Born in 1927, Sir Peter was due to retire in 1987 but was asked to remain in office beyond the normal retirement age. He has been director of GCHQ since 1983, having joined in 1948 almost straight from school when GCHQ was based at Eastcote in Middlesex. He was closely associated with the decision to ban trade unions at GCHQ. He rose to head of personnel, before taking over from Sir Brian Tovey (see below) in 1983.
Sir Peter was educated at the Lower School of John Lyon, in Harrow, and served in the RAF between 1945 and 1948. Sir Peter married in 1965, and lists his interests as the theatre, music (especially the opera) and gardening.
(*See: British Intelligence and Security Agencies (Defence Intelligence)*.)

Middleton, Sir Peter (Edward), KCB, Permanent Secretary, Her Majesty's Treasury
Tel: (Private Secretary) 01-270-4360

Born in 1934, Middleton was educated at Sheffield City Grammar School and Sheffield University. He did his national service in the Royal Army Pay Corp (1958–60). He joined the Treasury in 1962 as a senior information officer, and became a principal in 1964. From 1967 to 1969 he was assistant director of the Centre for Administrative Studies. From 1969 to 1972 he was private secretary to the Chancellor of the Exchequer; from 1972 to 1975, Treasury press secretary; in 1975, head of the Treasury's Monetary Policy Division; in 1976 he became Under-Secretary; and from 1980 to 1983 he was a Deputy Secretary. He assumed his current position in 1983.

One newspaper described Middleton on his appointment as 'the sharp-witted grammar school boy', with 'a reputation of not suffering fools gladly, held in high regard as an exceptionally lucid writer and speaker with a gift for press relations'.
(*See: Her Majesty's Treasury*.)

Nicholls, David Alan, CMG, Deputy Under-Secretary of State (Policy and Programmes), Defence Staff, Ministry of Defence
Tel: (Private Secretary) 01-218-3830

Educated at Cheshunt Grammar School and St John's College, Cambridge, and married since 1955 to Margaret Nicholls (they have two daughters), Nicholls entered the Admiralty in 1954, in which he remained until 1964. He was Assistant Principal in 1954, from 1958 to 1959 private secretary to a Parliamentary Secretary, and in 1959 Principal. From 1964 to 1975 he served in the new Ministry of Defence, from 1968 to 1969 as private secretary to the Minister of Defence for Administration and in 1969 as Assistant Secretary. From 1975 to 1957 he worked in the Cabinet Office and from 1977 to 1980 he was Assistant Under-Secretary of State at the MoD. From 1980 to 1984 he served at NATO as Assistant Secretary General for Defence Planning and Policy. He assumed his current post in the MoD in 1985. In this post, he also occupies the key position of British representative on the NATO High Level Group.

He lists his interests as 'sketching and printmaking'.
(*See: Defence Staff (MoD)*.)

Orman, Dr Stanley, Director-General, SDI (Strategic Defence Initiative) Participation Office, Ministry of Defence
Tel: 01-218-4239

Orman has both technical expertise in the production of nuclear weapons and their delivery systems and a detailed knowledge of the US market for for UK skills of potential application to SDI.

Born in 1935, Orman graduated with first-class honours in chemistry from Kings College London in 1957. In 1961 he entered the then Atomic Weapons Research Establishment (AWRE) at Aldermaston, where he was later, from 1978 to 1981, Director of Missiles. At Aldermaston - where he was described in the the house magazine as someone with a 'forthright approach and abundant energy'- he was one of the main influences on the Chevaline programme. (Chevaline was the new 'front-end' fitted to Polaris missiles in the 1970s with the aim of increasing their chances of a successful attack on Moscow.) From 1981 to 1982 he was Chief Weapons System Engineer Polaris in the Strategic Systems Executive, the department of the Navy Controllerate which deals with the UK's strategic nuclear force; 1982–4 Minister-Counsellor, Head of Defence Equipment, at the British Embassy in Washington DC where his main task was, in his own words,'not selling equipment but promoting US–UK co-operation and British involvment in defence R & D, which relates closely to the work of the SDI PO'. From April 1984 until appointed to lead the SDI PO he was Deputy-Director at Aldermaston.

About SDI, Orman has said:

> 'The whole of the history of warfare, which is the history of mankind is a struggle between offence and defence. Tanks used to be able to cut through infantry. Now portable weapons can destroy tanks, so the tables have been turned. The MoD's job is a constant reassessment of the threat and the ways of countering it. It's only by being involved in this research that we can have information to know whether improvements in Russia's ABM will reduce Trident's effectiveness. (*The Engineer*, 21/28 August 1986)
>
> [SDI] is not a fanciful, cloud cuckoo land idea because it does not go beyond known physical principles. There has been disproportionate attention paid to the vociferous minority of scientists who say it won't work. A lot of scientists are incredible experts in narrow areas. They find it difficult to take the blinkers off and look at the wider concepts. (*The Times*, 26 February 1987)
>
> I don't believe it's destabilizing because no single country could erect a total SDI barrier in a short period. I'm talking about decades. Before one side produced a highly effective system – and I don't mean an impenetrable barrier – the other side would have time to partially catch up. If you could say that in two to three years you could put up a total defence, that would be destabilising. But that's an impossibility...The whole game is to make sure that nobody sees an advantage in using nuclear weapons, which means that you design the system to cope with a mass launch of all Soviet missiles...Once you start placing parts of the system in space, better detection systems and new detector concepts can start being used, and the defences have far more time to cope with the attack. My perception is that the USSR sees the absence of weapons as a sign of weakness, capable of exploitation. The importance of SDI is that it can allow us to reduce the huge number of nuclear weapons in the world without seeming weak. (*The Engineer*, 21/28 August 1986)

(*See: Defence Scientific Staffs (MoD).*)

Oxburgh, Professor Ernest Ronald, FRS, Chief Scientific Adviser, Ministry of Defence

Born in 1934, Oxburgh was educated at the Liverpool Institute and Oxford. He received his PhD from the University of Princeton in 1960. He taught geology at Oxford from 1960 to 1978. From 1978 to 1988 he was Professor of Mineralogy and Petrology at Cambridge. He has been a visiting professor at the California Institute of Technology and at Stanford and Cornell universities. He is a member of the Geological Society of America and of the American Geophysical Union. His publications include *The Geology of the Eastern Alps*; he contributes to *Nature* and to the *Journal of Geophysical Research*. He lists his recreations as mountaineering, reading and theatre.
(*See: Defence Scientific Staffs (MoD).*)

Parry Evans, Air Marshal Sir David, KCB, CBE, Deputy Chief of Defence Staff (Programmes and Personnel)
Tel: (Personal Assistant) 01-218-6287

Born in 1935 into a military family, Parry Evans went to Berkhamsted School, and joined the RAF in 1956. From 1958 to 1970 he served in the Far East Air Force, the Coastal Command, the United States Navy and at the Royal Naval Staff College. Then in 1970 he moved to Headquarters Strike Command and served there for four years. In 1974–75 he was officer in command of 214 Squadron, then of RAF Marham until 1977. In 1977 he moved to the MoD, where he became director of defence policy in 1979. In 1981 he was appointed commandant of RAF Staff College for one year, and then moved on to be air officer commanding Nos 1 and 38 Groups of RAF Strike Command between 1982 and 1985. From 1985 to 1987 he was Commander-in-Chief RAF Germany and Commander of the Second Allied Tactical Air Force, before being appointed to his present post at the MoD.

Sir David is married with two sons and lists his hobby as rugby.
(*See: Defence Staff (MoD).*)

Pirnie, Rear Admiral I. H., CEng, IEE, Chief, Strategic Systems Executive, Sea Systems Controllerate, Ministry of Defence

Rear Admiral Pirnie was educated at Christ's Hospital before joining the Royal Navy at the age of 18 in 1953 as an electrical engineering cadet. After initial naval training, he read mechanical sciences at Cambridge. At the start of the Polaris project, in the 1960s, Pirnie joined the Submarine Service; after submarine training at *HMS Dolphin*, he competed the post-graduate guided weapon course at the Royal Military College of Science, before going to the US Guided Missile School in Virginia. He subsequently served in *HMS Resolution* and *HMS Repulse*, and as head of the weapons training at the Royal Naval Polaris School, Faslane. After promotion to commander in 1972, he attended a staff course at the National Defence College, Latimer. He then worked with the Engineering Branch working group, and subsequently on the naval staff dealing with strategic weapon systems. From 1979–81 Pirnie was at the Admiralty Underwater Weapons Establishment as the Assistant Director Weapon Systems, which included being the Weapon Systems Manager for the new 2400 SSK. Appointed to the Strategic Systems Executive in 1981, he served for three years in the early stages of the Trident programme, finishing up as the director of Naval Officer Appointments (Engineers), a post which he held for two years before taking up command of the royal Naval Engineering College, *HMS Thunderer*, in August 1986.

In March 1988 he was promoted to Rear Admiral and took up the post of Chief Strategic Systems Executive.
(*See: Systems Controllerates/ Procurement Executive (MoD).*)

Poole, R. J., Director, Defence Operational Analysis Establishment, Ministry of Defence

Poole took a first in electrical engineering at Adelaide University in 1951 and joined the Australian Department of Supply as a junior scientist. He came to the UK as a trainee and spent three years at the Admiralty Signals and Radar Establishment (ASRE), Portsdown, working on naval guided weapons. In 1953 he returned to Australia to work on guided weapons at Woomera. In 1957 he returned to ASRE to work on shipborne radar systems, moving in 1966 to lead the feasibility studies for the Sea Wolf guided weapon system. In 1980 he became Naval Scientific Adviser in the MoD Central Staff. He has been in his present post since 1986.

During his periods working on equipment development, Poole specialized in servomechanisms and automatic control systems, becoming an expert in very accurate radar tracking from a moving platform. He subsequently moved on to analytical studies of weapon and sensor performance and then to broader issues of equipment choice for the services and the operational analysis needed to support such choice.
(*See: Defence Scientific Staffs (MoD).*)

Pope, Geoffrey George, CB, FRAeS, Director, Royal Aircraft Establishment, Ministry of Defence

Born in 1934, Pope was educated at Epsom College and Imperial College, London. He joined the Royal Aircraft Establishment (RAE) in 1958, working in the Structures Department (1958–73); the Aerodynamics Department (1973–77); as group head of the Aerodynamics, Structures and Materials departments (1978–79); and as Deputy Director (Weapons) from 1979 to 1981. From 1981–2 he was Assistant Chief Scientific Adviser (Projects) in the MoD; from 1982 to 1984 Departmental Controller and Adviser (Research and Technology) in the MoD. He has published technical papers, mainly dealing with structural mechanics and optimum design of structures. He lists his recreations as music, photography and walking.
(See: Controllerate of Research and Development Establishments, Research and Nuclear Programmes/ Procurement Executive (MoD.)

Prior, Rt. Hon. James ('Jim') Michael Leathes, MP, Chairman, General Electric Company plc (GEC)

Jim Prior is Conservative MP for Waveney (where he enjoys a sizeable majority) and a farmer. He was born in 1927, the son of a prosperous Norwich lawyer. He was educated at Charterhouse public school and Pembroke College, Cambridge, where he got a first in estate management. In 1954 he married Jane Gifford, a London magistrate, and four years later he captured his present seat from Labour. His political career advanced when he became PPS to Edward Heath (from 1965 to 1970). He was Minister for Agriculture from 1970 to 1972, and for the next two years was Lord President of the Council and Commons Leader. When the Conservatives came back to power in 1979 he was made Employment Secretary for two years, and then Secretary of State for Northern Ireland until 1984. He opposed the restoration of hanging for terrorism in May 1982, introduced a 'forum for moderates' through a Northern Ireland Assembly. He admitted having made mistakes in handling a ban on pro-IRA US activists in 1984.

Prior is known as the most disarming of the senior mainstream Tories now assembled on the back-benches; he is a leading exponent of consensus and a pro-industry anti-monetarist. He is a director of United Biscuits, Barclays Bank, Barclays International and Sainsburys. He owns his 1,700-acre farm in partnership with Sir John Sainsbury. A life peerage was conferred on Mr Prior in 1987. He became Chairman of GEC in 1984. GEC has a long record of employing former government ministers and civil servants.

Jim Prior has three sons, David, Simon and Jeremy, and one daughter, Sarah. In his spare time he enjoys cricket, tennis, golf and gardening.
(See: Defence Contractors.)

Quinlan, Sir Michael (Edward), KCB, Permanent Under-Secretary, Ministry of Defence
Tel: (Personal Assistant) 01-218-2392

Born in 1930, Quinlan was educated at Wimbledon College and Oxford, where he took a first in Mods. He spent his national service (1952–54) as a flying officer with the RAF. He entered the Air Ministry as a civil servant in 1954. From 1956 to 1958 he was private secretary to successive Parliamentary Under-Secretaries of State for Air. From 1958 to 1968, with the rank of Principal, he carried out parliamentary, finance and air staff work. He was Assistant Secretary to the Director of Defence Policy between 1968 and 1970. From 1970 to 1973 Quinlan was seconded to the Foreign Office as Defence Counsellor to the UK delegation to NATO Headquarters in Brussels; and from 1974 to 1977 he was in the Cabinet Office as Under-Secretary. He returned to the MoD in 1977, and worked as Deputy Under-Secretary of State (Policy and Programmes) (DUS(P)) until 1980. Seconded to the Treasury as Deputy Secretary (Industry) from 1981 to 1982, Permanent Secretary at the Department of Employment from 1983 to 1988, Quinlan took up his present position April 1988.

Quinlan is married and has two sons and two daughters.
(*See: Permanent Under-Secretary (MoD).*)

Reffell, Vice Admiral Sir Derek (Roy), KCB, Controller of the Navy, Ministry of Defence
Tel: (Personal Assistant) 01-218-7767

Born in 1928, Reffell was educated at Culford School in Suffolk and at the Royal Naval College, Dartmouth. From 1946 to 1963 he served on various ships at home, in the Mediterranean, the West Indies and the Far East. In 1954 he qualified as a navigating officer, and as a Commander in 1963. He had command of *HMS Sirins* in 1966–1967, and from 1968 to 1969 he was Commander of the Britannia Royal Naval College, Dartmouth. He moved through various commands, becoming Director Naval Warfare in 1976. From 1979 to 1982 he was Assistant Chief of Naval Staff (Policy). He was Flag Officer Third Flotilla and Commander of Anti-Submarine Group Two in 1982–83, and then Flag Officer, Naval Air Command in 1983–84. He assumed his present position in 1984.

Reffell is married with one daughter and one son. He lists his recreation as wine-making.
(*See: Systems Controllerates/Procurement Executive (MoD).*)

Ridley, Robert George, Assistant Chief Scientific Adviser (Nuclear), Defence Scientific Staffs, Ministry of Defence
Tel: 01-218-7348

Born in 1932, Ridley received an honours degree in physics from Kings College, London, in 1953 and a PhD from Kings College in 1957. From 1957 to 1979 he worked at the Atomic Weapons Research Establishment at Aldermaston. From 1979 to 1982 he was Deputy Chief Scientific Officer, Defence Science (Nuclear), in the MoD and from 1982 to 1984 he worked again at Aldermaston. He assumed his current post in 1984.
(*See: Defence Scientific Staffs (MoD).*)

Robins, Ralph Harry, Managing Director, Rolls Royce plc

Born in 1932, Robins received a BSc at Imperial College, University of London. He joined Rolls Royce in Derby as a development engineer in 1955, and rose to become executive vice-president of Rolls Royce Inc. in 1971. Two years later he was managing director of Rolls Royce Industrial and Marine Division, and became commercial director of Rolls Royce Ltd in 1978.

He left to take up the chairmanship of International Aero Engines AG for a year in 1983, but returned in 1984 to become managing director of the company he had joined as a 23-year-old.

Robins is married, has two daughters and enjoys tennis, golf and music.
(*See: Defence Contractors.*)

Robson, Stephen Arthur, Under-Secretary, Defence Policy, Manpower and Material Group, Her Majesty's Treasury
Tel: 01-278-4813

Born in 1943, Robson was educated at Pocklington School and Cambridge, from which he received his PhD. He also has an MA from Stanford University, California. He joined the Treasury in 1969 and was private secretary to the Chancellor of the Exchequer from 1974 to 1976. He was seconded to Investors in Industry plc in from 1976 to 1978. He assumed his present post in 1987.
(*See: Her Majesty's Treasury.*)

Smith, Professor Roland, Chairman, British Aerospace plc

Professor Smith is chairman not only of British Aerospace, but also of Temple Bar Investment Trust, Readicut International, Hepworth Ceramic Holdings, Phoenix Properties and Finance, Senior Engineering and Kingston Oil and Gas. He is also a part-time professor of marketing at the University of Manchester Institute of Science and Technology.

He was born in 1928, the son of a Manchester police sergeant, and was educated at the universities of Birmingham and Manchester. At the age of 25 he was a flying officer in the RAF. He is known in industry for having a string of chairmanships, consultancies and directorships. 'What he loves doing', says a leading merchant banker,'is being on boards, and even more he loves being chairman – just loves it.'

His early career was chequered, even accident-prone. He took the chair at Barrow Hepburn, for example, in 1974. While he was in charge of Midland Aluminium the company had a £303,000 loss in 1975, and was taken over by Tube Investments.

He made his name at House of Fraser when it was fending off the takeover attempt by Lonrho. 'It is to his credit', wrote the *Financial Times*, 'that he gave more or less as good as he got, and stood up to Lonrho's relentless guerrilla tactics.' He revealed a talent for quotable phrases like 'we'll make the assets sweat'.

Roland Smith is the first chairman of British Aerospace who is not a government appointee. (The government retains a 'golden' share in British Aerospace which prevents foreign interests buying control of Britain's most important defence undertaking.) He took up the post in September 1987, and less than six months later announced a plan for a British Aerospace takeover of the Rover Group.This move would remove from government responsibility the problems of the car industry, which some commentators describe as the most troublesome post-war industrial issue in Britain.

Professor Smith is married and lists his recreation as 'walking'. He is proud of his skills in marketing and business development.
(*See: Defence Contractors.*)

Spiers, Donald Maurice, CB, Controller of Research and Development Establishments, Research and Nuclear Programmes (CERN), Ministry of Defence
Tel: (Personal Assistant) 01–218–3425.

Donald Spiers was born in 1934 and educated at Trinity College, Cambridge. He served in the Royal Engineers from 1952 to 1954 and in the Territorial Army from 1954 to 1967, receiving his Territorial Efficiency Decoration in 1966. From 1957 to 1960 he worked for the de Havilland Engine Co. Spiers joined the Air Ministry as a Senior Scientific Officer (SSO) in 1960. From 1960 to 1963 he carried out operational research on deterrence; in 1965 he went on to the Ministry of Defence (MoD) as a principal scientific adviser; from 1967 to 1970 he was scientific adviser to the Far Eastern Air Force (FEAF), Singapore; in 1970 he returned to the MoD, where he worked on research into aircrew and ground training. In 1972 he became Assistant Chief (Training) with the RAF, a post he kept until 1977.

In 1978 Spiers joined the Procurement Executive of the MoD as Assistant Director Military Aircraft Projects 2. In 1979 he was appointed Director of Aircraft Post Design Services and in 1981 Director General Aircraft 1. In 1984 he was promoted to Deputy Controller Aircraft. Spiers was appointed CERN in December 1986.
(*See: Controllerate of Research and Development Establishments, Research and Nuclear Programmes/ Procurement Executive (MoD).*)

Sprackling, Major-General Ian Oliver John, OBE, Director, Management and Support of Intelligence, Defence Intelligence Staff, Ministry of Defence
Tel: 01-218-3116

Born in 1936, Sprackling was educated at Bristol Grammar School, the Royal Military College of Science, the Royal College of Defence Studies, and the Royal Military Academy at Sandhurst. He became a second lieutenant in the Royal Corps of Signals in 1957. Between 1961 and 1975 he served in the Far East, in the UK and with the British Army on the Rhine in West Germany. From 1975 to 1977 he was a staff officer with the Sultan of Oman's Armed Forces. From 1977 to 1979 he was commanding officer, Electronic Warfare Regiment, British Army on the Rhine. He was attached to the Cabinet Office from 1979 to 1981. From 1982 to 1984 he was commander of Catterick garrison. In 1984 he was at the Royal College of Defence Studies and from 1985 to 1986 he was Director, Military Assistance Overseas. He assumed his present position in 1986. He lists his recreations as bridge, socializing, keeping fit and watching rugby.
(*See: British Intelligence and Security Agencies (Defence Intelligence).*)

Staveley, Admiral Sir William (Doveton Minet), GCB, First Sea Lord and Chief of the Naval Staff, Ministry of Defence
Tel: (Secretary) 01-218-2214; (Naval Assistant) 01-218-5395

Born in 1928, Staveley was educated at West Downs, Winchester and the Royal Navy Colleges at Dartmouth and Greenwich. He entered the Royal Navy as a cadet in 1942. His postings have taken him to the Mediterranean, Nigeria, Bermuda, the South Atlantic and Britain. From 1967 to 1970 he was Assistant Director, Naval Plans, Naval Staff. Between 1970 to 1972 he commanded *HMS Intrepid* in the Far and Middle East. From 1974 to 1976 he was Director of Naval Plans, Naval Staff; 1976–77, Flag Officer, Second Flotilla; 1977–78, Flag Officer, Carriers and Amphibious Ships, and NATO Commander of Carrier Striking Group Two. From 1977 to 1978 Staveley was Chief of Staff to the Commander-in-Chief, Fleet. He was then Vice Chief of the Naval Staff (1980–82). This was followed by three years (1982–85) as Commander-in-Chief, Fleet, and Allied Comander-in-Chief, Channel and East Atlantic. He assumed his current post in 1985. Staveley lists his recreations as gardening, fishing, shooting, riding, sailing and restoring antiques.
(*See: Chief of Defence Staff (MoD).*)

Stewart, (Bernard Harold) Ian (Halley) MP, Minister of State for the Armed Forces
Tel : (Private Secretary) 01-218-6385

Born in 1935, Stewart was educated at Haileybury School and Cambridge, where he got a first in classics. He did national service with the Royal Navy Volunteer Reserve from 1954 to 1956 and was subsequently a lieutenant commander with the Royal Naval Reserve. In 1959 he worked for a brokers firm, joining Brown Shipley Holdings and Co. Ltd in 1960, in which he rose to manager by 1966 and director by 1971.

Moving into the world of politics in the 1970s, he became Parliamentary Private Secretary to the Chancellor of the Exchequer in 1979, a job which he retained for four years. In 1983 he was Parliamentary Under-Secretary of State for Defence Procurement at the MoD, and from 1983 to 1987 Economic Secretary to HM Treasury. He is on numerous councils and trusts, has published books and papers on coins, and is interested in history, Homer, tennis and squash, both of which he plays.

Ian Stewart was Conservative MP for Hitchin from 1974 to 1983, and has been MP for Hertfordshire North since 1983. He married in 1966 and has one son and two daughters.
(*See: Ministers (MoD).*)

Stibbon, Lt-General John James, OBE, Master General of the Ordnance, Ministry of Defence

Born in 1935, Stibbon went to Portsmouth Southern Grammar School and on to the Royal Military Academy. He gained a BSc in engineering at the Royal Military College of Science and was commissioned to the Royal Engineers in 1954. From 1975 to 1977 he was commanding officer of the 28 Amphibious Engineer Regiment and was then appointed Assistant Military Secretary until 1979, when he took command of the 20 Armoured Brigade for two years. He was Commandant of the Royal Military College of Science between 1983 and 1985. He was then appointed Assistant Chief of Defence Staff Operational Requirements (Land Systems) before moving to his present post in 1987. He has been the Colonel Commandant of the Royal Army Pay Corps since 1985.

Married since 1957, Stibbon has two daughters and lists his hobbies as Association football, athletics, painting and palaeontology.
(*See: Systems Controllerates/Procurement Executive (MoD).*)

Thatcher, Rt Hon Margaret, MP, Prime Minister and First Lord of the Treasury
Tel: 01-270-3000

Born in 1923, in Grantham, Lincolnshire, Margaret Thatcher studied chemistry at Oxford University where she also devoted much of her time to the Oxford University Conservative Association. After Oxford, from 1947 to 1951, she worked in the research department of two industrial firms. She took up law in 1951 and was called to the Bar in 1954. She specialized in tax law.

In 1949 she was selected as Conservative candidate for Dartford in Kent, but failed to win the seat. She failed again in 1951. In 1959 she ran for Parliament in the north London constituency of Finchley, was elected, and has held the seat ever since. She was Shadow Minister of Education under Edward Heath, and received the Education portfolio in the Heath government of 1970 to 1974. In 1975 she was elected leader of the Conservative party. She has been Prime Minister since 1979.

The decision to replace Polaris with Trident was made by the first Thatcher government. Though a declared supporter of bilateral and multilateral disarmament, Mrs Thatcher opposes the inclusion of UK nuclear forces in arms talks, at least in the near future. After the Rejkyavik summit, when 50 per cent cuts in superpower arsenals were on the table, she insisted that the Trident programme would go ahead. In early 1988, during the NATO debate over nuclear disarmament after the INF Treaty, she declared herself opposed to full nuclear disarmament in Europe: 'I want a war-free Europe. A nuclear-free Europe, I do not believe, would be a war-free Europe.'

In the current discussions over possible restructuring of NATO, Mrs Thatcher, an ardent Atlanticist, has voiced criticism of the Franco–German moves towards closer military co-operation.

Mrs Thatcher has become involved in foreign policymaking and arms control negotiations. She stepped in to support the SDI programme following Geoffrey Howe's criticisms of it, but sought to ensure that European views were taken into account by negotiating the four 'Camp David points' on Star Wars (namely, that the USA would not seek superiority over the Soviet Union, that there would be no deployment of a space-based defence system without prior negotiations with Moscow, that the aim of SDI was to enhance deterrence, and that East–West arms negotiations would aim to achieve security at lower levels of offensive arms).

Mrs Thatcher is married and she and her husband, Denis, have two children, Mark and Carol.

(*See: Cabinet; Prime Minister.*)

Tombs, Sir Francis (Leonard), Chairman, Rolls Royce plc

Born in 1924, Tombs was educated in Walsall and at the Birmingham College of Technology. His first job was with Birmingham Corporation. He has gathered many engineering qualifications, and took himself back to London University for an honours degree in economics when he was 35 years old. Until 1957 he worked for two electricity authorities, and then for GEC for the next eight years as a 'problem solver' at various power plants. He climbed from director of engineering to chairman of the South of Scotland Electricity Board between 1969 and 1977, and for the next three years was chairman of the Electricity Council. He left the industry in disgust after both a Labour and a Conservative government had dithered about combining the electricity councils into one.

Lord Rothschild asked Tombs to become an adviser on energy matters and director of the family bank, an appointment which he eagerly accepted. Then he was asked to take on the chairmanship of the Weir Group, and achieved a remarkable turnaround of the nearly bankrupt company. In 1982 he became chairman of Turner and Newall and brought about an 'astonishing revival' of the company, making himself £1 million in share options in the process.

Tombs had a testing job on his hands when he became chairman of Rolls Royce in 1985. Fifteen years previously the most famous name in the world of engineering had collapsed in a spectacular bankruptcy, and was nationalized by the Heath government. Sir Francis took the company into profitability and saw it once again floated as a public company on the stock exchange.

Work on the Tornado aircraft, which carries nuclear weapons, has given the military division of Rolls Royce invaluable business. Work on the new European Fighter Aircraft starts at the end of the decade.

Sir Francis is described by a colleague as 'exceedingly firm, never flamboyant and always polite'. He has had a number of honorary degrees conferred on him and is chairman of the Engineering Council, and of ACOST. He is a former chairman of the Association of British Orchestras and lists his recreations as music, golf and sailing. He is married and has three daughters.
(*See: Defence Contractors.*)

Tovey, Sir Brian (John Maynard), KCMG, Defence and Political Adviser, Plessey Electronic Systems Ltd.

Born in 1926, Tovey was educated at St Edward's School, Oxford, and went on to St. Edmund Hall, Oxford, for one year. He later spent two years at the School of Oriental and African Studies, graduating in 1950 with a BA Hons. He saw service with the Royal Navy and subsequently the Army (with the Intelligence Corps and the Royal Army Educational Corps) in the intervening years (1945–48). In 1950 he joined the Government Communications Headquarters (GCHQ) as a junior assistant, becoming Principal in 1957 and moving up through the ranks of Assistant Secretary, Under-Secretary, Deputy Secretary, becoming Director of GCHQ in 1977, a post he kept until his retirement in 1983.

For two years after his retirement Tovey was defence systems consultant for Plessey Electronic Systems Ltd and Director of Plessey Defence Systems Ltd. In 1985 he was appointed to his present position of adviser to Plessey Electronic Systems on defence and political matters.

He lists his recreations as music, walking and history of art.
(*See: Defence Contractors.*)

Trefgarne, Lord David Garro (2nd Baron of Cleddau), Minister of State for Defence Procurement, Ministry of Defence

Born in 1941, educated at Haileybury (public school) and Princeton University in the USA, Trefgarne took his seat in the House of Lords in 1962. In 1977 he became Opposition Whip in the Lords, a post he kept until 1979. After the election of the Conservative government in May 1979, Trefgarne was appointed Lord-in-Waiting (Government Whip) and was also spokesperson in the Lords for the Foreign and Commonwealth Office (FCO) and the Department of Trade. From January to September 1981 he was Parliamentary Under–Secretary of State in the Department of Trade, where he had special responsibility for civil aviation, marine and shipping policy, in addition to speaking for the Department generally in the House of Lords. From September 1981 to April 1982 he was Parliamentary Under-Secretary in the FCO and from April 1982 to June 1983 he held the same post in the Department of Health and Social Security. He joined the MoD immediately thereafter, serving first as Parliamentary Under-Secretary of State for the Armed Forces and then, from 1985, as Minister of State for Defence Support. He was appointed to his current position in May 1986. Lord Trefgarne married Rosalie Lane in 1968 and they have three children.

Trefgarne's hobbies are photography and flying. He is probably the only British politician to have flown from Britain to Australia and back in a light aircraft (in 1963), a feat for which he won the Royal Aero Club Bronze medal. He has also been known to throw himself out of aeroplanes (with a parachute) to raise money for charity.
(*See: Ministers (MoD).*)

Vincent, General Sir Richard, KCB, DSO, Vice Chief of the Defence Staff, Ministry of Defence
Tel: (Military Assistant) 01-218-7657

General Sir Richard Vincent was born in 1931. He was commissioned in the Royal Artillery and has served in a variety of appointments in the United Kingdom, West Germany and the Far East. In 1980 he became commandant of the Royal Military College of Science in the rank of major-general. He was appointed Master-General of the Ordnance on promotion to Lieutenant General in 1983 (with responsibilities for the

procurement of land systems weapons and equipment for all three services). Promoted to General in 1986, he was appointed Vice Chief of the Defence Staff in October 1987. He has published in military journals. He is married and has one son and one daughter.
(See: Defence Staff (MoD).)

Walker, Lieutenant General Sir Antony, KCB, Deputy Chief of Defence Staff (Commitments), Ministry of Defence
Tel: (Personal Assistant) 01-218-6297

Walker was born in 1934 and educated at Merchant Taylor's School and the Royal Military Academy, Sandhurst. In 1954 he was commissioned into the Royal Tank Regiment. Walker joined 2 Royal Tank Regiment (2 RTR) and served in Münster and Libya before a period of secondment in 1961 to the Ghana Reconnaissance Squadron. He served briefly in the Congo as part of the Ghanaian contribution to the United Nations Force before returning to the UK and 2 RTR again. After a tour with the Regiment's squadron in the role of Royal Armoured Corps' Guided Weapons Squadron, he moved to regimental HQ in Northern Ireland as Adjutant. After attending Staff College, Camberley, in 1967, Walker was posted to Hong Kong. He returned to the UK in 1970. Between 1970 and 1985 he was posted to the UK, Cyprus, Northern Ireland and West Germany. He became Chief of Staff UK Land Forces in March 1985. He assumed his current post in March 1987.

Walker has two children from his first marriage. His recreations are bird watching, country sports, music, theatre and the practical study of wine.
(See: Defence Staff (MoD.)

Weinstock, Baron of Bowden (Arnold), Managing Director, General Electric Company (GEC) plc

Born in 1924, Weinstock received a degree in statistics at London University. Between 1944 and 1947 he was a junior administrative officer in the Admiralty and then moved into the world of finance and property development. In 1954 he joined Radio and Allied Industries Ltd, staying with them for nine years, becoming a director of GEC in 1961, and of Rolls Royce in the early 1970s. He is a trustee of the British Museum and the Royal Philharmonic Society, an Honorary Fellow of Peterhouse, Cambridge, and of the London School of Economics, and boasts a number of honorary degrees from various universities.

Baron Weinstock was knighted in 1970, and created a Life Peer in 1980. He is married with one son and one daughter and lists his hobbies as racing and music.
(See: Defence Contractors.)

Wilkins, Sir Graham John (Bob), Chairman, Thorn EMI plc

Born in 1924, Wilkins was educated at Yeovil School and University College, South West of England, Exeter. He has had many posts with the Beecham Group and is currently president of the Beecham group. He has published various papers on the pharmaceutical industry.
(See: Defence Contractors.)

Wright, Sir Patrick (Richard Henry), KCMG, Permanent Under-Secretary of State and Head of the Diplomatic Service Foreign and Commonwealth Office.

Born in 1931, Wright was educated at Marlborough and Oxford. He served in the Royal Artillery from 1950 to 1951. He joined the Diplomatic Service in1955. From 1956 to 1957 he was at the Middle East Centre for Arabic Studies. He was third secretary at the British Embassy in Beirut (1958–60) and private secretary to the Ambassador and later First Secretary at the British Embassy in Washington DC from 1960 to 1965. He spent the next two years as private secretary to the Permanent Under-Secretary of the FCO and then went to Cairo as First Secretary and Head of Chancery from 1967 to 1970. From 1971 to 1972 he was stationed in Bahrain and from 1972 to 1977 he was back in

London, first as Head of the Middle East Department in the FCO and then as private secretary to the Prime Minister with responsibility for overseas affairs. From 1977 to 1979 he was ambassador to Luxembourg and from 1979 to 1981 ambassador to Syria. He was Deputy Under-Secretary of State at the FCO from 1982 to 1984 and ambassador to Saudi Arabia from 1984 to 1986. He is married with two sons and a daughter and enjoys music, philately and walking.
(*See: Foreign and Commonwealth Office.*)

Younger, Rt Honourable George (Kenneth Hotson), MP, Secretary of State for Defence

George Younger's appointment as Secretary of State for Defence (SSD) in January 1986 apparently surprised observers, for two reasons: first, because he had just finished six-and-a-half years as Secretary of State for Scotland, a post which does not normally lead on to more important government positions; and, second, because he is at the 'wet' end of the Tory Party spectrum.

Born in 1931 the eldest son and heir of the 3rd Viscount Younger of Leckie, he first stood (unsuccessfully) for Parliament in the Labour seat of North Lanarkshire in the general election of 1959. Selected to fight the by-election at Kinross and West Perthshire in 1963, he had to stand down for Alec Douglas-Home who had disclaimed his earldom to become Prime Minister and was looking for a seat in the House of Commons. Younger was rewarded with the much less safe seat of Ayr in the 1964 general election, which he has held ever since. From 1965 to 1967 he was Scottish Conservative Party Whip and from 1970 to 1974 Parliamentary Under-Secretary of State for Development in the Scottish office, a portfolio which included industry, housing, planning and local government. He first entered the MoD in 1974, during Edward Heath's premiership, as Minister of State for Procurement. He continued there from 1975 to 1979 as Chief Opposition spokeman, a post with which he was 'rewarded' for having conducted himself with 'utter fairmindeness' in the party leadership battle in 1975 between Heath and Margaret Thatcher. After the Tory general election victory in 1979 he was appointed Secretary of State for Scotland, the prime candidate, Scottish Thatcherite Teddy Taylor, having lost his Parliamentary seat.

During his tenure in Scotland, Younger, 'ignoring the monetarist rhetoric of Whitehall... adopted a traditional interventionist Tory industrial policy, using his department's budgetary autonomy to slow down plant closures, while the new technology provided new jobs' (*The Observer*, 12 January 1986). In Cabinet he argued successfully against the closure of the Ravenscraig steel complex. His major political mistake was to underestimate the impact of Scottish rating revaluation, an issue which led to an explosion in the normally moribund Scottish Conservative Party.

Younger's popularity with the Prime Minister – despite his pursuit of a Macmillanite economic and social policy – seems to have been due to his ability to keep the lid on Scottish politics, a region in which the Tory party has traditionally been weak and which has been particularly badly hit by the economic recession. Certainly his open-mindedness in approaching Scottish plant closures earned him the respect even of his Labour critics.

In April 1986, Younger was one of only three Cabinet ministers (the other two were the Prime Minister and Foreign Secretary Sir Geoffrey Howe) who took the decision to allow US planes to fly from British bases to bomb Libya. He was reported as saying that this procedure was 'perfectly acceptable...: Nobody [in the Cabinet] has complained about it and I don't think they would' (*The Guardian*, 24 April 1986). Twelve hours before the attack, he said in a radio interview that he and his Cabinet colleagues were 'very dubious whether a military strike was the best way: it was liable to hit the wrong people and to create other tensions in the area' (*The Guardian*).

Younger was educated at Winchester (public school) and New College, Oxford. He did his military service in the Argyll and Sutherland Highlanders, serving with the BAOR in West Germany and in Korea. After university he worked in the family brewery for ten years, becoming a director in his mid-30s and eventually sales director for the wine and and spirits

division of Tennent Caledonian, which acquired the firm in 1960.
(*See: Ministers (MoD).*)

REFERENCES

Baylis, J., 1984, *Anglo-American Defence Relations, 1939–1984*, Macmillan, London.

Campbell, D., 1984, *The Unsinkable Aircraft Carrier, American Military Power in Britain*, Michael Joseph, London.

The Civil Service Year Book, 1988, 1988, HMSO, London.

Council for Science and Society, 1986, *UK Military R & D*, Oxford University Press, Oxford.

Counter Information Services, 1982, *War Lords, The UK Arms Industry*, Counter Information Services, London.

Edmonds, M., 1986, *The Defence Equation*, Brassey's, London.

Edmonds. M. (ed.), 1985, *Central Organizations of Defence*, Westview Press, Boulder Colorado/ Frances Pinter (Publishers), London

Hennessy, P., 1986, *Cabinet*, Basil Blackwell, Oxford.

Hobkirk, M. D., 1984, *The Politics of Defence Budgeting*, Macmillan/RUSI, London.

Levene, P., 1987, 'Competition and Collaboration: UK Defence Procurement Policy' in *RUSI Journal*, June 1987, Royal United Services Institute, London.

McLean, S. (ed.), 1987, *How Nuclear Weapons Decisons Are Made*, Macmillan/Oxford Research Group, London.

Miall, H., *Nuclear Weapons: Who's In Charge*, Macmillan/Oxford Research Group,London.

Pringle, P. & Arkin, W., 1983, *SIOP, Nuclear war from the inside*, Sphere Books Ltd, London.

Richelson, J. T. & Ball, D., 1985, *The Ties That Bind, Intelligence Cooperation Between the UKUSA Countries*, Allen & Unwin, London

Smith, D., 1980, *The Defence of the Realm in the 1980s*, Croom Helm, London

Smith, D. & Smith, R., 1983, *The Economics of Militarism*, Pluto Press, London.

The Central Organisation for Defence, 1984, Cmnd. 9315, HMSO, London.

Wilson, A., 1983, *The Disarmer's Handbook*, Penguin Books Ltd, Harmondsworth.

~4~

France

INTRODUCTION

France has been a nuclear power since the early 1960s. The first A-bomb was detonated on 13 February 1960, at Reganne, in the French Sahara. Yet it was not until the early 1970s that the deterrent force planned by de Gaulle in 1958 became operational. The first H-bomb was detonated in August 1968 and the first nuclear submarine, the *Redoutable*, left Cherbourg for its first operational mission in December 1971.

During the 1960s, the organization of the Armed Forces, weapons procurement and the defence sector of industry underwent revolutionary change. At first, only a handful of people supported de Gaulle in his plan for equipping France with a nuclear deterrent. These included Colonel Ailleret, General Buchalet, Perrin, and Guillaumat, who together secretly set up the administrative and industrial structures for building nuclear weapons. Part of the government and most of the armed forces were at best suspicious of and at worst opposed to the complete change in strategic thinking and command structures that would result from the introduction of such weapons. Consequently, a strong pioneering spirit and a sense of exclusiveness developed in the generation of people who had responsibility for this work. These same people either still hold the top jobs, or have only recently given them up. The individuals coming into decisionmaking posts today were working on the nuts and bolts of the new nuclear weapons systems in the early 1960s.

The strategic thinking behind the the French deterrent (formerly known as the *force de frappe* now as the *forces de dissuasion*) was also slow to develop. It was not until the mid-1960s that a small number of people put together a more or less coherent strategic rationale for the nuclear force. This was based on five principles: (1) the principle of deterrence of the strong by the weak (*dissuasion du fort par le faible*), i.e. that deterrence is effective once a minimum level of credibility (*seuil de crédibilité*) has been reached; (2) the notion of defence of the national sanctuary (*défense du sanctuaire national*) i.e. that nuclear weapons would only be used in the last resort when the national territory was threatened; (3) the political concept of independence from the two blocs (*indépendance vis-à-vis des deux blocs*), i.e. that France would no longer be part of the military structure of NATO and would make gestures towards the non-aligned group of nations; (4) the strategy of 'anti-city' targeting (*stratégie anti cités*); and (5) the idea that the French strategic deterrent would only be credible if all three of its constituent components (*composantes complémentaires*) were operational: the submarines, the bombers and the ground–launched missiles. Shortly afterwards another principle was added, namely that tactical nuclear weapons should be used as the 'ultimate warning' before a nuclear exchange, rather than as battlefield weapons.

By the time these basic 'Gaullist' principles were enshrined in the Defence White Book (*Livre blanc de la défense*) of 1972, visible cracks were already appearing in this strategic construction, and these cracks grew larger thereafter. The strategic situation changed in the mid–1970s. Right-wing politicians, among them President Giscard d'Estaing, came to power, who paid only lip-service to the Gaullist principles. The French nuclear forces were undergoing a major overhaul. The people working in nuclear weapons research, development and procurement, who often had a free rein in developing their own concepts, had little time for Gaullist strategy.

The nuclear deterrent force is now a *fait accompli*, imbedded into the French military and political landscape; but the technical and strategic potential of the new weapons, together with the new thinking about war which has emerged in the political generation which came to power after de Gaulle, have produced a complete lack of coherence in official strategy thinking in France.

Political events since 1981 have intensified this incoherence. In 1981, François Mitterrand was elected President of the Republic. There followed five years of socialist government from 1981 to 1986, and, from March 1986 until May 1988 the new phenomenon of *cohabitation* between the socialist President and the right-wing Prime Minister, Jacques Chirac, both of whom had real power. These developments allowed deep confrontations to exist, albeit in a state of apparently suspended animation behind a façade of national consensus on the nuclear deterrent.

The existence in France of a very bureaucratic political regime (with a strong and technocratic executive and a relatively weak parliament), dominated by a relatively homogeneous decisionmaking elite does not mean that there is little debate about future nuclear weapons. On the contrary, very heated debates take place, albeit muffled and hardly visible to the public. They are fuelled by the uncertainties of French nuclear strategy and by the conflicts between the corporate interests of the various institutions involved — the Délégation Générale pour l'Armement, the Commissariat à l'Energie Atomique, the Army, the Navy, the Air Force and the arms manufacturers. The same personnel are often exchanged among these institutions, forming a somewhat incestuous community in which confrontations over strategic and institutional policies take place using coded means of communication behind a veil of consensus and technocratic efficiency.

Current Issues

There is a certain irony in the fact that the recent focus of debate on the nuclear deterrent and procurement policy has been between a 'socialist' President, François Mitterrand, who now holds relatively orthodox 'Gaullist' views after having been the main parliamentary opponent of them for many years, and a right-wing Prime Minister, Jacques Chirac, and Minister of Defence, André Giraud, who were in principle the heirs of Gaullist strategic doctrine but who, in practice, have expressed views which are closer to the official nuclear strategy thinking of NATO.

'FLEXIBLE RESPONSE' VERSUS 'ULTIMATE WARNING'

President Mitterrand has put forward a policy based on the theory of pure deterrence applied to the defence of the 'national sanctuary' in which tactical nuclear weapons function not as battlefield weapons but as the 'ultimate warning' before strategic weapons are used (hence the euphemism for tactical weapons: *préstratégiques*, rather than *tactiques*). Giraud and Chirac, by contrast, when they were in power, presented a watered down version of NATO's 'flexible response' strategy and spoke of 'uncoupling' strategic and tactical nuclear weapons, in order to 'couple' conventional military forces with tactical nuclear weapons. On several occasions they hinted that the neutron bomb should be put into production.

The strategic debate in France since the early 1960s produced a number of concepts which were not put into practice. The best known of them is probably the *défense tous azimuts* (defence against all sides) suggested by General Ailleret, the Chef d'État Major des Armées (Army Chief of Staff), in 1965. This theory was never incorporated into official thinking, even though the media continued to use it as a synonym for the independent deterrent.

In 1976 President Giscard d'Estaing and his Supreme Chief of Staff, General Mery, proposed the concepts of 'frontline battle' (*bataille de l'avant*) and of 'enlarged sanctuary' (*sanctuaire élargi*). Both these concepts link the employment of nuclear weapons to the invasion of West Germany, rather than waiting for the front-line to reach the French border. A further move was made in a seminal defence document produced by the right-wing UDF party, in which it was argued that tactical nuclear weapons should be used to halt (*un coup d'arrêt brutal*) invading Warsaw Pact troops, rather than as an 'ultimate warning'.

Tactical nuclear weapons had in fact been conceived not as a weapon of warning, but as weapons for fighting on the battlefield. They had been produced as a result of an alliance between the Commissariat à l'Énergie Atomique (the CEA, which designs French nuclear warheads), and the Army, which wanted to recover a strategic role, having been deprived of its former primacy by the creation of a deterrent force based on the Navy's submarines and the Air Force's bombers and missiles.

The attempts of all the political leaders, and especially of Mitterrand, Chirac and Giraud, to maintain the appearance of consensus on nuclear weapons has been breaking down. In an interview in *Le Nouvel Observateur* (18–24 December 1987), François Mitterrand agreed that he was isolated internationally in his opposition to NATO's 'flexible response' doctrine. He added that ' French nuclear weapons, whatever their nature, strategic or prestrategic, are part of a whole. This whole is the autonomous strategy of nuclear deterrence, from which no part can be differentiated or placed under any authority other than that of the President of the Republic'. He insisted stubbornly that he agreed with Chirac. Chirac, however, had declared in a lecture given a few days earlier that 'An ultimate warning, if one is needed, will be diversified and staged in depth', and that 'there cannot be a battle of Germany and a battle of France'. Similarly, Giraud, the Minister of Defence, in an interview given in October 1987 to the right-wing paper *Le Figaro* hinted strongly that the NATO and US flexible response strategy was the only coherent way of defending Europe (16 October 1987). None of them, however, were willing to undermine the artificial consensus before the 1988 presidential election.

Many other issues are indirectly related to the issue of when and how tactical nuclear weapons would be used. One is how France should behave in relation to its allies, especially in Europe. Mitterrand favours bilateral or strictly European initiatives. A major bilateral initiative was taken in the autumn of 1987: the military co-operation provisions of the 1963 Franco-German Treaty were reactivated, with the creation of a Common Defence Council; this was followed by the decision to organize a Franco-German army brigade. The Force d'Action Rapide was set up in 1983 and took part in large-scale manoeuvres in West Germany in 1987, which demonstrated the French army's capacity to 'help' their German allies. Giraud, the former Minister of Defence, on the other hand, preferred better co-ordination of French resources with NATO, although the idea of a common command was still taboo.

THE MODERNIZATION OF THE FRENCH NUCLEAR ARSENAL

One of the main problems of French nuclear deterrence is the search for the elusive *seuil de crédibilité*: at what stage of development will French nuclear weapons be taken seriously by a potential aggressor and, in the short term, by the two superpowers? In this search for credibility, which sometimes smacks of the yearning of a second-ranking nation for world-power status, what counts is not so much the total megatonnage in the arsenal, but the capability of keeping up with new technical developments. The French deterrent has often been overtaken by such developments.

A number of first generation and second generation weapon systems are simply not 'credible' any more. This is the case with the current airborne strategic deterrent, the ageing Mirage IV. Even when updated for low altitude penetration flight and equipped with the sophisticated ASMP missile, the Mirage IV will not be a match for the advanced anti-aircraft missile systems of the 1990s; it will also be dependent on mid-air refuelling. Similarly, the Pluton tactical ground-launched missiles were obsolete as soon as they were commissioned, and even before commissioning no place for them had been found within the strategic thinking of French decisionmakers.

Another, even more important, reason for accelerated modernization of nuclear weapons systems is the efficiency of the Direction des Applications Militaires of the CEA, the Délégation Générale pour l'Armement of the Ministry of Defence, and of the various public and private arms manufacturers, in researching and developing new generations of weapons, sometimes years before officials and politicians are involved in the decisionmaking process. A well-known example is the description given of the ASMP missile and the neutron bomb in the CEA's Annual Report in 1973, years before they were officially approved for development. More recently, Alain Vidart, head of the Direction des Applications Militaires has spoken of 'special purpose nuclear weapons now being researched and developed at the CEA military *centres d'études'*. In a sense, the final stages of the decisionmaking process are already decided when the research and development stage has been completed. This does not mean, however, that conflicts do not emerge in the way new nuclear weapons systems are developed, ordered and deployed.

Recently, the two most important such conflicts concerned the future S4 strategic missile system, and the future Rafale aircraft (the French response to the Eurofighter) which would be used for tactical nuclear weapons deployment. The S4 debate gives a good indication of the issues currently being debated. The first studies on this mobile strategic missile system, then called SX, were launched in 1977. In 1981 the Defence Council took the decision to develop it. The problem is that these missiles with multiple warheads are expensive to develop and build. They are due to replace the land-based SSBS missiles on the Plateau d'Albion as well as the Mirage IV P-launched strategic missiles. As such, they would complement the SNLEs, the nuclear submarines; they are thus called the 'second component'. Former Minister of Defence Giraud, in his 1987 budget (presented in autumn 1986), decided that the cost of the S4 development was such that it would have to be compensated for by abandoning the retrofitting of one of the first generation SNLEs with new missiles. This move was opposed by the Navy and also by President Mitterrand who regards the submarine component as the ultimate, and only true, deterrent.

The Power of a Technocratic Elite in Decisionmaking Bodies

The top civil servants and officials who serve in French ministerial cabinets, departments and other governmental institutions, as well as the top managerial layer in public and private corporations which manufacture weapons systems, are all the products of a very small and elitist training system known as the *grandes écoles*. In the military weapons procurement world, one *grande école* dominates and this is the École Polytechnique, which is under the aegis of the Délégation Générale pour l'Armement of the Ministry of Defence.

Some 90 per cent of the decisionmakers whose biographies are presented in this chapter were educated at the École Polytechnique. This institution is directed by an army general, currently General Dominique Chevanat, and entry is dependent on success in an extremely selective examination process (called a *concours*, a competition). Graduates of the École Polytechnique, known as *les X*, are either 'bought out' by large companies (which reimburse the DGA for the cost of the students' studies), or are designated to follow complementary training in order to enter the special corps of civil servants or state engineers — called *corps de l'état*, or *grands corps*. The best known are the *ingénieurs des mines, des ponts et chaussées, des télécommunications*, and the *ingénieurs généraux de l'armement*, or IGA, who form most of the higher echelons of the Délégation Générale pour l'Armement. The CEA is mostly made up of *ingénieurs des mines*.

Another *grande école* which has a significant influence on decisionmaking in France is the École Nationale d'Administration (ENA). Graduates of the ENA, the so-called *énarques*, fill the ranks of ministerial cabinets and the highest levels of the civil service. But in the decisionmaking bodies concerned directly with military procurement (and especially with nuclear weapons procurement), the graduates of the École Polytechnique are in a majority. In a recent article, General Chavanat estimated (in *Armées d'Aujourd'hui*, no. 117, February 1987, SIRPA) that a quarter of all currently active *polytechniciens* are working in defence, directly or indirectly. Around 1,300 of them are employed by the Ministry of Defence, including around 1,000 *ingénieurs généraux de l'armement* (IGAs) working in the Délégation Général pour l'Armement (DGA); and around 270 are seconded to various sensitive posts, mainly in aerospace, electronics and in bodies such as the Directions des Applications Militaires (DAM) of the Commissariat à l'Énergie Atomique (CEA).

It is thus a relatively closed world, in which informal networks of co-operation and information develop to ease the working conditions of the system. As will be seen later, most top decisionmakers have come across each other in the various weapon procurement institutions and know each other very well. Not infrequently, people who were in high command posts in the armed forces a decade or less ago now hold positions of responsibility in large manufacturing firms. It would, however, be wrong to assume, because of the closeness of this highly professional elite, that the system runs smoothly and without conflicts. In fact there are rigid defences of individual and institutional power, and daily conflict. Unlike more public conflicts, however, these are highly coded and are between people of the same culture and same world, and of course rarely see the light of day.

The Main Institutions and Decisionmaking Bodies

In theory, there are five areas of responsibility in the decisionmaking process:

– *The political sphere*, headed by the supreme authority of the President, with the Conseil de Défense as the main instrument. The Prime Minister and other ministers (especially the Interior and Foreign Ministers) are also part of the system. Several small advisory administration bodies assist their work, especially the Secrétariat Général de la Défense Nationale (SGDN), and the various *cabinets* (private offices) of ministers. Parliament has singularly little impact in this sphere, with the exception of some indirect influence exerted through the vote on the Defence Budget and debates on defence programme law. These debates frame military equipment developments and budgets for the next four or five years. The permanent parliamentary committee on defence (the Commission Parlementaire de la Défense et des Forces Armées) also debates defence issues.

– *The Ministry of Defence*. The Minister himself has specific responsibilities, and is helped by several advisory bodies. But the most important part of the Ministry, as far nuclear weapons development and procurement are concerned, is the Délégation Générale pour l'Armement (DGA), a large and powerful administration, relatively autonomous from other central departments and administrations, which controls its own research centres, manufacturing and assembly plants (especially for tanks, guns and naval equipment), has close relationships with the private and public military equipment manufacturers, and helps them with exports.

– *The Commissariat à l'Énergie Atomique*, through its huge Direction des Applications Militaires (DAM) is entirely responsible for researching, developing, producing and maintaining nuclear warheads. (Delivery systems are the responsibility of the DGA and other bodies.) The DAM is a secretive department, hardly accountable in political terms, and practically autonomous in terms of research and development.

– *The weapons manufacturing industry*, which builds aircraft, parts, missiles, tankers, and electronic and communication equipment for nuclear weapons systems. Part of it is directly controlled by the DGA of the Ministry of Defence (the state arsenals), part is comprised of large-scale nationalized firms (such as Aérospatiale or AMD–BA) and private firms (for instance Matra, recently privatized).

– *The military*. The three services and the four all-powerful Chiefs of Staff have seen their organization, traditions and power base change dramatically since the early 1960s and the end

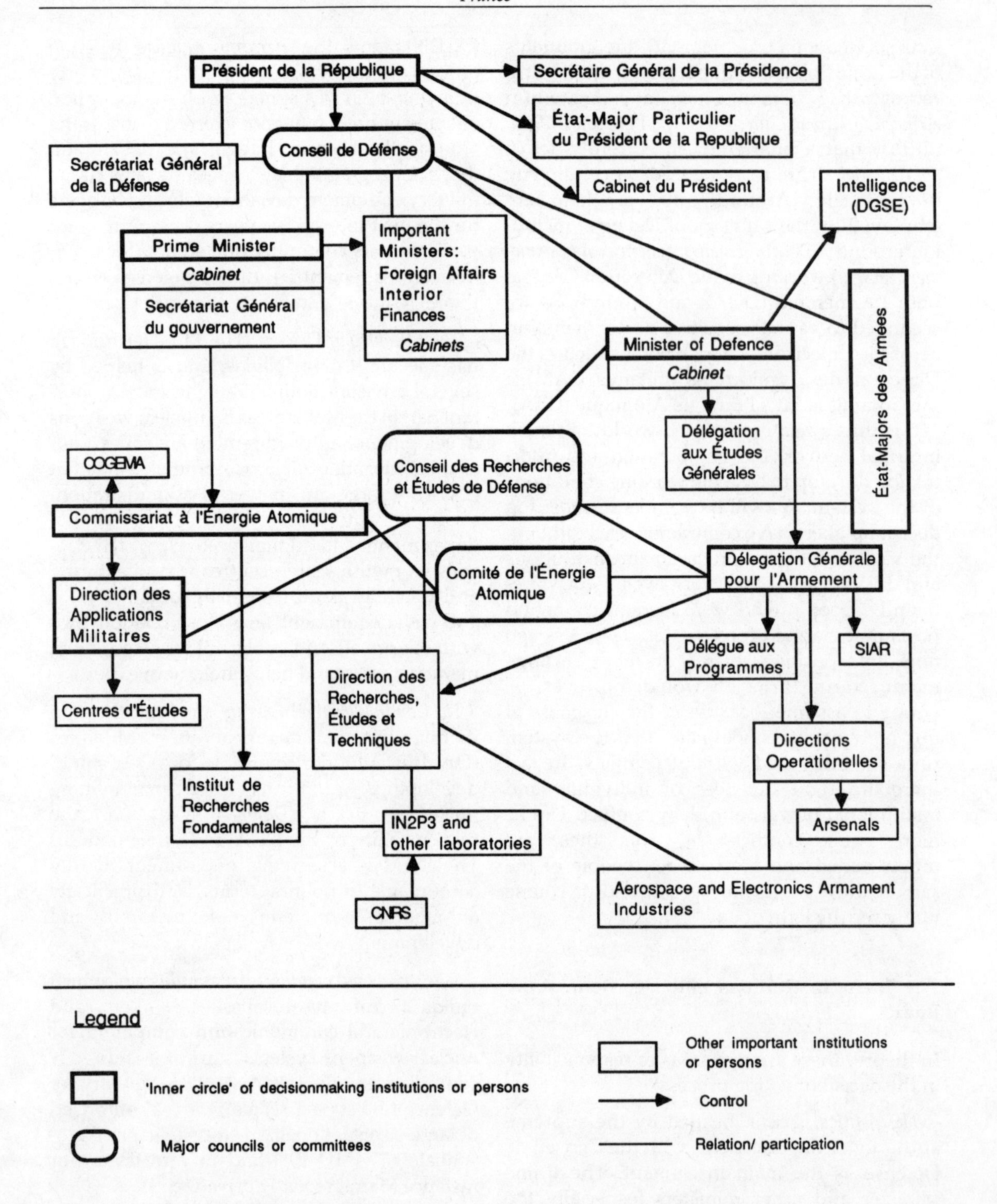

Figure 4.1 *Some of the main bodies and spheres of nuclear weapon decisionmaking in France*

of the colonial wars. The emergence of the nuclear deterrent was obviously a strong factor in this change, a deterrent that de Gaulle forced upon the military, but the use and control of which they would not now relinquish at any cost.

The five main sections which follow each cover one of the five areas outlined above. Some institutions which do not fit neatly into this classification, such as fundamental research institutions which are funded for defence work, are dealt with, when the need arises, in the context of these five areas.

The life-cycle of a weapons system typically divides into a number of stages. These include fundamental research, applications research, R & D, evaluation and production. Different decisionmaking organizations are involved at different stages of this process. The bodies in charge of the second and third stages, applications research and R & D, are those which in many instances control the system: they have the power to direct the key years of development work, which is increasingly costly. Once substantial sums have been spent and many different bodies are involved, it becomes increasingly unlikely that a system will be cancelled. Figure 4.1 gives an overview of the principal decisionmaking bodies that are covered in later sections, and of the main phases of development in which they are involved.

The various bodies, in theory, define their needs well in advance. But in many instances the requirements defined by the military, political or strategy-making authorities conflict. They also conflict with the requirements of the industries involved in weapons production, which often develop systems well in advance of an expressed military or strategic need.

In order to reconcile these conflicts, there are a number of main councils of co-ordination and decisionmaking which also have a central role in setting a clear direction for weapons development policy; several of them are shown in Figure 4.1. Besides the Délégation des Études Générales (formerly GroupeS), the Minister of Defence's strategic think tank and a very highly informed advisory body, there are three bodies of importance: first, the Defence Research and Studies Council (Conseil des Recherches et Études de Défense: CRED) which is presided over by the Minister of Defence, and makes R & D policy. It includes people such as the DGA, the four Chiefs of Staff of the Armed Forces, and the head of the DAM. Secondly, there is the Nuclear Energy Committee (Comité de l'Énergie Atomique), which advises the head of the CEA and co-ordinates R & D, partly for military purposes. Thirdly, there is the Defence Council (Conseil de Défense), which is the highest defence decisionmaking and co-ordinating body in France, identified as such in the constitution. It is chaired by the President, includes the Prime Minister and the Ministers of Defence, Interior, Finance and Foreign Affairs, the four Chiefs of Staff and the General Secretary of National Defence.

In addition there are various planning tools which provide a shared framework for defence planning. These include the annual defence budget which either directly or indirectly funds or stops the funding of projects; and the Annual Ministerial Guidelines (DMO) established within the Defence Ministry by the DEG (formerly GroupeS). These Guidelines range from strategic objectives down to single research objectives. They are incorporated in the Triennial Research and Studies Programmes which each relate to a theme of R & D, or in the Triennial Exploratory Development Programmes, which are more forward looking. It should be noted that the DMOs are not directly concerned with nuclear-warhead development, but with R & D on delivery and command systems.

A third vehicle for setting out defence plans is the *loi de programmation militaire*. This is a programme, normally covering five years, voted by Parliament, which fixes the budget lines for a number of equipment programmes and describes their development. It is usually rapidly superseded by events in military procurement, but nevertheless it provides an opportunity to air some of the main problems and to frame a sort of consensus. Currently, the sixth such law is in force, to apply from 1987 to 1991, with a revision in the 1989 budget.

Finally, when conflicts are not resolved by the co-ordinating councils or at lower levels, they reach the political level. This is addressed in the next section.

THE POLITICAL SPHERE

Since the French weapons procurement system is dominated by a narrow bureaucratic elite and powerful industries such as the CEA and Aérospatiale, it is easy to forget the central role played by the political process. However, it was a politician, de Gaulle, who broke the traditional patterns of the military hierarchy and the weapons industry to insist on nuclear weapons. More recently, considerable lobbying efforts by the CEA and DGA have not succeeded in getting the neutron bomb deployed, simply because it is not acceptable politically.

The politicians (who nowadays often come from the same mould as the technical and managerial leaders of weapons procurement institutions) play a central role in nuclear issues in a number of ways, even if the research and development stage does for all practical purposes shape many political decisions:

– they are responsible for the ultimate decisions about whether to maintain, and whether to use, nuclear weapons;

– they are decisionmakers on institutional structures and on budgets;

– they have the power of appointment;

– they are mediators between factions, lobbies and conflicting interests (evident recently in the Rafale case and on the aircraft carrier issue);

– they can block weapons systems, and influence broad strategic issues;

– they are a source for the legitimization of power, where nuclear weaponry is in a sense pre-digested for the whole society and where rhetorical talk has a definite purpose in making sense of the decisionmaking process.

The most important position is obviously that of the President of the Republic. Other important positions are those of the Prime Minister, who has special Constitutional defence prerogatives, the Minister of Defence and various other core ministers. Each has his own advisers and counsellors in his own private office, known as a *cabinet*. Then there are influential bodies which fall under the authority of politicians, for example the Secrétariat National de la Défense Nationale.

The Presidency of the Republic

A commentator has called the French President the 'nuclear monarch'. He is effectively the person who would press the so-called button, which is in fact an electronic code. He is also invested with considerable military powers through the Constitution; indeed the Constitutional change which modified the method of election of a French President came close on the heels of the first French nuclear bomb explosion.

The basic powers of the President are derived from Articles 5 and 15 of the Constitution. He is 'guarantor of national independence, of territorial integrity and of the respect of treaties. He is the chief of the armed forces and he chairs the councils and committees of national defence.' There are however some problems in defining the relative powers of the Prime Minister and the President, partly because of Article 19, which requires the Prime Minister's countersignature for most presidential acts, including defence, and partly because of Article 21 which designates the Prime Minister as 'responsible for national defence'.

The primacy of the role of the President has however become more and more accepted. Since 1962 his election has been by universal vote, giving him a national legitimacy which the Prime Minister lacks. Decrees passed in 1959, 1962 and 1964 have made his powers wider and less ambiguous. The decree dated 18 July 1962 interprets Article 21 of the Constitution to give the Prime Minister responsibility only for the means of defence — a restrictive interpretation. More significantly, the decree dated 14 January 1964 declares that nuclear forces can be engaged and launched only by a presidential order. Interestingly, this decree was attacked as unconstitutional at the time by a leader of the opposition — François Mitterrand. The President also chairs the Council of Ministers as well as the Defence Council, the two most senior decisionmaking bodies.

The President is advised by a number of key people, some who have power in their own right and some who are simply counsellors in his private *cabinet*. Among the most important are the Chief of Staff, the Chef de l'Etat-Major

Particulier du Président de la République. He is a very high-ranking officer, usually an admiral, a general or an air vice marshal, invested with the full confidence of his peers, and of the President. This post is usually a step on the way to the very top of the armed forces, as Chief of Staff or Joint Chief of Staff. The head of the President's private office, his Directeur de Cabinet, is his administrative right hand, knows all the files and often has to conduct delicate and discreet negotiations with other ministers. This post is not to be confused with another statutory function, that of Secrétaire Général de la Présidence de la République, usually filled by someone with political influence who also knows all the files. Other advisers are less easy to pin down in the sense of an organizational chart; they are often old political friends who have followed the President during his political career. Some are influential in defence matters and some are not.

The remaining body which is important in advising the President is the General Secretariat for National Defence, the Secrétariat Général de la Défense Nationale or SGDN. Its functions were defined by a decree passed on 25 January 1978. Formally the SGDN is responsible to the Prime Minister but, in practice, the President receives important support from this body.

(See biographies of: Attali (Special Adviser to President); Bianco (General Secretary of the Presidency); Fleury (Personal Chief of Staff); Ménage (Head of Private Office); Mitterrand.)

The Prime Minister and the Institutions of Government

THE PRIME MINISTER

The Prime Minister is chosen by the President, normally from the party that enjoys a parliamentary majority. According to the Constitution, the Prime Minister's function is to 'direct the work of the government' (Article 20). In defence matters, he is 'responsible for national defence...and for nominations to civil and military posts' (Article 21). The Prime Minister is also in charge of preparing the 'overall defence programme' (*ordonnance* 7 January 1959) and of overseeing the 'general organization of defence'.

Decree No. 62–808 of 18 July 1962 provides a more limited interpretation of the Prime Minister's powers with respect to defence matters than Article 21: the Prime Minister was now required merely to ensure 'the execution of government decisions'; the Cabinet and the Defence Council, rather than the Prime Minister, were now to be responsible for national defence.

The Constitutional changes of 1962, which introduced national presidential elections, increased the powers of the President relative to those of the Prime Minister. This was particularly the case in the area of defence. Decree No. 64–46 of 14 January 1964, which dealt with 'strategic air forces', gave the President sole control over the use of nuclear forces.

Until 1968 the view of the Prime Minister as the faithful executor of the President's policies predominated. The first sign of change came from Prime Minister Georges Pompidou, who presented himself as offering the only solution to France's problems even before de Gaulle had resigned as President. The second sign came in 1976 when Prime Minister Jacques Chirac resigned over policies of President Giscard d'Estaing, with which he did not agree. However, the full extent of the strain in the relationship between President and Prime Minister became evident in 1986, when a socialist President, Mitterrand, had to nominate a conservative Prime Minister, Chirac. Chirac announced loudly that he would not respect the tradition of leaving two spheres of policymaking, foreign affairs and defence, in the hands of the President; he would intervene in them to the full extent allowed by the Constitution. In addition, although the Prime Minister controls the government, the President chairs the Cabinet, and, according to the Constitution, 'nominates the members of government according to the proposal of the Prime Minister'. But that Cabinet follows policies devised by the Prime Minister rather than the President. The Prime Minister is a very influential member of the Conseil de Défense, and he controls the Joint Ministry Committee for Intelligence (Comité Interministériel du Renseignement). It is difficult to predict how power will be shared in future between the President and the Prime Minister, particularly in defence matters.

The Prime Minister's Advisers

As with the President's advisers, the Prime Minister's immediate collaborators can be separated into two groups: personal advisers, (members of the inner circle of old political friends, often in charge of difficult questions) and, in the other group, civil servants who form the official private office. For the Prime Minister, the most important of these is the Head of the Private Office (Directeur du Cabinet): often a member of a prestigious administration (such as the diplomatic corps or the *préfets*) who has gained a wide experience previously. He is in charge of organizing the Prime Minister's political manoeuvring and contacts and, therefore, will know of all the major decisions or problems, including those in the area of nuclear defence. Another close collaborator of the Prime Minister's staff is the Secrétaire Général du Gouvernement (SGG), whose role is a truly secretarial one concerning the Cabinet (Conseil des Ministres) in terms of preparation and follow-up. Usually, a relatively independent figure among high ranking civil servants is selected, often continuing from one government to another. The SGG participates in the Cabinet meetings (the weekly Conseil des Ministres) and most of the meetings of the inner Cabinet.

The Cabinet (Conseil des Ministres)

The Vth Republic Constitution expressly gives the Cabinet a number of defence responsibilities. The Cabinet, chaired by the President, is to 'determine and conduct the nation's policies' (Article 20). The government 'has the armed forces at its disposal'.

Does that mean that the government has a real say, as a collective institution, in nuclear defence policymaking and nuclear weapons procurement? The answer, in fact, is no: the Cabinet mostly deliberates on decisions which have already been taken either by the President or by the 'inner circle' of defence policymaking, which is the Conseil de Défense (Defence Council) — see below. However, the Cabinet is important in several respects: nominations to the highest army and administration posts are made there, as well as to the top jobs in the nationalized industries (including those in armament manufacturing); laws and important decrees affecting defence are finalized in Cabinet before being presented to parliament. There is a similar process for the budget and the programming laws on defence (see Parliament). In these respects, the important people within the Cabinet are probably exactly the same as those who are members of the Defence Council.

The Defence Council (Conseil de Défense)

The Defence Council is the highest power in defence policymaking in all its aspects — from strategic policymaking to weapons research and development. It was created by the Constitutional Decree No. 59–147 dated 7 January 1959, concerned with 'the general organization of defence'. The responsibility of the Defence Council is indeed to 'deal with the general direction of defence' (Article 7 of the decree). The decree dated 14 January 1964 also gives to the Defence Council the responsibility of taking decisions on the mission, the organization and the conditions of launching strategic nuclear forces. In case of crisis or war, the Defence Council would be the natural war cabinet, and many of its members would in fact directly have emergency powers: the President can engage the nuclear forces and can invoke Article 16 of the Constitution, which gives him total power of a quasi-dictatorial nature; the Cabinet can declare a state of siege (giving extra power to the military authorities) and can declare general mobilization.

The Defence Council is, therefore, the focal point of nuclear weapons policymaking, on two grounds: firstly, on the grounds of its composition — all its members having important responsibilities in their own right, and, secondly, because it is seen as the centre of power as a collective body.

The members of the Defence Council are:

– the President of the Republic, its chairman;

– the Prime Minister;

– the Minister of Defence, the Minister for Foreign Affairs, the Minister for the Interior, the Minister of Finance;

– the General Secretary for National Defence (Secrétaire Général de la Défense Nationale);

– the three Chiefs of Staff (Army, Air Force, Navy) and the Joint Armed Forces Chief of Staff.

The President can also request the presence of other decisionmakers or military leaders, depending on the subjects being covered. For instance the CEA's General Director might be called, or its Director of Military Applications, or the Ministry of Defence's General Delegate for Armament.

In any case, the presence of a person on the Council would be sufficient to insure his or her listing as a real decisionmaker, even if (as is the case of the Secrétaire Général à la Défense Nationale) this person is only there on a secretarial or advisory basis.

The Prime Minister can in some instances ask for a Conseil de Défense Restreint, which only groups some of the Defence Council members, but which is in principle still chaired by the President.

Is the Defence Council the real decisionmaking body on nuclear weapons matters? This Council might not be the initiator of most first development decisions; it intervenes mostly in two circumstances, either to start the construction of a weapon at the end of the research, development and integration process, or to resolve at the highest level some dispute between ministers, administrators or developers. But, because it is difficult for the Defence Council to follow every file, it is certain that the important R & D stages are in fact controlled by bodies such as the DRET and the CRED of the Délégation Générale pour l'Armement, and the DAM of the Commissariat à l'Énergie Atomique.

The Defence Council infrequently appears on the front page. Both cases occurring in recent years were related to changes in the political framework of weapons procurement. The first was the meeting of 30 October 1982, which announced an acceleration of the nuclear programme by the socialist President and government (through the construction of the new ground-launched tactical missiles Hadès, the decision to develop the new SX mobile ballistic missile and the construction of a seventh ballistic missile submarine) and signalled a relatively unexpected continuation of the deterrence strategy by Mitterrand. (He justified it as the response to new information on the international situation, made available to him in a number of Council meetings in 1981, especially on Soviet military reinforcement.)

More recently, on 30 October 1986, the Defence Council put the finishing touches to the new 6th Defence Programming law for 1987–91 established by the newly elected conservative Chirac government, replacing the 'socialist' programming law of 1984–88.

Under the Chirac government, small interministry committees comprised of the Prime Minister and two or three relevant ministers often took important decisions outside the usual councils. A typical case is the issue of the Rafale advanced fighter aircraft, on which Minister of Defence Giraud and the Navy were completely opposed to Prime Minister Chirac, the Air Force and the Dassault firm. After many incidents and changes of policy, the final decision to go ahead and build two supplementary prototype aircraft was taken in an interministerial committee on 28 January 1988.

THE SECRÉTARIAT GÉNÉRAL À LA DÉFENSE NATIONALE (SGDN)

This Secretariat is a central tool of co-ordination in defence policy, despite its lack of power. It was first created by Article 2 of Decree No. 62–808 dated 18 July 1962 concerning the organization of national defence, as a tool for the Prime Minister to implement defence policies decided by the government. The responsibilities of the SGDN were last established by a decree dated 25 January 1978. It is responsible for fulfilling functions for the Prime Minister and the President at several levels:

– to prepare and follow up the decisions taken by the Defence Council;

– to assist the Prime Minister concerning the general direction of defence policy (such as general thinking on strategic affairs, or co-ordination between ministries concerning civil and economic defence, or co-ordination of governmental command systems);

– to exercise various defence functions such as co-ordinating with the Ministry of Defence on defence-oriented scientific and technical research, secrecy policy, control of weapons export policy, etc., which all indirectly touch on nuclear weapons policy.

In terms of research, the SGDN controls the Comité d'Action Scientifique de la Défense, created in 1978, which co-ordinates at inter-ministerial level between eight relevant ministries on defence research. The Committee's function is specifically to liaise with the DGA and university research.

The SGDN has recently seen its functions concerning military and weapons secrecy being reinforced, especially in the field of electronic communication (see decree dated 28 October 1987).

The SGDN is made up of a great variety of personnel coming from all areas — from the army, the university or the armament engineers. With the exception of the present incumbent, the General Secretary has been chosen from the military, and his deputy is usually a diplomat.

Most of the work of this body is organized through other specialized agencies. For instance, its scientific and technical research co-ordinating role is carried out by the Comité d'Action Scientifique de la Défense, composed of eight members named by various ministers and intended to co-ordinate and keep in contact with research bodies and the DGA.

A second dependent body is the Institut des Hautes Études de Défense Nationale (IHEDN) — an annual think-tank attended by a hundred or so people from various professional origins, but all with defence links, and taking the form of a weekly seminar. Always an open forum in which various views could be aired, it is now even more important since the 'Gaullist' defence approach has been broken. The Prime Minister usually gives a lecture each year to the IHEDN, which has some weight in defence politics.

THE INDIVIDUAL MINISTERS

The ministers have a collective defence responsibility, through the Cabinet and, for four of them, through the Defence Council. These four ministers — Defence, Foreign Affairs, Finance, Interior — are important people in nuclear weapons matters in this respect. But, as in many countries, individual ministers are also important in defence matters because of their individual powers; for instance the Minister for Posts and Communications would be responsible for putting communication networks at the disposal of the armed forces in case of conflict. Specifically, every ministry in France is equipped with an Haut Fonctionnaire de Défense in charge of following up these specific defence responsibilities.

However, in terms of nuclear weapons development, few ministers have sizeable responsibilities. Apart from the four listed above the only other to be noted is the Minister for Industry, for two reasons: he is the minister in charge of the Commissariat à l'Énergie Atomique, one of whose departments is responsible for the procurement of radioactive materials and which can influence policies on uranium procurement and enrichment. (In France there is little separation between military and civil radioactive material procurement.)

The Foreign Office itself has very little influence directly on nuclear weapons policy and development. Its influence is largely indirect — the Minister for Foreign Affairs is part of the Defence Council, and traditionally a number of diplomats get jobs in defence-related posts, such as deputy secretary of the SGDN. Another area of influence is related to international negotiations on disarmament and on defence related treaties, areas covered by the Political Affairs Department, with two sections concentrating most of the work in this field: the Office of Strategic Affairs and Disarmament, and the Office of Atomic and Outer-Space

Affairs. But the Foreign Office has always been a lightweight in the defence politics of the Vth Republic. Under de Gaulle, the Foreign Minister was more of a servant fulfilling the President's wishes. After de Gaulle's resignation in 1969, foreign ministers gained more weight, but they still cannot be said to be important policymakers on nuclear issues.

The Ministry of Finance (which takes different titles according to the government — in the previous government it was the Ministry of the Economy, Finances and Privatizations and now it is the Ministry of the Economy, Finances and Budget) is far more important, albeit in a reactive rather than a policymaking way. Guardian of the financial orthodoxy and of the budgetary and taxation prerogatives of the executive, this ministry attracts some of the brighter products of ENA and the Polytechnique. In the best tradition, the ministry plays a sophisticated game of budgetary control of each spending ministry. Furthermore, the Vth Republic Constitution prevents the Assemblée Nationale from increasing public expenditure or significantly modifying the budget as presented to it by the government. All this makes the ministry a powerful administration.

The Ministry of the Interior has specific responsibilities concerning defence, largely in civil defence, for which it is the central organizing body and the co-ordinating organization between all the other ministers involved (these functions are described in the *ordonnance* of 1959). The Ministry also controls the counter-intelligence service (the Direction de la Surveillance du Territoire or DST) and the domestic intelligence services (the so-called Renseignements Généraux). It would obviously be responsible for law and order, and even population repression, in case of a crisis situation, for which it could ask for army support. However, in the case of an *état de siège* being declared by Parliament (a case which would occur in a war situation with a nuclear risk), the military authorities would take over the responsibilities of the Ministry of the Interior.

All the ministries — and not only those listed above — have specific defence responsibilities, organizing and preparing resources in their area in case of conflict. For instance, according to the 1959 *ordonnance*, the Minister of Finance is responsible for directing 'for purposes of defence the action of ministers responsible for producing, gathering and using various types of resources, as well as that of the country's industrial planning'. Every ministry receives the support of a Haut Fonctionnaire de Défense, originating from the DGA of the Defence Ministry, for the preparation of such defence functions.

(See biographies of: Bérégovoy (Minister of Finance); Dejean de la Batie (Deputy General Secretary of Defence); Denoix de Saint-Marc (Government General Secretary); Dumas (Minister of Foreign Affairs); Fougier (Secretary General of National Defence); Fouroux (Minister of Industry and Export); Huchon (Director of Prime Minister's Private Office) ; Joxe (Minister of Interior); Rocard (Prime Minister); Syrota (Minister of Industry).

The Parliamentary Institutions

One might ask why parliamentary institutions should be included in an account of nuclear weapons decisionmaking in France. The two chambers of the parliament — the Assemblée Nationale and the Sénat — have very few powers anyway, and especially few in defence.

The Constitution of the Fifth Republic limits the powers of the Assemblée in the two crucial areas of legislation and budgetary control. In the case of legislation, the control of the parliamentary agenda by the executive ensures that only government projects are examined and voted on. In the debate about the budget, amendments to bills may not increase the level of expenditure, nor transfer expenditures from one line item to another. A more general cause of weakness of the French parliament stems from the fact that, since 1962, popular legitimacy has been shared between the Assemblée Nationale and the President, since both are elected.

Another aspect of parliament's lack of power stems from the fact that the government is not constituted in such a way as to represent the parliamentary distribution of seats. De Gaulle's distaste for what he derogatorily called the 'game of the political parties' was such that, when he founded the Fifth Republic in 1958, he made sure that the executive could not be formed simply by proportional representation of parliament, as it had been during the Fourth Republic. Consequently, ministers have to resign their parliamentary seats when chosen, and some are not even MPs — they can be 'technical ministers', like Giraud, the Minister of Defence in the 1986–88 Chirac government, who has never held an elective mandate.

The period of *cohabitation*, however, gave Parliament a new feeling of importance, largely because Jacques Chirac, the Prime Minister, made the 1986 parliamentary elections a real test of French public opinion in order to limit Mitterrand's own legitimacy and power.

Within these evident limits, the French parliament has an influence on the political process of decisionmaking about nuclear weapons, in at least two respects: first, because it acts as a relay between the political class and the military and technocratic elite, from whom decision really originates; second, because it provides an ideological and rhetorical sounding board, through which deterrence policies and nuclear decisions are understood, or misunderstood, and accepted or not accepted by the public at large.

The role of being a relay, rarely questioning technocratic and industrial decisions, is performed by two devices: first, by the debates about and votes on defence budgets and *lois de programmation*; second, by the work of the defence committee of the Assemblée Nationale (Commission Permanente de la Défense Nationale et des Forces Armées.) A proper discussion of defence and nuclear weapons matters does not take place during the budget vote. MPs have neither the time nor the opportunity to look behind the misleadingly named titles and budgetary items, and mostly content themselves with restating their parties' policies. The main opportunity for discussing nuclear weapons policies — in terms of programmes and expenditure as well as in terms of strategic choices — is in the discussion of the *lois de programmation militaire* (also called *lois de programme*). These have a double function. On the one hand they represent a political commitment, and on the other they are an attempt to create a medium-term management tool. The *lois* describe the main weapons programmes either for development or construction, and present a financial evaluation of their costs. Such *lois de programme* were set up in the early days of the Fifth Republic in order to organize the considerable investment required by the new nuclear deterrent. The first two (1960–64 and 1965–70) were consequently limited in scope to the 'main programmes' (*programmes majeurs*) — mostly nuclear — and only covered capital expenditure rather than also planning for operating costs. The third *loi de programme* (1971–75) covered the whole amount of capital costs (*crédits d'équipement*) and the fourth (1976–82) covered the whole budgetary programme — *crédits de fonctionnement* (operating costs) as well as *crédits d'équipement*. The fifth *loi de programme* (1984–88), prepared by Charles Hernu of Mauroy's socialist government, similarly covered capital investments and operating costs for all programmes. The new *loi de programme* (1987–91), however, has returned to the pattern of the first two *lois* in only covering the main weapons programmes in some detail, and in only considering equipment expenditure. Furthermore, this *loi* only provides cost estimates in constant money, and is expected to be updated in 1989. It was prepared under rather difficult conditions. When the conservative coalition came to power in 1986 it promised to scrap the previous 1984–88 *loi de programmation* and to increase the defence equipment budget considerably (and in particular to speed up the modernization of the nuclear forces). However, conflicts soon arose between the Minister of Finance, Balladur, and the Minister of Defence, Giraud. Giraud also had to cover his flanks from the Assemblée Nationale, which was dissatisfied with the difficulties and uncertainties created by the scrapping of the previous *loi de programme* and by the delays this had created in some programmes.

There are few similarities between the Select Committee system of the British House of Commons and the French system of Commissions Parlementaires. The six Commissions depend for their information on the willingness of the administration to provide it, and they have very weak investigative powers and no power to compel an official or any individual to give evidence under oath. They do however represent a source of information for parliamentary debates and for the media. As such, the head of the defence committee and the main *rapporteurs* (MPs who take charge of a specific area and report on it) have an influence that is not negligible. Many influential politicians who do not have government or whip responsibilities make a point of being members of the defence committee. In the last Parliament before the 1988 elections, for example, the defence committee's members included Giscard D'Estaing, Fabius, Barre, Mauroy (one ex-president and three ex-prime ministers), Hernu (ex-Minister of Defence), Jospin (then general secretary of the Socialist Party) and Le Pen (leader of the Front National). A basic problem for the committee is that it has neither investigative researchers nor a secretariat, and it meets infrequently — in 1986, for instance, it only met for 57 hours.

(See biographies of: Boucheron (President Parliamentary Defence Committee); Fabius (President of the National Assembly).)

THE MINISTRY OF DEFENCE AND THE 'DÉLÉGATION GÉNÉRALE POUR L'ARMEMENT' (DGA)

The Ministry of Defence, and particularly its Délégation Générale pour l'Armament (DGA) is at the centre of the nuclear weapons decision-making process; it both initiates and takes fundamental decisions and co-ordinates the various elements of the decision making complex, liaising particularly with the Direction des Applications Militaire of the CEA and the major industrial contractors in the electronics and aerospace industries.

It should not be inferred from this that the minister himself is the most powerful figure in nuclear weapons procurement and development. The real power lies with the quasi-corporate DGA, which, institutionally and politically, is almost an autonomous organization. Its top personnel are continually exchanged with the Direction des Applications Militaires (DAM) of the CEA, and with the large defence contractors, either for temporary periods or after retirement (this is the so-called *pantouflage*).

The current structure of the defence ministry dates from the period when nuclear weapons were introduced into the French armed forces. Until after World War II, there had been no one governmental institution specifically concerned with procurement policy. The Army, Air Force and Navy each had their own ministry, and weapons procurement was organized through liaison between the arms manufacturers and the three military staffs. However, in 1951, in a first step towards integrating the procurement and defence organizations (or not, as some would say), a Ministry of Armaments was created, under a minister with the title of Deputy Minister of Defence.

The major change came in 1959 and in 1961. First, the three ministries of the armed forces were eliminated (their ministers had already been reduced to the rank of 'ministerial delegates' by the first government of the Fifth Republic) and a super-ministry of defence (under a 'minister in charge of armed forces', renamed 'Minister of Defence' in 1969) was created. According to Article 16 of the *ordonnance* No. 59–147 issued on 7 January 1959, this new ministry is responsible 'for the execution of military policy under the authority of the Prime Minister and especially for the organization, management, commissioning and mobilization of the entire armed forces as well as of the military infrastructure which they require.'

Decree No. 62–808 issued on 18 July 1962 specifically allocates to the Minister of Defence responsibilities for weapons procurement and equipment of the armed forces. Decree No. 62–811 (of the same date) specified the responsibilities of this minister and gave him three supporting officials: a 'general secretary for administration', in charge of general administration (this post was eliminated in the 1986 reform of the ministry), a Délegué Ministériel pour l'Armement (renamed Délégué Générale pour l'Armement in 1977) responsible for studies, research and arms manufacture, and a Chef d'État-Major des Armées (a post which had not existed previously) in charge of organizing the armed forces and their operational command.

The Délégue Générale pour l'Armement and the Chef d'État-Major des Armées play a particularly powerful role in the defence organization in general, and in the weapons procurement process in particular. Both are in the 'inner circle' of decisionmaking.

The placing together of all the military commands, the weapons procurement organization, military research, the intelligence services, and the strategic planning body under the single authority of the defence minister created a powerful instrument for the transformation of the defence industry and the military institutions. Responsibility for the whole of this sector was placed in the hands of the President by the Constitution of the Fifth Republic, the 1959 *ordonnance* and subsequent decrees. The concentration of power in the hands of the President, assisted by a dozen or so powerful people at the top of the defence ministry, was sufficient to wipe out the fierce resistance to de Gaulle's plans put up by some sections of the traditional military hierarchy.

In the 1960s, defence ministers were little more than faithful servants to President de Gaulle, who regarded defence policy as a private domain. Ministers such as Guillaumat (who had previously headed the CEA when it was secretly developing the nuclear bomb) and Messmer (Minister of Defence from 1960 to 1969) efficiently executed the tasks given to them under the 1959 *ordonnance*. Following de Gaulle's retirement in 1969, the new President, Pompidou, chose Michel Debré as his Minister of Defence. Debré preserved de Gaulle's approach to defence until 1973. Thereafter the ministry became relatively more autonomous, mainly because there was not such a close relationship between the President, the Prime Minister and the Minister of Defence. With Giscard d'Estaing as President, there was a tendency for ministers such as Soufflet, Galley, Bourges and le Theule to leave more freedom to their staff and to the DGA, which thus became powerful interest groups. Under Mitterrand, by contrast, and his defence ministers Hernu and Quilles, there was a return to the previous situation in which the minister was a faithful executive. When the period of *cohabitation* began in 1986, there was a break in the relationship between the defence minister and the president, with Giraud acting as lieutenant to Chirac, the prime minster.

The defence ministry is not a monolithic institution. Nor is the minister the ultimate centre of power in his ministry. Several departments and councils inside it have their own channels of communication with other centres of power (the intelligence bodies, for example, have direct links with the offices of the Prime Minister and the President). The relevant offices in the ministry are as follows:

1. The minister and his immediate colleagues in his *cabinet* (private office). The most important Cabinet member is the Directeur du Cabinet Civil et Militaire. Other colleagues include the Conseiller Scientifique. Under the minister's authority also are bodies with direct relevance to nuclear weapons procurement, such as the Conseil des Recherches et Études de Défense (CRED) and the Direction des Centres d'Expérimentations Nucléaires (DCEN), and the Direction aux Études Générales (formerly GroupeS); and of indirect relevance, such as the DGSE (the intelligence service) and the Controle Général des Armées). There is also a junior minister called the Secrétaire d'État auprés du Ministre but he has little, if any, influence over nuclear weapons procurement.

2. The *Chiefs of Staff* (Chefs d'État-Majors) *and their own services*. These are dealt with in the section on the armed forces.

3. *The Délégation Générale pour l'Armament* — the Délégué himself and his close associates, the DGA operational directorates, and all the important research and development bodies.

The next section describes the role of the Minister of Defence and the people and organizations around him, and the section after deals in more depth with the DGA.

The Minister of Defence and His Officials

The Minister of Defence's job is not an easy one. He has to co-ordinate the work of an enormous and highly bureaucratic institution, and manage the often conflicting pressures from the President, the Prime Minister, the Minister of

Finances, the armed forces and the weapons manufacturing corporations. This was particularly difficult during the years 1986–88 in the special conditions created by *cohabitation*. The then minister, Giraud, had a very heavy workload when he was appointed in 1986. He had to prepare a new defence budget for 1987, incorporating changed policies, and he also had to urgently prepare a new *loi de programmation* to replace that of the previous socialist government. At the same time, budget restrictions decided on by Balladur, the Minister of Economy and Finances, prevented the full programme of defence expenditure that the conservative coalition had promised. In addition, a number of very important decisions had to be made, in regard to the Rafale fighter, the nuclear-powered aircraft carrier, the ordering programme for the S4 ballistic missiles, the SNLE (ballistic missile submarines) retrofitting programme and SNLE-NG ordering.

In this context, the officials in the Minister of Defence's *cabinet* (office) play a crucial role. There are in fact two *cabinets*, one military and one civil. The top job here is that of the director of the civil and military *cabinet*, who supervises both sectors, and co-ordinates the work of the Minister, as well as organizing the contracts and meetings with which the Minister is concerned. This official negotiates behind the scenes to settle difficult issues. A second key official who is closely involved in problems related to weapons development is the Conseiller Scientifique (Scientific Adviser), who supports the Minister (but also the Délégué Général pour l'Armement) on matters of research policy.

An organization which comes under the Minister of Defence and can have an indirect impact on weapons development is the Direction Générale de la Sécurité Extérieure (DGSE), the intelligence agency. This agency has been relatively ineffective recently (see the biography of its director). Nevertheless, it can be important: after taking power in 1981 Mitterrand justified his new stance on nuclear weapons by saying that he based it on files on the Soviet threat presented to him by the DGSE.

Another body which comes under the Minister of Defence is the Direction des Centres d'Expérimentation Nucléaire, the military-controlled administration which manages the French nuclear test facilities in the Pacific in co-operation with the Direction des Applications Militaires of the CEA. Despite its involvement in bomb development, this organization is not actually involved in the nuclear weapons decisionmaking at a policy level. However the political weight of the director cannot be discounted. It is said that the sinking of the Greenpeace ship *Rainbow Warrior* was organized after a visit by the DCEN director to Charles Hernu, then Minister of Defence.

The Minister of Defence is also assisted by the Contrôle Général des Armées, a body composed of specially trained *contrôleurs*, who are present in all the organizations controlled by the Minister to check on the application of regulatory and policy decisions. Until recently, the Contrôle Général des Armées had a powerful influence (though it did not participate in decisionmaking). It was feared and listened to by industries and military bodies. Its control was exercised mostly a *posteriori*, but it also had the power to control *a priori* the Minister of Defence's own decisions and procedures. However its influence was severely curtailed in October 1987 when Giraud eliminated this power of *a priori* control.

The two bodies which are most important in relation to the decisionmaking process in nuclear weapons development are the Délégation aux Études Générales (DEG, formerly Groupe S)and the Conseil des Recherches et Études de Défense (CRED). The first is a long-term policy unit. The second is a policymaking committee responsible for defining the overall orientation of military research and development. Both are part of the inner circle of decisionmaking.

The Conseil des Recherches et Études de Défense replicates at the level of R & D the role held by the Conseil de Défense at the level of strategy and deployment policy. Its composition is at very high level: chaired by the Minister of Defence, it includes the Chiefs of Staff and the Joint Chief of Staff, the Délégué Général pour l'Armement, the director of the DEG, the Conseiller Scientifique, and other authorities concerned with defence research (probably the

CEA is also represented). CRED's role is to keep abreast of scientific developments which have military implications, to help prepare the defence R & D budget and to allocate this budget between the principal R & D efforts, particularly in regard to pre-development exploratory research. Because of its composition — every one of its members has a real voice in nuclear weapons development policy — and because of its pivotal position between the DEG and other institutions such as the DGA and DAM, CRED is a powerful committee whose work is likely to affect the course of nuclear arms development.

The Délégation aux Études Générales, until recently called the Groupe de Planification et d'Études Stratégiques, or GroupeS, is a highly important long-range strategic planning group. It is responsible for analysing future military trends, but its projections are translated into short-term directives and goals every year. It originated at the same time that the nuclear force was being developed during the early 1960s. At that time, the normal channels of strategic thinking in the military and the weapons procurement establishment were simply unable to carry out a wholesale recasting of French defence strategy. As a result, the Centre de Prospective et d'Évaluations (CPE) was created in February 1961 by Pierre Messmer, then Minister of Defence. This later became GroupeS. The CPE built a strategic model, which is still officially in existence. It was summarized in the 1972 White Paper on Defence, but was presented as early as 1965 or 1966 in two studies on the future mission of the armed forces, and a strategic model for France. Under the direction of General Poirier, the CPE at that time achieved its maximum influence, opposing ideas such as General Ailleret's *défense tous azimuts* (defence against all sides) and the Army Staff's idea of using tactical nuclear weapons as a kind of super-artillery. It was successful in both these clashes, but encountered continuing resistance from the three military service staffs (especially from the Army, later allied with the CEA, which redefined the link between tactical nuclear weaponry and conventional forces, in a way which contradicted the principles the CPE had espoused).

The influence of the DEG has certainly shrunk since the early 1970s. Nevertheless, it still occupies a central role, especially in forecasting technical military developments such as the nature of the future battlefield and in preparing applied research programmes. As such it is one of the rare informal links between the Ministry of Defence and the DAM in the CEA. It is informed of DAM's most secret development and has influence on them. The work of the DEG is expressed in a number of important policy documents which direct applied research — notably the Directive Ministérielle d'Orientation des Recherches (DMO: Annual Ministerial Guidelines). The purpose of the DMO is to determine priorities and rank the various applied research projects, within the framework of general defence policies and longer-term objectives. The DMO is prepared using five levels of analysis, which range from the global level of defence policy objectives and military force capabilities to the very detailed level of objectives of single research projects. According to the Ministry of Defence, the content of the directive is then incorporated into the Programme Pluriannuel des Recherches et Études (PPRE), a three-year research and studies programme established by the DGA (especially DRET), the Staffs and the DEG. The PPRE classifies the 1,500 or so research projects identified in the DMO into about thirty groups of responsibilities, covering broadly homogenous areas. This document is then submitted to the CRED for approval. The most promising projects are then incorporated into the PPDE (Programme Pluriannuel des Développements Exploratoires), a triennial exploratory development programme developed by the technical departments of the DGA, DRET and CRED. These involve technologies which have been successful at the pure research and applied research stages and which are considered worth exploring for weapons prototypes. In the PPDE, there are around some 150 projects running a year (there were 154 in 1982, for instance, and 149 in 1986). Little is known about how research outside the DGA comes to be included in the PPDE. Industrial and university laboratories obtain development finance from DRET, but industrial corporations also develop their own research directions (especially in sectors such as space, electronic, optics, etc.).

The DEG is not responsible for establishing programmes on nuclear explosives and warheads, but it has close contacts with the DAM. Its decisions have considerable impact on the development of launch vehicles, delivery vehicles, tracking and communication systems. It is a key element of the military technological complex. While it is meant to advise the Minister on behalf of the armed forces, it is always headed by an *ingénieur de l'armement* rather than by a soldier. Its director therefore belongs more to the weapons production community than to the army.

(*See biographies of: Blandin, Chevènement, Conzes, Curien, Gallois, Gillis, Lanxade, Mermet.*)

THE TOP RANKS AT THE DGA

The DGA: A Brief Account

The Délégation Général pour l'Armement is an enormous organization covering a unique range of political, research, industrial and training activities. It has a high degree of autonomy and manages its own personnel on corporate lines.

It is directly responsible for overseeing the entire procurement process for conventional arms and weapons systems and delivery systems for nuclear weapons, although not the bombs and warheads, which are the responsibility of the CEA. The DGA is responsible for implementing the decisions of the defence minister and other political authorities on armaments programmes (but there is strong evidence that the DGA also makes a strong input into political decisions on these programmes). The second task of the DGA is to prepare and programme future weapons systems requirements — in terms of research and development as well as industrial capability — adapting the armaments industry to predictable trends as well as performing the studies and research required for future systems. A third function of the DGA is to provide support to the whole armament industry, both public and private, in regard to the export markets which are very important to France.

This central organization was created by de Gaulle in 1961. It was then called the Délégation Ministérielle pour l'Armement and only changed its name to Délégation Général pour l'Armement in 1977. It was one of the central planks of the defence re-organization forced through by de Gaulle in order to convert French defence from conventional strategy forces to nuclear deterrent forces. It replaced a decentralized system under which the three armed services had their own technical directorates and weapons procurement departments. These three technical directorates became absorbed into five new operational directorates (see Figure 4.2).

The DGA is a highly centralized body whose economic weight, directly or indirectly, is considerable:

– It oversees the employment of around 290,000 people (in 1985) who work in the development and production of arms (73,100 of those are employed directly by the DGA).

– It has budgeting control over the entire material and equipment sector of the annual defence budget, including the funding of CEA development programmes and the manufacture of the nuclear warheads. This represents 51 per cent of the total defence budget (around 1.95 per cent of the GDP in 1987). The 1987 defence budget was FF169 billion — 3.79 per cent of GDP, 49 per cent of which went on operational costs and the rest on equipment costs. Of this total, nuclear forces (strategic and tactical) account for FF28.3 billion, i.e. 17 per cent (at least officially: a number of costs are transferred to other budgetary lines).

– The orders and contracts of the DGA account for 18 per cent of the business of the French electronics industry (and 55 per cent of its non-domestic, professional activities); 69 per cent of the aeronautics industry; for nearly 30 per cent of the state-funded R & D spending and 19 per cent of national R & D spending; and 46 per cent of the budget of the CEA (excluding its subsidiaries).

– It trains its own specialists and elite staff by

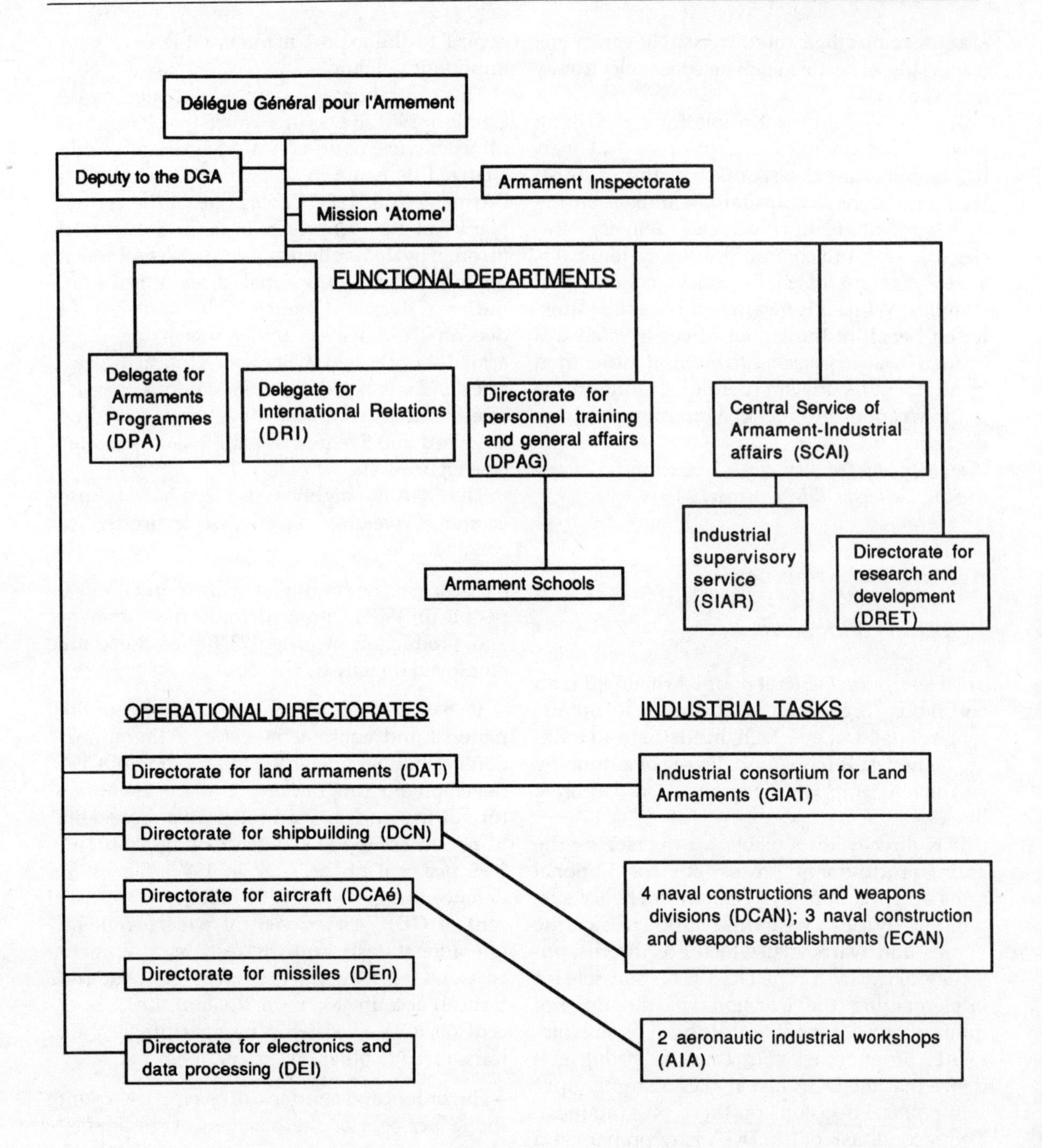

Figure 4.2 *Structure of the DGA* (Note: only full industrial units are included; testing centres, grounds, and services, and laboratories and technical documentation services are not included.)

managing not only its two Écoles de l'Armement which train *les X* to become *ingénieurs de l'armement*, but also the École Polytechnique itself, and the Centre des Hautes Études de l'Armement (CHEAr) which provides further training for senior armament engineers and senior officers at a conceptual and policy level as well as at a technical level.

This new centralized organization of weapons procurement was accompanied by a change in the professional organization of the armament engineers, who had previously been organized into eleven corps depending on the type of weaponry they were producing. A law of the 21 December 1968 regrouped them into two corps: *ingénieurs de l'armement* (who are found in all the responsible jobs) and *ingénieurs d'études et techniques d'armement* (who have a more practical role).

The scale and efficiency of the vertically integrated system has been demonstrated by the speed with which France has evolved from a nation defeated first in World War II and then in two colonial wars, to become a considerable nuclear power and, by the mid–1980s, the largest per capita arms exporter in the world. The DGA has played a central role in this process. It operates in close concert with large-scale autonomous state-controlled armament manufacturers and private firms, with which it shares expertise, R & D, and, most important, its own senior and junior personnel. *Ingénieurs de l'armement* (IGAs) move about frequently during their career: from operational directorates to functional units; or they are seconded for some years into the armaments industries (as technicians, or controllers), to the CEA (i.e. to DAM), and to governmental bodies (particularly the Ministry of Defence and the DEG). Furthermore, numerous IGAs, when retiring from their last DGA post, find themselves employed by the very firms with which they had been co-operating as clients, funders, R & D managers or providers of export assistance. Numerous examples of moves between these organizations can be found in the biographies pertaining to this section and the following two.

The IGAs control most of the posts in the DGA and the other key decisionmaking bodies in the government, with the exception of the military staffs. Admiral Sanguinetti, a retired admiral well known for his critical views, wrote recently: 'In the offices of the defence minister and the DGA, the armament engineers are sufficiently numerous to cater effectively for the private interests of their corporations.' He went on: 'Weapons are no longer produced according to defence doctrines which are thought out at the political level. It is the doctrines which are fitted, in a manner of speaking, to the use of the weapons being made.' (*Le Monde Diplomatique*, no. 409, April 1988.) What is the real power — in policy and political terms — of the DGA? The choice of the title, 'Délégation' is significant: the dictionary definition is, 'a commission which allows somebody to act in the name of another'. Effectivelyy, the DGA, by its sheer centralized weight and its permanency, has an overbearing power to act in the name of the Ministry of Defence. As Admiral Sanguinetti put it, 'It is exceptional for decisions to go back up to the level of the Minister of Defence, and when they do they are carefully prepared in advance, and there is as little risk, since the voice of the Delegate takes precedence over that of the armed forces'. However, in the case of nuclear weapons, this view of an overmighty DGA has to be qualified: the views of the DAM, on one hand, and those of the politicians and military staff on the other, do carry weight. The continous power struggles concerning the neutron bomb, the 'second components' and the SX missile, to give only a few examples, show that the DGA does not always get all its own way.

THE ORGANIZATION OF THE DGA AND THE CHANGES IN 1986

The current structure of the Délégation Général pour l'Armement is presented in Figure 4.2. Four layers in this structure can be distinguished: the senior managing posts (such as the Délégué himself and his deputy); the functional units (such as personnel and training, research and development), the operational directorates (five directorates for land armaments, shipbuilding, aircraft building, missiles and electronics and data processing) and the industrial tasks under the direct management of the DGA. There was a major reorganization of the top two layers of this structure in 1986.

According to former Minister of Defence Giraud, this reorganization was necessary in order to simplify and clarify the decision-making structure within the Ministry of Defence: 'The multiplication of the number of decisionmakers and the complexity of decision-making systems tend to result in a loss of accountability', he said (*Le Monde*, 7 May 1986). Others interpreted Giraud's move, which came less than two months after the change of government, as a way of getting rid of a number of 'undesirable' top officials. Indeed, these changes occurred at the same time as Emile Blanc was summarily retired as the Délégué Général pour l'Armement, and replaced by Jacques Chevallier.

At the apex of the DGA is the Délégué himself. He is among the highest ranking defence officials, on a par with the Chiefs of Staff of the Armed Forces. He is directly answerable to the Minister of Defence and is a member of the most important committees related to defence development, such as the Conseil de Recherches et Études de Défense (CRED) and the Comité de l'Énergie Atomique of the CEA. He is on the board of the major research institutes, and is represented on the management of all the major armament industries.

The Délégué has a number of advisers and deputies in his *cabinet* (private office). Amongst the current deputies, one has particular importance, as he is also head of the Mission 'Atome' directly responsible for co-ordinating programmes between the CEA and the DGA. This post is filled by a high-ranking *ingénieur général de l'armement* of wide experience. He 'aids the Délégué in expressing the technical side of things in terms a minister (of defence) can understand'.

Significant changes to the functional units were made in the reorganization of 1986, through Decree No.86–786, dated 27 June 1986. The departments most affected were the old Direction des Programmes et Affaires Industrielles (DPAI) and the Direction des Affaires Industrielles (DAI). The DPAI had been responsible for preparing and managing the DGA's programmes and for controlling the armaments industry, and the DAI was in charge of arms exports and international co-operation in arms procurement. The DAI has been replaced by the new Délégation aux Relations Internationales (DRI), headed by a Délégué, which has taken over the DAI's responsibilities for supporting and promoting French weaponry abroad. The DPAI was replaced by two new bodies, the Délégué aux Programmes d'Armement (DPA) and the Service Central des Affaires Industrielles (SCAI). The new Délégué aux Programmes d'Armement is now responsible for only two of the three functions of the old DPAI, namely 'plans, programmes, budget', and 'prices and market tenders'. The SCAI has been given responsibility for the 'industrial affairs' side (i.e. the control and supervision of public, nationalized and private weapons manufacturing firms, and the organization of collaborative programmes).

The two new *délégués* have a more central role in the DGA than their predecessors in the old structure. Both belong to the Délégué Général's own cabinet, and are on a par with his deputy (*adjoint*) and above his advisers (such as the head of the Mission 'Atome'). In particular, the Délégué aux Programmes d'Armement is central in the nuclear weapons decisionmaking system. He is the person, within the DGA, responsible for the planning, co-ordination and implementation of all the R & D, development and manufacturing programmes for new weapons. He prepares and oversees budgets and the capital expenditure schedules in the *lois de programmes*. He is in direct contact with the Minister of Defence, the four Chiefs of Staff, and the other operational and functional units of the DGA. He can also launch his own policy initiatives. He is a figure of central importance in the decisionmaking system.

The organization of the DPA is deceptively simple. It consists of very few people (not many more than a hundred), organized into two *missions*. One of these, the Mission Plan Programmes Budget is crucially important. It carries out the budgeting and programming of planned expenditure on behalf of the DGA and co-ordinates information on the requirements of the armed forces for materiel. It is consulted when new programmes are launched and monitors existing ones. It helps with programming research and is responsible for establishing the PPDE. It is also responsible for cost–benefit analysis and programming analysis within the DGA. It is organized into various *bureaux* (offices), each monitoring one type of equipment programme (such as missiles, aircraft, naval programmes and research).

Thus, this *mission*, known as the DGA/DPA/PPB, occupies a crucial position in the procurement process. Along with the DEG (formerly GroupeS) and the CRED, it is one of the four bodies directly responsible for relating military doctrine and requirements to the development of new weapons technology.

The other *mission*, the Mission Prix et Marchés, is of less importance, being concerned with marketing analysis, contract prices and tendering procedures.

The other new body created in 1986, the Service Central des Affaires Industrielles (SCAI) has been allocated the DPAI's old responsibilities concerning the *tutelle* (supervision) of armament industries. It is not a decisionmaking body, and its importance comes from the day-to-day control it exerts through its specialized arm, the Service de Surveillance Industrielle de l'Armement (SIAr), which has a *poste de contrôle* in each major manufacturing plant of military importance — some 300 in all, each with an engineer and small staff, helped by itinerant regional teams.

The SIAr is very powerful in non-nuclear armament matters, as it delivers quality insurance certificates to weapons. But the industries its engineers inspect are not directly involved in nuclear weapons. If the SCAI has some influence in this area, it is indirectly, through its advisory role with the Minister of Defence concerning his industrial policy. In particular, the SCAI's sub-directorate of armament industries, among other responsibilities, 'studies the ways in which the bodies participating in armament manufacturing fit in with the technical and economic developments and future weapons requirements (Ministerial Order (*arrêt*) 24 July 1986).

One other body helps the Délégué Général in his managerial tasks: the Inspection Générale de l'Armement. This body is made up of inspectors in aeronautics, naval engineering, missiles, etc., who undertake specialized studies and check whether the decisions of the DGA and the Ministry have been implemented.
(See biographies of: Arnaud (Assistant to the DGA); Barbery (Inspector General for Armaments at the DGA); Bénichou (Délégué aux Programmes d'Armement de la DGA); Chevallier (Director General of Weapons Production); Delaye (Assistant to the DGA); Le Febvre de Saint-Germain (Director of the Advanced College of Weaponry); Ramé (Director, SCIA).)

RESEARCH AND DEVELOPMENT INSIDE AND OUTSIDE THE DGA

The Role of DRET

DRET (the Direction des Recherches et Études Techniques) is 'overall programming co-ordinator, responsible for implementation of research' and 'studies preceding development', on all types of weaponry except direct R & D on nuclear warheads. In effect it covers all pre-development studies — from basic research through applied research to exploratory development. The basic research that DRET funds is mostly carried on in outside laboratories. The applied research is governed by the DMO issued by the DEG, and covers around 1,500 programmes called Objectifs Unitaires de Recherche (or OUR) selected in the Programme Pluriannuel des Recherches et Études (PPRE). In practice these are established by DRET, together with CRED and the DGA/DPA/PPB. The exploratory development projects which are included in the Programme Pluriannuel des Développements Exploratoires are closer to final weapon systems, and may include mock-ups. If successful, these exploratory developments become development projects.

Because of the high cost of the research and development phase of major military projects for a medium-sized country such as France, it is highly unlikely that a project reaching the stage of development will be abandoned. That explains why the R & D community in the French armament world is so powerful. Even if a new weapon has not been properly considered at the political level, or the strategic thinkers have failed to integrate the consequences of its development into their strategic frameworks, it is highly likely to be deployed once it has been developed, albeit at the cost of ambiguities, contradictions and weaknesses in the resulting policy framework. Examples of this tendency have been mentioned in the introduction.

DRET employs around 2,500 people, including 650 military personnel. At the top are 70–80 specialist engineering scientists organized in nine research groups of the Service des Recherches. Each research group specializes in a specific area (such as optics, signals, thermal engineering), and each group is familiar with all the laboratories and research in France in their area. They cover developments in their fields up to the stage of exploratory development. An overall view is provided by the group of people gathered around the director. DRET then collaborates with the DPA to develop the programme of confirmed developments, contracting them out to specialist outside firms and to the DGA's operational directorates.

Apart from the Service des Recherches, the central core of DRET is organized in a number of sub-directorates. The most important are the Sub-directorate for Co-ordination and Evaluation, which co-ordinates fundamental and exploratory developments as well as the exploitation of results, and the Sub-directorate for Nuclear, Biological and Chemical Defence. Besides the director of DRET and his immediate collaborators, an important figure is the Conseiller Scientifique (Scientific Adviser) who advises the Minister, the Délégué Général and the director of DRET. The Conseiller Scientifique is also the head of the Conseil des Recherches, which co-ordinates and checks the scientific validity of work done by the specialist engineers (described in the section on the Minister of Defence).

To undertake its various tasks, DRET has a number of support organizations. There is an enormous documentation centre (Centre de Documentation de l'Armement) in Paris, second in size only to that of the CNRS. There are also several subsidiary centres which help to develop and to test prototype weapons and equipment in the final phase of development for the operational directorates such as DAT and DEn. For nuclear weapons, the relevant centre is the nuclear unit at Arcueil.

An important body under the *tutelle* (supervision) of DRET, though it is formally independent, is the Office National d'Études et de Recherches Spatiales (ONERA). ONERA has its own laboratories, aerodynamic testing workshops and wind tunnels, and collaborates with SEP, Aérospatiale, and CNES (Centre National d'Études Spatiales) to develop ballistic missiles and other weapons.

DRET places a good deal of emphasis on collaboration with industry, public laboratories and university institutions; and the arms manufacturers also try hard to get their projects included in DRET's list of exploratory developments and confirmed development programmes.

Relationships with Outside R & D Bodies

DRET co-ordinates with the military through thirty-two *groupes de concertation* (co-ordinating groups) which meet twice a year and cover all the main areas of military R & D. Each group includes specialists from DRET, people from the relevant operational directorate (for instance, DEn for missiles), and people from the staff of the armed service which is the end-user for the weapon (for instance, for marine acoustic systems, a submarine staff officer from the Navy). This makes it possible to check the relevance of R & D to operational developments elsewhere in the DGA and to the military needs expressed by the potential user.

DRET's main collaborative effort is with bodies outside the Ministry of Defence. This is indicated by the proportion of the defence R & D annual budget which is spent outside the state sector. In 1986 the defence R & D budget amounted to FF22 billion — about 20 per cent of total national research and development funding and about 30 per cent of state funded R & D. Of this, FF13 billion went to the corporate sector (5 per cent), and FF9 billion to state establishments. These (by French standards) enormous R & D costs ultimately make up over 30 per cent of the final costs of weapons delivered to the armed forces.

It is difficult to know how much of this sum is controlled by DRET, and of this how much is attributable to nuclear systems. Around 30 per cent of the defence R & D budget is said to be in *études d'amont* (early studies up to, and including, exploratory developments). Of this, most is controlled by DAM. A good part of the R & D expenditure on missiles (which absorbs 15 per cent of total defence R & D funds) can be attributed to nuclear weapons systems, as well as part of defence R & D expenditure on aeronautics, electronics and shipbuilding (which absorb respectively 17 per cent, 28 per cent and 5 per cent).

DRET has a role in 'steering' the activities of non-military laboratories, for example in universities, towards military applications. Within the CNRS, whole sections work mainly on defence, directly or indirectly. Sometimes this is research of the most fundamental type, without immediate application, sometimes it has a more direct military purpose. Defence research clients often 'slice down' projects into various unrelated contracts, making the links difficult to establish.

In France, the Conseil National de la Recherche Scientifique (CNRS) is the major coordinator of all 'civilian' research, from humanities to physics and mathematics; it organizes and partly funds hundreds of affiliated laboratories. Many well-placed people (including in-house researchers) have no idea that the CNRS is engaged in work on behalf of the military. They are wrong — it has been for a long time. As early as 1939, the Caisse Nationale de Recherche Scientifique (which became the CNRS later the same year) filed patents for the use of nuclear fission, including some specifically for atomic bombs. The CNRS has always been heavily involved in fundamental nuclear and particle physics. Today nearly 25 per cent of the CNRS budget is devoted to nuclear-related research.

Among other laboratories two are specially interesting: the Collège de France, which has substantial facilities for nuclear physics research, and the École Polytechnique which provides several hundred researchers to the DRET for its research projects. Altogether,15 per cent of DRET's contracts go to the CNRS or university laboratories.

These research institutes also work under direct contract from the Direction des Applications Militaires (DAM) of the Commissariat à l'Énergie Atomique (CEA). The DAM also conducts fundamental research on nuclear matters through its six *centres d'études*. The DAM also benefits from the research and documentation of the Institut de Recherche Fondamentale (IRF), which is attached to the 'civilian' half of the CEA, and its four research centres.

As might be expected, the information flow in this process is strictly one way. DAM and DRET collect useful information from the Institut de Recherche Fondamentale and from the independent laboratories but share none of their own.

In conclusion, DRET is an unusual, but powerful, institution. It is both an operational directorate, undertaking many tasks itself, and also a policymaking body. Its director is a figure of key importance, usually with considerable experience in nuclear weapons administration, and represented on key committees such as CRED and the Comité de l'Énergie Atomique. For example, Victor Marçais, the current Director, was a former head of the DGA's Mission 'Atome', is a member of the Comité de l'Énergie Atomique, and is on the Boards of ONERA, COGEMA and Technicatome.

(See biographies of: Carpentier (President of the Administrative Council, ONERA); El Gammal (Technical Manger, ONERA); Lehmann (Director, Institute of Nuclear and Particle Physics); Marçais (Director, DRET).)

The Operational Directorates of the DGA

There are now five operational directorates under the DGA. The three old ones (Land Armaments, Shipbuilding and Aircraft) have been joined by the Missiles Directorate and, more recently, by the Electronics and Data Processing Directorate. The DGA not only establishes the framework for weapons development, it is also directly involved in the development and production of some types of military equipment and weapons. It has been said that the operational directorates suffer from a 'split personality', since they are both administrative and policy sector units (*puissances publiques*) and operational units (developing, producing and repairing material in their own fields).

Historically, the operational directorates evolved out of the technical services attached to each of the armed forces, and they have inherited their traditions and their skills; for instance the engineers of the *génie maritime* (shipbuilding engineers) had a pride which can now be found in armament engineers working in the DCN (Direction des Constructions Navales).

Two of these directorates have very sizeable manufacturing capabilities — the Shipbuilding and Land Armament Directorates (DCN and DAT); and the Aérospace directorate (DCAé) has two large-scale repair and maintenance workshops. These units will be briefly covered insofar as they are relevant to nuclear weapons systems in the section on the industrial sector.

The operational directorates are concerned with all types of weapons, and most of their activities are in the non-nuclear area. However, they play an important role in the development of delivery vehicles and other systems which form part of the nuclear infrastructure. For example, the DCN builds the ballistic missile submarines (the SNLEs and SNLE-NGs), the DEn controls the aerospace firms which build the nuclear missiles and the DEI collaborates with the electronic firms which develop and manufacture communication, guidance and satellite systems.

How do these Directorates relate to the other parts of the DGA and to the public and private manufacturing firms which liaise with them? The principle is relatively simple (see Collet 1988). The work related to weapon systems is organized into armament programmes, which are a set of operations deemed to fulfil a particular military need. These can be studies or research, developments, prototypes or series production. In all cases, the execution of a programme requires three participants: the staff of the armed service which will use the equipment, the DGA itself and the manufacturing firm or firms which will produce the weapon system. The programme consists of two stages: the development stage and the production stage.

Right at the beginning of the development stage, a DGA engineer is nominated as 'programme director' by the lead department (*direction menante*). He selects a partner from the Staff, the 'programme officer', who will liaise with him throughout and together they coordinate the work. In large programmes it is possible for the lead department to call for assisting departments (*directions coopérantes*). In all cases, the manufacturer is asked to provide prototypes which are then evaluated by the central technical services of the Staff.

In the case of important systems (such as nuclear weapons systems) which can include several separate programmes, a directing committee can be activated, with an 'overall programme director' (*directeur de programme d'ensemble*). Similarly, programmes which are of particlar interest — for strategic, industrial or financial reasons — can be declared a 'major programme' by the Minister of Defence, and then have to follow specific rules.

For all programmes (which are listed annually by the DGA in its *programme catalogue*), operations can be put in motion once the minister signs an authorization to start (*fiche de lancement*) and after the programme has been examined once again by a special commission. A cost limit is set for the duration of the programme (*autorisation de programme*) and another for expenditure in each year (*crédit de paiement*).

For *programmes d'ensemble* consisting of nuclear weapons systems (such as the new S4 ballistic missiles), the situation is made more complex by the fact that, to all intents and purposes, there are two lead departments — the CEA's Direction des Applications Militaires and the DEn, as well as several manufacturers (including Aérospiatiale, Thomson–CSF, and DAM's *centre d'études*). The one end-user, the Air Force's Strategic Air Forces, finds itself quite far removed from decisionmaking.

The best-known operational directorate is the Direction des Armements Terrestres (DAT), which supervises a large-scale manufacturing operation, the GIAT (see the section on the industrial sector). As far as nuclear weapons are concerned, DAT is only involved in the development of launch vehicles; it provided the

AMX 30 chassis for the Pluton tactical missiles, and it is working on the Hadès launching vehicles. If the new S4 ballistic missile is installed on mobile-launching vehicles, as seems likely, DAT will have developed them. DAT also develops and produces missiles, guns and ammunitions for the Army; it is thus likely to contribute to developments for neutron warheads in artillery.

A second, very important, operational directorate is the Direction des Constructions Navales (DCN) which designs and builds warships and naval weapons systems. Its major task for two decades has been the development, manufacture and maintenance of the nuclear submarine fleet, and especially the ballistic missile submarines (SNLEs, Sous-marins Nucléaires Lanceurs d'Engins). The industrial units which carry out this work are described in the industrial sector section. The construction of modern ballistic missile submarines is an exacting, expensive and technologically complex task, and the DCN collaborates closely with the the DAM on warheads, with the CEA's subsidiary Technicatome on nuclear propulsion units, and with other leading firms, on electronics, firing and other systems.

The operational directorate in charge of missiles, the Direction des Engins (DEn), was created in 1965. It plays a crucial part in the continued development of the nuclear force. Besides conventional missiles, the DEn has responsibility for two sectors that are relevant:

– it develops and supervises the manufacturing of strategic and tactical nuclear missiles;

– it carries out research on the military uses of space (at present working mainly on observation and communication satellites; this area of activity will become increasingly important as missiles, submarines and aircraft come to depend on satellites for guidance, communications and target recognition.)

The DEn has been responsible for all the land-based missiles (the SSBS — S-2, S-3 and soon the S4), the submarine launched missiles (MSBS — the M4 and the M5), the tactical missiles (Hadès and Pluton), the ASMP (the air-launched missile now fitted to the aircraft of the Force Aérienne Stratégique). In the space programme, the DEn is responsible for the development of the 'Syracuse' programme in collaboration with the CNES (Centre National d'Études Spatiales) and the Direction Générale des Télécommunications.

The DEn does not have its own production facilities: it only undertakes studies, carries out testing, and oversees development and production in collaboration with manufacturing firms which are at the forefront of French technological effort.

The DEn has three technical services and four 'establishments' at its disposal. The most important is the STen (Service Technique des Engins Ballistiques), responsible for the development of all long-range nuclear missiles and the satellite programmes. STen has a close relationship with manufacturers such as SNIAS and SEP, as well as with bodies such as ONERA and CNES.

The other two technical services are the Service Technique des Engins Tactiques (STET), which develops non-nuclear missiles, together with manufacturers such as MATRA or SNIAS (it was involved in the development of the Exocet, for example); and the Service Technique des Poudres et Explosifs (STPE) which supervises the SNPE (Société Nationale des Poudres et Explosifs) (see the section on the industrial sector) and has some involvement in nuclear matters, in so far as the SNPE is involved with studies of detonators and solid propellants for missiles.

The DEn's four establishments consist of a laboratory where aerodynamic systems and inertial guidance systems are developed in-house, and three rocket-testing sites. One of these sites, situated in Toulon, is for tactical, conventional missiles; the other two are for long-range and nuclear armed missiles. One of these is the CAEPE (Centre d'Achèvement et d'Essais des Propulseurs et Engins: Finishing and Testing Centre for Propellors and Missiles), which performs full-scale ground test firing of all strategic and tactical nuclear missiles, and as such is at the centre of DEn's development work. It liaises closely with the companies manufacturing missiles, such as SNIAS: half of the 1,000 or so people working at the CAEPE are employees of such firms. The second site is the Centre d'Essai des Landes (CEL) at Biscarosse along the Atlantic coast, where test launches of all nuclear missiles are carried out in the direction of the Azores. The CEL carries out a significant number of launches of nuclear missiles per year — including between five and ten ballistic missile launches. It has a whole range of tracking equipment at its disposal.

A fourth operational Directorate is the Direction des Constructions Aéronautiques (DCAé), responsible for overseeing and controlling the research, development and construction of all military aeronautic equipment. It is more an administrative and monitoring organ than a policy and decisionmaking body. The reason for this is that the aerospace industry in France is certainly the most successful of all the weapons industrial sectors, in both the domestic and the foreign markets. The aerospace industry is also the most vertically integrated of the armament industries, performing nearly all of its own developmental research and heavily involved in fundamental, exploratory and predevelopmental research as well as in post-construction evaluation. As such, the only role played by the DCAé, apart from that of official watchdog over the industry and technical coordinater of minor projects, is simply industrial support. State control tends to pass over the heads of the DCAé — the Délégué Général, Ministers, or, even the Prime Minister in the case of the Rafale ACE aircraft, talk directly to the administrators of the major companies.

The DCAé is organized around three technical services (Programmes Aéronautiques; Télécommunications et Équipement; Production, Prix et Maintenance), three flight test centres (Centres d'Essais en Vol), and two 'ground' test centres. It has also two aircraft and engine maintenance workshops, at Bordeaux and Clermont-Ferrand.

The last operational Directorate of the DGA is the most recently created and the smallest in terms of number of employees: the Direction de l'Électronique et de l'Informatique (DEI — known until recently as the SCTI: Service Central des Télécommunications et de l'Informatique). It employs just under 1,000 people. It plays quite an important part in the DGA's work: it studies and develops programmes for communication systems for the defence infrastructure and command software for weapon systems. It is also responsible for electronic safeguards for defence secrets. Together with large electronic firms such as Thomson–CSF, it develops systems for communications with nuclear forces, and for nuclear command and control.

The main body within the DEI is the CELAR (Centre Électronique de l'Armement). This organization tests electronic and data processing equipment, provides computing expertise and powerful data processing facilities to the armed forces and tests weapons systems in computer simulations. It employs nearly 700 of the DEI workers.

(*See biographies of: Bousquet (Director, Missiles Division, DGA); Cazaban (Director of Shipbuilding, DGA); Givaudon (Director, Directorate for Electronics and Data-Processing, DGA); Huet ((Deputy Director, DAT, DGA); Playe (Director, DAT, DGA); Sandreau (Director of Aeronautical Construction, DGA).*)

THE COMMISSARIAT A L'ÉNERGIE ATOMIQUE AND THE DIRECTION DES APPLICATIONS MILITAIRES

The CEA: Reactors and the Bomb

The French Atomic Energy Commission is the centre of all nuclear activity in France — except for the construction and operation of nuclear power plants. It is responsible either directly or through subsidiaries for most nuclear R & D (including all military R & D), for the production and handling of nuclear fuel at every stage of the fuel cycle, for the development of French nuclear reactor technology (including the PWRs which power nuclear submarines), and for the design, production, testing, handling and maintenance of all nuclear warheads, as well as for the research and development of future weapons (such as lasers and particle beams).

The CEA has grown from a tiny cluster of twelve people in 1945 to a large-scale industrial concern. The main company retains most of the

R & D activities and weapons-related work, while a separate holding company (CEA-Industries) groups together the various wholly-owned subsidiaries and affiliated bodies who work on the fuel cycle, data-processing, technological consultancy, etc. The CEA's current operating budget of the CEA (excluding the subsidiaries and affiliates) amounts to FF17.2 billion — of which FF14.8 billion are public subsidies. Military activities accounted for FF9.4 billion in 1986. Currently, the CEA employs 22,400 people, and the rest of the group another 15,000 (all figures for 1986). Military work provides around 8,850 jobs (nearly 40 per cent of the total).

The CEA was set up, in total secrecy, in 1945 and was made up of a small group of scientists who had returned from the USA. The bomb was one of the reasons why General de Gaulle (as he said later) established this organization. Despite the reluctance of some of its founders (such as Joliot-Curie, who was soon sacked for his pro-communist views), its military sector developed in great secrecy through the Bureau d'Études Générales and the so-called Reseau K (Network K), under the direction of Général Buchalet. The production of plutonium and the design of the bomb were pursued without the full knowledge of the political powers, up to the mid-1950s, when funding was officially allocated by the government of Félix–Gaillard. During this period, the CEA grew very fast, developing a fuel cycle for natural uranium, a power station design of the Magnox type (UNGG), and a number of civil research centres (*centres d'études*), many of which were also industrial plants.

The CEA is legally a 'public body'. It was placed under the direct control of the prime minister in the 1960s. The consequence of its *tutelle* (aegis) being so high in the state hierarchy was that it enjoyed great day-to-day autonomy, so long as it followed the broad policy direction of the government in power. Interestingly, neither the energy nor industry ministers (on the civil side of the CEA), nor the armed forces (on the military side) had any control over how the CEA used its funding. De Gaulle created this power-base in order to shake the power of the traditional military technicians and create a generation of nuclear pioneers for the *grandeur* of France.

But as early as 1967–68, de Gaulle was making changes which led him to disregard the CEA lobby. Since then, the CEA, still a powerful organization especially in respect to military uses of nuclear power, has suffered several identity crises and re-organizations.

A DIFFICULT TRANSITION FOR A SOUL-SEARCHING INSTITUTION

The first difficult period for the CEA was in the late 1960s, when de Gaulle gave Electricité de France the contract to build a PWR designed by the US company Westinghouse in preference to the CEA's own design. (The PWR, which used enriched uranium, was to become the design for future French power stations.) This was a heavy blow for the CEA, which was championing its own UNGG design (similar to the British Magnox reactor). As a result, the CEA's own monopoly on nuclear technology was shattered.

In 1970, the CEA found itself criticized from all sides, with a demoralized staff. The government, following the advice of a special commission, demoted the CEA and reduced the autonomy of its scientists. The CEA was no longer directly supervised by the prime minister but by the research minister, and the Haut-Commissaire (the chief scientist) lost his executive power to the Administrateur Général, an administrative appointee. The man chosen to be the new head, André Giraud (later to become defence minister in the Chirac government), used the experience he had acquired in the oil industry to make a success of this restructuring: he created a number of subsidiaries for operating the fuel cycle and industrial operations, and streamlined the R & D operations of the CEA itself.

A new identity crisis began to affect the CEA in the early 1980s. Most of its operations were becoming routine and there were very few new challenges in its traditional sphere which could allow it to build a new power base: the nuclear deterrent was in place as was a nuclear power capacity. A 1982 reform attempted therefore to

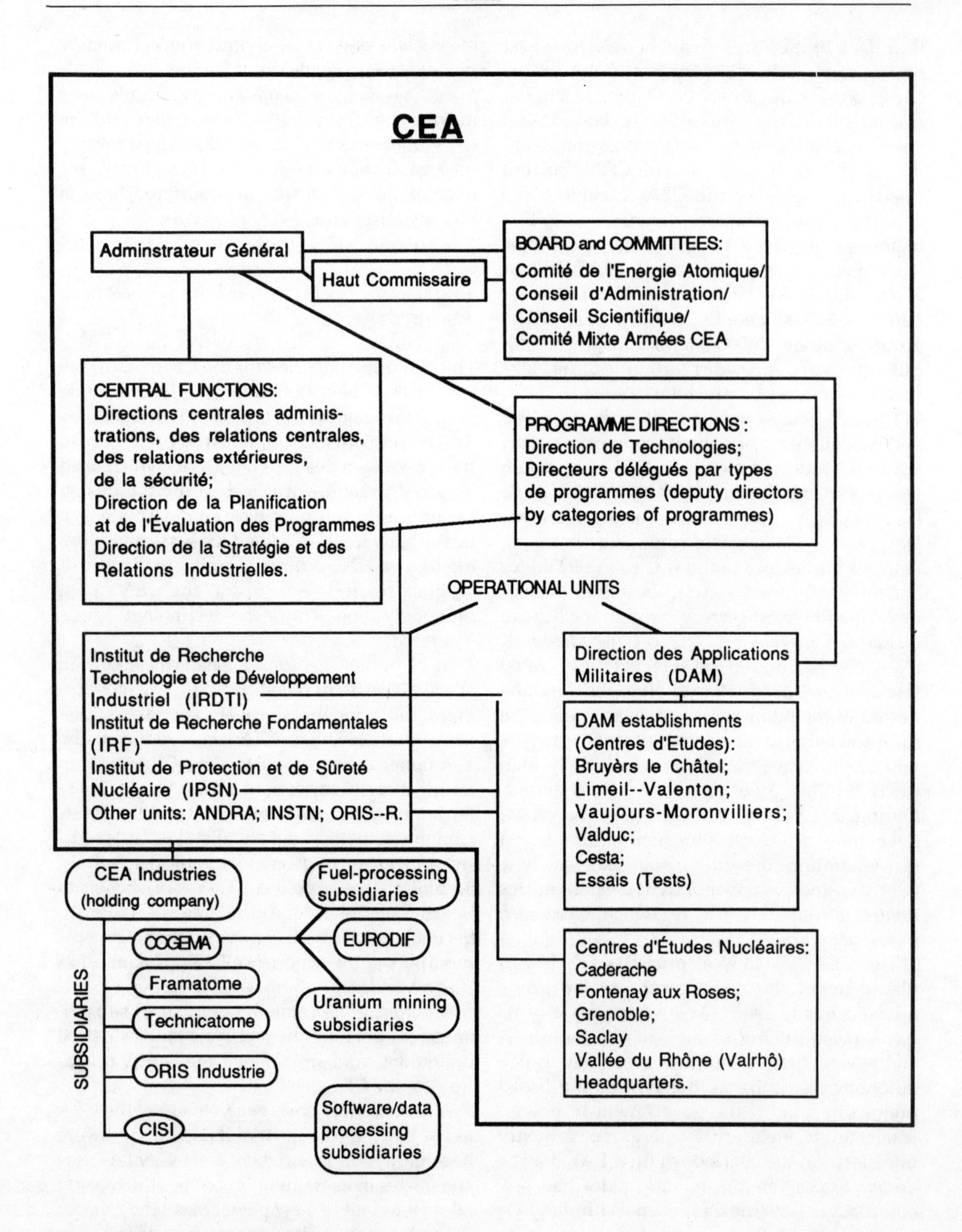

Figure 4.3 *Structure of the CEA group*

turn the CEA in a new direction, organizing its operational units into four institutes, one of which was the Institut de Recherche et Développement Industriel, intended to diversify the CEA's activities under the direction of the new administrator, Gérard Renon. By the mid-1980s, however, the CEA's problems had not disappeared: nuclear power was still beset with problems, Chernobyl cast its shadow, and the Superphoenix fast-breeder project had to be stopped for technical reasons and was proving to be uneconomical in a period of nuclear power overcapacity. In 1986, a new re-organization took place.

The new reform aimed at accelerating diversification and at decentralizing operational responsibilities. The resulting structure is shown in Figure 4.3. That this new structure was introduced in 1986, with a new man at the head of CEA, in the year when the Chirac government took power, led some commentators to conclude that the privatization of some of CEA-Industries was on its way.

The CEA Top Management

The top management of the CEA is headed by the Administrateur Général Délégué par le Gouvernement, a very powerful figure who has full executive control of the CEA and is also chair of the management boards of the CEA itself and of CEA-Industries, the 100 per cent holding company. The Administrateur Général and the board manage the CEA within the framework established by the Comité de l'Énergie Atomique. This Atomic Energy Committee is a powerful institution, comparable at its own level to, say, the CRED in the DGA. It is chaired by the Prime Minister or another minister (for example, those responsible for research, defence or industry). It includes people such as the Administrateur Général, the Haut Commissaire, the head of the DAM, and other leading figures. For instance, in the government Cabinet meeting of 2 December 1987, the following people were appointed to the committee: Renaud Denoix de Saint-Marc (Government General Secretary), General Schmitt (Chief of Joint Staff), Jacques Chevallier (director of DGA), Victor Marçais (director of DRET), Pierre Delaporte (chair of the board of directors of EdF), François Saglio (General Director of Industry in the Ministry of Industry), as well as the director of the École Normale Supérieure.

Another individual with significant weight is the Haut Commissaire. Until 1970 he was the real head of the CEA. Since then, he has been the scientific adviser of the Administrateur Général and the chair of a number of committees (notably the Conseil Scientifique, a scientific advisory committee, but also a number of committees concerned with safety).

The other top managers of the CEA basically head the main structures of the organization. The 1986 re-organization created four types of structures: the central functional directorates, which establish the general policy and fulfil central functions; the programme directorates, which are responsible for overseeing task-based programmes; the operational directorates, which organize the execution of the various programmes in specific areas of activity; and, finally, the research or production establishments in which the operations are physically performed.

In relation to nuclear weapons development and production, the Direction des Applications Militaires is responsible for most of the fundamental research, all the exploratory development, and the production and maintenance of the bombs themselves. It is treated separately below because of its importance. But other departments of the CEA are also relevant, either because of their managerial role or because their activities have a direct or indirect bearing on nuclear weapons development.

Of the central, functional directorates, two are of particular importance, as they help to define and plan the general strategy of the CEA: these are the Direction de la Planification et de l'Évaluation des Programmes (Directorate for Programmes Planning and Evaluation), which co-ordinates, and oversees the execution of, the various research, R & D and production programmes, and the Direction de la Stratégie et des Relations Industrielles (Directorate for Strategy and Industrial Relations), which is concerned with the industrial means and structures necessary to undertake programmes. Their respective directors have influence on the way the services, programmes and the departments of the CEA contribute to nuclear weapons development and to advanced weapons research.

The Direction des Technologies (Technology Directorate) has overall responsibility for all programme areas, such as waste management, the decommissioning of nuclear plants, life sciences, etc. The director of the Technology Directorate has a particular influence on the orientation of research applications.

Within the various non-military operational units, two have great importance in developing research directions and technological operations with direct or indirect relevance to the work of the Direction des Applications Militaires. The first of these is the Institut de Recherche Technologique et de Développement Industriel (IRTDI: Institute for Technological Research and Industrial Development), which, despite its specialization in the various aspects of the nuclear fuel cycle and nuclear reactors development, has an impact on the (militarily significant) fissile material production technology. It is also responsible for all aspects of technological diversification and innovation outside the nuclear field. The second important unit is the Institut de Recherche Fondamentale (Institute for Fundamental Research), which employs around 1,100 people and is responsible for advanced research in physics. It collaborates with civil laboratories and with the DAM's own researchers. The use of the Institute's research for long-term weapons development is unavoidable — especially within the nuclear physics and elementary particles physics departments.

The other operational units have little impact on the military activities of the CEA: the Agence Nationale pour la Gestion des Déchets Radioactifs (ANDRA), responsible for nuclear waste management, the Institut National des Sciences et Techniques Nucléaires (INSTN), a training institute for nuclear engineers, and the Institut de Protection et Sûreté Nucléaire, which is responsible for safety studies, procedures, technologies, etc.

(See biographies of: Capron (Deputy General Adminstrator, CEA); Cribier (Director, Institute for Fundamental Research); Ferrari (Director of Programme Planning and Evaluation, CEA) ; Mortier (Director, Strategy and Industrial Relations, CEA); Rapin (Director of Technology, CEA); Teillac (Commissioner for Atomic Energy, CEA).)

The Direction des Applications Militaires (DAM)

The Direction des Applications Militaires (DAM: Directorate of Military Applications) is essentially a nuclear bomb factory: the research and development and production of nuclear weapons is its *raison d' être*. Now that nuclear warheads are more sophisticated, its activities are probably more varied now than they were in the 1960s and recently it has been leaning towards 'star wars'-type research. Nevertheless, its basic function remains that of a research and production facility for nuclear weapons. It now employs around 8,900 persons directly (1986 figures); this represents some 40 per cent of total CEA jobs. Nearly all the top engineers who run it are *ingénieurs de l'armement* who spend part of their careers at the DGA in the Defence Ministry. The administrative structure of DAM, its internal budgeting and the details of its activities are strictly secret, although recently some details have trickled out following the reform of the CEA's structure in 1986 and in the documents released by the United States Department of Commerce in January 1987.

DAM is not responsible for the production of the weapons grade nuclear material it uses. The plutonium, tritium, lithium and highly enriched uranium are all produced by COGEMA. DAM simply places orders for the material it needs. The co-ordination of COGEMA's activities with the needs of the DAM takes place at the very highest level and is a function of the Administrateur Général.

As regards weapons R & D, DAM is almost entirely self-sufficient. While it works with 'civilian' CEA research establishments, such as the CEN of Grenoble, Saclay, Fontenay, etc., as well as with universities and other institutions outside the CEA, the flow of information is all one way. DAM has access to the results of research carried out anywhere in France, but shares none of its own. The 1986 re-organization may mean, however, that some collaboration at the technological level may perhaps develop with the outside world.

Since 1 January 1986, the directors of DAM's *centres d'études* have been given authority over the units situated in these centres; previously some of the most important units were controlled directly by headquarters. Moreover, the *centres d'études* have been asked to contribute to technological development in their regions. For example, Vergne, director of the Valduc centre d'études which produces nuclear bombs, signed a partnership agreement with a science park in the Burgundy region for the development and promotion of laser and electronic welding (*Inter Info* (internal journal of CEA), No. 210, March 1987).

Little is now known of what goes on within the walls of the six DAM *centres d'études*. Two of the three centres situated around Paris are prime nuclear weapons design centres (Bruyères le Châtel, and Vaujours–Moronvilliers). A third, Limeil-Valenton to the south of Paris is where DAM conducts advanced R & D for the high technology weapons of the future. Here, high energy laser programmes are developed such as the OCTAL and PHEBUS programmes for X-ray lasers.

Outside Paris, DAM has three other *centres d'études* which are predominantly production facilities for nuclear warheads although they also conduct R & D. Warheads are produced in series at the very important *centre d'études* of Valduc, in the north of Burgundy, in the Départment de Production d'Ensembles Nucléaires. This *centre d'études* also includes a Section d'Études de Criticacité et de Rayonnement (Section for the Study of Criticality and Radiation). Most of the nuclear material such as tritium and plutonium from COGEMA thus comes to Valduc; the secret military FBR reactor, Rachel, is also said to be located there.

Another important *centre d'études* is at Le Ripault, near the large town of Tours, in the Loire valley. As at Valduc, R & D, especially on implosion and detonation, is carried out at Le Ripault (it is probably here that the neutron bomb was developed). Ripault manufactures detonator units for warheads. Le Ripault is also the main centre for the maintenance of the existing stock of warheads, together with the sixth *centre d'études*, CESTA (Centre d'Études Scientifiques et Techniques d'Aquitaine) located at Le Barp, near Bordeaux. CESTA is where the instrumentation of nuclear warheads is developed, and where the engineering for weapons tests is carried out.

(See biographies of: Baleras (Deputy Director, DAM, CEA); Vidart (Director Military Affairs, DAM, CEA).)

Subsidaries with Military Activities

Most of the CEA's fuel cycle and non-nuclear activities have been hived off to commercial subsidiaries controlled by a holding group, CEA-Industries. Among the various companies in this group, a few have considerable military importance, although none of them has real decisionmaking power. The two most significant are COGEMA and Technicatome.

The main activities of COGEMA and its subsidiaries are uranium extraction and enrichment, fuel fabrication for nuclear plants, and fuel reprocessing. It produces military grade plutonium, highly enriched uranium, lithium and thorium.

COGEMA was created in the 1960s. It is now a giant international concern, wholly owned by CEA-Industries. Fuel processing forms a large part of its activities and nuclear materials for nuclear weapons use are produced at its plants in the Rhône Valley but the reprocessing plant at La Hague, near Cherbourg, is not directly involved

COGEMA is not particularly privy to the development or production of nuclear weapons. It simply fills orders for nuclear materials placed with it by the Direction des Applications Militaires of the CEA. Obviously, managers at COGEMA have a certain power in their specific field, but not at policy or development decisionmaking level.

Where, among all the COGEMA plants and establishments, are these military materials produced? In fact, the sources are widespread. Military-grade enriched uranium (90 per cent enrichment) is produced at the Pierrelatte enrichment plant which uses the gaseous diffusion facilities which have not been transferred to the EURODIF for low to medium enrichment levels for civilian purposes. Production of military grade plutonium entails the breeding of radioactive materials in nuclear reactors specially driven at a certain rate of reactivity for this purpose. The 'spent' material fuel is then reprocessed for plutonium extraction. Until recently, special reactors at the Marcoule plant were used: Celestin 1 and 2, and 'pile' G3. G3 is now decommissioned, and fuel from the Phoenix FBR and the Chinon 3 probably complement the material irradiated in Celestin 1 and 2. Spent fuel is then reprocessed in the UP1 workshop at Marcoule. UP1 has been modernized, with the new MAR-400 head-end installed.

Two other important products for nuclear bombs are also produced in the Rhône Valley: lithium-6 is produced at the Miramas COGEMA plant, and tritium is extracted at Marcoule (lithium is irradiated in the two Celestin reactors, and tritium is extracted in the special Atelier d'Extraction du Tritium).

Another important contribution of the CEA subsidiaries to the nuclear arsenal is the design and the manufacture of PWR reactors for nuclear-powered submarines: this activity is the responsibility of Technicatome, a company owned 90 per cent by the CEA and 10 per cent by Électricité de France. It specializes in all types of small and medium-sized reactors, including research and submarine reactors. Technicatome has built the reactors of the SNLEs, the current ballistic missile submarines, and is currently building the new ones for the SNLE–NG. It is also designing the propulsion unit for the nuclear-powered aircraft-carrier *Charles de Gaulle*.

(See biographies of: Bonnet (Managing Director, Technicatome); De Willocq (Managing Director, COGEMA).)

THE INDUSTRIAL SECTOR: PUBLIC AND PRIVATE MANUFACTURERS

Introduction

The French weapons manufacturing sector is a very large industry: in 1987 it accounted for 6 per cent of the GDP, 11 per cent of industrial exports and 17 per cent of exports of capital goods. It employs nearly 300,000 people and makes France the third-ranking power in terms of arms production. It is strongly oriented towards exports: these accounted for approximately FF35.2 billion in 1985, its peak period, some 30 per cent of its activities. (The total annual turnover of military activities of the two arsenal groups (GIAT, DCN) and the nine main weapons and equipment manufacturers (Thomson–CSF, SNIAS, AMD–BA, Matra, SNECMA, SNPE, Luchaire, Panhard and ESD) are currently around FF93 billion. The total sector turnover in 1986 was FF110 billion including FF8 billion accounted for in the production of nuclear bombs by the CEA's Direction des Applications Militaires. Estimates of the industry's total weight vary considerably — some experts claim that around one million jobs depend on the arms industry, directly or indirectly, through the extended use of subcontracting.

Whatever the exact size of the industry, the fact is that it has suffered a significant setback in 1986–87 and, despite some signs of recovery, notably in aerospace, it has not yet recovered the economic strength it had at the beginning of the 1980s. The current level of exports is at around FF27 billion. The consequences for employment are potentially important. As Henri Gonze, until recently 'Mr Export' at the DGA, said in early 1988: 'Our industry is geared up for sales of around FF100 to 110 billion, including FF45 billion in exports. If those exports fall to FF25 billion in the medium term, we will have to reduce our capacities by 20 per cent'. (*Science et Vie Économique*, No. 36, February 1988.) Some large companies, such as AMD–BA (the Dassault company), have already shed several thousand jobs in 1987, and the consequences for some of the 5,000 to 6,000 small to medium-sized sub-contractors could be significant.

What is the significance of the arms firms for nuclear weaponry? The situation is very different from that in the United States, where a limited number of large companies win contracts from the Pentagon for the development

Firm	Turnover (FF)/Nuclear-related employmentactivities		
Thomson–CSF (A subsidiary of the nationalized Thomson–Brant group)	Total turnover Arms Total employed – in military production	36.1 billion 24.5 billion 42,000 29,000	Electrical and electronics systems for all missiles (SSBS, MSBS, Pluton, Hadès, ASMP, etc.); electronic command and control systems
SNIAS (Aérospatiale (Société Nationale)	Total turnover Arms Total employed – in military production	25.4 billion 15.8 billion 34,200 17,100	Ballistic and tactical nuçlear missiles, general engineering (SSBS, Pluton, Hadès, ASMP)
DCN Arsenals	Total turnover (all military)	17 billion 28,400	Design and manufactures all warships, attack nuclear submarines, strategic missile submarines (SNLEs)
AMD–BA (Dassault) (Société nationalisé: state has 46% of shares and 55% of vote)	Total turnover Arms Total employed – in military production	15.6 billion 13.4 billion 16,600 12,600	Bomber and fighter aircraft with strategic and tactical nuclear roles (Mirage IV-A, Mirage 2000-N, Super-Etendard, Rafale)
MATRA (nationalized firm with subsidiaries Manutrin and Matra-Défense, privatized in January 1988)	Total turnover Arms Total employed – in military production	14.4 billion 5.2 billion 5,800 3,800	Missiles and electronics. Only nuclear weapons involvement is sub-contract with Hadés programme
GIAT	Total turnover (all military) Total employed	7.1 billion 17,000	Tanks, guns, ammunitions; Launch vehicles for tactical missiles
SNECMA	Total turnover Arms Total employed – in military production	10.2 billion 5.2 billion 14,400 8,800	Jet engines (ATAR, M53, M88) for nuclear-capable aircraft. Subsidiary SEP produces propulsion units for ballistic and'pre-strategic' missiles.
SNPE (Société Nationale des Poudres and Explosifs)	Total turnover Arms Total employed – in military production	2.9 billion 1.8 billion 6,900 4,800	Specializes in explosive and ammunitions; bomb detonator components for tactical and strategic missiles

Figure 4.4 *Major military equipment manufacturers and their nuclear-related activities (all figures for the end of 1986)*

of whole systems, and where there is a relatively strict *a posteriori* control by parliamentary bodies. In France the situation varies, depending on the type of material being built. For instance, nuclear submarines and their missiles are largely the responsibility of the Direction des Constructions Navales, which designs, tests, builds and maintains the ships and their armament (except for the nuclear reactors, which are the responsibility of the CEA subsidiary Technicatome and the warheads themselves, the responsibility of the CEA/DAM). But the land-based SSBS missiles on the Plateau d'Albion are built and commissioned through close collaboration between the Direction des Engins of the DGA, and Aérospatiale, the *maître d'œuvre*, both of which co-ordinate the work of a host of large and small companies as well as the R & D work of ONERA and CNES.

In the case of aircraft, particularly nuclear bombers and tactical fighters, it can be said that the development of new models is the result of intense lobbying at the highest level by Dassault, which goes over the head of the Direction des Constructions Aéronautiques and deals directly at the level of the Minister of Defence and Prime Minister.

So arms contractors are involved in the production of nuclear weapons systems in a variety of ways. But even where industries, public or private, take the lead in the development and production of equipment, the close relationship between the DGA and these companies is often further enhanced by the continuous flow of top staff and managers between the armed forces, the DGA and the weapons industry. Figure 4.4 summarizes the impact of the most prominent of these firms on the development and production of equipment for the nuclear forces.

The DGA Arsenals

As was explained in the section on the DGA, only two of the five operational directorates of the Délégation Générale pour l'Armement include sizeable industrial facilities: the Direction des Armements Terrestres (with its Groupement Industriel des Armements Terrestres or GIAT) and the Direction des Constructions Navales, which has its own shipyards, well known for the quality of their work.

The GIAT is not deeply involved in nuclear weapons development. The only impact it has in this sphere is as the supplier of launch vehicles for tactical, 'prestrategic', missiles such as Pluton and Hadès and as a subcontractor for some nuclear weapons equipment. For instance, the ATS, the GIAT factory at Tarbes, which is equipped with advanced machinery, is subcontracting work from SNIAS for parts of the Hadès prestrategic missile.

A future opportunity for GIAT will be the construction of the launch vehicles for the new S4 ballistic missiles. These missiles (nicknamed 'missiles on castors') could be deployed partly in silos in Haut Provence, and partly on mobile launchers deployed on trains or road vehicles.

The DCN arsenals are of a different order. Two of particular importance are the arsenals at Cherbourg and Brest. All the nuclear-powered submarines, both attack and strategic, are built, fitted and tested at Cherbourg. A new covered yard with high technology facilities has been installed specially for the construction of the second generation strategic submarines, the SNLE-NGs (Sous-marins Nucléaires Lanceurs d'Engins–Nouvelle Génération), the first one of which is currently being built. Moreover, the Cherbourg arsenal is in charge of reconditioning four of the first five SNLEs in order to modernize them and equip them with the new MIRVed M4 missiles. The Cherbourg arsenal employs 4,650 people (out of a total of 31,700 employed by the DCN). It is a large-scale industrial centre, with little call for outside expertise and industrial capabilities.

The Cherbourg arsenal, because it has a considerable impact on the design of a whole nuclear system, is the only industrial unit of the DGA which can be said to be influential, together with the central services of the DCN, in nuclear weapons decisionmaking.

Brest is the Atlantic base of the submarine deterrent force. The Brest DCN arsenal is in charge of the routine maintenance of the SNLEs. It employs 6,950 people. Another establishment, at Indret, repairs and maintains the non-nuclear parts of the submarines' propulsion units.

The Aerospace Industry: Missiles and Planes

The French aerospace industry is dominated by two international-scale companies: SNIAS (known as the Aérospatiale) and AMD–BA (Avions Marcel Dassault–Bréguet Aviation, known as Dassault). A number of other companies contribute specific systems components (for instance SNECMA makes jet engines, SEP propulsion units for missiles, Thomson–CSF electronics and avionics).

As has been noted, the military equipment industry is a complex sector, in which the administration, public R & D bodies, large public and private conglomerates and a large number of small and medium-sized subcontractors compete and combine to develop and produce military technology. This is illustrated by the fact that Dassault sometimes subcontracts Aérospatiale to manufacture parts for fighters, while Aérospatiale sometimes contracts establishments of the DAT to manufacture parts of nuclear missiles ordered by the DEn.

The aerospace industry is, of course, also deeply involved in the manufacture of civil aircraft. Aérospatiale obtains nearly half of its turnover from civil orders, although Dassault specializes mainly in military aircraft.

How do Aérospatiale, Dassault, SNECMA and SEP affect nuclear weapons procurement policy? It is necessary to distinguish lobbying for particular contracts from the more diffuse influence on policy that a particular group of industrialists can exercise. Dassault and Aérospatiale are undeniably extremely powerful as lobbies. However, they can also have an influence on policy, firstly, through the osmotic relationship between their management and R & D staff and the defence ministry's own professional staff and, secondly, through the contacts of their top managers with political figures and their immediate advisers. A number of the industrialist decisionmakers whose biographies are included here were fomerly in the DGA. For example, Henri Martre, current head of Aérospatiale, was formerly the Délégué Générale pour l'Armement, and Bernard Capillon, the current director of SNECMA, was previously Air Force Chief of Staff. There is also intense collaboration, at a more technical level, between the industrial firms and the R & D, testing and industrial development units in the DGA's own operational directorates, such as the DEn, the DCAé and even the DAT or the DEI. The skills and resources of public 'trade and industrial establishments' such as the ONERA (Office National d'Études et de Recherches Spatiales), are put at the disposal of Aérospatiale for projects in which this company is *maître d'œuvre* (project leader). This collaborative work is, however, carefully costed, and sophisticated costing and programming systems are used.

The way the various companies relate to the defence ministry depends upon their legal and commercial status. State companies are either 'public establishments', which are totally controlled by an administration (such as ONERA by DRET), or commercial firms whose shares are controlled by the state, either totally (in the case of nationalized firms, such as Aérospatiale) or in part (as in 'mixed economy' firms such as Dassault). In any case, commercial status companies are checked and controlled at two levels at least: in the boardroom, where state representatives (the so-called *commissaires du gouvernment*) make up either part or nearly all of the board and — in the case of totally nationalized companies — where the executive director is directly appointed by government cabinet; and, secondly, by technical or programme comptrollers (described in the section on the DGA).

The industries should not be seen as bodies which formulate policies on nuclear weapons procurement. But they do have influence at the level of technological and industrial choice. They are part of the weapons community, involved in its infighting, politicking and alliances. The trend, however, is likely to be towards a loss of autonomy and influence in the coming years: numerous commentators have emphasized the fact that the Rafale advanced fighter development is probably the last all-

French total aircraft development and that French industry is more and more involved in international collaborative efforts in missiles, planes and guns. The implications of this trend for the production of nuclear weapons and the associated infrastructure is still unclear. Many leading figures in France favour a European integration of some industries such as aerospace.

For instance, Henri Martre, chief executive of Aérospatiale, was reportedly very angry about British Aerospace's decision to diversify into car manufacture by acquiring Rover; he would like to see, ultimately, a merger of all the large European manufacturers still specializing in aircraft manufacture — such as BA, SNIAS, MMB — in order to compete with the US company Boeing. Diversification is seen as an obstacle to this ambitious plan.
(See biographies of: Betin (Deputy Manger, SEP) ; Calmon (Production Director, SNECMA); Capillon (President, Director General, SNECMA); Dassault (President, Director General, Dassault Aviation) ; Hugues (Director, Aquitaine Aérospatiale plant); Lachaume (Technical Director, SNECMA); Martre (Managing Director, Aérospatiale); Michot (Deputy Director, SNIAS); Poggi (Director of Propulsion, SNIAS); Revellin-Falcoz, (Vice-President of Research and Development, Dassault); Sollier (Director, SEP, Deputy Director, SNECMA).)

Electronics and Information Systems

Modern weaponry is increasingly being designed to incorporate 'intelligent' characteristics, such as continuous retargeting, contour following, multiple independently targetable warheads, satellite communications and command communications; and these are only the first stages in further developments. However, because electronics and information systems are only components of weapons systems, most electronics companies have no significant influence on decisionmaking, except in the case of the larger companies which design entire communication, command and targeting systems. In France, of the several companies which have a technological edge in armament electronics (Électronique Serge Dassault, CGE, Thomson–CSF) only Thomson–CSF has such a capability. The others act mostly as subcontractors, or are associated with developments under the authority of a *maître d'œuvre* (project manager), either of the main industrial manufacturer (generally Aérospatiale) or of the arsenals (DCn or DAT). But Thomson–CSF is in another league. It is a major exporter of military communications equipment (its equipment has been sold to the US Army, for instance). It has also contributed significantly to the development of ballistic missiles — it has just obtained the contracts for the electronics of the S4 ballistic SSBS missile. Thomson–CSF has always managed to fend off bids in this field by its competitor, Électronique Serge Dassault.

Thomson–Brant, the parent company, was nationalized in 1982 by Mauroy's socialist government and changed its name to Thomson SA. At that time the company was in poor shape: it was not particularly innovative and was spread over too many activities. The new managing director, Alain Gomez, pursued a policy of concentrating the company's interests in three sectors, namely armaments, domestic electronic products and electronic components, making acquisitions in these sectors and selling off the company's interests in others. (One of the new holdings, Thomson–RCA, became the third largest producer of colour TVs in the world).

This major reorganization left the company's armaments interests concentrated into two companies: Thomson Armements (specializing in missiles and similar hardware) and Thomson–CSF (communications, radar, guidance and command systems). The Chirac government intended to privatize Thomson; however, the defeat of Chirac at the presidential elections in May 1988 indefinitely postponed this project; Mitterrand now favours maintaining the status quo in the public sector.

Besides the electronics and aerospace manufacturers and the arsenals, there are a number of other arms companies and manufacturing firms which make some contribution to nuclear weapons sytems. However, none have a significant role, with the exception of the Société Nationale des Poudres et Explosifs (SNPE), which is one of the world leaders in explosives of all sorts as well as in detonating systems. It is associated with the development and construction of the nuclear deterrent in two ways: it carries out studies on detonators for DAM and the CEA, and it develops solid propellants for ballistic missiles, with SEP (Société Européenne de Propulsion), the subsidiary of SNECMA. The SNPE is under the administrative control of the DGA. The SNPE has recently been embroiled in a series of mini 'Irangates' which forced the resignation of its previous director. *(See biographies of: Cambier (Director, C3 Systems, Thomson–CSF); Clavelloux (Manager, Systems and Weapons Branch, Thomson–CSF); Gomez (Managing Director, Thomson–CSF); Philipponnat (Director of National Munitions Corporation).)*

THE ARMED FORCES

The Armed Forces and Nuclear Weapons

It is often said that the French armed forces have little say in the development, deployment and definition of rules of engagement of the nuclear forces, and that they simply obey orders coming from the political sphere or from the procurement sections of the Ministry of Defence, which are dominated by engineers. The nuclear deterrent was forced upon the French armed forces by de Gaulle during a period in the late 1950s and the 1960s, when the armed forces were also having to absorb the traumas of defeat in the wars of liberation in France's former colonies in South East Asia and Algeria.

The nuclear deterrent disrupted three fundamental aspects of military structure. It cut across traditional hierarchies and created new lines of command, with the President of the Republic becoming an operational commander. It destroyed the existing basis of strategic thinking (already weakened by guerrilla warfare in the colonial wars) and replaced it with concepts based on a 'strategy of means' rather than operational strategy. It destabilized the delicate equilibrium between the Army, the Air Force and the Navy, in particular weakening the Army. Two of the three components of the strategic deterrent were integrated into the Air Force (the land-based missiles and the nuclear bombers), and the third into the Navy (the ballistic missile submarines).

De Gaulle, himself an experienced military man and strategist, was deeply suspicious of the armed forces, particularly after the revolt of the generals in Algiers against the granting of independence to Algeria in 1962. De Gaulle forced radical changes on the entire armed forces, particularly the Army. This service (nicknamed *la grande muette* — the mute giant — because it obeys without protest) suffered the most severe effects of the reforms. Its numbers fell from 830,000 men in 1957 to 330,000 in 1964, a fall of 60 per cent.

The first institutional change introduced in June 1958 was the elimination of the secretaries of state for each of the three armed forces. In 1962 the military hierarchy was centralized through the creation of a Joint Armed Forces Chief of Staff and a Joint Staff, with the role of directing the overall strategy and coordinating the preparation and planning of all the armed forces. Another change which cut through the tradition was the creation of the Centre de Prospective et d'Évaluation in 1964 (the precursor of GroupeS and now DEG) at the Ministry of Defence to formulate nuclear strategy.

These changes circumscribed the pre-eminence of the three services in the management of their own military affairs. The introduction of nuclear forces did not, however, eliminate the lobbying power of the military services. On the contrary, in at least two respects, the military hierarchy has been quite successful in influencing events. First, the development of the 'pre-strategic' tactical nuclear forces has had as much to do with the determination of the Army to participate in these new forms of military power as with the development of strategic thinking. Second, strategic thinking is itself subject to the lobbying of specific interest groups in the armed forces. The case which best illustrates this is the way the Army staff (EMAT: État Major de l'Armée de Terre) developed the concepts of *bataille de l'avant* (forward battle) and promoted the use of nuclear tactical weaponry as battlefield artillery. It has been reported that

Presidents de Gaulle and Pompidou had to intervene firmly to prevent such positions becoming official.

Each armed force has now integrated nuclear weaponry into its own thinking and forges alliances with other institutions in the procurement system to lobby for particular weapons. For example the Army Staff, DAM and parts of the DGA lobbied jointly for rapid deployment of the neutron bomb. When the Chirac government came to power in 1986, it was assumed that deployment would proceed fairly quickly. However, Mitterrand's resistance prevented this development.

Conflicts regularly occur between the armed forces concerning potential weakening of their own part of the nuclear force. It is always instructive to read the yearly *ordres du jour* (standing orders) addressed by the various chiefs of staff to their troops explaining that they hold the most valuable share of these nuclear forces. Currently two debates are under way. One is about the planned abolition of the long-range strategic bombing forces based on Mirage IV-P squadrons, sometime in the 1990s: a rearguard lobby has been organized to promote the use of long-range bombers rather than develop the mobile S4 missile. The other is over the Navy's recently expressed concern that the Ministry of Defence (then under André Giraud) was limiting budgetary facilities for the retrofitting of older nuclear submarines with new missiles, in order to provide more funds for the development of the S4s and the tactical nuclear forces.

The Chiefs of Staff

There are four chiefs of staff: one for each of the three forces, and the Joint Chief of Staff. The Joint Chief of Staff (the Chef-d'État Major des Armées, a post created in 1962) has authority over the three chiefs of staff, except in relation to budgetary matters (these are decided by the Minister in liaison with the Committee of Chiefs of Staff, which is chaired by the Minister himself).

The responsibilities and powers of the four chiefs of staff were last established by Decree No. 82–138 dated 8 February 1982, which reaffirms the predominance of the Chef d'État-Major des Armées (CEMA) over the three others. In relation to nuclear weapons decisionmaking, the four chiefs of staff have three types of powers. First, they participate in the making of national policy as members of the Conseil de Défense, as members of the Conseil des Recherches et Études de Défense (CRED), and as participants in the planning of the defence budget and the *lois de programmation*. Secondly, they participate in long-term development policy by establishing strategic requirements for their own forces. Thirdly, they control the deployment and operational dispositions of the nuclear forces under their authority.

The most important figure in this regard is the Joint Chief of Staff (the CEMA), who would automatically become the 'Commander-in-Chief' of all the armed forces in wartime. He has his own staff, organized in six divisions and headed by a major general, and other services under him include two inspectorates and the Centre d'Exploitation du Renseignement Militaire (CERM: Centre for the Exploitation of Military Intelligence). He advises the government and the defence minister on military issues.

Even in peacetime, the Joint Chief of Staff has the authority to determine the operational duties of the Army, the Air Force and Navy Chief of Staffs and to co-ordinate their operations. For instance he directs manœuvres involving combined forces. In Article 5 of Decree No. 82–138, dated 8 February 1982, it is emphasized that 'the Joint Chief of Staff co-ordinates the proposals of the Delegate General for Armaments ('Délégué Général pour l'Armement'), of the chiefs of staff, and of the directors of inter-forces services in the areas of planning and programming'; and even more important, 'the Joint Chief of Staff proposes, after consulting with the chiefs of staff affected, the military characteristics of nuclear and space weapons and equipment and is consulted on the technical solutions studied by the Delegate General for Armaments'. As a consequence, the Joint Chief of Staff occupies a central role in the nuclear decisionmaking process in France, despite the fact that in most instances the characteristics of nuclear weaponry are a *fait accompli*, which pre-empts any autonomous decisions from the military sphere.

Therefore, the CEMA is an institution which upholds the basic principle established in 1958 of putting all the defence institutions under one chain of command, in response to the requirement for unity of doctrine and total co-ordination of forces in the nuclear era. Consequently, the policy-framing powers of the three service chiefs of staff have been curtailed, and they no longer control long-term developments and strategy. They do, however, have a strong lobbying presence in nuclear policy matters, and an operational role which is not negligible.

It is interesting to note that, since the early 1970s, the Joint Chief of Staff and the Naval Chief of Staff (Chef d'État-Major de la Marine, CEMM) as well as the Air Force Chief of Staff (Chef d'État-Major de l'Armée de l'Air, CEMAA) have been officers with long experience of nuclear forces — either as direct commanders or as aides to policymakers (for instance as President's Chief of Staff).

(See biographies of: Forray (Army Chief of Staff); Lerche (Air Force Chief of Staff); Louzeau (Navy Chief of Staff); Schmitt (Joint Chief of Staff).)

Commanding Officers of the Nuclear Forces

This final subsection deals with the direct command of operational nuclear forces. It is useful to recapitulate the structure of the French nuclear forces. Basically, there are two elements: the Forces Nucléaires Stratégiques and the Forces Nucléaires Pré-Stratégiques.

The Strategic Nuclear Forces are organized into two commands, the strategic airforce (Forces Aériennes Stratégiques, FAS) and the strategic deep-sea force (Force Océanique Stratégique, FOST).

The strategic airforce is itself made up of two of the three strategic components of the French nuclear deterrent, the airborne strategic component (*componante stratégique pilotée*), consisting of four squadrons of Mirage IV-P bombers, equipped with new ASMP missiles with 300 kt bombs (which replaced the free-fall 60 kt AN22 bombs), associated with in-flight refuelling cargo planes C135F; and the SSBS missiles based at the Plateau d'Albion (currently, eighteen missiles of the S3D type with 1 megaton warhead in hardened silos, to be replaced during the 1990s by S4 missiles partly in the same silos and eventually partly on mobile launching vehicles). The third component is the FOST submarines. There are six of the first generation and a new SNLE–NG is being built. Four of the first generation submarines are retrofitted with new MIRVed M4 missiles (sixteen of them, so-called MSBS missiles replacing single warhead M20 missiles). Each M20 missile had a 1 megaton warhead. The new M4 is equipped with six warheads of 150 kt each, and has a 4,000 km range. The last (6th) SNLE is armed with M4 missiles. The new SNLE–NG will be equipped with the new M5 MIRVed missile and will be operational in the mid-1990s.

The commanders of the two nuclear forces of the strategic deterrent (FAS and FOST) are important figures in the military hierarchy. The FAS Commander (*commandant*), whose functions are laid down in the well-known Decree No. 64–46 dated 14 January 1964 (which is the legal basis for giving the President the ultimate power to launch nuclear weapons), is involved in more than simply executing orders; in Article 4 of the decree, it is emphasized that the FAS Commander 'participates in the studies related to the definitions and conditions of use of the FAS; prepares operational programmes and establishes for this purpose the requirements of means which are necessary; prepares the forces for their mission; participates in establishing testing and experimental programmes for equipment'. Article 5 of the same decree gives the FAS Commander the responsibility of executing engagement orders given by the President of the Republic (and only by him), and this line of command, outside the normal hierarchial framework, gives him relative autonomy. The situation of the FOST Commander is similar.

The Forces Nucléaires Pré-Strategiques (tactical nuclear forces) are spread over the three armed forces. They consist of air-to-ground missiles and ground-to-ground missiles. The air-to-ground missiles are carried by five squadrons of Mirage 111E and Jaguar A fighters (these are being progressively replaced by Mirage 2000-N now armed with the AN52 25-kt bomb, soon to be replaced with ASMP missiles). These squadrons are part of the Force Aérienne Tactique (FATac). The Navy also uses the AN52 in two maritime squadrons of Super Étendards stationed on the *Foch* and *Clemenceau* aircraft carriers, which will also get the ASMP in the coming year. In the future it is planned that the Super Étendard and the Mirage 2000/Jaguars will be replaced by the Rafale advanced fighter. However, the Navy judges that its Super Étendards are now completely obsolete and would prefer to order F18 fighters soon, rather than wait until the late 1990s for the Rafale.

The last component of the so-called pre-strategic nuclear forces is made up of ground-to-ground missiles. Currently, the Pluton missiles are deployed, to be replaced by the new Hadès missiles from 1990 onwards. Pluton has a 120–150 km range, and is launched from an AMX30-derived vehicle. These missiles are curently organized in five regiments and they can be equipped with 25, 15 or 10 kt bombs. The future Hadès has a range of around 500 km. It is planned to organise the Hadès-based forces in one large unit which would be placed directly under the authority of the CEMA, rather than spread in five regiments under the three army corps as the Plutos now are. As in the case of the strategic nuclear weapons, only the President can order the firing of these weapons.

(*See biographies of: Merveilleux Du Vignaux (Commander, Strategic Naval Force); Vougny (Commander, Strategic Air Force).*)

BIOGRAPHIES

Arnaud, Emile, Chef de la Mission 'Atome', Adjoint au Délégué Général pour l'Armement (DGA) (Head of the 'Atom' Unit and Assistant to the Deputy General for Armaments)
Address: 14 rue St Dominique, 75997 Paris Armées

Emile Arnaud is a *polytechnicien* who became an 'engineer-general for armaments' (*ingénieur général de l'armement*). He now plays a central role in the whole nuclear weapons development and deployment system. Operating directly under the authority of the DGA, he is responsible for developing and co-ordinating the work of the DGA with the organizations responsible for developing and supplying nuclear material and bombs – primarily, the Directorate of Military Applications (DAM) of the Atomic Energy Commission (CEA). Arnaud is also important because he manages the funding of the DAM from the defence budget.

Emile Arnaud was a member of the *cabinet* (private office) of Charles Hernu, when Hernu was Minister of Defence. He then took the post of director of international affairs (Directeur des Affaires Internationales) at the Délégation Générale pour l'Armement (DGA), directly under the authority of the then Délégué, Emile Blanc. There he was mainly responsible for the DGA's policy of encouraging arms industry exports. He resigned from this post in May 1986 when the new Defence Minister, Giraud, took office. Arnaud was appointed to his current post on 1 October 1987, after having occupied for just over a year the post of deputy to Benichou (the DPA).
(*See: The Organization of the DGA and the Changes in 1986.*)

Attali, Jacques, Conseiller Spécial auprés du Président de la République
(Special adviser to the President)
Address: Palais de l'Elysée, 55 rue du Faubourg Saint Honoré, 75008 Paris

Jacques Attali is one of Mitterrand's closest advisers. He accompanies the President on many of his official journeys, and is present at the weekly government meetings (Conseil des Ministres) presided over by the President. The presence at these meetings of Bianco, the General Secretary of the Presidency, is normal, as well as that of the General Secretary of the Government. But Attali, as special adviser, should not by rights be there: the practice was started when the socialist government was in power, and Chirac did not dare to challenge it when he took over in March 1986.

One of twin sons born in 1943 into a shopkeeping family in Algiers, Attali is a *pied noir* (French colonials who lived for generations in Algeria before returning to France just before Algerian independence in 1962).

Attali is a clever intellectual who made the most of the elitism of the *grandes écoles*. Graduating top of the 1963 class of *les X* (the students of the École Polytechnique), he then entered the École Nationale d'Administration. He has a doctorate in economics and is an *ingénieur des mines*. Like Bianco, he is a Maître des Requêtes at the Conseil d'Etat, the top administrative court of law. He is also a professor at the Ecole Polytechnique, a seminar director at the ÉNA, and the director of several university research centres. He also finds the time to pursue a busy writing career, publishing numerous essays on economics, the philosophy of history and social sciences, etc. Amongst his best known books, published in several languages, are *Anti-économie* (1974), *La Parole et l'outil* (1975), *Noises: an Essay on the Political Economy of Music* (1977), and *The Three Worlds* (1981).

Although he is very close to Mitterrand, it is not likely that Attali is particularly influential in nuclear strategy and politics (despite the fact that Mitterrand's closest diplomatic and nuclear affairs adviser, Regis Debray, resigned some years ago). Attali is more interested in political economy. But his daily contacts must make him an extremely well-informed and influential figure, even indirectly. He is considered by many to be an intellectual maverick, slightly feared even by his colleagues for his brilliant and sometimes mischievous ideas. He

loves classical music and history. He married in 1981 and has two small children, a son and a daughter.
(*See: The Presidency of the Republic.*)

Baleras, Roger, Deputy Director (Directeur Adjoint) of the DAM (CEA)
Address: 31-33 rue de la Fédération, 75015 Paris

Roger Baleras is an 'engineer-general of armaments' (*ingénieur général de l'armement*); he was trained at the École Polytechnique and École Supérieure de l'Armement. In his present position his job is to manage the work of the so-called *centres d'études* of the Directorate of Military Applications (DAM), where bombs are developed and manufactured.

When speaking recently about the interaction between strategy and weaponry, he put a lot of emphasis on 'discreet' weapons with reinforced targeted effects, meaning neutron weapons which kill humans but leave buildings intact. He described developments of tactical 'discreet' weapons thus: 'In the area of tactical weaponry, the current potential of neutron weapons...will influence operational strategies. Because of their flexibility of use, they will make it possible to increase the efficiency of conventional forces and therefore make the threat of the strategic nuclear deterrent more credible.'(Ministère de la Défense et DGA, 'La DGA face aux défis de l'avenir', FEDN, 1987, Paris.) This statement illustrates the extent to which technological expertise is at the service of the theory of flexible response.
(*See: The Direction des Applications Militaires.*)

Barbery, Jean, Inspecteur Général de l'Armement, Délégation Générale pour l'Armement (DGA) (Inspector General for Armaments at the DGA)
Address: Centre Sully, 92210 Saint-Cloud

Jean Barbery was born on 8 June 1929 at Saint-Germain-En-Laye, near Paris, to a magistrate and a primary school teacher. He went to the École Polytechnique and specialized in naval engineering. He worked at the Lorient military shipyards, where he directed a construction programme for escort vessels and the construction of the well-known frigate, *Suffren*. In 1971, he was appointed sub-director of industrial affairs in the Directorate of Programmes and Industrial Affairs (Direction des Programmes et des Affaires Industrielles) (DPAI), and became its director in 1974. He thus occupied this powerful position before the recent reorganization, which separated the responsibilities of the deputy for weapons programmes (Délégué aux Programmes d'Armement) from those of the SCAI (Service Central des Affaires Industrielles de l'Armement); before June 1986 these had devolved on the DPAI. He handed on that job to Benichou in 1978, returning to his own specialization as director of shipbuilding. He took up his current position as Inspecteur Général de l'Armement in 1986.

Jean Barbery is married to a doctor. They have three sons.
(*See: Organization of the DGA and the Changes in 1986.*)

Benichou, Marcel, Délégué aux Programmes d'Armement de la DGA (Delegate to the Armaments Programme at the DGA)
Address: 14 rue St Dominique, 75997 Paris Armées

Marcel Benichou has a central role because he plans and co-ordinates all the development programmes with which the DGA is associated.

Having trained at the École Polytechniqe, he is now an 'engineer-general for armamennts' (*ingénieur général de l'armement*). He has held different responsibilities for planning DGA activities since 1978, when he was appointed deputy director for industrial affairs at the Directorate of Programmes and Industrial Affairs (Direction des Programmes et Affaires Industrielles: DPAI), becoming its director in December 1981. In 1986 the DPAI was reorganized and its tasks allotted to the Délégué aux Programmes (the post he then assumed) and the Service Central des Affaires Industrielles de l'Armament (SCAI), which supervises the armament manufacturing firms.

Marcel Benichou has also been a board member of AMD–BA (Avions Dassault) since 1982, and a board member (*membre du conseil de surveillance*) of the Société Nationale des Poudres et Explosifs (SNDE).
(*See: Organization of the DGA and the Changes in 1986*)

Bérégovoy, Pierre, Ministre de l'Économie, des Finances et du Budget (Minister of Finance)
Address: Ministère des Finances, 93 rue de Rivoli, 75056 Paris R.P.

Bérégovoy was born on 23 October 1925 near Rouen, where his parents owned a café. At 16 he started work as a metal worker for the railway company (during which time he joined the Resistance) and after that for the national gas company. A self-trained man, he progressed steadily there, and eventually in 1978 he became an adviser to the top management of Gaz de France. In 1979 he was nominated as deputy director of a Gaz de France subsidiary and got a seat in the national policy advisory body, Conseil Économique et Social.

During this time, he was politically active in the old socialist party (SFIO), leaving it as a protest against its colonial policy. A member of PSU (as was Rocard) up to 1967, he soon joined the socialist party (PSF) and became a faithful collaborator of Mitterrand and a member of the national secretariat of the party. But at the time he was never elected to the Assemblée Nationale – he was destined to become a 'technical' politician.

Just after the presidential election of 1981, Pierre Bérégovoy became the Secrétaire Général de la Présidence de la République (the post now held by Bianco) and made a very influential post of it – some members of the government at the time complained about that. In 1982, Bérégovoy crossed the river and took the difficult Ministry of Social Affairs, in which he had to resolve the constant problem of the social security and health insurance deficit. He was seen to be an efficient and thus became popular.

In the July 1984 formation of the new Fabius government, he was nominated as Minister for Economy and Finances, where he continued the austerity policy undertaken by his two predecessors (Delors and Fabius). His 'social-liberal' anti-inflationary policies coincided with a fall in the rate of inflation. He also undertook to modernize the French financial markets. Among his successes, he managed to get elected Mayor of Nevers (in the Niévre *département*, the old political base of Mitterrand himself) and *député* (MP), in the same town in 1986.

In 1988, he was one of the four or five runners-up tipped for the post of Prime Minister. Instead, he found himself back in his old job at 'rue de Rivoli' (soon to move to the new headquarters of the Ministry of Finance at Quai de Bercy).

Pierre Bérégovoy is married and has three children.
(*See: The Prime Minister and the Institutions of Government*)

Betin, Pierre, Directeur Général Adjoint de la Société Européene de Propulsion (SEP), (Deputy Manager SEP)
Address: Société Européenne de Propulsion, Tour Nobel, 3 avenue du Général de Gaulle, 92800 Puteaux

Born on the 21 November 1936 near Paris, the son of a post office manager, Betin went to the École Polytechnique and became an explosives engineer (*ingénieur des poudres*). In 1965, he joined the DTEn (precursor of the DEn, Directorate for Missiles) as head of the propellant division. In 1969, he became chief engineer at the SEP and from 1971 to 1984 he had various directorships of different departments. In 1985 he took on his current function of deputy general manager at SEP.

Betin has a number of hobbies, including genealogy and stamp collecting. He is married to a teacher,and has three daughters and a son.
(*See: The Aerospace Industry: Missiles and Planes.*)

Bianco, Jean Louis, Secrétaire Général de le Présidence de la République
(General Secretary of the Presidency of the Republic)

Address: Palais de l'Elysée, 55 rue du Faubourg Saint Honoré, 75008 Paris

Bianco was born on 12 January 1943 at Neuilly-sur-Seine, in the expensive Paris green belt. His father was an accountant. Bianco followed courses in political science at the 'Sciences Po', and then entered the elite École Nationale d'Administration. He is also an *ingénieur des mines* (one of the most prestigious *grand corps*) and holds a diploma in economics.

He has spent most of his professional life in town planning (especially of new towns) and in social affairs. From 1970 to 1979 he was deputy director of family, childhood and social services in the Ministry of Health. He was linked with the growing number of high-ranking civil servants who had left-wing tendencies during the 1970s. He is also a Maître des Requêtes at the Conseil d'Etat, the top administrative court of law. He became an adviser (*chargé de mission*) in the *cabinet* (private office) of Mitterrand when the latter became President in 1981.

Bianco was offered the post of general secretary of the Presidency when his predecessor, Pierre Bérégovoy, became Social Affairs Minister in June 1982. Bérégovoy was an influential figure in the Socialist Party (PS) and became an even better known as minister. As such he bestowed some glamour on the post of General Secretary in the Elysée Palace. The choice of Bianco could indicate a return to a situation where mainly bureaucrats occupy this post. A commentator has noted that it is difficult to assess which of the mixed bunch of advisers, civil servants and old friends (maverick figures such as Attali or, previously, Regis Debray) that surrounds the President, has real influence.

Bianco's post, and also the length of time that he has now served at the Elysée Palace, gives him the power which only an 'insider' has. He lives in an exclusive street in Paris. He has been married since 1971 and has two children.
(*See: Presidency of the Republic*.)

Blandin, Henri, Chef du Contrôle Général des Armées (Comptroller General of the Army)
Address: 14 rue Saint Dominique, 75997 Paris Armées

Born on 15 March 1925, Henri Blandin is the son of a trader in the Vendée. He became a naval officer after attending the École Navale in the late 1940s. After two years in submarines and other vessels and two years in Vietnam, he became a navy comptroller in 1958, a post he retained for almost ten years. In 1967, he began a sequence of tours as government commissioner (*commissaire du gouvernement*) in firms with important weapons contracts. In 1974 he became a director of the aircraft engines manufacturer SNECMA, before joining the General Administration of the Armed Forces (Contrôle Général des Armées) in 1975. He became successively deputy chief and head of the modernization office of the administration of the armed forces. He has been head of the Contrôle Général des Armées since 1981. In this post, he recently had to cope with a spate of scandals concerning sales of explosives and of military equipment. One particular scandal, the 'Affaire Luchaire', had political connections with Iran; Blandin had to intervene in the press, a rare occurrence for a comptroller general, in order to calm the uproar provoked by a report written by his immediate subordinate, Barba.

Henri Blandin has been married since 1945 and has three sons and a daughter. A true son of the French west coast, he enjoys sailing.
(*See: The Minister of Defence and his Officials*.)

Bonnet, Yves, Président Directeur Général de Technicatome (Managing Director, Technicatome)
Address:B. P. 18, 91190 Gif-sur-Yvette

Now aged 55, Yves Bonnet was a *polytechnicien* who became an *ingénieur de l'armement*. He worked first on nuclear submarine reactors under Chevallier. He then worked in the Direction des Applications Militaires (DAM) of the Commissariat à l'Énergie Atomique (CEA). He was Assistant Director before replacing J.-L. Andrieu as Managing Director.
(*See: Subsidiaries with Military Activities*).

Boucheron, Jean-Michel, Président de la Commission Permanente de la Défense Nationale et

des Forces Armées de l'Assemblée Nationale (President, Parliamentary Committee on National Defence and the Armed Forces)
Address: Assemblée Nationale, 75335, Paris

Boucheron represents a constituency in Britanny for the Socialist Party in the Assemblée Nationale. Elected in 1981, and again in1986, he was re-elected in 1988 in the first round. Previously a little known backbencher, he was nevertheless tipped for the post of President of the Committee on National Defence and the Armed Forces, of which he had previously been a member. It is still too early to know what influence Boucheron will be able to exert.

François Fillon, who held the post between 1986 and 1988, had few illusions about the Parliamentary Committee: in his book, *La Séance est Ouverte*, 'We have the opportunity of controlling the armed forces, of voting the defence budget, or of going to get information on the ground. We have power. However, if we criticize the smallest aspect of government defence policy we create a crisis. One must therefore act with caution'. In the same interview, Fillon noted the way the armed forces were trying to promote their interests: 'They call me incessantly in order to recommend such and such a plane or vehicle which would keep the French armed forces happy... It is one of the areas in which lobbies are most powerful and organized'.
(*See: The Parliamentary Institutions.*).

Bousquet, Jacques, Directeur, Direction des Engins, DGA (Director, Missiles Division, DGA)
Address: Tour DGA, 86 Boulevard Victor, 75996 Paris Armées

Born on 24 April 1934 in Montpellier in the south of France, Bousquet is the son of a company director. He went to the École Polytechnique, and two engineering schools, the École Supérieure d'Électricité and the École Nationale Supérieure d'Aéronautique (known as Sup'Élec and Sup'Aéro, respectively).

With this double qualification, he became an engineer in the technical division of air telecommunications at the DGA in 1960. In 1967 he joined the private office of the DMA as a technical adviser until 1971. After five years as director of the Bordeaux aircraft industrial workshop, he became deputy to the technical manager of aircraft construction (DCTA). In 1980 he returned to his original specialization by becoming deputy director (and in 1983 director) of the technical division of telecommunications and aircraft equipment (Service Technique des Télécommunications et des Équipements Aéronautiques (SSTE)). In 1986 he was appointed head of the Missile Division (Direction des Engins: DEn).

Bousquet cites music as his favourite pastime, and enjoys tennis and bicycling. He has been married since 1956 and has two sons.
(*See: The Operational Directorates of the DGA.*)

Calmon, Jean, Directeur, Technique et Production SNECMA (Production Director, SNECMA)
Address: SNECMA, 2 Boulevard Victor, 75274 Paris Cedex 15

The son of an insurance agent, Calmon was born on 31 December 1930. He graduated from the École Centrale (a well-known engineering *grande école*) and from the Centre d'Études Supérieures en Mécanique (a school of mechanical engineering). He has spent all his professional life at the SNECMA as an engineer: he was chief engineer on the Airbus (1967–70), on Concorde (1970–72) and on all engines for civil aircraft up to 1978. After a period as head of the chairman's private office, he took up his current position in 1975. He is also a professor in aircraft engineering at various specialized engineering institutes and a board member of, among other firms, Hispano Suiza, SEP and ONERA.

Calman has been married since 1956 and has one daughter. He likes travelling.
(*See: The Aerospace Industry: Missiles and Planes.*)

Cambier, Bernard, Directeur, Branche Systèmes de Détection, Contrôle et Communication, Thomson–CSF (Director, Command Control and Communication Systems, Thomson–CSF)
Address: 173 boulevard Haussmann, 75008 Paris

Aged 55 in 1988, Cambier has been an electronics specialist all his life. He is in charge of the radar and telecommunication work at Thomson-CSF, as well as the military computing and software divisions (through the subsidiaries Cimsa-Sintra and Sysera respectively). (*See: Electronics and Information Systems.*)

Capillon, Bernard, Président, Directeur Général, SNECMA (President, Director General, SNECMA)
Address: SNECMA, 2 boulevard Victor, 75274 Paris Cedex 15

Bernard Capillon was until very recently Air Force Chief of Staff and has now become head of SNECMA, a state firm which has been in some difficulty. He is thus an example of those senior people who leave the military procurement sphere to join the military production sphere. SNECMA has had to ally itself to the US aircraft engine manufacturer, General Electric, in order to survive in a world market which is particularly difficult for civil aircraft.

Bernard Capillon was born on 15 October 1929 in Tunisia, in the northern town of Bizerta. His father was a civil airline pilot. He went to secondary school in Paris. He attended the École de l'Air, and after graduating as a pilot was stationed in the USA. On his return from the USA, he was given the command of a squadron of fighters with the rank of lieutenant. Between 1957 and 1959 he commanded the prestigious Patrouille de France, the airforce aerobatics fighters squadron. He was given other commands, including that of Luxeuil from 1973 to 1975. After a period on the staff of the President of the Republic, during which he was promoted to general, he was deputy head of operations in the Air Force Staff until 1979, second-in-command of the Tactical Air Force between 1979 and 1981, commander of Air Defence at Taverny until 1982, and, in 1982, the youngest ever Air Force Chief of Staff at the age of 52. He held this post until 1986.

His appointment as Président Directeur Général (PDG) was reluctantly accepted by the staff at SNECMA, who would have preferred a professional manager rather than a former military man in this post. Capillon has many contacts at international level and is well informed on the technical side.

He is married with one son, and enjoys skiing and tennis.
(*See: The Aerospace Industry: Missiles and Planes.*)

Capron, Jean-Pierre, Administrateur Général Délégué du Gouvernement au Commissariat à l'Énergie Atomique (ÇEA) (Deputy General Administrator, Atomic Energy Commission)
Address: CEA, 31-33 rue de la Fédération, 75015 Paris

A number of people were shocked when Jean-Pierre Capron got this job in July 1986, just two and a half months after the right-wing coalition had gained power. The influential paper *Le Monde* even carried the front page headline: 'Change of Boss at Atomic Energy: French Style Spoils System'.

His predecessor in the post, Gérard Renon, had been an adviser to Mitterrand at the Elysée before taking the job of Deputy General Administrator, and then General Administrator. In this post, Renon managed to implement a number of reforms in a body which was losing its sense of purpose (see section on the CEA). He was relatively successful in helping to provide new direction for the CEA. But in June 1986 his contract was not renewed. In one of his previous posts as director of hydrocarbon fuels at the Ministry of Industry, Carpon was asked to resign by his minister, Fabius (soon to be Mitterrand's second socialist Prime Minister), after he had complained that Fabius did not want to speak to him about a scandal about which he knew more than anybody else.

Despite these problems, Jean-Pierre Capron has a good pedigree for the job. Still young (he was born on 15 September 1943), he graduated from the École Polytechnique and then from the École des Mines (a prerequisite for the top posts at the CEA). He began his career as an engineer in the minerals department of the Marseilles local authority, before taking various advisory posts in ministries and central administrations, for instance in the Treasury, and in the *cabinet* (private ofice) of Fourcarde, who was in turn

Minister of Finance and Minister of Equipment. He took the job of director of hydrocarbon fuels at the Ministry of Industry in 1978; this is an important post, since France is highly dependent on petrol and gas imports (and on the resolution of the oil crisis). After his departure in 1984, he then went to work in industry, first as director of planning with the Thomson group, the French electronics and electrical appliances conglomerate; and then as executive director of Technip, one of the largest engineering and consultancy firms in Europe.

Capron is said to be an austere, somewhat solitary, and brilliant top civil servant, with a deep commitment to his job. He has been married since 1965 and has three children.
(See: The CEA Top Management).

Carpentier, Jean, Président du Conseil d'Administration, ONERA (President of the Administrative Council, ONERA)
Address: ONERA, 29 avenue de la Division Leclerc, BP 72, 92322 Chatillon Cedex

Jean Carpentier was born on 13 April 1926 in northern France. His parents were both primary school teachers. Educated in the north, he went to Paris to attend the École Polytechnique. He then specialized as an aircraft engineer at the École Nationale Supérieure de l'Armement (IGA).

In 1961, after eleven years in the Air Engineering Technical Service, he joined the Direction de Recherches et Moyens d'Essai (DRME) of the Délégation Ministérielle pour l'Armement (DMA) as an engineer, becoming deputy director in 1972. In 1977, when the DMA became the Délégation Générale pour l'Armement (DGA), and the DRME became the Direction des Recherches, Études et Techniques (DRET), Jean Carpentier became the first director of DRET, a post he held until 1984, when he was appointed president of the administrative council of ONERA.
(*See: Research and Development Inside and Outside the DGA.*)

Cazaban, Henri, Directeur Direction des Constructions Navales, DGA (Director of Shipbuilding, DGA)
Address: DCN, 2 rue Royale, B.P.1, 75200 Paris Naval

Henri Cazaban was appointed to this post in early 1986. He went to the École Polytechnique and then specialized in shipbuilding engineering. He is an *ingénieur général de l'armement* (1st class), the highest category of weapons engineer. He sees the future of military shipbuilding in France in working collaboratively with other countries, and the licensing of foreign arsenals for advanced French designs.
(*See: The Operational Directorates of the DGA.*)

Chevallier, Jacques, Délégué Générale pour l'Armement, Délégation Générale pour l'Armement (Director General for Armaments)
Address: Ministère de la Défense, 14 rue Saint Dominique, 75007 Paris

As head of the DGA, Jacques Chevallier is one of the most powerful figures in the French weapons procurement system, especially with regard to nuclear weapons. He has held the two top jobs in the field of nuclear weapons development and production: before becoming head of the DGA, he was for a long time head of the Département des Applications Militaires (DAM) of the CEA, which develops and produces nuclear warheads.

He is extremely influential, even more so as he served under Giraud when the latter was head of the CEA, and then they were together at the Ministry of Defence in the Chirac government. He is a member of the Comité de l'Énergie Atomique. The satirical journal *Le Canard Enchaïné* described him as follows: 'with his slightly balding head, his small myopic glasses, and his lisp, Jacques Chevallier has a look similar to a Victorian cartoon scientist'.

Chevallier was one of the pioneers of the use of nuclear energy in France. Born on 28 December 1921, the son of a surgeon, he entered the École Polytechnique and afterwards specialized at the École Supérieure du Génie Maritime. It was not until he was thirty-eight that he entered the CEA, having first worked in various shipyards (Bizerte, Toulon), and then specialized in engine design at Indret. As the head of department there, he designed the power system for the prestigious cruiser *Colbert*. He was hired by the CEA in 1959 to head the newly formed nuclear powered systems group; its task was to build a nuclear powered submarine, following the unsuccessful attempts by the French Navy to design and build a natural uranium-fuelled submarine reactor. After the Navy's unsuccesful work, Guillaumat, the then Minister of Defence, called in the CEA to do the job. Chevallier went on to manage the design of a land-based prototype and then of the first-generation enriched-uranium PWRs, which now power the Redoutable-class ballistic missile submarine. Ironically, it was Chevallier, as an employee of the CEA, who introduced PWR technology into France, years before this technology was forced upon the French civil nuclear programme, against the opposition of the CEA of which Chevallier was then a top manager.

Chevallier stayed in this department until 1968, when he started a three-year period as managing director of COCEI, a high technology subsidiary of the CEA. In 1972, he was appointed head of DAM directly under the CEA administrator. His influence in this post was considerable. He revealed himself to be a firm supporter of new trends in nuclear weapons. He directed the development of the new generation of 'pre-strategic' and medium-sized warheads, putting a lot of effort into miniaturization and hardening of warheads. He also favoured neutron bombs; he is said to have declared once that 'the neutron bomb represents a real revolution in the field of weaponry; with regard to tanks, this new threat is comparable with that posed to the infantry by the invention of the machine gun'.

Chevallier is married, and is the father of four daughters and one son.

(*See: The Organization of the DGA and the Changes in 1986.*)

Chevènement, Jean Pierre, Ministre de la Défense Nationale (Minister of Defence)

Address: 14, rue St. Dominique, 75997 Paris Armées

Now aged 49, Chevènement attended the École Nationale d'Administration after having fought in the Algerian war of independence as a lieutenant in the Army. He became known as the co-author of a pamphlet against the bureaucratic elitism of the ENA, *L'Énarchie*, under the collective pseudonym of 'Mandrin'. After joining the Socialist Party, he became the leader of the CERES, the most important left-wing group within the PS which was well known for its centralizing, 'elitist' and technocratic blend of ideology, described at times as 'Stalinist' by its opponents.

The Mayor of Belfort, he has been an MP since 1973, and before 1981 he was an active member of the Public Accounts Committee (*commission du budget*) with special responsibility for reports on research (as a *rapporteur*). During these years he frequently opposed Rocard at all levels, and particularly when Rocard presented himself as a presidential candidate: Chevènement presented himself as the true 'republican socialist', as opposed to the social democrats who drew their inspiration from the United States.

After Mitterrand's victory at the 1981 presidential elections, he entered the first Mauroy government as Minister for Research and Technology, and in June 1982, the second Mauroy government as Minister for Industry, Research and Technology. This was the 'large' ministry he had desired in his quest for state-promoted industrial development. He had some success in influencing research policy, which saw a great increase in its budget, but he was not liked by the heads of the important nationalized industries for his constant interference.

However, in 1983, he openly criticized the lack of hard policies to counter unemployment and was himself attacked by Mitterrand. In May 1983, he resigned, claiming that, 'ministers have to keep quiet, and if they want to speak their mind, they have to resign!'. He continued to criticize the government, but in July 1984 he entered the Fabius government, a far more rightist and social democrat government than the one he had left a year and a half before, and which did not include any communists (Chevènement was a strong defender of the socialist-communist government alliance). He was appointed Minister of Education, a post in which he had to mop up the disastrous failure of the previous government's attempts to introduce a new law for private education funding and control. Surprisingly enough, Chevènement thrived in his new role, shelving the project and promoting a traditional and patriotic view of education: bringing back the 'three Rs' and 'civic education', a far cry from the original socialist ideas.

He is a well-known and outspoken supporter of the nuclear deterrent. He was one of the influential figures gathered together by Charles Hernu (Minister of Defence from 1981 to 1985, forced to resign after the Greenpeace affair) into the 'Convention pour l'Armée Nouvelle' which formulated the new Socialist Party defence policy at the end of the 1970s (and especially engineered the acceptance of the nuclear deterrent by a party which had been previously anti-nuclear). A true 'Jacobin' (i.e. of the centralist tradition), sometimes chauvinistic and concerned with a quasi-Gaullist vision of France's destiny, he recently declared, 'We must teach France to the French people again.... and give back to France the purpose of its destiny.' However, some other aspects of his thinking on nuclear strategy are worrying the top Army hierarchy: he is an ardent supporter of the airborne component of the deterrent (equipped with the new ASMP missile) and is suspected of wanting to scrap the Hadès 'pre-strategic' missiles, which are anyway not favoured by Mitterrand himself. A number of muted voices are now saying that if a parliamentary majority were obtained, the socialists would do just that.
(*See: The Minister of Defence and His Officials.*)

Clavelloux, Noël, Manager, 'Branche Systèmes et Armes', Thomson–CSF (Manager, Systems and Weapons Branch, Thomson–CSF)
Address: 173 boulevard Haussmann, 75008 Paris

Fifty-four in 1988, Noël Clavelloux attended the École Nationale des Arts et Métiers (general engineering school) and the École Supérieure d'Électricité. He was previously the manager of Thomson–Sintra, the subsidiary specializing in submarine activities.
(*See: Electronics and Information Systems.*)

Conzes, Henri, Délégué aux Études Générales (Research Director, Ministry of Defence)
Address: Ministère de la Défense, 14 rue St. Dominique, 75997 Paris Armées

The appointment of Henri Conzes as Délégué aux Études Générales, a new post created in André Giraud's last term as Minister of Defence before the resignation of the Chirac government, and replacing the post of Director of GroupeS, is difficult to assess: is it a promotion or side-step? Henri Conzes previously held an important operational post and is now in a strategy development post, which was important during the 1960s, but has lost some of its importance since.

Henri Conzes was born on 17 April 1939, went to the Polytechnique and became an armaments engineer. He is a typical example of the exchange between the Direction des Affaires Militaires of the CEA (in which he worked for a long time) and the DGA itself. In 1980 he was at the DGA in charge of the co-operation with NATO on weapons standards and policy. From May 1984 he worked as deputy director of the Direction des Affaires Internationales in charge, at the DGA, of international weapons co-operation, and the export policy of the French weapons manufacturing industries. At the time of the changes in the structure of the DGA in May 1986 (when Giraud took over the Ministry of Defence), he became the Délégué aux Relations Internationales (which now replaces the DAI). He stayed in this post until 1987, when he was replaced by his deputy, Bernard Retat, and was appointed as an adviser to André Giraud in his private office. He took up his present post between the rounds of the presidential election, in the first few days of May 1988.

During his time as Délégué aux Relations Internationales he had a high public profile, and promoted links between French manufacturers and foreign ones.
(*See: The Minister of Defence and His Officials.*)

Cribier, Daniel, Directeur, Institut de Recherche Fondamentale (Director, Institute for Fundamental Research)
Address: 31-33 rue de la Fédération, 75015 Paris

A scientist, Daniel Cribier took over this post in

January 1987 from the previous incumbent, Jules Horowitz, under whom he had served for several years as one of two deputy directors. (*See:The CEA Top Management*.)

Curien, Hubert, Président du Conseil Scientifique de Défense, Conseiller Scientifique du Ministre de la Défense (President, Defence Scientific Council, Scientific Adviser to the Minister of Defence)
Address: Ministère de la Défense, 14 rue Saint Dominique, 75700 Paris

Born in the eastern hills of the Vosges on 30 October 1924, Hubert Curien is a scientist who specializes in crystallography and the physics of solids. He was a student at the École Normale Supérieure, one of the most prestigious *grandes écoles*, and is a doctor of science.

After fighting in the war, Curien had a university career. He became a professor in 1960 and taught at the University of Paris VI. Since 1966, when he became one of the scientific directors of the Centre National de la Recherche Scientifique (CNRS) (the umbrella body which manages large chunks of public research in France), he has accumulated many important positions in research, research management and policy. In 1969 he became director general of the CNRS, and vice-president of ANVAR (a public agency for the marketing and efficient use of research). In 1970, he became a board member of ONERA, a member of the CASD (see SGDN, Prime Minister), and a member of the Comité de l'Énergie Atomique, posts which he kept until 1974, 1976 and 1976 respectively. In 1973 he was made the head of the Délégation Générale à la Recherche Scientifique et Technique, and director of the IGN and other bodies, where he held the highest responsibilities for research policy. In 1976, he became chairman of the board of the Centre National d'Études Spatiales. He continued to accumulate posts of this sort until 1984, when he was asked by Laurent Fabius, the young socialist Prime Minister, to become the Minister for Research and Technology. He stayed in this post until March 1986, working on the reorganization of public research bodies. He developed a three-year plan for research for 1986–88, but this was not put into practice as the government resigned in March 1986.

Hubert Curien came back into the limelight in autumn 1987, when he was appointed as scientific adviser to Giraud, then Minister of Defence. Curien was given a governmental post by Michel Rocard in May 1988, again as Minister for Research. He was not, however, given charge of the important field of space research, which was transferred to the Ministry for Post and Telecommunications.

Curien is married and has three sons.
(*See: The Minister of Defence and His Officials*.)

Dassault, Serge, Président Directeur Général des Avions Marcel Dassault–Bréguet Aviation (AMD–BA) (President, Director General, Dassault Aviation)
Address: 78, quai Marcel Dassault, 92214 Saint Cloud

The assumption by Serge Dassault of the post of Président Directeur Général (PGD) of the airplane manufacturing company created by his father just after World War II was strongly opposed by André Giraud, the then Minister of Defence. Serge Dassault won partly because he had the support of Prime Minister Jacques Chirac. The relations between Dassault and Giraud, having been merely antagonistic, then became completely hostile.

Born on 4 April 1925 in Paris, Serge Dassault attended the École Polytechnique and the École National Supérieure de l'Aéronautique. He then went to work for Dassault as director of air testing (he is also a pilot), and then as export director. In 1963 he created his own company with a friend, specializing in electronics, called Électronique Serge Dassault; he became its PDG in 1967. That same year, he became an administrative member of the board of AMD–BA.

When his father died in April 1985, the AMD–BA had been under the state control for more than three years. Minister of Defence Giraud wanted to separate the technical and policy control of the firm from the ownership control (AMD–BA is not nationalized and the

Dassault family is still powerful). This was forcefully opposed by Serge Dassault, who got the support of Jacques Chirac, the then Prime Minister and his friend. Serge Dassault was voted on to the board in October 1986. Dassault declared afterwards that 'the Minister of Defence has been badly informed and badly briefed. The minister continues to see the company from the outside, I from the inside...I will demonstrate to him that everything functions properly.' But, despite this official declaration, the relationship between the two men continued to be strained, for example with regard to the Rafale advanced fighter project.

Since he has become the PDG, the problems that Serge Dassault has to confront are considerable: foreign markets have dried up ; Serge Dassault closed four plants during the summer of 1987 which made 8 per cent of the work-force redundant (1,250 jobs). The future of the ACT–ACM advanced fighter project, the French competitor of the European advanced fighter project, and derived directly from the Rafale experimental plane, has officially been accepted, but it is a very expensive programme. The former Minister of Defence several times openly suggested combining it with the F-18 MacDonnell Douglas project in the USA, which is to be commissioned earlier and for this reason is preferred by the French Navy. Serge Dassault forcefully opposes the idea of the Navy having the F-18, declaring to the Defence Commission of the National Assembly that such an acquisition would ' mean the death warrant for the Rafale programme'.

Dassault, claimed by some as 'fragile' and shy, seems to have coped with the pressure of the job. He has been married since 1950 and has three sons and a daughter. He likes gentlemanly sports, such as golf, hunting and angling. Like his father, he is trying to get into politics: he has been elected as a local councillor but failed at the parliamentary elections in March 1986. Up to 1981, he was a member of the very right-wing CNIP party; he then created his own party, the Liberal party, which he dissolved in 1986. He is now very close to Chirac's RPR. He has also written several books on management.

(*See: The Aerospace Industry: Missiles and Planes.*)

Dejean de la Batie, Bernard, Secrétaire Général Adjoint de la Défense Nationale (Deputy General Secretary of Defence)
Address: 51 boulevard de Latour-Maubourg 75700 Paris

Dejean de la Batie has been in his post for only two years, but he has already seen three General Secretaries of Defence, the two first ones being powerful personalities – General Jacques de Barry and General Gilbert Forray – and now Fougiet, who has not yet had the time to make his mark.

As usual, the Deputy General Secretary is a civilian, Dejean de la Batie went to the École Nationale d'Administration (ENA) and has mostly been a diplomat (he held jobs as Embassy Councillor in Cairo, Bucharest, Rome, etc. before coming back to the Foreign Office central administration in 1982).

The son of a judge, he was born on 9 May 1927. He received a classical education and is married with two children. He lives on the Left Bank in Paris and has a love of horses.

(*See: The Prime Minister and the Institutions of Government.*)

Delaye, Michel, Adjoint au Délégué Général pour l'Armement (Assistant to the DGA)
Address: 14 rue Saint Dominique, 75997 Paris Armées

Born on 17 October 1934 in Cherbourg, Michel Delaye studied at the École Nationale Supérieure des Télécommunications after completing the École d'Armement and becoming an *ingénieur de l'armement*. He worked first in the telecommunications research and manufacturing section and in 1966 became head of the telecommunication and computing central service of the DMA. He became a technical adviser to the Délégué in 1970, and was in charge of aerospace and missiles until 1974.

In 1974, he took up the post of director of the missiles and propellors testing centre and in 1979 became deputy head of the technical service for ballistic missiles. In 1982 he became director of the very important Groupe de Planification et d'Études Stratégiques

(GroupeS) where he stayed until he took up his current post in 1986.
(*See: The Organization of the DGA and the Changes in 1986.*)

Denoix de Saint-Marc, Renaud, Secrétaire Général du Gouvernement) Government General Secretary)
Address: Hotel Matignon, 57 rue de Varenne, 75700 Paris

Born on 24 September 1938 at Boulogne sur Seine, near Paris, Denoix de Saint-Marc followed the usual top civil service training: he went to the Institut d'Études Politiques de Paris (Sciences Po) and the École Nationale d'Administration (ENA), from which he graduated in 1959. Like Chirac he is a member of the highest administrative court of law, the Conseil d'État (the General Secretary of the Government is always, by tradition, a member of the grand corps).

Before being appointed by Chirac in 1986, Denoix de Saint-Marc had been an adviser to the Minister of Justice since the 1970s. He is said to have been more involved than usual in the political work of the government and to have helped to short-cut the normal administrative routine of government decisionmaking. Under Chirac, many decisions were taken officially by the Prime Minister, and the Secrétariat Général du Gouvernment was stripped of its normal functions as a secretariat; but Denoix de Saint-Marc did participate in the formal interministerial and cabinet meetings. His predecessor, Jacques Fournier, was sacked in a move which caused surprise in government circles, as it smacked of a 'spoils system'. But, when Rocard became Prime Minister in May 1988, he announced that he would keep Denoix de Saint-Marc in his post, to prove that his '*ouverture*' style of government would not practise the 'spoils system'.
(*See: Prime Minister and the Institutions of Government.*)

de Willocq, François, Président Directeur Général, COGEMA (Managing Director, COGEMA)
Address: 2 rue Paul Dautier, 78140 Velizy Villacoublay

Born 13 September 1933, son of an engineer and industrialist, de Willocq attended the École Polytechnique and the École des Mines. He is an *ingénieur des mines*, the *grand corps* from which the CEA recruits its top grades.

De Willocq started his career in regional planning at DATAR; he soon entered the ministerial *cabinets* (private offices) of two ministers of planning and regional planning, Marcellin and de Bettencourt, respectively, then, in 1972, the cabinet of Prime Minister Jacques Chaban-Delmas.

Director of mining at the Ministry of Industry between 1975 and 1978, then administrator of Elf-Erap (the large state oil firm), de Willocq took up his current post at COGEMA in 1982. He is also a member of the Comité de l'Énergie Atomique and a member of the board of Eurodif. He is married with one son and one daughter.
(*See: Subsidiaries with Military Activities.*)

Dumas, Roland, Ministre des Affaires Étrangéres (Minister of Foreign Affairs)
Address: 37 Quai d'Orsay, 75700 Paris

Born in Limoges, in the centre of France, on 23 August 1922, Dumas was still young when war started. He participated actively in the Resistance. After the war he tried journalism, but trained as a lawyer. He quickly became a well-known figure, leading in court on such highly sensitive and celebrated cases as the assassinations of Prince de Broglie and Ben Barka, the case of the FLN networks, and the Markovich affair. He also defended Mitterrand in several scandals.

At the same time he attempted a political career, was elected to the Assemblée Nationale on a centre-left ticket in 1956, was beaten in 1958, re-elected in 1967, and was defeated in 1968. When he was re-elected in 1981, he had already become one of the close advisers and confidantes of Mitterrand.

In December 1983 he was nominated as Minister for European Affairs, but switched, in

June 1984, to the post of government spokesman in the new Fabius government, which was in fact a springboard for the post of Minister of Foreign Affairs, obtained in December of the same year. In 1986, when the Assemblée Nationale was re-elected with a right-wing majority and the government changed, he was elected as the president of the important Foreign Affairs parliamentary committee (Commission des Affaires Etrangères). He was replaced by Giscard d'Estaing, the ex-President, in 1987.

He is a pure 'Mitterrandist', a confidante of the President, and a man who, in contrast with his more extrovert predecessor Cheysson, never expresses his own political feelings. This secretive man has conducted - and is still conducting – many secret or confidential missions for the President abroad. But, far removed from the day-to-day management of his ministry, he is not particularly liked by the career diplomats. In Paris, he is a close neighbour of the Mitterrands (his flat is some houses away from Mitterrand's own private flat on the Left Bank) whom he regularly sees privately. He loves classical singing (he trained as a tenor in a music academy before taking up law).

(*See: Prime Minister and the Institutions of Government.*)

El Gammal, Maurice, Directeur Technique Général de l'ONERA (Technical Manager, ONERA)
Address: ONERA, 29 avenue du General Leclerc, 92320 Chatillon

Maurice El Gammal was born in June 1929 in Paris, the son of an engineer. He went to the École Polytechnique and also graduated from the École Nationale Supérieure de l'Aéronautique. He started his professional life in 1954 as an engineer at the Directorate for Aircraft Technology and Industry (DTIA), a predecessor of the DCAé. In 1964, he moved to ONERA, first as Directeur Scientifique des Matériaux (scientific director for materials), then in 1979 as planning and programming director and since 1984 as general technical manager.

El Gammal enjoys deep-sea diving. He is married with two sons.

(*See: Research and Development Inside and Outside the DGA.*)

Fabius, Laurent, Président de l'Assemblée Nationale (President of National Assembly)
Address: Hotel de Lassay, Paris

Laurent Fabius is the whiz-kid of French politics in the 1980s. In 1984, at the age of thirty-seven, he was youngest Prime Minister ever and he has now become the youngest president of the National Assembly since the late nineteenth century. In this respect, he is following the example of Jacques Chaban-Delmas, his predecessor in this post, a brilliant politician of the Gaullist mould who also started very young. Laurent Fabius is intellectually brilliant, has a prodigious memory and works hard. He is a distinguished son of a very rich family of the Parisian bourgeois. He is also very ambitious. His opportunity, and also his problem, has been to become the *conseiller du Prince* (adviser to the Prince), as *Le Monde* put it. He has fitted the mould at the right time, but he has not been able to shape it according to his own image (if he has any).

Born on 20 August 1946 in Paris, he studied at the Institut d'Études Politiques of Paris ('Sciences Po') and at university (studying literature at which he was *agrégé*) as well as at the two prestigous *grandes écoles*, the École Normale Supérieure and the École Nationale d'Administration (ENA). He completed ENA brilliantly and entered the Conseil d'État, the supreme administrative court, in 1973.

Fabius then joined the Socialist Party and became a member of Mitterrand's private office and his adviser. Admired by Mitterrand, he made himself a number of enemies in the Socialist Party by helping his protector to circumvent opposition in the Socialist Party (for instance in 1980 against Rocard). In 1978, he was elected MP of Normandy, a very safe constituency which had been given to him, in an area where he has been mayor since 1977.

He was re-elected without any problems in 1981. He was then appointed Minister responsible for the budget (under the authority of Delors, then Minister of Finances and now EEC

Commission President). In 1983, he became Minister for Industry and Research.

In these two jobs, Fabius was admired for his mastery of economics and technical questions. Although he was known to have a close relationship with Mitterrand, it was nevertheless a surprise when he was chosen as the new Prime Minister by Mitterrand in July 1984 following the resignation of Pierre Mauroy. Fabius was to put a new policy into practice — aimed at modernizing the economy and introducing social-democratic anti-inflationary policies. The Communists refused to participate in his government which they saw as having 'sold out to the bourgeoisie'.

After a year or so in power, Fabius got into difficulties. In the Rainbow Warrior affair, he found himself isolated even from Mitterrand, and other political problems put an end to the legend according to which he had had everything too easy in his life. He became relatively unpopular, and was seen as too cold and arrogant and lacking charisma.

In the 1986 legislative elections, he was re-elected and took an active part in parliamentary life. He was re-elected again in 1988. In May 1988 he stood for the post of General Secretary of the Socialist Party – vacated by Lionel Jospin, who had become Education Minister – but he lost to Pierre Mauroy. To an extent, his election as president of the National Assembly, a post which does not hold the same political prospects, is a second choice.

He is married with two children. He has, especially through his wife, Françoise Castro, an intensive social life in intellectual, avant-garde circles in Paris.
(*See: The Parliamentary Institutions.*)

Ferrari, Achille, Directeur de la Planification et de l'Évaluation des Programmes au CEA (Director of Programme Planning and Evaluation at the Atomic Energy Commission)
Address: 33 rue de la Fédération, 75015 Paris

Achille Ferrari was born on 3 July 1938 in Agen. He went to the École Polytechnique and, after university, started his career at an experimental research reactor at Cadarache in the early 1960s. After a period at the United States Atomic Energy Commission studying PWR safety (1965–66), he returned to France to head a CEA laboratory working on reactor safety. From 1970 to 1972 he was head of the management computing group at the Saclay CEN centre. He taught energy management in Milan for two years and then became assistant to the head of the economic affairs department of the CEA. In 1978 he became head of the CEA's programmes department (part of the Direction de la Planification et de l'Évaluation des Programmes). In 1981 he became deputy director for planning. He then briefly held the post of technical adviser to Jean-Pierre Chevènement, the socialist minister for research and technology, and later in 1982 he took up his current post.

Achille Ferrari sees the CEA and the DAM as being in the forefront of France's military effort. In early 1986 for instance, he spoke of developing a French Strategic Defence Initiative-type system based on directed energy weapons, arguing that the CEA, with its longstanding familiarity with particles, accelerators and lasers, had the necessary skills for such a project.

Ferrari enjoys sports, especially rugby, and is a music and theatre lover.
(*See: The CEA Top Management.*)

Fleury, Jean, General; Chef de l'État Major Particulier du Président de la République (Personal Chief of Staff of the President)
Address: Palais de l'Elysée, 55 rue du Faubourg Saint-Honoré, 75008 Paris.

If recent history is any guide, General Fleury has a bright future. His immediate predecessor in the job became First General Secretary of National Defence, and, five months later, Army Chief of Staff. The previous holder of the post became armed forces Joint Chief of Staff, the top military job.

General Jean Fleury took up his post on 31 July 1987, and shortly thereafter was promoted to the rank of Général de l'Armé de l'Air (Air Army general). Before coming to the Elysée Palace, he was in command of the very important Strategic Air Forces – the land-based

nuclear missiles at Plateau d'Albion and the Nuclear Air Bombers squadrons at the Taverny command centre. General Fleury thus has a considerable experience of and influence on nuclear matters. He is in charge of the black box containing the nuclear bomb codes which would activate the nuclear forces in war.
(*See: The Presidency of the Republic.*)

Forray, Gilbert, General, Général d'État Major de l'Armée de Terre (Army Chief of Staff)

Born on 6 February 1930 in Paris, Forray was a fellow student of General Schmitt at the Saint Cyr top military academy for officers. He served in fighting units in the Far East, in Algeria and more recently in Djibouti after having occupied several staff posts. Deputy Chief of Staff of the Army in 1979, he became director of the Coëtquidan officers training school in 1980.

In 1983 he took a more active post when he became the first commander of the Force d'Action Rapide, the newly created conventional fast deployment force which has become central to battlefield strategic thinking (especially in relation to Germany).

In 1985 he became Chief of Staff to the President of the Republic (replacing General Saulnier, who became Joint Chief of Staff) until 1987. He was then made head of the Secrétariat Général de la Défense Nationale (SGDN), a post he held for four months prior to taking up his present position.
(*See: The Chiefs of Staff.*)

Fougier, Guy, Secrétaire Général de la Défense Nationale (Secretary General of National Defence)

The nomination of Guy Fougier to this post is quite surprising. Not only was he nominated days after Rocard took over the position of Prime Minister, but he took a job which had been vacant since General Forray was made Army Chief of Staff in November 1987. And he is a civilian, whereas for decades a military officer had been chosen, often as a springboard to top staff jobs.

Born on 13 March 1932 in Paris, he came (as do so many top civil servants) from ENA, and spent most of his career in the *préfets* i.e. the special executive chief officers who direct the executive power of local authorities. However, he has also a long experience of ministerial private staff work; he was chief of staff of the Minister for Social Affairs between 1966 and 1969; technical adviser to the Minister for the Interior until 1971; a central administration director at the Ministry for the Interior until 1977; he took the job of general secretary of Paris in 1977 and regional posts of prefectures until 1983.

He took the very important post of police prefect of Paris in 1983. But, in March 1986, he resigned from his job as a protest against Charles Pasqua, then Minister for the Interior, who had queried the status and autonomy of the prefect function.
(*See: The Prime Minister and the Institutions of Government.*)

Fouroux, Roger, Ministre de l'Industrie, du Commerce Extérieure et de l'Aménagement du Territoire (Minister of Industry and Export)
Address:101, rue de Grenelle, 75700 Paris

Roger Fouroux is 61 years old (born on 21 November 1926 in Montpellier). He grew up in Tarbes, in the south west of France, a region whose distinctive local accent he has never lost. He was the son of a secondary school headmaster, a brilliant scholar, and went to two of the top *grandes écoles* (École Normale Supérieure, and the ENA). He got the *agrégation* (the top teaching diploma, equivalant of a PhD) in German.

He began his career as an Inspecteur des Finances, and in 1960 was briefly an adviser to the Minister for Education (who was then Louis Joxe, father of the current Minister for the Interior), in charge of private schools. But in 1961 he decided to leave the civil service and to go into industry. He started off as the administration director of Pont-à-Mousson, a very large pipe manufacturer. When this firm merged with St. Gobain, a leading glass manufacturer, he became financial director of the group.

In 1978 he was appointed executive manager of the group, which had then grown to be an international concern, and in 1980 he became the executive chairman.

He remained at his post when the group was nationalized by the new socialist government in 1981, despite his personal opposition to nationalization. He was to leave this post in 1986, however, to become the new director of the prestigious École Nationale d'Administration, the ENA, where he set himself the task of opening the school to industry and to the international world (he has a passion for education.) He leaves this post in order to take up his new ministerial duties.

He is a deeply religious man, a practising Catholic, who had been involved in education before taking the helm at the ENA. He is a true intellectual in the university mould. He is married and has six children.
(*See: The Prime Minister and the Institutions of Government*.)

Gallois, Louis, Directeur du Cabinet Civil et Militaire du Ministre de la Défense (Director of the Civil and Military Office of the Minister of Defence)
Address: 14 rue St. Dominique, 75997 Paris Armées

Born on 26 January 1944 at Montauban in the south west of France, Louis Gallois studied at the ENA, and on completion he started his career in the Ministère des Finances as *administrateur civil* (a top ranking civil servant, although second in rank to an *inspecteur des finances*), and was appointed a department head at the Treasury in 1972.

He was called by Jean-Pierre Chevènement, who had just been made Minister for Research and Technology in 1981, to be the head of his private office (Directeur de Cabinet), and he got the same post in the Ministry of Research and Industry in 1982. In 1983, when Chevènement was forced to resign by Mitterrand, Louis Gallois stayed in the Ministry of Research as Director General for Industry, a post which he left to work once again in the powerful post of Directeur de Cabinet with Chevènement at the Ministry of Defence.
(*See: The Minister of Defence and His Officials*.)

Gillis, Bernard, General, Directeur du Centre d'Expérimentation Nucléaire du Pacifique, Directeur des Centres d'Expérimentations Nucléaires (Director of the Experimental Nuclear Centre of the Pacific, Director of the Centre of Nuclear Experiments.)
Address: DIR-CEN, secteur postal 70080

General Gillis took up this post in November 1987, when the previous director, François Mermet, was made head of the secret services (DGSE).
(*See: The Minister of Defence and His Officials*.)

Givaudon, Pierre, Director, Direction de l'Électronique et de l'Informatique (DEI), DGA (Director, Directorate for Electronics and Data-Processing in the DGA)
Address: 2 bis, rue Lucien Bossourot, 75015 Paris

Givaudon is one of the most important people in the DGA at a time when his direction is more and more important for defining countermeasures and providing 'intelligent' work systems to weaponry. Pierre Givaudon was born on 15 May 1930 near Paris. He went to the École Polytechnique and specialized in weaponry at the École Nationale Supérieure de l'Armement, becoming an *ingénieur général de l'armement* some years later.

After fifteen years as an engineer in the Puteaux workshops, Givaudon spent a brief period as technical adviser to the Army Staff in 1970–71, then directed the Roland missile programme until 1976. After three years as director of the weapons joint programme co-ordinating office for France and West Germany, he became head of the weapons and weapons system department of DAT. In 1983, he became director of the Central Technical Weapons Establishment, which evaluates and specifies weapon systems being developed for DAT. He left this post to take up his current post at the DEI.

Givaudon is married with two sons and two daughters. He has also attended the Centre des

Hautes Études de l'Armement and the Institut des Hautes Études de Défense Nationale.
(*See: The Operational Directorates of the DGA.*)

Gomez, Alain, Président Directeur Général de Thomson–CSF (Managing Director, Thomson–CSF)
Address: 173 boulevard Haussmann, 75008 Paris

Alain Gomez is a prodigy of the French business establishment. Born on 18 October 1938 in Paris, he had a student life on the move: from Oran to London to Paris to get a degree in law; to Harvard, to get a management diploma; in Paris to get into the École Nationale d'Administration, from which he graduated in 1965.

He only stayed four years in the administration as Finances Inspector at the Treasury, and he joined the large chemicals and metal concern St. Gobain Pont-à-Mousson, first as deputy director then, in 1971, director of finances. From 1972 to 1982 he was PDG of a range of St. Gobain Pont-à-Mousson subsidiaries.

Gomez got his break in 1982 when he became administrator general (manager) of Thomson–Brant, and its PDG in 1982 also, before it became Thomson SA, and of Thomson CSF. He now controls a large civil and military electronics group – Thomson–CSF being the military wing of the group.

He has been married twice, the first to Francine Gomez, a forceful business manager in her own right. He re-married in 1986. His sport is cycling. He became known under the pseudonym of Jacques Mandrin (with two other bright young civil servants, one of them Chevènement) in 1967 when he wrote and published the pamphlet *L'Énarchie* – a critique of the technocratic power held in France by a narrow elite of civil servants trained in the same ENA mould.He likes business challenges – he declared recently, after reorganizing the top echelons of Thomson–CSF: 'I have dressed Thomson–CSF in battledress for the fight which is opening on the world armaments market'. It is strange to remember that years ago, before moving to management, he was, together with Chevènement, the founder of the CERES, the left tendency of the Socialist party, with strong centralist leanings.
(*See: Electronics and Information Systems.*)

Huchon, Jean-Paul,Directeur du Cabinet du Premier Ministre (Director of the Private Office of the Prime Minister)
Address: Hotel Matignon, 57 rue de Varenne, 75700 Paris

Born on 29 July 1946 in Paris, Huchon studied law and politics, and went to the ENA. He was an *administrateur civil* (a top civil servant) up until 1981.

He is a committed socialist: a PSU member at the same time as Rocard, he left to join the Socialist Party, and became a close adviser to Rocard. The relationship between Rocard and Huchon is so close that Huchon became deputy mayor of Conflons-Ste-Honorine when Rocard became mayor in 1977, and they wrote books on economics together.

In 1981 he followed Rocard as his *directeur du cabinet* (head of private office) when the latter became Minister for Planning, and again when he became Minister of Agriculture in 1983. Jean-Paul Huchon was then in charge of contacts with agricultural unions, a job in which he proved to be a skilled diplomat.

In January 1985, Rocard appointed him executive director of the Crédit Agricole, the large rural-based mutual bank (now one of the largest deposit banks). This was a strategic post. But in 1986 he was sacked by the new conservative Minister of Agriculture. Despite support from Mitterrand himself, he was not given another significant post. He then became adviser to the EXOR finance and property group's president.

A round and smiling person, with eclectic tastes (he is said to be a fan of rock music), he continued to work in tandem with Rocard, who called him back in May 1988.
(*See: The Prime Minister and the Institutions of Government.*)

Huet, Daniel, Directeur Adjoint de la Direction des Armements Terrestres, DAT, DGA (Deputy Director, DAT, DGA)

Address: DAT, 10 place Georges Clémenceau, 92210 Saint Cloud

Born on 16 February 1931 in Paris, son of a general practitioner, he is married with one daughter. He went to the École Polytechnique, École Nationale Supérieure de l'Armement and the Centre des Hautes Études de l'Armement.

He first worked as an engineer on the AMX tanks. In 1970, he started to go into managerial posts at the GIAT: deputy director of the orders section, head of the administration and finance section, and then in 1975, head of the marketing division. From 1980 to 1984 he was the *directeur général* (executive manager) of SOFMA, which builds weapons components, before taking his present job as deputy director of the DAT. He enjoys swimming and plays the piano.
(*See: The Operational Directorates of the DGA.*)

Hugues, Jean-Rémy, Directeur de l'Établissement d'Aquitaine de la SNIAS (Director, Aquitaine plant of Aérospatiale)
Address: Aérospatiale, 33165 Saint Médard-en-Jalles

Born 3 January 1927 in Algeria, married with four children, Hugues received his secondary education in Algiers before entering Sup-Aéro (École Nationale Supérieure de l'Aeronautique: the *grande école* which trains aeronautical engineers). He plays bridge and tennis.

He was a successful aeroplane designer (especially in his work as head of department for the design of the Vautour, one of the first French military jets) at a company (SNCASO) which was later absorbed into the SNIAS. From there, he moved to the missile-building company SEREB where he participated in the development of a first-generation satellite and the first-generation SSBS based at Plateau d'Albion. In 1970 he moved to Aérospatiale to be the director of the military missiles programme (directeur des programmes militaires ballistiques) and then director of the space and military ballistic programme during which time he supervised the development of the Ariane satellite launching rocket. In 1977 he became directeur of the Aquitaine plant of the Aérospatiale company, where he is still influential in rocket and missile design. In 1984 he became the *directeur* of Composites d'Aquitaine – a company which developed the new composite materials (carbon-metal-ceramics) which are becoming more and more important in air and space craft.
(*See: The Aerospace Industry: Missiles and Planes.*)

Joxe, Pierre, Ministre de l'Intérieur (Minister of the Interior)
Address: place Beauveau, 75800 Paris

Now aged 53, Pierre Joxe is the son of a well-known Gaullist *baron* (i.e. one of the companions of de Gaulle who supported his policy through parliamentary and governmental action). He went to the ENA, and after that worked at the Cour des Comptes (the supreme audit court, which audits all public sector budgets).

He is often seen as a leftist within the Socialist Party (PSF): he is a member of the CGT (the large communist-controlled trade union). He is an MP for Chalon-sur-Saône in Burgundy. He was briefly Minister for Industry, from May 1981 until July 1982, in the first Mauroy government, and then came back into the Fabius government as Minister for the Interior, where he replaced Gaston Deferre – a difficult act to follow. He continued to organize the policy of decentralization, and also implemented a modernization programme for the police, revealing himself to be an efficient administrator. As such, he was much appreciated by police staff, who now view his return positively. After the parliamentary elections of 1986, which saw the victory of the conservative alliance headed by Jacques Chirac, he became president of the socialist group of MPs at the National Assembly.

Raised in an old intellectual family with mixed Protestant and Jewish traditions, he is a workaholic, austere to the point of humourlessness, and he tends to make cutting remarks about people.
(*See: The Prime Minister and the Institutions of Government.*)

Lachaume, Pierre, Directeur Technique de SNECMA (Technical Director SNECMA)

Address: SNECMA, 2 boulevard Victor, 75015 Paris

Born in 1930, son of a public engineer, Lachaume studied at the École Polytechnique and 'Sup-Aéro'. He became an IGA and started to work at the testing centre for powering units between 1955 and 1963. He became head of the engine section of the DTCA (before it became the DCAé) until 1972. He then joined the SNECMA and held various responsible posts at the Villaroche plant. Since 1978 he has been the technical director of SNECMA and head of the Villaroche plant (since 1983). He is also a member of ONERA scientific and technical committee.

He is married with one son and one daughter. He lists as his leisure activities DIY, gardening and sailing.
(*See: The Aerospace Industry: Missiles and Planes.*)

Lallemand, Pierre, Directeur Scientifique, Direction de la Recherche, Études et Techniques d'Armement (DRET) (Scientific Director of the Directorate of Weapons Research, Studies and Techniques)
Address: Ministére de la Défense, 10 rue Saint Dominique, 75007 Paris

Lallemand is known as an academic. In fact, he was a professor of physics at the Ecole Normale Supérieur.
(*See: Research and Development Inside and Outside the DGA*)

Lanxade, Jacques, Chef du Cabinet Militaire du Ministère de la Défense (Head of the Military Office of the Ministry of Defence)
Address: 14 rue St. Dominique, 75997 Paris Armées

This vice-admiral used to command the French fleet in the Indian Ocean, and was responsible for the fleet intervention in the Iraq–Iran conflict. Before that, he was in command of a fleet in the Atlantic. Nominated to his present post by the previous Minister of Defence, André Giraud, he was confirmed in this post by Jean-Pierre Chevènement in May 1988.
(*See: The Minister of Defence and His Officials.*)

Le Febvre de Saint-Germain, Paul Ivan, Directeur du Centre des Hautes Études de l'Armement (CHEAr) (Director of the Advanced College of Weaponry)
Address: Centre des Hautes Études de l'Armement, École Militaire, 21 place Joffre, 75007 Paris

Although Le Febvre de Saint-Germain no longer holds an operational post, it is likely that he is still influential in the strategic and research work of the armaments community. He was born on 61 March 1936, the son of a farmer in Besançon, in the east of France. He was a student at the École Polytechnique, and specialized in the 'Sup-Aéro' *grande école* (École Supérieure de l'Aéronautique). He worked in the Direction de l'Aéronautique for some years, first in the power systems testing centre at Saclay, then in the technical air service until 1971.

He then went to work as a technical adviser at the DMA until 1979, and as representative (*chargé de mission*) in the private office of the Minister of Defence until 1975. He then became director of the Centre de Prospective et d'Évaluations' until 1982. He then moved to the DRET as deputy director and also became head of the Scientific and Technical Section of the CHEAr in 1985. In 1987, he was given the directorship of the CHEAr.

In an interview some years ago with the *Autrement* review, he revealed himself to be deeply fascinated by the long-term R & D process, insisting on the rationality of the whole system of weapon choice. Asked whether he had any moral problems in working on the nuclear bomb, he answered that the question was always at the back of his mind, but the bomb had brought peace for forty years. He is a committed Christian and has been married since 1959. He has four children and is a keen photographer.
(*See: The Organization of the DGA and the Changes in 1986.*)

Lehmann, Jean Claude, Directeur de l'Institut National de Physique Nucléaire et de Physique

des Particules (IN2P3) at the Centre National de la Recherche Scientifique (Director of the Institute of Nuclear and Particle Physics)
Address: CNRS, 15 quai Anatole France, 75007 Paris

Jean Claude Lehmann is a scientist and university teacher. Now the head of IN2P3, he has also been scientific director of the CNRS since 1981.

Born on 24 August 1939 in Paris, he holds a diploma of the École Normale Supérieure ('Normale Sup'), one of the most prestigious *grandes écoles*. He spent most of his professional career at the CNRS, while holding professional posts at the University of Paris VII. He was also scientific adviser to the Secretary of State for the Universities between 1971 and 1975. His influence in his current job is considerable and he has strong contacts with the CEA; for instance there is a joint venture between IN2P3 and the Institute of Fundamental Research (IRF) of the CEA – this is the GANIL (Grand Accelerateur National d'Ions Lourds) of which Cribier, head of the IRF, and Lehmann are respectively president and vice-president.

He is married, with two sons. He enjoys horse riding.
(*See: Research and Development Inside and Outside the DGA.*)

Lerche, Achille, Général d'Armée Aérienne, Chef de l'État Major de l'Armée de l'Air (Air Vice Marshal, Chief of Staff of the Air Force)
Address: 26 boulevard Victor, 75996 Paris Armées

Born 23 April 1932, Lerche entered the École de l'Air of Salon-de-Provence and then went to train in the USA in 1953, as did many young French fighter pilots. Between 1954 and 1963, he moved between the Cambrai airbase, in various commands, and being posted in Algeria.

In 1963, he was admitted to the 'Sup Élec' *grande école*, and specialized in electronics. In 1967, he took a post in programmes and equipment in the Air Force Staff, but in 1971 he entered the École Supérieure de Guerre Aérienne. He then took a post in the Minister of Defence's private office, which he left in 1975 in order to take the command of his old Cambrai airbase. Named head of general programmes at Air Force Staff, he was made an Air Vice Marshal in 1979, when he was nominated as *chef du cabinet militaire* of the Minister of Defence.

In 1981, he took command of communications in the Air Force, before taking command in the same year of the Second Region. In 1983 he was named Major Général de l'Armée de l'Air. He has 5,000 flying hours altogether.

He replaced Bernard Capillon in October 1986. He is a member of the Defence Council, and is pushing hard for the S4 missile concept. He said recently: 'The decision to continue the ground-launched missile component of the Plateau d'Albion, through the development of the S4 missile, will guarantee the complementarity [between the various elements of the deterrent forces] which is necessary to make our deterrent credible.'
(*See: The Chiefs of Staff.*)

Louzeau, Bernard, Amiral et Chef d'État Major de le Marine
(Admiral and Chief of Staff of the Navy)
Address: État Major de la Marine, 2 rue Royale, 75008 Paris

Born on 19 November 1929 at Talence near Bordeaux, where his father was an engineer, he graduated in 1949 from the École Navale, the ratings training school. He specialized in submarines and landing forces (he commanded such units in Vietnam). He obtained his first command in 1958, and after various staff posts and officer training periods (during which he became a Nuclear Specialist Engineer), he was given the command of the *Redoutable* in April 1967 – he supervised its commissioning and commanded it for its maiden mission in January 1972. In June of the same year, he joined the naval staff as head of long-term studies, then as deputy chief of staff to the President of the Republic between 1973 and 1976. He briefly commanded the missile-launching frigate *Suffren* in 1976, but soon came back to the staff as deputy chief of nuclear forces in 1978. In 1980 he was named deputy chief of staff in charge of operations for a brief period before receiving command in the same year of the Mediterranean fleet, which he held until 1984. Then he took command of the submarines and of FOST, the submarine component of the nuclear deterrent, for some months before becoming Major Général de l'État-Major des Armées (Major General of the Armed Forces Joint Staff) as well as president of the Space Study Group at the Defence Council. He then became Chief of Staff of the Navy on 30 January 1987, and as such a member of the Defence Council.

Admiral Louzeau is lobbying hard to replace the two existing conventionally-powered aircraft carriers by nuclear-powered ones. The development of the first one, the *Charles de Gaulle*, was slowed down by Giraud because of budgetary pressure, much to Louzeau's displeasure, although construction has already started. Louzeau sees such aircraft carriers as possible 'strategic' (i.e. carrying a nuclear deterrent) equipment. He wants proper catapults in order to get 'real planes' rather than vertical-landing Harrier jet aircraft (as he declared to *Défense Nationale* in July 1987). It is well known that he favours the replacement of the existing but ageing Crusader interception fighters by American F-18 fighters rather than waiting for the development of the proposed naval version of the Rafale, the ACM, developed by Dassault. Delicate negotiations are being conducted on this subject.

Admiral Louzeau has another preoccupation: maintaining the supremacy of the SNLE as the first component of the nuclear deterrent, especially in view of possible budgetary problems arising from the ordering of as many New Generation SNLE (SNLE–NG) as possible with multiple headed MIRV missiles (which Louzeau would like), together with the development and ordering of as many S4 ground-launched missiles to replace the silo-based Albion missiles (favoured by the Air Force which control them). For the moment, the S4, the so-called 'second component', has had budgetary priority and the retrofitting of one SNLE with new missiles has had to be abandoned.

Admiral Louzeau is married with two daughters and one son. He likes classical music and plays the violin. He is interested in astronomy. When away from the sea, he enjoys mountain climbing.

(*See: The Chiefs of Staff.*)

Marçais, Victor, Directeur de la DRET (Direction de la Recherche, Études et Techniques d'Armement) (Director, Directorate of Weapons Research, Studies and Techniques)
Address: Ministère de la Défense, 10 rue Saint Dominique, 75007 Paris

As the head of the organization within the DGA which directs and co-ordinates military weapons research, Victor Marçais exerts considerable influence, not only in the DGA but also in corporate and academic research institutions. Born in 1928, the son of a railway engineer, he went to the École Polytechnique and specialized as a naval engineer. He worked in the Cherbourg shipyard and took responsibility for the development of a number of conventional submarines. He then became responsible for the construction of the ballistic missile submarines, which followed the first, the *Redoutable*. In this task he worked with people like Chevallier, who built the nuclear reactors for the submarines.

He then extended his experience in the development of nuclear weapons, as head of the 'Atome' mission at the DGA (which was then directed by Martre who is now head of Aérospatiale). At the same time he was Councillor for National Defence at the Commissariat à l'Énergie Atomique and the nuclear affairs adviser to the Minister of Defence. He became Head of the DRET in 1984, and two years later became a member of the Conseil de l'Énergie Atomique attached to the CEA. This made him a powerful and experienced figure in several aspects of nuclear weapons decisionmaking – including the orientation of long-term and short-term research and development, which is a fundamental aspect of the French decision-making system.

He is also *administrateur* (member of the board) of several bodies including ONERA (which develops advanced missile technologies), COGEMA (which provides and reprocesses all nuclear material, including military) and Technicatome (the CEA subsidiary which builds the PWRs for the nuclear submarines).

In October 1986, giving a lecture on new technologies which will be important in the armaments field one or two decades hence, he noted the growing importance of the laser, stressing that: 'It is likely that in the next twenty years, it will be an absolutely necessary tool for any modern weaponry' (in 'La DGA face aux défis de l'avenir', FEDN, 1987). He also emphasised the future importance of other technologies such as infra-red and ultra-short-wave technologies, acoustics, etc., which will lead to more and more 'intelligent weapons' in the future.

He lists as his main sports: volley-ball, skiing and tennis.

(*See: Research and Development Inside and Outside the DGA.*)

Martre, Henri, PDG (Président Directeur Général) of Société Nationale des Industries Aérospatiales (Managing Director of Aérospatiale)
Address: 37 boulevard de Montmorency, 75781 Paris Cedex 16

Martre shows clearly the very close relationship between the DGA and the rest of the armaments industry. An IGA, he had been the head of the DGA for six years, and member of the Comité pour l'Énergie Atomique, when he was called by the Mauroy government to run Aérospatiale in 1983, where he replaced General Jacques Mitterrand, brother of the President (General Mitterrand had taken part in the development of the French nuclear deterrent; he had been the Commander of the Tactical Air Force, the airborne and land-based missiles deterrent).

Henri Martre was born on 6 February 1928 in the south west of France, son of a company director. He is now married with two children. A student at the École Polytechnique, he then specialized in telecommunications. Entering the DMA (before it became the DGA), he rose to the post of head of the industrial office at the central office of telecommunications and computing of the DMA.

But he really shot up in the hierarchy of the DGA in 1966 when he became deputy director, and in 1971 Programme Director of the Directorate of Industrial Affairs for Armaments. In 1974, he became deputy to the DMA. His nomination in 1983 as PDG of Aérospatiale was not a surprise, as he was already the state representative on the board of Aérospatiale and SNECMA before becoming the DGA.

Henri Martre expresses himself forcefully; as the DGA, in 1980, he pleaded for the full development of the neutron bomb. Since he has been head of the SNIAS, he has developed co-operative ventures (for instance the German MBB for helicopters, the Hermès spacecraft shuttle, and ship-missiles). He is also vice-president of Airbus Industries.

He expects that this collaboration policy will help to develop exports, which represented 6 per cent of orders for Aérospatiale in 1986. He is also reducing costs with some ruthlessness. He declared, when announcing 2,340 job losses in 1987, that 'fighting unemployment is not the function of the company. Our wish is to make a maximum turnover with as few people as possible'.

(*See: The Aerospace Industry: Missiles and Planes.*)

Ménage, Gilles, Directeur de Cabinet du Président de la République (Head of the Private Office of the President of the Republic)
Address: Palais de l'Elysée, 55 rue du Faubourg Saint-Honoré, 75008 Paris.

Gilles Ménage, who took up his new post on 27 June 1988, does not have a public image as bright as, say, Attali or Bianco among the close collaborators of the President. His function is to organize the details of the President's work. Part manager, part chamberlain, he is also a 'Mr. Fix-It' who knows of all the difficult questions and helps to resolve them internally. He replaces Jean-Claude Colliard, who went to work with Laurent Fabius at the Assemblée Nationale.

Born on 5 July 1943 near Paris, Ménage had a typical top civil servant's training: the Institute of Political Sciences of Paris followed by the ENA. He then entered the Prefecture. But, as a member of the socialist team, he was called to the cabinet as technical adviser as early as July 1981. He has been at the Elysée ever since.

When Colliard became director, Ménage replaced him as assistant director of the private office in July 1982. He now replaces him again. (*See: The Presidency of the Republic*)

Mermet, François, General; Directeur de la Direction Générale de la Sécurité Extérieur DGSE (Head of Secret Service).
Address: Ministère de la Défense, 14 rue Saint Dominique, 75007 Paris

The foreign intelligence service in France has had considerable problems recently, and General Mermet, previously a fighter pilot, is the fourth director in seven years who has tried to control and re-organize the institution and restore its morale. The DGSE (previously (SDECE) has been weakened by the *Rainbow Warrior* affair and by criticisms of its inefficiency and lack of control over its agents. Several of these have ended up in jail after being involved in drug trafficking, and the DGSE has had major problems in the Middle East, where a number of agents have been lost; indeed, the previous Minister for the Interior had to constitute his own special team to deal with the hostage crisis.

François Mermet was born on 21 March 1933, in the Alpine town of Chambéry. He is married with three sons. He trained as a pilot at the École de l'Air of Salon-de-Provence and became a fighter pilot in 1955. He soon took command of a fighter squadron. In 1969, he became wing commander. After a spell in the staff officers' training programme he was a military adviser at the Brussels embassy and then an Air Force General Inspector, before being given the command, in 1975, of an important airbase. In 1977, he joined the staff of the President of the Republic. In 1980, by then a general, he was appointed head of the nuclear forces department at the Joint Armed Forces staff. He then became director of the CENP until December 1987, when he was appointed the head of the secret services in place of General Imbot.
(*See: The Minister of Defence and His Officials.*)

Merveilleux du Vignaux, Michel, Vice Admiral,Commandant de la Force Océanique Stratégique (FOST) (Commander of the Strategic Naval Force)
Address: Centre Commandant Mille, 75998 Paris Armée

The FOST commander is from an old aristocratic family – one of his brothers is married to a Cossé-Brissac, and a cousin married a De France. In this family, there is a tradition of naval officers: one of his brothers is a vice-admiral, and his cousin is a frigate captain.

He is married with two sons and a daughter. (*See: The Commanding Officers of the Nuclear Forces.*)

Michot, Yves, Directeur Général Adjoint de la SNIAS (Deputy Director of the SNIAS)
Address: Aérospatiale, 37 boulevard de Montmorency, 75781 Paris Cedex 16

Aged 46, a *polytechnicien* and an *ingénieur général de l'armement*, Michot specialized in aeroplane engineering at the École Supérieure d'Aéronautique (Sup-Aéro). He started work at Aérospatiale, rising to become a main engineer in the Concorde design team. He then went to the DGA for several years as a technical adviser to the Délégué Général who was then Henri Martre. When Martre left, he directed the Mirage 2000 programme on the DGA side.

His recruitment at Aérospatiale in 1984 marked the start of Martre's reorganization of the Aérospatiale top management structure. He was Programme Director up to February 1987 when he was named Deputy Director.
(*See: The Aerospace Industry: Missiles and Planes.*)

Mitterrand, François, Président de la République (President of the Republic)
Address: Palais de l'Elysée, 55 rue du Faubourg Saint Honoré, 75008 Paris

In May 1989, François Mitterrand will be starting a second *septennat*, a seven-year term of office, and as President he is head of nuclear decisionmaking.

Born on 16 October 1916 he is the son of a railway official who built up a vinegar manufacturing concern in Jarnac, in the western region of the Charentes. He received the classical education one could then expect in provincial petit bourgeois circles and then went to Paris where he studied law and political sciences.

World War II saw him enrolled as a soldier. Injured and taken prisoner, he escaped at his third attempt and joined the Resistance - in which he helped to organize the National Movement of Prisoners. During this period, he met his future wife, Danielle Gouze, whom he married in 1944; they have two children, Jean Christophe and Gilbert.

Since the war his political career has been far-ranging. He started to the right of centre and slowly moved towards left-of-centre politics, actively participating in the murky political dealings of the 'IVth Republique' regime. From being de Gaulle's general secretary for prisoners of war during the 'Gouvernement Provisoire' of the summer of 1944 he went from strength to strength. A lawyer and a journalist, he created his own political party, the UDSR, and became minister eleven times in various posts. In these, he has alienated both the right (as Minister for Co-operation, he was associated with decolonization during a Mendès-France government) and the left (he was Minister for Justice when particularly repressive laws were passed against the Algerian nationalists). Now, as President, he sees his role as uniting left and right.

Turning to the detail, when de Gaulle came to power in 1958 and created the Vth Republic, Mitterrand revealed himself a consistent and constant opponent. He was elected a Sénateur (member of the second chamber of Parliament), and started to attack the personalization and concentration of power in the hands of de Gaulle. His well-known book *Le Coup d'état permanent*, published in 1964, attacked the constitutional change of having the President elected directly by universal vote rather than by an electoral college. In a series of bitter parliamentary speeches he also attacked what he called the 'double unconstitutionality' of the President's military nuclear role.

From the mid-1960s to the late 1970s he developed into a cunning politician, who managed to inherit the mantle of the decaying old socialist party (the SFIO) through the creation of a number of political clubs and organizations such as the Convention des Institutions Républicaines in which many of his future aides were groomed. At the Congrès d'Epinay in 1971 he became the leader of a new modern Socialist Party which was to provide him with a personal power base. He defended the idea of an alliance with the Communist Party, then a considerable force, which horrified the old socialists, and signed a 'Programme of the Union of the Left' in 1973. He came close to victory in the presidential elections in 1974, and pursued his work as leader of the opposition despite allegations by some on the left that he was a spent force, and despite challenges by people like Michel Rocard, and the breakdown of the 'Union of the Left' in 1977. With this history it was quite a shock for both right and left to see Mitterrand elected President in 1981.

After the March 1986 elections, with the narrow majority obtained by right-wing MPs in the Assemblée Nationale (National Assembly), the political equilibrium in France changed. Mitterrand had to find a way of working with a right-wing Prime Minister. He did so by adopting an Olympian attitude, placing himself 'above the political parties', somewhat as de Gaulle did. The message was that he unified the people in spite of divisions induced by politicians. This was also the message he put across in the Presidential election of April 1988.

During his long quest for power, Mitterrand has changed his position on the nuclear deterrent. It is now perhaps cruel to recall his statements in 1965 in which he claimed that the French nuclear bombs 'are extravagant expenditures. They cannot guarantee the security of France, on the contrary, they designate [France] as a target...'. In the twenty-five proposals of his 1965 presidential electoral platform, he presented a plan for stopping nuclear testing, for abandoning the manufacture of nuclear bombs and for converting military industry to civilian uses. On 10 August 1967, he reiterated this kind of declaration on the French deterrent. At a political rally, he declared that 'the left opposition solemnly warns the French public against the race for the nuclear bomb in which our country has been thrown by General de Gaulle. There is no more terrible danger for the survival of the human race. One must not hesitate to proclaim that the proliferation of nuclear weapons will lead to the proliferation of conflicts'.

It was in 1969 that Mitterrand started to shift his position on nuclear weapons in France: 'I said during my 1965 presidential campaign that I would scrap the French nuclear deterrent. I will not be able to say that in future. General de Gaulle's military policy has been approved by the French people who have re-elected him... Soon our nuclear weapons will be a reality. One cannot drown them as one might drown puppies'. But it was only in 1976–77 that Mitterrand and Charles Hernu, his future Minister of Defence, skilfully defeated anti-nuclear and pacifist opinion and persuaded the Socialist Party to endorse this view officially.

After being elected President in 1983 Mitterrand fitted comfortably into the mould of the Gaullist tradition. In his well-known TV interview on 16 November 1983 he said: 'I am, by the Constitution and the votes of the French people, the guarantor of national independence and of the integrity of national territory and I hold the function of Chief of the Armed Forces. I add that, since our strategy is based on deterrence... the key part of the deterrence strategy in France is the Head of State. It is myself'.

During the same period, Mitterrand defined his defence strategy with Hernu and Quilés, his two successive Ministers of Defence, along basic Gaullist lines. Since 1986 the prevailing political and military view has favoured a strategy closer to that of NATOs 'flexible response' doctrine, and this has left Mitterrand a somewhat isolated figure.

But he is used to that. Nicknamed 'the Florentine' or 'the Prince' (after Machiavelli), or, earlier in his political life, Rastignac or Sorel (well-known nineteenth-century French literary figures of young pushy adventurers in Paris), he is a secretive person who always keeps his cards close to his chest. During the IVth Republic regime, he was twice the most vilified and hated politician in France and went, as de Gaulle did in the 1950s, through a period of political isolation and self-doubt.

Mitterrand has almost become a Grand Old Man – often affectionately called 'uncle'. Not very tall, always wearing old-fashioned black hats, he is also said to be simple and very faithful to old friendships and to areas in which he has political or personal roots. He loves the countryside – indeed, his two best and well-known books of chronicles, *La Paille et le grain* ('Straw and Wheat', 1975) and *L'Abeille et l'architecte* ('The Bee and the Architect', 1978) are full of lyrical descriptions of rural landscapes. Each year he makes a pilgrimage to the Solutré hillcliff in south Burgundy with his Resistance companions. He spends his free time in his second home at Letche, in the pine forest in the Landes region, along the Atlantic south-west coast, where he walks his dogs and reads.
(*See: Presidency of the Republic.*)

Mortier, Denis, Directeur de la Stratégie et des Relations Industrielles, CEA (Director, Strategy and Industrial Relations CEA)
Address: 31–33 rue de la Fédération, 75015 Paris

Denis Mortier is one of the few non-engineers to hold an important post in the nuclear world. Still young at 48, he started his career working at the World Bank in Washington. Returning to France, he worked at the Institut de Développement Industriel (a public financing organization which assists with joint ventures and provides development capital for new firms). He then took a post with Eurodif (Société Européenne pour l'Enrichissement de l'Uranium). In 1978, he was appointed to the position of financial adviser to the CEA. He took on his present post in 1982. He declared in 1985 to the daily newspaper *Libération*: 'The CEA spirit is outstanding. I have never come across such a high concentration of intelligence'. He is also Directeur Général of CEA Industries.
(*See: The CEA Top Management.*)

Philipponnat, Bernard, General, Président Directeur Général de la Societé Nationale des

Poudres et Explosifs (SNPE) (President, Director General of National Munitions Corporation)

Born on 1 March 1926, volunteer in the army when he was 18 years old, Philipponnat rose through the ranks and is not a product of *grand écoles* or *écoles militaires*. After serving in the Vietnam and Algerian wars, he took command of a tank regiment and then an army division. He spent some time as the head of the French military mission in Saudi Arabia in 1972. In 1982 he was appointed commander of the French forces in West Germany until 1984, when he was named General Inspector of the Army.

His nomination as head of the SNPE was the direct consequence of a public scandal in 1987 and early 1988. It was revealed through a series of leaks that a kind of 'mini-Irangate' occurred in 1985–86 when, through a series of Italian, Swedish and Portugese intermediaries, explosives were sold to Iran and Iraq. When the customs investigated and proved the allegations, the previous holder of this position, the Army Comptroller Guy Bernardy, was asked by Minister of Defence Giraud to resign. General Philipponnat was appointed at the end of January 1988.

(*See: Electronics and Information Systems*).

Playe, Noël, Directeur de la Direction des Armements Terrestres, DGA (Director, Directorate for Land Weapons, DGA)

Address: 26 boulevard Victor, 75996 Paris Armées

Noël Playe, a first-class general weapons engineer (IGA), has been the director of the DAT since 1984. A son of a military family (his father was a general), he was born on 21 September 1930, and lived the life of a military child, following his father's career from town to town. He went to the École Nationale Supérieure de l'Armement after finishing at the École Polytechnique. He then did his national service in Algeria during the war of independence, mostly in active units.

He started his professional career at the land testing site of Angers and then he specialized in missiles, as the head of equipment at the Saharan missile-testing range of Colomb Béchar, until its closure after Algerian independence in 1962. He then became deputy director of the new missiles testing range installed in the Landes area, until 1968.

He then came back to central administration, as a technical adviser for the Délégué Ministériel pour l'Armement (previously called the Délégué Général pour l'Armement); he became head of the Systems Divisions, and deputy director of the GIAT, the industrial side of the DAT, for three years (1976–79). For a time he was in charge of the ARX–APX plant of the DAT. This was practical 'hands-on' experience before taking the jobs of deputy director in 1981, head of technical services a little later, and, in 1984, director of the DAT.

A keen gardener and a tennis enthusiast, he has been married since 1954 and has three children.

(*See: The Operational Directorates of the DGA.*)

Poggi, Jean, Directeur, Division des Engins Stratégiques et Spatieux, SNIAS (Director of Strategic and Space Propulsion, SNIAS)

Address: Aérospatiale, 37 boulevard de Montmorency, 75781 Paris Cedex 16

Jean Poggi is 'Mr. Strategic Missiles' at Aérospatiale. Born on 29 August 1926 at Toulon, son of an engineer, he went to the École Polytechnique, but, instead of furthering his studies in France, he went to the California Institute of Technology where he got an MSc in Aeronautics.

After some years at Sud Aviation and in the Sereb (both to be absorbed into SNIAS) he became technical manager in 1967 of the Setis (Société Européenne d'Études et d'Intégration des Systémes Spatiaux), then deputy manager until 1971. He then became a manager at SNIAS and programme manager at Euromissiles until 1974. He then went back to the core of SNIAS, to become the aircraft commercial manager until 1976, director of the Aérospatiale president's private office between 1977 and 1984, deputy general manager in charge of planning, programming and budgeting between 1982 and 1986, after which he took on his present responsibilities.

He is a fellow or a member of a number of scientific societies in the area of aeronautics and space sciences, and has also taught these subjects.
(See: The Aerospace Industry: Missiles and Planes.)

Ramé, Jean Benoît, Directeur du Service Central des Affaires Industrielles (SCAI), DGA (Director SCAI)
Address: 14 rue St Dominique, 75997 Paris Armées

Jean Benoît Ramé was born on 11 February 1938 at Versailles, near Paris, the son of a colonel. He studied at the École Polytechnique before specializing as a telecom engineer (a minor *grand corps*) at the École Nationale Supérieure des Télécommunications. Later, in 1980, he obtained the diploma of the Centre des Hautes Études de l'Armement (CHEAr).

He started his career as an engineer in the telecom section of the DTAT (one of the bodies later to become the Direction des Armements Terrestres) between 1962 and 1965. After several years as a deputy military attaché at the French embassy in Bonn between 1965 and 1971, he became head of the Industrial Co-ordination Office (Bureau de Co-ordination Industrielle) in the DPAI (Direction des Programmes et Affaires Industrielles) of the DGA, until 1975. He was then offered the job of technical adviser in the *cabinet* of then Minister of Defence, Yvon Bourges.

In 1979, he returned to the DGA, becoming responsible for anti-aircraft defence affairs in the DEn. In 1982, he was appointed deputy director of industrial affairs of the DGA, a post which he then left to become director of the SCAI. He was married in 1961 and he has six children: four sons and two younger daughters.
(See: The Organization of the DGA and the Changes in 1986.)

Rapin, Michel, Directeur des Technologies au CEA (Director of Technology, CEA)
Address: CEA, 31-33 rue de la Fédération, 75015 Paris

Born on 14 March 1932 in the south-west of France, the son of a civil servant, Rapin was married in 1955 and has two daughters.

He studied classics in Paris and Lyon, and went to university as well as to the École Centrale, one of the most prestigious engineering *grandes écoles*.

Michel Rapin is a specialist in metal technology. His whole career has been spent in the CEA's Institute of Technological Research and Industrial Development (IRDI): first as an engineer, then as Director of Metal Technology (Directeur de la Métallurgie), and, in 1978, as manager (*directeur délégué*) of nuclear energy applications. He became the director of IRDI in 1982, and presided over a significant expansion of applied research at the CEA. He took up his current post as Director of Technology in March 1987.

He also holds various other responsibilities as an engineering expert to the courts, and as professor of engineering at various engineering institutes in Paris. He is a board member (*administrateur*) of the holding company CEA-Industries which has various subsidiaries including a joint venture which builds the fast-breeder reactors, and Technicatome, the manufacturer of small PWR reactors.
(See: The CEA Top Management.)

Revellin-Falcoz, Bruno, Vice-Président pour les Affaires Techniques et la Recherche à Dassault (AMD-BA) (Vice President of Research and Development, Dassault)
Address: 78 quai Marcel Dassault, 92214 Saint-Cloud

Bruno Revellin-Falcoz has been the technical head of Dassault for several years. He worked on the development of the latest generation of Mirages, the Mirage 2000, and is the 'father' of the Rafale, the experimental advanced fighter developed by Dassault in competition with both the American F-18 and the European Advanced Fighter. The Rafale is the key to Dassault's survival as a major world military aircraft manufacturer, so Revellin-Falcoz is central to the organization's strategy and participates in the general debate on the future shape of nuclear tactical airborne force.

During the lifetime of Marcel Dassault, the firm's founder, Revellin-Falcoz was the technical general manager of the firm. When Marcel Dassault died, the Minister of Defence wanted to name him head of a group which would have had the real control of the company (Serge Dassault would only have been the chairman of a *conseil de surveillance* without executive power). This proposal was rejected by Serge Dassault and Jacques Chirac, and the compromise solution was to make Serge Dassault the PDG (chairman and general manager) of the firm, with four deputy chairmen, including Bruno Revellin-Falcoz.

(*See: The Aerospace Industry: Missiles and Planes.*)

Rocard, Michel, Premier Ministre (Prime Minister)

Address: Hôtel Matignon, 57 rue de Varenne, 75700 Paris

There is something vaguely ironic in seeing Mitterrand appointing as his Prime Minister the arch-rival who twice attempted to win the nomination of the Socialist Party for the presidential election against Mitterrand himself, and who criticized him for being 'archaic'. The reason, apart from the personal popularity of Rocard, is obviously that Mitterrand needs Rocard in order to conduct his policy of remoulding the French political landscape.

Born 23 August 1930 near Paris, son of Yves Rocard, a top scientist who was one of the fathers of the French nuclear bomb, Rocard studied law, political science and economics before entering ENA, where he completed his studies in 1958. He entered the top civil servant grade of Inspecteur des Finances, working in the forecasting division and then as the general secretary of the economic accounts commission of the Ministry of Finances.

He was a socialist militant in the 1950s but resigned in 1958 from the old socialist SFIO party. Member (under pseudonym, in order to protect his position of civil servant) of the Parti Socialiste Unifié (PSU) he became its general secretary in 1967 – and its presidential candidate in the 1969 elections. The PSU was an odd mixture, starting as a 'clean' social-democratic party in the early 1960s but moving at the end of the decade towards leftist politics – promoting libertarian self-management but including a strong 'Maoist' minority and largely made up of intellectuals. Michel Rocard looked quite 'odd' in this party, always reasoning and cold-headed in post-1968 politics. As *Le Monde* puts it, his position was quite schizophrenic. But he was known at national level, and popular in the media, especially on television. He even got a seat in the Assemblée Nationale in 1969 by-elections against a Gaullist.

But the beginning of the 1970s saw a low ebb of leftist politics, and Rocard lost his seat in 1973. In 1974, still in the PSU but no longer its general secretary and back as an Inspecteur des Finances, he supported Mitterrand's candidature in the presidential elections which saw Giscard d'Estaing elected. After that, Rocard joined the Socialist party with several PSU leaders and a number of trade-unionists, after nudges by Mauroy. Many in the Socialist Party already opposed Rocard; the Mitterrand and the Chevènement tendencies were particularly antagonistic to him.

In 1975 Rocard became a member of the Socialist Party's national secretariat, and in 1977 was elected Mayor of Conflans-Ste-Honorine. This same year, he asserted his own political views, opposing his decentralized, liberal/libertarian social democratic tradition to the centralist, elitist socialist tradition. He also asked for a complete overhaul of the 'Union of the Left' common programme (which governed the relationship between the Communists and Mitterrand). He survived by allying his group (the '*courant* Rocard') with Mauroy. He announced in 1980 his own candidature for becoming the socialist candidate at the 1981 presidential elections, if Mitterrand was not candidate. Mitterrand awaited this move, and announced his own candidature against Giscard. He was elected, and Rocard, despite his considerable popularity (he always topped the opinion polls at the time), looked a boyish and amateurish politician compared with the new President.

After this failure, he was to suffer in silence as Minister for Planning, without real powers compared to Delors and Dreyfus, Ministers of Finance and Industry, in what was a real snub for a man who commands a substantial following in the Socialist Party. In March 1983, he was nominated Minister of Agriculture – a politically more difficult and more rewarding post in which he did manage to rebuild bridges between the Socialist government and the agricultural trade unions as well as advancing difficult negotiations in Brussels.

But in April 1985 he resigned from his job, officially in protest against proportional representation introduced by the Socialist government, but many think that he was also distancing himself from this government in order to prepare his bid for the presidential election of 1988. Indeed, as early as May 1985, he hinted very strongly at such a scenario, stating that he had 'decided to go all the way'. In the following three years he smoothed his public image and cultivated his high popularity ratings and the Socialist Party had to cope with what was called the 'Rocard problem'. This time, he was careful not to pre-empt a decision by Mitterrand who, as before, was waiting until the last minute in order to unsettle the position of his adversaries. In February, Rocard and Mitterrand are said to have met and struck a deal, according to which Rocard would be the Prime Minister if an 'opening' was offered by Mitterrand to centre and right of centre political groups after his re-election. Rocard's political profile was ideally suited for the strategy. However, the lack of response of those centre politicians provoked the formation of a mostly Socialist government and the dissolution by Mitterrand of the existing Assemblée Nationale.

Rocard had expressed strong support for the nuclear deterrent and in the early 1980s had even talked in favour of the development and production of the neutron bomb. However he was now totally aligned to Mitterrand's own position.

A small sprightly man, he likes sailing and skiing. Remarried after a divorce, he has two children.
(*See: The Prime Minister and the Institutions of Government.*)

Sandreau, Jean, Directeur, Direction des Constructions Aéronautiques, DCAé, DGA (Director of Aeronautical Construction, DGA)
Address: DCAé, 26 boulevard Victor, 75996 Paris Armées

Jean Sandreau attended the École Polytechnique. Now a first class *ingénieur général de l'armement*, he has in fact spent a major part of his career in another directorate, the Direction des Engins, where he specialized in ballistic missiles, ending up as the director, in the early 1980s, of the Service Technique des Engins Ballistiques (which develops nuclear missiles). He joined the Direction des Constructions Aéronautiques in 1985. He is also a member of ONERA.
(*See: The Operational Directorates of the DGA.*)

Schmitt, Maurice, Général d'Armée, Chef d'État Major des Armées
(Joint Chief of Staff)
Address: 14 rue Saint-Dominique, 75997 Paris Armées

Born on 23 July 1930 in Marseilles, Schmitt trained at the top military school, the École des Cadres de Saint Cyr from which he graduated to serve in the *troupes de marine* (the ex-colonial corps) during the Vietnam war and the Algerian war of independence. He graduated in 1970 from the École de Guerre, which trains staff officers, and was appointed chief of staff of the armed forces in the French West Indies. He then took several commands (mostly in paratroop regiments) up to 1983 when he was promoted to Major Général de l'Armée de Terre. He reached the rank of Général de l'Armée and was appointed Army Chief of Staff in 1985, when he also became a member of the Defence Council (Conseil de Défense). He came to his current post in November 1987.

Many times decorated, General Schmitt has followed the same line as his predecessors as Army Chief of Staff, demanding more equipment and greater responsibilities for the Army in the continuous competition between the three forces, especially in nuclear matters. In an article in *Défense Nationale* in June 1987, he noted the growing concept of weapon systems set in battle situations, in which the coherence of the various mix of weapons being assembled

is more important than striking with an 'all or nothing' single weapon. He declared himself in favour of using tactical nuclear missiles in such future battlefields, and declared, true Army officer that he is nearly to the point of caricature, that 'firing equipment will again take precedence in battle. The Hadès nuclear missile will constitute the central element of this, and, in the domain of conventional fire power, the LRM, the Leclerc tank (the new generation AMX tank being developed by the GIAT), third generation vehicle or helicopter-launched missiles, and medium-range ground-to-air missiles, amongst others, will represent significant new steps'.
(*See: The Chiefs of Staff.*)

Sollier, Jean, Directeur, SEP, Directeur Général Adjoint, SNECMA (Director, SEP and Deputy Director, SNECMA)
Address: SNECMA, 2 Boulevard Victor, 75724 Paris Cedex 15

Born 9 March 1933 in Paris, son of a railway employee, Jean Sollier entered the École Nationale Supérieure de Télécommunications to become an engineer. He started to work for CSF in 1955, specializing in telecommunications, and in 1962 he joined SNECMA. In 1969 he directed the Concorde reactor programme. From 1972 to 1977 he took various responsibilities in SNECMA subsidiaries and in 1977 he became director of economic and financial affairs. He was named deputy director of SNECMA in 1979 (Directeur Général Adjoint), and, as a result, he also became a director of a number of subsidiary organizations, for example Hispano Suiza, and has been President of the SEP since 1986. In 1986 he was widely tipped to replace Jacques Benichou as the new head of SNECMA.

He has been married twice – he has a daughter and two sons from his first marriage and two daughters from his second. His interests are music and literature.
(*See: The Aerospace Industry: Missiles and Planes.*)

Syrota, Jean, Directeur des Matières Premières, Ministère de l'Industrie
Address: 101 rue de Grevelle, 75007 Paris

Born on 9 February 1937 in Paris, the son of an industrialist, Syrota was a student at the École Polytechnique before entering the grand corps of the Ingénieurs des Mines. He also studied mathematics at the University of Sciences in Paris.

Syrota began his professional career as a civil engineer, working in Metz, in the east of France, between 1964 and 1968. He then took a series of top assignments in energy efficiency and in enviromental protection. Until 1971 he was director of technical services for the prevention of industrial pollution at the Ministry of Industry; then until 1974 he was deputy head of the industrial enviromental department at the Ministry for the Enviroment and Nature Protection and head of the atmospherical problems department at the State Secretariat for Environment. He then became deputy secretary, then general secretary and vice–president, of the Consultative Committee on Energy use until 1978, at the same time becoming director of the Energy Savings Agency (Agence pour les Économies d'Énergie) between 1974 and 1978.

In further appointments Syrota headed departmental services, becoming director of Industrial Affairs in the General Directorate of Telecommunication in 1978, deputy chief executive of Telecommunications in 1980, and director of Industrial Commodities at the Ministry for Industry in 1981. He has taken numerous responsibilities: as a member of the Comité de l'Energie Atomique, government controller at COGEMA and AFME (French Agency for Energy Efficiency), President of the Industrial Commodities Fund (Caisse Française de Matières Premières), and so on. Syrota also controls uranium procurement.

He is married and he and his wife Liliane have two daughters. He has often been quoted in the press for criticizing inefficiencies at EDF.
(*See: The Prime Minister and the Institutions of Government.*)

Teillac, Jean, Haut Commissaire à l'Énergie Atomique, CEA (Commissioner for Atomic Energy, CEA)

Address: CEA 31-33 rue de la Fédération, 75015 Paris

Now aged 67, Jean Teillac has a doctorate in science. He is married and lives in a leafy suburb of Paris. He is a university professor, and has taught nuclear physics at Paris University since 1958. He has been Director of the Radium Institute and Director of the National Institute of Nuclear Physics and Particle Physics (IN2P3) at the Centre National de la Recherche Scientifique (CNRS). He became Haute Commissaire of CEA in 1975. He has been a member of the Comité de l'Énergie Atomique since 1981.

Another of his activities is at a European level; he is president of the council of the JET (Joint European Taurus) for the development of nuclear fusion energy, and of the European Nuclear Research Centre. He is also a member of the Conseil Économique et Social (the consultative national chamber made up of designated representatives of socio-economic and political pressure groups, which reports on proposed legislation and official reports).
(*See: The CEA Top Management*.)

Vidart, Alain, Directeur des Applications Militaires, DAM, CEA (Director, Military Affairs, DAM, CEA)
Address: CEA, 31-33 rue de la Fédération, 75015 Paris

Alain Vidart is 54 years old. He is married and has one son and two daughters. He went to the Polytechnique and, after École Supérieure de l'Armement, he became an IGA (*ingénieur général de l'armement*) and started to work for the DAM. He left in the early 1970s to work in private industry for some fifteen years. He returned to the DAM in 1985 and soon got the top job, replacing Chevallier who moved to the Ministry of Defence as the head of the DGA.

In a conference organized by the DGA in October 1986, Alain Vidart emphasized the fact that most weapons systems are unchangeable from an early stage in their development, because resource limitations do not usually allow parallel development of alternative technologies. This has long-term consequences. As Vidart said: 'in the weapons domain, the development of a weapon system and its operational lifetime can cover a period of about thirty years: ten years between the decision and the commissioning, followed by a useful lifetime of at least twenty years'. He also noted the importance of long-term studies and of co-operation between nations as well as between French military organizations. He recognized that 'it is true that recruitment to the DGA and even to armaments in general is somewhat lacking in diversity'.

More recently, in an article published in February 1988 in *Armement*, the DGA newspaper, he wrote that 'a new generation of nuclear weapons is just emerging'. Some are already practicable, such as the so-called 'directed-energy nuclear weapons', the neutron bombs, high-altitude electromagnetic bombs and ground-effect bombs. Others, according to Vidart, are being developed by the USA, by the USSR and by France: the X-ray laser, the anti-missile nuclear gun and the micro-wave gun. Some of these were originally part of the SDI programme, but are now being developed as weapons in their own right.

In early May 1988 it was announced that Alain Vidart had resigned from his post as Director of the Direction des Applications Militaires, in order to spend all his time as director of CISI, a post he has held for a year jointly with his DAM post. CISI is the software and data-processing consultancy subsidiary of the CEA. At the time of writing (May 1988) a replacement for Alain Vidart has not yet been announced.
(*See: The Direction des Applications Militaires*.)

Vougny, Général de Corps Aérien, Commandant des Forces Aériennes Stratégiques (FAS) (Air Force Commander of the Strategic Air Force)
Address: Commandement des Forces Aériennes Statégiques, 95150 Taverny

Vougny replaced the Général de Corps Aérien Jean Fleury, who became Chief of Staff of the President of the Republic in mid-1987. General Vougny was previously Commander of the Second Airspace Region (Deuxième Région

Aérienne) which covers the north, the west and the Paris region. His deputy is Général de Brigade Aérienne Jacques Fiori. The commander of the FAS headquarters at Taverny is the Général de Brigade Aérienne Gilbert Boury.
(*See: The Commanding Officers of the Nuclear Forces.*)

REFERENCES

Collet, A., 1988. *Les Industries d'armement*, coll. Qe Sais-je, No. 2387, Presses Universitaires de France, Paris.

Fillon, François, 1988. *La Séance est ouvert*, Ballard, Paris.

~5~
The People's Republic of China

Following the decision to develop its own nuclear bomb, taken in 1958 at the latest, China expended tremendous manpower and resources on producing its first atomic device, which was exploded on 16 October 1964. The effort continued with the detonation of a thermonuclear device in 1968. Currently, China has at least 100 land-based missiles and 100 nuclear bombs.

Changes in the outlook of the Chinese leadership since the death of Mao Zedong in 1976 have placed China on a new course of reform. In the countryside, the communes have been abolished in favour of agriculture conducted by family units. Factories have been told to run at a profit: government policy is to encourage individual responsibility. Industries have been encouraged to gear up for export, while consumerism has flourished. After thirty years of isolation, the government has declared an 'open door' to the West, inviting foreign firms to invest in China, and encouraging Chinese in all walks of life to learn from abroad.

China's post-Mao reformers see the building up of the economy as their main priority. Defence has to take second place. A report by the State Economic Commission in 1985 (merged with the State Planning Comission in April 1988 (*Xinhua News Agency*, 8 April 1988)) lamented the idle capacity in military industry while consumer goods were in short supply: despite its ability to produce jet fighters, China was unable to manufacture an airliner; despite its development of a nuclear bomb, China was paying foreign firms huge sums to import nuclear power technology.

Since 1985, many military airfields and harbours have been opened up to civilian use, and factories turned to produce civilian goods. In 1985, plants under the Ministry of Ordnance (now in the Ministry of Machine-Building and Electronics) produced, among other things, 500,000 motorcycles and 100,000 refrigerators for civilian consumers.

Since 1985, there has been a new emphasis on nuclear power generation; it is possible that less money and fewer resources are available for weapons development. China's nuclear programme began on the basis that national development would have to be sacrificed in the race to produce a bomb. This view appears to have been reversed in the mid-1980s. The reformers seem to have taken the view (partly from necessity) that a limited arsenal is a sufficient deterrent. Even China's carrier rocket technology is being used to earn hard currency: China is negotiating with the USA and with European customers to launch their satellites on the Long March 3 carrier rocket.

China has become a much more open country in the mid-1980s. 'Liberation of thinking', in public and academic life, is an essential part of the reform programme. Although criticizing Party rule is still a political offence, even such sensitive issues as nuclear accidents can now be openly discussed. There were demonstrations in Beijing in 1985 by students from the region of Xinjiang, in which China's nuclear test site, Lop Nor, is located, who claimed the tests had caused radiation sickness and deaths among the local population. Nuclear scientist Qian Xuesen, acting as spokesman for the Commission of Science Technology and Industry for

National Defence subsequently admitted that people had died as a result of the nuclear programme: 'A few deaths have occurred, but generally China has paid great attention to possible accidents. No large disasters have happened' (*The Times*, 12 May 1986). (The only known accident was in 1969, when about twenty workers were exposed to severe radiation after a pipe burst at a nuclear facility.)

There has been a conscious policy of making the decisionmaking process more open, of demystifying policy decisions and making the leaders more human. An anecdote from the National People's Congress in April 1988 contrasts with the reverence and awe in which previous leaders (especially Chairman Mao) were held. Returning to his place on the rostrum at the Congress, Central Military Commission Chairman Deng Xiaoping lit a cigarette. One delegate sent a note to the rostrum asking Deng to stop. Deng put the cigarette out. Communist Party Secretary General Zhao Zinyang asked the press to report this to discourage smoking.

This chapter introduces the organizations and individuals in China's 30-year-old nuclear weapons programme. Despite the increasing openness in public life, information on the programme is still — as it always has been — scarce; analysts have to rely on the occasional mention of the programme in Chinese publications and radio broadcasts monitored by the BBC and the US Joint Publications Research Service. Much more information has become available since the mid-1980s, yet much remains unknown. The Chinese rarely publish specific information on the nuclear decisionmaking process; usually the connections between organizations have to be inferred. Similarly, biographical information about those involved in the decisionmaking process is sometimes hard to come by.

THE PARTY, STATE AND ARMED FORCES

The most powerful political force in China is the Communist Party. It is the Party which takes major policy decisions. The decision to initiate a nuclear weapons programme would be taken by the Party leadership, particularly the five-man Standing Committee of the Politburo (see figure 5.1).

Part of the process of normalization after the Cultural Revolution (1966–76) has been a differentiation between the tasks of Party, State and military establishments, a distinction blurred under the older generation of guerrilla war veterans. As the veterans were persuaded to retire, they were replaced by technocrats and specialists. In the 1980s the People's Liberation Army's task was redefined purely in terms of national defence, contrasting with its political role in the Cultural Revolution.

The role of the Party, according to a speech by Zhao Ziyang in April 1988, is to exercise 'political leadership'; this means that 'it formulates political principles, indicates political direction, makes major policy decisions and recommends personnel for key parts in organs of state' (*Far Eastern Economic Review*, 31 March 1988). Decisions made by the Party are expressed as government policies through the State Council and the ministries under it, or through the Central Military Commission. The top State and military leaders (the Premier of the State Council, Li Peng, and the first Vice-Chairman of the Central Military Commission, Zhao Ziyang; Deng Xiaoping, Chairman of the Central Military Commission, is reported to be taking a back seat in favour of Zhao) are themselves members of the key Party body, the Politburo Standing Committee. Policies are transmitted down the system through ministry-level organizations (e.g., the Ministry of Defence, production ministries such as the Ministry of Aeronautics and Astronautics Industry and scientific establishments under the Chinese Academy of Sciences).

The reformers want to cut down on bureaucracy. To encourage initiative in industry, they have increased the power of the factory director; the Party secretary's view should be subordinate to commercial considerations. Not surprisingly, old Party habits of 'meddling in everything', die hard.

The military establishment is headed by the Central Military Comission (CMC), a State body, and its Party equivalent, the Military Affairs Commission (MAC). The CMC works

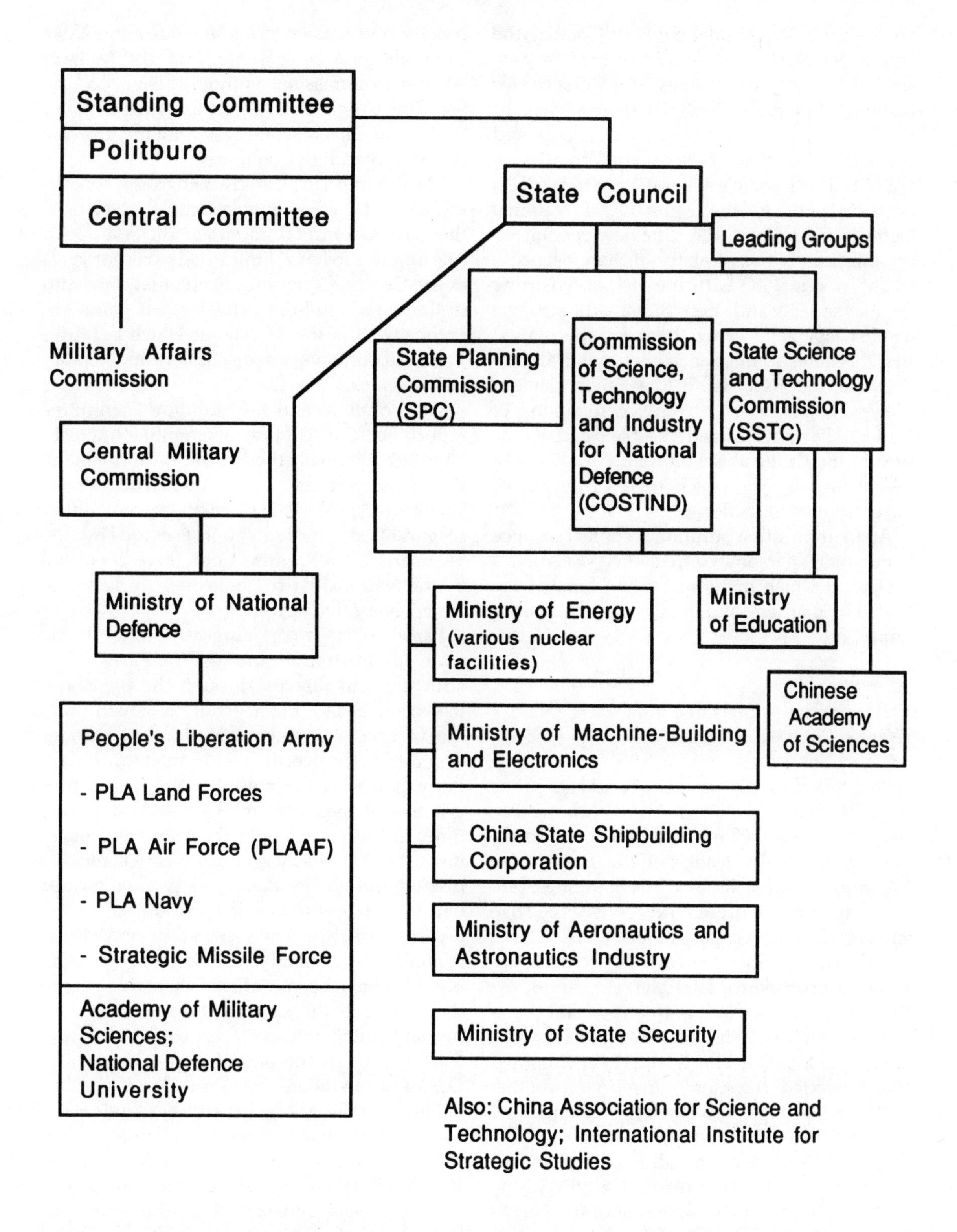

Figure 5.1 *The Party, the State and the Armed Forces in the People's Republic of China*

with organizations under the State Council (the Ministry of National Defence and the Commission of Science, Technology and Industry for National Defence (COSTIND)) and civilian-military bodies like the Ministry of Energy and the State Science and Technology Commission (SSTC). The People's Liberation Army (PLA) answers both to the Ministry of National Defence and to the CMC. One new specialized organization is the Ministry of State Security, established in 1983 with the task of 'ensuring China's security and strengthening the struggle against espionage'. There has been speculation that this ministry might become a political force such as the KGB is in the Soviet Union. However, China's current generation of leaders, having suffered disgrace and worse during the Cultural Revolution, is unlikely to accept any agency which tried to purge the Party from the outside.

Apart from the institutional contact in decisionmaking, personal connections (*guanxi*), in a society in which many of the top families are linked by marriage and family connections, are important.

The Communist Party of China

Address: Changanjie West, Beijing

At the top of the Communist Party is the five-man Standing Committee of the Politburo. The decision to start China's nuclear programme was taken by the leader of the Party (Mao Zedong) and the Politburo. The Standing Committee (in order of precedence) consists of Zhao Ziyang (General Secretary of the Party), Li Peng (Premier), Qiao Shi (Head of the Party's Organization Department), Hu Qili (Secretary of the Central Party Secretariat) and Yao Yilin (Vice-Premier and Minister of the State Planning Commission). The Thirteenth Party Congress which elected the Committee in November 1987 saw the departure of a large contingent of the old guard. Ye Jianying, Li Xiannian, Chen Yun and Deng Xiaoping all left the Standing Committee in favour of the new group. (Deng Xiaoping remained as Chairman of the Party's Military Affairs Commission and the State Central Military Commission (CMC). The Party constitution was specially amended to enable Deng to continue in charge of the Military Affairs Commission without being on the Standing Committee.) Of the five current members, only Zhao Ziyang was a member of the previous Standing Committee.

The Politburo itself is an inner group, consisting currently of seventeen people, elected by the Party's Central Committee. The Politburo's role appears to have diminished in recent years as the Central Committee Secretariat, made up of the Party's full-time officials, has gained in authority. It is the Secretariat which provides policy documents for discussion and shapes policy issues.

The Politburo and the Standing Committee report to the Central Committee, which, although nominally the highest authority in the Party, meets only once a year. The Central Committee rarely takes initiatives, but rather responds to proposals put forward by the Secretariat. The Central Committee is elected by the National Party Congress, which is convened every five years.

Party policy is communicated through the State administration, through the Party's own structure and directly through the press and television. Senior members of the government are invariably members of the Politburo or Central Committee: they reformulate and adapt Party policy as the policy or the formal programme of their own ministries. At the same time, within each ministry (indeed every institution) is a Party group, which will meet to discuss and absorb Party policy; these groups will be led by the senior Party official in the organization, the Party secretary or political commissar (in military organizations): inevitably there have been conflicts where this person has not been the same as the organization's formal head. The Party's thinking is also publicized through the official press: *The People's Daily* and the theoretical journal *Red Flag*.

The 46 million strong Party has undergone considerable change since the death of Mao in 1976. Despite the traumas of the Cultural Revolution (1966–76), when most of those now in power were vilified and abused, there has been no wholesale purging of 'leftist' activists, just as there was no wholesale debunking of

Mao. There was, however, a requirement for Party members to re-register, which enabled some Party branches to weed out opponents of reform. There have also been moves to broaden the Party by encouraging scientists and other intellectuals to join.
(See biographies of: Chi Haotian; Deng Xiaoping; Ding Henggao; Hu Qili; Hu Yaobang; Li Peng; Li Xuge; Qiao Shi; Qin Jiwei; Song Jian; Wang Hai; Yang Shangkun; Yao Yilin; Zhang Lianzhoug; Zhang Zhen; Zhao Ziyang; Zhou Guangzhao.)

The Central Military Commission (CMC)
Address: Changanjie West, Beijing

The CMC is the most senior military organization in China. In theory it is independent of both the Party apparatus and the administrative pyramid under the State Council. The Commission is elected directly by the National People's Congress: it does not report, as do other commissions and ministries, to the State Council, but to the National People's Congress.

The CMC has a parallel organization in the Party structure, the Military Affairs Commission (MAC, sometimes also referred to as the Central Military Commission). It appears that membership of the two commissions is identical and the two are often confused. The existence of both bodies has puzzled both Westerners and the Chinese public. An article in the *China Youth Daily* (*Zhongguo Qingnian Bao*) on 23 July 1983 explained that, despite membership of the two bodies being identical, the duplication was necessary to keep the Party and State structures separate. Suspended during the Cultural Revolution (1966–76), the CMC was re-established in June 1983. According to the Constitution, the CMC has the task of 'overseeing the armed forces'. It is responsible for formulating strategic policy and setting military priorities. It set the timetable of reform in the armed services (People's Liberation Army (PLA)), ordered manpower reductions and retirements, encouraged the transfer of military facilities to civilian use and implemented a reduced defence budget. The CMC holds a key position in deciding any new major weapons programme. The Commission also makes military appointments above the rank of division comrade and gives awards.

The CMC is chaired by Deng Xiaoping, his most official senior post. Former incumbents since 1949 were Mao Zedong (Party Chairman) and Hua Guofeng (Party General Secretary). In April 1988, Deng was reported (as Chairman of the Commission) to have submitted proposals on ranks and medals for the PLA to the National People's Congress Standing Committee, an indication that even the Commission wishes to be seen as accountable to the Congress.

According to some sources, the Commission controls the People's Armed Police (PAP). The PAP was established in 1982 to take over the functions of guarding the border and internal security from the PLA.
(See biographies of: Chi Haotian; Deng Xiaoping; Hong Xuezhi; Liu Huaqing; Yang Baibing; Yang Shangkun; Zhao Nanqi; Zhao Ziyang.)

The National People's Congress (NPC)
Address: (NPC Standing Committee), Great Hall of the People, Beijing
Tel: 656449

China's parliament, the National People's Congress (NPC), is usually convened once a year, when it elects a Standing Committee and the State Council (China's cabinet). The NPC Standing Committee acts for the Congress between its short sessions and issues most legislation.

The NPC, formerly dismissed as a 'rubber stamp' body, is emerging as an important forum for debate – even if that debate is limited (*Far Eastern Economic Review*, 7 April 1988). At the Seventh National People's Congress in April 1988, both Chinese and Western journalists were invited to see Chinese 'democracy' at work.

Among its other activities, the Seventh Congress voted on all the main State positions, including President, members of the CMC Premier and ministers. Voting was on the basis of candidates submitted by Zhao Ziyang as head of the Communist Party. While for key posts (such as in the CMC) there was no choice of candidates and delegates were not permitted to propose new candidates, there was a vote and the results were published. Eighteen of 2,877 delegates voted against Li Peng as Premier; 26 voted against Deng Xiaoping as Chairman of the Central Military Commission; 212 voted against, 77 abstained, in voting for Wang Zhen as Vice-President of the People's Republic of China (see: *BBC SWB*, 12 April 1988).

The Congress also considered a proposed restructuring of ministries in April 1988. While most proposals were approved, the Congress did not agree to the abolition of the Ministries of Railways and Communications in favour of a new Ministry of Transport. The proposal was dropped. Even if there was an element of stage-management in the process, the breadth of discussions reported in the Chinese press was a signal to ordinary Chinese that differences of opinion should be voiced. This was important in a society in which, both traditionally and under Communist rule, dissent has been equated with disloyalty.

The NPC has a variety of subcommittees, including one on foreign affairs, but it is largely concerned with China's internal politics. While it discusses economic and social issues, it is unlikely formally to debate China's nuclear policy or have any direct influence on a nuclear weapons programme.

The State Council

Address: Changanjie West, Beijing

The State Council is a cabinet of the ministers of all the ministries and equivalent bodies, chaired by the Premier. To assist co-ordination, the State Council has a number of 'Leading Groups' which bring together teams from different ministries to tackle issues which affect more than one ministry. Although their existence is rarely acknowledged, the groups perform an essential function in forming links between the self-contained ministries. The groups are usually chaired by a vice-premier and draw together ministers and vice-ministers from the ministries involved. The State Council Leading Group on Science and Technology, probably chaired by the premier, would act as ultimate arbiter on civilian research and development issues, and may discuss major military projects.

The restructuring in April 1988 reduced the number of ministries from 45 to 41. Of the 41 ministers appointed at that time, 33 were members of the Party's Central Committee (*Xinhua News Agency*, 12 April 88)

There are a number of commissions supervising the ministries; they include the State Planning Commission (SPC), the State Science and Technology Commission (SSTC) and the Commission of Science, Technology and Industry for National Defence (COSTIND). Ministries involved in the nuclear weapons programmes include the Ministry of Energy, the Ministry of Aeronautics and Astronautics Industry, the Ministry of Machine-Building and Electronics, the ministry-level China State Shipbuilding Corporation and the Ministry of National Defence. The State Environmental Bureau is also under the State Council.

Traditionally, ministries have behaved as totally independent structures. The factories, research institutes and trading corporations under each ministry have functioned quite independently of parallel activities run by the ministries. Co-ordination of activities is never easy, despite the presence of the supervisory committees.

(See biographies of: Dai Chuanzeng; Huang Yicheng; Li Peng; Qin Jiwei; Song Jian; Zou Jiahua.)

The State Planning Commission (SPC)

Address: 38 Yuetan Nan Jie Xichengqu, Beijing
Tel: 868521

The SPC formulates overall social and economic plans. In April 1988, the State Economic Commission, responsible for short-term plans, was amalgamated with it. The SPC acts as a co-ordinating body of all the ministries concerned with production. On the basis of bids from the ministries, it decides production priorities.

(See biography of: Yao Yilin.)

State Science and Technology Commission (SSTC)

Address: 54 Sanlihe Lu, Beijing
Tel: 8011860

The SSTC has responsibility for deciding the

priorities for China's research programme, and deciding budget allocations. Under the Commission are the Ministry of Education and the Chinese Academy of Sciences. Nuclear matters were formerly the concern of the Commission's Fifth Bureau. The direction taken by military research is mainly formulated by the Commission of Science, Technology and Industry for National Defence (COSTIND). However, the SSTC is involved where military and civilian research are intertwined.
(See biography of: Song Jian.)

Commission of Science, Technology and Industry for National Defence (COSTIND)
Address: Beijing, China

COSTIND works alongside the State Science and Technology Commission (SSTC), which has always been the junior partner, despite its broader scope. COSTIND allocates funds among the various defence research and development projects. Although the finance and other support for R&D is supplied through the ministries or institutes concerned, it is COSTIND which determines the relative importance of research topics and the size of the budget. COSTIND issues guidelines to the Academy of Sciences and Ministry of Education on research and training priorities.

COSTIND has taken on the tasks of the former National Defence Industry Office. It coordinates the distribution of equipment and supplies among the 900 or so factories and institutes involved in the nuclear programme. It exercises some direct supervision of the many factories under the Ministries of National Defence, Machine-Building and Electronics, Energy, Aeronautics and Astronautics, and other bodies as necessary.

The COSTIND Science and Technology Committee is believed to make a technical evaluation of new weapons systems proposed by the branches of the People's Liberation Army (PLA) (probably through the General Staff Headquarters of the PLA). COSTIND will pass a report to the Central Military Commission, which decides on major weapons programmes.

Under COSTIND is the Military Systems Engineering Committee, set up to apply systems analysis to China's defence needs, so that new weapons conform to China's strategic requirements. Also under COSTIND is the National Defence Science and Technology University in Changsha, Hunai, which is a major training centre in military technology.
(See biography of: Ding Henggao.)

Ministry of Energy
Address: Xinghua Lu Hepingli, Beijing
Tel: 446671

The Ministry of Energy was formed in April 1988 from the Ministries of Coal, Petroleum and Nuclear Industries. It has also taken over the power generation responsibilities from the Ministry of Water Resources (and Electric Power).

China began work on atomic energy in 1955. It currently has ten reactors in operation for research and military purposes, with reactors under construction at Daya Bay in Guangdong and Qinshan, near Shanghai, for power generation.

The former Ministry of the Nuclear Industry (MNI) and its predecessor, the Second Ministry of Machine-Building, controlled all stages in the production of nuclear weapons (as well as all civil nuclear activities) and it is assumed the new ministry has the same responsibilities (of, for example, the Science and Technology Committee of the MNI, which was believed to be responsible for assessing new developments and future projections for the industry). It has a major part in assigning development priorities in both military and civilian nuclear programmes. The ministry has uranium mines at Maoshan and Zhushan in Guangxi Province, Xiazhuang in Guangdong and Tacheng in Xinjiang.

The main nuclear separation plants are at Baotou in Inner Mongolia, Yumen in Gansu and Lanzhou in Gansu. The Lanzhou facility is said to produce weapons-grade uranium. It is supported by a related plant at nearby Helanshan. Warheads are manufactured at Huangyuan in Qinghai Province. Weapons are tested at Lop Nor in Xinjiang in western China.

The Nuclear Weapons Research Institutes in Beijing and Xining (Qinghai) are assumed to be under the administration of the ministry, as well as being affiliated, within the Institute of Atomic Energy, to the Academy of Sciences. Under the ministry is the China Nuclear Energy Industry Corporation, which deals with commercial imports and exports of nuclear-related materials, machinery and technology.
(See biographies of : Cheng Kaijia; Chen Nengkuan; Huang Yicheng; Jiang Shengjie.)

Ministry of Machine-Building and Electronics
Address: Sanlihe, Beijing
Tel: 868561

The Ministry of Machine-Building and Electronics was formed in April 1988 from the Ministry of the Electronics Industry and the State Commission of the Machine-Building Industry (itself an amalgamation of the former Ministry of Machine-Building and Ministry of Ordnance, formerly the First and Fifth Ministries of Machine-Building, respectively).

The ministry is responsible for research and development of basic weapons, from rifles to tanks, and for electronic components for more sophisticated systems.
(See biography of: Zou Jiahua.)

China State Shipbuilding Corporation (CSSC)
Address: 5 Yue Tan Bei Jie, Beijing
Tel: 890971

The CSSC was formed from the Sixth Ministry of Machine-Building in 1981. The Corporation, a major constructor in the world shipbuilding league, produces both civilian and military vessels. It is assumed to have been involved in the research, development and manufacture of nuclear-powered and nuclear-missile submarines.
(See biography of: Chai Shufan.)

The Ministry of Aeronautics and Astronautics Industry
Address: Andingmennei, Beijing
Tel: 444855

This ministry was set up by combining the Ministries of Aeronautics (or Aviation) Industry and Astronautics (or Space) Industry in April 1988 (formerly the Third and Seventh Ministries of Machine-Building, respectively). The aim of the restructuring was to increase coordination, especially in high-technology areas and to facilitate harmonization of military and civilian projects.

The ministry develops and produces a range of aircraft and missiles. The nuclear-capable B-6 Hong bomber is manufactured at Xi'an and Ha'erbin, the B-5 at Shenyang. Aircraft production, long biased towards military planes, is being turned to export and to civilian planes.

The ministry, which is also responsible for the R&D of ballistic missiles and satellites, manufactures strategic missiles, near Beijing and Shanghai. Missile test sites are at Shuangchengzi in Gansu and Wuzhai in Shanxi.
(See biography of: Lin Zangfang.)

The Ministry of National Defence
Address: Dianmen, Beijing
Tel: 667343

The ministry of National Defence reports to the State Council and the Central Military Commission (CMC). The Minister of National Defence, Qin Jiwei, is a member of the CMC.

The ministry, weakened by the attempted coup in 1971 by Minister Lin Biao, is likely to grow in importance as the regularization of the People's Liberation Army (PLA) proceeds. The ministry manages the military budget and plans the PLA's development, on instruction from the CMC. Under the ministry is the General Staff headquarters which links together the service branches of the PLA - the land forces, Navy, Air Force and Strategic Missile Force.
(See biography of: Qin Jiwei.)

The People's Liberation Army (PLA)
Address: PLA Headquarters, Beijing

The three-million strong PLA – which consists of four services: land forces; Air Force; Navy; and Strategic Missile Force – remains one of the world's largest military forces. However, it is on the whole poorly equipped and funds are only available for piecemeal modernization.

The PLA has changed dramatically in the 1980s. Under Deng Xiaoping's chairmanship of the Central Military Commission (CMC), the number of troops has been cut by one million by demobilization and retirement. In addition, the PLA construction corps of 30,000 men has become a civilian corporation, and border defence and militia have been separated from the main PLA.

The PLA is becoming more of a regular army. Ranks, abolished during the Cultural Revolution (1966–76), are expected to be restored in 1988 (*SWB*, 14 March 1988). Promotion through the ranks is not possible without attendance at a military academy. There has been an increased emphasis on specialization in warfare and on combined service manouevres. The drive to a greater professionalism follows high losses suffered by the PLA during its incursion into Vietnam in 1979. It also follows from the new strategy of flexible, conventional response to invasion rather than Maoist theories of guerrilla warfare, standard doctrine for some fifty years.

The PLA has had to accept a static defence budget since 1978, when the concept of subordinating defence to overall national development became national policy. While growth in State revenues kept military expenditure even in absolute terms, military expenditure fell from 17.7 per cent of the budget in 1977 to 11.9 per cent in 1985. There has been considerable dissatisfaction in the PLA over this. However, the declared military budget of Renminbi 21 billion in 1987 was matched by an equivalent Renminbi 20 billion (US $ 5.5 billion) from other budgets spent on military research and development (Tow, 1985).

It is assumed that, unlike other areas of defence (where the land forces, Air Force and Navy have acted with considerable independence), nuclear research, development and testing has been under the central co-ordination and control of the CMC and of the General Staff of the PLA. The most senior departments of the PLA concerned with operations are the General Staff Department, the General Political Department and the General Logistics Department.

THE PLA LAND FORCES

The development of specialized units (such as for chemical warfare) has been emphasized since the mid-1980s, but the land forces are still largely operating with equipment that is 20–30 years old. The land forces have until recent years been treated as infantry, under the strategic doctrine of fighting a campaign of attrition against any invasion.

THE PLA AIR FORCE (PLAAF)

The PLAAF has around 400,000 personnel. Since it became a centre for radical activism during the Cultural Revolution, it has repeatedly fared badly in budget allocations compared to the other services.

THE PLA NAVY

Though the PLA land forces are China's 'senior service', the PLA Navy is growing in importance. China now aims not only to protect inshore waters but also to be able to conduct long-range voyages to the South Pacific and Indian Oceans, to emphasize its status as an emerging global power and to protect its growing merchant shipping fleet. It is believed that the Navy has responsibility for testing and development of submarine-launched missiles (Muller, 1983; Hahn, 1986). The PLA Navy has around 240,000 personnel.

Research on nuclear-powered submarines started in October 1958 at the Atomic Energy Institute in Beijing. Work stopped from 1962–65 while resources were devoted to the atomic bomb. Work began again under Zhan Shengyang, Director of the newly-formed Submarine Nuclear Power Research Institute. The first sea trials took place in 1971.

THE STRATEGIC MISSILE FORCE

It is likely that all land-based nuclear weapons are under the control of the Strategic Missile Force, with units of the Force assigned to manage nuclear weapons under Air Force commands.

The Strategic Missile Force (still referred to by its previous title of Second Artillery) was formally established 1 July 1966. It is estimated to have over 100,000 personnel. Technical competence is high: the Force has one of the most extensive Chinese-character computer systems and recruits over 1,000 graduates a year (*SWB*, 1 August 1987).

Officer training for the Strategic Missile Force takes place at the Second Artillery College at Wuhan in Hubei and the Second Artillery Technical College at Xi'an in Shaanxi. Naval personnel may also be trained at the Navy Second Artillery College at Jinxi in Liaoning.

MILITARY INPUTS

Although budget restraints mean there will be only limited inputs of Western weapons, the PLA has imported key equipment and technology from the USA, Britain, France and Italy. The deals have involved advanced naval and aircraft engines, avionics, artillery ammunition, fire-control systems and helicopters.

ARMS EXPORTS

China's arms exports have grown fast in the 1980s. The China North Industries Corporation, the export arm of the Ordnance Ministry (and its successor, the Ministry of Machine-Building and Electronics), exported $5 billion of military equipment and supplies between 1983 and 1986, making China the world's fourth largest arms supplier. Sales have been boosted by the promise of immediate delivery from PLA stockpiles.

Sales are not restricted to the simple equipment. In 1985 there were reports that China was planning sales of CS5-2 intermediate-range missiles to Saudi Arabia. The China Nuclear Energy Industry Corporation, under the Ministry of Energy, offered in 1984 to store nuclear waste from Germany and elsewhere at its facilities in northwest China (*Far Eastern Economic Review*, 31 March 1988; *The Observer*, 12 March 1988).

THE ACADEMY OF MILITARY SCIENCES

The Academy, with around 1,000 research staff, is the PLA's most comprehensive research facility. A report in July 1987 said the Academy had published nearly 500 books and three times that number of research papers. Manuals issued by the PLA are usually prepared by the Academy.

NATIONAL DEFENCE UNIVERSITY

The University was formed in 1986 by merging the three central academies – the Military, Political and Logistics Academies. It is the highest training institute in the PLA; its basic task is to train commanders at an above army level for all services. It undertakes research on strategic issues and acts as an advisor to the Central Military Commission (*SWB*, 20 December 1985).

Within the University is the Institute for Strategic Studies, which researches international strategic relations, military strategy in general and as applied to China. It reportedly has little expertise on the detail of arms control. *(See biographies of: Chi Haotian; Li Xuge; Liu Lifeng; Wang Hai; Yang Baibing; Yang Guoliang; Yang Huan; Yang Shangkun; Zhang Lianzhoug; Zhang Zhen; Zhao Nanqi.)*

Chinese Academy of Sciences
Address: Sanlihe, Beijing
(Atomic Energy Institute)
Address: Fangshanqu , PO Box 275, Beijing
Tel: 868221

Under the State Science and Technology Commission (SSTC), the Academy of Sciences supervises the direction of research in China's premier institutes. The Academy has 80,000 researchers, technicians and other staff. It has around 110 institutes under its control, many of them the leading establishments in their fields. These include the Institute of Modern Physics, at Tuoli in Fangshan County near Beijing, which has been described in the Chinese press as a 'nuclear town'. In addition, there are several hundred institutes under local administration (for example the Nuclear Physics Institute in Shanghai), as well as institutes created by ministries.

The Academy is the formal sponsor of the Institute of Atomic Energy and the Institute of Mechanics (responsible for rocket development). The Institute of Atomic Energy is the main centre for nuclear weapons research. It may include the Beijing Nuclear Weapons Research Institute, which is assumed to be a sister institute of the establishment of the same name in Xining.
(See biographies of: Cheng Kaijia; Chen Nengkuan; Dai Chuanzeng; Qian Sanqiang; Zhou Guangzhao.)

Professional bodies
Address: c/o China Association for Science and Technology, Beijing

The China Association for Science and Technology is the umbrella body for a range of professional bodies, including the China Nuclear Society, the professional body for nuclear scientists and a forum set up to facilitate discussion between scientists, the China Nuclear Fusion and Plasma Physics Society, the China Nuclear Power Society, the China Mechanics Society, the Automation Society, the Systems Engineering Society, Mechanics and Automation Society, and the China Society of Isotopes.

Professional societies have become increasingly important in the 1980s. They provide, through conferences and publications, a means of exchanging information and ideas and facilitating discussion on research priorities. The societies also co-ordinate scientific exchanges. The Chinese Nuclear Society has exchange agreements with, among others, its US and European equivalents.
(See biographies of: Dai Chuanzeng; Jiang Shengjie; Peng Shilu; Qian Sanqiang; Qian Xuesen; Song Jian.)

The Institute of International Strategic Studies
Address: Beijing

The Institute aims to function as a non-governmental body, especially as a channel for foreign contacts and ideas. It is mainly funded by the Ministry of Defence. Under its Director, General Wu Xinguan (a strategic adviser to the Politburo), the Institute has held discussion sessions bringing together researchers from the PLA and academic institutions, an important function in China's compartmentalized society (*SWB*, 7 December 1985).

The Chinese People's Political Consultative Conference
Address: Changanjie West, Beijing

The Chinese People's Political Consultative Conference (CPCC) is a largely ceremonial forum in which China's remaining pre-1949 political parties, non-party individuals, and Communist Party members, are allowed to have some debate on national policies. Its Chairman is China's former president, Li Xiannian.

CASE HISTORY: FIRST ATOMIC DEVICE

China had begun some nuclear research in collaboration with the Soviet Union in the mid-1950s. By 1958, the Chinese were considering initiating their own programme, since it was unlikely that the Soviet Union would provide China with nuclear weapons. It was in part this failure to transfer nuclear technology which caused the Sino–Soviet split in 1961.

In June 1959 the Soviet Central Committee sent a letter refusing China the technology for a bomb. The Chinese Central Committee decided to produce one alone. The project, dubbed '596' after the date of the letter, was initiated by Liu Jie, Minister of the Second Machine-Building Ministry (then responsible for all nuclear matters, precursor of the Ministry of the Nuclear Industry). Zhu Guangya, Deng Jiaxian and other scientists were among the first to work on the project.

The ministry consulted the Central Committee before arranging for over a hundred scientists, from the Chinese Academy of Sciences and other bodies, to join them, probably at the Beijing Nuclear Weapons Research Institute.

The ministry reported on progress in September 1962. Chairman Mao Zedong and others approved the report; the Party Secretariat declared it feasible; it was discussed and approved by the Politburo. To ensure adequate co-ordination, a special Central Commission was formed, headed by Premier Zhou Enlai.

The Nuclear Weapons Research Institute, an Ordnance Ministry institute and the Lanzhou Institute of Chemical Physics produced detonators and explosives; a plant under the Ministry of Aviation produced the bomb's parts; the Institute of Mathematics and the Institute of Computing Technology (of the Chinese Academy of Sciences) contributed on the mathematics and methods of calculations; the Institute of Physics contributed to the theoretical design.

The first test took place on 16 October 1964 with Zhang Aiping (later Minister of National Defence) in command, Liu Xiyao (Vice-Minister of the Second Ministry) second in command (*SWB*, 27 June 1987).

CHINA AND ARMS CONTROL

China has signed neither the 1963 Partial Test Ban Treaty nor the 1968 Non-Proliferation Treaty (NPT), the latter on the grounds that it only curbs the 'horizontal' spread of nuclear weapons (to other countries) but does nothing to control the 'vertical' spread (of increasing weapons development within nuclear-capable countries). China has, however, undertaken to abide by the NPT and has strenuously denied providing Pakistan with military nuclear technology.

In 1986 China undertook not to conduct any further atmospheric nuclear tests (its last atmospheric test was in 1980.) China continues to carry out tests; its thirty-third took place on 5 June 1987.

In 1974 China signed the Treaty of Tlatelolco, which prohibits nuclear weapons in Latin America, and it supports the creation of a nuclear-free zone in the South Pacific. China has pledged never to be the first to use nuclear weapons and not to use nuclear weapons against non-nuclear states.

On disarmament, China calls on the superpowers to make the first moves. The Chinese view disarmament as an international problem and not just one to be left to the nuclear powers.

PEACE ORGANIZATION

China established the Chinese Peoples Association for Peace and Disarmament in 1985. The Association is affiliated to the Chinese Association for International Understanding. Both organizations have links with peace movements in the West, previously regarded by the Chinese government as wrongheaded.

THE ESTABLISHMENT OF CHINA'S NUCLEAR TESTING SITE

An Eyewitness Account

> In the early morning of 15 August [1958], a special mixed train slowly pulled itself into an unknown small railway station in the western part of China. This special train had started its journey in Shangqiu on 10 August. When we started, we had been told that a special mission was to be carried out. But not a word was disclosed as to our destination, what specific work we were engaged in or how long would it take. On 17 August, a survey team was formed in Dunhuang, and all-round survey work began on 20 August. In late August a meeting was held for cadres and Party members at a newly built cinema in Dunhuang, and the mission was made clear to us, that a range for the testing of atomic and hydrogen bombs was to be built.
>
> After three months hard work and struggle, by mid-November 1958, the point on the nuclear test range for the centre of explosions was determined. The command area and the living area had also been chosen.
>
> The commander arrived in mid-November. He made an analysis of the topography, the geological structure, the roads and water resources around the entire range, and the conditions of all locations within the range; he then came to the conclusion that it was not an ideal site for the range. The chief consideration was the problem of water resources and road conditions. In addition, the test range selected was too close to the main county town...and the command and living areas

would be polluted to a certain degree because of wind direction...

We went further westward, and arrived in the neighbourhood of Huangyanggou. There we spent two or three days making initial investigations of the topography, the landform, water resources, and the quality of the soil there...It was a marvellous site for nuclear tests.

In March 1959...the survey team and the hydrological team conducted a second comprehensive survey of the site for the test range...The third survey took place between winter 1959 and early spring 1960. That was an historic action which fixed the centre of the explosion of China's first nuclear test.

For technical reasons, there had to be a distance of 60 or 70km. between the command buildings and the centre of the explosion. At the same time, the explosion had to be directly in view when it took place. When the first pile was erected to mark the centre of the explosion, it was in view but only 50 km. from the command site, which was too close. Then we put up another pile at a distance of 90 km., to which we brought two carloads of firewood and lit it with oil, but we failed to spot it even with the help of a theodolite. Finally, we determined the position of the third and last pile on a height 70km. away, which met the requirements. In order to determine the ideal position for the erection of this ordinary pile, more that 1,000 fighters fought against the scorching heat and bitter cold; they lived in tents, drank bitter water, and worked in the deserted Gobi for exactly two years.

(*People's Daily*, overseas edn, 22 August 1985)

Twenty-six years later (mid-summer 1984) Guo Cheng visits China's nuclear testing ground

I departed by car from a place called Malan and headed for the ruins of the ancient city of Loulan. I happened to travel in the same car with Zhang Zhisan, an old friend of mine whom I had not met for a long time. The former commander of the nuclear testing base, Zhang Zhisan told me that the Lop Nor nuclear testing ground, with a total area of more than 100,000 sq. km., is as large as Zhejiang Province. Nowadays in the testing zone there is a highway network with a total length of more than 2,000 km. as well as various facilities for nuclear tests to be carried out on the ground, on towers, in the air, by missiles, in horizontal underground tunnels or in vertical shafts...

We drove for many hours along the road which oozed 'oil' under scorching sunshine. An odd scene finally presented itself before our eyes – dilapidated automobiles lay on rocks, armoured cars and aircraft had been turned into wreckage, dilapidated concrete buildings could be seen here and there and part of the surface looked like melted glaze. It looked as if a large-scale modern war had been fought in the depths of the desert some time ago!...

During my visit to the test areas people there were busy preparing for another nuclear test. Trucks carrying experimental equipment were speeding along the high roads; scientific and technical personnel were sweating away at their work in tents; and leading cadres of the base and various sections were giving commands at the test site. The quiet site was bustling with activity.

At the mouth of the shaft people were rehearsing the installation of an 'experimental product'. I saw that several base leaders in charge of technical work were directing the work there. All the technicians were working with rapt attention . It seemed that they were handling a real nuclear bomb rather than a dummy one.

(Miall, 1987, pp. 3–4)

BIOGRAPHIES

Chai Shufan, Chairman, China State Shipbuilding Corporation

Chai was born in Hubei province in 1905. He joined the Communist Youth League at the age of 12 and the Communist Party in 1927. He studied at the Sun Yat-Sen University in Moscow. He apparently took part in the Long March, but nothing is known of his activities during the Japanese War and the Civil War (1939–49).

In the 1950s and early 1960s, Chai was a Vice-Minister of the State Planning Commission (1957–59, 1961–67). After the Cultural Revolution he became a Vice-Minister of Foreign Trade (1973–78), which involved him in travel to the Middle East, South America and Europe, as well as Japan and Australia.

He subsequently became a Vice-Minister in the ministry responsible for shipbuilding, the Sixth Ministry of Shipbuilding. He became the Chairman when the ministry was converted into a corporation in 1981. Chai's wife is Chen Xin.

(See: China State Shipbuilding Corporation.)

Cheng Kaijia, Deputy Director, Nuclear Weapons Research Institute, Xining, China

Cheng Kaijia was among the second wave of about a hundred scientists and technicians sent to China's northwest in the early 1960s to accelerate China's nuclear programme. Zhu Guangya, Deng Jiaxian and others had conducted the initial research and development.

Cheng is a member of the Scientific Council (Mathematics and Science Department) of the Chinese Academy of Sciences. He was elected to represent Jiangsu Province at the National People's Congress in 1964 and as a representative of the armed forces (People's Liberation Army (PLA)) at the 1978 Congress.

(See: Ministry of Energy; Chinese Academy of Sciences.)

Chen Nengkuan Deputy Director, Nuclear Weapons Research Institute, Xining, China

Chen was among the one hundred or so scientists and technicians sent to China's northwest in the early 1960s to speed up the development of nuclear weapons.

Cheng is a member of the Scientific Council (Technical Science Department) of the Chinese Academy of Sciences. He was a delegate for Hunan Province to the 1964 National People's Congress and, in 1978, was a delegate to the Chinese People's Political Consultative Conference.

(See: Ministry of Energy; Chinese Academy of Sciences.)

Chi Haotian, Chief of Staff, People's Liberation Army (PLA)

General Chi Haotian replaced Yang Dezhi as Chief of Staff of the People's Liberation Army in November 1987. Chi is also a member of the Central Military Commission.

Chi, aged 62 in 1988, was born in Shandong. He was previously Deputy Political Commissar of Beijing, later Commissar of the Jinan Military Region (1985–87). In the late 1970s he served as Deputy Chief of Staff. His appointment as Chief of Staff was one of several designed to rejuvenate the military leadership.

Chi is a member of the Party's 175-man Central Committee.

(See: Communist Party of China; Central Military Commission; People's Liberation Army.)

Dai Chuanzeng, Member, Standing Committee of the China Nuclear Society

Dr Dai Chuanzeng is a former President of the Atomic Energy Institute. He studied at Liverpool University, receiving his doctorate in 1951.

Dai Chuanzeng is also a Deputy Director of the Nuclear Technology Inspectorate in the State Environmental Bureau (since 1985) and a member of the Mathematics and Physics Department of the Academy of Sciences.

He told a meeting of nuclear researchers at the Atomic Energy Institute in October 1985 that they were on a 'second round of pioneering', which involved civil instead of military research (as had been the case in the 'first round') as its main form. He urged scientists to expend more effort on the civil use of nuclear energy, on constructing nuclear power plants, studying other applications of nuclear technology, as well as on conducting basic research for national defence.

He attended the Chinese People's Political Consultative Conference in 1983.

(See: State Council; Chinese Academy of Sciences; Professional bodies.)

Deng Xiaoping, Chairman, Central Military Commission (CMC)

Deng Xiaoping has been the most important figure in Chinese politics since 1978, when the political climate changed following the death of Mao Zedong in 1976. Although he has relinquished most of his important posts, he remains Chairman of the Central Military Commission.

Deng Xiaoping was born in Guangian County, Sichuan Province, the eldest son of a landowner. After secondary school he went to France on a worker-student scholarship, reportedly studying at the University of Lyon. He joined the French branch of the Chinese Socialist Youth League in 1922 and the Chinese Communist Party in 1924. He also studied for a few months in Moscow before his return to China in 1926.

Deng then taught at the Xi'an Political and Military Academy, conforming with the Communist policy of co-operation with the Nationalists. The Academy was under the jurisdiction of the pro-Nationalist Feng Yuxiang, one of the warlords who established virtually independent states in China in the 1920s. Following the Nationalists' split with the Communist Party in 1927, Deng had to move to Shanghai, where he worked for the Party full-time.

In 1929–30 Deng helped to form the 7th Red Army in Guangxi, going on to be Political Director of the First Front Army during the Long March (1934–35). During the war against Japan (1939–45), he was Political Commissar of Communist forces in the Shanxi–Hebei guerrilla base, moving with them (expanded and reorganized as the Second Field Army) in campaigns against the Nationalist forces during the civil war 1946–49.

Deng moved with the army into southwest China, becoming Vice-Chairman of the southwest regional administration in 1950. In 1949 he had become a member of the Central People's Government, going on to be a Vice-Premier from 1952–66.

Deng's main career was as a Party man. Elected to the Central Committee in 1945, he became Secretary-General of the Party in 1954 and member of the Politburo in 1956.

During the Cultural Revolution (1966–76), Deng was attacked as the 'Number Two Capitalist Roader' (Liu Shaoqi being the 'Number One'). At a time when political survival meant unswerving loyalty to Mao Zedong Thought, symbolized in the Little Red Book of Mao's selected writings, Deng was infamous for his pragmatic approach, typified in the saying: 'It doesn't matter whether the cat is a white cat or a black cat, if it catches mice, it's a good cat'.

Although Deng himself survived the turmoil of the late 1960s unharmed, reappearing as a Vice-Premier and Central Committee member in 1973, his eldest son Deng Pufang was permanently disabled after apparently being thrown out of a window by Red Guards in 1968. Deng is Chairman of the China Disabled Persons' Federation, formed in 1988.

From April to November 1976 Deng again was criticized by the Maoists, only being restored to his position after the death of Mao and the arrest of the leading Maoists, who included Mao's wife Jiang Qing.

If the Third Plenum of the Eleventh Central Committee in October 1978 marked the beginning of Deng's road to reform, the Party Congress in October 1987 signalled the real beginning of his move to retirement. In 1987 Deng retired from the key centre of China's decisionmaking, the Standing Committee of the Politburo. More importantly, Deng has manouvered other octogenarians in the leadership into retirement.

One of Deng's major achievements has been to streamline what he dubbed China's 'bloated' armed forces. He has said that he wished to achieve this before handing on the CMC to a successor. As Chairman of the CMC, in January 1986 Deng commended Jiang Shaohua (about whom nothing further is known) and other personnel involved in a successful range test of a submarine-launched missile.

Deng married Zhuo Lin and had two sons and a daughter.

(See: Communist Party of China; Central Military Commission.)

Ding Henggao, Minister, Commission of Science, Technology and Industry for National Defence (COSTIND)

Ding, 57 in 1988, was formerly a researcher in the fields of precision machinery and optics. In 1982 he was appointed deputy head of the Science and Technology Department at COSTIND. In 1985 he was appointed Minister, in a move to place more technologists in top positions.

Ding became a member of the Communist Party's Central Committee in 1985. Ding's father-in-law is Nie Rongzhen, formerly a Vice-Chairman of the Central Military Commission.

(See: Communist Party of China; Commission of Science, Technology and Industry for National Defence (COSTIND).)

Hong Xuezhi, Deputy Secretary General, Central Military Commission

Hong Xuezhi was formerly head of the General Logistics Department of the PLA. Hong was born in 1913 in Jinzhai, Anhui Province. He joined the Party in 1928 and served with guerrilla armies until the mid-1940s, when he took part in the regular campaigns against the Nationalist forces.

Following his success in organizing logistics for the Chinese forces in Korea, Hong was promoted to the National Defence Council (in 1954) and to colonel-general (in 1955). Hong was subsequently made Director of the PLA Logistics Department, but was disgraced in 1959 as a follower of Marshal Peng Dehuai (who had denigrated Maoist policies). It was not until 1980 that he returned to the Logistics Department.

(See: Central Military Commission.)

Hu Qili, Member, Standing Committee of the Politburo of the Communist Party of China

Hu Qili was elected to the five-man Politburo Standing Committee in October 1987. As Secretary of the Party's Secretariat, Hu has been closely involved in persuading the Party's rank and file to support the process of reform, a process which involves a substantial dilution of Marxist doctrine and a loss of effective power by Party officials.

Hu, aged 59 in 1988, was born in Yulin in Shanxi in 1929. He is a graduate in mechanics from the prestigious Beijing University. Joining the Party in 1948, during the 1950s he was Secretary of the Communist Youth League at the University, Chairman of the National Students' Federation and a functionary in the Communist Youth League. Hu travelled extensively to the Third World countries as head of youth delegations.

Following his dismissal during the Cultural Revolution (1966–76), he became a Party Secretary in Ningxia (1972–77) reappearing as Secretary of the Youth League in 1978.

In 1980 he was elected Mayor of Tianjin, until his appointment as Director of the General Office of the Party and election to the Central Committee in 1982.

(See: Communist Party of China.)

Hu Yaobang, Member of the Central Committee, Communist Party of China

Hu Yaobang was Secretary-General of the Chinese Communist Party from 1982 to 1986. Despite his ousting from the leading post in the Party, he remains on its Central Committee. Hu was eased out of his post in 1986, apparently following concern in the wake of student demonstrations that the Party's ideas were being ignored.

Hu has had a reputation for outspokenness and, at times, for foolishness. Scurrilous Chinese, making a pun on his name, refer to him as 'Hu Shuohua', 'Talking Nonsense'. At one time he suggested that Chinese people should give up using chopsticks in favour of knives and forks, on the grounds that chopsticks were 'insanitary'. His open style and plain speaking reflected a new openness among Chinese leaders.

Hu was born in 1915 in Liuyang, Hunan Province. At the age of 12 or 13, he joined in the abortive Autumn Harvest Uprising in Hunan in 1927. By his late teens he was mobilizing youth to support the Jiangxi Soviet, one of China's early Communist-run areas. He took part in the Long March, a tactical retreat by the Communist forces to China's northwest.

In the 1940s Hu was a professional administrator in various military units. By 1949 he was on the Party's Central Committee. From 1952 Hu became Secretary of the New Democratic Youth League and First Secretary following its merger with the Communist Youth League in 1957 (until 1964). Hu became Vice-Chairman of the World Federation of Democratic Youth from 1953 to 1959, following his attendance at a conference in Bucharest in July 1953. Hu was also a member of the Executive Council of the China Federation of Trade Unions (1953–57).

Hu was also a Standing Committee member of the National People's Congress from 1954 to 1975. He was attacked as a 'capitalist roader' in January 1967, reappearing in public in 1972. In the 1970s he held administrative posts in the Chinese Academy of Sciences, the Party School and the Central Committee's Organization Department (responsible for administration).

Re-elected to the Central Committee in 1977, he became a member of the Politburo in December 1978, when the watershed Third Plenum of the 11th Central Committee began the reversal of Maoist policies. Hu became Secretary-General of the Party at a time when the Party chairmanship was abolished.

In November 1983 Hu Yaobang, who has made a number of foreign trips, visited Japan. Among topics of discussion with Japanese Prime Minister Nakasone was security in Asia, in particular the possibility that Soviet missiles targeted on Europe might be transferred to the Far East under any INF agreement between the Soviet Union and the United States. As a central figure in the Party machine, Hu will have been involved in the assessment of China's need for nuclear weapons. As a Central Committee member and former Secretary-General, he remains a figure of some influence.

Hu is married to Li Zhao, who has recently retired from working in the textile industry. They have four children in their 30s and 40s. They have five grandchildren.

(See: Communist Party of China.)

Huang Yicheng, Minister, Ministry of Energy

Huang was appointed Minister in the newly-formed Ministry of Energy in April 1988. Huang, 61 in 1988, was formerly a chief engineer in turbine manufacturing. Later he became Deputy Director of the Comprehensive Planning Bureau (responsible for co-ordinating overall strategy of the various sector bureaux) of the State Planning Commission. In 1982 he became a Vice-Minister of the Commission.

In 1984–85, he became more involved in planning China's energy development, for example as Deputy Director of the State Council Leading Group for the Development of Rural Energy.

(See: State Council; Ministry of Energy.)

Jiang Shengjie, Vice-President, China Nuclear Society

Jiang was also Director of the Science and Technology Committee in the Ministry of the Nuclear Industry (MNI) and, between 1980 and 1982, a Vice-Minister of the Nuclear Industry. It is uncertain whether Jiang retained his position following the integration of the MNI into the Ministry of Energy, formed in 1988.

Jiang, 75 in 1988, is a specialist in nuclear chemical engineering. He has represented Jiangsu Province at the National People's Congress.

(See: Ministry of Energy; China Nuclear Society.)

Li Peng, Premier, State Council

Li Peng formally became Premier in April 1988, following five years as a Vice-Premier since 1983. Li is a member of the five-man Politburo Standing Committee. He also has prime responsibility for reform of China's economy and trade, as Minister of the State Commission on the Restructuring of the Economic System.

Li was born in Chengdu, Sichuan Province, in 1928. His father, Li Shuoxun, was an early Communist, a participant in the Nanchang Uprising and other revolutionary activities. His father was executed by the Nationalists (Kuomintang) when Li Peng was only 3 years old: he was adopted by Zhou Enlai. It was Zhou who arranged for the 11-year old Li to go to secondary school in Changqing. Zhou Enlai, China's long-serving Premier, is seen by most Chinese as the steadying influence on the excesses wrought by Mao Zedong. Although Li has tried to play down his association with Zhou, it has undoubtedly been to his political benefit.

Li represents the earliest generation of Chinese to grow up under Communism. In the 1940s, Li studied at the National Science Academy in Yan'an, the backwoods capital of the Communists. He joined the Communist Party in 1945 at the age of 17. Li went on to study at the Zhangjiakon Industrial Institute and in 1948 was sent to the Moscow Power Institute. While in the Soviet Union, he was Chairman of the Association of Chinese Students there. Returning to China in 1955, Li became chief engineer and director of two power plants in northeast China and a Deputy Chief Engineer in the Northeast China Power Administration.

Unlike many of his future colleagues in power, he was apparently unscathed by the Cultural Revolution (1966–76). From 1966 he was Director of the Beijing Electric Power Administration. In 1979–83, he became Vice-Minister then First Vice-Minister in the Ministry of Water Resources and Electric Power.

Li has long been associated with China's plans to build nuclear power plants. It was Li, on an inspection tour of the nuclear plant under construction at Daya Bay near Hong Kong in Guangdong in May 1986, who sought to reassure public opinion that there would be no Chernobyl-type accident in China: 'Safety first and quality first must be the guiding principle for the construction and operation of China's nuclear power stations', he said.

From 1985, Li was not only a Vice-Premier but Minister of the State Education Commission.

Some Western analysts have interpreted Li's association with the Soviet Union as making him very pro-Soviet. Li once told a journalist who questioned him on this: 'I am a Chinese and a member of the Chinese Communist Party. I act only on the Party's line and in the interests of my country'.

Li is proficient in Russian, but has also taught himself some English. He is an avid reader. He and his wife have two sons and a daughter. Li is more diffident and less outgoing that his predecessor Zhao Ziyang.

(See: Communist Party of China; State Council.)

Li Xuge, Commander, Strategic Missile Force, People's Liberation Army (PLA)

Li Xuge became Commander of the Strategic Missile Force in 1985, following three years as Deputy Commander of the Force. Li Xuge is a member of the Communist Party's Central Committee. Li, aged 61 in 1988, formerly held the post of Deputy Chief of the Operations Department under the PLA General Staff Headquarters.

The Strategic Missile Force, formerly known as 'The Second Artillery' was formally established in 1966. Li is certainly in charge of all land-based missiles but it is not certain whether he has responsibility also for nuclear bombs carried by the Air Force, nuclear missiles in the Navy's submarines or any tactical nuclear weapons that China may possess.

In a rare interview with the China News Agency released on 28 May 1987, Li said that the Strategic Missile Force had built 'underground warehouses for storing thunderbolts' and could fulfil 'offensive, defensive and storage functions'. 'This means that it has established a self-contained defence system', he told reporter Guo Qingsheng. Li noted in the interview that a strategic nuclear capability was an important indicator of a country's national strength and its degree of defence modernization. China had developed nuclear weapons to end the nuclear monopoly of the superpowers, to deter other countries from starting a nuclear war against China, to protect the country's security and independence, and to uphold

world peace.
(See: Communist Party of China; People's Liberation Army.)

Lin Zangfang, Minister, Ministry of the Aeronautics and Astronautics Industry

Lin Zangfang was appointed minister of the newly-formed ministry in April 1988. Lin, aged 61 in 1988, was formerly a chief engineer and a senior official in the machine-building industry. He later became Vice-Minister of the State Economic Commission and Director of the Machinery Export Office of the State Council.
(See:Ministry of the Aeronautics and Astronautics Industry.)

Liu Huaqing, Deputy Secretary General, Central Military Commission.

Admiral Liu was Commander of the People's Liberation Army (PLA) Navy from October 1982 to February 1988.

Liu was born in Daun, Hubei, in 1917. At the age of 15, he joined a Communist guerrilla unit and served in various Communist armies. From 1946 to 1949, Liu was a political commissar in the land forces (PLA) before transferring to the Navy in 1950. He had risen to the rank of Rear-Admiral by 1958.

By 1967 he was a Vice-Minister in the Commission of Science, Technology and Industry for National Defence (COSTIND), a position he held for a period after the Cultural Revolution (c.1978). In 1968 he was criticized by Red Guards for having established a 'bourgeois kingdom' in the Commission.

In 1970 he became Deputy Political Commissar of the Navy and Deputy Chief of Naval Staff in 1972.
(See: Central Military Commission.)

Liu Lifeng, Political Commissar, Strategic Missile Force

Liu was apparently among the People's Liberation Army (PLA) delegates at the Thirteenth Party Congress in November 1987, where, in the PLA discussion group, he emphasized the need for political and ideological education to balance the emphasis on material development. Liu was a PLA representative at the 1983 National People's Congress.

Liu was Deputy Commander of the then Second Artillery from 1976 to 1980. From 1980 he was Deputy Political Commissar, until his promotion to Commissar in 1983.
(See: People's Liberation Army.)

Peng Shilu, Vice-President of the China Nuclear Society

Peng was born in Haifeng, Guangdong, in 1925. His father, the early Communist leader Peng Pai, was executed in 1929. From 1933 to 1935 Peng was a child prisoner. Later he attended St Joseph's English Institute in Hong Kong. He joined the Red Army in Guangdong in 1939. In the early 1940s he studied at the Communists' capital in Yan 'an.

After further education in Haerbin and Dalian, Peng spent seven years (1951–58) in Moscow, at the Chemical Engineering Institute and later at the Institute of Power Engineering. He became a teacher at the Chinese University of Science and Technology in 1960, pioneering a course on nuclear energy.

Peng was one of the two deputy chief engineers at the Submarine Nuclear Power Research and Design Institute who worked on the design of a submarine power plant from 1965–69. By 1969 he was the President of the Academy of Marine Architecture.

From 1981 to 1982, Peng was a Vice-Minister in the Sixth Ministry of Machine-Building, the precursor of the China State Shipbuilding Corporation. He became Chief Engineer and Deputy General Manager of the Corporation in 1982.
(See: Professional bodies.)

Qian Sanqiang, Honorary President, China Nuclear Society

Dr Qian Sanqiang is the 'father' of China's

hydrogen bomb. He is also Vice-President of the Chinese Academy of Sciences. Qian is a member of the Chinese People's Political Consultative Conference.

Qian Sanqiang was born in Zhajiang Province in 1912. His father was an activist in what became known as the May Fourth movement, China's first modern nationalist movement, named after anti-imperialist demonstrations on 4 May 1919.

After taking a degree in physics at China's premier scientific university, Qinghua (Tshinghua) University in Beijing, he joined the Academia Sinica (forerunner of the Chinese Academy of Sciences). Qian studied in Paris at the Curie Institute from 1937 to 1943, obtaining his doctorate in physics from the University of Paris in 1943 and, in 1946, a prize from the Academy of Sciences for his work on atomic fission. Qian remained in Paris until 1948, when he returned to Qinghua, where he had become head of the physics department by 1950.

Qian was head of the Atomic Energy Institute for twenty years from its foundation in 1958 until 1978 (except perhaps for a period during the Cultural Revolution (1966–76)), and of its precursor, the Institute of Modern Physics. Although criticized in the Cultural Revolution as a 'capitalist roader' and a 'secret agent', the importance of his work probably shielded him from the worst excesses.

From 1954 to 1961, Qian was Secretary-General of the Academy of Sciences; from 1961 to 1964, he held the lesser post of Deputy Secretary General. This apparent demotion may well have been because of his increasing involvement in the development of a hydrogen bomb in the early 1960s. Qian was head of a 'Neutron Physics Leading Group' that undertook the basic theoretical research into thermonuclear reactions. Qian was again known to be Secretary-General from 1975 until his appointment as a Vice-President of CAS in 1978.

Qian has represented China abroad since 1946, when he was attached to a UNESCO conference in Paris. He attended the Soviet-bloc World Peace Congresses in 1949, 1950 and 1953.

He was involved in the preparatory work in the establishement of the nuclear research centre in Dubna (near Moscow) in 1956 and was the senior Chinese delegate at a December 1960 meeting at Dubna of the countries involved in research.

He has been a delegate to the National People's Congresses elected in 1954, 1964 and 1978. He is not known to be a member of the Communist Party. Qian was appointed President of the University of Zhejiang in Hangzhou in 1979–84, a return to his native province.

Qian married He Cehui, who like him specialized in nuclear physics. She obtained her doctorate at the University of Shanghai.

(See: Chinese Academy of Sciences; Professional bodies.)

Qian Xuesen, Honorary President, China Mechanics Society

Qian Xuesen is regarded as the 'father' of Chinese rocketry. He has been the leading figure in the China Automation Society (since 1961) and in the China Society of Mechanics and Automation (since 1978). Qian is one of 28 vice-chairmen of the Chinese People's Political Consultative Conference.

Qian was born in Shanghai in 1912. His father was a businessman. After taking a degree in engineering at Jiaotong University in Shanghai, he went to the Massachusetts Institute of Technology (MIT) in 1935 to study aeronautics and aerodynamics. Moving to the California Institute of Technology (Caltech), he undertook research on jet propulsion, developing what became known as the 'Ch'ien Formula'. He received his doctorate at Caltech in 1938 and in 1946 became MIT's youngest professor.

Qian held a crucial position in the US defence research establishment in the 1940s. He was director of the rocket section of the US National Defence Scientific Advisory Board; it was Qian who, following Germany's surrender, supervised the removal of the research facilities at Peenemünde to the USA.

Refused a position by the Nationalist Government in 1947 on account of his youth, Qian became a professor at Caltech and later head of the Guggenheim Jet Propulsion Laboratory (1949–54).

Qian wished to return to China in 1950, but was refused permission by the US Government, since China was regarded as a hostile country. He was eventually allowed to return in 1955 (in exchange for nine Americans), with his family and nearly a ton of scientific material. The Chinese authorities welcomed the return of such a key scientist. He became the director of the newly-formed Institute of Mechanics in Beijing in 1956.

Qian has been a Vice-Chairman of the Commission of Science, Technology and Industry for National Defence (COSTIND)'s Science and Technology Committee.Qian joined the Communist Party in 1958. He was elected to the National People's Congress in 1958, 1964 and 1978.

In 1947 he married Jiang Ying, a teacher of music at the Central Conservatory. They have a son and a daughter.

(See: Professional bodies.)

Qiao Shi, Member, Standing Committee of the Politburo

Qiao Shi was elected to the Standing Committee of the Politburo in November 1987.

Qiao was born in 1924 in Dinghai, Zhejiang. Since joining the Communist Party in 1940, he has spent most of his life as a full-time Party official, in Shanghai, Hangzhou and the East China Bureau of the Party. By the early 1960s, he was associated with the prestigious Anshan Iron and Steel Plant; he became Director of the Research Institute of the Jiuquan Iron and Steel Company.

Qiao was Deputy Director of the Party's Liaison Department from 1978 to 1982, when he was elected to the Central Committee. He represented the Party on visits to Eastern Europe, France, Italy, Iran and North Korea.

Qiao was a Vice-Premier from 1986 to 1988. He is reported to have responsibility within the Party for security matters, including the People's Armed Police.

(See: Communist Party of China.)

Qin Jiwei, Minister of National Defence

Qin Jiwei was appointed Minister of National Defence in April 1988. He is also a State Councillor. He has been a member of the Central Committee since 1973 and became a full member of the Politburo in 1987.

Qin was born in a poor peasant family in Hangan County, Hubei Province, in 1914. In 1929, at the age of 15, he joined the Workers' and Peasants' Red Army, becoming a Party member in 1930. Qin took part in the Long March (1934–35) and was an officer in the Anti-Japanese (1937–45) and Civil (1946–49) Wars, serving for a period under Deng Xiaoping. He distinguished himself in the Korean War as Commander of the Chinese 15th Army, particularly in the battle of Shamkamryung Ridge in 1952.

Qin was criticized and deprived of his post during the early years of the Cultural Revolution, but was later appointed Commander of the Chengdan Military Area in Sichuan. On promotion to lieutenant-general in 1955, Qin studied for two years at the Nanjing Military Academy before becoming Commander of the Kunming Military Area in 1957.

In 1975 Qin was appointed Commander of the prestigious Beijing Military Region. In this position he succeeded in implementing planned troop reductions and in 1981 organized the first large-scale combined forces military exercise since 1949. Qin has considerable authority; his appointment may herald an increased importance for the Ministry of National Defence. Both Yang Baibing (Director of the PLA's Political Department) and Zhao Nanqi (head of the Logistics Department) have served under Qin in the Beijing Military Region.

Qin is married to Tang Xianmei.

(See: Communist Party of China; State Council; Ministry of National Defence.)

Song Jian, Minister, State Science and Technology Commission

Song Jian is also a State Councillor. Song was born in Rongcheng, Shangdong, in 1932. At the age of 14 or 15 he joined the Communist forces, becoming a Communist Party member in 1947.

Graduating from Haerbin Technical University in 1953, Song studied for eight years at the Bauman Polytechnic Institute at Moscow University. After his return to China in 1961, he applied his expertise in mechanics and cybernetics to the development of missiles, first at the Spaceflight Research Institute, and later at the New Rocket Research Institute. Song became Chief Engineer at the (then) Seventh Ministry of Machine-Building, responsible for rocket production, and renamed in 1981 the Ministry of the Space Industry. Song was a Vice-Minister at the Ministry from 1981 until 1984, when he became Minister of the State Science and Technology Commission .

Song, a prolific writer, has had a distinguished scientific career outside his main area of interest in rocketry. His research on population growth played an important role in the development of birth control policies in China in the 1980s. He became a Vice-President of the Population Science Society in 1984. Song has also held senior positions in a number of learned bodies, including the Automation Society (President) and the Systems Engineering Society.

Song became a full member of the Party Central Committee in 1984.

(See: Communist Party of China; State Council; State Science and Technology Commission.)

Wang Hai, Commander of the Air Force

Wang Hai was appointed Commander of the PLA Air Force (PLAAF) in July 1985 by the Central Military Commission and had previously been Deputy Commander of the PLAAF since 1982.

Wang, who was 63 in 1988, was born in Weihai in Shandong Province in 1925. Soon after he joined the PLA in 1946, he was sent to the Northeast Aviation Academy of the PLA. He was one of the first batch of pilots formally trained by the Communist forces.

Made a group commander of an air force brigade in 1950, he distinguished himself as a 'Grade One Combat Hero' in the Korean War; he was himself responsible for shooting down five enemy planes (in combat with the UN-sponsored forces operating from what became South Korea).

In 1969, he was head in a section of the Air Force training department. He became Commander of the Air Force in the Canton Military Region in 1975. A famous pilot, Wang is reputed to be popular in the Air Force. One story about him concerns his piloting of an F-7 jet fighter. When problems arose, he was ordered to eject. He angrily refused, insisting on landing the plane despite being unable to use the landing gear.

As Commander of the Air Force, Wang is responsible for the nuclear-capable aircraft. Wang has been tackling the task of trimming the 400,000 man force by 120,000 people. Wang is the fifth Commander of the PLAAF after Liu Yalou, Wu Faxian, Ma Ning and Zhang Tingfa, who is understood to have retired.

Wang Hai is a member of the 175-member Party Central Committee.

(See: Communist Party of China; People's Liberation Army.)

Yang Baibing, Director, General Political Department of the People's Liberation Army (PLA)

Yang Baibing was appointed Director of the General Political Department of the PLA in 1987. He is a member of the Central Military Commission.

Yang was from 1982 Deputy Political Commissar of the Beijing Military Regionthe PLA in 1987. He is a member of the Central Military Commission.

Yang was from 1982 Deputy Political Commissar of the Beijing Military Region, becoming Commissar in 1985.

(See: The Central Military Commission; People's Liberation Army.)

Yang Guoliang, Deputy Commander of the Missile Force

Yang was apparently a delegate at the Thirteenth Party Congress in November 1987, where he spoke in a discussion group of the PLA delegates. He said that reform of the PLA (i.e., the cut in numbers and in the defence budget) was inseparable from a change in strategic outlook (i.e., not expecting an imminent world war).

Yang was an alternative member of the Twelfth Central Committee (1985–87).
(See: People's Liberation Army.)

Yang Huan, Deputy Commander of the Strategic Missile Force.
(See: People's Liberation Army.)

Yang Shangkun, President of the People's Republic of China.

Yang Shangkun became President of the People's Republic of China in April 1988. He is also Permanent Vice-Chairman of the Central Military Commission. Yang is a member of the Party's 17-man Politburo, but not of its five-man Standing Committee. Although as President he holds a post that is largely honorific, as one of the few of the Party's old guard remaining, his views continue to carry a certain weight.

Yang was born in Tanguan, Sichuan Province, in 1904. He attended Shanghai University and joined the Communist Party in 1925. After studying in Moscow, he returned to China in 1931.

In 1931 Yang became a member of the Central Executive Committee of the Jiangxi Soviet, an early Communist area, and Director of the First Red Army's Political Department. As a returned student from Moscow, Yang may have been out of favour during the late 1930s and early 1940s, when Mao's idea of a Communism tailored to China (and independent of the Soviet Union) was important. Yang lead a political propaganda troupe in the northwest Communist areas.

Yang's Party career took off in 1943, when he became Secretary of the Party's North China Bureau and (in 1945) head of the General Office of the Central Committee (a post he held until 1966). He was elected to the Central Committee in 1956.

Yang was elected to the National People's Congress in 1964 and to its Standing Committee in 1965. Yang was criticized as a 'counter-revolutionary' in 1966. After years of obscurity during the Cultural Revolution (1966–76), in 1979 he was active in Guangdong Province, as Second Party Secretary and Vice-Governor. He became Executive Vice-Chairman of the new Central Military Commission on its re-establishment in 1983.

According to a report in the Hong Kong magazine Pai Hsing in September 1987, the reason behind Yang's removal from the Commission was his decision to bring troops into Beijing during student unrest earlier in the year. Yang did not, according to the report, consult the Commission's chairman Deng Xiaoping. Deng and his fellow reformers apparently thought the move rash and provocative. It was the People's Liberation Army (PLA) which restored order after the chaos caused by student and other youth rebels in 1968–69. The appointment of Zhao Ziyang as First Vice-Chairman of the Central Military Commission, higher in precedence than Yang as Permanent Vice-Chairman, in November 1987, already indicated that Zhao would have most authority on the Commission. Yang's election to the presidency also makes his becoming Chairman of the Commission less feasible.

Yang was married to the playwright Li Bozhao, who died in 1985.
(See: Communist Party of China; Central Military Commission; People's Liberation Army.)

Yao Yilin, Member, Standing Committee of the Politburo of the Communist Party of China

Yao Yilin was elected to the five-man Standing Committee in Ocober 1987. He is one of the three Vice-Premiers and the Minister of the State Planning Commission.

Yao, 70 in 1988, was born in Guichi, Anhui, in 1917. By 1935 he was a student at China's premier technical university, Qinghua, in Beijing, where he was involved in anti-Japanese demonstrations. It was probably in this period that he joined the Communist Party, since he held Party posts in the 1930s and 1940s, among them North China Bureau Secretary-General and Tianjin Party Secretary.

After Liberation in 1949, Yao served first as Vice-Minister, then, from 1960, as Minister of Commerce until he was criticized as a 'capitalist roader' in 1967. In 1973 he became a Vice-Minister of Foreign Trade, returning to the Ministry of Commerce in 1978. With his long involvement in China's internal and external trade, Yao has had considerable experience of the problems of China's economy; he is believed to have the main responsibility on the Standing Committee for the economy.

Yao became a full member of the Party Central Committee in 1977 and a member of the Politburo in 1982.

(See: Communist Party of China; State Planning Commission.)

Zhang Lianzhoug, Commander of the Chinese Navy

Zhang Lianzhoug was appointed Commander of the People's Liberation Army (PLA) Navy in February 1988 by the Central Military Commission. He had been Deputy Commander since July 1985.

Zhang, aged 57 in 1988, who joined the armed forces in 1947, has served as a submarine commander, the commander of a submarine detachment and Deputy Chief of Staff of the North China Sea (Beihai) Fleet. Zhang has under his command China's one nuclear-capable Xia-class submarine. The PLA Navy is currently expanding its role from inshore defence to more long-range operations. In political terms, Zhang is relatively junior. He was only elected a member of the Central Committee in October 1987, even then only as an alternate member.

Zhang's predecessor, Liu Huaqing, has become a Deputy Secretary-General of the Central Military Commission.

(See: Communist Party of China; People's Liberation Army.)

Zhang Zhen, President of the National Defence University

Born in 1907, Zhang received his military training in the Soviet Union in the mid-1930s. In the 1940s, he held a number of military commands in Eastern China.

After Liberation, Zhang was assigned to the General Staff Department of the People's Liberation Army (PLA) until his transfer in 1957 to the Nanjing Military Academy, where he stayed until 1967 (becoming its Commandant in 1963). He was Director of the PLA Logistics Department from 1978 to 1980 and a Deputy Chief of Staff from 1980 to 1985.

In 1982, Zhang was elected as an alternate member of the Party Central Committe. He resigned from the Central Committee and joined the Party Central Advisory Commission, a largely honorific post.

(See: Communist Party of China; People's Liberation Army.)

Zhao Nanqi, Member, Central Military Commission

Zhao is also Director of the PLA's General Logistics Department.

Zhao was born in Yanbian (Jilin) c.1935. In 1978 Zhao was First Party Secretary of Yanbian, a district inhabited mainly by the Korean ethnic minority, of which Zhao is a member. He became Deputy Governor of Jilin in 1980. In 1984 he became Political Commissar of the Jilin Military District until his appointment as Deputy Director of the General Logistics Department.

Zhao was a member of the Twelth Party Central Committee (1982–87).

(See: Central Military Commission; People's Liberation Army.)

Zhao Ziyang, Secretary General, Communist Party of China

Zhao Ziyang became Secretary-General of the Communist Party in 1987, following a two-year stint as China's Premier. He is also First Vice-Chairman of the Central Military Commission and has since 1980 been on the Standing Committee of the Politburo.

Zhao is arguably the second most powerful man in China after Deng Xiaoping; he has long been regarded as Deng's protégé. He faces two challenges: he must persuade the 46 million Party members that the Party should only concern itself with policy, not day-to-day administration; and he must remind the people of China, including Party members, that the Communist Party remains in ultimate control of the country. In the lead-up to the Seventh National People's Congress in April 1988, Zhao sought to show the public that the policies and leadership changes to be discussed at the Congress were the result of decisions made by the Party.

As First Vice-Chairman of the Central Military Commission (Deng Xiaoping is its Chairman), Zhao is responsible for ensuring that the military establishment respect Party policy on reducing military expenditure and restricting the role of the armed forces to defence issues, following over a decade of military primacy during the Cultural Revolution (1966–76). Although President Yang Shangkun remains as Permanent Vice-Chairman of the Commission, it is Zhao who is in line to take over the chairmanship when Deng Xiaoping steps down.

Zhao was born in 1918 in Huaxian, Henan Province, the son of a landowner. He attended secondary school, in Kaifeng and Wuhan and during this period joined the Communist Youth League (1932). Joining the Communist party in 1938, he was assigned work as a Party representative in the Hebei–Shandong Border Region, a Communist-led guerrilla base. In the mid-1940s he was involved in land reform in the region; he is likely to have experienced at first hand the problems involved in the Communists' first great rural reform: this set out to ensure every peasant a livelihood through the redistribution of landowners' property, but was in danger of alienating a large number of peasants whenever it turned into an attack on anyone who had any property.

After Liberation in 1949, Zhao's main work was as a Party functionary; for over twenty years, he was associated with the independently-minded province of Guangdong. By 1957, he was Party Secretary of the province, a post he may have held continuously until the Cultural Revolution attacks on him in 1967. In the early 1960s, he was the Party's man in the local military, as Political Commissar of the Guangdong Military Region. In 1967, Zhao was denounced as a member of the landowning class, labelled a 'capitalist roader' and paraded in a dunce's cap through the streets of Canton (Guangzhou).

In 1971–72, he was mentioned as Party Secretary and then Chairman of Inner Mongolia. He subsequently returned to Guangdong for two years, sometime holding the posts of First Party Secretary and Military Political Commissar, before his assignment (among other posts) as First Party Secretary of Sichuan Province from 1975 to 1980. During his four years in Sichuan (a province of 110 million people, the size of France) he introduced radical reforms in agriculture and industry, reducing political control in favour of material incentives, reforms that were later extended by Deng Xiaoping and his supporters throughout the country. Zhao became famous for his pragmatic, non-ideological approach. He earned the reputation as an achiever when the Chinese population had become tired of empty political rhetoric. A catchphrase about him became popular: 'If you want food, Zhao Ziyang is good' ('Yao chiliang, yao Zhao Ziyang').

Zhao represents a new generation of self-assured and relaxed Chinese politicians. He has a distaste for formality and is relaxed in his meetings with foreigners. Zhao set a precedent after the Thirteenth Party Congress in November 1987 by mixing with journalists at a reception, parrying awkward questions with apparent ease and frankness:

> *Reporter:* 'It is said you would rather be Premier than be the Party's General Secretary. Now that you are the Party's General Secretary, what is your feeling?'
>
> *Zhao:* 'Personally speaking, I still think that I am more suitable to assume the position of Premier. However, since I have now been elected General Secretary of the Party, I will try my best to do a good job in that post. As I said just now, there is no absolute freedom'.

and:

> *Reporter*: 'Mr. Zhao, I am a reporter from Japan. Please allow me to ask you a very personal

> question. I think you are wearing a very nice double-breasted suit. Could you tell me where it was made, in a foreign country or in Beijing?'
> *Zhao:* 'All my suits are made at home. I hope you will send a special news dispatch saying that all my suits are made in China and are very smart so that more Chinese-made garments will be exported to your country.' [Laughter]

As Premier, Zhao has been the principle spokesman on China's nuclear weapons policy. In 1983, during a visit to New Zealand, Zhao offered reassurances that China had 'no new or specific plans' for missile tests in the Pacific, a cause of concern for New Zealand. He expressed China's support for a nuclear weapons-free zone in the South Pacific.

It was Zhao who announced China's decision to halt atmospheric nuclear tests in March 1986. Marking the UN Year of Peace, Zhao said that China could have 'a major worldwide impact' on the question of world peace.

Zhao has been active in persuading the army to accept a reduced budget while China builds up its civilian economy and turns to the West for investment. Part of the process is transferring its military facilities and factories to civilian use. Zhao told a meeting of specialists in January 1986 that the defence industry could 'make a greater contribution to the country's modernization', it had not yet 'made the most of its potential'.

Zhao is married to Liang Boqi. He is a keen golfer and is Honorary Chairman of the Chinese Golf Society.

(See: Communist Party of China; Central Military Commission.)

Zhou Guangzhao, President of the Chinese Academy of Sciences (CAS)

Zhou Guangzhao was appointed President of the Chinese Academy of Sciences in January 1987.

Zhou, aged 58 in 1988, is from Changsha, Hunan Province. After graduating from the physics department of Qinghua University in 1951, he spent three years on postgraduate study at Beijing University.

In 1957 he was assigned to work in the Dubna Joint Nuclear Research Institute in the Soviet Union. He returned to China around 1960 to join in the development of China's nuclear weapons. He suffered some persecution and interruption of his research during the Cultural Revolution (1966–76). Zhou visited the USA as a visiting lecturer in 1981. He was appointed Vice-President of the CAS in 1984. Zhou has been a member of the Party Central Committee since 1982.

Since his appointment as President of the CAS, Zhou has underlined the importance of basic research in the development of the national economy. 'Scientists must be allowed to undertake research in the direction they feel most appropriate' he said, in March 1987, soon after his appointment. He cited academic democracy and free contention as 'the only two weapons for a flourishing science' (*SWB*, 18 March 1987).

(See: Communist Party of China; Chinese Academy of Sciences.)

Zou Jiahua, Minister, Ministry of Machine-Building and Electronics

Zou was appointed Minister of the newly-formed Ministry in April 1988. He is also a State Councillor. Zou was born in Shanghai in 1927. His father was a nationalist leader. Zou, who attended university, was at some time Chief Engineer and Director of the Shenyang No. 2 Machine Tool Plant. He became Director of the Machine Tool Research Institute of the (then) First Ministry of Machine-Building. Zou was also at some time Chief Engineer of the North-east Electric Power Administration and head of the Beijing Power Administration.

From 1983 to 1985, Zou was a Vice-Minister of the Commission of Science, Technology and Industry for National Defence (COSTIND) and, from 1985 to 1986, Minister of the Ordnance Industry. When the Ordnance Ministry was merged with the Ministry of Machine-Building in 1985, Zou became Minister of the new body, the State Commission for the Machine-Building Industry.

(See: State Council; Ministry of Machine-Building and Electronics.)

REFERENCES

Bartke, W., 1981 (1st edn), *Who's Who in the People's Republic of China*, Harvester Press, Brighton; 1987 (2nd edn), K. G. Saur, London.

Bullard, M.R., 1985, *China's Political-Military Evolution*, Westview, Boulder, Colorado.

China Phone Book, The, 1988, China Phone Book Co, Hong Kong.

Directory of Chinese Officials: Scientific & Educational Organisations, February 1985;

Directory of Chinese Officials: National Level Organisations, June 1985, (US Government) National Foreign Assessment Center.

Fieldhouse, R. W., 1986, 'Chinese nuclear weapons: an overview', SIPRI Yearbook 1986, Stockholm International Peace Research Institute, Oxford University Press, Oxford.

Gelben, H., 1979, *Technology, Defense and External Relations in China 1975-78*, Westview Studies, Boulder, Colorado.

Godwin, P., 1983, *The Chinese Defense Establishment*, Westview Studies, Boulder, Colorado.

Jencks, H., 1982, *From Muskets to Missiles: Politics and Professionalism in the Chinese Army 1945-81*, Westview Studies, Boulder, Colorado.

Joffe, E., 1988, *The Chinese Army after Mao*, Harvard University Press, Cambridge, Mass.

Johnson, A., 1986, *China and Arms Control*, Canadian Centre for Arms Control, Ottawa.

Kasumigaseki Kai, 1986, *Gendai Chugoku jinmei jiten*, Tokyo.

Lamb, M., 1984, *Directory of Officials and Organisations in China 1968-83*, ME Sharpe, New York .

Lewis, J. and Xue Litai, 1988, *China Builds the Bomb*, Stanford University Press, Calif.

Mackay, L., 1986, *China: A Power for Peace?*, Merlin Press, London.

Miall, H., 1987, *Nuclear Weapons: Who's in Charge?*, Macmillan/Oxford Research Group, London.

Nelson, H., 1987, *The Chinese Military System*, Westview, Boulder, Colorado.

Radiopress, 1987, *China Directory*, Radiopress, Tokyo.

Tow, W., 'Science & technology in China's defense', *Problems of Communism*, July-August 1985.

Whitson, W., 1972, *Military and Political Power in China in the 1970s*, Praeger, New York.

~6~

North Atlantic Treaty Organization

The North Atlantic Treaty Organization, NATO, is a military and political alliance constituted around the North Atlantic Treaty. The Treaty was signed in Washington DC on 4 April 1947 by twelve governments: those of Belgium, Canada, Denmark, France, Iceland, Italy, Luxembourg, Netherlands, Norway, Portugal, the UK and the USA. Since then, four more countries have acceded to the Treaty: Greece (1952), Turkey (1952), FRG (1954) and Spain (1982). Although there is a mechanism for withdrawing from the Treaty, no government has ever done so.

NATO is also a vast and diverse complex of political, military, administrative and executive bodies, with its headquarters in Brussels and with institutions and installations all over Europe and beyond. The organization is far more than the sum of its individual members: it has an independent identity as a fully matured inter-governmental organization, embracing hundreds of committees, employing thousands of personnel, with a never-static agenda of tasks to be fulfilled, plans to be designed, jobs to be carried out, goals to be designed (White, 1986, p.204).

Decisionmaking in NATO

NATO is an inter-governmental, not a supranational organization. It links its member states together, but has no compulsory binding power over them. The defence policies of the NATO nations are national responsibilities and, with a few exceptions (see below), all NATO military equipment is nationally produced. Decisions about research, development, testing and production of nuclear weapons systems are made in the NATO member states. The decisions which NATO fora make about deployment of nuclear weapons are the end stages of processes begun in the member countries. In the case of some dual-capable weapons platforms, NATO facilitates co-operation between national governments and firms (see Force Planning).

However, some NATO bodies have close links with national defence sectors and can influence the nuclear decisionmaking process before NATO's political decisonmaking fora become involved in it; though formally subordinate to NATO political bodies, they help shape the issues about which these bodies make decisions. An example of this is the influence which the staff at the Supreme Allied Headquarters (SHAPE) under the Supreme Allied Commander Europe (SACEUR) have on policy proposals made by staff at the US Department of Defence.

The equipment items for which NATO has complete responsibility include a range of Command, Control Communication and Intelligence systems (see NATO Infrastrucure Programme; Command Control Communications and Intelligence).

NATO decisionmaking is a process in which national governments and armed forces feed their policy preferences into the collective planning and consultation process. They do this through the Permament Representatives and the National Delegations (who participate in different NATO bodies in permanent session), National Military Representatives, the Military Committee (all of whom are part of the NATO machinery) and through various fora which stand partly outside the formal structure, such as the High-Level Group. Decisions taken by these bodies are passed up to ministerial meetings for ratification. NATO Supreme Commanders and their staffs and the permanent NATO staffs (the International Staff and the International Military Staff) are also participants in the nuclear weapon planning process). The bodies involved in this consultation process operate on the basis that decisions have to be formally endorsed not merely by majority, but by consensus, so that NATO decisons do not come into conflict with national views. The function of NATO consultations is therefore to negotiate between national representatives at various levels towards a position which attracts consensual support and where the problems of national–NATO conflict do not arise. By the time NATO adopts policies at ministerial level, the search for consensus should already have been completed. The theory and the reality of consensus politics are not the same. First, 'consensus' may actually not be 'positive'; decisions may be based on 'silent consensus', when countries with reservations remain silent during the final phases of deliberation and endorsement. Political pressures to stay silent, or the dangers of losing face with allies, may persuade countries to keep doubts to themselves. If strong dissenting views are maintained right up to the ministerial level these may be referred to in footnotes of NATO communiqués. The dissenting texts themselves are not readily accessible. In recent times, Greece, Spain and Denmark have been notable for their frequent expressions of formal dissent from the consensus position and in 1987–88 part of the West German government expressed public disagreement from the NATO position on removal under the INF treaty of ground-based medium-range missiles (see White, 1986, pp. 212–13).

Second, the principle of consensus obscures the different relative influence in the consultation process of the participating parties. Formally, all member countries participate on an equal basis: 'NATO is composed of sovereign nations which retain their independence in the field of foreign policy... all NATO Allies have equal rights and each has an equal voice at the Council' (*Facts and Figures*, 1981, p. 119) In practice, this principle of equality is necessarily undermined by the different relative economic, political and military status of each country. While Luxembourg's national delegation may have formal equal rights in NATO discussion and debates, its relative unimportance in almost every respect will limit the influence of its contributions to the Alliance consultation process.

The militarily most powerful, and therefore most influential, member of the Alliance is the United States. It is the USA which dominates the NATO nuclear consultation process. The commitment of its nuclear arsenal to the defence of Western Europe is the central military feature of the Alliance. The shape and size and the strategy governing the use of, and the targeting for, NATO's nuclear weapons are determined primarily in the USA (exceptions to this are the British nuclear arsenal, whose size and function are determined not solely by NATO requirements, the French nuclear arsenal and, in matters of strategy, the West German requirement for 'forward defence', i.e., that West German territory not be sacrificed in an East–West conflict). As we shall see below, most of the key players in the nuclear weapons decisionmaking process in NATO are still individuals and institutions either in the USA or which to some extent represent US interests in the Alliance.

THE STRUCTURE OF NATO

NATO is divided into a civil and a military organization, each of which is serviced by its own bureaucracy (see Figure 6.1).

Civil (political-diplomatic) structure

There are three fora which bring together representatives of NATO member states at different levels to discuss political and military matters.

THE NORTH ATLANTIC COUNCIL

Formally, the North Atlantic Council is the

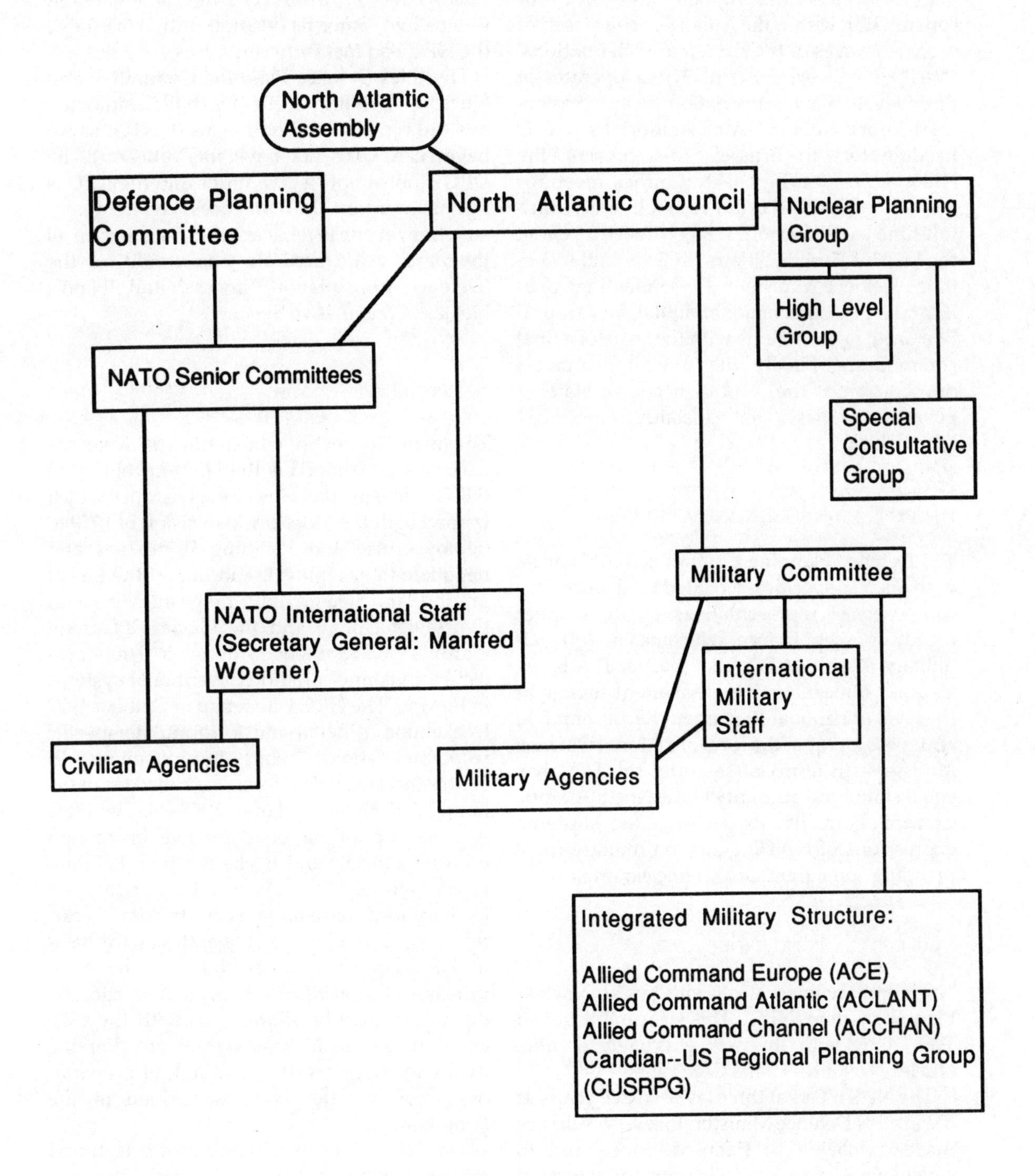

Figure 6.1 *The structure of NATO*

'highest decision making body and forum for consultation within the Alliance...composed of representatives of the sixteen member nations' (*NATO Handbook*, 1982, p. 31). It operates at three levels. First, each nation posts a Permanent Representative (Ambassador) to NATO headquarters in Brussels to represent the national position in weekly Council meetings and to conduct NATO diplomatic business on a full-time basis. Second, it meets twice a year at the level of Foreign Affairs Minister and sometimes Defence Ministers. These meetings usually take place in a national capital, last around two days, and conclude with the issue of a final communiqué. Finally, the Council also meets on occasion at the level of heads of state or government as, for instance, on 2–4 March,1988.

THE DEFENCE PLANNING COMMITTEE

The Defence Planning Committee (DPC) deals with matters specifically related to defence. It is composed of representatives of all member countries except France, which has no (official) military role in NATO. Like the North Atlantic Council, it meets both in permanent session at the level of national Permanent Representative and twice a year at the level of national Defence Ministers. In terms of seniority the DPC has equal status and authority to the North Atlantic Council. Formally, its decisions are supreme expressions of NATO policy on military force planning, procurement and nuclear affairs.

NUCLEAR PLANNING GROUP

Nuclear matters are dealt with by the Nuclear Planning Group (NPG). This was established in 1967 along with the now effectively defunct Nuclear Defence Affairs Committee.

The NPG meets at three levels: twice yearly at the level of Defence Minister, to review Alliance nuclear policies, to frame decisions and to consult on nuclear affairs; in permanent session at the level of Permanent Representative; and at the level of the NPG Staff Group under the auspices of the NATO Nuclear Planning Directorate, which is in the Defence Planning and Policy Division of NATO's International staff (see below). Since its creation until April 1988, the NPG had met forty-one times.

The titles Defence Planning Committee and Nuclear Planning Group are both somewhat misleading. Neither body plans (NATO, as we have seen, does not have this function); the DPC is not simply a committee and the NPG is not just a group. In both cases, constant consultation, at one level or another, is going on all the time. More accurate title would be the 'Defence Consultation Process' and 'Nato's Nuclear Consultative System'.

THE HIGH-LEVEL GROUP

The main forum in which nuclear weapons decisions are shaped is the High-Level Group (HLG). It was the High-Level Group which framed both the 'dual-track' decision of 1979 to deploy cruise and Pershing II missiles and negotiate their removal, and that of the Soviet ground-launched medium-range missiles, with the Soviet Union; and the Nuclear Planning Group's 1983 'Montebello' decision to 'modernize' various nuclear and conventional systems in Europe. The HLG was set up in October 1977 to examine in detail and to formulate specific recommendations about improvements in Nato's theatre nuclear forces, as called for in the Long Term Defence Plan of 1977–78. The HLG is made up of national defence or foreign ministry officials and is chaired by a US Pentagon official, the Assistant Secretary of Defence for International Security Affairs (currently Ronald Lehman). It operates on the basis of US leadership rather than on the Nato principle of consensus — though in practice the distinction may be slight if, as with the 1979 decision, all are in basic agreement. For the dual-track decision, the vast bulk of preparatory work for the HLG was done in the Pentagon.

The HLG does almost the entire technical preparatory work for the Nuclear Planning Group and has been known to meet the day before NPG meetings to hammer out final details of what the NATO ministers should discuss. It is commonly known as the 'nuclear

workhorse' of NATO. In short, the HLG is Nato's key nuclear affairs committee; in nuclear weapons matters the NPG, DPC and the North Atlantic Council function primarily to give legitimacy to its decisions. The HLG's major role in setting the NPG agenda and in determining the policies for ministers to approve has somewhat diminished the role and status of the Nuclear Planning Directorate Staff in Brussels. Where, previously, national defence ministers liaised via Brussels staff they now tend to liaise directly with each other within the HLG, bypassing the Brussels apparatus completely. It is widely acknowledged that the members of the HLG are in a better position anyway than Brussels staff to know what issues need to be discussed, to be aware of priorities, and to know what types of proposals are worth considering. HLG members are high in the decisionmaking apparatus, more in touch with the daily concerns of defence policymaking than are the Brussels personnel, who may be somewhat remote from them.
(See biographies of: Barth; Green; Karstad; Lopes Aleixo. For biography of UK HLG delegate (D. H. Nicholls) see Chapter 3; of US delegate (Ronald Lehman), Chapter 1.)[1]

SPECIAL CONSULTATIVE GROUP

The NATO special Consultative Group (SCG) is often regarded as the sister group to the High-Level Group. It too was set up to deal with the prominent nuclear issues of the late 1970s. It comprises senior foreign ministry officials from national capitals, and its mandate is to review and consult on the nuclear arms control policies of NATO. Unlike the HLG, the SCG has a high public profile and communiqués are usually issued after its meetings. The group is chaired by a senior official in the US State Department.

NATO SENIOR COMMITTEES

Since 1949 NATO Council has established a large number of subordinate committees which service the Council and frame policies which the Council or the DPC can then adopt. These committees, of which there are currently nineteen senior principal ones and hundreds more beneath, cover the whole range of NATO activities but, unlike, say, the Nuclear Planning Group, they do not meet at ministerial rank. They are generally open to all members of the Alliance, and there is broad national representation on most of them. NATO Council and the DPC cannot approve policies unless they have met with approval and endorsement at lower levels. If proposals cannot gain consensual support at the level of the relevant committee, their discussion in open session of the Council or DPC are liable to lead to discord or rancour—and will tend to be avoided. The relevant committees in the nuclear weapon decisionmaking process are the Defence Review Committee, the Conference of National Armaments Directors, the NATO Joint Communications Electronics Committee and the NATO Command, Control and Information System and Automatic Data Processing Committees (see below).

Civil bureaucracy

PERMANENT REPRESENTATIVES AND NATIONAL DELEGATIONS

Permanent Representatives (PRs) are appointed by their governments and are thus civil servants whose task is to act, under instructions from their capitals, as spokespersons for their governments. The committees they sit on include the North Atlantic Council and the Nuclear Planning Group (see above). They are usually career diplomats. The composition of the permanent delegation does not necessarily change with a new government. Its members with tasks relevant to nuclear weapons systems decisions include the National Armament Director's Representative. The size of national delegations varies from three (Luxembourg and Iceland), up through twenty (UK and France) to fifty (USA). Their average size is between twelve and seventeen.

Permanent Representatives (PR)
Address: NATO Headquarters, Evere, Brussels, Belgium
Tel: (Belgium)-2-241-0040 (for extensions, see individual biographies).

(See biographies of: Alexander; Benediktsson; Berg;

Borch; De Hoop Scheffer; de Ojeda; Fulci; Hansen; Keel; Robin; Scott; Thuysbaert; Vaz Pereira; Zacharakis.)[1]

SECRETARY GENERAL AND THE INTERNATIONAL STAFF

Secretary General
Address: NATO headquarters, Evere, Brussels, Belgium
Tel: (Belgium)-2-241-0040 x5596; (Directeur du Cabinet) 2-241-0040 x 5593

The Secretary General, who has always been a European, is the senior member of the International Staff, for the effective functioning of which he is ultimately responsible (See Figure 6.1). The Secretary General (currently Manfred Woerner) is not a politician but a civil servant: however, as a civil servant of an alliance of sovereign nations he represents no government and so is not empowered to undertake diplomatic ventures, say, to the Warsaw Pact. For the same reason, he is not answerable to anybody for NATO decisions: 'Je n'éxiste pas', as the former Secretary General, Lord Carrington, put it succinctly. The Secretary General may arbitrate inter-Alliance disputes; he can conciliate, initiate ideas, and will normally maintain a prominent public profile as an Alliance figurehead. He chairs the North Atlantic Council and the Defence Planning Committees, the Nuclear Planning Group and various other NATO senior committees. He is aided in his work by a Deputy Secretary General (Marcello Guidi).
(*See biographies of: Guidi; Woerner.*)

The International Staff
Address: NATO Headquarters, Evere, Brussels, Belgium
Tel: (Belgium)-2-241-0040

The function of the NATO International Staff (IS), the Brussels-based bureacracy whose personnel is drawn from the member states, is to support the work of the North Atlantic Council, the Defence Planning Committee, the Nuclear Planning Group and the NATO senior committees (see Figure 6.2). Its work is divided among five Divisions: Political; Defence Planning and Policy; Defence Support; Infrastructure, Logistics and Council Operations; and Scientific Affairs. Each Division is led by an Assistant Secretary General, who is also that Division's linkperson with the Secretary General, national delegations, the Military Authorities and the other divisions of the International Staff.

Political Division

The Political Division, which is lead by the Assistant Secretary General for Political Affairs (Henning Wegener), has three directorates; the Political Directorate, which prepares the political discussions of the Council and the Political Committee and supports the political work of the Secretary General; the Economic Directorate which has similar functions with regard to economic questions with a political or defence implications for NATO; and the Information Directorate, which is NATO's public relations department.

The Assistant Secretary General for Political Affairs is Chairman of the Political Committees.
(*See biography of: Wegener.*)

Division of Defence Planning and Policy

The Division, which is headed by the Assistant Secretary General for Defence Planning and Policy (ASGDPP) (Michael Bell), is organized into three Directorates:

(1) Directorate of Force Planning and Policy, which concerns itself primarily with conventional defence matters: together with national delegations it prepares papers and business concerned with the Defence Review (see below), including the analysis of national defence programmes; advises the Defence Planning Committee on politico–military and military–economic matters; prepares studies on NATO defence for the Executive Working Group; and maintains a computerized data base of information on NATO and Warsaw Pact forces;

(2) the Directorate of Nuclear Planning, which services the Nuclear Planning Group (see

Nuclear Planning Group and High-Level Group); and

(3) the Directorate of Civil Emergency Planning, which prepares plans for use of civil resources in 'support of the Alliance defence effort' ; and would co-ordinate the transition of peacetime economies to an emergency footing.

The Assistant Secretary General for Defence Planning and Policy is Chairman of the Defence Review Committee (DRC) Chairman of the 'Alerts' Committee, Chairman of the Ad Hoc Group on Military Assistance to Portugal and Turkey, Deputy Chairman of the Executive of the Executive Working Group (EWG) (which supervises the Long-Term Defence Plan) and Deputy Chairman of the Senior Civil Emergency Planning Committee (SCEPC); he also supervises the work of the Nuclear Planning Group (NPG) Staff Group (see above).
(*See biography of: Bell.*)

Defence Support Division

The Division is organized into four Directorates:

(1) the Directorate of Armaments and Defence Research, which is responsible for promoting NATO standardization in weapons systems concepts and requirements and in national research, development and production programmes;

(2) the Directorate of Command, Control, and Communications, which co-ordinates and encourages co-operation in NATO's civil and military communications: it services the NICSMA, the NJCEC (see: C3I), and the Council Operations and Exercises Committee and the Civil Communications Planning Committee;

(3) the Directorate of Air Defence, which is responsible for co-ordinating work done on the Alliance Air Defence system: it supports the NATO Air Defence Committee; and

(4) the Directorate of Planning and Support, responsible for overall planning of activities in support of armaments cooperation.

The Assistant Secretary General for Defence Support (ASGDS) (Mack F. Mattingly) is the permanent chairman of the Conference of National Armaments Directors (CNAD) and 'advises the Secretary General, the North Atlantic Council, the Defence Planning Committee, the Military Committee, and any other NATO bodies on all matters related to armaments research, development, production and procurement, air defence systems, and command, control and communications systems'.
(*See biography of: Mattingly.*)

Division of Infrastructure. Logistics and Council Operations

This division, led by the Assistant Secretary General for Infrastructure, Logistics and Council Operations, has three directorates which are responsible for advising NATO bodies on matters relating to logistics and infrastructure; preparing proposals relating to infrastructure programmes and overseeing such programmes.

Science Affairs Division

Headed by the Assistant Secretary General for Scientific Affairs and Environmental Affairs, this division advises NATO bodies on scientific, technological and environmental matters and plans and implements the international programme work of the Science Committee and the Committee on the Challenges of Modern Society.

Civil Agencies

There are a number of civilian institutions which provide permanent specialised support and advice on NATO planning. For example, large multi-national agencies exist in the Netherlands to manage the NATO Airborne Early Warning System (AWACS), in Munich to supervise the joint Anglo-German–Italian Tornado aircraft programme, and in Brussels to supervise civil-military communications projects (for some of the military agencies which advise NATO, see Command, Control, Communications and Intelligence (C3I)).

North Atlantic Assembly

This is the inter-parliamentary organization of

NATO member countries. It provides a forum where elected representatives in domestic assemblies can debate NATO matters.

Military structure

THE MILITARY COMMITTEE
Address: NATO Headquarters, Evere, Brussels, Belgium.
Tel: (Belgium)-2-241-0040 (for individual extensions, see below).

Formally, the Military Committee (MC) is the 'highest military authority in the Alliance' (*NATO Handbook*, 1982, p. 33). The two Supreme Commanders (Europe and Atlantic), the Commander-in-Chief Channel and the Canada–US Regional Planning Group are all responsible to it. Fifteen Military Agencies serve under it. It meets on two levels. First, five times a year at the level of Chief of Staff of fourteen of the sixteen member nations: twice at Nuclear Planning Group meetings; twice at Defence Planning Committee meetings, and once on its annual tour of inspection of two NATO countries. Second, in permanent session at NATO HQ in Brussels at the level of the permanent Military Representatives of the Chiefs of Staff. France, which withdrew from the Integrated Military Structure in 1966, is represented in NATO by a military mission; Iceland, which has no armed forces, may be represented on the Committee by a civilian.

The Military Committee is answerable to the North Atlantic Council. Its peacetime task is to recommend to the Council and to the Defence Planning Committee measures considered necessary for the common defence area. Its chairman (Admiral Sir John Fieldhouse) is elected from among the Chiefs of Staff for a two-year period which can be extended. His task is to co-ordinate suggestions put forward by the Chiefs of Staff and introduce them into Alliance politics.

It has been argued that the function of the Military Committee has not been to provide collective military assessment of politically considered military matters (e.g., the Montebello decison) but rather to act as a sounding board for the political authorities as they try to reach acceptable common positions on military and strategic matters; and it does not appear to function as a separate nuclear policy consultation group; it is also widely recognized that the voice of the Supreme Allied Commander Europe (SACEUR) is more authoritative than that of the Chairman of the Military Committee, even though the latter is technically senior in the NATO hierarchy. National Military Representatives are stationed at SHAPE, SACEUR's headquarters, rather than at NATO headquarters in Brussels.

Below are listed the current members of the Military Committee at Chief of Staff and at National Military Representative level. Some biographies are provided in the biographies sections.[1]

Chiefs of Defence Staff

Bisogniero, General R. (Italy) (Tel: x2562); **Correia, Lieutenant-General H. J. S. P.** (Portugal) (x2583); **Craig, Air Vice Marshal D.** (UK) (x3060); **Crowe, Admiral W. J.** (USA), (x5824); **Eide, General V.** (Norway) (x4523); **Gysemberg, Lieutenant-General M. J. L.** (Belgium) (x2500); **Huyser, Lieutenant-General G. L. J.** (Netherlands) (x2576); **Kouris, General N.** (Greece) (x2554); **Ley, Colonel N.** (Luxembourg) (x5648); **Manson, General P. D.** (Canada) (x2507); **Puigcerver Roma, General G.** (Spain) (x2569); **Thiede, S. E., Admiral** (Denmark) (x2520); **Torumtay, General N.** (Turkey) (x2593); **Wellershoff, Admiral D.** (West Germany) (x2546).

National Military Representatives

Bernard, Lieutenant-General V. (Italy) (x2562); **Carter, Admiral P. F.** (USA) (x5824); **Evraire, Lieutenant-General, R. J.** (Canada) (x2507); **Granviken, Lieutenant-General A.** (Norway) (x 4523); **Heck, Lieutenant-Colonel J. P.** (Luxembourg) (x5648); **Herweijer, Lieutenant-General A.** (Netherlands) (x2576); **Juliam, Lieutenant-General P.** (Belgium) (x2500); **Karliaftis, Lieutenant-General E.** (Greece)

(x2554); **Knight, Air Chief Marshal Sir M.** (UK) (x 50260); **Pardon da Santayana, General J. R.** (Spain) (x2569); **Paulino Correia, Lieutenant-General H. J. da S.** (Portugal) (x2583); **Sorenson, Major-General N. H.** (Denmark) (x2520); **Tandecki, Lieutenant-General H. P.** (West Germany) (x2546); **Uger, Vice-Admiral F.** (Turkey) (x2593);
(See biographies of: Evraire; Fieldhouse; Granviken; Herweijer; Paulino Correia. For biography of UK Chief of Defence Staff (Craig), see Chapter 3; of US Chief of Defence Staff (Crowe), Chapter 1.)

Military bureacuracy

THE INTERNATIONAL MILITARY STAFF

This Brussels-based military bureaucracy, numbering currently some 150 officers, 150 other enlisted personnel and 100 civilians, provides staff support to the Military Committee (see Figure 6.1). It is headed by a Director of three-star rank (i.e. a Lieutenant-General or Air Marshall) who must be a different nationality to the Chairman of the Military Committee. The Chairman is assisted by seven flag or general officers, six Assistant Directors and the Secretary of the International Military Staff (IMS). The IMS has six divisions: Intelligence; Plans and Policy; Operations; Management and Logistics; Command, Control and Communications Systems; and Armaments Standardization and Interoperability. These cover the whole range of NATO military activity, including nuclear planning. WIthin these divisions Military Committee policies are both framed and implemented.

Integrated Military Structure

The task of planning military operations is that of the NATO military commanders and their staffs inside the NATO Integrated Military Structure. In 1950–51 the NATO Council endorsed the idea of an Integrated Military Structure for all the armed forces assigned to missions in the NATO area. Until that time, the armed forces of member states had been commanded and organized on a purely national basis; and Nato's military profile amounted to no more than a US military guarantee, via its nuclear superiority and its regular forces in Europe, to its Western European Allies. Following the vital 1950–51 decisions the Alliance structure was transformed. Today, Nato's command structure and war-time planning are fully integrated between member states. Nato's geographical area is divided into four military command regions:

Allied Command Europe (ACE), which covers the land area extending from the North Cape to North Africa and from the Atlantic to the eastern border of Turkey, excluding the United Kingdom and Portugal, the defence of which is not the responsibility of any single major NATO Command.

Allied Command Atlantic (ACLANT), which extends from the North Pole to the Tropic of Cancer and from the coastal waters of North America to those of Europe and Africa, including Portugal, but not including the Channel and the British Isles.

Allied Command Channel (ACCHAN), which extends from the southern North Sea through the English Channel.

Canada US Regional Planning Group (CUSRPG), which covers the North American area.

A supreme commander is appointed to each of the three main commands: Supreme Allied Commander Europe (SACEUR) (General John Galvin); Supreme Allied Commander Atlantic (SACLANT) (Admiral Frank Kelso); Allied Commander in Chief Channel (CINCHAN) (Admiral Sir Julian Oswald) respectively. Within each main command a subordinate hierarchy of regional military commands has been created.

SUPREME ALLIED COMMANDER EUROPE (SACEUR)

Address: Supreme HQ, Allied Powers Europe, Casteau, Belgium
Tel:(Belgium)-32-65-445000 X4113

To date, SACEUR has always been a US General (currently General John Galvin). He has a dual role as SACEUR and as Commander-in-Chief, United States Europe Command (CINCEUR). As CINCEUR, he is in charge of the 300,000-strong US forces in Europe. CINCEUR's area of command includes all of ACE and extends into most of Africa and part of the Middle East. SACEUR's headquarters, the Supreme Headquarters Allied Powers Europe (SHAPE), is near Mons in Belgium. His wartime role is officially described as follows: 'SACEUR is responsible for the defence of Allied countries situated within his Command area (i.e. NATO-Europe) against any attack. In time of war he would command all land, sea and air operations in this area. Internal defence and defence of coastal waters remain the responsibility of the national authorities concerned but the Supreme Commander would have full authority to carry out such operations as he considered necessary for the defence of any part of the area under his command.' (*Facts and Figures*, 1981, p.106.)

In peacetime, SACEUR has a number of roles to play. He must organize, train and equip the North Atlantic forces permanently assigned to his command (e.g. the NATO air defence aircraft and the associated network of ground-based radar and communications installations). Most of Nato's forces are under national command, so in respect of them SACEUR's role is to develop plans and assess forces rather than exert direct control. Formally, he makes 'recommendations to the Military Committee about such matters as the instruction, training, equipping and support of his forces and, indeed, on any military questions which affect his ability to carry out his responsibilities in peace and war' (*Facts and Figures*, 1981, p.106). However, observers agree that SACEUR's voice carries more weight in NATO on military matters than does that of the Chairman of the Military Committee (see Military Committee). He also has the right of direct access to the Chiefs-of-Staff of any of the NATO powers and to Defence Ministers and Heads of Government.

As the single most powerful military figure in the Western alliance, SACEUR also has an important *political* role to play. General Bernard Rogers, who held the post from 1979 to 1987, described himself as 'a soldier assigned to a political mission, to do what I can in the deterrence of war'.

SACEUR's role can involve high-level diplomacy with European allies, reassuring them of the US commitment to their defence. At the same time, as a *European* commander, he represents the interests of the Western European allies in Washington. He also has the influence to effect changes in NATO policy; in addition, there may be conflict between his responsibilities as CINCEUR and those as SACEUR. The interpretation of SACEUR's role differs with each incumbent (and depends on the political climate within and without NATO). General Rogers provided an example of the scope for political action which the post provides. He participated publicly in many of the major military–political debates of the 1980s in the Western Alliance: for example, he expressed reservations about the Strategic Defence Initiative (SDI) and campaigned actively for the European Defence Initiative (EDI); he also argued in favour of keeping Nato's nuclear threshold high through increased spending on conventional forces of 4 per cent per annum by NATO members. Most controversially, however, he voiced public concern about President Reagan's proposals at the Reykjavik Summit (October 1986) to eliminate all ballistic missiles within ten years, and about the elimination of Nato's short-and medium-range land-based missiles in the INF agreement of December 1987; he said the latter have him 'gas pains'.

In the view of some US officials Rogers exceeded the bounds of soldierly propriety in openly voicing disquiet about the Reykjavik proposals. It is widely thought that displeasure within the Reagan administration at his opposition to the INF deal was a major reason for recommending his replacement. West European political and military leaders, by contrast, were big admirers of Rogers': Field Marshal Bramal described him as 'one of the finest Supreme Commanders' and European governments supported his reappointment. The then General Secretary, Lord Carrington, commented, 'Invariably the American in this job ends up being seen in Washington as too pro-European and has to be replaced'.

SACEUR also has influence to effect changes in NATO policy: for example, under Rogers, NATO moved its public posture towards a greater emphasis on conventional defence, e.g., by making use of 'emerging technologies' (ET), especially through deployment of accurate conventional weapons capable of 'deep strike' several hundred miles into the enemy's rear. The (perceived) conflict between CINCEUR and SACEUR responsibilities came to the fore during the US air raids on Libya in April 1986, when much of European opinion accused Bernard Rogers of allowing NATO facilities to be (mis-)used by the US forces.
(See biography of: Galvin.)

SHAPE STAFF

SHAPE'S staff includes three major nuclear weapons sections: Nuclear Operations, Nuclear Policy and Nuclear Concepts. SHAPE staff have had an important influence on nuclear weapon deployment decisons in NATO-Europe: the Long-Term Defence Programme (LTDP) of 1977–79, point ten of which, the call for a review of Nato's theatre nuclear weapons posture, helped shape the 1979 'dual-track' decision, was a product of the work of the Pentagon and the SHAPE staff; and the SHAPE staffs's Nuclear Requirements Study of 1980–85 produced proposals for the battlefield nuclear weapon 'improvements' called for at the 1983 Montebello meeting of the Nuclear Planning Group.

SUPREME ALLIED COMMANDER ATLANTIC (SACLANT)
Address: Norfolk, Virginia, 234511 USA
Tel: (USA)-804- 445 X3200

SACLANT (Admiral Frank Kelso) has always been an American. He is nominated by the US President and then 'appointed' by the Defence Planning Committee. Like SACEUR, he has right of direct access to the Chiefs-of-Staff and to defence ministers and heads of government. Politically, SACLANT carries less weight than SACEUR; his tasks are confined primarily to operational matters.
(See biography of: Kelso.)

COMMANDER-IN-CHIEF CHANNEL
Address: Maritime Headquarters, Northwood, Middlesex
Tel: (UK)-(0)9274-26161 X488

The primary function of the Channel Command is to protect merchant shipping in its area. It is always a British appointment. It has been described as 'a minor command that was carved out of ACLANT and allocated to the British on order to satisfy Churchill's aspirations for British importance in NATO' (Phillips, 1984)
(See Biography of: Oswald.)

NATO'S INFRASTRUCTURE PROGRAMME

NATO's Military Commands are responsible for proposing additions to NATO's Infrastructure programme — the fixed installations which are responsible for the deployment and operation of the armed forces, such as airfields, signals and telecommunication installations (including NATO Air Defence) and military headquarters. These are the only items of NATO's inventory which are not the responsibility of member nations (see Command, Control, Communications and Intelligence (C3I)).

WEAPONS PRODUCTION AND FORCE PLANNING IN NATO

As NATO is not a supranational organization, responsibility for weapons production and equipping forces is a national one. Conventional force planning — which will include decisions about some *dual-capable* weapons platforms and delivery vehicles and other material essential for the effective functioning of NATO's nuclear arsenal — is a constant process of proposals, reviews and agreements. Formally, the outcome of this process is determined by negotiations and compromise between NATO requirements and national force plans and defence industry capabilities; in practice, it is the latter, shaped by domestic political and economic constraints, which have greater weight in determining what NATO is able to deploy. NATO's role in this field is thus mainly one of advice and co-operation. Only in the - albeit vital — areas of communications, airborne early warning and control, and common infrastructure works (see above) is NATO directly involved in the research, development and production of equipment.

A feature of the system whereby NATO's armaments are produced nationally has been the high cost of weaponry (partly because of short production lines) and continuing non-'interoperability' in certain areas (as each industry produces equipment according to national specifications). These two factors — though particularly the continuing steep increase in equipment costs — have underscored the need for collaboration in defence production among NATO countries (though whether such co-operation can actually reduce costs significantly is unclear). There is also a growing *political* requirement, at a time of increasing pressure on the US defence budget, to enlarge Europe's contribution to NATO through either trans-Atlantic or West European collaboration. It seems probable, therefore, that NATO bodies involved in the collaboration process will play a more important role in the coming years.

NATO fora which advise on and co-ordinate production of equipment

CONFERENCE OF NATIONAL ARMAMENTS DIRECTORS

The Conference of National Armaments Directors (CNAD) is one of the principal committees of the North Atlantic Council, to which it reports (see NATO Senior Committees). It is Nato's main civilian body concerned with defence equipment. All members of the Alliance, including France, take part in its work. The CNAD provides a forum for exchanging information on operational concepts, national equipment programmes, technical and logistical matters, as well as stimulating long-term research. The five 'Main Groups' under the CNAD are: the Naval Armaments Group; the Army Armaments Group; the Airforce Armaments Group; the Defence Research Committee; and the Tri-Service Group on Communications and Electronics Equipment (TSGCEE). The NATO Industrial Advisory Group (NIAG) is not officially designated as a Main Group but is considered as having equal status; it provides advice and assistance to the CNAD and the Main Groups.

CNAD has another approximately 250 groups, many of which are exploring co-operative possibilities in conventional force production. The CNAD meets at two levels: at that of National Armament Directors (NADs) and regularly at the level of the National Armaments Directors' Representatives (NADREPS). NADREPS are part of the NATO member country's National Delegation to Brussels and meet to carry out the CNAD's regular work under the Chairmanship of the Assistant Secretary General for Defence Support of the International Staff.

THE JOINT PROCUREMENT PROCESS

Typically, military requirements are first agreed between countries taking part in a specific equipment project. In some cases, NIAG will carry put a pre-feasibility study from the technical point of view. In the next phase, governed by a Memorandum of Understanding (MOU), industries of the participating countries carry out a wider feasibility study. This leads to a NATO operational requirement being agreed by the countries concerned and the preparation of a new MOU for the project definition, development and production phases. NATO then establishes a NATO Steering Committee to complete the work and monitor development of the project. Industrial firms set up their own organization (Klepsh, 1978, p. 28). Current and recent NATO joint procurement projects with dual capability include the Tornado; F-16; the NAVSTAR satelite system; the SP-70 and FH-70 howitzers; and the Multi-Launch Rocket System (MLRS).

COMMAND CONTROL COMMUNICATIONS AND INTELLIGENCE (C3I)

C3I systems provide the means by which to communicate with nuclear weapons units of the armed forces, and to direct their use. These systems are the 'central nervous systems' of the nuclear warfare establishment: without them the weapons are inert bits of technology, their military custodians unable to receive commands about what to do: with them the weapons can fulfil the missions for which they are intended, and they can serve — in theory — the ends which the political leadership desires in war.

In the early years of the Alliance, NATO's strategic communications depended mainly on national post-office circuits. In the late 1960s, 'it became clear that a new approach was required to support the revised strategy of flexible response and the increased emphasis being placed on crisis mangement.' (*Facts and Figures*, 1981, p.179.) The programmes involved here are complex, expensive and technically formidable, but they aree largely away from the political limelight. C3I systems are the hidden; unglamorous side of the nuclear establishment. Few politicians, or members of the public, choose to understand the technologies involved, or their precise purposes. Many of the most important prógrammes are funded over many years, are concealed deep within military requests full of acronyms and weird technical terms; in Europe, if not in the US, C3I has a low budgetary and political profile. But the fact remains that C3I is at least as significant to nuclear deterrence and to nuclear warfare as specific weapons systems (McLean, 1986, p.220). Some observers have argued that improved C3I is an essential element of new 'warfighting' strategies such as Follow on Force Attack (FOFA) and Airland Battle (ALB).

NATO has several agencies devoted to the technical work on C3I problems which help shape the Alliance's requirements for this equipment. These include:

– The NATO Joint Communications-Electronics Committee (NJCEC), established in 1969, which regularly brings together senior national military and civilian representatives of the Alliance member nations to co-ordinate and consult on civil and military Communications-Electronic matters. As a NATO Senior Committee it reports to the North Atlantic Council and the Defence Planning Group.

– The NATO Command, Control and Information System and Automatic Data Processing Committee (NCCDPC), established in 1970, which is in charge of development of a NATO Command, Control and Information System supported by automatic data processing. Its work included recommending policies concerning command, control and information, initiating the overall organization of NATO's Command, Control and Information System, and identifying which aspects of the system require standardization. The system is part of NATO's infrastructure programme. The NCCDPC, one of NATO's senior committees and with a permanent staff drawn from the NATO International Military Staff, reports to the North Atlantic Council, or to the Military Committee on military matters.

– The NATO Integrated Communication System Organization (NICSO), established in 1971. The NATO Integrated Communications System is the Alliance's basic communications system. It is one of the largest NATO infrastructure projects. Completion is set for 1995. NICSO is responsible for planning and implementing the system. It reports to the NJCEC.

There are a further nine agencies which provide the Military Committee with technical advice, the permanent staffs all but one of which are drawn from the NATO International Military Staff. In addition, the International Military Staff has its own Command, Control and Communications division and the staff under SACEUR at SHAPE includes a Nuclear Command and Control Division of high-level military and scientific experts. As in other areas of nuclear activity, these SHAPE personnel probably carry most weight in nuclear decision-making in this field.

BIOGRAPHIES

Alexander, Sir Michael, Permanent Representative of the United Kingdom to NATO
Tel: 2-241-00-40 x50226

Born in 1936, Alexander was educated at, among other places, St Paul's school and the University of Cambridge. He served in the Royal Navy from 1955 to 1957. He entered the diplomatic service in 1962. Early appointments included Moscow (1963–65) and the Office of the Political Adviser, Singapore (1965–68). After returning to the Foreign Office he was, in 1972–74, assistant private secretary to the Secretary of State for Foreign and Commonwealth Affairs. From 1974 to 1977 he was with the UK delegation to the Geneva Conference on Security and Co-operation in Europe (CSCE) and later with the UK mission to Geneva. He served with the Foreign Office between 1978 and 1979 and was then appointed Private Secretary (Overseas Affairs) to the Prime Minister, Margaret Thatcher. From 1982 until his NATO appointment in February 1987, Alexander was ambassador to Austria and, from April 1985, head of the UK delegation to the Mutual and Balanced Force Reduction (MBFR) talks in Vienna.

Alexander is a champion fencer (he won a silver medal as a member of the UK Epée team at the 1960 Olympic games) and lists his recreations as reading history and watching or participating in sport of any kind. He is married and has two sons and one daughter.
(*See: Permanent Representatives and National Delegations.*)

Barth, Dirk J., Head of Dutch Delegation to the NATO High-Level Group

Born in 1943, Barth studied modern history at the University of Utrecht. He entered the Dutch Ministry of Defence in 1971 as civil officer in the Department of General Policy Affairs. In 1984 he became deputy director of this department. From 1984 to 1986 Barth was appointed to the office of Director-General Material, before becoming director of the Department of General Policy Affairs.

Barth is married with two children.
(*See: High-Level Group.*)

Bell, Michael, Assistant Secretary General for Defence Planning and Policy (ASGDPP)
Tel: 2-241-0040 x2050.

Mr Bell was appointed ASGDPP in September 1986. Born in September, 1941, Mr Bell studied philosophy and ancient history at Oxford University and then spent a year as a research associate at the Institute for Strategic Studies in London. He joined the UK Ministry of Defence (UK MoD) in 1965, where his appointments included assistant private secretary to the Secretary of State for Defence (1968–69) and private secretary to the Permanent Under-Secretary. From 1977 to 1979 he was on secondment to HM Treasury. From 1982 to 1984 Bell was Assistant Under-Secretary of State (Resources and Programmes) at the UK MoD, where he was concerned with programme planning and resource allocation, and from 1984 until his appointment to NATO was Director General of Management Audit in the Ministry of Defence, where he was responsible for internal audit, staff inspection and central management services. In this post he led the team charged with the planning and implementation of the major MINIS reorganization at the MoD (see Chapter 3).
(*See: The International Staff.*)

Benediktsson, Einar, Permanent Representative of Iceland to NATO
Tel: 2-241-0040 x5500

Mr Benediktsson was appointed Iceland's Permanent Representative in November 1986. Mr Benediktsson has held the following posts: Administrator, Organization for European Economic Cooperation (OEEC) (1956–60), the forerunner of the Organization for Economic Cooperation and Development (OECD); temporary Deputy Head of the Icelandic delegation to

the OEEC and NATO (1960); Head of Section, Ministry of Economic Affairs and subsequently Ministry of Commerce in Reykjavik (1961–64); appointed Head of Section, Ministry for Foreign Affairs in 1964; Counsellor of Paris embassy and Deputy Head of OECD Delegation (1964–68); Head of Section, Ministry of Foreign Affairs (1968–70); and Permanent Representative to international organizations in Geneva with the rank of Minister Plenipotentiary and subsequently that of Ambassador (1970–76). From 1976 to 1982 he was Iceland's ambassador in Paris, its Permanent Representative to OECD and UNESCO, and was also accredited as ambassador to Spain, Portugal and Cape Verde. From 1982 to 1986 he was Iceland's ambassador in London and was also accredited as ambassador to Ireland, the Netherlands and Nigeria.
(*See: Permanent Representatives and National Delegations.*)

Berg, Eivinn, Permanent Representative of Norway to NATO
Tel: 2-241-0040 x4502

Eivinn Berg was appointed Norway's Permanent Representative in September 1984. He entered the Foreign Office in 1957 and early in his career served with the Consulate General in Chicago and with the Foreign Ministry in Oslo. From 1963 to 1966 he was a member of the Norwegian Delegation to the European Free Trade Association, to the European Headquarters of the UN and to other international organizations in Geneva. From 1966 to 1968 he was Director of Department at EFTA and returned to the Foreign Ministry in Oslo (1968–70).

Between 1970 and 1973 Mr Berg was posted to the Brussels embassy and to the mission to the European Communities. He took a second leave of absence from the Foreign Ministry in 1973, when he became Director of International Affairs at the Head Office of the Norwegian Shipowners' Association in Oslo. He was appointed Deputy Director General at the Ministry of Foreign Affairs (Department of External Economic Affairs) in 1978 and Director General of the same department in 1980. From 1981 to 1984 he was State Secretary to the Foreign Ministry.
(*See: Permanent Representatives and National Delegations.*)

Borch, Otto Rose, Danish Permanent Representative to NATO
Tel: 2-241-0040 x4136

Borch was appointed Denmark's Permanent Representative to NATO in December 1983. The early years of his career were spent at the Ministry of Foreign Affairs, to which he later returned, first as Head of Section (1959–61), then as Head of Division and then (1976–78) as Under-Secretary of State. He has also been posted to Bonn (1954–59), to NATO (then in Paris) from 1964–67, to the United Nations as Permanent Representative (1967–68) – during which period he served as Denmark's Representative on the Security Council – and to Washington as Denmark's ambassador (1974-83).
(*See: Permanent Representatives and National Delegations.*)

De Hoop Scheffer, Jakob G. N., Permanent Representative of The Netherlands to NATO
Tel: 2-241-0040 x4441

Born in 1924, De Hoop Scheffer joined the Dutch Ministry of Foreign Affairs after studying law at the University of Leiden. In 1953 he became an officer in the diplomatic service. He served in Jakarta, Bonn, Berlin, Bagdad, Jerusalem, Athens, Paris and Brussels. In the period 1961–64 he was private secretary to the Minister and State Secretary for Foreign Affairs. In 1972 he became Special Ambassador and in 1973 Roving Ambassador and chief of the European Affairs Department. He assumed his current position in 1981.

De Hoop Scheffer is married to Carola Furnée.
(*See: Permanent Representatives and National Delegations.*)

de Ojeda, Jaime, Permanent Representative of Spain to NATO
Tel: 2-241-004- x3937

Mr de Ojeda was appointed Spain's Permanent Representative in January 1983. Early in his career, Mr de Ojeda was in charge of Politico-Military Affairs in the Directorate-General for North America at the Ministry of Foreign Affairs in Madrid (1960–62). He served in Washington from 1962 to 1969, and then returned to the Directorate-General for North America (1969–73). In 1973 he was appointed to the Peking Embassy, where he held the post of Minister Counsellor until 1976. In 1976–79 he was Consul General in Hong Kong and Macao. He was Deputy Director General for Western Europe at the Ministry of Foreign Affairs in 1981–82. In 1982 he was appointed Deputy Permanent Representative to the North Atlantic Council.
(*See: Permanent Representatives and National Delegations.*)

Evraire, Lieutenant-General Richard J., Military Representative of Canada to the Military Committee of NATO
Tel: 2-241-0040x 2507

Born in 1938 in Ottowa, Evraire joined the Royal Canadian Infantry Corps, Regular Officer Training Plan, in 1954 and attended the Collége Militaire Royal de S. Jean (CMR), Quebec, and Royal Military College, Kingston, Ontario. He obtained a BSc in civil engineering from McGill University in 1960. Upon graduation from university, he was assigned to the 1st Battalion of the R22e Régiment at Camp Valcartier, Quebec, remaining there until August 1962. He then joined the Royal Canadian School of Infantry, Camp Borden, Ontario, as commander, anti-tank wing, weapons division. On completion of a course at the Canadian Army Staff College in 1966, he was promoted major and assumed command of C Company, 2nd Battalion, Royal 22e Régiment, based at Werl, West Germany. In December 1968 he was appointed personal assistant to the Chief of Personnel at Canadian Forces Headquarters, Ottawa. Evraire was promoted to Lieutenant-Colonel in 1970. In 1971 he was assigned to the United Nations Military Observer Group, serving as military observer and staff officer, operations, in India and Pakistan. In July 1971 he was appointed commanding officer, 1st Battalion, Royal 22e Régiment, based at Lahr, West Germany. In 1973 he became senior staff officer, operations, at 4 Canadian Mechanized Brigade Group Headquarters, Lahr. He was promoted colonel in 1975 and in the same year became commandant of CMR. In1978 he was promoted Brigadier-General and assumed command of the Canadian Contingent United Nations Middle East. In 1979 he was appointed Director General, Management Services, at National Defence Headquarters, Ottawa. In 1982 he assumed command of 4 Canadian Mechanized Brigade group, Lahr. In 1984 he was promoted to the rank of Major-General and appointed commandant, National Defence College, Kingston. In 1986 he was appointed Chief, Land Doctrine and Operations at National Defence Headquarters, Ottawa, and in 1988 he was promoted to Lieutnenant-General and assumed the appointment of Candian Military Representative to the NATO Military Committee.
(*See: The Military Committee.*)

Fieldhouse, Admiral Sir John, CGB, Chairman of the Military Committee of NATO

Sir John Fieldhouse assumed the post of chair of the NATO Military Committee in December 1988. He was previously UK Chief of the Defence Staff, a post he took up in November 1984. Before that he had been Chief of the Naval Staff.

Born in Leeds, Yorkshire, in February 1928, the son of SIr Harold Fieldhouse KBE CB, Fieldhouse has been in the Navy since adolescence. He began his naval career in 1941 as a Cadet at the the Royal Naval College, Dartmouth; served as a Midshipman on *HMS Nigeria* and *HMS Norfolk*; then on the East Indies Station; and entered the submarine branch as a sub-lieutenant in 1947. The next six years were spent serving in HM submarines

Thule, *Astute*, *Aeneas* and *Totem*, and in 1956 he took his first command, HM submarine *Acheron*. He subsequently commanded HM submarines *Tiptoe* and *Walrus* and finally the nuclear-powered Fleet Submarine *HMS Dreadnought*. In 1966 he attended the Joint Services Staff College at Latimer before joining the aircraft carrier *HMS Hermes* as the Executive Officer. In December 1967 he was promoted to captain and later moved to Faslane in Scotland to command the newly formed 10th Submarine Squadron of Polaris submarines. He served in frigates and destroyers from 1970 to 1972, first as commanding officer of *HMS Diomede* and Captain Third Frigate Squadron and then as commander of the NATO Standing Naval Force Atlantic in the rank of commodore.

Fieldhouse joined the British Ministry of Defence (MoD) as Deputy Director of Naval Warfare in February 1973 and assumed the Director's post the following November. In December 1974 he became Flag Officer Second Flotilla as a Rear Admiral and then Flag Officer Submarines and Commander Submarines Eastern Atlantic in November 1976. He was appointed Controller of the Navy as a Vice-Admiral in 1979 and took up the appointment as Commander-in-Chief Fleet, Commander-in-Chief of the NATO Eastern Atlantic Area and Allied Commander-in-Chief Channel in May 1981. He was promoted Admiral in July 1981 and was made a CGB in the Queens Birthday Honours List 1982. During the Falklands campaign (Operation Corporate), he was commander of the Task Force, and was subsequently made a GBE.

Admiral Fieldhouse was appointed First Sea Lord and Chief of the Naval Staff, and First and Principal Naval Aide-de-Camp to Her Majesty the Queen on 1 December 1982. He was promoted to Admiral of the Fleet on 2 August 1985 upon relinquishing his appointment as First Sea Lord. Fieldhouse's appointment as UK Chief of the Defence Staff was interpreted by some observers as his reward, from Prime Minister Thatcher, for masterminding the Falklands campaign – the success of which gave Mrs Thatcher the 'Falklands Factor' in the landslide 1983 general election. 'By rights [the job of Chief of Defence Staff] should have gone to the air force. But it was her personal wish that Fieldhouse should get the job', one MoD source said at the time (*Sunday Times*, 1 September 1987).

Fieldhouse was Chief of the Defence Staff in one of the most difficult periods for the British armed services since 1945: with defence spending falling in real terms, there was pressure from MPs for a defence review. The cost of the Trident weapons system made Trident a central factor in the defence debate. Fieldhouse, was a strong supporter of Trident, which he defended as 'an unrepeatable best buy' (Sunday Times, 1 September 1987).
(*See: Military Committee.*)

Fulci, Francesco Paolo, Permanent Representative of Italy to NATO
Tel: 2-241-0040 x4741

Mr Fulci was appointed Italy's Permanent Representative in September 1985. Mr Fulci entered the Foreign Service in 1956. He has served in New York, Moscow, Paris and Tokyo and was ambassador to Canada from 1980 to 1985. At the Italian Ministry of Foreign Affairs he has had posts in the Economic and Political Affairs General Directorates and in the Cabinet of the Foreign Minister as Liaison Officer with Parliament. In 1976–80 he headed the Cabinet of Mr Fanfani, President of the Italian Senate. He holds three degrees in law: Doctor of Law (cum Laude), University of Messina (1955); Master of Comparative Law, Columbia University, New York (1955); and Diploma of the Hague Academy of International Law (1955).
(*See: Permanent Representatives and National Delegations.*)

Galvin, General John R., Supreme Allied Commander Europe (SACEUR)
Tel:(Belgium)-32-65-445000 X4113

General John Galvin succeeded General Bernard Rogers as SACEUR and CINCEUR at the end of June 1987. Fifty-eight in 1987, Galvin received a Bachelor of Science degree from the US Military Academy at West Point in 1954 and a Master of Arts from Columbia University in 1961. Before taking up his current posts, he had served nearly nine years in Europe in a variety of command and staff positions in US Army Europe, the US European Command and SHAPE, including Commanding General VII Corps, US Army Europe, Stuttgart, West Germany (1983–85) (during which he learnt German and insisted that his staff do so as well). From 1969 to 1970 he was Battalion Commander with the 1st US Cavalry in Vietnam. Decorations from that period include a silver star, the 'soldier's medal', awarded only for saving a life at the risk of one's own.

From 1985 to 1987 Galvin was Commander-in-Chief US Southern Command (Quarry, Panama). He took over from General Paul Gorman after the Southern Command had grown in response to a perceived Soviet-inspired threat to America's 'backyard', particularly in Grenada and Nicaragua as well as Cuba. He is a strong supporter of the US-backed Contra rebellion in Nicaragua and appears to subscribe to the Domino Theory view of Soviet foreign policy. He believes, says The TImes, 'that Nicaragua, Cuba and the Warsaw Pact forces are bent on subverting and intimidating their neighbours rather than marching across their borders. Larry Birns, Director of the Council of Hemispheric Affairs, a US liberal advocacy group opposed to the Reagan Administration's Nicaragua policies, claimed that his attitudes had alarmed even Latin American generals and said 'I'm glad to get him out of the region...he's an absolute cold warrior'.

A US State Department official said of him: 'He gets very high marks for diplomacy as well as military ability'. He is 'regarded as a tough soldier with firm views about the global communist threat and a sophisticated diplomat who could help to reassure Western Europe about the US commitment to its defence'.

General Galvin will probably need all his diplomatic skills in his current post. The problems he faces include the disparity of views between the USA and Western Europe on SDI, arms control, US troops in Europe, East-West relations and trade and economic issues. These problems are exacerbated by the growing cost of defence which is causing Nato-Europe countries to review their level of military commitment to the alliance.

Unlike General Rogers, Galvin endorsed the 'double-zero' INF treaty: 'I can carry out my mission of deterrence and defence with the nuclear capability and the conventional capability that is left in Europe after the Treaty is ratified' (*Channel 4 News*, 23 November 1987). He has opposed the replacement of cruise and Pershing II missiles, describing the 'idea' of 'so-called "compensatory adjustments"' as 'dead in the water' (*Channel 4 News*). Like Bernard Rogers, however, he has supported the implementation of the 'modernization' programme agreed to at the 1983 meeting of the NATO Nuclear Planning Group at Montebello, which includes the introduction of a new battlefield Lance nuclear-tipped missile, a new 'stand-off' nuclear missile to be fired from aircraft at long range, and various conventional systems. He said that these 'buttressing measures' would be sufficient to sustain the credibility of NATO strategy (*Financial Times*, 16 September 1987). He is adamant that flexible response and forward defence, based on the triad of strategic nuclear weapons, theatre nuclear arms and conventional forces, remain the best strategy for NATO. Flexible response is not invalidated by the withdrawal of ground-launched medium-range missiles under the INF deal, he believes (*Financial Times*, 11 February 1988).Galvin is also an enthusiastic backer of air mobility for army, which is central to the US Army AirLand Battle doctrine, which calls for striking at the rear echelons of Warsaw Pact if they try to invade Western Europe.

Galvin has also expressed support for Franco-German moves towards closer military co-operation. In describing this co-operation as a 'very good development', he was echoing the views of a group of influential US Senators, including Senate Armed Services Committee chairman Sam Nunn, who said in early February 1988 that the joint Franco-German brigade and Defence Council would strengthen the European pillar of the alliance. (UK Prime Minister Margaret Thatcher, by contrast, has doubts about the compatability of the Franco-German moves with multilateral co-operation within NATO.) (*Financial Times*, 11 February 1988.)

Galvin has a sceptical view of glasnost' and perestroika in the Soviet Union: 'I haven't seen any change in the Soviet Union that makes me feel optimistic...the perestroika - the re-organization – that I see doesn't have anything to do with military power. The real question in the Soviet Union has always been one of military power. The Soviet Union in the last three or four years has out-produced all of the sixteen countries of NATO in military equipment. The Soviet Union still has a doctrine which is offensive doctrine, with a training in which they are trying to train to a level of command and control of large units moving very rapidly in the offensive over long distances. This is an offensive orientation...they make great sacrifices to the quality of life in the Soviet Union, in order to maintain a very high military force and not one iota of that has changed under Mr Gorbachev...particularly in the military.'

(*See: Supreme Allied Commander Europe (SACEUR).*)

Granviken, Lieutenant-General Alf, Norwegian Military Representative to the Military Committee of NATO.

Tel: 2-241-0040 x4523

Born in 1932, Granviken joined the Royal Norwegian Air Force (RNOAF) in 1951. He received his pilot training with the USAF at Craig Air Force Base and followed this with Combat Crew Training at Luke Air Force Base. He completed Air Force Academy in 1956. In the period 1961-63 he served as the commander of the RNOAF Fighter Weapons School. He attended RAF Staff College in 1964. In 1965 he was appointed squadron commander of the First Norwegian F-5 Squadron, before joining the RNOAF Staff College as instructor in 1968. From 1971 to 1974 he commanded the Operations Group at Bodoe Main Air Station. He then joined the RNOAF staff responsible for Operational Requirements/Requirements Fighter Operations. In the same period he was largely occupied with the F-16 project, acting as one the operational advisers to the Multinational Steering Committee. In 1976–77 he attended the National Defence College. He was then appointed station commander at Sola Main Air Station. In 1979 he was commander of the Rugge Main Air Station. In 1981 he was promoted to major-general and appointed Commander Allied Air Forces North Norway. In June 1984 he was appointed Chief of Staff at Headquarters Defence Command. He assumed his present position on 1 January 1988.

Graviken and his wife Annelise have two sons and one daughter. His interests are fishing, swimming and skiing.

(*See: Military Committee*)

Green, Lorne Edmond, Canadian Head of Delegation to High-Level Group

Tel: (Ottowa)-992-3988

Born in 1946, Green received an MA in international relations in 1968 from Dalhousie University, in Halifax, Nova Scotia. In the same year he worked in the Africa and Middle East Division at the UN General Assembly, moving in 1969 to the Canadian International Development Agency. In 1971–73 he was second secretary at the Canadian embassy in Islamabad, Pakistan and from 1973 to 1975 he worked in the Defence Relations Division of the Department of External Affairs. From 1973 to 1979 he was head of the press office at the Canadian High Commission in London, and from 1979 to 1980 deputy director of the United Nations Social and Humanitarian Affairs Division. In 1981 he became departmental assistant in the Office of the Secretary of State for External Affairs and in 1982 he joined the Disarmament Division in the Department of External Affairs. In this post he was responsible for arms control issues relating to the UN Conference on Disarmament and was the Canadian representative to Working Group III at the United Nations Second Special Session on Disarmament. From 1982 to 1986 he was Counsellor to the Canadian delegation to NATO, in which post he was Canadian representative to the Nuclear Planning Group Staff Group and a member of the Canadian delegation to the Special Consultative Group. He became head of the Canadian delegation to the High-Level Group in 1986, when he was

appointed Director, Nuclear and Arms Control Policy in the Department of National Defence. Officially, he is 'responsible for all conventional and nuclear arms control issues in the Department of National Defence with the objective of ensuring that arms control and defence efforts complement each other as elements of Canadian security policy.' He is married with two children and lists his interests as skiing, tennis, canoeing and European period furniture.
(*See: High-Level Group.*)

Guidi, Marcello, Deputy Secretary General, NATO
Tel: 2-241-0040 x5585

Fifty-nine in 1988, Marcello Guidi entered the Italian diplomatic service in 1954. After a period of service at the Ministry of Foreign Affairs in Rome, he was assigned to the Italian Consulate in Toulon in France. Following another tour of duty at the Foreign Ministry, Guidi was then transferrred to the Italian embassy in Washington DC, where he served as First Secretary until 1964. He then served in Libya as Counsellor of Embassy in Tripoli until 1968 and subsequently in The Netherlands at the Italian embassy until 1970. From 1971 to 1975, Guidi was head of the Secretary General's Bureau at the Ministry of Foreign Affairs. In 1976 he was appointed ambassador to Ethiopia and served in Addis Ababa until 1979, whereupon he returned to the Foreign Ministry to take up new duties as Head of Protocol. Before becoming Deputy Secretary General at NATO in January 1986, he was ambassador in Tokyo.
(*See: Secretary General.*)

Hansen, N., West German Permanent Representative to NATO
Tel: 2-241-0040 x5229

Mr Hansen was appointed West Germany's Permanent Representative to NATO in October 1985. Mr Hansen has spent most of his career abroad on Foreign Office duties: From 1954 to 1955 he served with the Trade Mission in Austria, from 1958 to 1961 he was in the embassy in Lisbon, Portugal, from 1961 to 1965 in the embassy in Bern, Switzerland, and from 1965 to 1968 at the Consulate in New York. In the period 1973–79 he was again posted to the United States, first in New York with the Permament Mission to the United Nations and then in Washington, where he was Minister Plenipotentiary at the embassy. From 1981 to 1985 he was West Germany's ambassador to Israel. His domestic appointments at the Foreign Ministry have included: Personal Assistant to the Foreign Minister (1955–58); Head of Section in the Political Division (1968–73); and Head of the Planning Staff (1979–81).
(*See: Permanent Representatives and National Delegations.*)

Herweijer, Lieutenant-General Arie, Dutch Military Representative to the Military Committee of NATO
Tel: 2-241-0040 x2576

Born in 1935, Herweijer completed military academy in 1955. He then served as a lieutenant and captain in the infantry until he was promoted to major and attached to Army HQ. In 1968 he was admitted to the Higher Military School, an institute of higher education for the most promising officers. After he had sucessfully completed his course there in 1970, he served as staff officer for the commander of the territorial forces. He then returned to the Higher Military School after completing a course at the US Army Command and General Staff College. In the period 1978–87 he was for several years the commander of an infantry battalion and, with the rank of colonel, and later brigadier-general, supervised the Department of Operations for the Staff of Defence and Army. In 1987 he was appointed to his current position and promoted to lieutenant-general.

Herweijer is married and has two sons and two daughters.
(*See: Military Committee.*)

Karstad, Arne, Norwegian Representative on the High-Level Group

Born in 1942 in Narvik, Karstad graduated from

the University of Oslo in 1969 with a degree in political science, history and sociology. In the period 1970–71 he was on the foreign desk of the *Arbeiderbladet*, the major Labour Party newspaper and was its Bonn correspondent from 1972 to 1974. He served as civilian secretary of the National Defence Review Commission from 1974 to 1978. From 1978 to 1982 he was deputy chief editor at the Labour Party's News Agency. In 1982 he became foreign editor of Norsk Telegrambyråo, the Norwegian News Agency.

Karstad has attended courses at the National Defence College in 1971, 1977 and 1985. He was secretary of the Council on Arms Control and Disarmament of the Labour Party in 1980–81 and has been a member of the Labour Party's Foreign Policy Council since 1977. He was appointed State Secretary in the Ministry of Defence in May 1986.
(*See: High-Level Group*.)

Keel, Alton, Permanent Representative of the United States of America to NATO
Tel: 2-241-0040 x73230

Alton Keel was appointed the USA's Permanent Representative (PR) in February 1987. Unlike most of his fellow PRs, he is not a career diplomat. In 1970 he received a Doctor of Philosophy in engineering physics from the University of Virginia and began his professional career at the Naval Surface Weapons Center, White Oak Laboratory, Maryland, in 1971. He became manager of the laboratory's Hypervelocity Research Facility in 1972, and Scientific Staff Assistant to the Associate Technical Director in 1976. In 1977, Keel was selected as a Congressional Science Fellow by the American Institute of Aeronautics and Astronautics, and served as a Defense and Technical Advisor to the Tactical Air Power Sub-committee of the Senate Armed Services Committee. In 1978, he became a professional staff member of the same Committee and, two years later, was appointed the senior professional staff member for tactical warfare conventional force preparedness and assessment of the five-year defence plan.

In 1981, Dr Keel was appointed by the President and confirmed by the Congress as the Assistant Secretary of the Air Force for Research, Development and Logistics. In this position, he chaired the Air Force Systems Acquisition Review Council, served as Chairman of the F-16 Multinational Steering Committee for the European Participating Governments, and was the US National Delegate for the Board of Delegates of the NATO Advisory Group for Aerospace Research and Development (AGARD).

In 1982, he became Associate Director for National Security and International Affairs, Office of Management and Budget, in the Executive Office of the President. His responsibilities there included national defence, foreign policy and assistance, international trade policy and international economic and financial policy. From February to August 1986, Dr Keel served as the Executive Director of the Presidential Commission on the Space Shuttle Challenger accident. In September 1986, he agreed to serve the President as his Acting Deputy Assistant for National Security Affairs and, in November of that year, became Acting Assistant for National Security Affairs, a post which he held until 2 January 1987.
(*See: Permanent Representatives and National Delegations*.)

Kelso, Admiral Frank B. II, Supreme Allied Commander, Atlantic (SACLANT)

Kelso was appointed SACLANT by the Defence Planning Committee in June 1988. In addition to this position, Kelso holds the post of Commander-in-Chief, US Atlantic Command. He was previously Commander-in-Chief, US Atlantic Fleet and Deputy Commander-in-Chief, US Atlantic Command.
(*See: Supreme Allied Commander Atlantic (SACLANT)*.)

Lopes Aleixo, Rui, Portugese Representative to the High-Level Group

Born in 1947, Lopes Aleixo graduated in history from the University of Lisbon in 1970. He entered the Ministry of Foreign Affairs in 1975.

He became Secretary of the Portugese embassy in London in 1980, and its First Secretary in 1984. Since September 1987 he has been diplomatic adviser to the Minister of Defence. He was appointed Portugese High-Level Group Representative in March 1988.
(*See: High-Level Group.*)

Mattingly, Hon. Mack F., Assistant Secretary General for Defence Support (ASGDS)

Former US Senator Mack F. Mattingly was appointed ASGDS in 1987. He served in the USAF from 1951 to 1955 and with the IBM Corporation from 1959 to 1979. He was elected to the US Senate in 1980 for the State of Georgia. In the Senate he was a member of the Senate Committee on Appropriations and Chairman of its Sub-committee on Military Constructions, and of the Senate Committee on Banking, Housing and Urban Affairs. He actively supported efforts to increase armaments co-operation and collaborative projects in the Atlantic Alliance. While continuing to support joint conventional defence procurement among NATO countries, Mattingly has argued that, in the light of increasing conventional equipment costs and of potential 'inflexibility' in Alliance strategy caused by the Warsaw Pact's 'predominant conventional strength', this must take place within a NATO Conventional Armaments Planning System. Such a system would prioritize the defence needs of the Alliance, rather than, as at present, allowing these to be determined by the technological and industrial 'push' of the various national defence industries (*NATO Review*, 5/1987).
(*See: International Staff.*)

Oswald, Admiral Sir Julian J. R., Commander-in-Chief Channel
Tel: (UK) – (0)9274-26161 X488

Admiral Sir Julian Oswald was appointed Commander-in-Chief Channel (CINCHAN), Commander-in-Chief Eastern Atlantic Area (a subordinate command within Allied Command Atlantic) and Commander-in-Chief Fleet (a UK national appointment) in May 1987.

Admiral Oswald has spent his whole career in the Navy. He joined the Royal Navy at the age of 13 and has served in seven vessels, including *HMS Vanguard*, the Navy's last battleship, *HMS Verulam*, an anti-submarine frigate and *HMS Newfoundland*, a cruiser. He has also served in the Ministry of Defence, in both the Directorate of Navy Plans and, twice, in the Defence Policy Staff. In September 1982, on promotion to Rear Admiral, he became Assistant Chief of the Defence Staff (Programmes) and, in January 1985, Admiral Oswald became Assistant Chief of Defence Staff (Policy and Nuclear). Other appointments have included Flag Officer Third Flotilla and Commander Anti-Submarine Warfare Striking Force. In January 1986 he was promoted to Vice-Admiral and, in May 1987, Admiral, following his NATO appointments and the UK national appointment.
(*See: Commander-in-Chief Channel.*)

Paulino Correia, Lieutenant-General Helder José da Silva, Portugese Military Representative to the Military Committee
Tel: 2-241-0040 x2583

Born in 1934, Paulino Correia graduated from Military College in Lisbon in 1952, entered the Military Academy (Aeronautical Course) in the same year and was commissioned as a second lieutenant in 1956. In the first two years of his career he was assigned to the flight training squadrons as an instructor pilot and in 1958 moved to Anti-Submarine Warfare (ASW) operations in which he participated as an aircraft commander on several NATO maritime exercises. Promoted to captain in December 1960, he served in Angola as a squadron commander and marked up 2, 200 flight hours in light bombers and COIN aircraft. After this tour of duty in Africa, he was promoted to major and attended the Air Force General Staff course. He was then appointed instructor in the Air Staff College and in the Army Staff College. In May 1968 he attended the Air Command and Staff Course at the Air University at Maxwell Air Force Base (AFB) in the USA. From 1972 to 1974 he was Air Base Commander at Tete AFB in Mozambique. Promoted to colonel in 1974, he was appointed executive assistant to the Chief of Air Staff in the same year. In 1975 he was appointed Chief of the Air Force Reorganization Working Group. In 1977 he was promoted to major-general and director of the Air War Course. In 1981 he was promoted to lieutenant-general and appointed Assistant Chief of General Staff for Operations. He has been in his current post since October 1987.

Paulino Correia has several military decorations and awards, including the Distinguished Service Medal (Gold). He is married and has two children.

(*See: Military Committee.*)

Robin, Gabriel, French Permanent Representative to NATO
Tel: 2-241-0040 x5409

Mr Robin was appointed France's Permanent Representative to NATO in March 1987. He joined the Central Administration of the Foreign Ministry in 1958, having worked as a (*lycée*) school teacher from 1953 to 1956 and studied at the École Nationale d'Administration in Paris from 1956 to 1958. Between 1961 and 1963 he served with the French Permanent Representation to the European Communities in Brussels and then returned to Paris on appointment as a Technical Adviser in the Private Office of Prime Minister Couve de Murville (January–June 1969). After his appointment as Assistant Director for Western Europe in the Foreign Ministry, M. Robin was posted to the London embassy (1972–73) before returning to Paris as Diplomatic Adviser to President Pompidou (December 1973). Head of Cultural and Technical Cooperation at the Foreign Ministry in May 1974, he was Technical Adviser to President Giscard d'Estaing from 1974 to 1979. In the period 1979–81 he was a Political Director at the Foreign Ministry, from which he went to the Center for International Affairs at Harvard University.

(*See: Permanent Representatives and National Delegations.*)

Scott, Gordon, Permanent Representative of Canada to NATO
Tel: 2-241-0040 x4201

Born in 1941, Gordon Scott received his BA at McGill University in 1962 and his PhD at the Massachusetts Institute of Technology in 1966 (subject: RAF War Plans and British Foreign Policy, 1935–40). In the same year he joined the Defence Research Board in Ottawa and in 1967 the defence liaison department in the Department of External Affairs. From 1968 to 1970 he was a member of the Canadian delegation to NATO. In 1970 he was appointed special adviser to the Minister of National Defence; in 1972 Director, Planning Development in the Privy Council Office; in 1973 Director, Machinery of Government; and in 1976 Senior Assistant Secretary Machinery of Government. In 1978 he was appointed Deputy Secretary to the Cabinet (Plans); in 1979 Deputy Under-Secretary, Management and Planning (External Affairs); in 1980 Associate Secretary to the Cabinet; in 1981 Secretary in the Ministry of State for Social Development; and in 1984 Associate Secretary to the Cabinet and Deputy Clerk; in 1985 Deputy Minister, Political Affairs, External Affairs. He was appointed to his current post in 1985.

(*See: Permanent Representatives and National Delegations.*)

Thuysbaert, Prosper, Permanent Representative of Belgium to NATO
Tel: 2-241-0040 x4086

Thuysbaert became Belgium's Permanent Representative on the North Atlantic Council at the end of 1987. Fifty-six in 1987, he entered the Belgian diplomatic service in 1958 and, early in his career, served in Luxembourg, Paris and Tel Aviv. He was appointed adviser to the Minister for Foreign Trade in 1964 and, the following year, became a counsellor with the Belgian delegation to the European Communities. In 1970, he served as adviser to the Foreign Minister, subsequently being appointed deputy head of the Minister's private office. He became deputy head of the Prime Minister's

private office in 1977, returning to the Foreign Ministry in 1980 as head of the private office of the Minister for External Relations (as the Foreign Minister's title had then become) in 1981. In 1983, Thuysbaert was promoted to ambassador and appointed Director General for Political Affairs in the Foreign Ministry. He became Permanent Representative to Geneva organizations in 1985, a post he kept until taking up his position as Permanent Representative to NATO.
(*See: Permanent Representatives and National Delegations.*)

Vaz Pereira, Antonio, Permanent Representative of Portugal to NATO
Tel: 2-2241-0040 x5311

Mr Vaz Pereira was appointed Portugal's Permanent Representative in April 1984. He began his foreign service career in 1952 and was subsequently posted to Rio de Janeiro (1957–61) and London (1961–65). He was Counsellor with the Ministry of Foreign Affairs (1965–67) and then served as Consul-General in Johannesburg. He was appointed Deputy Director General for Political Affairs, at the rank of Minister, at the Ministry of Foreign Affairs in 1970.

From 1974 to 1977 Mr Vaz Pereira was ambassador to Denmark, subsequently (1977–79) serving as ambassador to Mozambique. From 1979 to1984 he was Director General for Political Affairs in Lisbon.
(*See: Permanent Representatives and National Delegations.*)

Wegener, Dr Henning, Assistant Secretary General for Political Affairs (AGSPA)

Dr Wegener was appointed ASGPA in 1986. He entered the West German Foreign Service in 1965. He served in Port-au-Prince, Haiti (1962–63); the Political Division of the Foreign Office in Bonn (1964–65); Jakarta, Indonesia (1965–69) and Paris (1969–71). He returned to the Foreign Office in 1971 (Multilateral Affairs). Between 1974 and 1977 he was with the Permanent Mission to the United Nations and other international organizations in Geneva; from there he went back to Bonn, where he served, on secondment from the Foreign Office, as adviser on foreign and security policy matters to the right-wing Christian Democratic Union (CDU), and subsequently as director of the CDU International Office. From 1981 until his NATO appointment, he was Head of the Federal German Delegation to the Conference on Disarmament at Geneva; to the First Committee of the UN General Assembly; the UN Disarmament Commission; the Review Conference of the Nuclear Non-Proliferation Treaty; and to other disarmament-related conferences. He was chairman of the UN Disarmament Commission for 1986. From 1985 to 1986 he was appointed by the UN Secretary General to serve as a member of an Expert Group to produce a UN Study on the Implications of Deterrence.
(*See: International Staff.*)

Woerner, Manfred (Dr Jur), Secretary General of NATO

Manfred Woerner was appointed NATO Secretary General in December 1987 and took up his post in June 1988. He is the first West German to hold the post. Woerner was born in September 1934. He studied at the universities of Heidelberg, Paris and Munich, was a (CDU) Christian Democratic Union State Parliamentary Advisor in Baden-Wuerttemberg from 1962 to 1964, and was elected to the West German Bundestag (Parliament) in 1965. He was West German Minister of Defence from 1982 to 1988. He is a reserve pilot in the Luftwaffe.

In contrast to normal practice, whereby the Secretary General is chosen after private talks between heads of government, Mr Woerner was, for a time, competing for the post against Mr Klare Willoch, the former Norwegian Prime Minister. Mr Willoch presented himself as a candidate in August 1987, but withdrew at the end of November in recognition of the growing support for the West German. Mr Woerner was understood to have the particular support of the USA and the UK. But he is also a controversial figure. He was a critic of the INF negotiations on the grounds that the removal of

ground-based medium-range missiles might harm NATO's strategy of flexible response. He also opposed (unsuccesfully) the removal – as part of the INF deal – of West Germany's Pershing 1A missiles carrying US nuclear warheads.
(See: Secretary General.)

Zacharakis, Christos, Permanent Representative of Greece to NATO

Mr Zacharakis was appointed Greece's Permanent Representative in February 1986. From 1965 to 1966 he served with the Consulate General in New York and from 1966 to 1969 with the Copenhagen embassy. He then went to the Consulate General in Istanbul, Turkey (1969–71), thereafter serving with the Greek Delegation at NATO Headquarters (1971–74). From 1974 to 1975 he was Consul-General in Alexandria, Egypt, and from 1975 to 1978 Counsellor with the embassy in Nicosia, Cyprus, subsequently returning to the Ministry of Foreign Affairs in Athens. He was appointed ambassador to Nicosia in 1979 and, in 1981, promoted to Minister Plenipotentiary.
(See: Permanent Representatives and National Delegations.)

NOTES

1. Biographies of NATO personnel are included where available. NATO headquarters and national defence ministries did not provide biographical material for some personnel (Chiefs of Defence Staff, some Permanent Representatives, National Military Representatives and High-Level Group members) and for these, unfortunately, only names are listed.

REFERENCES

Facts and Figures, 1981, NATO Information Service, Brussels.

NATO Handbook,1986, NATO Information Service, Brussels.

McLean, S., 1986, *How Nuclear Weapons Decisions Are Made*, Macmillan/Oxford Research Group, London.

Phillips, S., 1984, 'Who's Who and What's What in Nato', in *Journal of European Nuclear Disarmament (END Journal)*, No. 9, April–May 1984.

White, A., 1986, 'North Atlantic Treaty Organisation', in *How Nuclear Weapons Decisions Are Made*, Scilla McLean (ed.), Macmillan/Oxford Research Group, London.

~7~

Warsaw Treaty Organization

Two main problems confront the researcher trying to shed light on the nature of nuclear decisionmaking within the Warsaw Treaty Organization (WTO). The first of these is the secretive nature of the organization on many matters, not simply those of nuclear weapons development and deployment policy. As one Western commentator has put it: 'with an alliance such as the Warsaw Pact, whose workings proceed behind a veil of secrecy, the greatest caution, even humility, is necessary' (Brown, 1984).

The second problem concerns the comparative unimportance of nuclear weapons decisionmaking for intra-alliance politics in the WTO. While nuclear weapons and attempts to control or cut their numbers inevitably play a role in WTO politics in the sense that so much of East–West diplomacy is focused upon these tasks, there are important differences to be seen if we compare the WTO with NATO. By contrast with NATO, the WTO has only one nuclear power, with no middle-rank powers such as France and Britain, and apparently (though opinions differ) little evidence of any arrangements analogous to those within NATO whereby European armed forces have indirect access to US-owned nuclear warheads for their own weapons systems.

The asymmetries between the two alliances are not complete, and later sections of this chapter will assess the evidence for a degree of partial Eastern European integration innto the Soviet nuclear weapons infrastructure ('Eastern Europe' here refers to the Soviet Union's six WTO allies — Bulgaria, Czechoslovakia, German Democratic Republic (GDR), Hungary, Poland, and Romania). A more general political point can, however, be made to the effect that nuclear weapons do not play the kind of role within the WTO which makes concepts such as 'extended deterrence' and 'flexible response' so crucial to an understanding of NATO. The asymmetry is partly a geographical one, in the sense that the proximity of the Soviet Union to Eastern Europe has meant that Soviet domination of the region has been ensured primarily by conventional military means, by contrast with the hegemony-enhancing symbolism of US nuclear 'coupling' within NATO. There is also an asymmetry in the fact that the Soviet Union plays a more dominant role within the WTO than does the USA within NATO in terms of military forces and expenditure, as well as nuclear weapons.

One cannot, therefore, give an account of the WTO as a mirror-image of NATO institutions, and very little can be said about major decisions on the design, development and manufacture of nuclear weapons in the Eastern bloc, since these functions are prerogatives of the Soviet Union. Nevertheless, the structures of the WTO itself do have some involvement in questions of nuclear deployments, foreign policy aspects of deployments, and to some extent of financial considerations. This chapter gives a brief history of the WTO since its formation in 1955; outlines of the WTO's political and military institutions and their relationship to nuclear weapons infrastructure; some concluding comments on the relationship between these structures and recent East–West diplomacy; and some biographical information on leading figures in WTO structures (for fuller examination of all these aspects, see Holden, 1988).

HISTORY OF THE WTO

The Warsaw Treaty was signed in Warsaw on 14 May 1955, by the representatives of Albania, Bulgaria, Hungary, the German Democratic Republic (GDR), Poland, Romania, the Soviet Union, and Czechoslovakia. The immediate reason for the formation of the WTO at that time was the formal accession to NATO, a few days earlier, of the Federal Republic of Germany (FRG). Before 1955, the Eastern European states were linked to each other by bilateral treaties and through the mulitlateral economic organization COMECON (or CMEA, Council for Mutual Economic Assistance).

The text of the treaty emphasizes the parties' view of the threat to European security caused by West Germany's remilitarization and reintegration into the Western bloc. It commits its signatories to mutual assistance 'in the event of an armed attack in Europe in one or several states that are signatories of the treaty', to the establishment of a joint command for their armed forces, and to working towards the prohibition of nuclear weapons and the establishment of a collective security system in Europe (see treaty text in Mal'tsev, 1986, p. 9; English text in Mackintosh, 1969).

In addition to the perceived threat from West Germany there were a number of other factors at work which prompted the formation of the alliance in 1955. At that time, the post-Stalin manoeuverings for power within the Soviet leadership were unresolved, and different groups saw the alliance as important for different reasons: to some it was a vehicle for strengthening the socialist bloc, to others, more of a bargaining chip for managing relations with the West as tentative moves were made towards improving East–West relations. An alliance was also seen as a way of managing Soviet control of Eastern Europe at a time when Stalinist methods of direct control were having to be eased, and of managing military co-operation more efficiently than formerly. In addition, the withdrawal of Soviet forces from Austria in 1955, under the terms of the Austrian State Treaty, created problems for the legitimization of the Soviet military presence in Hungary and Romania. Soviet writers also cite Western alliances (ANZUS: Australia New Zealand United States; SEATO: South East Asia Treaty Organization) as contributory factors – a good indication of the WTO's function in a global political role as well as a regional military one.

Since 1955 there have been a succession of political crises in Eastern Europe which have served to illustrate the fragility of Soviet–Eastern European relations and the degree to which the WTO has functioned as a mechanism for internal political control. Paradoxically, however, the institutions of the WTO itself have rarely been used to resolve these crises. In 1956, the Soviet Union re-established its authority in Hungary through the use of its own troops. Although Imre Nagy announced Hungary's withdrawal from the WTO at the height of the crisis, the Soviet Union's subsequent citing of the Warsaw Treaty as a justification for its intervention was unconvincing, since the Treaty expressly forbids the use of force and interference in its signatories' internal affairs. There seem to have been bilateral consultations between the Soviet leadership and other WTO leaders, but no co-ordination of policy through WTO channels. Events in Poland at the same time were resolved without Soviet intervention.

Between 1955 and the Czechoslovakian crisis of 1968, developments took place in the military organization of the WTO which had implications for nuclear policy within the alliance. Both Soviet and Eastern European forces were equipped with nuclear-capable short-range weapons systems (missiles and aircraft), and trained in multilateral exercises for combat in nuclear conditions. Although evidence on this period is rather sparse, it does not appear that the Eastern Europeans were themselves equipped with nuclear warheads or trained to use them. However, there is evidence that both Czechoslovakia and Romania felt that decisions taken at this time on military planning were made with insufficient consultation by the Soviet Union of its allies. It is hard to find evidence of whether or how these issues were discussed within WTO institutions, and most commentators treat it as a question of Soviet strategy. At any rate, unhappiness with aspects of WTO policy certainly emerged in Czechoslovakia and Romania, and there is evidence that Czechoslovakia resisted pressure in the early 1960s for Soviet troops and nuclear-capable missiles to be stationed in Czechoslovakia (see Wolfe, 1970; Rice, 1984).

In 1968 the force which occupied Czechoslovakia was multinational, but overwhelmingly composed of Soviet troops. Before the intervention itself, pressure was put on the Czechoslovakian leadership by a series of meetings between WTO leaders, but none of these were technically meetings of WTO bodies. Any WTO meeting would have had to involve Romania, and Romania would not have endorsed any preparations for intervention. The intervention led Albania formally to withdraw from the WTO, although she had been estranged from the Soviet Union since 1961.

Romanian unhappiness with the alliance had been growing since the early 1960s, and grew out of a mixture of economic grievances and discontent over Soviet domination of the military alliance. Romania refuses to allow foreign troops on its soil, does not participate in multilateral exercises, makes regular calls for mutual bloc dissolution, and has resisted pressure for increased defence spending. Although these Romanian gestures of independence may be of limited practical significance because of Romania's lack of strategic importance to the WTO, it does seem likely that the reorganization of WTO institutions which took place after 1968 was partly prompted by Soviet concern that insufficient consultation within the alliance could lead to renewed Eastern European unhappiness and repetitions of the Czechoslovakian crisis.

Several additional bodies were created after 1968 which gave Eastern European leaderships more opportunity to discuss military and foreign policy, although this did not amount to giving them a veto over Soviet policy. The reforms did not, however, prevent occasional public differences of opinion, such as occurred over defence spending at the 1978 meeting of the WTO's Political Consultative Committee (PCC – see below). The imposition of martial law in Poland in December 1981 illustrated yet again the seriousness of internal political problems within the WTO, although it could be argued that in some respects the imposition of a 'solution' by domestic military force was preferable to Soviet intervention.

During the 1983–87 period, the question of nuclear deployments on Eastern European territory acquired a symbolic political importance it had previously lacked. In a step described as a countermeasure to NATO's deployment of cruise and Pershing II missiles in Western Europe, 'operational-tactical' missiles (Shorter Range Intermediate Nuclear Forces (SRINF), in NATO's categorization) were deployed in the GDR and Czechoslovakia (Other simultaneous countermeasures were the stepping-up of Soviet submarine deployments off US coasts and the lifting of a moratorium on further SS-20 deployments in the Soviet Union). There was evidence that both the GDR and Czechoslovakian leaderships were uncomfortable about these deployments, which were based on bilateral agreements between the Soviet Union and the two countries, and collective WTO bodies themselves seemed reluctant to express much enthusiasm for the Soviet measures (for a more detailed account, see the author's chapter in Mclean, 1986).

These Eastern European deployments were frozen in April 1985, just before the Warsaw Treaty was renewed for twenty years, with an option to renew it for a further ten years after that, to the year 2015 (statement in Mal'tsev, 1986, p. 378; and *Soviet News*, 1 May 1985). With the signature of the INF Treaty in Washington in December 1987, this episode in the WTO's history seems to be closed, though short-range nuclear weapons still remained on Eastern European territory (see below).

Political and military institutions

Figure 7.1 shows the principal WTO institutions divided into 'political' and 'military' categories. The categories may be misleading if interpreted too literally, and it should be not be assumed that there is a 'military' or 'political'

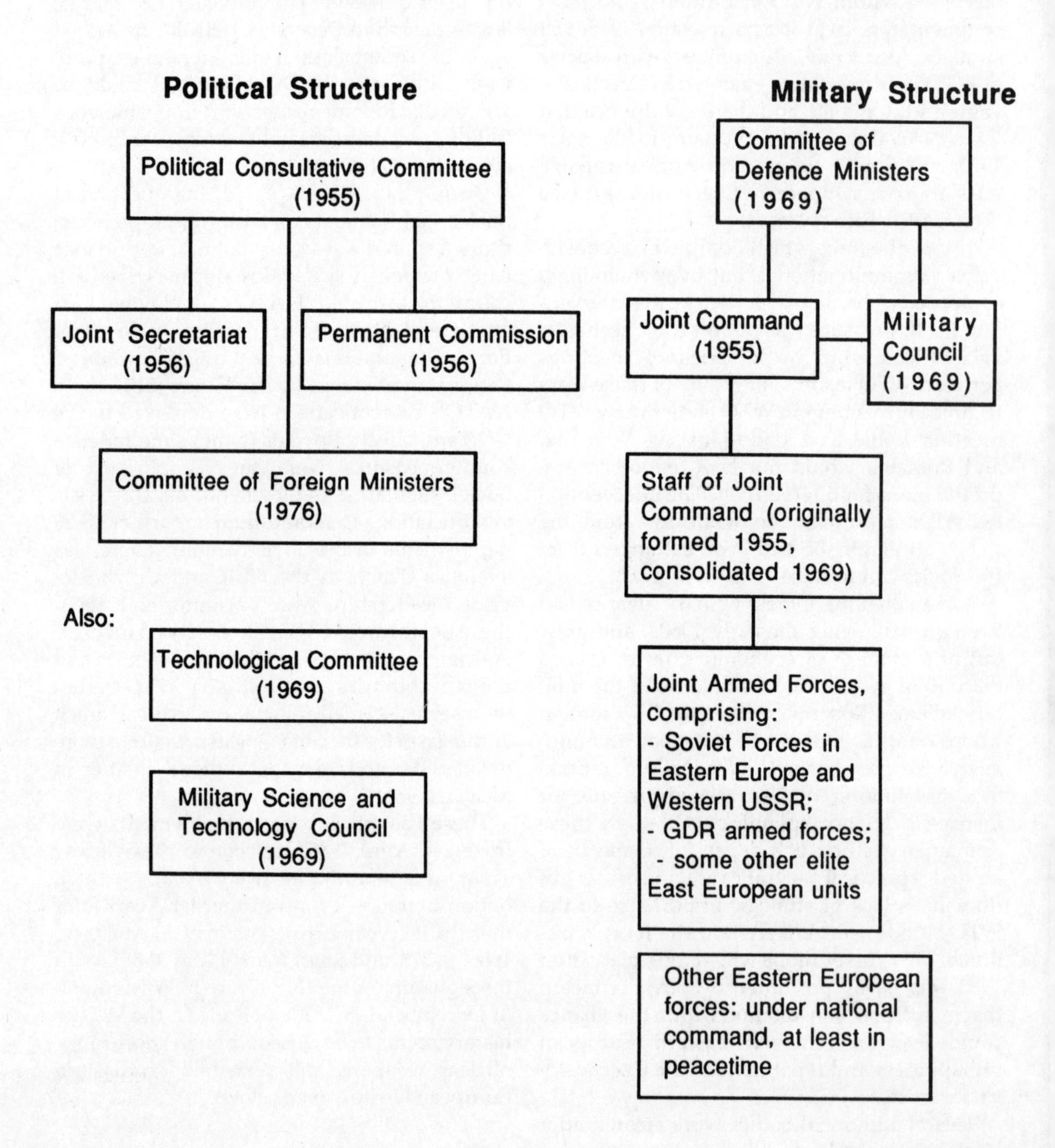

Figure 7.1 *Principal WTO institutions (figure reproduced from Chapter 3 of Holden, G., 1988)*

essence to any institution, since there is no clear dividing-line between the functions.

Political Structure

The WTO's chief body, the Political Consultative Committee (PCC), was set up by the Warsaw Treaty itself, with powers to create additional bodies as required. The PCC's functions are as follows, according to the *Sovetskaya Voennaya Entsiklopediya* (Soviet Military Encyclopaedia: 1986, Vol. 2, p. 21): 'At sessions of the PCC the most important foreign policy questions are discussed, decisions are worked out collectively on international questions which affect the interests of all participants in the (Warsaw) Treaty, and the most important problems connected with the strengthening of defence capability and carrying out of the obligation of the states parties to the Warsaw Treaty to collective defence are examined.'

The PCC thus has a wide politico-military remit. Its membership has been identified by a Soviet source as: General or First Secretaries of the respective parties, the heads of state or their deputies, ministers of defence and foreign ministers, plus the Commander-in-Chief (C.-in-C.) of the WTO forces and the General Secretary of the PCC (Savinov, 1986, p. 23). The PCC's power to create additional bodies was used to set up the Permanent Commission (PC) and Joint Secretariat (JS) in 1956, and later, in 1976, the Committee of Foreign Ministers (CFM). The Permanent Commission apparently provides recommendations on foreign policy to the PCC, and the Secretariat is thought to prepare the PCC's agendas. The PCC remains the senior body, and it is presumably here that the C.-in-C. reports on the work of the military bodies. The PCC is also responsible for appointing the organization's Commander-in-Chief, Chief of Staff, and General Secretary. This latter office has not traditionally been as publicly visible as NATO's Secretary General, but has been more noticeable in recent years when there have been proposals for direct talks between the incumbents of the two posts. It appears that the WTO post is held by a deputy foreign minister of the country responsible for hosting the next regular PCC meeting.

The PCC's role in co-ordinating diplomatic activity among the WTO member-states has not always been evident when crises have arisen, as the resort to bilateral mechanisms in 1956 and 1968, and again in 1983, indicated. A cluster of meetings of the CFM and Committee of Defence Ministers (CDM — see below) in late 1981 seems to have been associated with preparing the ground for the imposition of martial law in Poland, but the statements of these committees are more frequently used to put common foreign policy positions before a world diplomatic audience. In May 1987 a commission was set up to deal with disarmament questions, and this body may become more important in European disarmament diplomacy in the aftermath of the signature of the INF Treaty.

There has been a general trend within the WTO towards increased consultation in the additional bodies which have been formed, which suggests that the Soviet Union has increasingly had to bargain with its allies to achieve its goals in intra-bloc and external policy. The creation of additional bodies in the military sphere suggests that something similar has happened there as well, but it does not follow that there has been a relaxation of ultimate Soviet control over the WTO's military structure: if anything, the reverse seems to be the case.

Military Structure

The Warsaw Treaty itself set up the Joint Command (JC) and Joint Armed Forces, and also a Staff located in Moscow to work with the Commander-in-Chief. Both the Command and Staff are multinational, but Soviet officers serve as representatives to defence ministries in Eastern Europe, and the WTO's C.-in-C. and Chief of Staff positions have always been held by Soviet officers. The current incumbents are: C.-in-C. Marshall V. G. Kulikov (since 1977; predecessors: I.S. Konev, 1955–60; A. A. Grechko, 1960–67; I. I. Yakubovskii, 1967–76); Chief of Staff General A. I. Gribkov (since 1976; predecessors: A. I. Antonov, 1955–62; P. I. Batov, 1962–65; M. I. Kazakov, 1965–68; S. M. Shtemenko, 1968–76; see Volkogonov, 1985, pp. 28–9). The WTO C.-in-C. is one of three Soviet First Deputy Ministers of Defence.

There was a major reorganization in March 1969, when a PCC meeting in Budapest set up four further bodies: the Committee of Defence Ministers (CDM), the Military Council (MC), and two technical bodies, the Technological Committee (TC) and the Military Science and Technology Council (MSTC). This reorganization seems to have been partly a response to the grievances expressed by Romania and Czechoslovakia about insufficient consultation in WTO fora, and in particular to the protocol problem that Eastern European defence ministers sat on the PCC as subordinates (deputy C.-in-C.s) to a Soviet C.-in-C. who was only a Deputy Soviet Defence Minister. Thus the reorganization may not have had operational military significance, but it did improve the Eastern Europeans' access to fora in which they could discuss policy.

The CDM is composed of the seven defence ministers plus the C.-in-C. and Chief of Staff, while the Military Council and Joint Command appear to have closely similar memberships (C.-in-C., Chief of Staff, deputy C.-in-C.s who are usually deputy defence ministers). The MC probably also includes additional officers with particular responsibilities such as air defence. The division of labour between the various military bodies is that the CDM is the senior body which, with advice from the MC, supervises the work of the Command and its Staff. The Staff's main work is concerned with the preparedness of the WTO's troops and fleets, in particular with the preparation of manoeuvres, while the MC is principally concerned with questions of arms, equipment, and combat readiness, and the Command itself is largely occupied with the integration of units into the Joint Armed Forces (see below).

The two military-technical institutions also set up in 1969 are rarely publicized, but some unexpected light has recently been shed on them by Polish sources. According to a Polish publication cited by Michael Checinski (Checinksi, 1987), the Military Science and Technology Council is an advisory body charged with analysing developments in enemy military technology and coordinating WTO research, while the Technological Committee acts as the Council's executive organ. Both bodies are subordinate to the Military Council, and the head of the MSTC sits on the Military Council. The tasks carried out via this structure seem to include co-ordination of WTO arms production and supply, with a degree of co-ordination with the COMECON Military-Industrial Commission (set up in 1956) and with the national military-industrial planning mechanisms.

It has been suggested that the possibility of increased economic leeway for Eastern European states within COMECON may even affect the sphere of military industry, but this does not affect the basic feature that these WTO technical institutions are, as far as is known, limited to conventional weaponry, with no likelihood that nuclear policy would ever come into their purview. Thus, while increased pressure for collaboration in military technology may affect both NATO and the WTO in future, this seems unlikely in the WTO's case to spill over beyond traditional conventional concerns. Most of the Western studies of Soviet nuclear weapons acquisition have concentrated on missiles of intermediate-range and above, but none of the limited amount of work done on tactical-range weapons has found evidence of the involvement of anything other than the central Soviet institutions in making decisions on systems to be deployed on Eastern European territory (a relevant recent study is Evangelista, 1986). It therefore seems most useful to pay some attention to the mechanisms for deployment of nuclear weapons and for military command within the WTO.

NUCLEAR WEAPONS AND MILITARY COMMAND

The involvement of Eastern Europe in the Soviet nuclear infrastructure can be dated from the late 1950s and early 1960s, a time when a 'nuclearization' of Soviet military thinking was under way and Khrushchev was adopting the view that nuclear weaponry would be decisive in any future war. In a move which paralleled the proliferation of tactical and shorter-range nuclear-capable systems within NATO, systems such as the Su--7 aircraft and FROG and SCUD missiles were introduced into both the Soviet and the Eastern European forces. It has always been a matter of some dispute whether nuclear warheads for Soviet systems were actually stored on Eastern European territory, although there has been fairly widespread acceptance that none of the Eastern European armies themselves had access to warheads for their own systems. Bill Arkin (Arkin, 1982) has suggested that the GDR was involved in nuclear preparations of some sort, and has provided (with Richard Fieldhouse) the most detailed breakdown of Soviet and domestic facilities in Czechoslovakia, the GDR, Hungary and Poland which have been involved in any way with support for nuclear-capable systems (Arkin and Fieldhouse, 1985, Appendix B).

There is no evidence available of discussions taking place in WTO fora either of the nuclearization of strategy, or of the specific deployments of particular systems, though, as already mentioned, it is thought that particular pressure was put on Czechoslovakia before 1968, when there were no Soviet troops in the country. From the late 1960s onwards the first generation of short-range nuclear-capable systems was replaced by a later generation (including the MiG-27, Su-17/20, Su-24 aircraft, and nuclear-capable artillery of several types), though the earlier systems remained in service with Eastern European forces. By 1983 (and before the 'counterdeployments' to cruise and Pershing) a number of these systems were being forward-deployed into Eastern Europe (Arkin and Chappell, 1983).

Some of these weapons re-emerged into the limelight in mid-1987 at a time of concentrated East–West diplomacy over systems of below-INF range, but even though some of the standard Western sources held the position that there was a technical possibility of Soviet warheads being available for the Eastern European systems, this did not really become a live issue in the INF negotiations themselves (See *The Military Balance*, 1987–88, pp. 207–9). The Soviet Union itself has recently become more explicit about the nuclear capability of some of its tactical systems in Eastern Europe, notably artillery (*Disarmament and Security Yearbook*, Vol. 1, 1986, p. 192).

Even though the Eastern European armies have probably not had access to nuclear weapons, they have been trained for combat in a war in which the use of nuclear weapons owned by the Soviet Union could in theory be initiated from Eastern European territory, and to that extent Eastern Europe has therefore been in a position analogous to Western Europe's in relation to the USA. Multilateral exercises within the WTO began in the early 1960s and were supervised by the Joint Command, but once again it is not known at what level, if any, their strategic basis was discussed in WTO fora. The WTO command structure itself may not in fact have any wartime responsibilities, and may be limited to the peacetime tasks of training, exercises, etc. This is not a point on which much evidence can be adduced, but in 1968 the multinational WTO force which occupied Czechoslovakia was commanded not by the WTO C.-in-C., but by General Pavlovskii, the Commander of Soviet Ground Forces.

In normal peacetime circumstances the Joint Armed Forces of the WTO are thought to comprise the Soviet forces in Eastern Europe and some at least of those in the western Soviet military districts, plus the GDR's entire armed forces and other elite units such as the Polish Navy (integrated into a United Baltic Navy) and Polish airborne division. The WTO's air defence system has also been integrated into a single system directly from Moscow, but other Eastern European units are said to remain under national command through the agency of the deputy defence ministers who sit on the Joint Command. Whether this would remain the case in the event of war is questionable, and a number of Western commentators have considered that, in wartime, command authority would pass directly into the hands of the Soviet High Command.

Romanian forces remain unintegrated into this system, and under the national doctrine of 'homeland defence by the entire people' are committed only to the defence of national territory, under Romanian command at all times (see Volgyes, 1982, Ch. 4). However, it has recently been argued that trends within WTO command-and-control are likely to lead towards a much closer integration of all Eastern European forces into WTO and/or Soviet commands by the mid-1990s, so that the WTO will move closer towards being the kind of supranational organization it has always claimed not to be (Smith and Meier, 1987; Petersen, 1987). The late Soviet Defence Minister, Marshal Ustinov, made some comments in 1982 (see *Pravda*, 12 July 1982) about the implications of the Soviet No First Use declaration for command-and-control of nuclear weapons, but any changes which are in progress affecting Eastern European forces are less likely to be a direct result of changes in nuclear planning, and more a consequence of the broader reorganization of Soviet and WTO forces into Theatres of Military Operations or TVDs, which has now been in progress for something like ten years (on the TVD structure, see Erickson, 1985; Fitzgerald, 1986).

This aspect of recent developments in the WTO may have some interesting implications for the command responsibilities borne by particular individulals. At present the three most important figures are Marshal V. G. Kulikov (C.-in-C. of the WTO); General A. I. Gribkov (WTO Chief of Staff); and Marshal N. V. Ogarkov (former Soviet Chief of General Staff, now believed to be in command of the Western TVD covering Central Europe) (for biographies of Kulikov and Gribkov, see end of chapter; for biography of Ogarkov, see chapter 2.)

The careers of Kulikov and Ogarkov, in particular, have run in fairly close parallel, but some aspects of their careers shed some interesting light on the role of factionalism in the Soviet armed forces (see Cockburn, 1983, Ch. 4). Kulikov was apparently a protégé during the 1960s–70s of Andrei Grechko, then Minister of Defence. His appointment as Chief of General Staff in 1971 owed much to Grechko's patronage, but on Grechko's death Kulikov did not, as expected, succeed him as Minister of Defence. This job went to Ustinov, and in January 1977 Kulikov was appointed C.-in-C. of the WTO. Simultaneously Nikolai Ogarkov, who had lost out to Kulikov in the 1971 reshuffle, became Chief of General Staff, and although the WTO C.-in-C. had previously outranked the Chief of Staff, it emerged that this order had now been reversed, even though Kulikov and Ogarkov were both promoted to Marshal at the same time. It has been suggested that differences over *détente* and arms control lay behind this factionalism, rather than inter-service rivalry, since both Kulikov and Ogarkov had made their careers in the Ground Forces.

The question of their relative status arose again in 1984, when Ogarkov lost his post as Chief of Staff, possibly because he had argued too insistently for increased resources for the military, particularly for advanced conventional weaponry. Ogarkov's dismissal, however, seemed not to amount to complete disgrace, since comments by the then Politburo member Grigorii Romanov confirmed the suspicion of a number of Western commentators that he had been moved to a command post in the crucial Western TVD, where his geographical area of responsibility would overlap to a considerable extent with Kulikov's WTO command. The likelihood that TVD commands have now been set up in peacetime makes the overlap even more marked, and suggests that the putative closer integration of Eastern European forces will be directly into a Soviet command structure. This would leave Marshal Kulikov (along with General Gribkov) as a rather peripheral figure whose responsibilities are little more than those of the commander of a peacetime Soviet military district, despite Kulikov's apparent renewed superiority over his old rival, Ogarkov. As far as control over nuclear weapons is concerned, Ogarkov as TVD commander is probably responsible for the short-range weapons deployed in the WTO's 'Northern Tier' in the GDR, Czechoslovakia, and Poland, and Kulikov's duties are likely only to extend to their peacetime maintenance and security.

CONCLUSION

The WTO's own role in Soviet nuclear weapons policy has been seen in this chapter to be relatively unimportant, but not entirely negligible. The 1983 'counterdeployments' in the

GDR and Czechoslovakia became important again for a brief period in mid-1987, as already mentioned, and in 1988 the possible denuclearization of Central Europe has once again become a live issue.

During the negotiations which preceeded the conclusion of the INF Treaty on a basis which included some, though not all, of the 'counterdeployments' missiles (SS-22s and 23s, but not 21s), it appeared as though the FRG's Pershing-Ia missiles, with US warheads allotted to them, would become a stumbling block. Some Westerners argued that there were already equivalent missiles on the Eastern side which should be included, but the argument was weak since no convincing evidence had ever been produced to suggest that the Soviet Union seriously contemplated attaching Soviet warheads to its allies' missiles. On the Soviet side, Gorbachev and Foreign Minister Shevardnadze raised the possibility that the Soviet Union would consider doing that if the Pershing-Ias were not included, but this looked more like an 'endgame' negotiating gambit than a serious threat (see Gorbachev, 1987, p. 247). In the end the issue was decided by a combination of fudge and climbdown by the the West German Chancellor Helmut Kohl, as had always been probable.

The conclusion of the treaty necessitated arrangements with the deployment countries on inspection of their territory to verify the missiles' removal. Although some indications were seen that some Czechoslovakian leaders had doubts about the (undeniable) concessions made by the Soviet Union to obtain the treaty (*International Herald Tribune*, 17 November 1987), the GDR and Czechoslovakia probably had no more ultimate say in the agreement to remove the missiles than in their original deployment. The Soviet Union announced that it was consulting with its allies over the inspections (Bessmertnykh, 1987), and then signed an agreement with the two governments immediately after the Washington summit, on the same day as a WTO general secretaries' meeting endorsed the conclusion of the treaty (*Soviet News*, 16 December 1987). This agreement was later elaborated in the form of inspection agreements between the USA and the GDR and Czechoslovakia (for the US–Czechoslovak agreement, see Krasnaya Zvezda, 6 January 1988) and Erich Honecker of the GDR welcomed the treaty with the words: 'We have never made it a secret that the deployment of additional nuclear weapons in both West and East was not welcomed with joy in our country.' (*Panorama DDR*, 1987.)

The Czech General Staff also gave the INF Treaty its approval (*Arms Control Reporter*, December 1987, p. 403. B. 597) and the Memorandum of Understanding attached to the treaty provided detailed information on the location of the SS-22s and 23s in the GDR and Czechoslovakia. The 'counterdeployments episode' itself was thus almost over, though attention then shifted to the possibility of further denuclearization and a 'Triple-Zero' option (*The Guardian*, 7 January 1988). With this refocusing of attention on to nuclear weapons in Central Europe, the WTO may continue to be involved in its traditional, though limited, manner in the development of Soviet nuclear policy.

BIOGRAPHIES

Gribkov, General Anatolii Ivanovich Chief of General Staff, Warsaw Treaty Organization
Address: c/o Ministry of Defence, 34 Naberezhnaya M. Thoreza, Moscow, USSR

Born 23 March 1919; entered army, 1938; member of CPSU since 1941; graduate of Frunze Military Academy and (Voroshilov) General Staff Military Academy (1942 and 1951); wartime posts as General Staff representative on various fronts; postwar service with General Staff and then in Leningrad Military District (Commander, 1973–6); Chief of General Staff of WTO troops (1st. Deputy Chief of General Staff of Soviet Army and Navy), 1976 to present; candidate member of Central Committee of CPSU, 1976–81, full member, 1981 to present (*Great Soviet Encyclopedia*, 1982, p.389; Lewytzkyj,1984, p.114).

Kulikov, Marshal Viktor Georgievich Commander-in-Chief, Warsaw Treaty Organization
Address: c/o Ministry of Defence, 34 Naberezhnaya M. Thoreza, Moscow, USSR

Born 5 July 1921; entered army, 1939; member of Communist Party of Soviet Union (CPSU) since 1942; graduate of Frunze Military Academy and (Voroshilov) General Staff Academy (1953 and 1959); posts in Kiev Military District during and after war; C.-in-C. of Soviet Group of Forces in Germany, 1969–71; Chief of General Staff of Armed Forces of the Soviet Union, 1971–77; C.-in-C. of WTO, January 1977 to present; member of Central Committee of CPSU, 1971 to present (*Great Soviet Encyclopedia*, 1976, p.559; Lewytzskyj, 1984, p.181).

REFERENCES

Arkin, W.M., 1982, 'Nuclear weapons in Europe', in Kaldor, M., and Smith, D. (eds), *Disarming Europe*, Merlin Press, London.

Arkin, W.M., and Fieldhouse, R.W., 1985, *Nuclear Battlefields: Global Links in the Arms Race*, Ballinger, Cambridge, Mass.

Arkin, W.M., and Chappell, D., 1983, 'The impact of Soviet theatre nuclear force improvements', *ADIU Report*, Vol. 5, No. 4, July–August.

Bessmertnykh, A., 1987, *New Times*, No. 4, 23 November 1987.

Brown, J.F., 1984, 'The future of political relations within the Warsaw Pact', in Holloway, D., and Sharp, J. M. O. (eds), *The Warsaw Pact: Alliance in Transition?*, Macmillan, London.

Checinski, M., 1987, 'Warsaw Pact/CMEA military- economic trends', *Problems of Communism*, Vol 36, No.2.

Cockburn, A., 1983, *The Threat: Inside the Soviet Military Machine*, Hutchinson, London.

Disarmament and Security Yearbook, 1986, Volume 1, 1987, Institute of World Economy and International Relations, USSR Academy of Sciences, Moscow.

Erickson, J., 1985, 'The implications of Soviet military power', *Catalyst*, Vol.1, No.2, Summer 1985.

Evangelista, M., 1986., 'Technological innovation and the arms race: a comparative study of Soviet and American Decisions on tactical nuclear weapons', doctoral dissertation, Cornell University.

Fitzgerald, M.C., 'Marshal Ogarkov on the modern theater operation', *Naval War College Review*, Vol. 39, No.4, Autumn 1986.

Gorbachev, M., 1987, *Perestroika: New Thinking for Our Country and the World*, Collins, London.

Great Soviet Encyclopedia, Vols 13, 18, 30 (trans. of 3rd Soviet edition), 1976, 1978, 1982, Macmillan, New York.

Holden, G., 1988, *The WTO and Soviet Security Policy*, Basil Blackwell, Oxford.

Lewytzkyj, B. (ed.), 1984, *Who's Who in the Soviet Union*, K. G. Saur, Munich.

Mackintosh, M., 1969, *The Evolution of the Warsaw Pact*, Adelphi Paper No. 58, International Institute for Strategic Studies, London.

McLean, S. (ed.), 1986, *How Nuclear Weapons Decisons Are Made*, Macmillan/Oxford Research Group, London.

Mal'tsev, V. F. (ed), 1986, *Orgsnizatsiya Varshavskogo Dogovora 1955–85, Dokumenty i Materialy*, Izdatel'stvo Politicheskoi Literatury, Moscow.

Military Balance, The, 1987–1988, 1987, International Institute for Strategic Studies, London.

Petersen, P.A., 1987, 'Soviet offensive operations in central Europe', *NATO's Sixteen Nations, Vol. 32*, No. 5, August 1987.

Rice, C., 1984, *The Soviet Union and the Czechoslovak Army, 1948–83: Uncertain Allegiance*, Princeton University Press, Princeton, NJ.

Savinov, K. I., 1986, *Varshavskii Dogovor – Faktor Mira, Shchit Sotsializma*, Mezhdunarodnye Otnosheniya, Moscow.

Smith, D. L., and Meier, A.L.,1987, *'Ogarkov's revolution: Soviet military doctrine for the 1990s'*, International Defense Review, July 1987.

Sovetskaya Voennaya Entsiklopediya (Soviet Military Encyclopedia) 1976, Voennoe Izdatel 'stvo, Moscow.

Volgyes. I., 1982, *The Political Reliability of the Warsaw Pact Armies: The Southern Tier*, Duke Press Policy Studies, Durham, NC.

Volkogonov, D .A. (ed.), 1985, *Armii Stran Varshavskogo Dogovora*, Biblioteka Ofitsera, Voenizdat, Moscow.

Wolfe, T., 1970, *Soviet Power and Europe 1945–70*, Johns Hopkins University Press, Baltimore, Md.

Name Index

Post-holders included in the Biographies sections are not listed below unless their names appear in other sections of the book.

Subject Index